Digital Preservation and Documentation of Global Indigenous Knowledge Systems

Tlou Maggie Masenya
Durban University of Technology, South Africa

A volume in the Advances in Information Quality and Management (AIQM) Book Series

Published in the United States of America by
    IGI Global
    Information Science Reference (an imprint of IGI Global)
    701 E. Chocolate Avenue
    Hershey PA, USA 17033
    Tel: 717-533-8845
    Fax: 717-533-8661
    E-mail: cust@igi-global.com
    Web site: http://www.igi-global.com

Copyright © 2023 by IGI Global. All rights reserved. No part of this publication may be reproduced, stored or distributed in
any form or by any means, electronic or mechanical, including photocopying, without written permission from the publisher.
Product or company names used in this set are for identification purposes only. Inclusion of the names of the products or
companies does not indicate a claim of ownership by IGI Global of the trademark or registered trademark.
                    Library of Congress Cataloging-in-Publication Data

Names: Masenya, Tlou, 1972- editor.
Title: Digital preservation and documentation of global indigenous
    knowledge systems / edited by Tlou Maggie Masenya.
Description: Hershey, PA : Information Science Reference, [2023] | Includes
    bibliographical references and index. | Summary: "The overall objective
    of this book is to determine how indigenous knowledge can be documented
    and digitally preserved to benefit indigenous knowledge owners and their
    communities, and be accessible for future generations. It aims to
    provide the best practices, innovative strategies, theoretical and
    conceptual frameworks, and empirical research findings regarding digital
    preservation and documentation of indigenous knowledge systems,
    worldwide"-- Provided by publisher.
Identifiers: LCCN 2023003358 (print) | LCCN 2023003359 (ebook) | ISBN
    9781668470244 (h/c) | ISBN 9781668470282 (s/c) | ISBN 9781668470251
    (ebk)
Subjects: LCSH: Ethnoscience. | Digital preservation. | Cultural
    property--Protection.
Classification: LCC GN476 .D54 2023 (print) | LCC GN476 (ebook) | DDC
    001.089--dc23/eng/20230303
LC record available at https://lccn.loc.gov/2023003358
LC ebook record available at https://lccn.loc.gov/2023003359

This book is published in the IGI Global book series Advances in Information Quality and Management (AIQM) (ISSN:
2331-7701; eISSN: 2331-771X)

British Cataloguing in Publication Data
A Cataloguing in Publication record for this book is available from the British Library.

All work contributed to this book is new, previously-unpublished material. The views expressed in this book are those of the
authors, but not necessarily of the publisher.

For electronic access to this publication, please contact: eresources@igi-global.com.

Advances in Information Quality and Management (AIQM) Book Series

Siddhartha Bhattacharyya
RCC Institute of Information Technology, India

ISSN:2331-7701
EISSN:2331-771X

Mission

Acquiring and managing quality information is essential to an organization's success and profitability. Innovation in information technology provides managers, researchers, and practitioners with the tools and techniques needed to create and adapt new policies, strategies, and solutions for information management.

The **Advances in Information Quality and Management (AIQM) Book Series** provides emerging research principals in knowledge society for the advancement of future technological development. This series aims to increase available research publications and emphasize the global response within the discipline and allow for audiences to benefit from the comprehensive collection of this knowledge.

Coverage

- IT Innovation and Diffusion
- Electronic Commerce Technologies
- Human and Societal Issue
- Web Services and Technologies
- Decision Support and Group Decision Support Systems
- Knowledge Management
- Emerging Technologies Management
- Business Process Management and Modeling
- Supply Chain Management
- Mobile Commerce

IGI Global is currently accepting manuscripts for publication within this series. To submit a proposal for a volume in this series, please contact our Acquisition Editors at Acquisitions@igi-global.com or visit: http://www.igi-global.com/publish/.

The Advances in Information Quality and Management (AIQM) Book Series (ISSN 2331-7701) is published by IGI Global, 701 E. Chocolate Avenue, Hershey, PA 17033-1240, USA, www.igi-global.com. This series is composed of titles available for purchase individually; each title is edited to be contextually exclusive from any other title within the series. For pricing and ordering information please visit http://www.igi-global.com/book-series/advances-information-quality-management/73809. Postmaster: Send all address changes to above address. Copyright © 2023 IGI Global. All rights, including translation in other languages reserved by the publisher. No part of this series may be reproduced or used in any form or by any means – graphics, electronic, or mechanical, including photocopying, recording, taping, or information and retrieval systems – without written permission from the publisher, except for non commercial, educational use, including classroom teaching purposes. The views expressed in this series are those of the authors, but not necessarily of IGI Global.

Titles in this Series

For a list of additional titles in this series, please visit: www.igi-global.com/book-series

Information Literacy Skills and the Role of Social Media in Disseminating Scholarly Information in the 21st Century
C. Baskaran (Alagappa University, India) and S. Dhanavandan (Central University of Tamil Nadu, India)
Information Science Reference • © 2023 • 236pp • H/C (ISBN: 9781668488058) • US $215.00

Library and Media Roles in Information Hygiene and Managing Information
Collence Takaingenhamo Chisita (Durban University of Technology, South Africa & University of South Africa, South Africa) Alexander Madanha Rusero (University of Johannesburg, South Africa) Ngoako Solomon Marutha (University of South Africa, South Africa) Josiline Phiri Chigwada (Chinhoyi University of Technology, Zimbabwe) and Oluwole Olumide Durodolu (Department of Information Science, University of South Africa, South Arica)
Information Science Reference • © 2022 • 268pp • H/C (ISBN: 9781799887133) • US $215.00

Using Information Technology Advancements to Adapt to Global Pandemics
Efosa C. Idemudia (Arkansas Tech University, USA) Tiko Iyamu (Cape Peninsula University of Technology, South Africa) Patrick Ndayizigamiye (University of Johannesburg, South Africa) and Irja Naambo Shaanika (Namibia University of Science and Technology, Namibia)
Engineering Science Reference • © 2022 • 276pp • H/C (ISBN: 9781799894186) • US $270.00

Mass Communications and the Influence of Information During Times of Crises
Mohammed Nasser Al-Suqri (Sultan Qaboos University, Oman) Jamal Mattar Alsalmi (University of Nizwa, Oman) and Obaid Said Al-Shaqsi (Media Training Center, Oman)
Information Science Reference • © 2022 • 307pp • H/C (ISBN: 9781799875031) • US $215.00

Social Justice Research Methods for Doctoral Research
Robin Throne (University of the Cumberlands, USA)
Information Science Reference • © 2022 • 397pp • H/C (ISBN: 9781799884798) • US $215.00

Encyclopedia of Information Science and Technology, Fifth Edition
Mehdi Khosrow-Pour D.B.A. (Information Resources Management Association, USA)
Engineering Science Reference • © 2021 • 1966pp • H/C (ISBN: 9781799834793) • US $2,145.00

Handbook of Research on Managing Information Systems in Developing Economies
Richard Boateng (University of Ghana, Ghana)
Business Science Reference • © 2020 • 695pp • H/C (ISBN: 9781799826101) • US $295.00

701 East Chocolate Avenue, Hershey, PA 17033, USA
Tel: 717-533-8845 x100 • Fax: 717-533-8661
E-Mail: cust@igi-global.com • www.igi-global.com

List of Reviewers

Michael Asuquo, *University of Calabar, Nigeria*
Monicca Bhuda, *University of Mpumalanga, South Africa*
Josiline Chigwada, *Chinhoyi University of Technology, Zimbabwe*
Collence Chisita, *Durban University of Technology, South Africa*
Bryan Chrstiansen, *USA*
Petros Nhlavu Dlamini, *University of Zululand, South Africa*
Nkululeko Fuyane, *University of Bringhton, UK*
Sarah Kaddu, *Makerere University, Uganda*
Tom Kissock-Mamede, *University of Cambridge, Cambridge*
Jeffrey Kurebwa, *Bindura University of Science Education, Zimbabwe*
Lungile Luthuli, *University of Zululand, South Africa*
Jane Madireng, *University of Limpopo, South Africa*
Ngoako Solomon Marutha, *University of South Africa, South Africa*
Mehluli Masuku, *National University of Science and Technology, Zimbabwe*
Jannatul Mawa, *Monash University, Australia*
Mpilo Mthembu, *University of Zululand, South Africa*
Ignitia Motjolopane, *University of North West, South Africa*
Tinashe Mugwisi, *National University of Science and Technology, Zimbabwe*
Sam Mutsagondo, *University of Zimbabwe, Zimbabwe*
Nkholedzeni Sidney Netshakhuma, *University of Mpumalanga, South Africa*
Godian Okenjom, *University of Calabar, Nigeria*
Valentine Joseph Owan, *University of Calabar, Nigeria*
Adefemi Oluwaniyi Owoputi, *Durban University of Technology, South Africa*
Mousin Omarsaib, *Durban University of Technology, South Africa*
Notice Pasipamire, *National University of Science and Technology, Zimbabwe*
Sulaiman Patel, *Durban University of Technology, South Africa*
Janet Petters, *University of Calabar, Nigeria*
Mampilo Phahlane, *University of South Africa, South Africa*
Mogiveny Rajkoomar, *Durban University of Technology, South Africa*
Nina Olivia Rugambwa, *Kyambogo University, Uganda*
Alexander Rusero, *Harare Polytechnic, Zimbabwe*

Vusi Wonderboy Tsabedze, *University of Eswatini, Eswatini*
Tahleho Tseole, *National University of Lesotho, Lesotho*
Godfrey Tsvuura, *Zimbabwe Open University, Zimbabwe*

Table of Contents

Preface xix

Acknowledgment xxiv

Chapter 1
Reviving Indigenous Clay Pot Production for Students' Entrepreneurial and Vocational Inspiration ... 1
Janet S. Petters, University of Calabar, Nigeria & Ultimate Research Network, Nigeria
John Asuquo Ekpenyong, University of Calabar, Nigeria & Ultimate Research Network, Nigeria
Valentine Joseph Owan, University of Calabar, Nigeria & Ultimate Research Network, Nigeria
Michael Ekpenyong Asuquo, University of Calabar, Nigeria & Ultimate Research Network, Nigeria

Chapter 2
Valorization and Digital Preservation of Indigenous Knowledge Systems in South African
Indigenous Communities: Best Practices in the Digital Transformation Era 27
Tlou Maggie Masenya, Durban University of Technology, South Africa

Chapter 3
Students' Entrepreneurship Development Through Indigenous Palm Wine Production and
Alcohol Distillation: The Case of Yala-Obubra Community 43
Valentine Joseph Owan, University of Calabar, Nigeria & Ultimate Research Network, Nigeria
John Asuquo Ekpenyong, University of Calabar, Nigeria
Mercy Valentine Owan, University of Calabar, Nigeria & Ultimate Research Network, Nigeria
Joshua Nkpokpo Owan, Independent Researcher, Nigeria
Aidam Benjamin Ekereke, University of Calabar, Nigeria

Chapter 4
Supporting Digitization of Traditional Medicinal Knowledge Through Technologies in KwaZulu-
Natal, South Africa 68
Petros Nhlavu Dlamini, University of Zululand, South Africa

Chapter 5
Opportunities and Challenges in Digitization of Indigenous Knowledge and Implication for
Educational Management in the Nigerian Context 87
    Michael Ekpenyong Asuquo, University of Calabar, Nigeria
    Godian Patrick Okenjom, University of Calabar, Nigeria
    Ovat Egbe Okpa, University of Calabar, Nigeria
    Ameh Eyiene Eyiene, University of Calabar, Nigeria

Chapter 6
Promotion and Preservation of Indigenous Knowledge Systems and the Traditional Environmental
Knowledge of Garo Communities in Bangladesh 105
    Jannatul Mawa, Monash University, Australia

Chapter 7
Challenges and Opportunities of Preserving African Indigenous Knowledge Using Digital
Technologies: The Case of Bogwera 123
    Kealeboga Aiseng, Rhodes University, South Africa

Chapter 8
Efficacy of Acquiring and Transferring Indigenous Medicinal Knowledge Among Its Owners and
Practitioners in uMhlathuze in KwaZulu-Natal, South Africa 142
    Nokwanda Charity Khanyile, University of Zululand, South Africa
    Petrus Nhlavu Dlamini, University of Zululand, South Africa
    Tlou Maggie Masenya, Durban University of Technology, South Africa

Chapter 9
Agricultural Indigenous Knowledge Systems Practiced in Gutu Rural District of Zimbabwe 159
    Jeffrey Kurebwa, Bindura University of Science Education, Zimbabwe

Chapter 10
Enhancing African Indigenous Knowledge Collection Management in Ugandan Public University
Libraries: Lived Experiences of Senior Library Staff 178
    Nina Olivia Rugambwa, Kyambogo University, Uganda
    Francis Adyanga Akena, Kabale University, Uganda
    Claire Clement Lutaaya Nabutto, Makerere University, Uganda
    Grace Kamulegeya Bugembe, Makerere University, Uganda

Chapter 11
Turbulences in Repackaging Traditional Knowledge in an Era of Sovereignty: Case of Uganda
and Zimbabwe 196
    Collence Takaingenhamo Chisita, Durban University of Technology, South Africa
    Sarah Kaddu, Makerere University, Uganda

Chapter 12
African Indigenous Knowledge on the Cloud: The Role of Libraries, Archives, and Museums 219
    Madireng Monyela, University of Limpopo, South Africa

Chapter 13
Electronic Documentation of Nigerian Indigenous Arts and Crafts for Historical Research
Engagements and Tourism.. 236
Valentine Joseph Owan, University of Calabar, Nigeria & Ultimate Research Network, Nigeria
David Adie Alawa, University of Calabar, Nigeria
Kinsley Bekom Abang, University of Calabar, Nigeria
Mercy Valentine Owan, University of Calabar, Nigeria & Ultimate Research Network, Nigeria
Felicia Agbor-obun Dan, University of Calabar, Nigeria
Delight Omoji Idika, University of Calabar, Nigeria
Daniel Clement Agurokpon, University of Cross River State, Nigeria

Chapter 14
Indigenous Livestreaming in Brazil: A Methodological Case for Reflective Distant Witnessing...... 262
Tom Kissock-Mamede, University of Cambridge, UK

Chapter 15
Decolonising and Humanising Pedagogies in South African Postgraduate Education: Lessons
From Indigenous Knowledge Systems.. 282
Mothusiotsile Edwin Maditsi, North-West University, South Africa
Monicca Thulisile Bhuda, University of Mpumalanga, South Africa

Chapter 16
Integration of Indigenous Knowledge Into Library and Information Science Teaching Practices: A
Systematic Review of the Global Literature 303
Mousin Omarsaib, Durban University of Technology, South Africa
Nalindren Naicker, Durban University of Technology, South Africa
Mogiveny Rajkoomar, Durban University of Technology, South Africa

Chapter 17
The Application of OAIS Model as a Framework for Digital Preservation of Indigenous
Knowledge Systems: The Roles of Educational Managers.. 322
Godian Patrick Okenjom, University of Calabar, Nigeria
Michael Ekpenyong Asuquo, University of Calabar, Nigeria

Chapter 18
Indigenous Research and Data Management in Electronic Archives: A Framework for African
Indigenous Communities 342
Valentine Joseph Owan, University of Calabar, Nigeria & Ultimate Research Network, Nigeria
Joseph Ojishe Ogar, Federal University Ndufu-Alike, Nigeria
Patience Okwudiri Nwosu, Taraba State University, Jalingo, Nigeria
Victor Ubugha Agama, University of Calabar, Nigeria & Ultimate Research Network, Nigeria
Anjali Verma, Government Degree College, Lahar, India
Favour-Ann Kyrian Nwoke, Alex Ekweme Federal University, Nigeria

Chapter 19
Time Travel and Paradoxes: Could Libraries Be an Alternative?... 363
    Adebowale Jeremy Adetayo, Adeleke University, Nigeria

Compilation of References 377

About the Contributors 434

Index.. 439

Detailed Table of Contents

Preface xix

Acknowledgment xxiv

Chapter 1
Reviving Indigenous Clay Pot Production for Students' Entrepreneurial and Vocational Inspiration ... 1
Janet S. Petters, University of Calabar, Nigeria & Ultimate Research Network, Nigeria
John Asuquo Ekpenyong, University of Calabar, Nigeria & Ultimate Research Network, Nigeria
Valentine Joseph Owan, University of Calabar, Nigeria & Ultimate Research Network, Nigeria
Michael Ekpenyong Asuquo, University of Calabar, Nigeria & Ultimate Research Network, Nigeria

This book chapter provides a comprehensive overview of indigenous clay pot production, including its definition, importance, and history. It explores how clay pot production is practised in different parts of Africa, such as Ghana, Tanzania, and Nigeria, and its significance in various cultures. The chapter examines the types of clay used in pot production, different techniques used, and traditional tools and equipment employed. Moreover, the chapter highlights the potential of clay pot production for students' entrepreneurship and vocational career development. It delves into the challenges of pursuing a career in clay pot production, such as the limited market for pottery products, access to raw materials, learning curve, physical demand, business challenges, and creative isolation among others. Through case studies, the chapter shows how clay pot production has aided entrepreneurial success despite these challenges. This chapter is a valuable resource for anyone interested in understanding the world of clay pot production and its potential for economic and cultural development.

Chapter 2
Valorization and Digital Preservation of Indigenous Knowledge Systems in South African
Indigenous Communities: Best Practices in the Digital Transformation Era 27
Tlou Maggie Masenya, Durban University of Technology, South Africa

Indigenous knowledge is considered as the most important resource for indigenous communities and the society at large. However, concern over the loss of this vital knowledge has thus raised a need to preserve and document it in digital formats. But how can this irreplaceable knowledge be valorised, documented, and preserved for the benefits of indigenous communities, in this technology-driven dispensation era? Best practices, initiatives and strategies must thus be implemented in different parts of the world to safeguard indigenous knowledge systems. Digital preservation has become a popular method for valorising and enhancing long-term access to indigenous knowledge in the digital transformation era, characterized by globalization and digital knowledge-based economy. This chapter thus aimed at changing the phrase "history was written by the victors" by making it possible for indigenous communities and relevant stakeholders worldwide to preserve their knowledge, history, wisdom, and culture using digital technologies.

Chapter 3
Students' Entrepreneurship Development Through Indigenous Palm Wine Production and
Alcohol Distillation: The Case of Yala-Obubra Community..43
 Valentine Joseph Owan, University of Calabar, Nigeria & Ultimate Research Network, Nigeria
 John Asuquo Ekpenyong, University of Calabar, Nigeria
 Mercy Valentine Owan, University of Calabar, Nigeria & Ultimate Research Network, Nigeria
 Joshua Nkpokpo Owan, Independent Researcher, Nigeria
 Aidam Benjamin Ekereke, University of Calabar, Nigeria

This chapter used a qualitative approach to investigate and describe the palm wine production and alcohol distillation practices of the indigenous people of the Yala-Obubra community in Cross River State, Nigeria. The chapter involved palm wine tappers and alcohol distillers (n = 10). A focus group discussion was held with the respondents, with audio recordings and notes for data collection. The study documented several practices in palm wine production and alcohol distillation and discovered declining palm tree population, climate change, high cost of production, lack of access to credit and social amenities, and stealing as some challenges faced in producing palm wine and distillation of alcohol. The chapter recorded some economic opportunities in the indigenous production of palm wine and distillation of alcohol, and discussed the relevance of these two traditional practices in promoting entrepreneurship among students. The implications of this study's findings were discussed for the promotion of sustainable production and preservation of these traditional practices in Nigeria.

Chapter 4
Supporting Digitization of Traditional Medicinal Knowledge Through Technologies in KwaZulu-
Natal, South Africa 68
 Petros Nhlavu Dlamini, University of Zululand, South Africa

This chapter aimed to examine the terminology of traditional medicine and the urgency for supporting local knowledge through technology in medical libraries. The chapter was informed by three research objectives which are: categories of traditional medicinal knowledge practitioners available in rural areas; types of traditional medicinal knowledge digitized in medical libraries; and technologies for digitizing traditional medicinal knowledge in medical libraries. The approach for the investigation was a desktop literature review. The study used academically recognized journals, books, and databases as its primary sources of literature. The author also strongly drew on his prior experience in the field, as he had already published several publications on indigenous knowledge. The author also presumptively conducted an electronic search of published literature, heavily depending on the Web of Science, using the institutional repositories of universities, Google Scholar, and Medline.

Chapter 5
Opportunities and Challenges in Digitization of Indigenous Knowledge and Implication for
Educational Management in the Nigerian Context 87
 Michael Ekpenyong Asuquo, University of Calabar, Nigeria
 Godian Patrick Okenjom, University of Calabar, Nigeria
 Ovat Egbe Okpa, University of Calabar, Nigeria
 Ameh Eyiene Eyiene, University of Calabar, Nigeria

This chapter focuses on opportunities and challenges in digitizing indigenous knowledge with implications for educational management in the Nigerian context. Digitization provides an avenue for safeguarding and sharing traditional knowledge that may be at risk of being lost or marginalized. By converting indigenous knowledge into digital formats, it can be documented, archived, and easily accessed by future generations, thereby contributing to the preservation of cultural heritage. Specifically, this chapter addresses the overview of indigenous knowledge, digitization of indigenous knowledge, management of indigenous knowledge in the digital age, opportunity in the digitization of indigenous knowledge and challenges of digitization of indigenous knowledge.

Chapter 6
Promotion and Preservation of Indigenous Knowledge Systems and the Traditional Environmental Knowledge of Garo Communities in Bangladesh.. 105
    Jannatul Mawa, Monash University, Australia

Together with other indigenous groups living in Bangladesh, Garo people are considered to be an ethnic group originating from Tibet who have inherent knowledge about nature and biodiversity. Garo people depend on diverse ecosystems for their food, economic, cultural, social, and spiritual existence, and having an intricate relationship with nature has enabled the community to know different plants, herbs, and the use of these plants as foods as well as the technique of how to protect and conserve these plants. In this context, this chapter aims to discover, document and preserve Garo people's traditional environmental knowledge such as climate indicators, traditional medicine and housing techniques. This chapter further explored Garo's people role during seasonal activities and in preserving relevant portions of the traditional knowledge system.

Chapter 7
Challenges and Opportunities of Preserving African Indigenous Knowledge Using Digital Technologies: The Case of Bogwera 123
    Kealeboga Aiseng, Rhodes University, South Africa

Most indigenous knowledge systems, practices, and values disappear due to the influence of technology, human migrations, climate change, globalization, death, memory loss, and civilization. Therefore, indigenous knowledge systems will disappear if they are no longer used. This is because many traditional practices and activities within indigenous knowledge systems that have been used are essential coping and living strategies and are now in danger of disappearing. The chapter investigates how social web technologies, social media platforms, and online video tools can digitize, share, and preserve indigenous knowledge for the current generations that need to be more knowledgeable about these systems and future generations. With the example of bogwera, the chapter studies the role that digital technologies can play in protecting and preserving indigenous knowledge systems in the Taung community in North West, South Africa.

Chapter 8
Efficacy of Acquiring and Transferring Indigenous Medicinal Knowledge Among Its Owners and Practitioners in uMhlathuze in KwaZulu-Natal, South Africa 142
    Nokwanda Charity Khanyile, University of Zululand, South Africa
    Petrus Nhlavu Dlamini, University of Zululand, South Africa
    Tlou Maggie Masenya, Durban University of Technology, South Africa

Most of the population in Africa is still dependent on indigenous medicinal knowledge for treating and managing ailments. However, it is still not yet understood how this valuable knowledge is acquired and transferred from one generation to the next. The aim of this chapter was to assess the process of acquiring and transferring indigenous medicinal knowledge among its owners and practitioners. The study adopted a qualitative research approach. The findings revealed that indigenous medicinal knowledge is acquired in many different ways including visions, dreams and vigorous training and it is transferred to specially chosen children and trainees through vigorous training.

Chapter 9
Agricultural Indigenous Knowledge Systems Practiced in Gutu Rural District of Zimbabwe........... 159
    Jeffrey Kurebwa, Bindura University of Science Education, Zimbabwe

This chapter focused on the agricultural Indigenous knowledge systems (AIKS) used in Zimbabwe with specific reference to Gutu rural district. The study relied on qualitative methodology while data was collected using key informant interviews and documentary searches. The study findings indicated that a number of AIKS systems are used in the Gutu rural district. These include pest and disease management, food/grain storage and preservation, soil fertility management, and weather prediction. This study also identified several challenges associated with the documentation of AIKS, and among others include methodology, access, intellectual property rights, and the media and formats in which to preserve knowledge. The chapter concludes that Indigenous knowledge is in danger of disappearing because of global changes, and the capacity and facilities needed to document, evaluate, validate, protect, and disseminate such knowledge are lacking in most developing countries such as Zimbabwe.

Chapter 10
Enhancing African Indigenous Knowledge Collection Management in Ugandan Public University Libraries: Lived Experiences of Senior Library Staff.. 178
    Nina Olivia Rugambwa, Kyambogo University, Uganda
    Francis Adyanga Akena, Kabale University, Uganda
    Claire Clement Lutaaya Nabutto, Makerere University, Uganda
    Grace Kamulegeya Bugembe, Makerere University, Uganda

Various studies in library and information science have emphasized that indigenous knowledge management is still a neglected area and a challenge in the discipline of information management. However, the rationale for this neglect and driving challenges in university libraries has not been documented from the practitioner's perspective. This chapter shares lived experiences from experienced senior staff of public University libraries in Uganda regarding the management of African Indigenous knowledge collections. The study uses the theoretical lens of Wilson's information behavior model interpolated with participants' views to gain insight into the perspectives of the practitioners. The findings revealed challenges in lack of appropriate metadata descriptors to accommodate this knowledge, biased knowledge organization tools that are incompatible with African indigenous knowledge metadata characteristics, and limited funding in university libraries for research and indigenous knowledge collection development.

Chapter 11
Turbulences in Repackaging Traditional Knowledge in an Era of Sovereignty: Case of Uganda and Zimbabwe.. 196
    Collence Takaingenhamo Chisita, Durban University of Technology, South Africa
    Sarah Kaddu, Makerere University, Uganda

Traditional or Indigenous systems have always been the bedrock of Africans' socioeconomic and political livelihoods before the dawn of colonialism in developing countries like Uganda and Zimbabwe.

Indigenous practices are important to people's daily lives. This chapter looks to strengthen classical African systems and methods for decoloniality. The study explored traditional knowledge with a focus on its meanings and critical features, reviewed the laws protecting traditional knowledge in Uganda and Zimbabwe, and how libraries can contribute to preserving such classical knowledge in Zimbabwe and Uganda. It explored the factors that affect the preservation of traditional and proposed strategies to enhance conventional conservation by libraries in Zimbabwe and Uganda. An Afrocentric paradigm underpins the chapter, and data were collected from the literature review and the researchers' personal experiences as members of indigenous communities.

Chapter 12
African Indigenous Knowledge on the Cloud: The Role of Libraries, Archives, and Museums 219
 Madireng Monyela, University of Limpopo, South Africa

Indigenous knowledge is knowledge that people have of their local environment acquired through the accumulation of experiences, informal experiments, and observation rooted in particular places and practised as culture. This kind of knowledge is not documented as it is tacit and transferred though oral tradition. Being largely uncodified, it is constantly changing and forgotten as people adapt to changing circumstances due to beliefs, intercultural settings, and colonisation. Therefore, it faces a danger of fading. Libraries, archives, and museums (LAM) should be proactive in their approach and should ensure that indigenous knowledge, although based on orality and oral traditions, should be managed and preserved just like other documentary materials that are grounded in western codified knowledge schemes and create sustainable strategies to preserve it for future use.

Chapter 13
Electronic Documentation of Nigerian Indigenous Arts and Crafts for Historical Research Engagements and Tourism... 236
 Valentine Joseph Owan, University of Calabar, Nigeria & Ultimate Research Network, Nigeria
 David Adie Alawa, University of Calabar, Nigeria
 Kinsley Bekom Abang, University of Calabar, Nigeria
 Mercy Valentine Owan, University of Calabar, Nigeria & Ultimate Research Network, Nigeria
 Felicia Agbor-obun Dan, University of Calabar, Nigeria
 Delight Omoji Idika, University of Calabar, Nigeria
 Daniel Clement Agurokpon, University of Cross River State, Nigeria

Indigenous arts, crafts, and culture are critical components of the world's diverse cultural heritage. Unfortunately, preserving this rich heritage remains challenging for most developing countries, especially with the increasing use of electronic media and the marginalisation of indigenous communities. This chapter discussed digital documentation strategies for Nigerian indigenous arts, crafts, and cultures to support future historical research engagements and tourism. It begins by examining indigenous arts, crafts, and cultures, such as stone carving, bronze and brass, weaving, pottery, etc. It tackled the importance and challenges of electronic documentation of these indigenous arts for historical research and tourism. Some case studies of successful electronic documentation of indigenous arts, crafts, and cultures in other societies were reviewed. Lessons were drawn from such previous efforts to shape future initiatives. It was concluded that documenting and preserving indigenous arts, crafts, and cultures is crucial for promoting and preserving cultural heritage.

Chapter 14
Indigenous Livestreaming in Brazil: A Methodological Case for Reflective Distant Witnessing...... 262
    Tom Kissock-Mamede, University of Cambridge, UK

This chapter explores how livestreaming is a means to advocate for Indigenous rights and seeks to understand how Indigenous communal organizing is disseminated to distant others, focusing on researchers. Using video data analysis (VDA), it empirically explores a livestream on Instagram by the Huni Kuin showing a food distribution program. The key findings show that livestreams have both epistemological insights and rifts regarding the information that can be gained from distant witnessing. It argues that indigenous streaming is a positive, however, it's vital to remain reflexive as researchers when examining Indigenous livestreams. It postulates that we should understand streams as a form of witnessing rather than observation and sets out best practices for conducting empirical research on them. It conceptualizes a methodology for cataloguing livestreams by expanding on VDA and amalgamating it with critical auto-ethnographic reflections as a distant researcher. It concludes we should be sharing spaces as solidarity witnesses, and provision testimony in a form of knowledge transfers.

Chapter 15
Decolonising and Humanising Pedagogies in South African Postgraduate Education: Lessons
From Indigenous Knowledge Systems...282
    Mothusiotsile Edwin Maditsi, North-West University, South Africa
    Monicca Thulisile Bhuda, University of Mpumalanga, South Africa

Indigenous knowledge systems (IKS) have been marginalized in higher education institutions that have mostly followed Western paradigms of teaching, learning, and research. The prevalence of western pedagogies and worldviews has prompted certain stakeholders, such as the #FeesMustFall movement, to ask for the decolonization and humanization of South African higher education institutions' curricula. This chapter employed a qualitative document analysis (QDA) method to investigate how IKS could be used as a foundation for decolonizing and humanizing pedagogies at South African universities. It used Ubuntu's indigenous philosophy to elicit meaning, understanding, and case studies in which Ubuntu enshrines norms and values commensurate with African worldviews and epistemologies in order to humanize pedagogies. The study concludes that IKS is a social capital that can change the way universities design and apply pedagogies for teaching, learning, and research. The indigenous pedagogical praxis is the link between decolonization and humanization of higher education.

Chapter 16
Integration of Indigenous Knowledge Into Library and Information Science Teaching Practices: A
Systematic Review of the Global Literature 303
    Mousin Omarsaib, Durban University of Technology, South Africa
    Nalindren Naicker, Durban University of Technology, South Africa
    Mogiveny Rajkoomar, Durban University of Technology, South Africa

Indigenous knowledge is an emerging theme in humanistic scholarly conversations. Therefore, the purpose of this study was to present a global perspective of teaching practices related to indigenous knowledge in the Library and Information Science (LIS) field as it lends itself to a humanistic approach. The aim was to identify how indigenous knowledge is integrated into the LIS curriculum. Preferred Reporting Items for Systematic Reviews and Meta-Analyses methodology was used to review the literature. Key findings revealed that integrated teaching practices and indigenous knowledge are still emerging topics at LIS schools. The study recommends academics from LIS schools earnestly contribute to global literature by sharing their knowledge on teaching practices 'vis-a-vis' indigenous knowledge. Globally, this would ensure LIS academics tread common ground in integrating indigenous knowledge into the curriculum by using appropriate teaching practices. Ultimately, developing future LIS graduates as custodians of indigenous knowledge in industry.

Chapter 17
The Application of OAIS Model as a Framework for Digital Preservation of Indigenous
Knowledge Systems: The Roles of Educational Managers.. 322
Godian Patrick Okenjom, University of Calabar, Nigeria
Michael Ekpenyong Asuquo, University of Calabar, Nigeria

In a world faced with increased and emerging technology, indigenous knowledge systems seem to be en route to extinction. This is resulting from lack of preservation practices by knowledge experts. This kindled the interest of the researchers to discuss how the OAIS model can be applied in the preservation of indigenous knowledge system and the roles educational managers can also play. The chapter vividly discussed the concept of digital preservation, approaches to digital preservation, components constituting framework for digital preservation and application of the OAIS model as framework for digital preservation of indigenous knowledge systems. The model used as framework for digital preservation of indigenous knowledge system discussed in this chapter is the open archival information system (OAIS) reference model. This model discusses the basis for preserving indigenous knowledge system for a long time and providing necessary access to knowledge holders without restrictions. Appropriate conclusion was made for the study.

Chapter 18
Indigenous Research and Data Management in Electronic Archives: A Framework for African
Indigenous Communities 342
Valentine Joseph Owan, University of Calabar, Nigeria & Ultimate Research Network, Nigeria
Joseph Ojishe Ogar, Federal University Ndufu-Alike, Nigeria
Patience Okwudiri Nwosu, Taraba State University, Jalingo, Nigeria
Victor Ubugha Agama, University of Calabar, Nigeria & Ultimate Research Network, Nigeria
Anjali Verma, Government Degree College, Lahar, India
Favour-Ann Kyrian Nwoke, Alex Ekweme Federal University, Nigeria

This chapter introduces a framework for indigenous research and data management in electronic archives that aligns with indigenous worldviews and practices. It discusses indigenous communities' challenges in owning and controlling their data and the need for a culturally relevant framework for managing indigenous data in electronic archives. The proposed eight-step framework emphasises community control, data sovereignty, and ethical data management practices; and includes key components such as community engagement, informed consent, and culturally relevant metadata standards. Best practices for data sharing and partnership building with non-indigenous institutions are also discussed, as well as the steps for implementing the framework and the role of stakeholders in the process. Evaluation metrics for measuring the framework's success are proposed. The chapter concludes by emphasising the importance of community control and ethical data management practices in preserving and protecting indigenous cultural heritage and identity in electronic archives.

Chapter 19
Time Travel and Paradoxes: Could Libraries Be an Alternative?.. 363
Adebowale Jeremy Adetayo, Adeleke University, Nigeria

The purpose of this chapter was to gain a deeper understanding of the paradoxes surrounding time travel, and to explore how students view libraries as a source of knowledge for both the past and the future. A survey research design was adopted, and the results were analyzed using descriptive statistics. Of the 384 surveyed, the findings revealed that students occasionally use libraries for research purposes, both for exploring the past and envisioning the future. This indicates support for libraries as a viable alternative solution to the paradoxes of time travel. Although students held the belief that time travel will be possible in the future, they also expressed support for government funding of libraries, to make them more suitable for historical and futuristic research. Therefore, it is recommended that government funding be made available to libraries, with the aim of equipping them with state-of-the-art technologies that will enhance their suitability for research.

Compilation of References 377

About the Contributors 434

Index 439

Preface

Indigenous knowledge, deeply rooted in the cultural fabric of local communities, holds immense value as a vital resource. Passed down through generations via oral traditions, traditional practices, and demonstrations, it has been the foundation of agriculture, education, healthcare, and various other societal activities for centuries across the globe. Yet, the steady erosion of indigenous knowledge within indigenous communities is a cause for concern. Factors such as death, illness, memory loss, and the pressures of modernization, colonization, and globalization threaten its existence, leading to an irreplaceable loss.

Recognizing the urgency to preserve and document indigenous knowledge, organizations like the United Nations Educational, Scientific and Cultural Organization (UNESCO) and the World Council of Indigenous People have emphasized the need for formal, standardized, and sustainable practices and policies in this domain. Indigenist thinkers have also highlighted the recovery, promotion, and safeguarding of indigenous knowledge systems as integral to the decolonization of indigenous communities and nations. In the era of digital globalization and a knowledge-based economy, digital preservation has emerged as a popular method for valorizing, safeguarding, and ensuring long-term access to indigenous knowledge.

The purpose of this edited reference book, *Digital Preservation and Documentation of Global Indigenous Knowledge Systems*, is to explore how indigenous knowledge can be effectively documented and digitally preserved to benefit knowledge owners, their communities, and future generations. It aspires to present best practices, innovative strategies, theoretical and conceptual frameworks, and empirical research findings from around the world related to the digital preservation and documentation of indigenous knowledge systems.

This book will serve as a valuable resource for students, academics, researchers, information professionals, knowledge managers, records managers, indigenous knowledge owners, indigenous communities, librarians, archivists, computer scientists, Information Technology specialists, data curators, sociologists, anthropologists, and policy makers in fields such as Library and Information Science, Information Systems, Informatics, Archival Science, Information Technology, Computer Science, Social Science, and Anthropology. Its comprehensive coverage aims to provide state-of-the-art knowledge in preserving and documenting indigenous knowledge systems.

Topics addressed in this book include global initiatives for digital preservation and documentation of indigenous knowledge systems, digitization, digital curation, and digital preservation challenges and opportunities. It explores strategies, techniques, tools, systems, and technologies for the preservation and documentation of indigenous knowledge. Furthermore, the book delves into barriers and enablers of indigenous knowledge sharing, indigenous knowledge sharing techniques and strategies, decolonization of indigenous research, indigenization, and decolonization of indigenous knowledge in an educational context, as well as indigenous knowledge in healthcare, agriculture, and indigenous languages.

Preface

Recognizing the vital role of memory institutions such as libraries, archives, and museums, this book explores their significance as repositories for indigenous knowledge, ensuring proper documentation and preservation. It further examines the role of cultural heritage institutions, Indigenous Knowledge Documentation Centres, and cultural heritage agencies in promoting, protecting, documenting, and preserving indigenous knowledge systems. Additionally, the book explores the role of digital libraries in digitization, preservation, and dissemination of indigenous knowledge, as well as the custodial responsibilities of research institutions and the potential of knowledge repositories and institutional repositories in managing, preserving, and enhancing access to indigenous knowledge.

This book also highlights the interconnection between indigenous knowledge and sustainable development, addressing the importance of protecting and safeguarding the world's cultural and natural heritage in line with the Sustainable Development Goal 2030. Furthermore, it explores the impact and implications of policies and protocols in the protection and promotion of indigenous knowledge. The intersection of indigenous knowledge systems with the Fourth Industrial Revolution (4IR) technologies, climate change, frameworks for digital preservation, web-archiving, and the wider implications of indigenous knowledge preservation are also examined.

By bringing together diverse perspectives and expertise, this book endeavors to reimagine innovative preservation and knowledge sharing strategies. It calls for a collective effort from cultural heritage institutions, agencies, governments, indigenous communities, and all stakeholders to act now to safeguard, document, and preserve indigenous knowledge systems. Failure to do so risks the loss of our cultural heritage and the onset of a new dark age in history.

We hope that this book will serve as a catalyst for change, inspiring effective mechanisms for sharing, documenting, and preserving the rich tapestry of indigenous knowledge. May it contribute to sustainable development, ensure long-term access to this invaluable resource, and honor the wisdom of indigenous communities for generations to come.

Organization of this Book

Chapter 1: This chapter provides a comprehensive overview of indigenous clay pot production, exploring its definition, history, and cultural significance. It examines clay pot production practices in different parts of Africa, delving into the types of clay used, techniques employed, and traditional tools and equipment utilized. The chapter also addresses the potential of clay pot production for students' entrepreneurship and vocational career development, discussing challenges and case studies that showcase entrepreneurial success in this field. It serves as a valuable resource for understanding the world of clay pot production and its potential for economic and cultural development.

Chapter 2: This chapter explores the need to preserve and document indigenous knowledge in digital formats. It discusses the importance of indigenous knowledge and the challenges it faces, highlighting the role of digital preservation in valorizing and enhancing access to this knowledge. The chapter focuses on global initiatives, best practices, and strategies for safeguarding indigenous knowledge systems in the digital era. It emphasizes the use of digital technologies to preserve knowledge, history, wisdom, and culture of indigenous communities worldwide.

Chapter 3: This chapter investigates the practices of palm wine production and alcohol distillation among the indigenous people of the Yala-Obubra community in Nigeria. It examines the techniques and challenges associated with these traditional practices, such as declining palm tree population and climate change. The chapter also explores the economic opportunities presented by palm wine production and

xx

Preface

alcohol distillation, discussing their relevance to promoting entrepreneurship among students. It highlights the implications for sustainable production and preservation of these traditional practices in Nigeria.

Chapter 4: This chapter focuses on the terminology and digitization of traditional medicine. It examines the categories of traditional medicinal knowledge practitioners available in rural areas and the types of traditional medicinal knowledge digitized in medical libraries. The chapter also discusses the technologies used for digitizing traditional medicinal knowledge and draws on prior experience and literature in the field. It contributes to the understanding of managing and preserving indigenous knowledge in the context of traditional medicine.

Chapter 5: This chapter explores the opportunities and challenges of digitizing indigenous knowledge with implications for educational management. It provides an overview of indigenous knowledge, the digitization process, and the management of indigenous knowledge in the digital age. The chapter discusses the opportunities presented by digitization for preserving and sharing traditional knowledge, along with the challenges associated with methodology, access, intellectual property rights, and media formats. It emphasizes the importance of digitization for preserving cultural heritage and enhancing access to indigenous knowledge.

Chapter 6: This chapter focuses on the traditional environmental knowledge of the Garo people, an ethnic group in Bangladesh. It aims to discover and document their traditional knowledge related to climate indicators, traditional medicine, housing techniques, and their role during seasonal activities. The chapter highlights the intricate relationship between the Garo people and nature, emphasizing the importance of preserving and conserving their traditional knowledge.

Chapter 7: This chapter explores how social web technologies, social media platforms, and online video tools can be used to digitize, share, and preserve indigenous knowledge. It specifically examines the role of digital technologies in protecting and preserving indigenous knowledge systems in Taung, with a focus on the example of bogwera. The chapter highlights the potential of digital technologies in safeguarding indigenous knowledge and emphasizes the need for active engagement and participation in the preservation process.

Chapter 8: This chapter investigates the process of acquiring and transferring indigenous medicinal knowledge among its owners and practitioners. It employs a qualitative research approach, exploring various ways in which this knowledge is acquired and transferred, including visions, dreams, and vigorous training. The chapter sheds light on the methods and practices associated with indigenous medicinal knowledge and its transmission across generations.

Chapter 9: This chapter focuses on the Agricultural Indigenous Knowledge Systems (AIKS) used in the Gutu Rural District of Zimbabwe. It explores various AIKS systems, including pest and disease management, food/grain storage and preservation, soil fertility management, and weather prediction. The chapter examines the challenges associated with documenting AIKS, such as methodology, access, intellectual property rights, and media formats. It emphasizes the need to preserve and disseminate indigenous knowledge to ensure its sustainability in the face of global changes.

Chapter 10: This chapter discusses the management of African Indigenous Knowledge (AIK) collections in university libraries in Uganda. It presents the challenges faced in appropriately organizing and developing metadata descriptors for AIK, along with limited funding for research and collection development. The chapter highlights the importance of documenting and preserving AIK within university libraries and proposes strategies to overcome the challenges faced.

Chapter 11: This chapter explores the preservation of traditional knowledge in Zimbabwe and Uganda, focusing on the Laws protecting traditional knowledge in both countries. It discusses the role of libraries

xxi

in preserving and promoting traditional knowledge, drawing on Afrocentric perspectives. The chapter examines factors affecting the preservation of traditional knowledge and proposes strategies to enhance conservation efforts. It emphasizes the importance of libraries in safeguarding and preserving traditional knowledge for future generations.

Chapter 12: This chapter addresses the need to manage and preserve indigenous knowledge in libraries, archives, and museums. It discusses the challenges faced in preserving tacit and oral knowledge, emphasizing the importance of proactive approaches. The chapter calls for sustainable strategies to ensure the preservation of indigenous knowledge alongside other forms of codified knowledge, highlighting the vital role of cultural heritage institutions in this endeavor.

Chapter 13: This chapter explores digital documentation strategies for Nigerian indigenous arts, crafts, and cultures to support historical research engagements and tourism. It examines different indigenous arts, such as stone carving, bronze and brass, weaving, and pottery, discussing the importance and challenges of electronic documentation. The chapter draws lessons from case studies of successful electronic documentation in other societies and emphasizes the preservation and promotion of cultural heritage through digital means.

Chapter 14: This chapter examines how livestreaming can be utilized as a means to advocate for indigenous rights and disseminate indigenous communal organizing. It focuses on a livestream on Instagram by the Huni Kuin, showcasing a food distribution program. The chapter explores the epistemological insights and challenges associated with distant witnessing through livestreams. It provides best practices for conducting empirical research on indigenous livestreams and emphasizes the importance of sharing spaces as solidarity witnesses.

Chapter 15: This chapter investigates how Indigenous Knowledge Systems (IKS), specifically Ubuntu philosophy, can be integrated into pedagogies to decolonize and humanize South African higher education. It explores the use of indigenous pedagogical praxis to link decolonization with the humanization of higher education. The chapter emphasizes the potential of IKS as a social capital that can reshape teaching, learning, and research practices in universities.

Chapter 16: This chapter presents a global perspective on teaching practices related to indigenous knowledge in the field of Library and Information Science (LIS). It identifies how indigenous knowledge is integrated into the LIS curriculum, emphasizing the need for academics to share their knowledge and experiences. The chapter explores the emerging topics of integrated teaching practices and indigenous knowledge in LIS schools and calls for common ground in integrating indigenous knowledge through appropriate teaching practices.

Chapter 17: This chapter introduces a framework for indigenous research and data management in electronic archives, aligning with indigenous worldviews and practices. It discusses the challenges faced by indigenous communities in owning and controlling their data and presents the Open Archival Information System (OAIS) model as a framework for digital preservation of indigenous knowledge systems. The chapter emphasizes community control, data sovereignty, and ethical data management practices, providing steps for implementing the framework and evaluating its success.

Chapter 18: This chapter explores the paradoxes surrounding time travel and how libraries can serve as a source of knowledge for both the past and the future. It presents the results of a survey investigating students' views on libraries as a resource for historical and futuristic research. The chapter highlights the importance of government funding to equip libraries with advanced technologies that enhance their suitability for research and address the paradoxes of time travel.

Preface

Chapter 19: This chapter proposes a culturally relevant framework for managing indigenous research and data in electronic archives. It discusses the challenges faced by indigenous communities in owning and controlling their data and emphasizes community control, data sovereignty, and ethical data management practices. The chapter explores best practices for data sharing and partnership building with non-indigenous institutions, highlighting the importance of preserving and protecting indigenous cultural heritage and identity.

Tlou Maggie Masenya
Durban University of Technology, South Africa

Acknowledgment

First and foremost, I would like to thank the Almighty God, the Lion King of Judah who gave me wisdom and strength to make this book a reality. I would also like to acknowledge and thank all the authors, researchers and academics for making a valuable contribution to this book "Digital Preservation and Documentation of Global Indigenous Knowledge Systems" by sharing their valuable insights, knowledge and considerable expertise". Without their contribution, this book would not have become a success. This book went through a vigorous blind-peer review and editing by professionals in accordance with the best research practices and global ethical standards. The accomplishment of this intellectual discourse would therefore not have been possible without the support and commitment of reviewers drawn from different countries but not limited to Nigeria, Uganda, Australia, Swaziland, Zimbabwe, Botswana, Swaziland, Brazil, Lesotho, United Kingdom and South Africa. I appreciate the reviewers' thoughtful comments, and efforts towards strengthening the quality of the book and for the priceless commitment and dedication that added value to the book. I am greatly indebted to IGI-Global development team for their persistent help, technical and managerial support throughout all the stages of editing and publishing this book. Special thanks to my family for their constant love, motivation, patience and unwavering support, and I am forever grateful for immeasurable sacrifices they have made throughout my academic career and research journey.

Tlou Maggie Masenya
Durban University of Technology, South Africa

Chapter 1
Reviving Indigenous Clay Pot Production for Students' Entrepreneurial and Vocational Inspiration

Janet S. Petters
University of Calabar, Nigeria & Ultimate Research Network, Nigeria

John Asuquo Ekpenyong
University of Calabar, Nigeria & Ultimate Research Network, Nigeria

Valentine Joseph Owan
University of Calabar, Nigeria & Ultimate Research Network, Nigeria

Michael Ekpenyong Asuquo
University of Calabar, Nigeria & Ultimate Research Network, Nigeria

ABSTRACT

This book chapter provides a comprehensive overview of indigenous clay pot production, including its definition, importance, and history. It explores how clay pot production is practised in different parts of Africa, such as Ghana, Tanzania, and Nigeria, and its significance in various cultures. The chapter examines the types of clay used in pot production, different techniques used, and traditional tools and equipment employed. Moreover, the chapter highlights the potential of clay pot production for students' entrepreneurship and vocational career development. It delves into the challenges of pursuing a career in clay pot production, such as the limited market for pottery products, access to raw materials, learning curve, physical demand, business challenges, and creative isolation among others. Through case studies, the chapter shows how clay pot production has aided entrepreneurial success despite these challenges. This chapter is a valuable resource for anyone interested in understanding the world of clay pot production and its potential for economic and cultural development.

DOI: 10.4018/978-1-6684-7024-4.ch001

INTRODUCTION

Research has shown a growing concern among African scholars about the need to return to indigenous arts (Mugovhania, 2012; Ndubuisi, 2022; Zondi, 2021). The recognition of the gradual extinction of the history, knowledge, relevance, and practice of African traditional art and culture in modern African society may occasion this. For instance, it is argued that poor documentation of the rich and cherished art and cultural heritage of the African people has hindered the growth of African culture and the poor practice of indigenous art among Africans (Ekong, 2018). This cultural impoverishment affects indigenous art's historical, social and technological relevance and the economic and entrepreneurship opportunities associated with ancient African artefacts. It is also obvious that most of the works on African indigenous art and craft are merely artistic writing which only focuses on presenting to students their historical antecedents, styles, and techniques and neglects their economic potential (Elebute & Odokuma, 2016). Pottery is one of the indigenous arts that has been in practice for ages and is still relevant in modern society due to the wide usage of pots within traditional African settings. For instance, it is reported that clay wares are used for traditional religious rituals, traditional worship, cooking, eating, fetching and preserving water, and storing and preserving food items and clothes in ancient traditional Sub-Saharan African society (Busari & Odetoyinbo, 2021). Umoru-Oke (2017) argued that indigenous clay pots have innate functions in African culture which cannot be replaced by modern synthetic products such as rubber, enamel, and plastics and that indigenous pottery is an ongoing, dynamic and viable art used in many Yoruba communities in Nigeria to empower young girls in modern times. Contrary to the view of potters that indigenous clay pot art is no more financially rewarding due to modernity (Ayuba, 2009), one cannot deny the fact that clay pots still have many uses and functions in contemporary society. In the Niger Delta region of Nigeria, the 'evwere" is used to quickly thicken banga soup and speed up the cooking time for any soup, stew, or broth (Ugboma, 2021). Researchers have argued that cooking with indigenous clay pots, which are produced from natural materials, makes food taste better, healthier, and juicier than cooking with modern cookware because it almost preserves all the micronutrients present in the food (Khan & Banerjee, 2020; Saxena et al., 2021).

There are huge entrepreneurial opportunities for clay pot art in modern society. It is not enough to expose students to the historical perspective of indigenous arts and analyse their styles and techniques to promote their knowledge, practice and relevance in modern society. Students should be made to see entrepreneurial and economic opportunities in indigenous arts and develop indigenous vocational skills for self-reliance (Major & Leigha, 2019). Okonkwo (2014) reported that more than eighty (80) per cent of students interviewed had the perception that ceramics education is not economically viable and thus may not guarantee vocational opportunities in society. This may be because the indigenous traditional arts curricula do not provoke entrepreneurial and vocational inspirations among students but merely analyse the arts' antecedent, history, relevance and practice.

Therefore, this chapter aims to present a detailed process of traditional indigenous clay pot production from real-time studio experience and the vocational and entrepreneurial opportunities it can provide students in modern society. The chapter starts by defining indigenous clay pot production and explains the importance of indigenous clay pot production. It also presents a brief history of indigenous clay pot production, indigenous clay pot production in different parts of the world, uses of indigenous clay pots in various cultures, types of clay used in indigenous clay pot production, different techniques in indigenous clay pot production, traditional tools and equipment used in indigenous clay pot production and the benefits of indigenous clay pot production to vocational career development. The chapter also presents the challenges faced in indigenous clay pot production, opportunities available in indigenous clay pot production, strategies to address challenges and take advantage of opportunities. Lastly, the chapter reviews some case studies on how indigenous clay pot production can spur entrepreneurship and vocational careers among students.

DEFINITION AND IMPORTANCE OF INDIGENOUS CLAY POT PRODUCTION

Indigenous clay pot production is an ancient traditional art commonly referred to as pottery (Asmah et al., 2013). It is also called Earthenware (Abbacan-Tuguic & Galinggan, 2016). Research has shown that indigenous clay pot production is an aspect of industrial art called "Ceramics art", a branch of fine and applied arts concerned with producing wares from clay and subjecting them to heat treatment for permanence (Esosuakpo, 2020). Indigenous pot production is one of the earliest complex technologies involving changing clay into ceramic, known as pottery (Okwoche & Okonkwo, 2021). Indigenous clay pot production is described as a traditional pottery made by firing a fashioning plastic clay into an object of desirable shapes under a particular temperature to produce permanent pots used for different cultural, social and personal purposes (Okwoche & Okonkwo, 2021). It is also defined as the traditional or cultural art that involves changing clay into pots and earthenware in response to the people's social, economic and technical demands based on the development of several different civilisations from ancient to modern society (Olasebikan, 2022). No wonder indigenous clay pot production has names according to cultural differences and the origin of the art. For instance, it is called Isan pottery by Ekiti people in Ekiti State, Nigeria (Olasebikan, 2022), Mambong Pottery in Malaysia (Tajul et al., 2011), Zulu pottery in South Africa (Olalere, 2019), Sirigu traditional pottery and Mpraeso pottery in Ghana (Kusimi et al., 2020; Navei, 2021), and *Okpasi Ikoror* pottery by Yala people in Cross River State, Nigeria, among others.

Scholars across the globe have widely documented the importance of indigenous clay pot production. The importance of this ancient traditional industrial art ranges from maintenance of traditions, cultural artifacts, and indigenous knowledge (Kaari & Ombaka, 2019; Olasebikan, 2022), providing opportunities for inculcating in younger generation of women the spirit of industry and traditional technology development (Esosuakpo, 2020; Olalere, 2019), providing cultural tourism opportunities for traditional communities (Asmah et al., 2016; Navei, 2021; Yussif et al., 2018), providing opportunities for rural women to contribute to the socio-economic development of their country (Busari & Odetoyinbo, 2021), providing alternative source of livelihood for marginalised population (Elebute & Odokuma, 2016), and provide entrepreneurship and vocational or career opportunities for rural people in modern society (Pal, 2021). This implies that indigenous clay or traditional pot production has sociocultural, socio-economic, vocational and entrepreneurship potentials in modern society. The importance of indigenous clay pots in Africa includes history, culture, symbolism, technology, education and art (Asante et al., 2015).

INDIGENOUS CLAY POT PRODUCTION IN DIFFERENT PARTS OF AFRICA

This section discusses the processes and procedures used in the production of indigenous clay pots in different African contexts.

Ghana

In Ghana, indigenous or traditional clay pot production at Mpraeso pottery has been adequately documented by Kusimi et al. (2020). The process follows a sequence of activities called *"chaine operatoire"*. This process involves extraction, processing, forming, drying, firing, sorting or packing, and transportation or utilisation.

Extraction: Potters mined clay material from Nkawkaw, Oframase, or Amanfrom, while the "amodine" (local sand) is mined from Nkorkrokumah.

Procession: The clay material is purified to remove all debris, after which it is soaked in water for a day or two to form a wet clay slurry so that the potter can easily work with the cleaned clay material. The potter adds filtered local sand called amodine and mixes it properly to smoothen, soften, and make the clay material plastic to prevent cracks when firing. The mixed clay material is then purged, pinched, wedged, and kneaded until the desired texture is obtained (see Figure 1).

Forming: The potter places the kneaded clay on a piece of board and on a potter's, wheel called *dua* made locally, rolls the kneaded clay into a rod-like form, and coils it into a circular shape. The potter then walks around the dua to smoothen and cut the edges of the clay while moulding the pot. The potter uses a piece of fabric called ntomago dipped in water to give the pot perfect smoothening (see Figure 2).

Drying: The sun-drying of the pots is done two times. The first time is immediately after moulding. The inside and the outside of the pots are further smoothed using sabroba to beat and flatten the base, sikyie to polish both the inside and outside, kwaboba to give further a fined polishing texture, dadwe to create designs, and finally, ahwenie and sapo to smooth the pots further and prepare them for the second sun-drying (see Figure3).

Firing, sorting/packing, and transportation/utilisation: Pots are open-fired on low-temperature in the backyards of the residence of the potters, using firewood and sawdust. The sawdust is meant to give

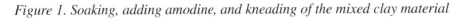

Figure 1. Soaking, adding amodine, and kneading of the mixed clay material

Figure 2. The forming process in clay pots manufacturing

Figure 3. Drying and smoothening process of clay pots manufacturing

the pots a black colour. After the firing process, the pots are sorted out from the fire and are ready for sale (see Figure 4).

Tanzania

In Tanzania, the indigenous or traditional clay pot production is documented by Mteti (2016), specifically in Kisi and Pare of Southern Highland and North-East highland of Tanzania. In Tanzania, pottery art was originally meant for women. However, with the introduction of the potter's wheel, men started venturing into the vocation. Pot production has three processes (clay extraction and transportation, clay preparation, pot making, firing, decoration, and marketing) with sub-activities in each stage.

Clay extraction and transportation: The potters travel kilometres to extract clay materials from farmlands, transport the clay materials to their homes, store the materials in their homes and preserve the

Figure 4. The firing and sorting processes in clay pots manufacturing process

materials either in bags or spray them on the ground and cover them with other substances to prevent theft (see Figure 5).

Clay preparation: The potters take time to remove impurities like pebbles, rocks or leaves from the extracted clay material. The clay is soaked in water and, at the same time, kneaded using hands while removing impurities such as stones and other unwanted substances. After proper mixing, the clay material is heaped at the potting area, which can be potter's wheels for modern technology or pieces of board placed on bare ground for traditional technique.

Pot making: The potters start moulding the pot by forming a lump of clay with a hole in the centre. The lump of clay is placed on a ring on a banana leaf for the traditional approach, while the modern approach is made on the potter's wheel. In the case of Tanzania, traditionally, pots are made in two halves (the top and the base), and then the top and base are joined together to form a pot. Scraping of the base is done until it is perfectly smoothened (see Figure 6).

Figure 5. Storage of clay materials at home

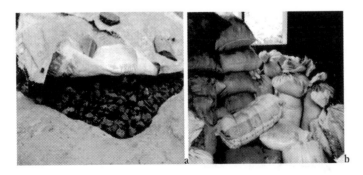

Figure 6. Traditional and modern pot making in Tanzania

Pot firing: The potters in Kisi and Pare adopt an open firing technique just as those in Ghana under controlled temperatures. While Pare potters prefer to use small twigs of tree species called Mathanzu in Kipare to fire the pots, potters in Kisi use firewood from a tree known as 'Nguti' to fire theirs. It is reported that the moder firing approach adopted uses a kiln for black colouration (see Figure 7).

Decoration and marketing: This process is done after firing in modern pot production in Pare, while for Kisi, it is done before firing. The potters use both traditional designs and modern designs. In Pare, after firing the pots, they are immediately covered with leaves of a nkasha tree to give the pots a bright colour (see Figure 8). However, potters in Kisi decorate their pots at the end of the shaping process while the clay is still malleable. The finished products are moved directly to the consumers or distributed through a third party.

Figure 7. Firing of pots after moulding

Figure 8. Decoration of pots using leaves of a Nkasha tree

Nigeria

In Nigeria, indigenous clay pot production at Ebo Yala pottery in Cross River State has also been properly documented by Okwoche and Okonkwo (2021). The production techniques are the same as that of Ghana and Tanzania, even though the processes at Yala pottery are thoroughly reported. The process starts with clay collection, clay preparation, pot making,

Clay collection and storage: Traditionally, the soil texture meant for clay pods is known and called "Ome". The "Ome" soil belongs to the clay soil family found in selected environments or farmland in the Yala kingdom, while some are collecting the brink of the river bank. A shovel, hoe, knife or spade is used to dig the clay. The collected clay material is taken home for the stage (see Figure 9). The clay material is stored either in bags or bowls to avoid hardening.

Clay preparation: Just as in other countries, the clay is prepared through cleaning, pulverisation, mixing, and kneading. At the cleaning stage, the potter uses bamboo or a shell to slice the clay and remove

Figure 9. Clay collection and storage in Yala

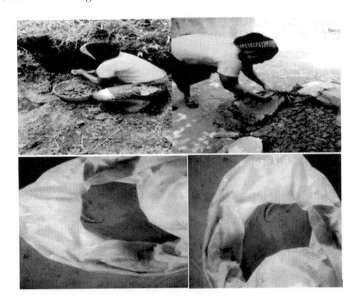

Indigenous Clay Pot Production for Students' Vocational Inspiration

the particles not needed in the clay, such as stone, water, dirt or decomposed materials. Immediately after this stage, the clay is pulverised (pound) with a wooden pestle and sieve. The sieved clay is then mixed with sand to make it plastic. After pulverising the clay, the kneading process starts. The potter can use his hand, wood or bamboo to knead the clay while adding dried husk gently until the desirable clay texture is obtained. The potter has to cover the kneaded clay with wet gumming bags to maintain its softness and wetness (see Figure 10).

Clay pot making: This stage involves forming or fashioning the pots. It can be done using hand-finger-forming or wheel-forming approaches. The potter places a sizable roll of clay and uses an anvil to beat it to an elongated flat mass to form the pot's base. Similarly, the potter uses the same approach to form the body (IbeyiIbeyi). When the pot base attains some hardness, the potter soaks it again in water to soften the surface. Then the thick part of the lower body is gently beaten with bamboo, and the anvil is held from inside with the right hand while rotating it on the concave base. The next stage involves forming the neck. The same pattern is used as both the shortened end of the circular plates are drawn together and are roundly pressed to fix with each other and transform into an undifferentiated mass by pressing with the fingertips. The last process here is smoothening. The potter uses an old local sponge made from a sack bag soaked inside the water to smooth the surface and then leaves them to dry under the sun. All these processes are presented in Figure 11).

Pot decoration and sun drying: Like the Kisi potters in Tanzania, Ebo Yala potters decorate their pots before drying and firing. It is reported that decoration uses an impression, roulettes, maise cob, bamboo, rope, and shell. The most popular ones are roulette (glazed) hand painting, slip painting, engraving and patterns (Okwoche & Okonkwo, 2021). After decorating or fashioning the pots, they are exposed to mild sunlight in the shade under controlled temperature for 2-3 days. This process is intentionally designed to protect the pots from damage due to excess heat (see Figure 12).

Pot firing: Firing and marketing are the last stages in the Yala pottery pot production process. Firing helps to transform the plastic clay into plastic. The Ebo Yala pottery firing process is called "bonfire firing". They use specific firewood called "iginibe" with the help of mall twigs of the stick (ochi) in

Figure 10. Clay preparation by Yala potters

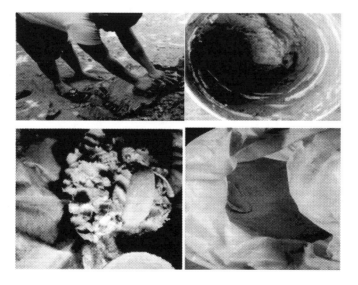

Indigenous Clay Pot Production for Students' Vocational Inspiration

Figure 11. Clay making by Yala potters

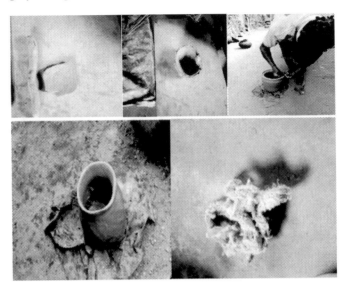

Figure 12. Clay pot decoration and sun drying by Yala potters

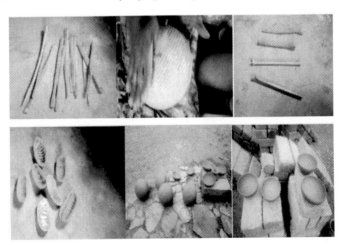

Yala. To start the firing process, the firewood logs are lined up round on the ground with the clay pots placed on them, beginning from the middle until all the pots are arranged properly. The potters covered the arranged pots with banana leaves and grasses and then hit the fire (see Figure 13). The pots are taken to their local markets and sold to people from neighbouring communities.

Pot colouring, dying and marketing: After the firing process, the pots are set up for colouring and dying. The report states that Yala potters colour their pots using pigment extracted from Yede. They do this by dipping their fingers into the prepared colour or dye and drawing curved lines on the pots, including signs and symbols such as dots, flower drawings, and slashes. After the colouring and dying processes, the pots are taken to their local weekly markets and sold to people from Ogoja and other neighbouring communities (see Figure 14)

Figure 13. Pot colouring, dying and marketing in Yala

Figure 14. Pot firing in Yala

IMPORTANCE OF INDIGENOUS CLAY POTS AND CLAY POTS PRODUCTION IN VARIOUS CULTURES

Research has indicated that in Kenya, indigenous clay pots are used for cooking, brickmaking, and plastering floors and walls and are major sources of livelihood for rural women (Kaari & Ombaka, 2019). The same source reported that many rural people in Kenya prefer to cook with indigenous clay pots because of the belief that the food cooked from clay pots tastes different compared to conventional utensils. In Kenya also, indigenous art is used as a national model of poverty reduction among rural women by empowering them through training and financial support (Ongachi et al., 2017). It is reported that rural farmers in Kenya prefer to store seeds in indigenous clay pots for incubation before planting because clay pots produce higher seed quality than those stored in polythene bags (Maina et al., 2017). In India, apart from the ceremonial use of clay pots for cooking food, storing water, and religious and smoking purposes, which are common to all cultures, indigenous clay pots were also used as traditional tiles before the emergence of modern building practices (Panda et al., 2019; Rao & Lal, 2010). Another interesting use of indigenous clay pots is among the traditional Akans of Ghana, where these pots are produced in different special forms and used for serving food during Marriage Rites, Puberty Rites, Death and Burial rituals, and traditional rituals (Ancestral Veneration and Shrines) among others (Adjei et al., 2015).

To date, Kalinga people in the Philippines are still using indigenous clay pots for rice cooking (ittoyom), vegetable/meat cooking (oppaya), and water storage (immosso) pots (Abbacan-Tuguic & Galinggan, 2016). The Kalinga people believe that globular clay pots are far more advantageous than other organic containers because the heat has little or no effect on the containers and their contents, and they protect the food from moisture and pests. In Nigeria, water pot (àmù), cooking pot (ape ìdáná), money box (kóló), local stove (àdògán), flower pot (ìkòkò òdòdó), frying pot (àlàtí/ agbada), herbal pot (orù), local oil lamp (fìtílà), plate (àwo ebo), soup pot (àsèje), placental pot (agbébi), sieve (ajere), and coal pot (kólùpótù) are still produced and used by the Yoruba people. Among the Akwa Ibom people, 'indigenous clays pots such as 'abang mmong' (water pot), 'Oko Ibibio' (cooking pot), 'Usan Ibibio' (bowls), 'Oko ata' (basin), 'etok oko' (small cooking pot), 'etok abang' (small water pot), 'oko ukot' (Palm wine pot) and 'abang isong' (big ceremonial pot for communal palm wine drinking) are still common (Peters, 2021). Like the rural Kenyan women, Akwa Ibom rural women in Nigeria believe that food cooked from indigenous pottery pots has a unique good taste which differs from food cooked from enamel or aluminium pots. The importance of indigenous clay pot production and the use of clay pots among different cultures is inexhaustive. In many cultural settings like the Philippines, pot making has been developed into modern usage and modified into ceramics for different modern uses.

TECHNIQUES USED IN INDIGENOUS CLAY POTS PRODUCTION

The techniques used for indigenous pot production are peculiar to different cultures. In Nigeria, the Yoruba people adopt three common techniques: direct, indirect and coiling moulding techniques (Fatuyi, 2018; Nanashaitu, 2017). When a potter uses the direct moulding technique, the pots are moulded without a pre-mould. The direct technique involves the following process: opening, coiling, consolidating the rim, expanding the belly, shaping the pot, scraping the pot and lastly, smoothening the pot. On the other hand, the indirect technique is used when the potter places the base of the pot upside down and involves rolling clay into a ball, making it into a flat surface, moulding on pre-mould, coiling, rim forming, smoothening and smoothening of the outer surface. Similarly, the coiling technique, known in Yoruba as 'ooran', involves building up the pot wall with superimposed rolls of clay coils until the desired shape of the pot is achieved (see Figure 15).

In Tanzania, two techniques are applied by potters: the traditional technique and the modern technique (Mteti, 2016). In the traditional technique, the lump of clay is placed on a ring placed on a banana leave, and the potter keeps using their hand to shape the lump of clay until the desired shape is formed. In this technique, pots are made in two halves (the top and the base), and the potter gradually adds clay to join the top and base to form a pot. In the modern technique, the potter applies the potter's wheel, where the lump of clay is placed on the wheel and gradually added to form desired pot (see Figure 16). This implies that techniques for making clay pots can be direct, indirect, coiling, traditional and modern.

Figure 15. Direct, indirect and coiling techniques of making clay pots in Yoruba

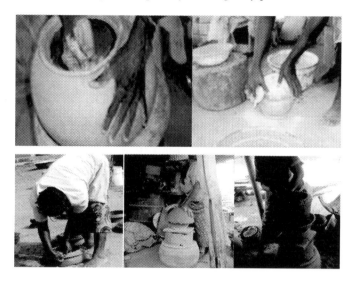

Figure 16. Traditional and modern techniques of making clay pots in Tanzania

TRADITIONAL TOOLS AND EQUIPMENT USED IN INDIGENOUS CLAY POT PRODUCTION

Indigenous clay pot production is a traditional craft that has been practised for thousands of years around the world. The process of making clay pots involves various traditional tools and equipment. Traditional tools and equipment used in clay pot production are crucial in preserving cultural heritage, promoting sustainability, and enhancing artisanal skills. Using traditional tools and techniques, potters also reduce their environmental impact by using local and natural materials and minimising energy consumption. Additionally, the continued use of traditional pottery-making tools and techniques helps preserve traditional knowledge and skills passed down from generation to generation. This section discusses some traditional tools and equipment used in indigenous clay production.

- **Clay**

Clay is the main and most important raw material used in the traditional craft of clay pot production. It is a naturally occurring material composed of fine-grained minerals that can be moulded into various shapes when wet and hardened through firing. Clay is typically sourced from local deposits and is usually prepared by digging it out of the ground and refining it through washing, sieving, and drying. This process helps to remove any impurities, such as stones, organic matter, or debris, that might interfere with the quality of the clay. Once the clay has been refined, it can be used in pot production. The clay is typically mixed with water to form a workable paste that can be moulded into various shapes using a potter's wheel or hand tools. One of the most important properties of clay is its plasticity, which is the ability to be moulded and shaped without cracking or breaking (Bao et al., 2021; Tran Ba et al., 2016). This property makes clay ideal for making pottery, allowing potters to create various shapes and designs. Clay is also highly porous, which means that it can absorb water. This property is important in clay pot production because it allows the pots to "breathe," which helps to regulate the temperature and humidity of the contents inside. The type of clay used depends on the region and the intended use of the pots. Once the pots have been shaped and decorated, they are fired in a kiln to harden the clay and make it durable.

- **Potter's Wheel**

The potter's wheel is a traditional tool and equipment for clay pot production. It shapes and moulds clay into various forms, including bowls, plates, cups, and vases. The potter sits at the wheel and uses their hands to shape the clay as it spins on the platform. Using the potter's wheel in clay pot production dates back thousands of years and has been an essential tool for potters worldwide (Méry et al., 2007). It allows them to create symmetrical and consistent shapes, which would be difficult to achieve by hand alone. The process of using the potter's wheel involves several steps. First, the potter takes a lump of clay and centres it on the wheel by pressing it firmly onto the centre of the platform. Then, using their hands, the potter applies pressure to the clay as it spins, shaping it into the desired form. The potter's wheel allows for a wide range of shapes and sizes to be created, from small cups to large vases (Berg, 2007). Once the pot has been shaped on the wheel, it is typically allowed to dry and harden before being fired in a kiln.

- **Clay Cutter**

A clay cutter is a traditional tool used in clay pot production designed to cut the clay into specific sizes and shapes for use in pottery making. Clay cutters are typically made of wire or thin metal blades attached to a handle or frame. A clay cutter is essential for preparing clay on the potter's wheel (Müller, 2007). After removing them from the wheel, the clay cutter is also used to trim and shape the edges of pottery pieces. There are different clay cutters, each designed for a specific purpose. The wire clay cutter, for example, is used to slice through blocks of clay to create even-sized pieces. On the other hand, the metal blade clay cutter is used to trim and shape the edges of pottery pieces. Using clay cutters in clay pot production is an important part of traditional craft. It

Indigenous Clay Pot Production for Students' Vocational Inspiration

allows potters to work with clay efficiently and effectively, ensuring that each piece of pottery is of a consistent size and shape. Without clay cutters, the process of pottery making would be more time-consuming and less precise.

- **Rolling Pin**

Using a rolling pin in clay pot production allows potters to create flat, even slabs of clay that can be used to make various pottery pieces (Triplett, 2000). While rolling pins are commonly associated with baking, they have also been used as a traditional tool and equipment in clay pot production. In pottery making, a rolling pin is typically used to flatten and shape slabs of clay into various forms (Peterson & Peterson, 2003). The rolling pin used in pottery is usually made of wood. It is designed to be sturdy and durable, with a smooth surface allowing easy clay rolling. For example, slabs of clay can be rolled into sheets and then cut and shaped into plates, bowls, or other forms. In addition to shaping the clay, a rolling pin can also be used to create textures or patterns on the surface of the clay. By rolling the clay over a textured surface, such as a piece of fabric or a carved block, the rolling pin can leave impressions that add visual interest to the finished pottery piece. While other tools, such as the potter's wheel and clay cutters, are also essential in pottery making, the rolling pin is a versatile tool that offers unique opportunities for creativity and expression.

- **Hand Tools**

Hand tools are essential to pottery making, and traditional clay pot production relies heavily on various hand tools. In addition to the potter's wheel, clay cutter, and rolling pin, various hand tools are used as traditional tools and equipment in clay pot production. These tools include spatulas, knives, and wooden ribs, among others. Spatulas are flat, thin tools used to smooth and shape the surface of the clay. They are especially useful in creating curves and contours on the surface of a pot. Spatulas come in various shapes and sizes, including straight, curved, and angled, to allow for a range of manipulation.

Knives are used to cut and shape the clay into specific forms. A sharp blade can be used to trim excess clay from a pot, while a serrated blade can be used to create texture on the surface of the clay. Knives come in various shapes and sizes and can be metal or plastic.

Wooden ribs are flat tools made of wood or plastic used to smooth and shape the surface of a pot. They are especially useful in creating curves and contours and can compress and smooth the clay as it is being shaped. Wooden ribs come in various shapes and sizes and can be used inside and outside a pot.

Wire and loop tools play a crucial role in creating clay pots. Wire tools are primarily used for cutting clay. A wire tool consists of two wooden handles with a wire between them, and it is used to cut through the clay. This tool is used to remove the clay from the potter's wheel after it has been shaped, and it can also be used to trim excess clay from the pot. Loop tools are used to shape the clay. A loop tool consists of a metal blade with a loop at one end and a wooden handle at the other. This tool scrapes clay from the pot's surface, creating different shapes and textures. Loop tools can also be used to smooth the clay pot's surface. By gently scraping the surface of the clay, the potter can create a smooth surface that is perfect for decorating. Both wire and loop tools can create fine details in the clay. For example, wire tools can create lines or grooves in the clay, while loop tools can create intricate patterns and designs.

Indigenous Clay Pot Production for Students' Vocational Inspiration

- **Kiln**

A kiln is an essential traditional tool used in clay pot production. It is a furnace or oven for drying, baking, and firing clay objects at high temperatures. Kilns have been used for thousands of years to create pottery and ceramics (Bienkowski & Millard, 2010), and they have evolved, but the basic principles of their operation have remained the same. The kiln plays a critical role in shaping and transforming raw clay into functional and decorative objects in clay pot production (Zola et al., 2020). Before the clay pots are fired in the kiln, they are shaped by hand or with the help of a potter's wheel. The raw clay pots are left to dry in the open air or a shaded area until they are leather-hard. Once the pots are dry enough, they are loaded into the kiln, which is heated to temperatures ranging from 500°C to 1300°C (McClellan & Dorn, 2006). The firing process can take anywhere from a few hours to several days, depending on the size of the kiln and the thickness of the clay pots. The kiln's temperature gradually increases during the firing process, causing the clay pots to undergo physical and chemical changes. At around 600°C (Ashby, 2013; Wroe, 1994), the clay begins to transform into a hard and durable material known as ceramic. At higher temperatures, the clay vitrifies, meaning it becomes glass-like, and the glaze applied to the pots melts, fusing to the surface of the clay and creating a smooth, glossy finish.

- **Glazes**

Glaze is a traditional tool used in clay pot production to create a smooth and glossy surface on clay objects. It is a mixture of finely ground minerals and chemicals suspended in water, which is applied to the surface of the clay pot before firing in the kiln. The glaze provides a protective coating on the clay pot, preventing water from penetrating the surface and making it more durable (Maltoni et al., 2012). It also enhances the beauty of the clay pot by adding colour, texture, and lustre to the surface. Glazes come in various colours and textures; potters can create their custom glazes by mixing different minerals and chemicals in various proportions (Rice, 2015). Applying glaze to the clay pot is a crucial step in the pottery-making process. The potter must ensure that the glaze is applied evenly and smoothly to avoid bubbles, drips, and other imperfections that can affect the final appearance of the pot. Once the glaze is applied to the clay pot, it is fired in the kiln at high temperatures, causing the glaze to melt and fuse to the surface of the clay (Levy et al., 2022). This process creates a smooth, glossy finish and a layer of protection on the pot. In addition to enhancing the beauty and durability of the clay pot, a glaze can also be used to create specific effects on the surface, such as crackling, crystallisation, and speckling. These effects can be achieved by manipulating the glaze's composition and the kiln's firing temperature.

- **Decorating Tools**

Traditional clay pot production often involves various decorating tools that can be used to create unique and intricate designs on the surface of the pots. The most common tools used in pottery decoration include brushes, stamps, and carving tools. Brushes are commonly used in pottery decoration for painting designs onto the surface of the pots. These brushes are often made from natural materials like bamboo, animal hair, or plant fibres, which can provide a variety of textures and effects on the pot's surface. Different brush sizes and shapes can create fine details or larger patterns. Stamps are another common decorating tool in pottery production. These can be carved from wood, clay, or stone to create repeating patterns or designs on the pot's surface. Stamps can be used to create a variety of textures and

Indigenous Clay Pot Production for Students' Vocational Inspiration

shapes and can be used to create intricate designs quickly and easily. Carving tools create designs by carving into the pot's surface. These tools can include knives, chisels, and other sharp instruments that can be used to create intricate patterns and textures. Different tools, such as fine lines or deeper grooves, can create different effects. Overall, these tools are essential in traditional clay pot production and can help to create unique and intricate designs on the surface of the pots. The skilful use of these tools can result in beautiful and functional pottery that is not only aesthetically pleasing but also durable and long-lasting.

- **Drying Racks**

Drying racks are essential tools in traditional clay pot production, where they are used to dry newly formed pots before they are fired. In this process, freshly made clay pots are placed on the drying rack, allowing them to air dry evenly and gradually to prevent cracking and warping during firing (Peterson & Peterson, 2003). In traditional clay pot production, drying racks are typically made from natural materials such as bamboo or wooden poles, ropes, and netting. The racks are designed to be simple and efficient, allowing for good airflow around the pots to facilitate drying. The drying racks come in different sizes and shapes, depending on the size and shape of the pots being made. For instance, small drying racks may be used for small pots, while larger ones may be used for bigger pots. Some drying racks are also adjustable, allowing the size to be modified to fit different pots (Orton & Hughes, 2013). To use the drying rack, the freshly made pots are carefully placed on the racks to allow for adequate airflow around each pot. The racks are placed in a well-ventilated area to ensure the pots dry evenly.

POTENTIALS OF INDIGENOUS CLAY POT PRODUCTION FOR STUDENTS' ENTREPRENEURSHIP AND VOCATIONAL CAREER DEVELOPMENT

Indigenous clay pot production has a long and rich history, with various communities and cultures developing unique styles and techniques. There has been a renewed interest in traditional pottery recently, with many people seeking handmade and artisanal products. This has increased the demand for traditional clay pots, creating opportunities for individuals and communities to reap many benefits. One of the key benefits of traditional clay pot production is the development of vocational skills. To produce high-quality clay pots, individuals must learn various skills, including pottery throwing, glazing, and firing. These skills can be acquired through vocational or technical schools, apprenticeships, or self-directed learning. Vocational training programs can provide students with a solid foundation in the basics of pottery production, including techniques for shaping, trimming, and finishing clay pots.

Additionally, the demand for traditional pots for domestic and decorative purposes and for cooking and serving indigenous dishes in hotels and restaurants creates job opportunities (Adebimpe, 2015). Therefore, individuals can start their businesses and become self-employed, selling their pottery creations and contributing to the economic development of their communities. Starting a pottery business involves much more than just creating pottery. Individuals must learn to manage finances, develop a marketing strategy, and understand customer needs and preferences. These skills can be honed through practical experience and mentorship from experienced potters. Furthermore, entrepreneurial studies have been introduced into the Nigerian education system, equipping students with the skills and drive to establish successful enterprises in traditional industries such as pottery (Anthony-Euba & Towobola, 2014). These educated graduates are expected to introduce improved technologies to traditional indus-

17

tries, like pottery making, which would reduce failure rates and, in turn, positively impact the national economy. Furthermore, using better tools in traditional pottery making will result in less strenuous work for potters, enabling them to be more creative (Alimba & Mgbada, 2003).

Moreover, indigenous clay pot production can help preserve culture and heritage. Pottery making has been an essential part of many cultures for thousands of years, with unique styles, techniques, and designs that reflect the history and traditions of the community. By learning and practising this craft, individuals can help keep these traditions alive and pass them down to future generations, thus strengthening cultural identity and creating a sense of belonging within the community. In many indigenous communities, pottery-making has been a communal activity that brings people together and strengthens social bonds. By learning and practising this craft, individuals can connect with others in their community, build relationships, and create a shared identity (Nortey & Bodjawah, 2018). This can promote social inclusion and create a more vibrant and cohesive society.

The production of traditional clay pots can also promote sustainability and environmental stewardship. Traditional pottery techniques often use locally sourced materials and natural methods, which can promote sustainability and reduce the industry's environmental impact. By incorporating these practices into modern production methods, individuals can create more eco-friendly and sustainable pottery, thus contributing to a more environmentally responsible industry. As an example, a study has shown that the creation of artisanal products such as clay pots can impact changes in land use and cover, and the existence of traditional governance organizations can aid in establishing a link between producers and markets to encourage more enduring management of territorial resources like the tropical dry forest, which is ecologically valuable but frequently disregarded (Lira et al., 2022).

The tactile nature of pottery production can also help individuals develop their fine motor skills and hand-eye coordination. Pottery making is an art form, and individuals can express their creativity by designing and producing unique clay pots. The process of creating pottery can be therapeutic and meditative, providing a means of relaxation and stress relief. In addition to vocational and entrepreneurial skills, students pursuing a traditional clay pot production career can develop their creative expression. Pottery making is an art form, and students can express their creativity by designing and producing unique clay pots. Creating pottery can be therapeutic and meditative, providing relaxation and stress relief for students. Additionally, the tactile nature of pottery production can help students develop their fine motor skills and hand-eye coordination.

CHALLENGES ASSOCIATED WITH PURSUING A CAREER IN INDIGENOUS CLAY POT PRODUCTION

Despite the numerous benefits of traditional clay pot production, there are also challenges associated with pursuing a career in this field. It has been stated that potters are facing several challenges in their profession, including a lack of access to working capital and outdated equipment (Adebimpe, 2015; Ogunyoku et al., 2011). Other challenges that individuals interested in a career in clay pottery may face include the following:

- **Limited Market for Pottery Products**

Indigenous Clay Pot Production for Students' Vocational Inspiration

While there is a growing demand for handmade and artisanal products, the market for traditional clay pots is still relatively small. This means that individuals who want to make a living from producing pottery must be creative and innovative in marketing and selling their products. This may involve developing a strong online presence, targeting niche markets, or collaborating with other artists and designers to create unique and distinctive products.

- **Access to Raw Materials**

The availability and cost of clay and other materials used in pottery production can vary depending on the location. In some areas, individuals may be able to source materials locally, while in others, they may need to import materials from other regions or countries. This can also increase production costs and impact a pottery business's profitability.

- **Learning Curve**

One of the most significant challenges of pursuing a career in clay pottery is the steep learning curve. It takes time and effort to master the art of clay pottery. A potter must learn to understand the properties of clay and how to use various tools, techniques, and firing methods to create functional and decorative pottery. This requires significant practice, experimentation, and patience.

- **Physical Demands**

Working with clay pottery is physically demanding. A potter must be able to knead, shape and mould clay for extended periods. It can be strenuous and requires stamina and good physical health.

- **Business Challenges**

The business side of pottery making is also challenging. Potters have to manage the cost of materials, production, marketing, and sales. Building a successful pottery business requires financial management skills and balancing creative expression with commercial viability.

- **Creative Isolation**

Pottery making can be a solitary activity that can be challenging for some people. Potters need to spend significant time alone, working on their craft. This can be isolating and require self-motivation and discipline to maintain focus and productivity.

- **Environmental Concerns**

Pottery making can also pose environmental challenges, especially during the kilning process, which usually involves heating moulded objects in a local furnace. Nearby grasses, microorganisms or animals useful to humanity are killed due to heat from the furnace. Potters need to be mindful of the environmental impact of their materials and production methods. They must choose sustainable materials and firing methods to minimise their carbon footprint and reduce waste.

- **Competition**

The pottery market can be highly competitive. Potters must thus be able to create unique and compelling designs to stand out in a crowded market, and they must also be able to market their products effectively to reach potential customers.

- **Financial Stability**

Like many creative professions, pursuing a career in pottery can be financially unstable. Potters may experience financial instability due to the seasonal nature of their work and the ups and downs of the market. It may be necessary to have a secondary source of income to supplement their pottery income.

CASE STUDIES ON HOW INDIGENOUS CLAY POT PRODUCTION HAS AIDED THE ENTREPRENEURIAL SUCCESS

Despite these challenges, there are many success stories of students who have pursued careers in indigenous or traditional clay pot production. For example, in India, the Khurja Pottery Cluster in Uttar Pradesh has become a hub for traditional clay pot production, with over 200 small and medium-sized enterprises producing various pottery products (Craft Ghar, n.d). Government initiatives have supported the cluster to promote traditional crafts and provide local artisans with training and business development services.

Another case study was presented by Yadav and Goyal (2015) concerning Mansukhbhai Prajapati, whose family was involved in traditional clay pottery in rural India. Mansukhbhai Prajapati, from rural India, dropped out of school and returned to his family's traditional business of clay pottery after facing setbacks in his education and career. While working at a brick roof tiles factory, Prajapati developed a machine to create more efficient clay products. He experimented with different types of clay to create innovative products like the Mitticool clay refrigerator, nonstick clay tawa, and clay pressure cooker. The Mitticool clay refrigerator gained attention for providing a low-cost alternative to traditional refrigeration by using natural evaporation to keep food and drinks cool without electricity. This made it ideal for rural areas with unreliable or unavailable electricity. Prajapati's success improved his financial situation and positively impacted his community, and he also received several awards, including recognition from the President of India, and inspired many seeking to impact their communities positively.

Between 2003 and 2013, the Sri Lanka project collaborated with Ashram International Charity in the UK to empower women through craft revival (Anjum, 2013). Artisanal potters worked with a modern ceramic factory to produce items for export, using traditional making methods such as throwing on the wheel or beating. In contrast, the factory provided glazing, firing, packaging, and shipping to Europe. The project adhered to fair trade principles, paying potters 30% more for their work than they would locally (Anjum, 2013). The project positively impacted craft revival, women's empowerment, lifestyle, and health and safety at the pottery. One of the ranges produced by the potters, called Matti, won the House Beautiful Gold Award for Best Tableware range in 2011 and was sold by retailer Jamie at Home.

CONCLUSION AND RECOMMENDATIONS

In conclusion, this chapter has provided valuable insights into indigenous clay pot production. It has highlighted the importance of indigenous clay pot production in various cultures, examined the different techniques and traditional tools used in the process, and explored the potential of pottery as a source of entrepreneurship and vocational career development for students. Moreover, the chapter has addressed the challenges of pursuing a career in indigenous clay pot production and provided case studies of successful entrepreneurs. These case studies demonstrate that despite the challenges, indigenous clay pot production can be a viable source of economic development in African countries and other regions where pottery is practised. Overall, this chapter has significant implications for students, scholars, and pottery enthusiasts interested in understanding the world of indigenous clay pot production. It highlights the potential of pottery as a source of economic and cultural development and underscores the importance of preserving traditional techniques and knowledge in the field. The chapter provides a foundation for future research and scholarship on pottery, entrepreneurship, and vocational career development in African countries and beyond.

REFERENCES

Abbacan-Tuguic, L., & Galinggan, R. (2016). Earthenware: The art of traditional pottery of Pasil Kalinga. *International Journal of Advanced Research in Management and Social Sciences*, 5(6), 774–784. http://bitly.ws/BkCv

Adebimpe, O. (2015). Pottery production, an entrepreneurship perspective for job creation and poverty alleviation. A case study of Dada pottery, Okelele, Ilorin, Kwara State, Nigeria. *Journal of Economics and Sustainable Development*, 6(2), 172–178.

Adjei, K., Asante, A. E., & Adu-Gyamfi, V. E. (2015). Life, death and eternity: The role of pottery in some cultural practices among the Akans of Ghana. Online International Journal of Arts and Humanities, 4(4), 55-61. https://bit.ly/3LKP0Fh

Alimba, J. O., & Mgbada, J. U. (2003). Socio-economic consequences of technological change on the rural non-farm Igbo women entrepreneurs of south-eastern Nigeria: Implications for farm and non-farm linkages. *ATPS Working Paper Series No. 40*. African Technology Policy Studies Network. https://www.africaportal.org/documents/17076/working_paper_series_40.pdf

Anjum, M. (2013). *Artisanal craft pottery in South Asia (and Ethiopia) and the potential for expanding markets locally and globally* [Doctoral dissertation, Royal College of Art, United Kingdom].

Anthony-Euba, P., & Towobola, W. (2014). Entrepreneurship for sustainable development: A Case for present-day Ìjàyè pottery tools genre. *Journal of Poverty. Investment and Development*, 5, 112–117.

Areo, A. (2014). Women involvement in handmade pottery and marketing concept strategy. *Journal of Economics and Sustainable Development*, 5(6), 150–159. https://core.ac.uk/download/pdf/234646323.pdf

Asante, E. A., Opoku-Asare, N. A., & Wemegah, R. (2015). Indigenous pottery at Sirigu: Dialogue on materials, methods and sociocultural significance. *Craft Research*, *6*(1), 31–56. doi:10.1386/crre.6.1.31_1

Ashby, M. F. (2013). *Materials and the environment* (2nd ed.). Elsevier.

Asmah, A. E., Frimpong, C., & Asinyo, B. K. (2013). Enhancing the Value of Indigenous pottery products with surface decoration methods & macramé. *Arts and Design Studies, 8*, 1-9. http://bitly.ws/BkCvhttp://bitly.ws/Bm5x

Asmah, A. E., Mateko, M. M., & Daitey, S. T. (2016). Tourist art: A prime phase of Sirigu art. *European Journal of Research in Social Sciences, 4*(2), 1–14. http://bitly.ws/BmyD

Ayuba, Z. (2009) *Adaptation of aspect of Garin Bah traditional pottery into contemporary ceramic* [M. A thesis, University of Nigeria, Nsukka]. http://bitly.ws/BbIY

Bao, X., Huang, Y., Jin, Z., Xiao, X., Tang, W., Cui, H., & Chen, X. (2021). Experimental investigation on mechanical properties of clay soil reinforced with carbon fiber. *Construction & Building Materials, 280*, 122517. doi:10.1016/j.conbuildmat.2021.122517

Barnett, W. K., & Hoopes, J. W. (1995). *The emergence of Pottery. Technology and innovation in ancient societies*. Smithsonian Institution Press.

Berg, I. (2007). Meaning in the making: The potter's wheel at Phylakopi, Melos (Greece). *Journal of Anthropological Archaeology, 26*(2), 234–252. doi:10.1016/j.jaa.2006.10.001

Bienkowski, P., & Millard, A. (2010). *Dictionary of the ancient near east*. University of Pennsylvania Press.

Burrison, J. A. (1997). The living tradition of English country pottery. *Folk Life, 36*(1), 25–39. doi:10.1179/043087797798238198

Busari, D., & Odetoyinbo, O. (2021). Homegrown; Home inspired: The resilience of traditional hand-built pottery production in Ìjàyè, Abéòkúta, Southwest Nigeria. *African Identities, 2021*, 1–17. doi:10.1080/14725843.2021.1940839

Craft Ghar. (n.d.). *Khurja Pottery and Ceramics & Jaipur Blue Pottery*. Craft Ghar. https://www.craft-ghar.com/blogs/handicrafts-of-india/khurja-pottery-and-ceramics-jaipur-blue-pottery

Ekong, C. E. (2018). Rethinking the preservative relevance of pottery to the development of Nigeria. *Humanities Report, 8*(1), 59–72.

Elebute, A., & Odokuma, E. (2016). Arts and crafts as veritable sources of economic empowerment for marginalised people in Nigeria. *International Journal of Development and Economic Sustainability, 4*(3), 11–24. http://bitly.ws/B9Le

Esosuakpo, S. (2020). Restructuring ceramic production for wealth creation, security and sustainable development through the construction of Kick Wheel. *UJAH: Unizik Journal of Arts and Humanities, 21*(4), 118–134. doi:10.4314/ujah.v21i4.7

Fatuyi, O. A. (2018). Technological Shift and Consequences for Pottery Practices in South-Western Nigeria. *International Journal of Sciences*, *7*(06), 93–102. doi:10.18483/ijSci.1284

Kaari, M. F., & Ombaka, O. (2019). Indigenous knowledge and applications of clay among rural communities in western Kenya. *International Journal of Development and Sustainability*, *8*(4), 264–283. https://isdsnet.com/ijds-v8n4-01.pdf

Khan, D., & Banerjee, S. (2020). Revitalising ancient Indian clay utensils and their impact on health. *International Journal of All Research Education and Scientific Methods*, *8*(7), 357–360. https://www.researchgate.net/publication/343678519

Kusimi, Donkor, A. K., Ayivor, J. S., Kyeremeh, K., & Kusimi, J. M. (2020). The lifecycle of pottery art processes and production in Mpraeso, Ghana. *Dearte*, *55*(3), 70–94. doi:10.1080/00043389.2020.1805849

Levy, M., Shibata, T., & Shibata, H. (2022). *Wild clay: Creating ceramics and glazes from natural and found resources*. Bloomsbury Publishing.

Lira, M. G., Davidson-Hunt, I. J., & Robson, J. P. (2022). Artisanal products and land-use land-cover change in indigenous communities: The case of mezcal production in Oaxaca, Mexico. *Land (Basel)*, *11*(3), 387. doi:10.3390/land11030387

Maina, Gohole, L. S., & Muasya, R. M. (2017). Effects of storage methods and seasons on seed quality of jute mallow morphotypes (Corchorus olitorius) in Siaya and Kakamega counties, Kenya. *African Journal of Food, Agriculture, Nutrition and Development*, *17*(3), 12395–12412. doi:10.18697/ajfand.79.16035

Major, N. B., & Leigha, M. B. (2019). Indigenous skills and entrepreneurship education: A critical blend for sustainable development in Nigeria. *Brock Journal of Education*, *7*(2), 140–148. http://bitly.ws/Bb2R

Maltoni, S., Silvestri, A., Maritan, L., & Molin, G. (2012). The medieval lead-glazed pottery from Nogara (north-east Italy): A multi-methodological study. *Journal of Archaeological Science*, *39*(7), 2071–2078. doi:10.1016/j.jas.2012.03.016

McClellan, J. E. III, & Dorn, H. (2006). *Science and technology in world history: An Introduction*. JHU Press.

Méry, S., Anderson, P., Inizan, M. L., Lechevallier, M., & Pelegrin, J. (2007). A pottery workshop with flint tools on blades knapped with copper at Naushaero (Indus civilisation, ca. 2500 BC). *Journal of Archaeological Science*, *34*(7), 1098–1116. doi:10.1016/j.jas.2006.10.002

Mteti, S. H. (2016). Engendering pottery production and distribution processes among the Kisi and Pare of Tanzania. *International Journal of Gender and Women's Studies*, *4*(2), 127–141. doi:10.15640/ijgws.v4n2a11

Mugovhania, N. G. (2012). The androgynic pedagogic approach in the study and teaching of performing arts in South Africa. *Journal of Sociological Studies*, *2*(12), 908–917. http://bitly.ws/B9nk

Müller, K. (2007). *The Potter's Studio Handbook*. Quarry Books.

Nanashaitu, U. (2017). The indigenous Yoruba pottery: Processes and products. *Research on Humanities and Social Sciences, 7*(20), 52–63.

Naveᵢ, N. (2021). Cultural tourism potentials of Daɲi traditional pottery art. *International Journal of Innovative Research and Development, 10*(9), 153–165. doi:10.24940/ijird/2021/v10/i9/JUL21044

Ndubuisi, C. (2022). The Oye-Ekiti Christian art workshop and the fusion of the European Catholic tradition and Nigerian indigenous art in three Lagos churches. *Art in Translation*, 1-25. https://doi.org/doi:10.1080/17561310.2022.2120343a

Nortey, S., & Bodjawah, E. K. (2018). Designers' and indigenous potters' collaboration towards innovation in pottery production. *Journal of Desert Research, 16*(1), 64–81. doi:10.1504/JDR.2018.091153

Ogunyoku, T. A., Nover, D. M., McKenzie, E. R., Joshi, G., & Fleenor, W. E. (2011). Point-of-use drinking water treatment in the developing world: Community acceptance, project monitoring and revision. *International Journal for Service Learning in Engineering. Humanitarian Engineering and Social Entrepreneurship, 6*(1), 14–32. doi:10.24908/ijsle.v6i1.3207

Okonkwo, I. E. (2014). Students' perception of ceramics education in Nigeria tertiary institutions. *African Research Review, 8*(2), 217–234. doi:10.4314/afrrev.v8i2.13

Okwoche, A. S., & Okonkwo, E. E. (2021). Contemporary Process of Pottery Making in Yala Local Government of Cross River State. *American Journal of Aerospace Engineering, 8*(1), 1–8. doi:10.11648/j.ijmpem.20210601.11

Olalere, F. E. (2019). Effects of ecological process on indigenous pottery as a cultural tourism product: A case of Zulu pottery. *African Journal of Hospitality, Tourism and Leisure, 8*(5), 1–11. http://bitly.ws/BmuMa

Olasebikan, M. K. (2022). Socio-economic impacts of pottery business to the people of Isan Ekiti from 1960-2000. *Sapientia Global Journal of Arts. Humanities and Development Studies, 5*(3), 73–80.

Ongachi. (2017). Traditional pottery techniques towards poverty eradication in Emuhaya constituency, Vihiga County, Kenya. *International Journal of Economics, Commerce and Management, 5*(12),868-877. http://bitly.ws/BSag

Orton, C., & Hughes, M. (2013). *Pottery in archaeology*. Cambridge University Press., doi:10.1017/CBO9780511920066

Pal, S. K. (2021). Reviving Pottery Industry by Solving Problems: A Study in a Developing Economy. *IOSR Journal of Business and Management, 23*(7), 44–49. http://bitly.ws/BmWP

Panda. (2019). Traditional clay pottery of Odisha, India. *Indian Journal of Traditional Knowledge, 18*(2), 325–332. http://bitly.ws/BSfo

Peters, E. E. (2021). Implication of early pottery practice by women in Nigeria: A focus on women pottery practice in Akwa Ibom state. *Academicia: An International Multidisciplinary Research Journal, 11*(1), 474–481. doi:10.5958/2249-7137.2021.00067.7

Peterson, S., & Peterson, J. (2003). *The craft and art of clay: a complete potter's handbook.* Laurence King Publishing.

Rao, T. Y., & Lal, B. S. (2010). Rural artisans-indigenous technology: An empirical study on village potters in Warangal. *Indian Journal of Development Research and Social Action, 5*(1), 309–317.

Rice, P. M. (2015). *Pottery analysis: A sourcebook.* University of Chicago press.

Saxena, S., Saini, S., Samtiya, M., Aggarwal, S., Dhewa, T., & Sehgal, S. (2021). Assessment of Indian cooking practices and cookwares on nutritional security: A review. *Journal of Applied and Natural Science, 13*(1), 357–372. doi:10.31018/jans.v13i1.2535

Tajul. (2011). Local Genius of Mambong Pottery in Kelantan, Malaysia. *International Journal of Humanities and Social Science, 1*(21), 147–155. http://bitly.ws/Bmbh

Tran Ba, L., Le Van, K., Van Elsacker, S., & Cornelis, W. M. (2016). Effect of cropping system on physical properties of clay soil under intensive rice cultivation. *Land Degradation & Development, 27*(4), 973–982. doi:10.1002/ldr.2321

Triplett, K. (2000). *Handbuilt ceramics: pinching, coiling, extruding, molding, slip casting, slab work.* Lark books.

Ugboma, J. (2021). *Thicken Soups in a Flash with a Nigerian Evwere Clay Pot.* http://bitly.ws/BbMV

Umoru-Oke, N. (2017). Apprenticeship system in indigenous Yoruba pottery art of Nigeria. *International Journal of Small Business and Entrepreneurship Research, 5*(4), 29–34. http://bitly.ws/BbzI

Wroe, F. C. R. (1994). Microwave-assisted firing of ceramics. In *Proceedings of the Institute of Energy Conference held in London, UK,* (pp. 43-53). IEEE. 10.1016/B978-0-08-042133-9.50007-1

Yadav, V., & Goyal, P. (2015). User innovation and entrepreneurship: Case studies from rural India. *Journal of Innovation and Entrepreneurship, 4*(1), 1–20. doi:10.118613731-015-0018-4

Yussif, I., Adu-Gyamfi, V. E., & Tabi-Agyei, E. (2018). Documentation of some identified traditional pottery decorative techniques in Northern Ghana. *Asian Research Journal of Arts & Social Sciences, 6*(3), 1–11. doi:10.9734/ARJASS/2018/41149

Zola, F. C., Colmenero, J. C., Aragão, F. V., Rodrigues, T., & Junior, A. B. (2020). Multicriterial model for selecting a charcoal kiln. *Energy, 190,* 116377. doi:10.1016/j.energy.2019.116377

Zondi, N. B. (2019). *A dissection of the Protection, Promotion, Development and Management of Indigenous Knowledge Systems Act 6 of 2019: substantive issues and foreseeable consequences for creative industries in South Africa* [Minor Dissertation, University of Cape Town]. http://hdl.handle.net/11427/36221

ADDITIONAL READING

Akudago, J. A., Mounkeila, B., Guemnin Boutchueng, O., Obatsa, L. N., & Ausel, J. (2016). Innovation and lessons learnt in design and pilot implementation of clay-bodied bio-sand filters in Niger. In *Proceedings of the 39th WEDC International Conference, Kumasi, Ghana, 2016* (Refereed Paper 2507, pp. 1-6). Water, Engineering and Development Centre (WEDC).

Barua, P., Ahsan, R., Islam, M. T., Tasnim, N., & Hasan, M. A. (2022). Eco-friendly Entrepreneurship to Promote Plastic Alternatives. *Notitia-časopis za ekonomske, poslovne i društvene teme, 8*(1), 35-51.

Heierstad, G. (2017). *Caste, entrepreneurship and the illusions of tradition: Branding the potters.* Anthem Press.

Mwiandi, F. K., & Ombaka, O. (2017). Assessment of indigenous knowledge and practices on the use of clay among rural communities in Meru, Kenya. *International Journal of Development and Sustainability, 6*(11), 1701–1720.

Mwiandi, F. K., & Ombaka, O. (2019). Indigenous knowledge and applications of clay among rural communities in western Kenya. *International Journal of Development and Sustainability, 8*(4), 264–283.

KEY TERMS AND DEFINITIONS

Entrepreneurship: In the context of this chapter, it refers to the act of starting a business or a series of businesses with the goal of creating a benefit to humankind, indigenous communities and society at large, and it focuses on helping communities or the environment through their products and services. It is one of the resources economists categorize as integral to production and the other three being land or natural resources, labor and capital.

Indigenous Arts: It is an expression of Indigenous people's identity, culture, spirituality and relationships to their indigenous communities and countries.

Indigenous Clay Pot Production: It is described as a traditional pottery made by firing a fashioning plastic clay into an object of desirable shapes under a particular temperature to produce permanent pots used for different cultural, social and personal purposes.

Indigenous Pottery: It is made by forming plastic clay into objects of required shapes and firing them to appreciable temperatures in the open or in pits to induce reactions that lead to permanent changes, including increase in strength, hardening and setting their shape.

Traditional Tools: Refers to the equipment, instruments, or devices that have been used historically or traditionally in a particular craft or trade, such as the tools used in indigenous clay pot production.

Chapter 2

Valorization and Digital Preservation of Indigenous Knowledge Systems in South African Indigenous Communities:
Best Practices in the Digital Transformation Era

Tlou Maggie Masenya
Durban University of Technology, South Africa

ABSTRACT

Indigenous knowledge is considered as the most important resource for indigenous communities and the society at large. However, concern over the loss of this vital knowledge has thus raised a need to preserve and document it in digital formats. But how can this irreplaceable knowledge be valorised, documented, and preserved for the benefits of indigenous communities, in this technology-driven dispensation era? Best practices, initiatives and strategies must thus be implemented in different parts of the world to safeguard indigenous knowledge systems. Digital preservation has become a popular method for valorising and enhancing long-term access to indigenous knowledge in the digital transformation era, characterized by globalization and digital knowledge-based economy. This chapter thus aimed at changing the phrase "history was written by the victors" by making it possible for indigenous communities and relevant stakeholders worldwide to preserve their knowledge, history, wisdom, and culture using digital technologies.

DOI: 10.4018/978-1-6684-7024-4.ch002

Copyright © 2023, IGI Global. Copying or distributing in print or electronic forms without written permission of IGI Global is prohibited.

INTRODUCTION

Indigenous knowledge is largely tacit and stored in people's minds and unequally shared in the communities where it had been generated. It is thus important to note that indigenous knowledge is becoming extinct due to the lack of adequate methods or techniques to preserve and share it. Digital preservation is thus regarded as one of the modern techniques for ensuring sustainable knowledge access and increasing knowledge sharing. Although indigenous knowledge may have ancient origins, however, it is relevant in the day-to-day lives of indigenous people and their communities, worldwide. This vital knowledge is used by indigenous communities as a basis for making decisions pertaining to food security, human and animal health, education, natural resources management and other vital activities (Gorjestani, 2000). Kaya and Seleti (2013) also noted that the wealth of knowledge that elders and other knowledge holders in African local communities still possess and demonstrates the vibrant intellectualism to which African researchers and intellectuals should turn. However, in the African context, the indigenous researchers and academics have still not done enough to redress this travesty of disseminating indigenous knowledge in ways that have no relevance for the original knowledge holders (Keane, Khupe & Seehawer, 2017), and are also conducting a research that is not benefitting the indigenous knowledge owners and their communities.

In most cases, indigenous knowledge is owned by an individual researcher or institution which limits who has access to this knowledge and how it can be used. indigenous knowledge holders, and their communities are getting any credit, recognition or compensation from that appropriation. For the past decades, indigenous knowledge has been transmitted orally from one generation to the other. As highlighted by Sithole (2007) the indigenous knowledge is mostly disseminated and preserved through various family histories, taboos, symbols, rituals, dances, festivals, poetries, folk stories, drama and other knowledge sharing methods. However, traditional cultures, history, languages, ancient knowledge and wisdom as well as many of our past lessons are slowly fading away among indigenous communities worldwide, as a result of decolonization, westernization, modernization and globalization. Most of young generations in African countries have also seen no relevance of this vital knowledge as they embraced western knowledge and civilisation. Therefore, this irreplaceable resource has rarely been recorded and is at the risk of being extinct for future generations, if there is little effort made towards valorizing and preserving. It might also end-up diminish with its owners and this will have a negative impact on lives of communities who depend or benefit from it (i.e. for economic empowerment, agriculture, social transformation, health benefits etc.)

A concern over the loss of indigenous knowledge has thus raised a need to preserve and document this knowledge in digital formats. Thus, more efforts should be made by reimagining new strategies and adopting digital technologies for promoting, managing and preserving this knowledge to ensure sustainable access and effective knowledge sharing. Digital preservation has become a popular method for valorising, safeguarding and enhancing long-term access to indigenous knowledge in the digital transformation era, characterized by globalization and digital knowledge-based economy. The rapidly increasing use of emerging new technologies thus creates opportunities in the valorisation, preservation and sharing of indigenous knowledge among indigenous communities, in digital and social media platforms. Digital preservation is perceived as the planning, resource allocation and application of preservation methods and technologies necessary to ensure continued access to digital materials of enduring value. Duranti (2010) also described digital preservation as the whole of the principles, policies, rules and strategies aimed at prolonging the existence of a digital object by maintaining it in a condition suitable for use,

Valorization, Preservation of Indigenous Knowledge in South Africa

either in its original format or in a more persistent format, while protecting the object's identity and integrity, that is, its authenticity. Increasing number of institutions and organization worldwide are actively adopting innovative technologies and digital preservation systems in creating, organizing, storing, managing, disseminating, preserving and enhancing access to their vital knowledge, and to extend their relevance in the digital era.

The rapidly increasing use of social media platforms also creates opportunities to form local and international partnerships that can facilitate the process of creating, managing, preserving and knowledge sharing. However, the high rate of information illiteracy and the exclusion of indigenous knowledge from Western education add to the information gap experienced in indigenous communities in African countries including South Africa. African indigenous knowledge should thus be incorporated in education curriculum and be differentiated from Western values and culture inherited from colonialism. This chapter thus looked at best practices, technologies and strategies adopted in different parts of the world to valorise and preserve indigenous knowledge systems for the benefits of indigenous communities and for future generations in South Africa. The chapter was therefore guided by four research objectives which were to:

- Establish the importance of indigenous knowledge in indigenous communities
- Determine the use of digital technologies and social media platforms in preserving and sharing indigenous knowledge
- Determine the role of digital library as digital repository and archive for preserving and sharing indigenous knowledge
- Determine the strategies for promotion and valorization of indigenous knowledge

THEORETICAL FRAMEWORK

Ontological-based knowledge modelling framework and social capital theory were used as a guide or roadmap for applying best indigenous knowledge management and preservation strategies and practices.

Ontological-Based Knowledge Modelling Framework

Indigenous knowledge has been affirmed as critical resource which brings development in every human endeavour, and it is also critical to sustainable development of indigenous communities and society at large. Effective knowledge sharing and management has thus become crucial. As noted by Kozhakhmet and Nazri (2017) one of the most important purposes of knowledge management is to systematically influence knowledge sharing or transfer, creation and application thereby creating value. Likalu, et al. (2010) described knowledge sharing or transfer as the process in which knowledge is shared or communicated to other individuals or groups within the organisations through workshops, seminars, conferences, classrooms, meetings, face-to-face interactions or the use of technologies. It is the design and transmission of knowledge within an organization or between organizations to enhance learning and productivity of workers, which is essential in the overall success of the organization (Gaura, Hongjia & Baoshan, 2019). As stated by Sagsan (2009) knowledge sharing requires the prerequisites mechanisms that allow teams, departments and groups to share their tacit and explicit knowledge through technological and social communication infrastructure channels.

Ontologies have gained immense importance as one of the widely used methods to represent and share knowledge in several domains such as software engineering and enterprise modelling (Happel, Maalej & Seedorf, 2010; Tebes et al., 2019). Taye (2010) described ontologies as shared and common understanding of a domain that can be communicated across people and application systems and are also being used for intelligent information integration, information retrieval, knowledge management, web standards, online databases and multi-agent systems. The role of ontology in knowledge management processes thus aids in knowledge creation, acquisition, storage, transfer and application together with performance improvement (Haron & Hamiz, 2014). Ontological-based knowledge modelling framework offers a mechanism for transforming implicit knowledge, which is in experts' s domains into explicit models and also provides sensible structures of information, to make domain hypothesis explicit, to provide categorization structure and to enable reuse of domain knowledge (Haron & Hamiz, 2014). This framework represents the knowledge in a manner which knowledge management systems can facilitate, whereby software applications such as e-services can exchange data and make such data transactions interoperate independently of their internal technologies by sharing an ontology (Vassev, Hinchey & Gaudin, 2012). Knowledge management systems are designed to allow users to access and utilize the rich sources of information and knowledge stored in different forms, and also to support knowledge creation and knowledge transfer within organizations (Chimalakonda & Nori, 2020). The application of knowledge ontology and modelling framework will develop a clear path pertaining the adoption of knowledge management systems in support of knowledge management and sharing (Liana, 2011).

Social Capital Theory

Bhandari and Yasonobu (2009) described social capital as a collective asset in the form of shared norms, values, beliefs, trust, networks, social relations and institutions that facilitate cooperation and collective action for mutual benefits. Social capital refers to connections among individuals-social networks and the norms of reciprocity and trustworthiness that arise from them (Putnam, 2007). It consists of trustworthy networks and social relations that enable collaboration among individuals within the organizations or communities and it is closely related to civic engagement, participation in voluntary organisations and social connections which fosters sturdy norms of reciprocity and trust. It is a productive resource that facilitates production and make possible to achieve certain ends that would be impossible in its absence (Bhandari & Yasonobu, 2009), and inheres in the structure of relations between and among actors.

The values of social capital theory thus lie in its ability to transfer and facilitate other forms of capital beneficial for individuals and organizations. This theory examines how social relationships once formed can benefit individuals and organizations beyond their original context of creation. The whole notion of social capital theory is centred on social relationships and its major elements include social networks, civic engagement, norms of reciprocity etc. Social capital benefits not only those involved but also by-standers and society at large, and as a system, this theory feeds on itself "trusting relationships help build other trusting relationships". As stated by Putnam (2007) economies with high levels of social capital are top performers on social and economic indicators such as health, social integration, national wealth, democracy etc. Coleman (1990) proposed three forms of social capital which can be used by indigenous communities to achieve their ends, namely: level of trust (as evidenced by obligations and expectations), information channels and norms and sanctions that promote the common good over self-interest. The following are three types of social capital by Gittell and Vidal (1998):

- **Bonding social capital** describes close relationships among family, friends, neighbourhood, ethnicity and social group people sharing specific traits.
- **Bridging social capital** refers to relationships between strangers or people that have sporadic relationships (i.e in business meetings or conferences) and between people that might offer different points of views and information and with whom contact might be of advantage in future situations. This type of social capital describes connections that link people across a cleavage that typically divides society (such as race, or class, or religion) and associate that 'bridge' *between* communities, groups, or organisations.
- **Linking social capital** involves creating social relationships with leaders or government officials to leverage their power and influence.

METHODOLOGY

This chapter adopted a qualitative research approach, a desktop-based research. Literature search on the valorisation and digital preservation of indigenous knowledge systems in South African indigenous communities was conducted using Google Scholar, Web of science and Scopus databases. The search terms and phrases included "digital preservation of indigenous knowledge in indigenous communities", "digital technologies and digital preservation of indigenous knowledge", "social media platforms and knowledge sharing", "strategies for valorisation of indigenous knowledge", "digital library and digital preservation of indigenous knowledge", digital libraries and knowledge sharing". Conducting a literature review can thus assist to develop a conceptual definition of a construct based on shared meaning and describe what theories, models and frameworks were used to explain relationships between concepts, as stated by Ngulube (2017). Ontological-based knowledge modelling framework and social capital theory were used as a guide for applying best indigenous knowledge preservation practices and their implications on the implementation of knowledge sharing systems and strategies.

FINDINGS FROM LITERATURE REVIEW

The findings were discussed under the following themes, in line with the research objectives:

THE IMPORTANCE OF INDIGENOUS KNOWLEDGE IN INDIGENOUS COMMUNITIES

World Council of Indigenous Peoples (WCIP) (1998) described indigenous knowledge as the summation of knowledge and skills possessed by people belonging to a particular geographic area which allows them to derive value from their natural setting. Indigenous knowledge is held by any community, whether it is a rural or urban community and it is based on experiences, practices and information that have been imparted by local people and merged into their way of life (Chisenga, 2002). As noted by Chisenga (2002) it is difficult to communicate indigenous knowledge to those who do not share nor understand the language, tradition and cultural experiences involved Agrawal (1995) outlined the characteristics of indigenous knowledge using a system of knowledge framework, namely:

- Indigenous knowledge is embedded in a particular community and exclusive to that community whereby community members are dependent on this knowledge for survival.
- There are no contradictions in what the indigenous people believe or no conflicting ideas in their belief system.
- Indigenous people are committed to and practice their knowledge systems on a daily basis and there are no contradictions in what they believe or no conflicting ideas in their belief system.
- Indigenous people conform to the rules and laws that are governed by the elders in the community and these laws do not change over time to suit a situation as they are deeply rooted in their belief system.

This knowledge has been the basis for agriculture, health care, education and the wide range of other activities that sustain a society and its environment in many parts of the world for many centuries (Senanayake, 2006). It has been estimated that 80% of Africans use medicinal plants or traditional medicine, compared to 60% of the world's population in general, as reported by World health Organization (WHO) (2008). In South Africa, particularly, there are over 24 000 variety of indigenous plants, which play an important role in the daily lives of many indigenous communities (Boikhutso, 2012). Most of indigenous people in African countries are using indigenous plants for self-medication and for the treatment of a wide variety of diseases such as cancer, diabetes, malaria, diabetes and Human Immunodeficiency Virus (HIV) (Nyumba, 2006) and some of the medicinal plants are exploited pharmaceutical companies. However, in most cases, indigenous communities are using traditional medicines because they have no choice as most of them not have access to health care services (Boikhutso, 2012). Indigenous food also contributes a great deal to the livelihood, self-reliance and well-being of indigenous communities, as stated by Matenge et al. (2011), whereby indigenous crop production provides these communities with food resources produced from cereals, groundnuts, sorghum, melons, pumpkins etc. Indigenous communities in India were also able to leverage indigenous and global knowledge locally, and build a network of practitioners that engaged the agricultural administration and research in a dialogue of partners (Gorjestani, 2000). Sithole (2007) noted that documenting this vital knowledge will help ensure that communities are not disadvantaged because of the unique beliefs and folkways that pattern their lives. Documentation and preservation are thus an acceptable way to validate and grant indigenous knowledge protection from bio piracy and other forms of abuse (Sithole, 2007).

THE USE OF DIGITAL TECHNOLOGIES AND SOCIAL MEDIA PLATFORMS IN PRESERVING AND SHARING INDIGENOUS KNOWLEDGE

The oral transmission or passing down of indigenous knowledge orally or through generations by word of mouth suggests the importance of documenting, managing and preserving it digitally for fear of it being lost. Proper knowledge management, preservation and sharing is likely to be enabled by digital technologies which open up new possibilities, foster better opportunities, explore new modes of communication, helps overcome geographical remoteness by ensuring faster communication and provide more access to information and knowledge and enabling users to create and share information and ideas, generate content, collaborate and interact with each other in virtual communities and networks. Digital world has revolutionised opportunities for and the nature of networking and communication through the application and adoption of digital technologies. These innovative technologies have the ability to document and preserve indigenous knowledge for long-term benefits and that may also contribute to possible exploitation of this knowledge for promoting local communities to their struggle against poverty. It is thus crucial to understand how different populations or communities use digital technologies and social media platforms in order to explore their potential to improve social and health outcomes.

As also pointed out by Chisenga (2002) indigenous knowledge in African communities needs to be codified into electronic formats for both audio and video to make it widely accessible through global infrastructure. The use of digital tools is viewed as the appropriate technique to preserve indigenous knowledge and can enhance access to indigenous knowledge in the local communities In January 2004, the African Union Heads of State and Government adopted a declaration that calls on the African countries to prioritize Information Technology (IT) as a vehicle for driving Africa's development agenda (Department of Arts & Culture, 2019). Yunnus and Yummus (2017) also proposed the use of digital technologies to capture and document indigenous knowledge by citing the example of the Campbell Collections library, which uses digitisation to preserve and disseminate important African artefacts to the global community via the web. The use of digital technologies and social media platforms in preserving and sharing indigenous knowledge has thus been recommended by several scholars (Chisenga, 2002; Hunter, 2005). These technologies can be used to strengthen and encourage cultural diversity and to preserve and promote the language, distinct identities and indigenous knowledge of local people and nations in a way that they determine the best means to advance these objectives (World Summit on the Information Society, 2003).

The use of social media technologies in introducing indigenous knowledge can be viewed as a viable and foundational way of preserving, managing and sharing indigenous knowledge and can also lure the young generations to learn more about their cultural practices. Some of the libraries and information centres are known for posting audio feeds and videos of indigenous knowledge to social media and communication technologies, in this digital world. Lemma and Hoffmann (2005) further observed that the more the small scale adapt digital technologies to their indigenous practices the more they innovate and improve their indigenous techniques, skills and practices, As also stated by Hunter (2005) the use of digital technologies and social media platforms can assist in preserving and sharing indigenous knowledge for the future generation, to promote effective cost dissemination of indigenous knowledge, to create easily accessible indigenous knowledge information systems, to provide a platform for advocating for improved benefit from indigenous knowledge systems of the poor and to promote integration of indigenous knowledge to formal and non-formal training and education and enhance access to indigenous knowledge in the local communities.

Social media platforms thus cover range of digital platforms which enable connections with other people of similar interests and backgrounds and allow creation of a profile, uploading and sharing of media such as pictures and video as well as various ways to interact with other users and ability to setup groups including Facebook, LinkedIn, YouTube, Flickr, etc. Social media platforms such as Facebook offers features for building virtual communities among dispersed indigenous peoples. The study of San Nicolas-Rocca and Parrish (2013) shows the extent of sharing and preserving indigenous knowledge among the Chamorro peoples through social media platforms and revealed that Facebook belongs to the top social networking websites that are used by Chamorros people to learn and share cultural or indigenous knowledge. Virtanen (2015) also noted that Facebook has become a major domain of communication and expression among Brazilian Amazonian indigenous groups. However, such use of digital technologies and social media platforms seems not appropriate for South African indigenous communities whereby people rely on indigenous knowledge for their daily living.

DIGITAL LIBRARY AS DIGITAL REPOSITORY AND ARCHIVE FOR PRESERVING AND SHARING INDIGENOUS KNOWLEDGE

A number of memory or cultural heritage institutions and archives around the world are increasingly adopting new emerging technologies and social media platforms, in this digital era, in an attempt to ensure long-term preservation of their indigenous knowledge systems (Corcoran & Duane, 2018). The majority of cultural heritage institutions including the academic libraries in South Africa have also developed knowledge repositories and implemented their own digital preservation systems, technologies and open source software or proprietary systems in an attempt to address the digital preservation conundrum (Masenya 2018). Examples of systems and technologies mostly used by cultural heritage institutions in managing and preserving information and knowledge digitally are Preservica, Repository of Authentic Digital Record (RODA), DSpace, Eprints, ETD-db, Greenstone, Fedora, Archivematica, Archeevo, just to name a few (Masenya 2018). Bountouri (2017) described Archivematica as a free and open software which supports Metadata Encoding and Transmission Standards (METS), Preservation Metadata: Implementation Strategies (PREMIS), Dublin Core, Badgit specification and other recognised standards to ensure trustworthy, authentic, reliable and system-independent Archival Information Packages (AIPs) for storage in a preferred repository.

Preservica is one of digital preservation system that has contributed to the development of many important standards such as PRONOM persistent unique identifier and OAIS (Preservica, 2016), and it is widely implemented by business, archives, libraries, museums and government, which focuses on the processes and systems needed to keep valuable digital assets accessible and readable for the long-term. Preservica also supports many different file format migrations which can be carried out not only during the initial ingest but also at any point in future (Preservica, 2016). The emergence of these modern technologies is thus transforming traditional libraries into virtual or digital libraries. Digital libraries appeared as a new mechanism and a solution for managing scholarly production, dissemination and preservation of Indigenous knowledge in various institutions and organizations, worldwide. IFLA/UNESCO (2010) described the mission of the digital library as to give direct access to information resources, both digital and non-digital, in a structured and authoritative manner and thus to link information technology, education and culture in a contemporary library service.

Digital preservation action must thus be at the heart of any future digital library research agenda, given the core dependency of digital libraries on guaranteeing the authenticity, integrity, interpretability and context of the digital material across systems, time and context (Ross, 2007). Ross (2007) pointed out that if we think more carefully about digital libraries we easily observe that they may be libraries by name, but they are archives by nature and the content they hold does not really need to be held elsewhere because net-based services mean it can be provided from a single source wherever and whenever it is wanted. Mdhluli et.al. (2021) described the digital libraries as having the potency to brood an environment that permits indigenous peoples to engage and allow the osmosis of ideas about agriculture, medical care and soil conservation. The study contducted by Mdhluli et.al. (2021) on managing, preserving and sharing indigenous knowledge through digital libraries revealed that the Vhavenda youth in Limpopo noticed that the advent of a digital library in preserving, managing and sharing indigenous knowledge is a way to go to restore the cultural heritage that is unknown to them. Mdhluli et.al. (2021) further noted that the development of digital libraries was labelled by the youth as an appropriate measure that has the potential of breeding new opportunities for information agencies, including schools and libraries, to partner with rural communities, national governments and social entrepreneurs to create, manage and preserve knowledge and skills that are unique to communities in Limpopo. The majority of developing countries, worldwide are thus increasingly creating digital libraries of indigenous or traditional knowledge to prevent misappropriation of this knowledge through commercial patents. For example, India has developed a Traditional Knowledge Digital Library that contains information on 36,000 formulations used in Ayurveda (Fredriksson, 2021). Other South Asian countries such as Bangladesh, Bhutan, Maldives, Nepal, Pakistan and Sri Lanka that are members of the South Asian Association for Regional Cooperation (SAARC) (1985) also developed digital library aimed at providing a uniform system for organising, disseminating and retrieving traditional knowledge seamlessly across regions or countries. This digital library contains information on traditional medicine including materials used for treatment i.e. plants, animal products, minerals, their generic or specific method of preparations or designs, their dosage, mode and time of administration and their therapeutic action or application. The SAARC (1985)'s digital library will also promote research on novel drugs, enhancing the region's share of the global herbal medicine market and helping set the international agenda on intellectual property rights.

STRATEGIES FOR PROMOTION AND VALORIZATION INDIGENOUS KNOWLEDGE

Indigenist researchers have advocated for the implementation and adoption of anticolonial strategies as important process in decolonizing, promoting and preserving indigenous communities (Masenya, 2022). Therefore, engaging in anticolonial strategies for the promotion, valorization and protection of indigenous knowledge systems means that academics, indigenous knowledge owners, political leaders of indigenous nations and settler governments will be dismantling the colonialism in all of its current manifestations. Decolonization or Africanization of indigenous knowledge education, developing partnerships, collaboration and participatory opportunities, and analysis and reframing of indigenous knowledge systems policy trajectory have been identified as some of the anticolonial strategies for promotion, valorization and safeguarding of indigenous knowledge.

- **Colonization and Africanization of indigenous knowledge education and curriculum**

The call for Africanisation of knowledge, students and academics are demanding a shift from Eurocentric knowledge systems. Indigenous knowledge has been discredited in the science world although it is considered an inspiring source of strategies for sustainable development. Modern science and technologies thus need to find ways and means for accommodating and using the multi-dimensional framework of indigenous knowledge (Lodhi & Miculecky, 2011). As noted by Mothibe and Sibanda (2019) the curriculum in South African universities is still influenced and geared towards a Western and conventional education system and model. The education system continues to favour western knowledge over indigenous knowledge (Wilson, 2004). Africa thus has a long history of actions of rebuttal to colonial education and trying to achieve curriculum transformation (Motsa, 2017), and a series of curriculum reforms have been implemented in South Africa particularly, since the 1990s. However, there has also been a general disregard of indigenous knowledge system amongst academics and scientists, and as a result, the value of primary knowledge was strategically rejected among academics (Mji, 2019). Therefore, teaching of indigenous knowledge can be a viable tool in the decolonisation and Africanisation of the curriculum. Africanisation is understood as a process of restoring the original living or people's science that has been negatively affected by colonialism and it entails salvaging what has been stripped from the continent. As noted by Ramose (2004) all aspects of indigenous people's live were affected with the most dangerous trend being that Africans were voluntarily and, in many cases, were forced to abandon their entranced knowledge systems under the impression of it being labelled barbaric, backward and ungodly. Bovill (2017) further noted that curricular structures need to include space for innovation, creativity and ensuring relevance to learners and one way of achieving this is to decolonize curriculum. Although African knowledge systems have a rich heritage in that they have shaped and defined the way of life for African people for many centuries, however, for many decades, the African values have been marginalised by an education system in favour of Western values only. In the past years, South African government have been calling for Higher Education Institutions (HEIs)to revise their curriculum to better prepare students for the rapidly changing world and to respond to changing economic and societal needs. Rhodes University and University of Cape Town are among HEIs in South Africa which responded to the call for the decolonization and Africanization of curriculum, and appointed central curriculum committee to coordinate decolonization process within the institutions.

The United Nations Drafting Declaration (2007) on the rights of indigenous people further stated that indigenous individuals, particularly children have the right to all levels and forms of education of the state and when possible, to an education in their own culture. In line with the call for Africanization of the curriculum, there is also an acceptance and recognition of the importance of teaching medical or health science students in higher institutions of learning about traditional medicine (Mothibe & Sibanda, 2019). Higher Education Institutions (HEIs) thus need to decolonize their curriculum by redesigning or redeveloping their courses and innovative pedagogical strategies. However, quality decolonized education is guided by pedagogical principles and methods developed in participation with indigenous communities and based on their culture and tradition (King & Schielmann, 2004).

- **Developing partnerships, collaboration and participatory opportunities**

As noted by Council of Canadian Academies (2015) many organizations and insitutions including memory institutions (Libraries, Archives and Museums) (LAM), worldwide are working to establish partnerships and collaboration in addressing the challenges posed by the digital environment. LAM use collaboration strategies to advance digital preservation work and take advantage of resources in the larger library and digital preservation community. A framework for realizing opportunities for adapting to the digital age by Council of Canadian Academies (2015) outlined participatory and collaborative opportunities as factors for adapting to the digital age. Memory institutions are retaining their relevance in the digital era by encouraging a participatory culture, contributions from communities, from simple tagging activities to sharing of historical knowledge and also designing of preservation systems and software by expert volunteers (Council of Canadian Academies, 2015). Therefore, by reaching out to the communities they serve, memory institutions are not only maintaining relevance and satisfying the expectations of communities, but they are building collaborative networks while also taking advantage of volunteers who can help them in designing preservation systems adapt to the digital age.

As stated by Council of Canadian Academies (2015) collaboration among communities and memory institutions may allow them to become involved in exciting activities that enhance their visibility and to undertake large projects that they could not otherwise resource on their own. Collaborative initiatives are essential for developing and maintaining relationships between memory institutions and various communities, and provide an opportunity for indigenous communities to increase their exposure. For

Valorization, Preservation of Indigenous Knowledge in South Africa

example, as also noted by Council of Canadian Academies (2015), aboriginal communities in Canada are collaborating with museums to create culturally sensitive content management systems to support access to their cultural heritage and facilitate self-representation. Furthermore, the Council of Canadian Academies (2015) provides factors supporting the realization of digital opportunities including the prioritization of digital opportunities and developing new business models for these opportunities, the promotion of standardized Information and Communications Technologies (ICTs) infrastructure, managing partnerships, managing the cloud and managing the various copyrights.

- **Analysis and reframing of indigenous knowledge systems policy trajectory**

The majority of governments departments in South Africa have enacted laws and policies governing the preservation of indigenous knowledge, which are making provision for the establishment of national institutions with responsibility for implementing measures that serve to ensure the promotion and protection of the indigenous knowledge. The Department of Science and Technology (DST) (2004) in South Africa approached the cabinet in pursuit of formulation of indigenous knowledge policy and Acts aimed at promoting and protecting indigenous knowledge. The Protection, Promotion, Development and Management of Indigenous Knowledge Act 6 of 2019) aimed at regulating the equitable distribution of the benefits of the use of indigenous knowledge, protecting the indigenous knowledge from unauthorized use and misappropriation, and providing guidance in the documentation of indigenous knowledge. DST (2016) also developed the National Recordal System (NRS) aimed at recording indigenous knowledge and bridge the chasm between indigenous knowledge systems production and other Western knowledge systems. Although protocols for handling indigenous knowledge help to uphold its interests by developing standards for ethical professional practice, however, they do not provide any legal framework for those who want their cultural and intellectual property rights protected. Developing standards for ethical professional practice among indigenous communities is important as it is about managing risks associated with breaches of intellectual property rights. South African intellectual property systems do not provide effective protection to indigenous knowledge, although most of the indigenous knowledge systems in cultural heritage institutions remains subject to relevant copyright laws.

As noted by Msuya (2007) most of indigenous knowledge systems in developing countries such as South Africa are not legally protected and as a result, much of this knowledge is open to bio-piracy and it can be used without the consent of the indigenous knowledge owners. For example, the lengana plant has been patented for medicinal purposes in African countries and there was no recognition or compensation given to the indigenous communities that shared this knowledge with the global world. Much of indigenous knowledge were collected without the consent of the indigenous owners and the custodial organizations or institutions are now facing the challenges of determining ownership and seeking the direction from the owners on the future of such knowledge. There is therefore a need to reframe indigenous knowledge systems policy to protect indigenous knowledge and their communities, although as compared to other countries, South Africa has emerged as the only country that has instituted the web-based portal of the national heritage resources known as National Heritage Repository, hosted by National Research Foundation (NRF).

South Africa need to also put in place a number of indigenous knowledge policy for the protection of indigenous knowledge and the rights of indigenous knowledge owners, that should also work as decentralized service structures, making it easier to protect and manage indigenous knowledge within indigenous communities. Indigenous knowledge holders and their communities, indigenous researchers, academics, memory and cultural heritage institutions, traditional and political leaders in governments and other relevant stakeholders thus need to be prepared to dismantle the colonialism and bio-piracy by engaging in anti-colonial strategies and policies for the protection and preservation of indigenous knowledge. However, South African government need to ensure that the indigenous knowledge policy and protocols are easily located and be understood by indigenous researchers, academics and indigenous knowledge owners and their communities.

CONCLUSION AND RECOMMENDATIONS

This chapter viewed digital preservation as a viable strategy to safeguard and provide long-term access to indigenous knowledge, in this digital transformation era. The policy frameworks and strategies were also analyzed in this chapter in order to understand the promotion, valorization and preservation of indigenous knowledge for the benefit of indigenous holders and their communities. So far, indigenous knowledge policies, laws and standards have been enacted by various government departments in South Africa in promoting and preserving indigenous knowledge and the recognition of this knowledge is increasingly becoming part of the sustainable development agenda. National and local initiatives, projects and programs are also developed in an attempt to safeguard this irreplaceable knowledge. However, some substantial challenges remain as some of the policies and protocols are not easily located and also not well understood by indigenous researchers, indigenous knowledge owners and their communities. Memory institutions should also prioritize the documentation and preservation of indigenous knowledge and developing digital preservation policy that can serve as a guide. Indigenous communities should also build consultation, partnerships and collaborative networks with various memory institutions, non-governmental organizations and indigenous researchers as this may result in developing digital preservation projects that communities can also use as tools for sustainable development. There is also a need to strengthen the capacities of local authorities including traditional healers, community leaders or elders at their native places as intermediaries to support indigenous communities to manage, preserve and share their indigenous knowledge. As in most cases indigenous knowledge handed down orally from generation to generation, due to weak communication some time it is imposable to transfer exact knowledge. Recommendations suggest that digital technologies be adopted by indigenous knowledge owners and their communities as a strategy to preserve and disseminate indigenous knowledge for long-term accessibility and for use of future generations. Memory institutions should educate or provide training to indigenous knowledge owners on the application of new emerging technologies to valorize, manage and preserve their knowledge. Indigenous knowledge systems policy and laws should also be reviewed by South African government to ensure that they meet international requirements for the safeguarding and preservation of indigenous knowledge. A sui generis approach should be adopted and be used as a guideline to protect and preserve indigenous knowledge systems in South Africa.

REFERENCES

Agrawal, A. (1995). Dismantling the Divide between Indigenous and Scientific Knowledge. *Development and Change*, *26*(3), 413–439. doi:10.1111/j.1467-7660.1995.tb00560.x

Bandhari, H., & Yasunobu, K. (2009). What is Social Capital? A Comprehensive Review of the Concept. *Asian Journal of Social Science*, *37*(3), 480–510. doi:10.1163/156853109X436847

Boikhutso, D. N. (2012). *Methods of Indigenous Knowledge Preservation in South Africa*. Tshwane University of Technology.

Bountouri, L. (2017). Archives in the digital age: standards, policies and tools. United Kingdom: Chandos Publishing (Oxford) Ltd.

Bovill, C. (2017). A Framework to Explore Roles Within Student-Staff Partnerships in Higher Education: Which Students Are Partners, When, and in What Ways? *International Journal for Students as Partners, 1*(1). Advance online publication. doi:10.15173/ijsap.v1i1.3062

Chimalakonda, S., & Nori, K. V. (2020). An ontology-based modeling framework for design of educational technologies. *Smart Learn. Environ., 7*(1), 28. doi:10.118640561-020-00135-6

Chisenga, J. (2002). Indigenous knowledge: Africa's opportunity to contribute to global information content. *South African Journal of Library and Information Science, 68*(1), 16–22.

Coleman, J. S. (1990). *Foundations of social theory*. Harvard University Press.

Corcoran, N., & Duane, A. (2018). Using Social Media to Enable Staff Knowledge Sharing in Higher Education Institutions. *AJIS. Australasian Journal of Information Systems, 22*. Advance online publication. doi:10.3127/ajis.v22i0.1647

Council of Canadians Academies. (2015). Leading in the digital world: Opportunities for Canada's memory institutions. The expert panel on memory institutions in the digital revolution. Canada: Ottawa.

Department of Science and Technology (DST). (2004). *Indigenous Knowledge Systems*. DST.

Department of Science and Technology (DST). (2016). Protection, promotion, development and management of indigenous knowledge systems bill. South Africa: Pretoria.

Duranti, L. (2010). The long-term preservation of the digital heritage: A case study of universities' institutional repositories. *JLIS.it. 1*(1), 157–168.

Fredriksson, M. (2021). India's Traditional Knowledge Digital Library and the Politics of Patent Classifications. *Law and Critique*. Doi.org/10.1007/s10978-021-09299-7 PMID:36915708

Gaura, A. S., Honjia, M. A., & Baoshan, G. E. (2019). MNC strategy, knowledge transfer context and knowledge flow in MNEs. *Journal of Knowledge Management, 23*(9), 1885–1900. doi:10.1108/JKM-08-2018-0476

Gittell, R. J., & Vidal, A. (1998). *Community organizing: Building social capital as a development strategy*. Sage Publications, Inc. doi:10.4135/9781452220567

Gorjestani, N. (2000). Indigenous knowledge for development: Opportunities and challenges. *The UNCTAD Conference on Traditional Knowledge in* Geneva. The World Bank.

Happel, H., Maalej, W., & Seedorf, S. (2010). *Applications of Ontologies in Collaborative Software Development*. . doi:10.1007/978-3-642-10294-3_6

Haron, H., & Hamiz, M. (2014). An Ontological Framework to Preserve Malay Indigenous Health Knowledge. *Journal of Computational and Theoretical Nanoscience, 20*(1), 226–230.

Hunter, J. (2005). The Role of Information Technologies in Indigenous Knowledge Management. *Australian Academic and Research Libraries*, *36*(2), 109–124. doi:10.1080/00048623.2005.10721252

IFLA/UNESCO. (2010). *Manifesto for Digital Libraries*. National Library of the Netherlands.

Kaya, H., & Seleti, Y. N. (2013). African Indigenous Knowledge Systems and Relevance of Higher Education in South Africa. *International Education Journal: Comparative Perspectives*, *12*(1), 30–44.

Keane, M., Khupe, C., & Seehawer, M. (2017). Decolonizing methodology: Who benefits from indigenous knowledge research? *Educ. Res. Soc. Change*, *6*(1), 12–24. doi:10.17159/2221-4070/2017/v6i1a2

King, L., & Schielmann, S. (2004). *The Challenge of indigenous education: practice and perspectives. Project: Indigenous education*. UNESCO.

Kozhakhmet, S., & Nazri, M. (2017). Governing Knowledge Sharing Behavior in Post-Soviet Kazakhstan. *Journal of Workplace Learning*, *29*(3), 1–18. doi:10.1108/JWL-06-2016-0053

Lemma, M., & Hoffmann, V. (2005). The Agricultural Knowledge System in Tigray, Ethiopia: Empirical Study about its Recent History and Actual Effectiveness. *The Global Food and Product Chain: Dynamics, Innovations, Conflicts, Strategies, Tropentag 2005*. Stuttgart-Hohenheim. http://www.tropentag. de/2005/proceedings/node152.html#2487

Liana, R. (2011). An Ontology-Based Framework for Modeling User Behavior. A Case Study in Knowledge Management. *IEEE Transactions on Systems, Man, and Cybernetics. Part A, Systems and Humans*, *41*(4), 772–783. doi:10.1109/TSMCA.2011.2132712

Likalu, M., Abdulla, R., Selamat, M. H., Ibrahim, H., & Nor, M. Z. M. (2010). A framework of collaborative knowledge management system in open source software development environment. *Computer and Information Science*, *3*(1), 81–90. doi:10.5539/cis.v3n1p81

Lodhi, S & Miculecky, P. (2011). *Motives and modes of indigenous knowledge management*.

Masenya, T. M. (2018). *A Framework for preservation of digital resources in academic libraries in South Africa*. [PhD thesis, University of South Africa].

Masenya, T. M. (2022). Decolonization of Indigenous Knowledge Systems in South Africa: Impact of Policy and Protocols. [IJKM]. *International Journal of Knowledge Management*, *18*(1), 1–22. doi:10.4018/ IJKM.310005

Matenge, S. T. P., Van der Merwe, D., De Beer, D., Bosman, M. J. C., & Kruger, A. (2012). Consumers' beliefs on indigenous and traditional foods and acceptance of products made with cow pea leaves. *African Journal of Agricultural Research*, *7*(14), 2243–2254.

Mdhluli, T. D., Mokgoatšana, S., Kugara, S. L., & Vuma, L. (2021). Knowledge management: Preserving, managing and sharing indigenous knowledge through digital library. *Hervormde Teologiese Studies*, *77*(2), a6795. doi:10.4102/hts.v77i2.6795

Mji, G. (2019). *Opting for a walk without limbs: the avoidance of Stellenbosch University to be an African University*. Stellenbosch University Library Auditorium.

Mothibe, M. E & Sibanda, M. (2019). *African Traditional Medicine: South African Perspective.* InTech. . doi:10.5772/intechopen.83790

Motsa, Z. (2017). When the lion tells the story: A response from South Africa. *Higher Education Research & Development, 36*(1), 28–35. doi:10.1080/07294360.2017.1249070

Msuya, J. (2007). Challenges and opportunities in the protection and preservation of indigenous knowledge in Africa. *International Journal of Information Ethics, 7,* 1–8.

Nduka, S. C., & Oyelude, A. A. (2019). Goge Africa: Preserving Indigenous Knowledge Innovatively through Mass Media Technology. *Preservation. Digital Technology & Culture, 48*(3-4), 120–128. doi:10.1515/pdtc-2019-0007

Nyumba, J. B. (2006). *The role of the library in promoting the application of indigenous knowledge (ik) in development projects.* IFLA.

Ogundipe, O. O. (2005). *The Librarianship of Developing Countries: The Librarianship of Diminished Resources.* Ikofa Press.

Preservica. (2016). *How Preservica works.* Preservica. http://preservica.com/ preservica-works.

Putnam, R. (2007). E pluribus Unum Diversity and community in the twenty-first century. *Scandinavian Political Studies, 30*(2), 137–174. doi:10.1111/j.1467-9477.2007.00176.x

Ramose, M. B. (2004). *In search of an African identity.* South African Journal of Education.

Ross, S. (2007). *Digital Preservation, Archival Science and Methodological Foundations for Digital Libraries, Keynote Address at the 11th European Conference on Digital Libraries (ECDL).* Budapest: HATII at the University of Glasgow.

Sagsan, M. (2009). Knowledge management discipline: Test for an undergraduate program in Turkey. *Electronic Journal of Knowledge Management, 7*(5), 627–636.

San Nicolas Roca, T., & Parrish, J. (2013). *Using Social Media to Capture and Convey Cultural Knowledge: A Case of Chamorro People. System Sciences (HICSS), 2013 46th Hawaii International Conference.* IEEE. 10.1109/HICSS.2013.593

Senanayake, S. G. (2006). Indigenous knowledge as a key to sustainable development. *Journal of Agricultural Science, 2*(1).

Sithole, J. (2007). The challenges faced by African *libraries and information centres in documenting and preserving indigenous knowledge. IFLA Journal, 33*(2), 117–123. doi:10.1177/0340035207080304

Taye, M. M. (2010). Understanding Semantic Web and Ontologies: Theory and Applications. *Journal of Computing, 2*(6).

Tebes, J. K., Champine, R. B., Matlin, S. L., & Strambler, M. J. (2019). Population health and trauma-informed practice: Implications for programs, systems, and policies. *American Journal of Community Psychology, 64*(3-4), 494–508. doi:10.1002/ajcp.12382 PMID:31444915

Thomas, A., & Gupta, V. (2022). The role of motivation theories in knowledge sharing: An integrative theoretical reviews and future research agenda. *Kybernetes*, *51*(1), 116–140.

Vassev, E., & Hinchey, M. (2015). Knowledge Representation for Adaptive and Self-aware Systems. In: Wirsing, M., Hölzl, M., Koch, N., Mayer, P. (eds) Software Engineering for Collective Autonomic Systems. Lecture Notes in Computer Science. Springer, Cham. doi:10.1007/978-3-319-16310-9_6

Virtanen, P. K. (2015). Indigenous social media practices in Southwestern Amazonia. *AlterNative: An International Journal of Indigenous Peoples,* 11, 4, 350.

World Council of Indigenous Peoples (WCIP) (1998). *World Council of Indigenous Peoples Report.* WCIP.

World Health Organization (WHO). (2008). [- *Primary Health Care: Now More Than Ever.* Geneva.]. *World Health Report.* WHO.

Yannus, F. (2017). Preservation of indigenous knowledge by public libraries in Westcliff. Chatsworth, Durban. University of Western Cape.

KEY TERMS AND DEFINITIONS

Digital Preservation: It is aiming to ensure the protection or safeguarding of knowledge of continuing value through the application of preservation strategies, methods and technologies necessary to ensure that this knowledge remains accessible and usable by present and future generations.

Digital Transformation: It create innovative ways for organizations to improve their business practices and processes through the application and integration of new emerging digital or innovative technologies

Indigenous Knowledge: It is regarded as tacit knowledge that exists in the minds of indigenous people and community elders which is passed from one generation to the other through the word of mouth.

Indigenous Communities: distinct social and ethnic groups that share collective cultural values, unique languages, beliefs and possess invaluable knowledge of practices for the sustainable management of their natural resources.

Knowledge Sharing: It is the process in which knowledge is shared or communicated to other individuals or groups within the organisations through community of practices, storytelling, oral tradition, face-to-face interactions or the use of digital technologies.

Chapter 3

Students' Entrepreneurship Development Through Indigenous Palm Wine Production and Alcohol Distillation:
The Case of Yala–Obubra Community

Valentine Joseph Owan
https://orcid.org/0000-0001-5715-3428
University of Calabar, Nigeria & Ultimate Research Network, Nigeria

John Asuquo Ekpenyong
https://orcid.org/0000-0002-1477-2605
University of Calabar, Nigeria

Mercy Valentine Owan
University of Calabar, Nigeria & Ultimate Research Network, Nigeria

Joshua Nkpokpo Owan
Independent Researcher, Nigeria

Aidam Benjamin Ekereke
University of Calabar, Nigeria

ABSTRACT

This chapter used a qualitative approach to investigate and describe the palm wine production and alcohol distillation practices of the indigenous people of the Yala-Obubra community in Cross River State, Nigeria. The chapter involved palm wine tappers and alcohol distillers (n = 10). A focus group discussion was held with the respondents, with audio recordings and notes for data collection. The study documented several practices in palm wine production and alcohol distillation and discovered declining palm tree population, climate change, high cost of production, lack of access to credit and social amenities, and stealing as some challenges faced in producing palm wine and distillation of alcohol. The chapter recorded some economic opportunities in the indigenous production of palm wine and distillation of alcohol, and discussed the relevance of these two traditional practices in promoting entrepreneurship among students. The implications of this study's findings were discussed for the promotion of sustainable production and preservation of these traditional practices in Nigeria.

DOI: 10.4018/978-1-6684-7024-4.ch003

Copyright © 2023, IGI Global. Copying or distributing in print or electronic forms without written permission of IGI Global is prohibited.

INTRODUCTION AND BACKGROUND

Over the years, there has been a persistent cry in Nigeria among stakeholders due to the issue of unemployment among youths. A significant portion of the unemployed people have graduated from different tertiary institutions in Nigeria (Owan et al., 2022a). In the past, different scholars have advocated for restructuring the tertiary education curriculum to improve students' entrepreneurial skills for job creation (Eje et al., 2021; Owan et al., 2021; 2022b). However, the unemployment situation keeps worsening with each passing year. Recently, Oseni and Oyelade (2023) analysed available World Bank data on unemployment from 1981 to 2020 and revealed that the average proportion of the labour force in Nigeria was 76.77%, with the lowest and highest values falling between 71.7% and 79.35% respectively. In contrast, the rate of employment growth was only 17.45% annually. This substantial difference explains why the compensation for employees is low, with a growth rate of only 35.96%. At the time of writing, Nigeria's unemployment rate stood at 41% (Osabohien, 2023).

The high unemployment rate has created a need for university students to devise new strategies to generate income and create self-employment opportunities. It has been argued that no government can employ all its citizens (Ekaette et al., 2019; Odigwe & Owan, 2019), although highly developed and industrialised nations have small unemployment rates. One way that Nigerian students and graduates can leverage to free themselves from the burden of unemployment and poverty is to consider developing entrepreneurial skills and mindset. Some studies have shown that the entrepreneurship activities of students are critical in poverty reduction (Lee & Rodríguez-Pose, 2021); however, students' behavioural changes were required (Si et al., 2015).

From the preceding, it is imperative for students to consider venturing into different initiatives to enhance their earnings and liberate themselves from poverty. This qualitative research paper discusses the importance of indigenous practices such as local palm wine production and alcohol distillation in enhancing students' entrepreneurship development. Palm wine is a traditional beverage very common in Nigeria, like most African countries that grow palm (Akinrotoye, 2014). It is a whitish liquid consumed throughout the tropics (Uzogara et al., 1990). However, it must be noted that fermented palm wine can produce spirits through a distillation process. The distillation process involves heating the fermented palm wine to a high temperature to produce steam, which is then condensed into liquid form, resulting in a more concentrated and potent alcoholic beverage. Although both can be termed alcoholic drinks, palm wine is different from the spirit produced from it in several regards. First, palm wine is a mildly alcoholic beverage, with an alcohol content ranging from 2% to 6% (Lal et al., 2003). In contrast, the alcohol produced from palm wine is much stronger, with an alcohol content of around 40% to 43% (Tagba et al., 2018). Palm wine has a sweet, slightly sour taste, with a fruity aroma that is often compared to that of champagne. Unfermented palm wine is clean, sweet, colourless syrup, which is mainly sucrose (Okafor, 1975). The alcohol produced from palm wine, however, has a more intense flavour and a stronger, more pungent aroma. Palm wine is produced by tapping the sap of palm trees and collecting it in containers. The alcohol produced from palm wine is made by fermenting it and then distilling it. The alcohol from palm wine is durable and can be bottled for export to other countries. On the contrary, palm wine is a perishable product typically consumed locally and regionally.

Nevertheless, through the pasteurisation process (boiling fresh palm wine up boiling point of 70 to 75°C) followed by refrigeration, palm wine can have a long-lasting duration (Ikegwu, 2014). Pasteurising palm wine at 75°C for 45 minutes and packaging it for up to 24 months with no preservatives does not affect the nutrients or deteriorate the content (Obahiagbon & Oviasogie, 2007). This suggests that pasteurised palm wine and distilled alcohol can be good sources of income for those practising the trade, particularly in rural areas where formal employment opportunities are limited.

Despite the importance of traditional palm wine production and alcohol distillation practices, which have the potential for entrepreneurship development in Africa, these practices are often overlooked and undervalued by policymakers, investors, and other stakeholders. This is partly due to the perception that such traditional practices are obsolete and that modernisation and formalisation are necessary for economic growth and development. Unfortunately, this perspective overlooks the potential of these two traditional practices to drive entrepreneurship and economic growth in Africa, particularly when combined with modern techniques and technologies. For instance, some youths see such practices as occupations for poor or hopeless individuals. Others tend to believe that these practices are meant for those in rural localities. The high rate of rural-urban migration in Nigeria due to the quest for white-collar jobs and employment opportunities (Olorunfemi, 2023) has further limited youth participation in agriculture-related activities such as palm wine production and distillation (Ovharhe et al., 2022).

Producing palm wine and distilled spirits requires complex and expensive scientific procedures. This involves selecting raw materials, milling and mashing to create a fermentable mash, fermenting with yeast, and distilling to separate alcohol from water and impurities. Thus, different devices and machines will be required for production. These might be very expensive for a beginner to afford. However, it is common knowledge that there are traditional approaches to palm wine and distilled spirits production that are less expensive to follow. Nevertheless, the indigenous processes involved in palm wine production and alcohol distillation is not easily accessible since only very few people possess such information. Moreover, the knowledge of these practices cannot be easily accessed from the existing literature or the Internet since such techniques have not been previously documented. Therefore, it is important to extract such information from the few individuals possessing them and document them electronically to guide against its extinction and pass it on to newer generations interested in it. Along these lines, this chapter aims to provide a comprehensive overview of indigenous palm wine production and alcohol distillation practices in Africa and to explore the implications of these practices for entrepreneurship development.

Research Objectives

The objectives of this chapter are to:

- Identify the steps and materials required to tap palm wine in the context of the Yala-Obubra Community;
- Reveal the causes of poor taste in the palm wine of some tappers in the community;
- Uncover the reasons for differentiated drunkenness patterns among different palm-wine consumers;
- Identify the materials and processes involved in indigenous alcohol distillation practices in the community;
- Reveal the challenges facing traditional palm-wine production and distillation of alcohol in the community.

LITERATURE REVIEW

Empirical studies continue to explore ways in which the indigenous palm wine or the yeast associated with it can be used for the production of other useful substances such as vinegar, juice and medicine (Akinrotoye, 2014; Samuel et al., 2016). This interest has been driven by several factors, including the recognition of the potential of indigenous practices to create jobs, generate income and support local development, the increasing demand for high-quality and authentic African products in both local and international markets and the growing awareness of the need to preserve and promote African cultural heritage (Owan et al., 2020).

Studies on entrepreneurship has been conducted to identify ways in which palm wine and alcohol distillation can improve the livelihoods of rural individuals. For instance, Scholtes (2009) found that small-scale ethanol production shows promise for supplying energy in remote areas and establishing related value chains, particularly in rural Africa, for purposes other than transportation. Given the easy integration of sugarcane cultivation and ethanol production through small-scale distilleries, smallholders engaged in cane production can benefit significantly from this approach. Similarly, McCoy et al. (2013) discovered that alcohol production serves as an adaptive livelihood strategy for women in agriculture, allowing them to maintain control over income and support their households, but it also exposes them to increased vulnerability through risky sexual behaviours). Another study discovered that palm wine is a major source of livelihood across the various rural communities studied (Macie & Martins, 2019). Studies on entrepreneurship have shown that income can be generated from numerous sources. For example, Odigwe et al. (2018) identified baking and computer business operations as two sources of income generation for students. Another study identified farm enterprises as a sustainable source of vocational venture for students (Francis et al., 2019). The challenges hindering entrepreneurship in Nigeria have been extensively researched, and there is a general agreement among scholars that several factors hinder students from venturing into different vocational activities. These factors include poor entrepreneurial culture, limited access to funds, a weak knowledge-based economy with low competitiveness, insufficient entrepreneurial education resources, a lack of practical entrepreneurship programs in school curricula, negative societal attitudes towards technical and vocational education, inadequate teaching and learning facilities, government insensitivity towards enterprise creation and expansion strategies, ineffective program management in certain areas, inadequate parental care, erosion of family values and discipline, and political manipulation of youth organisations (Babatunde et al., 2021).

Nevertheless, previous studies have not adequately paid attention to the processes involved in tapping palm wine or traditional alcohol distillation. Although various methods are used across contexts, the non-documentation of these processes in the literature leaves a gap that should be filled. Traditional methods of palm wine and alcohol production need to be documented to strengthen entrepreneurial opportunities and sustain such practices from extinction. Bridging these gaps, the current study was designed to highlight the processes involved in the traditional production of alcohol and the challenges rural producers face.

CONTEXT OF YALA-OBUBRA COMMUNITY

Yala-Obubra community, also known as Nkum Okpambe, is in Obubra Local Government Area of Cross River State, Nigeria. Nkum Okpambe, a Yala tribe of the larger Idoma nation predominantly known for hunting, fishing and crop farming, are extremely peaceful, loving, hospitable and enterprising. The community's people represent a diplomatic melting point between their fellow Obubra and Ikom neighbours. The community is bounded to the north by the cross river, south by the Ofumbongha community, east by the Okosora community and West by the Obokpa community, all in Cross River State.

The community is rich in cultural practices and celebrates different festivals, such as the new yam festival and Okpambe fishing festival, with two massive lakes under their belt. There are numerous stone monoliths, including Lechor Olikplikpo, a mysterious stone that measures just arm's length but comparatively longer than anyone that dares to measure their height with it. However, at the time of writing, the community lacked government presence and social amenities such as motorable roads and electricity. Consequently, most of its indigenes pass through what may be regarded as "hell" to access urban areas. Mostly, the people are farmers, palm wine tappers, fishermen, hunters and artisans. Farmers in this community cultivate cash crops like rice, oil palm, corn, oranges, plantain and cocoa, and food crops like yam, cocoa yam, vegetables and so forth. The population of inhabitants of this community is approximately 3000; however, due to rural-urban migration, half of this population is always found in the community (Independent National Electoral Commission, 2022).

Regarding tourism potential, the community has beautiful sand beaches, a peaceful and serene environment, and a rich cultural heritage. The community also has over 500 natural and artificial fishponds in major lakes. This community was chosen because some of the most experienced palm wine producers and alcohol distillers can be found there. Secondly, the alcohol produced from this part of the country is adjudged the best against the ethanol produced in other regions.

RESEARCH METHODOLOGY

This study adopted qualitative research methods based on the philosophy of interpretivism. Interpretivism is a research philosophy that emphasises the importance of understanding human behaviour and social phenomena from the perspective of the individuals involved (Alharahsheh & Pius, 2020). The interpretive philosophy was considered appropriate for this study because it enabled the researchers to understand the social and cultural significance of palm wine production and alcohol distillation activities from the perspective of the community members involved. The researchers followed the ethnographic case study design in this study. "Ethnographic case studies employ ethnographic methods and focus on building arguments about the cultural, group, or community formation or examining other sociocultural phenomena" (Schwandt & Gates, 2018: 344).

Study Participants

The participants of this study were 10 palm wine tappers (producers) and alcohol distillers in Yala-Obubra, a rural community in Obubra Local Government Area of Cross River State, Nigeria. These participants were carefully chosen due to their years of experience in the activities. The eligibility criteria were that a potential participant is a resident of the Yala-Obubra community, producing palm wine and alcohol, with over 10 years of experience. This cut-off in the age range was to recruit individuals with at least a decade of experience. Participants who are residents of the community that produce only palm wine without alcohol, regardless of their years of experience, were excluded. It is impossible to find rural alcohol producers that do not tap palm wine.

Data Collection and Analysis

The researchers assembled the 10 participants in a hall with chairs arranged semi-circularly. This arrangement enabled the participants to see each other and engage in eye contact and nonverbal communication. After all the participants were seated, the researchers introduced themselves and the purpose of the study thereof. They also explained the nature of the focus group discussion and obtained the participants' informed consent to participate in the study. The researchers began the focus group discussion with an icebreaker activity to help the participants feel comfortable and encourage open discussion. The researchers took notes using notebooks during the discussion to record key points, themes, and ideas, whereas audio recordings of the entire conversation were made through sound recorders. The researchers moderated the entire process by asking follow-up questions, clarifying participants' responses, and encouraging further discussion. Upon completion, the researchers thanked the participants for their time and input and provided an opportunity for them to ask any questions they had. The researchers transcribed the audio recording of the focus group discussion and analysed the data. The researchers used the information from the discussion to identify key themes to develop insights and draw conclusions.

Verifiability and Trustworthiness

Note-taking is a valuable process in qualitative research, as it allows the researcher to capture important points that may not be captured by audio or video recordings. This process allows the researcher to record data in real-time, enabling them to capture a comprehensive discussion account. While note-taking is an important instrument for data collection in qualitative research, there is no need for formal validity and reliability tests, as note-taking is a subjective process that depends on the researcher's interpretation and understanding of the discussion (Hussein, 2022). In the current study, the researchers enhanced validity by ensuring that the notes were taken by one of the co-authors, who was knowledgeable about palm wine production and alcohol distillation and the participants' culture. This enabled the researchers to record the nuances of the discussion and avoid misinterpretation accurately.

Ethical Considerations

The researchers obtained informed consent from all participants before conducting the focus group discussion and recording any audio. The researchers ensured that the participants knew their participation was voluntary and that they could withdraw at any time without consequence. During the focus group discussion, the researchers ensured that all participants were given equal opportunities to express their opinions and that no one was discriminated against based on their tribe, religion, or other personal characteristics. The researchers also ensured that the data collected was used only for the study and was not shared with any third-party individuals or organisations without the explicit consent of the participants. Lastly, the researchers acknowledged the participants' contributions to the study by allowing them to review the findings and provide feedback.

RESULTS OF THE STUDY

The results from the focus group discussion were organised under the following themes in line with the objectives of this study.

Demographic Information

Regarding the demographic characteristics of the respondents, all the participants were males, as the activities are exclusively male-dominated, with an average age of 46.9 years and an average experience of 15.8 years. In terms of education, 30% (n = 3) had no formal education; 20% (n = 2) completed primary education; 40% (n = 4) completed secondary education, whereas 10% (n = 1) completed university education.

Indigenous Palm Wine Tapping Processes in Yala-Obubra

The participants were asked to discuss the steps involved in tapping palm wine according to their traditional methods. The various responses of the participants were synthesised. According to the respondents, the steps involved in palm wine production are:

Selection of mature palm trees: According to the participants, this process involves looking for suitable palm species, checking for mature trees with good health and suitability, and planning for sustainability by avoiding tapping trees that are too young. The tapper goes into the farmland (field) and selects or picks out all the mature palm trees ready for felling based on the numbers or quantities desired for that tapping season. This process is called *ikoro olala.*

Clearing the surrounding area: This process involves using a machete by the tapper to eliminate all grasses, shrubs or other materials that might hinder the next process. Thus, the tapper ensures that the area around the tree is cleared of any obstacles that may hinder the felling process. This process is known and called *Ebeh Onghongho Sigah Ikiro.*

Felling of the palm trees: The third stage is called *Ikiro Ofufu.* It requires falling axes, knives, and hoes for digging. In this stage, the tapper cuts the base of the palm tree using a sharp machete or axe, ensuring that the cut is deep enough to allow the tree to fall in the desired direction. The tapper must ensure that he digs in a manner that allows for the palm tree to fall in the desired direction. In some cases, once the cut is made, a rope could be used to pull the tree in the desired direction to ensure that it falls safely. These could be done by hired or self labour.

Pruning: This is called *Ikiro Opraprah.* The process involves using a sharp machete to cut the fronds and expose the tapping points. The tapper should ensure not to cut too much of the frond to avoid damaging the tree. Thus, the palm fronds are cut out, kept clean, and ready for tapping. Again, this process requires hiring or self labour.

Clearing/cleaning of the road (tracts): In this stage, the tapper keeps the tracts leading to the various felled palm trees clean. This is done to avoid disturbances during tapping and movement from one point to another. The process involves using sharp machetes and can involve both self and employed labour. This process is called *okpolo ongbhogho.*

Heating the cut edges of the pruned palm tree: This step involves the use of prepared bundles of dry palm rods with fire at one end to activate the fresh liquid (palm wine) basically for effective (maximal) production, good taste and prevention of palm-weevils (pests) attack and invasion that can ruin the production process. The fire on the dry palm rods is pointed around the trunk (*Okor*) of the pruned palm tree. The cylindrical trunk represents what is left after pruning all the palm fronds from their crown shafts. This is where the clay pot (*Ukpasi ikiro*) or polythene bag (*waterproof*) is suspended for the collection of palm wine.

Tapping proper: This is the process wherein the tapper cuts off the fermented surfaces of the pruned edge of the palm tree's trunk. Once this is done, clay pots or polythene bags are suspended from collecting all the saps dropping from the palm tree. In Yala-Obubra, this is done two times daily (morning and evening). Tapping requires the use of a very sharp knife to enhance the cutting process and make the surface of the edge of the palm tree trunk to be very clean. In using the machete during this stage, the tapper should not strike the knife; instead, he should use the levering process. Levering involves using the machete as a lever to force it into the topmost edge of the trunk. To do this, the machete is placed against the desired position on the edge of the pruned palm tree trunk, and then pressure is applied to the handle and top region of the knife to push the blade into the palm tree.

Palm wine collection: This stage requires using clay pots (*Ukpasi ikiro*)/polythene bags to collect extracted saps. In this stage, the trimmed edges of the pruned palm are covered with clay pots or polythene bags (depending on what is available or preferable). The clay pots or polythene bags serve as the mechanism where the tapper collects the fresh liquid (palm wine). As a note, the participants discussed that the choice between the use of clay pots or polythene bags depends on several factors such as availability, cost, the quantity of production and the demand of the end-users or consumers of the palm wine.

For availability, they explained that clay pots are sometimes inaccessible due to their very low production in the Yala-Obubra community. They added that a clay pot is sold at the rate of N500, making it very expensive compared to polythene bags sold at the rate of N50. The disparity in the price also affects the preference of most tappers who opt for polythene. They also advised that clay pots are recommended for small-scale production and the use of polythene for large-scale production. During cultural events such as festivals (*Ogbuk*), naming ceremonies (*liyi ojoje*), child dedications (*oyi oyigiyigi*), or hirings (*leligha*), special requests can be made for palm wine collected through clay pots; however, the price is usually different from that collected with polythene bags. In terms of quality, all the participants rated palm wine produced using clay pots to be of higher quality than that produced using polythene bags.

Regarding the quality between the two palm-wine collection methods, some study participants revealed the following:

Participant 4: *The difference between waterproof wine and the one from clay pot (Ukpasi Ikoro) is very clear. The wine from a clay pot is always very cool and fresh, whereas waterproof wine is always very hot. When you drink the two, you will taste the difference without anyone telling you.*

Participant 8: *Palm wine collected through clay pots has a wider acceptance among consumers than those collected from waterproofs. Most drinkers complain of stomach aches after consuming palm wine tapped using waterproof. Because of this, anytime I use waterproof to tap, I struggle to sell up to 40 litres of palm wine in a day. However, whenever I use clay pots, people rush to buy them.*

Participant 3: *Because of the low acceptance of waterproof collected palm wine, I do not make commercial sales of fresh palm wine whenever I use waterproof. I only supply fresh palm wine when not producing in large quantities. Usually, when I produce in large quantities, like most other tappers here, I aim to convert fresh palm wine to alcohol after fermentation. Waterproofing is preferred in this case* *due to the cost associated with having to buy many clay pots that are very delicate. Nevertheless, when the number of palm trees I felled is like 10 or anything less, I use my clay pots, and during that time, fermentation to alcohol is not done; I only supply palm wine sellers or people with occasions or based on special requests.*

Causes of the Poor Taste of Palm Wine from Some Tappers

Respondents were asked to discuss why some palm wine products yield a poor or sour taste. After deliberations among the participants, the following factors were noted as causes of poor palm wine taste. These included individual differences in tapping approach, poor maintenance culture of the tapping instrument such as knife, sharpening, washing (cleaning) of the pots, invasion of certain insects like Agàyankpa, Edangblan and bees, tapping period (intervals), i.e., tapping two times daily (morning and evening) at inappropriate time schedules.

Reasons for Differential Drunkenness Patterns among Palm Wine Consumers

Participants were further asked to explain why some palm wines are more potent in promoting drunkenness among individuals consuming the same quantity. According to the participants, the toxicity of palm wine is based on the following factors: the soil texture, the age (maturity) of palm trees, the tapping season (rainy or dry season, but the latter is recommended) and the tapping apparatus (e.g., polythene bags, clay pots). The participants also mentioned personal factors such as blood group, the nature (ability) of the individual drinking the palm wine and family traits. The researchers visited the palm wine production site of Participant 5, aged 64 years, with over 20 years of experience in palm wine production and alcohol distillation. Subsequently, the following photographs were taken to substantiate the writing.

Indigenous Alcohol Distillation Practices in Yala-Obubra

There are a series of tapping processes that lead to the extraction of alcohol in Yala-Obubra, as revealed by this study's participants. The processes which were thoroughly discussed include:

Collection of palm wine: This is the process whereby the "tapped" fresh palm wine is collected to a central point to prepare for the distillation process. It requires several containers, such as pots, drums (both plastics/tin), and gallons of different sizes. Figures 5 and 6 show how palm wine has been collected into different containers.

Fermentation: the fresh palm wine is stored in the container for about 1-2 weeks before the distillation processes based on the boast of fresh palm collected daily by the tapper. Fermentation duration lasts between 1-3 weeks for proper and good alcohol. The tapper learns that the stored wine is ready for distilling by observation and the amount of yeast that settles at the bottom of the stored containers. Figure 7 shows palm wine undergoing fermentation at a production site.

Materials required: Several apparatus/equipment is needed here, which are locally produced or made available by the tapper. These include boiling pots/drums, water, firewood, distilling pipes, receivers, funnels, corks, crushed cassava or rotten plantain/tissue or soak gari, carved wooden boats, sharp pointers, and stone of big sizes. The pots/boiling drums serve as an instrument for heating the palm wine to change of stage, i.e., liquid-gas. Fire/firewood provides the heating effects for cooking/boiling procedures. The cork connects the distilling pipes to the pots or boiling drums. A carved wooden boat

Figure 1. Front view of a pruned palm tree producing fresh palm wine

Figure 2. Back view of pruned palm tree producing fresh palm wine

serves as the condenser that aids change of state (that is, palm-gas-alcohol). Crushed cassava, gari or rotten plantain tissue serve as seals that prevent evaporation (escape of gaseous alcohol to the atmosphere. Stones serve as locally made triple stands where the boil pods or boiling drums are placed. Dry

Figure 3. Pruned palm tree producing wine with cleaned Rafias on top of it

Figure 4. Pruned palm tree producing palm wine fitted with polythene bag

woods serve as sources of fuel for heating that aid temperature change. Receivers are for the collection of distilled spirits after condensation. In the olden days, empty bottles, calabash, and pots were used; however, gallons are common nowadays. The funnel prevents waste during high wind or breeze and aids the safe collection of alcohol. The pointer helps to direct the flow of alcohol into the receiver, whereas the cotton wool is used for filtration.

Figure 5. Palm wine collected and stored in containers

Figure 6. Collected palm wine undergoing fermentation

Figure 7. Left view of palm wine undergoing heating

Alcohol Distillation: The distillation of palm wine typically involves using a pot still, a simple device consisting of a large pot with a lid, a tube or pipe to carry the vapour, and a condenser (a canoe-like object) to cool and collect the distilled liquid. The pot is filled with fermented palm wine and heated at a regulated temperature over a fire. As the liquid is heated, the alcohol and other volatile compounds evaporate and rise through the tube or pipe. The vapour is then directed through the condenser, which cools the vapour and causes it to condense back into a liquid. The resulting liquid is collected in a container and can be further distilled to increase its alcohol content. The process can be repeated several times until the desired alcohol concentration is reached. However, it is important to note that the traditional distillation process for palm wine can be risky and potentially dangerous. This is because impurities can be present in fermented palm wine, producing toxic compounds like methanol. Additionally, using open flames and other heat sources can pose a fire hazard if not used properly. To mitigate these risks, it is recommended that only experienced individuals carry out the distillation process and that proper safety measures are taken, such as using a well-ventilated area and ensuring that the steel is free from contaminants. Figures 8 to 12 display some of these procedures.

Challenges to Traditional Palm Wine Production and Distillation of Spirits In Yala-Obubra

The participants identified the following challenges in their palm wine production and alcohol distillation practices.

Declining palm tree population: One of the major challenges to traditional palm wine production is the declining population of palm trees. Palm trees are the primary source of palm wine, and as the number of trees decreases, the availability of palm wine also decreases. This is especially so because, in the Yala-Obubra community, the destructive approach to palm wine tapping is prevalent. This means that as a palm tree is felled and wine is tapped off it, that tree ceases to exist. The recent surge in palm oil prices also challenges indigenous palm wine tappers. Buttressing this point, participant 2 said:

One of our biggest problems right now is having access to land with plenty of mature palm trees. God planted most of the palm trees used for tapping, and we were only born to meet and harvest them. Some of us, like me, have finished tapping all the mature palm trees in our family forest; I now buy from community members willing to sell.

Moreover, participant 9 added:

Recently, there has been a massive increase in the price of palm oil. As a result, many people are no longer selling their palm trees for wine production. They prefer to harvest palm fruits and process them into oil which they sell at very good prices. Palm kernel is now a hot cake; almost all oil producers sell palm oil and its associated kernel. This gives them extra income, and by comparison, it seems rational to produce palm oil rather than palm wine which destroys the trees.

Climate change: Climate change has also been identified as a challenge to traditional palm wine production in the Yala-Obubra community. Changes in temperature and rainfall patterns can affect the production of sap and the growth of palm trees, leading to reduced yields. For instance, participant 7 favoured the dry season as the best time for palm wine production, with the highest yield. Participant 7 added that:

During the dry season, the wine comes out very well when taping. You will tap a few palm trees and have production in relatively large quantities, but during the rainy season, palm wine is expensive because of low production. Only a few individuals tap during that time.

High cost of production: The high cost of production is another challenge to traditional palm wine tappers. The equipment and materials needed for palm wine production and alcohol distillation are expensive, making it difficult for small-scale producers to compete with larger commercial producers. Most participants, who do not have palm trees on their private or family lands, attested to buying them at a high cost from community members willing to sell. Participant 6 felt the following regarding the high cost of production:

Before now, we used to buy litre 20 at the rate of N350 and litre 25 at the rate of N500, but today, if you go to our market, you cannot afford them any longer. An empty litre 20 is now sold for N1800, while 25 litres is sold at N2000 or N2200. In a tapping season, you may need ten of these gallons. Then, for alcohol production, you need big rubbers (Baba Sala or Buta) for the fermentation of palm wine. The of these depend on the size of the rubber, but the smallest and cheapest one out there is not less than N14,000 Naira, and you may need about four to five depending on the number of palm trees felled. These rubbers when my father used to tap, we used to buy these for less than N10, but Nigeria has changed.

Lack of access to credit: Small-scale producers also faced challenges accessing credit to invest in their operations. This limits their ability to purchase palm trees, equipment and materials needed for production and ultimately limits their ability to grow their businesses. Study participants also complained about a lack of government support to expand their businesses. Most participants (n = 6) are unaware of the possibility of accessing credit facilities. The lack of awareness and knowledge about financial support opportunities led to traditional alcohol distillers not taking advantage of credit opportunities. Without access to credit, traditional alcohol distillers could not invest in their businesses, leading to low productivity and limited income. This, in turn, made it difficult for them to repay debts and enjoy a better living amidst family responsibilities. Instead, some participants (n = 5) indicated that they borrow monies from informal credit facilities such as moneylenders, relatives, *Osusu*, age grades and other community-based committees to finance their businesses at a very high (50%) interest rate.

Lack of social amenities: Lack of social amenities was discussed as one of the most threatening challenges faced by traditional palm wine producers and alcohol distillers. Social amenities refer to basic public facilities and services such as electricity, clean water, sanitation, and transportation. When collecting this data, the Yala-Obubra community had no motorable road or means of transportation and electricity. The citizens only generated electrical power through privately-owned generators. Since transportation is crucial for producers to transport raw materials and finished products to markets, this presented a big threat to them. Some respondents discussed how they could not visit neighbouring and distant markets to sell their products. Participant 8 said:

For us here in Yala-Obubra, the road is our biggest problem. Every year, politicians come here to campaign that we vote for them, but when they emerge victorious, we only see them again after four years in the next election season. Because of no motorable roads, many buyers of palm wine or alcohol do not enter our village. The few that manage to enter our community take monopolistic and sometimes oligopolistic advantage of the people by offering very low prices for our products. Since we do not have a choice, we sell our products at whatever fees they are willing to pay. It is quite understandable because the lack of a good road network to our community makes buyers spend so much on transportation to get here.

Participant 5 added that:

We suffer here a lot due to the lack of roads and electricity. As my brother has already said, buyers from outside treat us as they like since they know we have no other options but to do their bidding. Another big problem for us here is no light. I have heard from some of my friends that palm wine can be boiled and refrigerated to maintain freshness; we cannot practice such here because there is no light to power our fridges. Do we even buy fridges in this community? No one buys such because it will be a waste of money.

Stealing: Traditional alcohol production often involves using valuable raw materials and equipment, which can make them a target for theft. The participants indicated that theft could occur at various stages of the production process, from collecting raw palm wine materials to the final distillation of alcohol. They said the theft could occur at the production site or home during storage. For example, the participants generally agreed that community members sometimes visit their site to steal fresh palm for drinking. Other times, they target other resources such as pipes, fermenting rubbers, etc. Participant 4 emphatically stated that:

Stealing happens to us almost every season, from fellow tappers to community members. For example, there was a time when a tapper from this community stole my distillation pipe. This distillation pipe was rated the best in town due to its thickness and ability to promote condensation with a limited wa-

ter supply. Many tappers considered me lucky to own such a pipe; it was inherited from my father, my friend is here now, and he can testify. We searched the entire place and visited all alcohol production sites looking for the pipe. Fortunately, we found the pipe in the hand of a tapper who claimed to have bought it from an undisclosed man.

DISCUSSION OF FINDINGS

The traditional process of tapping palm wine in Yala-Obubra involves selecting mature palm trees, clearing the area, felling the trees, pruning the fronds, clearing the tracts, heating the cut edges of the trunk, tapping the fermented surfaces, and collecting the sap in clay pots or polythene bags. This finding aligns with the results obtained by Mba et al. (2019), which also revealed that the traditional tapping process employed by palm wine tappers involves cutting open or felling palm trees to collect the sap for fermentation. The result also supports Apeh and Opata's (2019) finding that in Igboland, particularly in Enugu State, three methods of palm wine production are used -inflorescence, bud and felling methods. Under the felling method (like the approach practised by Yala-Obubra tappers), the cited researchers explained that the oil palm tree is either cut down or uprooted and tapped at the bud. In the case of a felled tree, the leaves are removed to expose the inner part of the bud, which is then left for two to four weeks. Subsequently, a chamber with dimensions of approximately 15 cm x 15 cm is created on the bud and covered with leaves to shield it from direct sunlight, which may cause drying. After an additional three days, a hole is drilled through the chamber below the bud, where a funnel is attached. The wine seeps into the chamber, flows through the hole, collects in the funnel, and fills the gourd or pot beneath the bud.

The current study further discovered that the choice between clay pots and polythene bags as methods of palm wine collection depends on availability and cost, with clay pots being preferred for small-scale production. Palm wine collected with clay pots is considered higher quality and more widely accepted by consumers. This finding aligns with the position of Apeh and Opata (2019) that the quality of palm wine could be affected by production methods. However, the authors revealed, through a comparison of three production methods, that the inflorescence method was superior, followed by the bud and felling methods. The authors added that proficiency and skill are essential for effectively executing each of these techniques, as they demand significant training and dexterity. This finding has implications for small-scale producers who can prioritise using clay pots for palm wine collection to meet consumer preferences and increase their market share.

The poor taste of palm wine from some tappers can be attributed to various factors identified by the participants. These factors include differences in tapping approaches among individuals, inadequate maintenance of tapping instruments such as knives, lack of proper cleaning of pots, infestation by insects like Agàyankpa, Edangblan, and bees, and tapping at inappropriate intervals or time schedules. These findings highlight the importance of proper tapping practices, instrument maintenance, and hygiene measures to produce high-quality palm wine with desirable taste characteristics. Addressing these factors can improve palm wine quality and consumer satisfaction in the community.

According to the participants, the differential patterns of drunkenness among palm wine consumers can be attributed to various factors. These factors include the soil texture, age (maturity) of palm trees, tapping season (preferably dry season), tapping apparatus (polythene bags or clay pots), personal factors such as blood group, individual's nature or ability to handle alcohol and family traits. This finding varies from the results obtained by Mbadiwe et al. (2021), showing that the gender and age of consumers were

Figure 8. Right view of palm wine undergoing heating

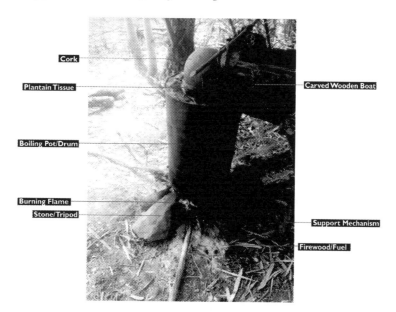

Figure 9. A canoe-like device used for condensation

associated with differential alcohol patterns among youths. The variation in the results of the cited and the present study is understandable since the former focused on factors specific to consumers. In contrast, the current study focused on producer-related factors responsible for differences in drunkenness patterns among consumers. Thus, understanding these factors can help consumers make informed choices, and tappers produce palm wine with desired characteristics.

Figure 10. Top view of the condenser with water inside for cooling the pipes

Figure 11. Alcohol collection point

The indigenous alcohol distillation practices in Yala-Obubra involve a series of processes. These include the collection of palm wine into various containers, fermentation of the palm wine for 1-2 weeks, and using locally made apparatus such as boiling pots, distilling pipes, and receivers. The alcohol distillation process utilises a pot still, where fermented palm wine is heated, causing the alcohol and volatile

Figure 12. Closer view of the alcohol collection process

compounds to evaporate and then condense back into a liquid using a condenser. However, it is important to note that traditional distillation methods can be risky, and precautions should be taken to ensure safety. These processes are at variance with the ones reported by Hue et al. (2022) in Vietnam, where alcohol is produced using glutinous rice and indigenous herbs. The author reported that rice and specific forest leaves are used to culture wine starters known as "banh men la" by the local community. After alcoholic fermentation and distillation, the product is white wine or "ruou trang." These processes also misalign with those reported by Asrani et al. (2019) in India, where people use medicinal plants to produce alcoholic drinks because these plants have special properties. In addition to medicinal plants, people use fruits, vegetables, grains, and herbs to make these beverages. One similarity between all the studies cited and the current one is that fermentation played a key role in alcohol production. Nevertheless, the indigenous alcohol distillation practices in Yala-Obubra hold cultural and traditional significance, reflecting the community's rich heritage and resourcefulness. These practices involve using locally made apparatus and highlight the community's adaptability. However, it is important to prioritise safety measures and promote education to prevent accidents and ensure the well-being of the distillers.

In Yala-Obubra, traditional palm wine production and alcohol distillation face several challenges. These include a declining palm tree population due to destructive tapping practices and the preference for palm oil production, the impact of climate change on palm wine yields, the high cost of production and lack of access to credit for small-scale producers, the absence of social amenities such as electricity and transportation, and the issue of theft at various stages of the production process. These challenges jeopardise the sustainability of traditional practices and call for interventions to support the producers and preserve their cultural heritage. The challenges faced by traditional palm wine producers and alcohol distillers in Yala-Obubra have multiple underlying reasons. The declining palm tree population results from destructive tapping practices and the shift towards palm oil production, driven by economic factors. This agrees with the result of Mba et al. (2019) that the practice of palm wine tapping results in many palm trees becoming unproductive or dying, and there is a lack of emphasis on tree planting, further exacerbating the negative impact on the palm tree population. This study discovered that climate change contributes to the situation by affecting palm wine yields. The result also agrees with the results of Nwashindu and Onu (2019) that the risk of death associated with climbing tall palm trees, environmental factors such as cold or swampy plantations, malaria sickness of the tappers and attacks from wild animals are other challenges affecting palm wine production. Other challenges identified in the current study include the high cost of production, lack of access to credit, absence of social amenities, and incidents of theft pose additional threats. Addressing these challenges is crucial to ensure the sustainability of traditional practices, support the livelihoods of producers, and preserve the cultural heritage of Yala-Obubra.

IMPLICATIONS OF THE FINDINGS FOR STUDENTS' ENTREPRENEURSHIP DEVELOPMENT

Palm wine production and alcohol distillation are economic opportunities that can foster entrepreneurship development and drive sustainable economic growth. The two economic activities have been practised for centuries in many rural communities worldwide, and they offer significant opportunities for income generation, employment creation, value addition, and innovation. The importance of palm wine production and alcohol distillation for entrepreneurship development is that they offer opportunities for students to learn practical skills and gain hands-on experience in various areas, including agriculture, food processing, chemistry, and business management. For example, producing palm wine requires knowing how to tap and collect sap from palm trees, how to ferment and age the sap to create the desired flavour and alcohol content, and how to package and market the finished product. Similarly, alcohol distillation involves understanding the chemical processes involved in separating and concentrating ethanol and how to design and operate distillation equipment, manage fermentation processes, and comply with regulatory requirements.

In addition to these technical skills, palm wine production and alcohol distillation also require entrepreneurial skills such as marketing, sales, leadership and financial management. Students who engage in these activities must learn to identify and target potential customers, develop effective marketing strategies, negotiate with suppliers and distributors, manage cash flow and inventory, and comply with legal and regulatory requirements. By gaining experience in these areas, students can develop valuable skills and knowledge that will serve them well in many career paths.

Another reason palm wine production and alcohol distillation are important for entrepreneurship development is that they can provide income and economic opportunities for students and their communities. According to Apeh and Opata (2019), palm wine production is a significant means of generating income and employment opportunities for rural farmers. In many regions where these practices are common, they have long been important sources of income and employment, particularly for small-scale producers and entrepreneurs. By learning how to produce and sell these products, students can create their income streams and contribute to the economic development of their communities. Moreover, they can leverage technology and social media platforms to reach a wider market and increase their income. Many producers and alcohol distillers explained that the business has a huge income generation and recommend that people without better-paying jobs engage in them. Some tappers have trained their wives, children and other dependents up to the university level using proceeds from these two indigenous practices. Others have built houses, bought cars and motorcycles, and recorded other achievements as palm wine tappers. Therefore, these two practices can generate income for students, especially unemployed graduates, as they wait for better employment opportunities.

CONCLUSION AND RECOMMENDATIONS

This study used a qualitative approach to investigate and describe palm wine production and alcohol distillation. The study's findings revealed several steps involved in producing palm wine and distilling alcohol. Palm wine tappers and alcohol distillers in the Yala-Obubra community face various challenges in the production process. Palm wine production and alcohol distillation are important economic activities with good entrepreneurship potential for students and graduates. Therefore, higher education students and graduates can consider these as alternative sources of income generation and poverty eradication rather than rely solely on white-collar jobs. The study underscores the importance of preserving and promoting traditional practices in Nigeria. The traditional practices of palm wine production and alcohol distillation offer significant socio-economic benefits that could contribute to the country's development. The following recommendations were made to help address the challenges facing palm wine producers and alcohol distillers in the Yala-Obubra community.

- Tappers in Yala-Obubra need to adopt sustainable methods of palm tree management that promote the longevity of the trees. Since palm oil production was discussed as the reason for the lack of access to palm trees for tapping, destructive approaches to palm wine production should be discouraged. This can include tree pruning instead of felling, controlled tapping methods that allow trees to recover and planting new palm trees to increase the population.
- The impact of climate change can be mitigated by adopting climate adaptation strategies such as planting drought-tolerant palm tree varieties, implementing rainwater harvesting, and using irrigation to ensure adequate water supply during dry seasons.
- The government and other organisations can financially support traditional palm wine producers and distillers by offering low-interest loans and grants to purchase equipment and materials, expand their businesses, and improve their livelihoods.
- Providing social amenities such as motorable roads, electricity, clean water, sanitation, and transportation will greatly benefit traditional palm wine producers and distillers in the Yala-Obubra community.
- Alcohol producers can use traditional fencing around the production site or hire a security guard to monitor the site. This can help producers minimise theft risk and protect their valuable raw materials and equipment.

REFERENCES

Akinrotoye, K. P. (2014). Effects of fermented palm wine on some diarrhoeagenic bacteria. *Elite Research Journal of Biotechnology and Microbiology*, 2(1), 4–14.

Alharahsheh, H. H., & Pius, A. (2020). A review of key paradigms: Positivism vs interpretivism. *Global Academic Journal of Humanities and Social Sciences*, 2(3), 39–43.

Apeh, A. A., & Opata, C. C. (2019). The oil palm wine economy of rural farmers in Nigeria: Evidence from Enugu Ezike, south-eastern Nigeria. *Rural History*, *30*(2), 111–128. doi:10.1017/S0956793319000062

Asrani, P., Patial, V., & Asrani, R. K. (2019). 14 - Production of Fermented Beverages: Shedding Light on Indian Culture and Traditions. In A. M. Grumezescu & A. M. B. T.-P. & M. of B. Holban (Eds.), Production and management of beverages (pp. 409–437). Woodhead Publishing. https://doi.org/ doi:10.1016/B978-0-12-815260-7.00014-6

Babatunde, S., El-Gohary, H., & Edwards, D. (2021). Assessment methods in entrepreneurship education, challenges and opportunities in developed and developing nations: A comparative study of Nigeria and England. *Education + Training*, *63*(7/8), 1092–1113. doi:10.1108/ET-12-2020-0368

Eje, A. E., Udie, E. A., & Vincent, C. A. (2021). Making Agricultural Education more Practicable: The need for its curriculum restructuring in Nigeria. [AJRD]. *Academic Journal of Research and Development*, *15*(2), 52–64.

Ekaette, S. O., Owan, V. J., & Agbo, D. I. (2019). External debts and the financing of education in Nigeria from 1988 – 2018: Implication for effective educational management. [JERA]. *Journal of Educational Realities*, *9*(1), 1–14. doi:10.5281/zenodo.4320606

Francis, O. M., Ifeanyieze, F. O., Ikehi, M. E., Ojiako, C. C., Okadi, A. O., Nwankwo, C. U., & Ekenta, L. U. (2019). Vocational agriculture and entrepreneurship aspirations among university students in Nigeria. *International Journal of Training Research*, *17*(3), 220–237. doi:10.1080/14480220.2019.1690744

Hue, N. V., Chung, N. D., Hang, V. T. T., Be, P. T., & Nga, T. T. P. (2022). Factors affecting the fermentation process of Vietnamese traditional wine ("men la" wine) using" Ba Nang" wine starter. *African Journal of Food, Agriculture, Nutrition and Development*, *22*(5), 20317–20330. doi:10.18697/ajfand.110.21480

Hussein, H. (2022). Interview Method. In M. R. Islam, N. A. Khan, & R. Baikady (Eds.), *Principles of social research methodology*. Springer. doi:10.1007/978-981-19-5441-2_14

Ikegwu, J. U. (2014). The value of palm wine tapping in the food production practices of Igbo-land: a case study of Idemili south local government area, Anambra state. *Research on Humanities and Social Sciences, 4*(6), 49-54. https://iiste.org/Journals/index.php/RHSS/article/view/11891

Lal, J. J., Sreeranjit, K. C. V., & Indira, M. (2003). Coconut palm. In B. Caballero (Ed.), *Encyclopedia of Food Sciences and Nutrition* (2nd ed., pp. 1464–1475). Academic Press. doi:10.1016/B0-12-227055-X/00263-7

Lee, N., & Rodríguez-Pose, A. (2021). Entrepreneurship and the fight against poverty in US cities. *Environment and Planning A. Environment & Planning A*, *53*(1), 31–52. doi:10.1177/0308518X20924422

Macie, P., & Martins, A. R. O. (2019). Malazi, the palm wine tapper. In D. Pullanikkatil & C. Shackleton (Eds.), *Poverty reduction through non-timber forest products. Sustainable Development Goals Series*. Springer. doi:10.1007/978-3-319-75580-9_17

Mba, E. H., Ekpo, A. S., Ozim, E. C., & Oladeinde, S. O. (2019). Assessment of traditional palm wine tapping practice: Effect on vegetation in Nasarawa State, Nigeria. *International Journal of Environment and Climate Change*, *9*(12), 841–851. doi:10.9734/ijecc/2019/v9i1230165

Mbadiwe, N., Adikaibe, B. E., Achor, J., Okoye, O., Onodugo, O., Anyim, O., Ijoma, U., Orah-Okpala, C., Ugwu, C., & Onodugo, N. (2021). Alcohol use in selected low-income neighbourhoods in Enugu, Southeast Nigeria. *Annals of Medical and Health Sciences Research, 11*, 1555–1560.

McCoy, S. I., Ralph, L. J., Wilson, W., & Padian, N. S. (2013). Alcohol production as an adaptive livelihood strategy for women farmers in Tanzania and its potential for unintended consequences on women's reproductive health. *PLoS One, 8*(3), e59343. doi:10.1371/journal.pone.0059343 PMID:23527167

Nwashindu, V., & Onu, A. (2019). Palm wine economy and labour migrants of mgbowo community of Igbo society. *International Journal of Research in Arts and Social Sciences, 12*, 202–228.

Odigwe, F. N., Offem, O. O., & Owan, V. J. (2018). Vocational training duration and university graduates' job performance in Cross River State, Nigeria. *International Journal of Current Research, 10*(7), 72024–72028. doi:10.5281/zenodo.4320545

Odigwe, F. N., & Owan, V. J. (2019). Trend analysis of the Nigerian budgetary allocation to the education sector from 2009 – 2018 with reference to UNESCO'S 26% Benchmark. *International Journal of Educational Benchmark, 14*(1), 1–14. doi:10.5281/zenodo.4458703

Okafor, N. (1975). Preliminary microbiological studies on the preservation of palm wine. *The Journal of Applied Bacteriology, 38*(1), 1–7. doi:10.1111/j.1365-2672.1975.tb00493.x

Olorunfemi, S. O. (2023). The Ado of Rural-Urban Migration: Implication on Food Security in Akutupa-Kiri, Kogi State, Nigeria. In A. A. Popoola, H. H. Magidimisha-Chipungu, & L. Chipungu (Eds.), *Handbook of Research on Managing the Urban-Rural Divide Through an Inclusive Framework* (pp. 167–187). IGI Global. doi:10.4018/978-1-6684-6258-4.ch010

Osabohien, R. (2023). ICT adoption and youth employment in Nigeria's agricultural sector. *African Journal of Economic and Management Studies.* doi:10.1108/AJEMS-03-2022-0111

Oseni, I. O., & Oyelade, A. O. (2023). Effect of capital expenditure on unemployment rate in Nigeria. *African Journal of Economic Review, 11*(3), 1–12.

Ovharhe, O. J., Ebewore, S. O., & Alakpa, S. O. E. (2022). Rural-urban migration of farmers in Delta and Edo States, Nigeria: Policy implications. *Migration and Development, 11*(2), 163–173. doi:10.108 0/21632324.2020.1806601

Owan, V. J., Agurokpon, D. C., & Udida, U. J. (2021). Curriculum restructuring and job creation among Nigerian graduates: The mediating role of emerging Internet applications. *International Journal of Educational Administration, Planning, &* [IJEAPR]. *Research, 13*(2), 1–16. doi:10.5281/zenodo.5886422

Owan, V. J., Duruamaku-Dim, J. U., Okon, A. E., Akah, L. U., & Agurokpon, D. C. (2022a). Joint mediation of psychosis and mental stress on alcohol consumption and graduates' job performance: A PLS structural equation modeling. *The International Journal of Learning in Higher Education, 30*(1), 89–111. doi:10.18848/2327-7955/CGP/v30i01/89-111

Owan, V. J., Emanghe, E. E., Denwigwe, C. P., Etudor-Eyo, E., Usoro, A. A., Ebuara, V. O., Effiong, C., Ogar, J. O., & Bassey, B. A. (2022b). Curriculum management and graduate programmes' viability: The mediation of institutional effectiveness using PLS-SEM approach. *Journal of Curriculum and Teaching*, *11*(5), 114–127. doi:10.5430/jct.v11n5p114

Owan, V. J., Ndibe, V. C., & Anyanwu, C. C. (2020). Diversification and economic growth in Nigeria (1981–2016): An econometric approach based on ordinary least squares (OLS). *European Journal of Sustainable Development Research*, *4*(4), em0131. Advance online publication. doi:10.29333/ejosdr/8285

Samuel, O., Lina, J., & Ifeanyi, O. (2016). Production of vinegar from oil-palm wine using Acetobacter aceti isolated from rotten banana fruits. *Universal Journal of Biomedical Engineering*, *4*(1), 1–5. doi:10.13189/ujbe.2016.040101

Scholtes, F. (2009). *Status quo and prospects of smallholders in the Brazilian sugarcane and ethanol sector: Lessons for development and poverty reduction*. University of Bonn, Center for Development Research (ZEF). http://hdl.handle.net/10419/88388

Schwandt, T. A., & Gates, E. F. (2018). Case study methodology. In N. K. Dezin & Y. S. Lincoln (Eds.), *The Sage handbook of qualitative research* (5th ed., pp. 341–358). Sage publications.

Si, S., Yu, X., Wu, A., Chen, S., Chen, S., & Su, Y. (2015). Entrepreneurship and poverty reduction: A case study of Yiwu, China. *Asia Pacific Journal of Management*, *32*(1), 119–143. doi:10.100710490-014-9395-7

Tagba, P., Osseyi, E., Fauconnier, M. L., & Lamboni, C. (2018). Aromatic composition of" sodabi", a traditional liquor of fermented oil palm wine. *Advance Journal of Food Science and Technology : AJFST*, *14*(1), 15–22. doi:10.19026/ajfst.14.5421

Uzogara, S. G., Agu, L. N., & Uzogara, E. O. (1990). A review of traditional fermented food condiments and beverages in Nigeria. Their benefits and possible problems. *Ecology of Food and Nutrition*, *24*(4), 267–288. doi:10.1080/03670244.1990.9991145

ADDITIONAL READING

Akudago, J. A., Mounkeila, B., Guemnin Boutchueng, O., Obatsa, L. N., & Ausel, J. (2016). Innovation and lessons learnt in design and pilot implementation of clay-bodied bio-sand filters in Niger. In *Proceedings of the 39th WEDC International Conference, Kumasi, Ghana, 2016* (Refereed Paper 2507, pp. 1-6). Water, Engineering and Development Centre (WEDC).

Barua, P., Ahsan, R., Islam, M. T., Tasnim, N., & Hasan, M. A. (2022). Eco-friendly Entrepreneurship to Promote Plastic Alternatives. *Notitia-časopis za ekonomske, poslovne i društvene teme*, *8*(1), 35-51.

Mwiandi, F. K., & Ombaka, O. (2017). Assessment of indigenous knowledge and practices on the use of clay among rural communities in Meru, Kenya. *International Journal of Development and Sustainability*, *6*(11), 1701–1720.

KEY TERMS AND DEFINITIONS

Distilled Spirits: These, also known as hard liquor or alcoholic beverages, are produced by distilling fermented grains, fruits, or vegetables. Examples include whiskey, vodka, gin, rum and brandy, which typically have higher alcohol content than beer or wine.

Entrepreneurship: Entrepreneurship refers to designing, launching, and running a new business venture in the face of uncertainty and risk to create value, generate profits and achieve sustainability. Entrepreneurship drives economic growth, creates jobs, fosters innovation, and addresses social challenges.

Fermentation: The process by which microorganisms such as yeast break down sugars into alcohol, carbon dioxide, and other byproducts. In palm wine production, fermentation converts sap from palm trees into an alcoholic beverage.

Indigenous Practices: This refers to traditional knowledge, skills, and techniques passed down through generations in a particular community or culture. These practices are often closely tied to the local environment and resources and are shaped by social and cultural factors.

Palm Wine Production: This refers to the process of extracting sap from the trunk of palm trees, which is then fermented to produce a beverage with low alcohol content. This practice is common in many parts of Africa and plays an important cultural and economic role in many communities.

Chapter 4

Supporting Digitization of Traditional Medicinal Knowledge Through Technologies in KwaZulu-Natal, South Africa

Petros Nhlavu Dlamini
University of Zululand, South Africa

ABSTRACT

This chapter aimed to examine the terminology of traditional medicine and the urgency for supporting local knowledge through technology in medical libraries. The chapter was informed by three research objectives which are: categories of traditional medicinal knowledge practitioners available in rural areas; types of traditional medicinal knowledge digitized in medical libraries; and technologies for digitizing traditional medicinal knowledge in medical libraries. The approach for the investigation was a desktop literature review. The study used academically recognized journals, books, and databases as its primary sources of literature. The author also strongly drew on his prior experience in the field, as he had already published several publications on indigenous knowledge. The author also presumptively conducted an electronic search of published literature, heavily depending on the Web of Science, using the institutional repositories of universities, Google Scholar, and Medline.

INTRODUCTION

According to statistics, more than 85% of African people depends on the services and goods of traditional medical expertise, science, and technologies for both the provision of healthcare and for problems relating to the social, economic, and local community (James, et al., 2018). Indigenous knowledge (IK), and particularly traditional medical knowledge, is making a significant contribution to the primary healthcare of rural community residents who cannot pay the costs of mainstream medicine. The lack

DOI: 10.4018/978-1-6684-7024-4.ch004

Copyright © 2023, IGI Global. Copying or distributing in print or electronic forms without written permission of IGI Global is prohibited.

of trained medical professionals in rural areas and the inadequate and underfunded hospitals and clinics further worsen this issue. Due to these, traditional healthcare providers became the only known, convenient, respectable, and reasonably priced source of healthcare (Mokhesi & Modjadji, 2022). One of the significant contributions of indigenous knowledge to human health in recent years has been the utilisation of plants for medicine manufacturing and illness treatment in various traditional medicinal systems. The use of plant-based medications or products to treat illnesses or as curative agents, either alone or in combination with other treatments, is on the rise. It is estimated that traditional/folk medicine contains up to 75% of the plant-based medicinal agents utilised globally (Prakash, et al., 2021). In India, natural resources account for over 70% of all synthetic medicine discoveries, and several other synthetic equivalents have been created using prototype molecules obtained from plants. According to Noronha et al., (2020), there is a growth in the use of plants in the development of medications to treat chronic illnesses, and more than 60% of cancer treatments on the market or in clinical trials are based on natural ingredients. As noted by Nugraha et al., (2019), currently, nearly 80% of cardiovascular, immunosuppressive, anti-cancer, and anti-microbial medications come from plant sources. One and seventy-seven (177) anticancer medicines have been licensed, and more than 70% of those are based on natural substances or their imitations. Approximately 121 of the prescription medications currently in use are plant-based, accounting for around 25% of all drugs found on the market.

Between 2005 and 2007, thirteen medications with a natural origin were approved in the US; currently, more than 100 drugs based on natural products are undergoing clinical studies. Additionally, it was calculated that just 11 per cent of the 252 total medications on the WHO's list of essential medications was derived from plants (Sen & Chakraborty, 2017). Local communities' concerns, particularly those of the underprivileged rural communities, have been greatly helped by indigenous knowledge. Indigenous knowledge (IK) is essential to the survival of local communities since it makes a significant contribution to knowledge about global development. Masango (2020) emphasised that indigenous knowledge has been used by traditional medical practitioners to create a variety of medicines as well as to identify valuable experiences and preserve them over generations through a highly sophisticated information system. Indigenous knowledge (IK) is also playing a significant role in the documentation of traditional medicines. Davenport and Kalakota (2019) noted that complex health management systems have been developed and are being utilised to address several societal health problems through the use of information systems for documenting traditional medical practices.

The truth is that without the transmission of indigenous knowledge, there would not be any modern practitioners of traditional medicine (Bibi, 2022). For instance, in the face of the potential for a global pandemic, scientists are searching for a variety of tolerant solutions, and they get this knowledge by talking to residents about the various strategies for battling the pandemic without losing any lives. Armed with the advantage of local expertise, these researchers return to their labs with their experimental drugs and engage in diverse activities by looking for solutions to address pandemic problems (Ansah, 2022). Herbs used in traditional medicine that are frequently used with orthodox treatments in developing nations are currently gaining popularity in the west. Traditional medicine is "the totality of knowledge, skills, and practices based on the theories, beliefs, and experiences indigenous to different cultures, whether explicable or not, used in the preservation of health and the prevention, diagnosis, improvement, or treatment of physical and mental illness," according to the National Library of Medicine.

The accumulated body of local knowledge that is transmitted orally through Traditional Health Practitioners (THPs) and knowledge holders has been incorporated into traditional medicine in a significant way, combining physical, mental, emotional, and social well-being (Mothibe & Sibanda, 2019). A holistic approach to treatment is used by TM which frequently combines herbal remedies and physiotherapy with elements of African spirituality (Kristoffersen, et al., 2019). In African TM, the illness is frequently viewed as the breakdown of intricate physical, social, and spiritual ties. Therefore, a diagnosis starts with an examination of both human and supernatural interactions. For instance, when the ailment is mystical, ritual diagnosis is a fundamental part of the traditional healing process for re-establishing social and emotional equilibrium (Adu-Gyamfi & Anderson, 2019). Particularly, the philosophical clinical care embedded in African traditions, culture and beliefs has contributed to making TM practices acceptable and hence highly demanded by the population (Agbor & Naidoo, 2016), estimated by the WHO about 80% of people.

As much as traditional medicine is essential in the lives of indigenous people, it cannot be ignored that there is a steady demise of indigenous knowledge systems, including traditional medical knowledge (Dlamini & Ocholla, 2018). The beginning of colonization, which portrayed African cultural traditions as inferior and was strongly opposed by the colonial masters, contributed to this in part (Ocholla, 2007). The result is that indigenous culture has suffered severely as a result of the adoption of western cultural practices. Africa has given more attention to Western medicine and even information centres in Africa have accommodated western knowledge compared to local medicinal knowledge. Libraries and archives are generally regarded as the guardians of knowledge and cultural legacy; they house illustrations, photographs, and other documentation treasures like manuscripts, documents, books, and audiovisual materials.

It is recent that indigenous medicinal knowledge is drawing much attention in libraries where its preservation and documentation is taken very seriously. According to the conditions in each country, the knowledge of traditional medicines, therapies, and practices is being respected, protected, promoted, and shared broadly and effectively by traditional medical libraries and non-specialised libraries. This is accomplished through deliberate documenting of the already-known information (Anyaoku, Nwafor-Orizu & Eneh, 2015). The key strategy for conserving knowledge is documentation. Moreover, books, periodicals like newspapers and journals, material medica, various media for preservation, such as multimedia recordings, and information and communication technologies can all be used to collect and preserve traditional medical knowledge. An illustration of a digitalisation initiative to preserve traditional medical knowledge is the Indian traditional knowledge digital library system. The names of hundreds of traditional Indian remedies are listed in this digital database, along with details about each one, in both local and translated Western languages (Anyaoku, Nwafor-Orizu & Eneh, 2015; Khanyile & Dlamini, 2021).

The literature that this study reviewed on supporting traditional knowledge through digital preservation of traditional medicine is underpinned by Afrocentric Model by Asante (1991) (1994). Afrocentric Model (AM) was conceived by Asante (1991) and the purpose of this model is to promote African culture and the way Africans should live without being forced to depend on foreign knowledge with its traditions. Burbanks (2014:13) adds that Afrocentricity is the in-depth analysis and interpretation of the economy, culture, history, philosophy, politics, language and society from a conceptual, methodological and theoretical framework that puts into the spotlight Africa and honors the agency of African people and their originality. The Afrocentric paradigm is a revolutionary shift in thinking of African people offered as an adjustment to black disorientation and lack of agency of African people. The Afrocentrism asks the question, "What would African people do if there were no white people?" Asante (1991:172). Alternatively, what natural responses or reactions would occur in the relationships, education, religion, culture and historical points for African people if there had not been any interference from Western colonialism or enslavement? Asante (1991:172) further explains that Afrocentricity responses to this

Digitization of Traditional Medicinal Knowledge in KwaZulu-Natal

question by involving the central role of the African subject within the context of African history and its people, thereby eliminating Europe from the centre of the African reality. Minishi-Majanja (2012) adds that lacking the indigenous knowledge context of your working environment makes you lack an understanding of the environment you are operating in.

The application of Afrocentric Model on the other hand promotes the use of indigenous knowledge where traditional medicine become the main medicine for African people. Asante (1991) highlighted that African intellectuals should assist Africa in closing the gap produced by more than four hundred years of dominance and marginalization of African people's knowledge systems. Thiong'o (1986), in his key book on "Decolonizing the mind," expressed this problem in an effective manner. African traditional knowledge should not just be considered a "alternative" form of knowledge, but also one of many. African knowledge should be used by African people to help Africa stand on her own without relying in western knowledge. It can be said that Afrocentric model is one of the core models supporting the promotion and use of local knowledge to benefit African people. The chapter was informed by four research objectives which were to:

- Determine the categories of traditional medicinal knowledge practitioners available in rural areas.
- Establish the types of traditional medicinal knowledge digitised in medical libraries.
- Determine the technologies for digitising traditional medicinal knowledge in medical libraries.
- Determine the digital preservation processes of traditional medicinal knowledge.

METHODOLOGY

The chapter adopted a desktop literature review which provides insightful information for indigenous medicinal knowledge. This chapter utilised various databases to review articles and book chapters on indigenous medicinal knowledge while also relied on researcher's experience after producing multiple studies on indigenous knowledge. An electronic search of published literature utilising the institutional repositories of universities, Google Scholar, Journal Storage, and Medline, largely depending on the Web of Science was presumptively conducted. As noted by Herrera-Franco et al. (2020) the literature review on indigenous knowledge and indigenous medicinal knowledge is approximately more than 5,000 publications, publishing years, document kinds and sources. However, this chapter focused on literature review on indigenous medicinal knowledge, and it achieved a degree of quality assessment of the included studies by restricting itself to just peer-reviewed literature.

Search Process

While acknowledging the various terminology for indigenous medicinal knowledge, the chapter adopted used terms like indigenous knowledge, traditional medicinal knowledge, traditional medicinal knowledge practitioners, types or forms of traditional medicinal knowledge, and types of ICTs for digitising traditional medicinal knowledge. These keywords produced a massive body of literature on supporting the digitisation of traditional medicine. To ensure exhaustivity and inclusivity, the precise phrases "traditional medicinal knowledge" was used in an advanced search. The following criteria were used to narrow the search:

Table 1. Criteria

Eligible studies inclusion criteria
• Open-access articles only
• Final papers
• Language: English
• Book chapters
Exclusion criteria
• Duplicate articles
• Articles that are not full texts
• Articles that did not answer the research questions.

To ascertain whether the included articles fit the established criteria, the full texts of each article was independently examined. The current study thus includes articles for review that fit the criteria.

CATEGORIES OF TRADITIONAL MEDICINAL KNOWLEDGE PRACTITIONERS AVAILABLE IN RURAL AREAS

This section delves the various local traditional practitioners that the traditional medical community takes into consideration. It is important to note that the Traditional Health Practitioners Bill of 2003 permitted traditional doctors (traditional health practitioners) to recommend medication and sick leave to patients, much like western physicians. Charlatans (false healers who use human body parts to create mixtures (muti) and declare to be able to cure a range of ailments) are not permitted to work under the license (Sagan, 2013). The Traditional Health Practitioners Act (22 of 2007) was enacted by the government of South Africa to ensure that traditional doctors in South Africa have the same legal rights as other medical professionals and that all medical professionals are compliant with Department of Health regulations. The Traditional Health Practitioner Bill (2003) was approved by Parliament in 2003. The Bill's objectives were to acknowledge South Africa's traditional healthcare system, establish a framework for ensuring their effectiveness and quality, and provide patients with remedies in the event of malpractice (Sagan, 2013; Masoga & Shokane, 2020).

Traditional Medical Practitioners (TMP) deal with their patients considerably differently than contemporary medical professionals, utilising a more patient-centred communication style to find common ground with the ill (Chisaka, 2019). Given sociological and economic considerations, TM is an essential resource for healthcare in developing nations and it positively affects the provision of primary healthcare to the local population because, typically, TM appears to be more accessible and less expensive than pharmaceutical drugs for the majority of patients living in Africa. Generally, the experiences have been field-tested for millennia, and the dialect and culture of the area have formalized the locals' interaction with their ecological systems (Tyburski, 2021). The understanding, prevention, and treatment of diseases are said to consider a patient's internal and external environments by the holistic approach of TM techniques. Contrary to contemporary medicine, Traditional Chinese Medicine (TM) frequently employs natural ingredients, which have the benefit over manufactured substances due to their inherent capacity to produce gentle healing effects and cause fewer adverse effects (Yuan et al., 2016).

The cornerstone of disease treatment, however, depends on the molecular correspondences between the clinically active substances and their biological targets in both TM and alternative medicine (AOM). Traditional knowledge is generally shared in an unstructured manner because it is essentially tacit. Additionally, there are certain disparities between the therapeutic knowledge linked with medicinal plants and the healing powers firmly embedded in the collective imagination due to the lack of scientific data supporting the efficacy of TM techniques (Haque et al., 2018). To improve and widen the lengthy history of usage of these medicines, it is also necessary to formalise the most widely utilised information for TM. The necessity of formalising traditional medical knowledge should be emphasized since it can aid in the discovery and development of new conventional and alternative treatments (Haque et al., 2018). As such, there are many categories of traditional medicinal knowledge found in Africa and their categories are not limited to, 1) those who practice without appealing to supernatural forces, such as herbalists, traditional birth attendants, and bonesetters; and 2) those who do, whether or not they employ material remedies (priest healers, faith healers, diviners, cult healers etc. (Amzat et al., 2008; Dlamini, 2016).

It is noteworthy that people in rural areas, including some urban dwellers, consult different categories of traditional healers (iZinyanga) not limited to herbalists (abesebenzisi amakhambi), diviners (sangomas), spiritualists (imimoya), and prophets (abaprofethi) and faith healers (abaphilisi bokholo), as well as community elders (abadala bomphakathi), for guidance when they are ill, to determine whether the cause of their problems is caused by the displeasure of their ancestors, and to determine whether a person is destined to become a sangoma (traditional healer). The patient is then expected to instructions as directed by the traditional healer (iZinyanga) (Viriri & Mungwini, 2009; De Lange, 2017). Some of the offices of traditional medicinal practitioners are briefly discussed as follows:

- **DIVINERS (IZANGOMA)**

A diviner (isangoma) uses bones to consult ancestors in order to diagnose the cause of sickness or ailment. The diviner gives the patient medicine after identifying the disease's underlying causes. Should the treatment not work, the patient is then directed to a herbalist (umsebenzisi amakhambi), who will treat and manage the ailment using herbs like plants and roots. However, if the treatment is unable to reduce the symptoms of the condition the patient is then directed to a Western treatment regimen (Westerlund, 2006; Singh, Baijnath & Street, 2020). In the case of an unexplained illness, diviners make their diagnosis through listening, observation, and experience as well as with the assistance of the ancestors, who communicate with them by throwing bones. Another technique a diviner uses to speak with the amadlozi (ancestors) is prediction, which is used to assess the impact of illness and therapeutic rites or mechanics. This ceremony entails praying, dancing, going into a trance, throwing bones or shells, and using mirrors, water, and palm reading (Hakim, 2010; Mothibe, & Sibanda, 2019). In a nutshell, the diviners may employ various physiological, psychological, and spiritual factors to diagnose their patients' misfortunes or ailments by using divination to communicate with their own ancestor spirits (and those of their patients). As they identify and categorise illness, as well as its cause and origin, according to African belief systems, diviners are regarded as spirituality experts.

- ### FAITH HEALERS AND PROPHETS (ABATHANDAZI)

The faith healers and prophets (abaprofethi) utilise water and visions to treat diseases that have natural origins. Faith healers and prophets are an example of syncretism, a rewriting of conventional Christianity to fit in with established culture. Therefore, even if they are not exactly conventional healers, prophets do share some traits with them. Faith healers identify and treat illness using prayer, candlelight, or water. Patients who are healed frequently become members of the church where the healer also belongs (Masoga & Shokane, 2020; Mokgobi, 2014).

- ### HERBALIST (INYANGA)

As stated by Masoga and Shokane (2020), an herbalist in Zulu is called inyanga. Because plants are mostly employed as traditional medicine in Africa, herbalists frequently use them to treat symptoms and diseases. Community members in Africa contact herbalists before turning to western doctors. Herbalists are increasingly preferred due to the expensive cost of western medicines and the difficulty in accessing western services; for many Africans, this makes them their only option for medical care. It is argued traditional medicine is cheaper compared to western medicine and African people rely in their own medicine because it has no side effects (Mapara, 2009). In a nutshell, herbalists approach healing through the administration of appropriate herbs and plant material. The herbalist knows a lot about plants, herbs, insects, animals and birds, however, a genuine herbalist uses only plants to treat and manage ailments or diseases.

- ### TRADITIONAL SURGEONS

Traditional surgeons are often men who are qualified, accredited, trusted, experienced, and recognised to circumcise boys (Mokgobi, 2014). Traditional surgeons have extensive expertise performing circumcisions, and because of their competence, the community has faith in them. The requirement that traditional surgeons register with the Department of Health in order to conduct traditional male circumcision is one example of the adjustments the government has undertaken in South Africa (Kepe, 2010). According to WHO (2008:29) traditional surgeons use special plants that cause a wound to heal quickly, and boys stay on the mountain for some time until the healing process begins.

- ### TRADITIONAL BIRTH ATTENDANTS

Traditional birth attendants are elderly women with extensive experience in giving birth who also offer care and counselling to expectant mothers as well as possible maternal and childcare (Hassim, Heywood & Berger, 2007). Traditional birth attendants (TBAs) have traditionally been the primary carers for women during childbirth throughout Africa. Pregnant women in Africa, like many low and middle-income nations, continue to give birth at home or with TBAs. According to the World Health Organization, a traditional birth attendant (TBA) is "a person who assists a mother during childbirth and who initially acquired her skills by delivering babies herself or through apprenticeship to other traditional birth attendants" (Abdul-Mumin, 2016; Ohaja & Murphy-Lawless, 2017). It is believed that TBAs have

Digitization of Traditional Medicinal Knowledge in KwaZulu-Natal

had very little education and training that would allow them to be integrated into the wider healthcare system, however, they are known to have culturally inherited herbal remedies to support women prior to, during, and after childbirth.

TYPES OF TRADITIONAL MEDICINAL KNOWLEDGE DIGITISED AND PRESERVED IN MEDICAL LIBRARIES

The application of traditional medical knowledge in Africa to manage and treat illnesses and diseases is progressing gradually but certainly. In light of this, a few African countries (for instance, Ghana, Nigeria, South Africa, and Zambia) have established national herbal pharmacopoeias in order to document beneficial medicinal methods and to further ensure their safety, efficacy, and quality (McGaw et al., 2022). Several plants may have qualities that are comparable to those of medications, according to certain theories. Unfortunately, no comprehensive scientific evaluation of their biological roles has been done (WHO, 2013). Many individuals think that because medicinal herbs are natural, they are safe from risks associated with unproven preparations or are less likely to hurt something. However, if the product or treatment is subpar, applied incorrectly, or used in concert with other medications, TM and its practice could have negative effects and be hazardous.

There are numerous possible reasons why TMP negative effects occur, and these include erroneous labelling, adulteration, misidentification, adulteration with toxic or dangerous substances, overdosage, improper use of herbal remedies by patients or healthcare professionals, and the use of herbal remedies and other pharmaceuticals together (Kaggwa, 2022). It is therefore advisable that patients need to learn more about these issues and proceed cautiously. Also, traditional practitioners need to receive better training, and cooperation and communication between them must be encouraged. As mentioned earlier, this section discusses the different types herbal or medicinal plants that are used by traditional healers. In that light, the table below shows some of the African traditional plants that are used to treat a variety of ailments.

As the table above demonstrates, local plants are frequently used to treat a variety of diseases that might harm the community. The table illustrates that the native population has its own plants that are utilised in the neighborhood to treat particular diseases. According to claims, indigenous knowledge is frequently employed to treat a wide range of illnesses for the benefit of the members of the community. Further examples of traditional medicine are as follows:

- A mixture of warm water and the roots of the usongo tree, which must be drunk three times each day, is used to treat diarrhea (isifo sohudo).
- Hot water mixed with the roots of the sekatapohwana tree would be given to a patient experiencing stomach pain. A traditional healer can also blend warm water and the barks of the leshogwa tree.
- A diviner uses dried chicken breast and holy water to prevent heartburn and nausea. After giving delivery, a lady will receive phate ya ngaka and makwati a mosetlha to cleanse the womb.

PACKAGING OF TRADITIONAL MEDICINE FOR CONSUMPTION IN AFRICA

Packaging of traditional medical knowledge has become common in African communities, and this is to benefit consumers. According to De Vaus (2014), packaging of medicinal plants and herbs is one of

Table 2. Commonly used traditional plants and their indigenous use(s) in African communities

Common Name (local name)	Part of plant used	Medicinal uses
Pterocarpus soyauxi (padouk, or camwood)	Ground stem (Isiqu esiphansi)	Childbirth, marriages
Milicia excelsa (Iroko)	Most sacred tree species	Sacrifices to appease gods
Nauclea diderrichii (bilinga)	Bark, root, and wood or trunk	Fevers, stomach problem
Canarium schweinfurthii (aiele)	Fruits, popular in local market	Resin is burnt as incense start fires or as "bush candle"
Lophira alata (azobé or ironwood)	Trunk	Medicine for back pain, toothache
Costus afer	Stem and juice	Coughs, sore throats, eye infection
Emilia coccinea	Entire plant	Anti-poison, jaundice, snakebite
Eremomastax speciosa	Leaves	Purify and strengthen blood
Aframomum spp	Leaves	Spice for food, coughs, magnifiers in medicinal mixtures
Piper guineensis	Leaves	Spice for food, treat hangovers, stomach problems, build strength
(Garcinia kola) Bitter Kola	Seeds	Digestive agent, poison antidote, protects microsomal enzymes against phalloidin
Bush Pepper	Seeds	Mix with others to treat cough, chest pain spleen for children
Araceae (Ihlukwe)	Leaves and rhizomes	Leaves used for wounds, sores and boils. Ground leaves applied to parts affected
Bombacaceae (Isimuku)	Bark	Asthma and skin disorders
Celastraceae (Umhlawazizi, umhlwazi)	Leaves	Coughs, asthma and other respiratory conditions, relief sleeplessness
Geraniaceae	Roots	Gonorrhoea, diarrhoea, dysentery, colds and lung infections
Lamiaceae	Leaves	Colds, influenza, liver problems and piles
Velloziaceae (Isiphemba, isiqumama)	Root, whole plant and bark	Dried leaves are smoked to stop nose bleeding
Zingiberaceae (Isiphepheto, indungulo)	Rhizomes	Asthma and dysmenorrhea
African potato (leraka)	Root	Treatment of patients with symptoms of HIV/AIDS

(Source: Eyong, 2007; Hutchings, et al., 1996; Van Wyk, 2011)

the ways of increasing its popularity and use among African people. It can be argued that packaging traditional medicinal knowledge is meant to maintain the identity, strength, and quality of the product and avoid contamination. Its packaging materials must effectively provide stability and shelf-life for medications (Saha, 2011). According to Oppong (2018), the introduction of packaging of herbal medicines has led to the rise of use of local medicine. Packiging is meant for the product to be confined, identified, characterized, protected, show, advertise, and for the goal of making the product clean and marketable (Agariya et al. 2012). This means that just like modern pharmacies, custodians of traditional medicine are packaging their products for attraction to attention and to make their products dignified in the community. The package catches and holds the attention of new buyers and help current customers recognize the brand. Nowadays, traditional medicine is packaged in a way that it fulfils and brings customers' inner satisfaction through a well-designed package (Robertson, 2013). It means the package itself is eye-catching as it displays the product's contents and effectively convey to the customer the satisfaction the product gives. The diagram below demonstrates how packaging of traditional medicine is done in Africa.

The diagram above demonstrates that the product's ingredients, use, and instructions, as well as the results of use, must all be clearly indicated to the consumer on the packaging. All additional pertinent information must be communicated to the potential buyer either directly or indirectly through the design. Direct descriptions of the product, its attributes, advantages, and application strategy must be on the box. More crucially, packaging features like shape, color, design elements, and graphics can be employed to subtly convey to customers the inherent qualities of the product. To help the user get clear instructions on dosage, on the product, printed information on the label relating to the contents, usage instructions, and required legal information must be readable, clear, and understandable (Oppong, 2018).

TECHNOLOGIES FOR DIGITISING TRADITIONAL MEDICINAL KNOWLEDGE IN MEDICAL LIBRARIES

Digital medical libraries are platforms that give their users or customers cohesive access to a sizable and well-organised digitised information. For the predictable future, the digital libraries have included both printed and digitised content. These kinds of libraries provide a comprehensible, consistent view of as many of these repositories as possible in order to fully exploit the opportunities that are offered by the materials that are in digital formats (Venkanna, 2018; Cocq, 2022). The goal of digital libraries is to develop information systems that provide access to a coherent collection of material, more and more of which will be in digital format as time goes on. Digital technology based on artificial intelligence is of

Figure 1. Packaging of traditional medicine in Africa (Robertson, 2013)

importance in medical libraries. According to Cocq (2022), medical libraries are motivated to use digital technologies to digitise traditional medicinal knowledge that has been missing in medical libraries. This is a response to the loss of indigenous knowledge, which has compelled organisations and information centres in the documentation using the readily available technologies (Dlamini & Ocholla, 2018). This means that medical libraries are taking advantage of technology to document and safeguard traditional medicinal knowledge. Since indigenous knowledge more especially traditional medicinal knowledge has been missing in medical libraries, it is not surprising that medical libraries are now taking advantage of the neglected knowledge to benefit its users and researchers. They believe that if the information is made available to the public, the information needs of clients will be met. Therefore, it is necessary to explore types of technologies that are suitable for digitising traditional medicinal knowledge. These serve as the foundational knowledge for the documenting of indigenous knowledge.

The use of technology in medical practices is expanding, and efforts are being made to incorporate it into complementary and alternative medicine which is otherwise regarded as Traditional Medical Practices (TMP) (Khan, 2021). Ilo (2012) posits that the use of technology for acquisition, preservation and accessibility of indigenous knowledge like traditional medicine in medicinal libraries is a step-by-step process, requiring various kinds of facilities to ensure that the knowledge is made available to customers. Kennedy and Davies (2006) stress the value of using digital technology for traditional medicinal knowledge gathering, storing, analyzing, and retrieval. This is an indication that gathering traditional medicinal knowledge from its owners is the first step to ensure that the knowledge is safeguarded from getting lost.

According to Dlamini and Ocholla (2018), Khanyile and Dlamini (2021), several technologies are used to collect, capture, and save data on indigenous knowledge (traditional medicine), such as the herbs and roots used for curing and managing ailments. The fundamental obstacles to the purchase, preservation, and accessibility of indigenous resources in libraries have been removed by the development of new technologies. Dlamini and Ocholla (2018) highlighted that storage devices like flash drives, hard drives, mobile phones, CDROMs, and computer hard drives as well as social media networks have made the work of libraries easier. This means that preservation of traditional medicinal knowledge encompasses all information-delivery mediums, including official digital systems, microforms, compact discs, videodiscs, and other non-book media, in addition to the traditional book.

Several techniques are used by libraries to get information. Equipment for audio, visual, or audio-visual purposes is among the main gadgets. Dlamini and Ocholla (2018) highlighted that indigenous knowledge can be captured or recorded using video camera, smartphones and voice recorders. The two authors also revealed in their study that indigenous knowledge (traditional medicine) can also be stored in various ICT tools like smartphones, computers, tape or voice recorder, video or digital camera, internet (Facebook, YouTube), just to mention a few. Lastly, indigenous knowledge in medicine can also be disseminated using several ICTs which are not limited to Internet (e.g. Facebook, YouTube, Twitter and many more), smartphones, laptops and desktop computers.

DIGITAL PRESERVATION PROCESSES

Broadly speaking, one of the common contemporary techniques in the twenty-first century is digitisation of information. According to Akinwale (2012), Masenya and Ngulube (2019), digitisation is the process of codifying information or knowledge such that it may be accessed globally and over an extended period of

Digitization of Traditional Medicinal Knowledge in KwaZulu-Natal

time. However, digital preservation is considered as the process of keeping information materials like digital surrogates made when analog materials are converted to digital format and those that are born digital and were not in analogue format before. Moreover, the relevance of digitisation has been related with institutional repositories in various libraries, particularly academic libraries. It must be mentioned that digitisation involves a special process (Shimray & Ramaiah, 2018). As such, the process of digitisation includes selection, evaluation of requirements and priorities, planning for prototypes to be digitised, gathering and forming metadata, creating data assortments, and presenting digital assets to delivery systems and storage facilities (Brown, 2008).

Apart from digitisation, there is digital preservation. According to Chen (2007), digital preservation refers to the process of digitising rare, sensitive materials and artefacts using computers, electronic devices, mobile phones, digital cameras, recorders, and displays. The purpose of the digital preservation activities is to safeguard and sustain bit items, which are prone to being lost or damaged (Kastellec, 2012; Ilo, 2012). The following is an explanation of the process of digital preservation:

- **Planned action**: it involves the identification of a subject for digitisation; Analysing the legal standing of a thing; an assessment of the resources needed; complete the criteria that will be used; an explanation of the methods and deadlines for the quality mechanism; and assessment of risks, hazards, including current and upcoming weaknesses.
- **Preparation for digitalisation**: this depicts deciding which object should be digitalised; a review of the digital materials' quality; digitalisation of the materials; any preparation needed prior to digitalisation; compilation of both structural and descriptive metadata; and research in the literature and archives.
- **Procedure of digital conversion**: the procedure of digital preservation is not limited to digitalising particular materials; the availability of skilled personnel and specialised tools; quality control and development of digital masters.
- **Process after digitisation**: the process after digitisation encapsulates metadata regulator related to long-term preservation; adherence to information on distribution and repository structures, as well as data collection and management; the development of online-accessible metadata and digitised copies; evaluation and valuation of the undertaking; and quality control.

It must be noted that once digital preservation has been accomplished, it is therefore categorised into the following categories of access (Ruusalepp & Dobreva, 2013):

- Long-term preservation: which refers to ongoing access to digital materials, or at least to the information contained in them, indefinitely;
- Medium-term preservation: which refers to ongoing access to digital materials beyond changes in technology for a defined period of time but not indefinitely; and
- Short-term preservation: which refers to access to digital materials for a defined period while use is anticipated but does not extend beyond the foreseeable future, or until it becomes impossible to access them due to technological limitations.

DISCUSSIONS OF FINDINGS

In examining and assessing literature review on the process of supporting traditional knowledge through digital preservation of traditional medicine in medical libraries, the following issues emanated. The literature has shown that rural people rely on indigenous knowledge (IK) more especially traditional medical knowledge for their medical conditions. As such, traditional medicine is making a significant contribution to the primary healthcare of rural community residents who cannot afford to pay for the western or mainstream medicine. It is based on such sentiments that the reviewed literature has demonstrated that rural communities have several categories of traditional healers. These categories of traditional healers are not limited to herbalists (abesebenzisi amakhambi), diviners (sangomas), spiritualists (imimoya), and prophets (abaprofethi), faith healers (abaphilisi bokholo), traditional birth attendants, traditional surgeon and community elders (abadala bomphakathi) (De Lange, 2017; Singh, Baijnath & Street, 2020). Additionally, the custodians of traditional medicine are well informed about their own situations, their resources, what works and what does not work, and how one changes, impacts other parts of their system (Rajasekaran, 1993; Mothibe & Sibanda, 2019). In other words, the traditional healers are considered traditional doctors of rural communities who play different roles when dealing with certain ailments, just like modern doctors who are specialists in certain illnesses.

The reviewed literature has also demonstrated that indigenous knowledge in traditional medicine like herbs or plants, roots, stems, barks and leaves are highly used to deal with certain ailments. It cannot be ignored that some traditional healers only use holy water to cleans their patients when they are sick and such knowledge is gotten from spiritually (through dreams and visions from the ancestors) (Masoga, 2017). As demonstrated in Table 1.1, it was discovered that plants are used by traditional healers for different purposes depending on the type of illness affecting a patient. The plants presented on Table 1.1 are an indication that medical libraries have huge role to play in the digitisation of traditional medicine. It became evident that modern technologies can be of great help if used properly to manage tacit knowledge.

CONCLUSION AND RECOMMENDATIONS

The introduction of digital libraries is too significant in the management of traditional medicinal knowledge through the use of modern technologies. It is indisputable that local knowledge like traditional medicine has a role to play in expanding libraries' collection of resources. African medicinal knowledge is essential to medical libraries, yet its acquisition, protection, and accessibility are still under danger. It is critical that medical libraries should develop the personal skills necessary to use modern technologies if they want to perform exploits. Ilo (2012) and Mdhluli et al. (2021) advise that librarians should be encouraged to acquire computer and ICT-related abilities, so that they are familiar with best practices. They will be able to use ICT tools and use them effectively in the gathering and sharing of indigenous knowledge like traditional medicine. The study showed that modern technologies are capable of making indigenous knowledge (traditional herbs accessible to the public, but collaboration is key between medical libraries and owners of indigenous knowledge. To ensure that indigenous medicinal knowledge is available in medical libraries for the present and future generations, it is necessary to have a strong working relationship between librarians and owners of traditional medicine in the communities that have extensive knowledge to share it with the libraries.

REFERENCES

Abdul-Mumin, K. H. (2016). Village midwives and their changing roles in Brunei Darussalam: A qualitative study. *Women and Birth; Journal of the Australian College of Midwives, 29*(5), 73–81. doi:10.1016/j.wombi.2016.04.002 PMID:27105748

Adu-Gyamfi, S., & Anderson, E. (2019). Indigenous medicine and traditional healing in Africa: A systematic synthesis of the literature. *Philosophy. Social and Human Disciplines, 1*, 69–100.

Agariya, A. K., Johari, A., Sharma, H. K., Chandraul, U. N. S., & Singh, D. (2012). The role of packaging in brand communication. *International Journal of Scientific and Engineering Research, 3*(2), 1–13.

Agbor, A. M., & Naidoo, S. (2016). A review of the role of African traditional medicine in the management of oral diseases. *African Journal of Traditional, Complementary, and Alternative Medicines, 13*(2), 133–142. doi:10.4314/ajtcam.v13i2.16

Akinwale, A. A. (2012). Digitisation of indigenous knowledge for natural resources management in Africa. *Proceedings of the AERN Summit.* SCECSAL. https://www.scecsal.org/publications/papers2016/034_sraku_latey_2016.pdf

Amzat, J., & Abdullahi, A. A. (2008). Role of traditional healers in the fight against HIV/AIDS. *EthnoMed., 2*(2), 153–159.

Ansah, E. K., Moucheraud, C., Arogundade, L., & Rangel, G. W. (2022). Rethinking integrated service delivery for malaria. *PLOS Global Public Health, 2*(6), e0000462. https://www.ncbi.nlm.nih.gov/pmc/articles/PMC10021790/. doi:10.1371/journal.pgph.0000462 PMID:36962405

Anyaoku, E. N., Nwafor-Orizu, O. E., & Eneh, E. A. (2015). Collection and Preservation of Traditional Medical Knowledge: Roles for Medical Libraries in Nigeria. *Journal of Library and Information Science, 3*(1), 33–43. https://obianujunwafor-orizu.com/collection-and-preservation-of-traditional-medical-knowledge-roles-for-medical-libraries-in-nigeria/. doi:10.15640/jlis.v3n1a2

Asante, M. K. (1991). The Afrocentric idea in education, spring. *The Journal of Negro Education, 60*(2), 170–180. doi:10.2307/2295608

Bibi, F., Abbas, Z., Harun, N., Perveen, B., & Bussmann, R. W. (2022). Indigenous knowledge and quantitative ethnobotany of the Tanawal area, Lesser Western Himalayas, Pakistan. *PLoS One, 17*(2), e0263604. https://journals.plos.org/plosone/article?id=10.1371/journal.pone.0263604. doi:10.1371/journal.pone.0263604 PMID:35192648

Brown, A. (2008). *Digital preservation guidance Note 1: Selecting file formats for long-term preservation.* CDN. https://cdn.nationalarchives.gov.uk/documents/selecting-file-formats.pdf

Burbanks, S. (2014). *Afrocentricity published in the encyclopaedia of identity.* https://www.researchgate.net/publication/268148430

Chen, S.-S. (2007). Digital preservation: Organisational commitment, archival stability, and technological logical continuity. *Journal of Organizational Computing and Electronic Commerce, 17*(3), 205–215. doi:10.1080/10919390701294012

Chisaka, J. W. (2019). *The use of traditional herbal medicines among palliative care patients at Mulanje Mission Hospital, Malawi.* Master's thesis, Faculty of Health Sciences, University of Cape Town, South Africa]. https://open.uct.ac.za/handle/11427/31511

Claire, C., Lefebvre, V., & Ronteau, S. (2020). Entrepreneurship as practice: Systematic literature review of a nascent field. *Entrepreneurship and Regional Development, 32*(3-4), 281–312. doi:10.1080/0898 5626.2019.1641975

Cocq, C. (2022). Revisiting the digital humanities through the lens of Indigenous studies—Or how to question the cultural blindness of our technologies and practices. *Journal of the Association for Information Science and Technology, 73*(2), 333–344. doi:10.1002/asi.24564

Davenport, T., & Kalakota, R. (2019). The potential for artificial intelligence in healthcare. *Future Healthcare Journal, 6*(2), 94–98. doi:10.7861/futurehosp.6-2-94 PMID:31363513

Dlamini, P. (2016). *The use of information and communication technologies to manage indigenous knowledge in KwaZulu-Natal, South Africa.* [PhD, Dissertation, Department of Library and Information Science, University of Zululand, South Africa]. https://uzspace.unizulu.ac.za/server/api/core/bitstreams/f6a73311-71d8-4bd0-8652-c9655efad417/content

Dlamini, P., & Ocholla, D. N. (2018). Information and communication technology tools for managing indigenous knowledge in KwaZulu-Natal Province, South Africa. *African Journal of Library Archives and Information Science, 28*(2), 137–153.

Eyong, C. T. (2007). Indigenous knowledge and sustainable development in Africa: Case study on Central Africa. *Tribes and Tribals, Special, 1*, 121-139. https://www.researchgate.net/publication/208152935_Indigenous_Knowledge_and_Sustainable_Development_in_Africa_Case_Study_on_Central_Africa

Hakim, G., & Chishti, M. (2010). *The traditional healer's handbook: a classic guide to the medicine of Avicenna.* Healing Arts Press.

Haque, M., Chowdhury, A. B. M., Shahjahan, M., Harun, M., & Dostogir, G. (2018). Traditional healing practices in rural Bangladesh: A qualitative investigation. *BMC Complementary and Alternative Medicine, 18*(1), 1–15. doi:10.118612906-018-2129-5 PMID:29448941

Hassim, A., Heywood, M., & Berger, J. (2007). *Health and democracy: A guide to human rights, health law and policy in post-apartheid South Africa.* ALP. http://www.alp.org.za/publications/healthanddemocracy/Chapter7.pdf

Herrera-Franco, G., Montalván-Burbano, N., Carrión-Mero, P., Apolo-Masache, B., & Jaya-Montalvo, M. (2020). Research trends in geotourism: A bibliometric analysis using the scopus database. *Geosciences, 10*(10), 379. doi:10.3390/geosciences10100379

Hutchings, A., Scott, A. H., Lewis, G., & Cunningham, A. B. (1996*). Zulu medicinal plants: An inventory.* University of Natal Press. https://pubs.acs.org/doi/10.1021/np970084y

IIo, P. I. (2012). Acquisition, preservation and accessibility of indigenous knowledge in academic libraries in Nigeria: The place of ICT. *Ikenga: International Journal of Institute of African Studies, 14*(1), 468–487.

James, P. B., Wardle, J., Steel, A., & Adams, J. (2018). Traditional, complementary and alternative medicine use in Sub-Saharan Africa: A systematic review. *BMJ Global Health*, *3*(5), e000895. doi:10.1136/bmjgh-2018-000895 PMID:30483405

Kaggwa, B., Kyeyune, H., Munanura, E. I., Anywar, G., Lutoti, S., Aber, J., Bagoloire, L. K., Weisheit, A., Tolo, C. U., Kamba, P. F., & Ogwang, P. E. (2022). Safety and efficacy of medicinal plants used to manufacture herbal products with regulatory approval in Uganda: A cross-sectional study. *Evidence-Based Complementary and Alternative Medicine*, *2022*, 1–21. doi:10.1155/2022/1304839 PMID:35463071

Kastellec, M. (2012). Practical limits to the scope of digital preservation. *Information Technology and Libraries*, *31*(2), 63–71. doi:10.6017/ital.v31i2.2167

Kennedy, G., & Davis, B. (2006). *Electronic communication systems* (4th ed.). McGraw-Hill.

Kepe, T. (2010). Secrets that kill: Crisis, custodianship and responsibility in ritual male circumcision in the Eastern Cape Province, South Africa. *Social Science & Medicine*, *70*(5), 732–740. doi:10.1016/j.socscimed.2009.11.016 PMID:20053494

Khan, M. S. A., & Ahmad, I. (2019). Herbal medicine: current trends and future prospects. In *New look to phytomedicine* (pp. 3–13). Academic Press., doi:10.1016/B978-0-12-814619-4.00001-X

Khanyile, N. C., & Dlamini, P. (2021). Preservation of traditional medicinal knowledge: Initiatives and techniques in rural communities in KwaZulu-Natal. *Library Philosophy and Practice*, 1-19. https://digitalcommons.unl.edu/libphilprac/4824

Kristoffersen, A. E., Broderstad, A. R., Musial, F., & Stub, T. (2019). Prevalence, and health-and sociodemographic associations for visits to traditional and complementary medical providers in the seventh survey of the Tromsø study. *BMC Complementary and Alternative Medicine*, *19*(1), 1–11. doi:10.118612906-019-2707-1 PMID:31711478

Mapara, J. (2009). Indigenous knowledge systems in Zimbabwe: Juxtaposing postcolonial theory. *The Journal of Pan African Studies*, *3*(1), 30–68.

Masango, C. A. (2020). Indigenous knowledge codification of African traditional medicine: Inhibited by status quo based on secrecy? *Information Development*, *36*(3), 327–338. doi:10.1177/0266666919853007

Masenya, T. M., & Ngulube, P. (2019). Digital preservation practices in academic libraries in South Africa in the wake of the digital revolution. *South African Journal of Information Management*, *21*(1), a1011. doi:10.4102ajim.v21i1.1011

Masoga, M. A. (2017). Critical reflections on selected local narratives of contextual South African indigenous knowledge. In P. Ngulube (Ed.), *Handbook of research on theoretical perspectives on indigenous knowledge systems in developing countries*. IGI Global. doi:10.4018/978-1-5225-0833-5.ch014

Masoga, M. A., & Shokane, A. L. (2020). Socio-economic challenges faced by traditional healers in Limpopo province of South Africa: Conversations from below. *Alternative*, *00*(0), 1–8. doi:10.1177/1177180120956718

McGaw, L. J., Omokhua-Uyi, A. G., Finnie, J. F., & Van Staden, J. (2022). Invasive alien plants and weeds in South Africa: A review of their applications in traditional medicine and potential pharmaceutical properties. *Journal of Ethnopharmacology*, *283*, 114564. doi:10.1016/j.jep.2021.114564 PMID:34438034

Mdhluli, T. D., Mokgoatšana, S., Kugara, S. L., & Vuma, L. (2021). Knowledge management: Preserving, managing and sharing indigenous knowledge through digital library. *Hervormde Teologiese Studies*, *77*(2), a6795. doi:10.4102/hts.v77i2.6795

Minishi-Majanja, M. K. (2012). *Educating a changeling: The paradox of library and information science in Africa*. Inaugural Lecture, University of South Africa. https://uir.unisa.ac.za/bitstream/handle/laugural%

Mokgobi, M. G. (2014). Understanding traditional African healing. *African Journal of Physical Health Education Recreation and Dance*, *20*(2), 24–34. PMID:26594664

Mokhesi, T., & Modjadji, P. (2022). Usage of Traditional, complementary and alternative medicine and related factors among patients receiving healthcare in Lesotho. *The Open Public Health Journal*, *15*(1), e187494452202090. doi:10.2174/18749445-v15-e2202090

Mothibe, M. E., & Sibanda, M. (2019). African traditional medicine: South African perspective. *Traditional and Complementary Medicine*, 1-27. https://www.intechopen.com/chapters/65475

Noronha, M., Pawar, V., Prajapati, A., & Subramanian, R. B. (2020). A literature review on traditional herbal medicines for malaria. *South African Journal of Botany*, *128*, 292–303. doi:10.1016/j.sajb.2019.11.017

Nugraha, A. S., Damayanti, Y. D., Wangchuk, P., & Keller, P. A. (2019). Anti-infective and anti-cancer properties of the Annona species: Their ethnomedicinal uses, alkaloid diversity, and pharmacological activities. *Molecules (Basel, Switzerland)*, *24*(23), 4419. doi:10.3390/molecules24234419 PMID:31816948

Ocholla, D. N. (2007). Marginalized knowledge: An agenda for indigenous knowledge development and integration with other forms of knowledge. *International Journal of Information Ethics*, *7*(9), 237–247.

Ohaja, M., & Murphy-Lawless, J. (2017). Unilateral collaboration: The practices and understandings of traditional birth attendants in southeastern Nigeria. *Women and Birth; Journal of the Australian College of Midwives*, *30*(4), 165–e171. doi:10.1016/j.wombi.2016.11.004 PMID:27889258

Oppong, P. K. (2018). *The influence of packaging and brand equity on over-the-counter herbal medicines in Kumasi, Ghana. (Doctor of Philosophy, School of Management, IT and Governance)*. University of KwaZulu-Natal., https://ukzn-dspace.ukzn.ac.za/handle/10413/17127

Prakash, S., Kumar, M., Kumari, N., Thakur, M., Rathour, S., Pundir, A., & Mekhemar, M. (2021). Plant-based antioxidant extracts and compounds in the management of oral cancer. *Antioxidants*, *10*(9), 1358. doi:10.3390/antiox10091358 PMID:34572990

Rajasekaran, B. (1993). A framework for incorporating indigenous knowledge systems into agricultural research, extension, and NGOs for sustainable agricultural development. *Studies in Technology and Social Change 21*. Ames, IA: Technology and Social Change Program, Iowa State University. http://www.iss.nl/ikdm/IKDM/IKDM/1-3/articles/rajasekaran.html

Robertson, G. L. (2013). *Food packaging: Principles and practice* (3rd ed.). CRC Press.

Ruusalepp, K. I., & Dobreva, M. (2013). *Innovative digital preservation using social search in agent environments: State of art in digital preservation and multi-agent systems.* Durafile. http://www.durafile.eu

Sangha, K., Baijnatha, H., & Street, R. (2020). Spirostachys Africana: A review of phytochemistry, traditional and biological uses and toxicity. *Indilinga, 19*(2), 176–188.

Sen, S., & Chakraborty, R. (2017). Revival, modernization and integration of Indian traditional herbal medicine in clinical practice: Importance, challenges and future. *Journal of Traditional and Complementary Medicine, 7*(2), 234–244. doi:10.1016/j.jtcme.2016.05.006 PMID:28417092

Shimray, S. R., & Ramaiah, C. K. (2018). *Digital preservation strategies: an overview.* www.researchgate.net/publication/327221006_Digital_Preservation_Strategies_An_Overview/link/5b80da10a6fdcc5f8b6592f4/download

Singh, K., Baijnath, H., & Street, R. (2020). Spirostachys Africana: A review of phytochemistry, traditional and biological uses and toxicity. *Indilinga, 19*(1), 176–188.

Thiong'o, N. (1986). *Decolonising the mind: The politics of language in African literature.* J. Currey.

Tyburski, E., Mak, M., Sokołowski, A., Starkowska, A., Karabanowicz, E., Kerestey, M., Lebiecka, Z., Preś, J., Sagan, L., Samochowiec, J., & Jansari, A. S. (2021). Executive dysfunctions in schizophrenia: A critical review of traditional, ecological, and virtual reality assessments. *Journal of Clinical Medicine, 10*(13), 2782. doi:10.3390/jcm10132782 PMID:34202881

Van Wyk, B. E. (2011). The potential of South African plants in the development of new medicinal products. *South African Journal of Botany, 77*(4), 812–829. doi:10.1016/j.sajb.2011.08.011

Venkanna, E. (2018). Perspectives of digital libraries in medical education. *IJARIIE,* 4(1), 2395-4396. http://ijariie.com/AdminUploadPdf/PERSPECTIVES_OF_DIGITAL_LIBRARIES_IN_MEDICAL_EDUCATION_ijariie7279.pdf

Viriri, A., & Mungwini, P. (2009). Down but not out: Critical insights in traditional Shona metaphysics. *The Journal of Pan African Studies, 2*(9). https://www.academia.edu/7946155/Down_But_Not_Out_Critical_Insights_in_Traditional_Shona_Metaphysics

Westerlund, D. (2006). *African indigenous religions and disease causation.* Brill. https://brill.com/display/title/12074

WHO (World Health Organization). (2013). *Traditional medicine definitions.* WHO. www,synergy.com.kurt.

World Health Organisation. (2008). *Male circumcision policy, practices and services in the Eastern Cape Province of South Africa: Case study.* WHO. https://www.malecircumcision.org/sites/default/files/document_library/South_Africa_MC_case_study_May_2008_002_0.pdf

Yuan, H., Ma, Q., Ye, L., & Piao, G. (2016). Traditional medicine and modern medicine from natural products. *Molecules (Basel, Switzerland), 21*(5), 559. doi:10.3390/molecules21050559 PMID:27136524

KEY TERMS AND DEFINITIONS

Afrocentric Model: is a theory that situates Africa's and the African diaspora's experiences and peoples within their own historical, cultural, and social framework.

Indigenous Knowledge: refers to the vast collection of indigenous people's local knowledge, which encompasses customs, traditions, traditional ecological knowledge, spiritual beliefs and local language.

Local Knowledge: is a collection of both old and new knowledge that indigenous people receive by interaction with elderly people, scenery, culture, and other elements of their immediate environment.

Medical Libraries: the establishment of libraries responsible for digitising traditional medicinal knowledge to meet the needs of their customers.

Traditional Medicine: refers to medical systems that were created before the advent of modern medicine and are based on cultural practices and beliefs that have been passed down from one generation to generation.

Digital Preservation: The administration and safeguarding of digital information for the purposes of preserving its trustworthiness, authenticity, and long-term accessibility.

Chapter 5

Opportunities and Challenges in Digitization of Indigenous Knowledge and Implication for Educational Management in the Nigerian Context

Michael Ekpenyong Asuquo
University of Calabar, Nigeria

Godian Patrick Okenjom
https://orcid.org/0000-0003-1212-2163
University of Calabar, Nigeria

Ovat Egbe Okpa
University of Calabar, Nigeria

Ameh Eyiene Eyiene
University of Calabar, Nigeria

ABSTRACT

This chapter focuses on opportunities and challenges in digitizing indigenous knowledge with implications for educational management in the Nigerian context. Digitization provides an avenue for safeguarding and sharing traditional knowledge that may be at risk of being lost or marginalized. By converting indigenous knowledge into digital formats, it can be documented, archived, and easily accessed by future generations, thereby contributing to the preservation of cultural heritage. Specifically, this chapter addresses the overview of indigenous knowledge, digitization of indigenous knowledge, management of indigenous knowledge in the digital age, opportunity in the digitization of indigenous knowledge and challenges of digitization of indigenous knowledge.

DOI: 10.4018/978-1-6684-7024-4.ch005

Copyright © 2023, IGI Global. Copying or distributing in print or electronic forms without written permission of IGI Global is prohibited.

INTRODUCTION

There is no doubt that the arrival of missionaries in Nigeria was to introduce the Christian Religion and subsequently convert the indigenous people of Nigeria from their traditional practices to Christianity (Nwadialor, 2021; Akinwumi, 1988). Nigeria is naturally and culturally blessed with indigenous knowledge systems as evidenced by various practices and languages used in expressing diverse identities and cultural and historical information of people and their communities. For instance, Nigeria, as an independent country, has various native languages (Ndiribe & Aboh, 2022). Although Afolayan (1984) identified Hausa, Igbo and Yoruba as the three major and majority indigenous languages in Nigeria, however, Nigeria has more than four hundred (400) indigenous languages such as Edo, Efik, Fulfude, Idoma Igala, Ijo, Kanuri, Nupe, Tiv. These are regarded as minority indigenous languages (Adegbite, 2003). From the inception of the indigenous communities in Nigeria, traditional practices remain useful in conserving cultural practices, economic activities, indigenous laws and sustainability of local empowerment (Jimoh, 2012). In addition to diverse indigenous languages in Nigeria, other traditional practices by indigenous natives of Nigeria manifest in their traditional worshipping, medicine, fishing, weaving, crafts, and masquerading (Ekpe et al., 2016). Palm wine tapping, locally made pots, doors, chairs and tools are common among the Efiks. The Efik people are known for their traditional practices, such as palm wine tapping, making locally made pots, doors, chairs, and tools. They also have a rich dance, music, and storytelling culture, passed down from generation to generation. All these were transferred from one generation to another.

It is common knowledge that each community in Nigeria is associated with one traditional practice or the other. For instance, the Calabar community in the southern region of Cross River in Nigeria is popularly known for Ekpe and Nnabo masquerades during important traditional ceremonies. Again, In the 1880s, the Efik and Ibibio people of Nigeria practiced the killing of twins during the pre-colonial periods. Giving birth to twins was considered an abomination and a curse to society. The killing of twins at birth was a traditional practice in Nigeria that was eliminated by a Scottish missionary named Mary Slessor. This practice was believed to bring misfortune to the community, and Slessor worked tirelessly to convince the people that twins were not evil. The arrival of Missionaries and the emergence of the colonial government and its operations in Nigeria brought about a new way of life that influenced the Nigerian natives (Ugwu, 2017). As such, in many African countries and Nigeria in particular, educational programmes and activities are based on Western thinking and the belief system as opposed to existing indigenous knowledge (IK) (Kaya & Seleti, 2013). The predominance of foreign practices introduced by the colonizers in Nigeria tends to make the indigenous people of Nigeria foreigners in their environment. Although the foreign ideology seemed to be forced on the natives, the Nigerian natives are still conscious of the practices of their immediate environment (Eyong, 2007). It is common knowledge that, prior to the arrival of the colonial masters, indigenous knowledge in each of the various traditional and ethnic groups in various geographical areas in Nigeria had already been in existence. Man's awareness of his environment provokes him to start activities using available natural resources (Maurya, Ali, Ahmad, Zhou, Castro, Khane & Ali, 2020). The indigenous community members ' skills and knowledge in local farming, trading, craft work, fishing, wine tapping, blacksmithing, traditional medicine and animal rearing have since been attributed to the traditional ways of knowing how to carry out economic activities (Agu, 2013).

AN OVERVIEW OF INDIGENOUS KNOWLEDGE

Indigenous knowledge is a term used to refer to the knowledge, skills, and practices developed and passed down by Indigenous people over generations. It is often based on a deep understanding of the natural environment and the local community. This knowledge can be used for various purposes, such as agriculture, healthcare, and resource management (Ojei & Owojuyigbe, 2019), and it is evidenced in indigenous people's unique culture and tradition in a specific society. Hunter (2005) observed that indigenous knowledge is the cornerstone for the decision-making process concerning food, security, the health of man and animals, and indigenous community members' management of educational and natural resources. Indigenous knowledge is often stored in the minds of Indigenous people. It is expressed through physical practices, such as storytelling, singing, ceremonies, dancing, farming, and other traditional ways of doing things (Wane, 2008). This knowledge is often passed down from generation to generation through oral tradition, and it can be a valuable resource for development. The value of indigenous knowledge and the importance of digitizing it to revitalize cultural heritage and preserve it for future use has been recognized by communities and organisations worldwide (Hunter, 2015). As a result, centers for indigenous knowledge are being set up to preserve this valuable knowledge. Generally, we view knowledge as the ideas in people's minds that are highly valuable to the owners due to their competitive advantage. Knowledge is invisible, intangible and could be associated with the global sharing problem (Sokoh & Okolie, 2021). Nevertheless, digital tools facilitate the easy dissemination of knowledge in contemporary society. In this context, we view IK as skills, experiences, and insights acquired outside the formal education system. This knowledge can improve, transform, sustain and empower communities for sociocultural and economic aspirations (Engdasew, 2022; Camacho et al., 2016). Indigenous knowledge is the knowledge that indigenous community members accumulate for themselves over generations of living in a particular environment (Rÿser 2011). Ideas, information, understanding and skill that an individual acquires through local training, experiences, common sense, observation and intuition are of indigenous knowledge. The importance of indigenous knowledge has made it a path to follow as a crucial tool for human development (Oluwatoyin, 2015).

Scholars have x-rayed why indigenous knowledge should not be in danger of extinction. For instance, the inclusion of indigenous knowledge in social work academies has been stressed (Dumbrill & Grren, 2008). Indigenous knowledge is still being adopted by farmers, even with the merits associated with the mechanization of agriculture. Ebhuoma and Simatele (2019) documented that indigenous knowledge is still used for soil fertility management, pest and disease control, weeding, harvesting, and other post-farming activities. They also stated that research on indigenous knowledge in the educational system is a conscious response to the sustainability of cultural identities, heritage, and practices. Indigenous knowledge is a crucial tool for sociocultural and economic growth and development, especially regarding the sustainability of cultural heritage. The significance of indigenous knowledge has informed research on the issues of cultural heritage, tradition, and religion in the preschool curriculum and how to pass on this knowledge from one generation to another (Reimers, 2022).

Other studies attempted to address the teaching and learning approaches that could promote learning experiences in cultural and traditional heritage and knowledge-related courses (Chin et al., 2018; Kim et al., 2019). The importance of knowledge in an individual's life and a nation at large is crucial in actualizing national and sustainable development in a digitalized setting. Again, to avoid the danger of IK from depletion, many countries have already taken action to maintain specific legislation in this direction (Byron, 2022). It has also been noted that to regress the indigenous knowledge trend from depletion, IK's transparency in the educational system becomes crucial (Nnama-Okechukwu & McLaughlin, 2022); hence, efforts to digitize indigenous knowledge need attention.

DIGITIZATION OF INDIGENOUS KNOWLEDGE

Digitization may be associated with a wide range of meanings based on the context in which it is used. From our perspective, digitizing indigenous knowledge converts tacit indigenous knowledge to explicit indigenous knowledge. It also involves making indigenous knowledge available on the internet for easy retrieval, access and utilization for teaching, learning, research, decision-making and general management of educational organizations (Whaanga et al., 2015). Digitization is the application of emerging information and communication technologies (ICT) to conserve sources of information and knowledge. In this case, information and knowledge are documented in electronic format to make such information available to all and sundries around the globe (Ifijeh et al., 2015).

The digitization of indigenous knowledge aims to preserve valuable ideas, practices, and information from indigenous cultures on the internet so that they are accessible to everyone around the world (Whaanga et al., 2015). It involves managerial, financial and technological efforts to ensure that knowledge is always accessible, stored, utilized and protected from extinction (Nekesa & Oyelude, 2016). Ifijehet al.,2015) averred that digitization plays a vital role in the dissemination, preservation, visibility, accessibility and utilization of valuable knowledge and information. In this context, we look at digitization as utilizing information and communication technologies to preserve valuable practices, knowledge, ideas and information. Globally, studies with respect to digitization in educational system abound in literature (Colombari & Neirotti,2022; Decuypere et al., 2021; Ljungqvist & Sonesson, 2022; Mertala, 2020; Vlieghe, 2016). This is an indication that the area of digitization is not relatively new in the literature. Thus, digitization has brought significant alternatives in knowledge acquisition, creation, access, storage, sharing and utilization (Shiri, Howard, & Farnel, 2022). Digitization of indigenous knowledge aims at making cultural heritage accessible to all indigenous people irrespective of the time and geographical location of the users. This makes the expression of indigenous knowledge freer than in the era of the non-existence of digitization. Digitizing indigenous knowledge and cultural heritage has received the attention of scholars over the years (Ghimire, 2021; Taylor & Gibson, 2017). The digital era is characterized by innovation in how people access knowledge at their disposal, communicate acquired knowledge and demonstrate feedback at any time in the knowledge-driven world time in the knowledge-driven world (Höchtl, Parycek & Schöllhammer, 2016).

Nevertheless, studies addressing opportunities and challenges of digitization of indigenous knowledge with implications for educational management in the context of the Nigerian environment are scarce (Boamah, 2018 &Nicholas, 2022). For instance, existing studies in relation to digitization (Singh et al., 2019; Taylor & Gibson, 2017; Bollweg et al.,2020) emphasized the sales profession, popularization of heritage via digital access and barriers of digitization in retail outlets, respectively. The forgoing studies did not focus on digitizing indigenous knowledge with implications for educational management. Nevertheless, specific studies have addressed challenges and opportunities associated with digitization in maritime logistics (Fruth & Teuteberg, 2017) and food supply (Kittipanya-Ngam & Tan, 2020) with-

Opportunities, Challenges in Digitization of Indigenous Knowledge

out focusing on the educational system. Digitization of Indigenous Knowledge entails the utilization of digital technologies for the preservation of indigenous knowledge and to enhance its easy dissemination, access, retrieval and utilization (Singh et al., 2019; Nicholas, 2022)

Educational activities and programs are constantly being shaped by new technologies (Flessa & Huebner, 2021). In no small measure, digitization is tremendously facilitating quick and easy access to information and knowledge in all human societies. In time past, the physical or traditional methods were the only approach through which man had access to relevant knowledge and information. The traditional method of knowledge and information sharing had its challenges, where users of knowledge and information had to travel from one location to another in search of knowledge and information (Johnson, Jacovina, Russell & Soto, 2016). Fortunately, this limitation was nipped in the bud through the process of digitization arising from the advent of digital tools. No doubt, in the digital era, there is a tremendous transformation in how people interact with the world around them. Advantages attributed to digitization in developed countries include incremental economic growth, while in less developed countries, the reverse is the case (Ghimire, 2021). The economic growth of many countries is a function of digitization, as evidenced in employment and poverty reduction, improved quality of life and access to public services and educational programmes and activities in particular. It is common knowledge that digital technologies facilitate business communication, communication in educational and non-educational organizations and information and knowledge sharing at a faster rate (TariqZafar, 2019).

Aspiration for cultural heritage accessibility calls for digitization in this regard. Digitization, in the literature, is gaining momentum worldwide due to increased technological development and advancement. Expansion of educational opportunities and access to online teaching and learning facilities have been attributed to the application of digital tools in the educational system. Digitization converts analogue data sources into digital forms and file (McKnight et al.,2016; Greenhow & Askari, 2017; Palvia et al., 2018 Morgan; Amhag & Stigmar, 2019; 2020; Williamson et al., 2020; Kim,2020; Ritter & Pedersen, 2020). It changes analogue information streams into digital forms (Brennen & Kreiss, 2016) and this means that digitization entails using digital technologies to convert traditional and analogue information into digital forms. This could be facilitated through the processes of making indigenous knowledge available in hard copy (paper records), photographs, maps and figures for scanning and onward uploading to the internet and ensuring that they are saved in Portable Document Format (PDF) for wider dissemination and easy retrieval, access and utilization for teaching, learning research, decision-making and general management in the educational system (Ruhaimi, Yatin, & Fadzil, 2018). The digitization of indigenous knowledge requires digital tools, a product of information and communication technology advances. These tools are used in various educational settings, including distance, face-to-face and hybrid learning, to support a range of educational purposes. Digital technologies are now an integral part of the educational system, and there is a growing focus on how they can be used to facilitate teaching, learning, and school management (Amhag et al., 2019). Digital tools are emerging technologies that educational institutions use to enhance teaching, learning, and school management. Asuquo et al. (2021) identified YouTube, Edmodo, Facebook, WhatsApp, Blogging, Telegram, Digital Whiteboard, Wechat, EasyBib, projector, and Zoom as some of the digital tools that are used for various purposes in the educational system. Asuquo et al. (2022) also stated that all digital tools are essential for knowledge management in educational systems at all levels.

MANAGING INDIGENOUS KNOWLEDGE IN THE DIGITAL AGE

The importance of knowledge in the life of an individual and the society at large is crucial in achieving economic growth and development of a nation (Ghirmai, 2010). A country's economic, political, sociocultural, and technological standards are all based on the accumulated knowledge of its human resources. This is why scholars from different areas of specialization emphasize the need for knowledge management in every organization across the globe (Asrar-ul-Haq & Anwar, 2016; Zaim et al., 2019;). Knowledge management entails sharing, storage, and utilization and its subsequent impact on every activity and programme (Zaim et al.,2019). It is a common idea that knowledge not managed properly in terms of sharing, storing, and utilizing becomes extinct, particularly the tacit knowledge in a person's mind. Ghirmai (2010) described knowledge as the lifeblood of a country, and as such, it remains a prerequisite asset for the survival of a country in the present dynamic and competitive world. As every other resource is being managed in the school system, so does it apply to knowledge. Scholars have stressed that implementing information systems is a significant role in knowledge management (Al-Emran et al.,2018).

The emergence of technological tools has revolutionized how we access, store, edit, process, share, disseminate, and utilize information and knowledge in the modern world (Haleema, Javaida, Qadri & Sumanc, 2022). Owing to the merits associated with indigenous knowledge, one wonders about the accessibility, storage and easy retrieval of this knowledge at any time and place when the need arises. No doubt, through digital tools, storage, easy access, and collection of indigenous educational materials become easier (Lata & Owan, 2022). As the ideas regarding indigenous knowledge increase, so does the number of interested users who wish to utilize indigenous knowledge for one reason or another, irrespective of place and time. Nevertheless, the greater proportion of the indigenous knowledge in practice by the indigenous community members is not documented (Nelson, 2015). This may be attributed to the accessibility, collection, and storage of authentic and reliable information concerning indigenous knowledge and the tradition of people appearing to be a herculean task (Whaanga et al., 2015). Resiliency in indigenous knowledge deformation is crucial concerning practices handed down in the past by the indigenous traditionalists. Indigenous knowledge is an important societal resource that needs conservation to enhance the sustainability of indigenous practices for peaceful co-existence and balance in the future (Holtorf, 2018). Recognizing this, Nigeria's National Policy on Education (2006) stresses promoting cultural heritage.

Generally, the existence of knowledge takes both tacit and explicit forms (Kumar, 2017). In most cases, indigenous knowledge is not documented because it exists in the mind of the indigenous people and is expressed through various practices, demonstrations and the belief system. Indigenous knowledge is unique based on traditional skills and know-how, fishing, planting, worshipping, traditional medicinal ideas, belief systems, and other practices. Globally, indigenous knowledge remains essential for indigenous communities and the advancement of scientific knowledge (Ghimire, 2021). Indigenous knowledge in tacit form is the knowledge that an individual carry in his or her mind to discharge assigned responsibilities and deal with societal challenges (Dortheimer & Margalit, 2020; Hwang, 2022; Wylie & Kim, 2022). Tacit knowledge is the form of intuition, individual personal belief and experiences. It is not found in a document and, as such, may result in the extinction of knowledge. To avoid this, it is necessary to document indigenous knowledge and make it explicit for future generations. Indigenous knowledge in explicit form is knowledge in written form. As the world is going digital, efforts to ensure that tacit knowledge is documented becomes critical (Carlucci, Kudryavtsev, & Bratianu, 2022; Liu, Li,

Opportunities, Challenges in Digitization of Indigenous Knowledge

He, & Zhang, 2022; Andriani, Christiandy, Wiratmadja, & Sunaryo, 2022). Documentation, preservation, dissemination, accessibility and utilization of indigenous knowledge, irrespective of time and place, are paramount in a digital era (Mahwasane, 2017).

OPPORTUNITIES IN THE DIGITIZATION OF INDIGENOUS KNOWLEDGE

Preserving indigenous materials and practices will not be achieved without digitization for the accessibility of knowledge beyond a given geographical area (Ghimire, 2021). Digitization has made dissemination, visualization, collection and access to information easier (Lata & Owan, 2022). The availability, functionality, and utilization of digital tools positively impact educational institutions' effectiveness in knowledge production and sharing. As a result, digital transformation has become a priority for governments, non-governmental organizations, and researchers. There is a growing effort to digitize these systems to improve global competitiveness (Whaanga et al., 2015). Digital tools have profoundly impacted how we process, communicate, disseminate, access, and utilize knowledge (Ingram & Maye, 2020). Digitization has significantly enhanced teaching, learning, research dissemination, and university management. Digital tools have made accessing and sharing information easier, collaborating with others, and delivering and receiving feedback. This has led to more efficient and effective teaching, learning, research dissemination, and university management (Asuquo et al., 2022).

Digitization of indigenous knowledge is associated with diverse opportunities. For instance, the educational system in Nigeria can take advantage of digitizing indigenous knowledge to remain competitive in the global setting. Scholars have expressed advantages associated with digitization. Such advantages include access to archival (historical) information and data, preservation of valuable archival contents and information, provision for remote access, provision of primary sources of information for research, and availability of digital images of the original picture and contents (James-Gilboe,2005). Digitization enhances excellent chances to collect, store, and analyze accurate user data and personal messages (Lata & Owan, 2022). It has also been noted that applying digital technologies in education increases students' creativity, communication skills and effective information delivery (Fahm, 2022).

Again, digitization enhances effective and efficient preservation and widespread indigenous knowledge (Ghimire, 2021). Digital tools have properties that make things work freely in all directions. For instance, digital tools have been widely used for uploading and downloading educational information globally. The application of digital tools in education has opened up new possibilities for the running and management of education organizations, their programmes and activities, as well as communication among individuals and groups (Parashar, Hulke, & Pakhare, 2018; Pfister, Lehmann, 2022), the utilization of digital tools facilitate the storage of an organization's data, data processing, access to knowledge and information, retrieval, text editing, sharing of ideas, virtual teaching and learning, and asynchronous and synchronous e-learning (Ardolino et al., 2018; Amhag, Hellström, & Stigmar, 2019). With asynchronous e-learning, for instance, knowledge can be accessed by logging in to an e-learning environment at any time to download documents and send messages to the targeted audience, while a synchronous e-learning environment facilitates the feeling of real-life participation in teaching-learning processes with the application of videoconferencing (Shintani, 2016; Stuart, O'Donnell, Scott, O'Donnell, Lund, & Barber, 2022).

A well-digitized educational system uses digital tools to improve the dissemination and access to educational information, service delivery, teaching and learning processes, information security, work stress minimization, students' academic experiences, and administrative decision-making (Williamson, Eynon & Potter, 2020). It is no longer news that digital technologies have already made significant progress in the culture of the people by way of international access to local knowledge (Taylor & Gibson, 2017). It facilitates knowledge communication and accessing remote knowledge from worldwide sources (Starkey, 2020). This removes the constraints of time and distance with respect to knowledge. In most cases, digital tools are also used to assist in performing activities in educational institutions. Emerging digital tools enhance the effectiveness of school managers by enabling effective information management, programme coordination and decision-making process and the ability of the human resource to access and analyze effectively and efficiently. Scholars have highlighted the advantages of digital tools in educational management. These include effective teaching and learning, instant connection with others, immediate access to information, information retrieval enhancement, ease data analysis, promotion of students centered in learning, reinforcing of referencing rules, information storage, editing of information, facilitating online teaching and learning, online payments, enhancement of research skills, freedom to upload lectures at one's comfort, increased access to research materials, promotion of Webinar among faculties (Asuquo et al., 2022).

There are many other benefits of digitization. For instance, digital tools facilitate speed in data processing, information delivery and information exchange and enhancement of qualitative and quantitative information accuracy. With digital tools, many people can link up at a specific time or otherwise through the internet or websites to directly share or exchange information within and outside an organization. The digital tool enhances the rapid processing of data. Irrespective of the quantity of data, such data can be processed briefly with Information and Communication Technology (ICT). In the digital age, emerging digital tools allow for the easy handling of a large amount of information. In this age, educational institutions have computerized their system to simplify record-keeping and general management functions (Noaman et al., 2017). Other advantages that are associated with digitization are discussed below:

- *Availability of information:* Access to various sources of knowledge and information has since been made easier for users around the globe with the help of digital tools. School administrators, teachers, researchers, and students surf/browse the net for needed educational information.
- *Improvement in the principles and methods of instruction:* Digital tools raise the standard of instruction by providing opportunities for learners to explore and discover solutions to problems rather than waiting for their teachers (Awada, 2016). Digitization promotes student-centred learning. Students can independently surf the internet in search for current educational materials or information instead of seeing their teachers as the only sources of information.
- *Digital tools extend teachers' and learners' experience:* Internet connectivity makes it possible to demonstrate what is not practically available in the immediate teaching and learning environment. What is done in real-life situations in any part of the globe can be brought and demonstrated in the classroom through internet connectivity. For instance, video conferencing, zoom, teleconferencing and webinars extended teachers' and students' experience.
- *Provide easy access to online learning and teaching materials:* Digital tools in teaching and learning processes make it easier for teachers and students with internet connectivity to interact at any time, irrespective of location (Amhag et al., 2019; Mcknight et al., 2016). This indicates that internet connection makes the whole world a global village. Access to online learning and teaching materials has been improved and sustained through emerging digital facilities.

Opportunities, Challenges in Digitization of Indigenous Knowledge

- *Facilitate information effectively*: Digital tools are crucial tools that facilitate available information concerning staff salaries, students' charges, pension and gratuity. Even so, in Nigeria, digitization of indigenous knowledge may not be effective when poor planning, inadequate information, and communication technological tools prevail. The success of digitization is contingent upon a good management process in terms of planning, organizing, directing, staffing, and coordinating, as well as a proper budgeting system.

CHALLENGES OF DIGITIZATION OF INDIGENOUS KNOWLEDGE

Notwithstanding the benefits of digitization, in a less developed country like Nigeria, it has been observed that digitization of operations and processes in the educational system appears to be low and, in some cases, not practicable (Akpan & Ibidunni, 2021; Adedoyin & Soykan, 2020). James-Gilboe (2005) identified difficulties in scanning due to large sizes of images and long texts as challenges of digitization. Other scholars averred that inadequate funding constitutes a major challenge that slows down digitization processes (Chikodi & Obidike, 2015). In addition, poor technical know-how, poor internet connectivity and lack of sound administrative policies and guidelines have also been identified as challenges facing digitization by Chikodi and Obidike (2015). Besides, other challenges, as discussed in this context, include:

- **Unstable electricity/power supply**: Poor power supply strangles the functionality and application of digital tools in teaching, learning and general school management in Nigeria. It is rare to have a constant power supply in many areas of Nigeria. This challenge remains chronic and, as such, negatively affects the digitization process in the school system.
- **Conservative attitude exhibited by most educational administrators:** School administrators are the major key players in facilitating the implementation of digital tools in teaching, learning and general school management. However, many school administrators follow bureaucratic procedures in their leadership, and introducing innovation, a global best practice in the school system, becomes difficult. By implication, many school administrators' negative attitudes and leadership challenges concerning adopting information and communication technology (ICT) appear to deviate from the global best practice in the digital era. This attitude, in no small way, limits both the students' and teachers' access to and utilisation of emerging technologies.
- **Inadequate digital resources:** The challenges of digitization faced by many schools in Nigeria are manifested in many areas. These challenges, according to Fahm et al. (2022), include inadequate needed and genuine software, insufficient information and communication (ICT) tools in the instructional activities in the classrooms, challenges associated with slow speed and poor internet connectivity, poor capacity building programmes to develop digital skills in both staff and students, inadequate technical know-how to support and sustain digitization and poor administrative support.
- **Inadequate technical experts to handle the maintenance aspect of digital facilities:** Poor maintenance culture has been observed as the major challenge concerning information and communication technologies. Where digital tools are available in little proportion compared to the number of users, maintenance challenges are the major setback. Other challenges include organizational culture, incompetency in using available ICT facilities to enhance or improve teaching

95

and learning, institutional policy, and poor internet penetration and connectivity. Nevertheless, regular upgrading of the digital facilities, provision of a trained and skilled workforce in ICT, and regular training on how to use digital facilities effectively constitute ways to effective digitization (Chikodi Mole & Obidike, 2015).

- **Organizational culture:** Organizational culture entails values, norms, belief systems, and attitudes that may not have been expressed but shape people's behaviour and how things are done. It is all-pervasive because it indicates communication between management and staff within educational organisations and outsiders. Arguably, understanding, meaning and knowledge are still disseminated devoid of digital tools in many educational organisations in Nigeria.

THE IMPLICATION OF DIGITIZATION OF INDIGENOUS KNOWLEDGE FOR EDUCATIONAL MANAGEMENT

Arguably, the history of educational management as a process is said to be as old as when man became aware of what was transpiring in his immediate environment. To sustain indigenous or traditional practices, man ensures that such cultures are preserved and passed from generation to generation. Digitization of indigenous knowledge facilitates cultural conservation, economic dependence and involvement of community members in the planning processes and development (Hunter, 2015). Digitization of indigenous knowledge has diverse implications for educational management. For instance, digitization and preservation of indigenous knowledge are crucial in the resuscitation of exterminated traditional knowledge and activities and in improving economic self-reliance and sustainability of indigenous community members in educational institutions' planning and decision-making processes (Awada, 2016; Nyiringango, 2019). Another implication of the digitization of indigenous knowledge for educational management is that effectiveness in adapting digital tools in educational management by the educational stakeholders is a sure way to improve and sustain the quality of teaching, learning and general school management to promote economic growth and development. By implementing efficient management strategies, the school will promote opportunities for additional training and development programs aimed at enhancing the use of digital tools by both teachers and students. Possessing management skills, including human, technical, and conceptual abilities, is essential for future school administrators to effectively oversee various aspects of the institution, such as student and staff management, fostering positive relationships with the school community, developing instructional materials and curriculum, managing school operations, and handling overall responsibilities within the school (Yusufali, 2021). School administrators who demonstrate effective management practices can influence teachers and students, working towards achieving educational objectives in the digital era by employing emerging digital tools. These objectives become feasible when every teacher and student acquires fundamental knowledge, skills, and competencies in utilizing digital tools to access, download, upload, document, share, and disseminate knowledge regardless of time and location.

The effective accomplishment of managing the educational system to achieve educational goals can also be determined by the manifestation of indigenous values and the development of morally upright and independent thinking abilities in every student, enabling them to perform civic responsibilities. However, several challenges hinder the practical implementation of educational programs and activities, making them more theoretical. These challenges include insufficient basic digital facilities, underutilization of available digital resources, inadequate maintenance of facilities, and a lack of personnel with digital skills. These challenges deviate from global best practices. In order to promote digitization in the educational system, it is crucial for the local, state, and federal governments, as well as institutional managers, to recognize and address the obstacles that hinder digitization in schools. By doing so, they can enhance the educational system's effectiveness (Onyango & Ondiek, 2021). To digitalize indigenous knowledge, the Nigerian government should be actively involved in increasing awareness of the digitization of teaching, learning and general school management. This could be achieved through adequate funding of the educational sector. Existing government policies, programmes, activities, and actions about digitization should be made known to all school managers. These can be facilitated through the mass media, workshops, conferences and seminars. These programmes (workshops, conferences and seminars) will train teachers and school managers on digitization as a prerequisite in the digital era. These programmes will provide a platform for experts on digitization to exchange ideas on best practices to address the challenges of digitization in the school system. Institutional repositories should be made functional by the school management.

Provision of basic education facilities in line with the demands in the digital era, employment of a competent number of programme instructors, organization of capacity building/training for instructors, provision and maintenance of basic digital tools, replacement of worn-out digital facilities and provision of adequate digital facilities for every staff member and students are the management responsibility in promoting digitization of indigenous knowledge in the school system (Instefjord & Munthe, 2016). Governments at various levels should establish appropriate funding mechanisms for raising school managers' awareness of digitization. Such funds should be included in budgetary provisions annually. If digitization of indigenous knowledge is made part of the educational curriculum in Nigeria, it will reduce ignorance about indigenous knowledge. In each of the States in Nigeria, the State government should maintain an official website to provide information on indigenous knowledge of the Nigerian natives. Ministry of Education should develop teaching and learning materials in the field of digitization of indigenous knowledge for educational institutions and how this knowledge is acquired as well as how it could affect our lives, skill acquisition, poverty alleviation, economic growth and development, prosperity, our health, our welfare and how everyone could support the digitization of indigenous knowledge at all levels of education in the digital era. Researchers have recognized that educational management is crucial in facilitating quality improvements in academic activities and programs (Ekpoh & Asuquo, 2018). Educational management has helped in the identification of deficiencies and the way forward. Educational management promotes programmes that meet the expected minimum academic standards. It ensures that educational programmes at all levels are brought to the knowledge of the public, thereby encouraging the students to enrol in such programmes. The digitization of indigenous knowledge in the conventional school system has serious implications for educational management in Nigeria. It results in preserving cultural heritage and the accessibility, application and utilization of indigenous knowledge by agricultural education students and other employability skills for self-reliance and economic growth and development. To achieve the goals of education in Nigeria in terms of developing and promoting Nigerian languages, art and culture in the context of the world's cultural heritage (FRN, 2008), the digitization of indigenous knowledge should be taken seriously by all stakeholders at the management cadre in all educational levels. To this end, education funding in Nigeria should be given serious and adequate attention to facilitate the resources needed to implement educational programmes and activities effectively. Improvement in education funding is imperative if the digitization of indigenous knowledge is to be guaranteed and sustained in the Nigerian educational system. Therefore, the minimum budgetary allocation of 26%, as recommended by UNESCO, should be implemented.

CONCLUSION AND RECOMMENDATION

In the modern era, educational organisations worldwide are experiencing a significant impact from the emergence of digital tools. These tools have become essential for educational institutions to gain a competitive edge in the information and communication technologies era. They have transformed various activities and programs within educational organisations, leading to substantial teaching, learning, and administration changes. Embracing digital tools has become crucial for educational institutions to keep up with the evolving technological landscape and to ensure they remain relevant in today's digital age. Education, as an essential sector in every society, is boosting its activities, programmes and general management by application of emerging digital technological facilities to meet students' demands in particular and that of society in general. Undoubtedly, the present era is when information and communication technologies are pervasive. Adapting to this new environment necessitates the digitization of IK for preservation, easy dissemination, easy access and retrieval, and utilization of IK for teaching, learning and research. It is recommended that school management in educational organisations at all levels in the digital era should identify with and promote opportunities for the digitization of educational activities despite the prevailing challenges.

REFERENCES

Adedoyin, O. B., & Soykan, E. (2020). Covid-19 pandemic and online learning: The challenges and opportunities. *Interactive Learning Environments*, 1–13. doi:10.1080/10494820.2020.1813180

Adegbite, W. (2003). Enlightenment and attitudes of the Nigerian elite on the roles of languages in Nigeria. *Language, Culture and Curriculum*, *16*(2), 185–196. doi:10.1080/07908310308666667

Afolayan, A. (1984). The English language in Nigerian education as an agent of proper multilingual and multicultural development. *Journal of Multilingual and Multicultural Development*, *5*(1), 1–22. doi:10.1080/01434632.1984.9994134

Akpan, I. J., & Ibidunni, A. S. (2021). Digitization and technological transformation of small business for sustainable development in the less developed and emerging economies: A research note and call for papers. *Journal of Small Business and Entrepreneurship*, 1–7. doi:10.1080/08276331.2021.1924505

Al-Emran, M., Mezhuyev, V., Kamaludin, A., & Shaalan, K. (2018). The impact of knowledge management processes on information systems: A systematic review. *International Journal of Information Management*, *43*, 173–187. doi:10.1016/j.ijinfomgt.2018.08.001

Amhag, L., Hellström, L., & Stigmar, M. (2019). Teacher educators' use of digital tools and needs for digital competence in higher education. *Journal of Digital Learning in Teacher Education*, *35*(4), 203–220. doi:10.1080/21532974.2019.1646169

Amhag, L., Hellström, L., & Stigmar, M. (2019). Teacher educators' use of digital tools and needs for digital competence in higher education. *Journal of Digital Learning in Teacher Education*, *35*(4), 203–220. doi:10.1080/21532974.2019.1646169

Ardolino, M., Rapaccini, M., Saccani, N., Gaiardelli, P., Crespi, G., & Ruggeri, C. (2018). The role of digital technologies in the service transformation of industrial companies. *International Journal of Production Research, 56*(6), 2116–2132. doi:10.1080/00207543.2017.1324224

Asrar-ul-Haq, M., & Anwar, S. (2016). A systematic review of knowledge management and knowledge sharing: Trends, issues, and challenges. *Cogent Business & Management, 3*(1), 1127744. doi:10.1080/23311975.2015.1127744

Asuquo, M. E., Ekpoh, U. I., & Udeh, K. V. (2022). Politics of managing university education with emerging technologies in the covid – 19 pandemic era: Perspectives of academic staff in Cross River State, Nigeria. *Global Journal of Educational Research, 21*(2), 87–97. doi:10.4314/gjedr.v21i2.1

Awada, G. (2016). Effect of WhatsApp on critique writing proficiency and perceptions toward learning. *Cogent Education, 3*(1), 1264173. doi:10.1080/2331186X.2016.1264173

Boamah, E. (2018). Relative advantages of digital preservation management in developing countries. *New Review of Information Networking, 23*(1-2), 83–98. doi:10.1080/13614576.2018.1544088

Bollweg, L., Lackes, R., Siepermann, M., & Weber, P. (2020). Drivers and barriers to the digitalisation of local owner-operated retail outlets. *Journal of Small Business and Entrepreneurship, 32*(2), 173–201. doi:10.1080/08276331.2019.1616256

Brennen, J. S., & Kreiss, D. (2016). Digitalisation. *The international encyclopedia of communication theory and Philosophy*, 1-11. https://doi.org/ doi:10.1002/9781118766804.wbiect111

Byron, I. P. (2022). The protection of traditional knowledge under the sui generis regime in Nigeria. *International Review of Law Computers & Technology, 36*(1), 17–27. doi:10.1080/13600869.2021.1997086

Camacho, L. D., Gevaña, D. T., Carandang, A. P., & Camacho, S. C. (2016). Indigenous knowledge and practices for the sustainable management of Ifugao forests in Cordillera, Philippines. *The International Journal of Biodiversity Science, Ecosystem Services & Management, 12*(1-2), 5–13. doi:10.1080/21513732.2015.1124453

Chikodi Mole, A. J., & Obidike, N. A. (2015). Overcoming challenges of electronic collection development in university libraries: A study of three Nigerian university libraries. *Library Collections, Acquisitions & Technical Services, 39*(3-4), 73–81. doi:10.1080/14649055.2016.1231564

Chin, K. Y., Lee, K. F., & Chen, Y. L. (2018). Using an interactive ubiquitous learning system to enhance authentic learning experiences in a cultural heritage course. *Interactive Learning Environments, 26*(4), 444–459. doi:10.1080/10494820.2017.1341939

Colombari, R., & Neirotti, P. (2022). Closing the middle-skills gap widened by digitalisation: How technical universities can contribute through Challenge-Based Learning. *Studies in Higher Education, 47*(8), 1585–1600. doi:10.1080/03075079.2021.1946029

Decuypere, M., Grimaldi, E., & Landri, P. (2021). Introduction: Critical studies of digital education platforms. *Critical Studies in Education, 62*(1), 1–16. doi:10.1080/17508487.2020.1866050

Development in Ethiopia. Ethiopian. *Journal of Social Sciences and Humanities, 18*(1), 121–144. doi:10.1314/ejossah.v18i1.5

Dumbrill, G. C., & Grren, J. (2008). Indigenous Knowledge in the Social Work Academy. *Social Work Education*, *27*(5), 489–503. doi:10.1080/02615470701379891

Ebhuoma, E. E., & Simatele, D. M. (2019). 'We know our Terrain': Indigenous knowledge preferred to scientific systems of weather forecasting in the Delta State of Nigeria. *Climate and Development*, *11*(2), 112–123. doi:10.1080/17565529.2017.1374239

Ekpoh, U. I., & Asuquo, M. E. (2018). Management techniques and sustainability of post-basic education in Calabar Education Zone of Cross River State, Nigeria. *African Journal of Studies in Education*, *12*(2), 39–53. https://scholar.google.com/scholar?cluster=8570829484364958859&hl=en&oi=scholarr

Fahm, A. O., Azeez, A. L., Imam-Fulani, Y. O., Mejabi, O. V., Faruk, N., Abdulrahaman, M. D., Olawoyin, L. A., Oloyede, A. A., & Surajudeen-Bakinde, N. T. (2022). ICT enabled Almajiri education in Nigeria: Challenges and prospects. *Education and Information Technologies*, *27*(3), 3135–3169. doi:10.100710639-021-10490-7 PMID:34539214

Federal Republic of Nigeria (FRN). (2008). *National Policy on Education*. NERDC Press.

Fenton, J. A. (2016). Masking and money in a Nigerian metropolis: The economics of performance in Calabar. *Critical Interventions*, *10*(2), 172–192. doi:10.1080/19301944.2016.1205364

Fruth, M., & Teuteberg, F. (2017). Digitization in maritime logistics—What is there and what is missing? *Cogent Business & Management*, *4*(1), 1411066. doi:10.1080/23311975.2017.1411066

Ghimire, P. (2021). The digitalisation of Indigenous Knowledge in Nepal—Review Article. *Acta Inform. Malays*, *5*(2), 42–47. doi:10.26480/aim.02.2021.42.47

Greenhow, C., & Askari, E. (2017). Learning and teaching with social network sites: A decade of research in K-12 related education. *Education and Information Technologies*, *22*(2), 623–645. doi:10.100710639-015-9446-9

Höchtl, J., Parycek, P., & Schöllhammer, R. (2016). Big data in the policy cycle: Policy decision making in the digital era. *Journal of Organizational Computing and Electronic Commerce*, *26*(1-2), 147–169. doi:10.1080/10919392.2015.1125187

Holtorf, C. (2018). Embracing change: How cultural resilience is increased through cultural heritage. *World Archaeology*, *50*(4), 639–650. doi:10.1080/00438243.2018.1510340

Hunter, J. (2005). The role of information technologies in indigenous knowledge management. *Australian Academic and Research Libraries*, *36*(2), 109–124. doi:10.1080/00048623.2005.10721252

Ifijeh, G., Iwu-James, J., & Osinulu, I. (2015). From binding to digitization: Issues in newspaper preservation in Nigerian academic libraries. *Serials Review*, *41*(4), 242–249. doi:10.1080/00987913.2015.1103153

Instefjord, E., & Munthe, E. (2016). Preparing pre-service teachers to integrate technology: An analysis of the emphasis on digital competence in teacher education curricula. *European Journal of Teacher Education*, *39*(1), 77–93. doi:10.1080/02619768.2015.1100602

James-Gilboe, L. (2005). The challenge of digitization: Libraries are finding that newspaper projects are not for the faint of heart. *The Serials Librarian, 49*(1-2), 155–163. doi:10.1300/J123v49n01_06

Jimoh, S. O., Ikyaagba, E. T., Alarape, A. A., Obioha, E. E., & Adeyemi, A. A. (2012). The role of traditional laws and taboos in wildlife conservation in the Oban Hill Sector of Cross River National Park (CRNP), Nigeria. *Journal of Human Ecology (Delhi, India), 39*(3), 209–219. doi:10.1080/09709274.2012.11906513

Kim, J. (2020). Learning and teaching online during Covid-19: Experiences of student teachers in an early childhood education practicum. *International Journal of Early Childhood, 52*(2), 145–158. doi:10.100713158-020-00272-6 PMID:32836369

Kim, S., Whitford, M., & Arcodia, C. (2019). Development of intangible cultural heritage as a sustainable tourism resource: The intangible cultural heritage practitioners' perspectives. *Journal of Heritage Tourism, 14*(5-6), 422–435. doi:10.1080/1743873X.2018.1561703

Kittipanya-Ngam, P., & Tan, K. H. (2020). A framework for food supply chain digitalisation: Lessons from Thailand. *Production Planning and Control, 31*(2-3), 158–172. doi:10.1080/09537287.2019.1631462

Kolawole, O. D. (2015). Twenty reasons why local knowledge will remain relevant to development. *Development in Practice, 25*(8), 1189–1195. doi:10.1080/09614524.2015.1078777

Lata, N., & Owan, V. J. (2022). Contemporary trends and technologies in research libraries: An overview. In T. Masenya (Ed.), *Innovative technologies for enhancing knowledge access in academic libraries* (pp. 40–56). IGI Global., doi:10.4018/978-1-6684-3364-5.ch003

Ljungqvist, M., & Sonesson, A. (2022). Selling out education in the name of digitalisation: A critical analysis of Swedish policy. *Nordic Journal of Studies in Educational Policy, 8*(2), 89–102. doi:10.108 0/20020317.2021.2004665

Mahwasane, N. P. (2017). Library support and the innovative application of Indigenous knowledge systems. *Journal of Sociology and Social Anthropology, 8*(2), 77–81. doi:10.1080/09766634.2017.1316952

McKnight, K., O'Malley, K., Ruzic, R., Horsley, M. K., Franey, J. J., & Bassett, K. (2016). Teaching in a digital age: How educators use technology to improve student learning. *Journal of Research on Technology in Education, 48*(3), 194–211. doi:10.1080/15391523.2016.1175856

Mertala, P. (2020). Paradoxes of participation in the digitalisation of education: A narrative account. *Learning, Media and Technology, 45*(2), 179–192. doi:10.1080/17439884.2020.1696362

Morgan, H. (2020). Best practices for implementing remote learning during a pandemic. *The Clearing House: A Journal of Educational Strategies, Issues and Ideas, 93*(3), 135–141. doi:10.1080/00098655 .2020.1751480

Ndiribe, M. O., & Aboh, S. C. (2022). Multilingualism and marginalisation: A Nigeria diversity approach. *International Journal of Multilingualism, 19*(1), 1–15. doi:10.1080/14790718.2020.1818752

Nekesa, A. W., & Oyelude, A. A. (2016). Standing Conference of Eastern, Central, and Southern African Library Associations XXII 2016. *The International Information & Library Review, 48*(3), 228–231. do i:10.1080/10572317.2016.1205430

Nicholas, G. (2022). Protecting Indigenous heritage objects, places, and values: Challenges, responses, and responsibilities. *International Journal of Heritage Studies, 28*(3), 400–422. doi:10.1080/1352725 8.2021.2009539

Nnama-Okechukwu, C. U., & McLaughlin, H. (2022). Indigenous knowledge and social work education in Nigeria: Made in Nigeria or made in the West? *Social Work Education,* 1–18. doi:10.1080/026 15479.2022.2038557

Noaman, A. Y., Ragab, A. H. M., Madbouly, A. I., Khedra, A. M., & Fayoumi, A. G. (2017). Higher education quality assessment model: Towards achieving the educational quality standard. *Studies in Higher Education, 42*(1), 23–46. doi:10.1080/03075079.2015.1034262

Nyiringango, G. (2019). *Assessing Changes in Knowledge about and Self-efficacy for Neonatal Resuscitation Among Rwandan Nurses and Midwives after a Mentorship Process* (Doctoral dissertation, The University of Western Ontario (Canada).

Onyango, G., & Ondiek, J. O. (2021). Digitalisation and integration of sustainable development goals (SGDs) in public organisations in Kenya. *Public Organization Review, 21*(3), 511–526. doi:10.100711115-020-00504-2

Palvia, S., Aeron, P., Gupta, P., Mahapatra, D., Parida, R., Rosner, R., & Sindhi, S. (2018). Online education: Worldwide status, challenges, trends, and implications. *Journal of Global Information Technology Management, 21*(4), 233–241. doi:10.1080/1097198X.2018.1542262

Parashar, R., Hulke, S., & Pakhare, A. (2018). Learning styles among first professional Northern and central India medical students during digitization. *Advances in Medical Education and Practice, 1-5,* 1–5. Advance online publication. doi:10.2147/AMEP.S182790 PMID:30588146

Pfister, P., & Lehmann, C. (2022). Digital value creation in German SMEs–a return-on-investment analysis. *Journal of Small Business and Entrepreneurship,* 1–26. doi:10.1080/0827633 1.2022.2037065

Reimers, E. (2020). Secularism and religious traditions in non-confessional Swedish preschools: Entanglements of religion and cultural heritage. *British Journal of Religious Education, 42*(3), 275–284. doi:10.1080/01416200.2019.1569501

Ritter, T., & Pedersen, C. L. (2020). Digitization capability and the digitalisation of business models in business-to-business firms: Past, present, and future. *Industrial Marketing Management, 86,* 180–190. doi:10.1016/j.indmarman.2019.11.019

Shintani, N. (2016). The effects of computer-mediated synchronous and asynchronous direct corrective feedback on writing: A case study. *Computer Assisted Language Learning, 29*(3), 517–538. doi:10.10 80/09588221.2014.993400

Shiri, A., Howard, D., & Farnel, S. (2022). Indigenous digital storytelling: Digital interfaces supporting cultural heritage preservation and access. *The International Information & Library Review, 54*(2), 93–114. doi:10.1080/10572317.2021.1946748

Singh, J., Flaherty, K., Sohi, R. S., Deeter-Schmelz, D., Habel, J., Le Meunier-FitzHugh, K., Malshe, A., Mullins, R., & Onyemah, V. (2019). Sales profession and professionals in the age of digitization and artificial intelligence technologies: Concepts, priorities, and questions. *Journal of Personal Selling & Sales Management, 39*(1), 2–22. doi:10.1080/08853134.2018.1557525

Starkey, L. (2020). A review of research exploring teacher preparation for the digital age. *Cambridge Journal of Education, 50*(1), 37–56. doi:10.1080/0305764X.2019.1625867

Stuart, J., O'Donnell, A. W., Scott, R., O'Donnell, K., Lund, R., & Barber, B. (2022). Asynchronous and synchronous remote teaching and academic outcomes during COVID- 19. *Distance Education, 43*(3), 408–425. doi:10.1080/01587919.2022.2088477

Taylor, J., & Gibson, L. K. (2017). Digitization, digital interaction and social media: Embedded barriers to democratic heritage. *International Journal of Heritage Studies, 23*(5), 408–420. doi:10.1080/13527258.2016.1171245

Vlieghe, J. (2016). Education, Digitization and Literacy training: A historical and cross-cultural perspective. *Educational Philosophy and Theory, 48*(6), 549–562. doi:10.1080/00131857.2015.1044928

Wane, N. N. (2008). Mapping the field of indigenous knowledge in anti-colonial discourse: A transformative journey in education. *Race, Ethnicity and Education, 11*(2), 183–197. doi:10.1080/13613320600807667

Whaanga, H., Bainbridge, D., Anderson, M., Scrivener, K., Cader, P., Roa, T., & Keegan, T. T. (2015). He Matapihi Mā Mua, Mō Muri: The ethics, processes, and procedures associated with the digitization of indigenous knowledge—The Pei Jones collection. *Cataloging & Classification Quarterly, 53*(5-6), 520–547. doi:10.1080/01639374.2015.1009670

Williamson, B., Eynon, R., & Potter, J. (2020). Pandemic politics, pedagogies and practices: Digital technologies and distance education during the coronavirus emergency. *Learning, Media and Technology, 45*(2), 107–114. doi:10.1080/17439884.2020.1761641

Yusufali, S. S. (2021). A Values-Based, Holistic Approach towards School Mission in a US Islamic School. Retrieved from https://ir.lib.uwo.ca/oip/204

Zaim, H., Muhammed, S., & Tarim, M. (2019). Relationship between knowledge management processes and performance: Critical role of knowledge utilization in organisations. *Knowledge Management Research and Practice, 17*(1), 24–38. doi:10.1080/14778238.2018.1538669

KEY TERMS AND DEFINITIONS

Digitization: Digitization is the process of ensuring that tacit indigenous knowledge is converted to explicit indigenous knowledge and subsequently making them available on the internet or online database. With digitization, indigenous knowledge is converted into such digital items as still images, videos, audio and texts.

Educational Management: Educational management is the control of all educational resources for the purpose of improving, achieving and sustaining educational goals and objectives.

Indigenous Knowledge: Indigenous knowledge is the traditional knowledge of the natives of a given geographical area. It is evident in the culture of the indigenes of a particular community.

Tacit knowledge: It is any knowledge, information, skill and ability that an individual has gained through experience which is often quite challenging to explain, communicate, or simply put into words.

Traditional practices: These are various economic, religious and sociocultural ways of doing things by indigenous community members of a particular ethnic group.

Chapter 6

Promotion and Preservation of Indigenous Knowledge Systems and the Traditional Environmental Knowledge of Garo Communities in Bangladesh

Jannatul Mawa
Monash University, Australia

ABSTRACT

Together with other indigenous groups living in Bangladesh, Garo people are considered to be an ethnic group originating from Tibet who have inherent knowledge about nature and biodiversity. Garo people depend on diverse ecosystems for their food, economic, cultural, social, and spiritual existence, and having an intricate relationship with nature has enabled the community to know different plants, herbs, and the use of these plants as foods as well as the technique of how to protect and conserve these plants. In this context, this chapter aims to discover, document and preserve Garo people's traditional environmental knowledge such as climate indicators, traditional medicine and housing techniques. This chapter further explored Garo's people role during seasonal activities and in preserving relevant portions of the traditional knowledge system.

INTRODUCTION AND BACKGOUND

The Adivasi worldview has been and remains underpinned by a system of knowledge which understands a forested environment as a sacred domain, demanding care and careful harvesting so as not to create disharmonious relations between deities and humans (Bleie, 2005).

DOI: 10.4018/978-1-6684-7024-4.ch006

Copyright © 2023, IGI Global. Copying or distributing in print or electronic forms without written permission of IGI Global is prohibited.

Jointly with other indigenous groups residing in Bangladesh, also known as the Garos are deemed to be an ethnic group deriving from Tibet (Gain, 1995). The estimated Garo population is about 0.1 to 0.13 million people (Burling 1997; Drong, 2004 & Islam 2008, cited in Muhammed et al, 2011) spread across India and Bangladesh. Garo people of Bangladesh call themselves 'Mandi'. As stated by Bal (2007), around 100,000 of Garo people who live in Bangladesh are residing mostly in the northernmost part of the Mymensingh district within a few kilometres of the Indian border. Smaller settlements of Garo people are also found in other parts of Bangladesh such as in the Modhupur forest near Durgapur, Bhaluka, and Haluaghat, and other small groups live in Sunamganj, Sylhet and Joydebpur (Sangma, 2010) while other groups live in Dhaka. The Garos have intrinsic knowledge about nature and biodiversity, and the social, economic, cultural and religious rituals of these people are involved in a circle of the ecosystems. Garos thus depend on the varied environments for their food, economic, cultural, social and spiritual existence. Having an extravagant association with the surrounding nature has facilitated Garo communities to know different plants, herbs and the use of these plants as foods, and they also know the technique of how to protect and conserve these plants. In this context, this chapter aims to discover and document Garo people's traditional environmental knowledge such as climate indicators, traditional medicine and housing techniques and explore their role during seasonal activities and in preserving relevant portions of the traditional knowledge system.

TRADITIONAL KNOWLEDGE AND VALUES OF GARO PEOPLE

Garo people have a matrilineal family system where property owners and transferring authority are inherited by women (Biswas et al, 2015), and as noted by Majumdar (1978), these people were shifting cultivators, conceiving and practising *jhum* – shifting agriculture. In the pre-colonial period, women in Garo matrilineal communities played a major role in *jhum* production. Women's responsibility was to collect the forest resources while men looked after the land and household (Sangma, 1998). The youngest daughter of the family inherited the property, a form of ultimogeniture (Bal, 2007). The husband of the youngest daughter had custody of the land but no authority to dispose of the land without the consent of his wife and it was also his responsibility to look after his wife's parents until their death (Bal, 2007). Garo people are one of the two matrilineal societies in Bangladesh whose traditional practice includes the inheritance of property through the female line. Being organised in a matrilineal society, Garo children take their mother's title and belong to her kinship group (Sangma, 2010).

The whole Garo community is divided into five major *Chatchi* clans, namely: *Sangma, Marak, Momin, Shira* and *Abetty*, and each of them is different from the others. In Bangladesh, most of the Garo people belong to *Sangma, Marak,* and *Momin* groups. A *Chatchi* is also separated into sub-groups, each of them known as *Machong* (Das & Islam, 2005). A *Machong* is also divided into small groups, each of them known as a *Mahari* and the people in a *Mahari* is related by blood, and all of these levels of clan and sub-clan down to the immediate family are bound by the matrilineal family systems and their kinship ties are very strong (Jengcham, 1994). In the studied areas, Garo people continue following these kinship, tradition and habitation regulations. A significant portion of the Garo community practices their traditional religion called *Sangsarek* (Muhammed et al, 2011). Most Garo people also converted to Christianity, as is typical across indigenous and tribal populations in the region where Christian missionaries were a key actor during the colonisation of the region by European colonial powers, and tribal peoples amalgamated their traditional beliefs with new Christian forms. However, there are still several

Indigenous and Environmental Knowledge of Garo Communities

vestiges of antiquated theories present in the studied communities. As portrayed in the existing narrative, the adherents of the *Sangsarek religion* consider that there are several non-existent Gods that can symbolize ecological energies, plants and creatures.

Garo people also have a rich cultural heritage and a deep connection with the natural environment. The Garo people possess a traditional or indigenous knowledge system that is closely intertwined with their surroundings and plays a vital role in preserving the ecosystem. The following are some key aspects of the Garo people's knowledge system and their role in environmental conservation:

- **Traditional Ecological Knowledge (TEK):** The Garo people have accumulated a vast body of knowledge about their local ecosystem through generations of observation and experience, and they possess an intricate understanding of the behavior, habitats, and ecological interactions of various plant and animal species in their surroundings. This traditional ecological knowledge, passed down orally from elders to younger generations, forms the foundation of their sustainable practices.
- **Forest Management:** The Garo people have developed unique forest management systems that prioritize sustainable resource utilization, and they have a deep respect for the forest and consider it a sacred entity. Traditional practices such as rotational shifting cultivation, known as jhum cultivation, are employed to maintain a balance between agricultural needs and forest preservation. The Garo people selectively harvest timber, non-timber forest products and medicinal plants, ensuring the regeneration of the forest.
- **Biodiversity Conservation:** The Garo people have an intricate understanding of the biodiversity in their region and the importance of its preservation, and they have identified and protected sacred groves, which are patches of forests considered sacred and left undisturbed. These groves act as sanctuaries for a diverse range of plant and animal species, serving as biodiversity hotspots and gene banks for future generations.
- **Water Resource Management:** The Garo people have a deep understanding of water resource management, and they have developed traditional systems for rainwater harvesting, stream diversion and irrigation to ensure the sustainable use of water for agricultural purposes. These practices promote water conservation and help maintain the ecological balance of the region.
- **Traditional Laws and Customs:** The Garo people have a well-defined system of customary laws and practices that govern the use of natural resources. These laws regulate hunting, fishing and the collection of forest products to prevent overexploitation. The community elders and leaders play a crucial role in enforcing these regulations and ensuring the sustainable management of resources.
- **Cultural Practices and Rituals:** The Garo people's cultural practices and rituals are deeply intertwined with nature and its conservation. Festivals such as Wangala and Rongchu Gala celebrate the harvest season and express gratitude to the deities and spirits of the land. These festivals also serve as reminders of the importance of maintaining a harmonious relationship with nature and the need to protect the environment.

Overall, the Garo people's knowledge system is rooted in their deep connection with the natural environment. Through their traditional practices, customs, and sustainable resource management techniques, they play a significant role in preserving the biodiversity and ecological balance of their surroundings. However, it's important to note that the challenges of modernization and external influences

TRADITIONAL REMEDY USED BY GARO PEOPLE

Consistent with *Sangsarek's* opinions, besides the Gods that rheostat natural spectacles, there are some *mitde* who are accountable for explicit human diseases. When they bite a person, the person indentures an ailment. Throughout the ancient, they were able to comprehend which *mitde* had bitten a person after referring the traditional therapist. As stated by Jengcham (1994:78)

There used to be a priest in every Garo village to worship and provide herbal medical treatment. The Garos used to call him "Khamal'. Generally, the elder respectable persons used to be selected as the 'Khamal' who receives different matras from different Gods in his dreams, and with those mantras, he worships the Gods and gives treatments to sick people. With these mantras and local herbs, he works for the public welfare of the villagers but this is not his profession and he does not take money for these treatment […] Otherwise this Khamals or priests are like ordinary farmers of the village.

In Durgapur, people described one technique used by the *Khamal* to recognise which *mitde* pretentious the sick people. It is comprised of sagging three filaments from a bow and articulating numerous names of diverse *mitdes* in sequence. When the filaments unexpectedly started to wobble, the name that was being told in that instant was measured to be the name of the remorseful *mitde*. In Haluaghat, people alleged in the historical *Simma mitde* used to distress their people, one was cured by slaughtering a hen. These days, Garo people desire to use herbal treatments to heal several bites from deities. Similarly, if *Mitde* reasons a disease that makes people's body agitation. Garo people heal the person by taking the liquid from the tree named *Chishik* and using it to massage his body. Likewise, *Hashi midte* sources fever and body shaking, in this case the treatment is the fluid from the *Hashi* tree. Jengcham (1994) revealed a myth about the system deities would spread to Garo people the surreptitious remedial and magic possessions of plants.

The story is about a young man called Delong who lives in the Garo hills, instead of getting married, he preferred to pass his days wandering in the forest while studying and discovering different kinds of plants. One day, he decided to visit a mysterious hill where he entered the palace of the Queen of the magic plants, who showed him her enchanted garden and explained to him the use of many unknown plants, herbs and roots. When Delong left to return to his village, she gave him many roots and herbs as a gift, promising to give and teach him more the next time he visited her again. Delong planted all the medicinal plants she gave him in his village and explained to a friend how to grow and use them. The second time he went to visit the enchanted hill, he brought his friend with him, but the guardian girls of the magic palace did not allow his friend to enter, as only unmarried boys are allowed. The friend therefore went back to the village and Delong entered the garden. From that day onwards, Delong never returned to the village but his friend started practising and spreading the knowledge he transmitted to him.

In the observed Garo communities, the knowledge of medicinal plants is still collected by males and females and pragmatic furthermost of the period at the domestic level. Herbal medications equipped from

Indigenous and Environmental Knowledge of Garo Communities

extracts of precise plants and yaps originating in the forest are used today not only to indulge the bite of the *mind* but also of snakes, leeches and insects. In cases when bugs bite, people use an assorted liquor of ginger, garlic and lime on their physique. When bitten by the *sinnaru* (millipede) people use to do a message with the sweet pumpkin on the belly; in the case of a scorpion bite, they use rice beer. People also know how to make a plaster with the pedigrees of traditional plants to heal a broken leg. Forest tree leaves and cortex are also used by Garo people to formulate extracts that are drunk when people have been condemned or terrified by spirits(*miming*) or bad wind. Participants from the research areas also revealed that some of the therapeutic plants which are used as a compress to cure the attack of bad wind by massaging the body of the sick person are *nursing, makbul khacchi, wak pantra and tulshi*. When the occurrence of a spirit or bad wind has more solemn significance, and the therapy generally used at the household level is not working, people recourse to *Ghashanta Chikitsok*, who is a person with the knowledge on how to unambiguously use *Ghashanta*, a remedial plant. This is also used to cure explicit illnesses such as jaundice, pneumonia, cholera, chickenpox, puerperal fever and stomach problems. Apart from herbal medicine, another traditional method used to cure people attacked by bad wind is called *Mansi*, However, people do not rely on this ritual when they have normal diseases, in which case they can go to an allopathic doctor.

Research further revealed that people reminisce that they used to go to the consecrated Banyan tree to bestow their oblations (like pigeons, candies, and flowers). At present, still some people exercise this tradition when confronted by a bad wind or a spirit while sleeping. In inference, Garo people comprehend corporeal and psychological well-being and illness is still linked to olden mores. The practice of herbal remedies from the wilderness is immobile and generally used by the observed people. Occasionally the term of an illness still resembles the designation of the tree used to treat it. Separately after the traditional individual masculine therapist accessed when the illnesses are predominantly solemn, equally males and females repeat natural remedies on daily basis. Yet again, the timberland has conventionally frolicked a dominant part in the life of the Garo people. The forest is concurrently a dwelling for roughly evil spirits which grounds illnesses and the foundation of the herbal medications mandatory to treat these diseases along with the habitation of the deified Banyan Sapling. However, as a sign of the desertion of the forest, assembling herbal remedies is becoming more and more problematic. Furthermore, the enhancement of transportation and thus elevated entree to marketplaces has adopted the dissemination of allopathic medicine among the Garo people.

NATURAL NEEDLES USED BY GARO PEOPLE

Garo people are still entirely trusting on traditional approaches to comprehending climate behaviour. One of our participants said, "When the frogs cry that means the rain is coming". Partha (2018) further stated that:

It indicates the conception and base of ecological thought and practices of the rural people of Bangladesh.

Garo people also deliberate to perceive the moon, and if there is a red colour sphere adjacent to it, then there will be rain. The beginning of flood is designated by the infrequent behaviour of snakes, and when many snakes cross the road numerous times it means there will be flooding. Garo people perceive natural rudiments not only to envisage climatic behaviour but also other conceivable proceedings that could distress their lives. For example, if the wild hen makes the sound *wang* somebody will certainly die soon. During a lunar eclipse, no one is permitted to have a meal since it is alleged that this would reason a calamity. Precisely, pregnant women are not permitted to see this spectacle or else their children are in danger of becoming blind. People used to bang the plates and make noises so that the eclipse would not last long. Throughout the *Sangsarek* period, a hen would be slaughtered during the wedding ceremony to comprehend whether the new couple would have a happy life or not. This research thus found such fascinating information from the research areas. Again, during the *Wangala* festival amongst *Sansarek* Garos, a prophecy about the impending harvest is completed by perceiving the path occupied by the smoke of the exasperate scorched in the house of the traditional leader. Through the same festival, in Durgapur, the prediction about a decent or bad harvest is done by perceiving the intestines of the slaughtered hen. Dreams are a significant apparatus that links Garo people with their environment, consenting them to comprehend what weather will perhaps ensue. As stated by Jengcham (1994: 73):

The Garos usually see dream which is consistent with their daily life. For example, their dreams are often about the forest, elephant, tiger, wild swine, fish etc. That means most of the time their dreams are about nature. For example, if anyone dreams of a tiger that means that there will be a drought or very hot weather. If anyone sees a drinking party, that means there will be heavy rain.

The research participants revealed this same clarification of dreams and they also mentioned that the dreams are also the language used by Gods to transmit to the Garo traditional healer, *Khamal*, knowledge of how to heal people. In observation of Garo communities, it has been found out how the adjacent atmosphere has an unfathomable denotation for the Garo communities and how their traditional knowledge is interrelated and constructed on practical or emblematic contacts with the existing existences that form a part of the forestry ecosystem. The desertion of the forest, the transformation in climate patterns and the overview of other peripheral interferences are donating to the commotion of these exchanges between the Garo and their environment.

ECOLOGICAL EXPERTISE AND CULTURAL TRANSMISSION

The indigenous knowledge of women and men farmers, forest-dependent people and fishers can be a valuable entry point for localised adaptation. The different knowledge of women and men must be acknowledged by making sure that all local knowledge is gathered and treated equally. This means recognising the advantages of and capitalising on locally adapted crops, fish and livestock, farming systems, soil, water and nutrient management, agroforestry systems and wildfire management. It is also important to note that local knowledge about less obvious resources, such as small crops, forest food and medicinal plants is often held only by women (FAO, 2012: 29). Indigenous people's knowledge systems of the surrounding natural environments are getting further consideration in the global investigation along with development and climate change deliberations.

As stated by Galloway (2010:23)

There is a growing appreciation that indigenous traditional knowledge offers information and insight that complements conventional science and environmental observations and provides a holistic understand-

Indigenous and Environmental Knowledge of Garo Communities

ing of environmental, natural resources and culture. This had led to increasing collaborative efforts to document traditional knowledge.

In Bangladesh, there is still a lot to explore concerning the ecological knowledge of indigenous people. Burling (1997:189, 190) emphasizes the Garo people's knowledge about the living things in the forest.

Garo people know which leaves can be eaten, which bits can be useful as oral medicines, and which can be rubbed on the skin to smooth a rash. This knowledge is unsystematic and unrecorded but enormous. Without formal instruction, they all acquire the extensive technical skills needed for survival and have words for times of the day and night, for maths and seasons, for times past and time future. Without ever having seen a compass they orient themselves easily by the compass points. Occasionally, however, they deal with time and space in ways that strike the outsider as wonderfully imaginative.

However, it is hard to cover Garo's ecological knowledge in a very short period. This chapter also focuses on Burling's thoughts about Garo's ecological knowledge which is crucial for this study. The participants from the study mentioned their knowledge of modes of harvesting hunting, processing and consuming animals, bushes, wild vegetables, tubers and other edibles. It is well known that indigenous women play a vital role in accumulating and making foods naturally available in the forest. Apart from the food available in the forest, the Garo people used to cultivate other harvests in the fields. Prior ecological knowledge associated with the *jhum* system, was restarted in Sunamganj. Participants mentioned that, "We prepared the land and throwing the seeds, the crops are automatically growing after the rain", and they stated that through the harvest period, women collected paddy together with the other crops. Women used to get the seeds from the forest and they are still doing that. This exemplifies the fundamental traditional role women had as being the repository for techniques of seed conservation and stewards of biodiversity. At present, they still reserve a small portion of the paddy, corn, garlic and onion seeds in a mud pot near their bamboo bed for the following year. Women also preserve the ancient expertise of assembly rice wine(*chu*) which is made with an exact local variety of rice through a complicated procedure. Drinking rice wine is an integral part of their society and culture. Garo people distributed this rice wine to welcome visitors and social events.

The conditions for the cultural transmission of Garo ecological knowledge have been immensely battered by consecutive waves of deviations. Many of the traditions are about to collapse since many of the Garo traditions are related to forests. However, with the growing compression of natural properties, joint with losses of biodiversity, the traditional system of knowledge is becoming less pertinent, as the conditions for its imitation are being demolished. In the observed areas, it has been found that Garo traditional culture, is lost or in the process of being lost due to environmental dilapidation and other external pressures. However, the research found a reminiscence thriving with folklore and myths. Also, some Garo research participants particularly Catholics, are still practising their own culture and tradition and transmitting it to the young generation. Garo people in observed areas are still using natural climate indicators and traditional practices to call the rain or chase the storm away while Garo women are still using herbal medicine and transmit to the young generation. However, the choice of permanent migration to cities and different countries as a response to environmental degradation and climate variability, will likely interest more Garo people. This migration represents a potential threat to traditional knowledge transmission ecosystem conservation.

RECOGNISE AND DEFEND THE SETTINGS OF TRADITIONAL KNOWLEDGE SPREAD

As indigenous knowledge has an imperative part to endure and preserve biodiversity, the settings of its cultural transmission (rituals, songs, dance, myths and legends) should be of certain worth and constant. Methodical indication provisions that the areas in which indigenous peoples live, anchor remarkably high levels of biodiversity and that human cultural assortment is related to the enduring meditations of biodiversity. In Durgapur for example, people should be delighted to remain enthusiastic about the traditional periodic festival (*pohela boishak*) and invite Garo neighbours to assist with this event. In the villages where traditional festivities are no longer experienced, ingenuities like the revival of the *Wangala* festival should be endorsed. They have a significant part to substitute communal solidity and provide Garo people with the chance to perform their songs and dances and diffuse it to the young people. Besides, the joint assignation, which the carnival of traditional rituals comprises is essential to reintroduce communal bonds that are an imperative source when a community has to experience diverse kinds of hardships. As the fount people of traditional myths, folklores and natural pointers are dwindling in numeral and getting older, new ways of transmitting the knowledge to the youth should be discovered (such as drawing competitions among children, cultural exchanges). Garo people should appraise the possibility of revitalising the *Nokpante (Garo traditional bachelor's dormitory).* These days, some villagers still have houses for teenagers, but these are only considered simple dormitories used when the youths return from school or seasonal jobs to visit the village. Communities should imitate the prospect of restoring the role of *Nokpante* as a place to organise cultural programs dedicated to the young generations and for the determination of holding communal, collective meetings in case of emergencies. This would also allow women to participate, involving them as local promoters of traditional culture (Rahman, 2006).

KNOWLEDGE SHARING STRATEGIES USED AMONG GARO COMMUNITY MEMBERS

The Garo community cultural heritage and traditional knowledge that is often shared and transferred among community members through various strategies. The following are some common methods employed by the Garo people for sharing and transferring indigenous knowledge:

- *Oral Tradition:* The Garo community has a strong tradition of oral storytelling and passing down knowledge through generations. Elders, considered repositories of wisdom, share their knowledge through verbal narratives, songs, chants, and folk tales. This method ensures the preservation and transmission of cultural and historical information.
- *Community Gatherings:* Community gatherings, such as festivals, fairs, and social events, provide opportunities for knowledge sharing. These events often involve cultural performances, rituals, and ceremonies where community members actively participate and exchange traditional knowledge, skills, and practices.
- *Apprenticeship and Mentoring:* The Garo community values intergenerational learning and encourages younger members to learn from experienced individuals. Apprenticeship models are often employed, where younger community members work closely with skilled elders to acquire specific knowledge and skills related to farming, craftsmanship, traditional medicine, or other areas of expertise.

Indigenous and Environmental Knowledge of Garo Communities

- *Rituals and Ceremonies*: Rituals and ceremonies play a significant role in the Garo community, serving as important platforms for the transmission of indigenous knowledge. During these events, cultural practices, traditional songs, dances, and rituals are performed and knowledge related to spirituality, healing practices, and social customs is shared.
- *Elders' Councils:* The Garo community often has a council of respected elders who act as custodians of traditional knowledge and they convene to discuss community matters, resolve conflicts, and share their wisdom with younger members. These councils serve as important knowledge-sharing platforms, allowing for the transfer of cultural, social, and governance-related knowledge.
- *Informal Interactions and Daily Life*: Indigenous knowledge is also shared through informal interactions within the community and during daily activities. Discussions, conversations, and observations during work, household chores, and community engagements provide opportunities for community members to exchange practical knowledge, traditional practices, and cultural values.
- *Song and Dance*: Music and dance are integral to Garo culture and are used as a means of transmitting knowledge. Traditional songs and dances often contain narratives, historical accounts, and moral lessons, effectively passing on indigenous knowledge in an engaging and memorable way.
- *Community-Based Organizations:* Several Garo community-based organizations and cultural institutions actively promote the preservation and dissemination of indigenous knowledge. These organizations organize workshops, seminars, exhibitions, and training programs to facilitate knowledge sharing among community members, especially the younger generation.

It is important to note that the strategies employed for knowledge sharing may vary among Garo communities in Bangladesh. However, the oral tradition, intergenerational learning, and cultural events remain common threads in preserving and transferring indigenous knowledge within the Garo community.

CHALLENGES OF SHARING INDIGENOUS KNOWLEDGE

Sharing indigenous knowledge can be accompanied by various challenges, and the Garo people, an indigenous community in Bangladesh, face similar obstacles. Some challenges include:

- *Cultural Appropriation:* Indigenous knowledge is often vulnerable to cultural appropriation, where outsiders exploit or misuse traditional knowledge without proper understanding or acknowledgement. The Garo people may face the risk of their knowledge being commodified or misrepresented by external entities.
- *Intellectual Property Rights:* Indigenous communities, including the Garo people, often struggle with protecting their intellectual property rights. Existing legal frameworks may not adequately address the unique nature of indigenous knowledge, leading to potential exploitation and lack of control over its use.
- *Language and Communication Barriers:* Indigenous knowledge is predominantly transmitted orally and passed down through generations in native languages. As globalization and modernization advance, the younger generation may face language barriers or a lack of interest in learning traditional practices, hindering effective sharing and preservation of indigenous knowledge.
- *Socioeconomic Factors:* Socioeconomic factors, such as poverty, limited access to education, and lack of resources, can impede the sharing of indigenous knowledge. The Garo people, like

many other indigenous communities, may struggle with inadequate infrastructure, limited connectivity, and economic marginalization, making it challenging to document and share their knowledge widely.

- *Power dynamics and Marginalization*: Indigenous communities often face marginalization and discrimination within larger societal structures. Power dynamics can inhibit the Garo people from freely sharing their knowledge, as their perspectives and contributions may not be valued or given due recognition in mainstream society.

THE ROLE OF GARO PEOPLE AND OTHER RELEVANT STAKEHOLDERS IN DOCUMENTING AND PRESERVING THE INDIGENOUS KNOWLEDGE

Despite these challenges, the Garo people play a crucial role in the preservation and dissemination of their indigenous knowledge. They can actively contribute to addressing these challenges through:

- *Community-led Initiatives:* The Garo people can initiate community-led projects and organizations aimed at documenting, preserving, and sharing their indigenous knowledge. By taking the lead in these efforts, they can ensure that their knowledge is shared in a culturally appropriate and respectful manner.
- *Education and Awareness:* Educating both the Garo community and the wider society about the importance and value of indigenous knowledge is vital. By promoting awareness and understanding, the Garo people can foster a greater appreciation for their knowledge and discourage cultural appropriation.
- *Legal Advocacy:* The Garo people can advocate for stronger legal frameworks that protect indigenous intellectual property rights. They can collaborate with legal experts and organizations specializing in indigenous rights to ensure their knowledge is safeguarded and respected.
- *Technology and Digital Platforms*: Embracing technology and digital platforms can provide the Garo people with tools to document and share their knowledge more effectively. Creating digital archives, websites, or social media platforms can help reach a wider audience while maintaining control over the dissemination of their knowledge.
- *Collaboration and Partnerships:* Collaborating with researchers, scholars, and organizations that value indigenous knowledge can promote cross-cultural understanding and provide opportunities for the Garo people to share their knowledge on a broader scale. Establishing partnerships based on mutual respect and benefit is essential in preserving and promoting indigenous knowledge.

The Garo people, like other indigenous communities, thus have a vital role in ensuring their knowledge is preserved and shared and by actively engaging in these efforts and overcoming the challenges, they can contribute to the rich tapestry of indigenous knowledge and foster cultural diversity and understanding. Sharing indigenous knowledge can present several challenges, including issues related to cultural sensitivity, intellectual property rights, language barriers, and the potential for misappropriation. Other relevant stakeholders, such as cultural or memory institutions, play a crucial role in documenting and preserving indigenous knowledge while addressing these challenges.

Indigenous and Environmental Knowledge of Garo Communities

- ***Documentation and archiving:*** Cultural or memory institutions, such as museums, libraries, and archives, can collaborate with the Garo people to document and preserve their indigenous knowledge. These includes recording oral histories, collecting artefacts, and creating digital archives.
- ***Educational initiatives:*** These institutions can develop educational programs and exhibitions to showcase the cultural heritage of the Garo people. They can create spaces where indigenous knowledge can be shared, appreciated, and learned by people from different backgrounds.
- ***Research and collaboration:*** Cultural institutions can engage in collaborative research projects with the Garo people to document their knowledge systems, practices, and traditional ecological knowledge. This can help bridge the gap between academic research and indigenous knowledge.

Other relevant stakeholders like the government plays a crucial role in creating policies that recognize and protect indigenous knowledge, and they can support initiatives for the documentation, preservation, and promotion of Garo indigenous knowledge. Non-governmental organizations (NGOs) can work closely with the Garo people to provide resources, technical support, and advocacy for the preservation and sharing of indigenous knowledge. They can also facilitate capacity-building programs and promote community-led initiatives. Academic institutions: Universities and research institutions can collaborate with the Garo people in conducting research, documenting traditional knowledge, and integrating indigenous perspectives into academic curricula. Media and communication platforms: Media organizations can provide platforms for the Garo people to share their stories, knowledge, and experiences. This includes print media, television, radio, and digital platforms, helping to amplify indigenous voices and raise awareness about their culture. By acknowledging and addressing the challenges, and through collaboration among the Garo people, cultural institutions, government agencies, NGOs, academic institutions, and media organizations, indigenous knowledge can be effectively documented, preserved, and shared, ensuring its cultural and ecological value is safeguarded for future generations.

THE PROMOTION AND PROTECTION OF INDIGENOUS KNOWLEDGE AMONG GARO COMMUNITY IN BANGLADESH

The promotion and protection of indigenous knowledge among Garo communities in Bangladesh is crucial for preserving their cultural heritage and ensuring their sustainable development. Indigenous knowledge refers to the unique knowledge, skills, practices, and beliefs developed and passed down through generations within indigenous communities.

- *Preserving Cultural Heritage:* Indigenous knowledge is deeply intertwined with the cultural heritage of the Garo communities and it encompasses their traditional ecological knowledge, agricultural practices, medicinal knowledge, craftsmanship, storytelling, rituals, and spiritual beliefs. By promoting and safeguarding indigenous knowledge, we can ensure the preservation of their cultural identity and heritage and it allows future generations to connect with their roots, fostering a sense of pride, belonging, and cultural continuity.
- *Sustainable Development:* Indigenous knowledge often contains valuable insights into sustainable resource management, biodiversity conservation and resilient livelihood systems. The Garo

115

communities have developed intimate knowledge of their local ecosystems, including forest resources, water management, and sustainable agricultural practices. By recognizing and integrating indigenous knowledge into development initiatives, we can promote sustainable practices that are aligned with the ecological balance of the region. This approach can enhance food security, mitigate climate change impacts, and ensure the well-being of both the Garo communities and the environment they depend on.

- *Community Empowerment:* Recognizing and valuing indigenous knowledge empowers the Garo communities by acknowledging their expertise and contributions. It provides opportunities for them to actively participate in decision-making processes, collaborate with external stakeholders, and shape policies that affect their lives. By involving the Garo communities in the promotion and protection of their indigenous knowledge, their voices can be heard, and their rights can be respected. This empowerment enhances their capacity to maintain control over their own development and make informed choices that align with their values and aspirations.

- *Cultural Diversity and Social Cohesion:* Preserving indigenous knowledge among the Garo communities contributes to the broader cultural diversity of Bangladesh. Indigenous knowledge systems are often deeply rooted in local landscapes, ecosystems, and social structures. By safeguarding indigenous knowledge, we celebrate the richness of diverse cultural perspectives and foster social cohesion. This recognition and appreciation of indigenous knowledge can also promote intercultural dialogue and understanding among different communities in Bangladesh, contributing to a more inclusive and harmonious society.

In conclusion, the promotion and protection of indigenous knowledge among Garo communities in Bangladesh hold immense importance for preserving cultural heritage, ensuring sustainable development, empowering communities, and fostering social cohesion. By valuing and integrating indigenous knowledge, we can pave the way for a more equitable, inclusive, and sustainable future for the Garo communities and the nation as a whole. Indigenous knowledge refers to the wisdom, practices, and understandings developed by indigenous peoples over generations, based on their deep connection with the land, nature, and their cultural heritage. Here are some reasons why it is important to value and integrate indigenous knowledge:

- *Cultural Preservation:* Indigenous knowledge carries the traditions, beliefs, and values of the Garo communities. By recognizing and valuing this knowledge, we preserve their unique cultural heritage, ensuring its transmission to future generations.

- *Environmental Stewardship:* Indigenous communities often possess a profound understanding of local ecosystems and sustainable resource management. Integrating their knowledge can help promote sustainable practices, protect biodiversity, and mitigate the negative impacts of development and climate change.

- *Holistic Perspective:* Indigenous knowledge systems often emphasize a holistic view of the world, recognizing the interconnectedness of all living beings. By integrating this perspective into decision-making processes, we can foster a more comprehensive understanding of complex issues and promote sustainable solutions that consider social, economic, and environmental aspects.

- *Social Equity:* Indigenous knowledge is rooted in the lived experiences and struggles of indigenous communities. By incorporating their knowledge, we acknowledge their rights, experiences, and contributions, promoting social justice and creating more inclusive policies and practices.

Indigenous and Environmental Knowledge of Garo Communities

- *Community Empowerment:* Recognizing and respecting indigenous knowledge empowers indigenous communities to actively participate in decision-making processes that affect their lives. It enhances their self-determination, strengthens their sense of identity, and enables them to contribute their expertise to sustainable development initiatives.
- *Knowledge Exchange:* Indigenous knowledge systems hold valuable insights that can complement and enhance mainstream scientific knowledge. Encouraging collaboration and knowledge exchange between indigenous knowledge holders and other stakeholders can lead to innovative and inclusive approaches to tackle complex challenges.

To pave the way for a more equitable, inclusive, and sustainable future, it is essential to involve indigenous communities as equal partners in decision-making processes, respect their rights and traditional practices, and ensure their active participation in policy development, education, and resource management. Therefore, by valuing and integrating indigenous knowledge, we can tap into a wealth of wisdom that can benefit not only the Garo communities but also the entire nation by fostering a more sustainable and harmonious relationship with the environment and promoting social justice. Indigenous knowledge refers to the traditional knowledge, practices, and beliefs of indigenous peoples, which are often closely tied to their natural environment and cultural identity.

IMPACT OF POLICIES, PROCESSES AND PROTOCOLS ON INDIGENOUS KNOWLEDGE SYSTEMS

The impact of policies, processes, and protocols on indigenous knowledge systems among Garo communities in Bangladesh can vary. While some initiatives have aimed to promote and protect indigenous knowledge, challenges and gaps remain. Here are some key aspects:

- *Legal Recognition*: The Constitution of Bangladesh recognizes the rights of indigenous communities and ensures their protection. However, implementation gaps and lack of effective enforcement mechanisms often limit the practical realization of these rights.
- *Land Rights:* Land rights are crucial for indigenous communities to maintain and practice their traditional knowledge systems. However, land disputes, encroachment, and limited access to ancestral lands pose significant challenges to the Garo communities' ability to sustain their traditional practices.
- *Education and Awareness:* Promoting indigenous knowledge among Garo communities requires integrating it into formal and non-formal education systems. While efforts have been made to include indigenous content in the curriculum, more comprehensive measures are needed to ensure the transmission of traditional knowledge to younger generations.
- *Cultural Preservation:* Cultural preservation initiatives, such as festivals, cultural events, and museums, play a vital role in promoting and safeguarding indigenous knowledge. However, resource constraints and limited support hinder the effective implementation of such initiatives.
- *National Initiatives and Mechanisms:* In Bangladesh, several national initiatives and mechanisms have been established to promote, protect, document, preserve, and share indigenous knowledge. These include:

- *Ministry of Chittagong Hill Tracts Affairs*: This ministry focuses on the development and welfare of indigenous communities, including the Garo people. It plays a vital role in formulating and implementing policies related to indigenous knowledge and cultural preservation.
- *National Indigenous Cultural Festival:* The government organizes an annual National Indigenous Cultural Festival to showcase the cultural diversity of indigenous communities, including the Garo. This event provides a platform for indigenous peoples to share their knowledge, traditions, and practices.
- *Indigenous Knowledge Documentation Centres:* Efforts have been made to establish documentation centres to collect, preserve, and digitize indigenous knowledge, including the knowledge of Garo communities. These centres aim to create repositories of traditional knowledge accessible to researchers, policymakers, and the general public.
- *Indigenous Peoples Development Fund:* The government has established the Indigenous Peoples Development Fund to support development initiatives of indigenous communities. This fund can be utilized for projects that focus on promoting and protecting indigenous knowledge.

Despite these initiatives, challenges persist in effectively promoting and protecting indigenous knowledge among Garo communities. It requires sustained efforts, inclusive policies, active community engagement, and collaboration between government agencies, indigenous organizations, and civil society to ensure the preservation and promotion of indigenous knowledge for the long-term benefit of the Garo community.

FUTURE RESEARCH DIRECTIONS

Future research directions related to the Indigenous Garo people's knowledge system of the surrounding natural environment and their role in preserving it could encompass several areas of investigation. Here are a few potential research directions:

- Documentation and Preservation of Traditional Knowledge: Indigenous communities, including the Garo people, possess a wealth of traditional knowledge about their local ecosystems, biodiversity, and sustainable resource management practices. Future research should focus on documenting and preserving this knowledge to prevent its loss. This could involve working closely with the Garo community to record oral histories, traditional practices, and indigenous ecological knowledge.
- Indigenous Resource Management Practices: The Garo people have likely developed effective resource management practices over generations. Research can explore these practices and assess their sustainability and applicability in contemporary conservation efforts. Investigating the ecological impact of traditional Garo practices, such as shifting agriculture, agroforestry, and community-based governance systems, can help bridge the gap between traditional wisdom and modern conservation strategies.
- Climate Change Resilience and Adaptation: Understanding how the Garo people's knowledge system and traditional practices contribute to their resilience in the face of climate change is crucial. Research can explore the adaptive strategies employed by the Garo community to cope with changing environmental conditions. This may include examining their traditional agricultural

Indigenous and Environmental Knowledge of Garo Communities

techniques, land-use patterns, and indigenous forecasting methods to assess their effectiveness in adapting to climate-related challenges.

- Community-Based Conservation Initiatives: Investigating the Garo people's active involvement in conservation initiatives can provide valuable insights into community-based approaches to natural resource management. Research can explore the Garo community's role in biodiversity conservation, forest protection, and the establishment of community-managed conservation areas. Understanding the socio-cultural factors that motivate and sustain such initiatives can inform the development of collaborative conservation models elsewhere.

- Traditional Ecological Knowledge and Modern Science Integration: Research can explore opportunities for integrating traditional ecological knowledge held by the Garo people with modern scientific approaches. This interdisciplinary approach can enhance understanding of local ecosystems, biodiversity, and sustainable management practices. Collaborative studies between Garo elders, researchers, and conservation practitioners can facilitate the exchange of knowledge and promote culturally sensitive conservation strategies.

- Indigenous Rights and Environmental Governance: Examining the legal and policy frameworks surrounding the rights of the Garo people in their traditional lands is essential. Research can explore how indigenous rights are recognized, protected, and implemented in relation to environmental governance. This can help identify gaps and barriers that need to be addressed to ensure effective participation of the Garo community in decision-making processes affecting their natural environment.

These research directions can contribute to a comprehensive understanding of the Indigenous Garo people's knowledge system, its role in preserving the surrounding natural environment, and its relevance for contemporary conservation and sustainability efforts. It is crucial to conduct such research in collaboration with the Garo community, respecting their cultural protocols, and ensuring the benefits of the research are mutually beneficial and sustainable.

CONCLUSION AND RECOMMENDATIONS

"While adaptation and change are a normal part of cultural transmission, the sustainability of cultural ways of life depends heavily on the maintenance of some strong continuities when the means to support and sustain cultural continuity is destroyed, we suggest that the destruction is not just immoral and/or illegal; it lessens the diversity and therefore the adaptive capacity of humanity as a whole (Johnston B.R. et al., 2012).

Inherited land signifies the substance of Garo culture. By reviewing the ancestral lives in Garo communities, it is understandable that the Garo people have developed the ability to survive in very hard conditions, constantly adapting to their changing surroundings. The self-sufficiency and eco-lifestyle that characterised Garo communities in the past have to be an object of specific consideration by both Garo people and development interferences, discovering accurate ways to endorse and revitalise it. This existence should also be supplemented by predictable scientific know-how, recognising that new scientific knowledge is also needed. Traditional *jhum* cultivation, agroforestry, soil management practices and seed conservation should be encouraged and capitalised on. Garo women's traditional knowledge regarding periodic assortment should be accredited. To provide chances for the imminent Garo generations to acquire and exercise their traditional health knowledge, the example of the traditional healer should be followed; plants and herbs that cannot be found anymore in the forest should be planted in the yards. A communal crusade should be endorsed by local leaders. The use of herbal medicines has to be transmitted to the young generations. The *Nokpante* could be the right location to congregate remedial workshops with the local youths. Furthermore, Traditional Garo leaders should be aware of the possibility of the ancient tradition of communal works and encourage the organisation of collective initiatives to preserve this traditional practice active; possible initiatives could be medical plant collection and transplantation, water and firewood storage. The Indigenous Garo people possess a rich and intricate knowledge system that is deeply rooted in their understanding of the surrounding natural environment. This knowledge system encompasses various aspects, including their traditional ecological knowledge, spiritual beliefs, and sustainable practices. Their role in preserving the natural environment is fundamental and has proven to be crucial for maintaining the ecological balance and the well-being of both humans and nature.

The Indigenous Garo people have developed a profound understanding of the local ecosystems, including forests, rivers, and wildlife. Their traditional ecological knowledge, passed down through generations, enables them to identify and utilize the natural resources in a sustainable manner. They possess a holistic perspective that recognizes the interconnectedness of all living beings and their environment, emphasizing the need for balance and harmony. The Garo people's knowledge system is deeply intertwined with their spiritual beliefs. They perceive nature as sacred, viewing every component of the ecosystem as imbued with spiritual significance. This spiritual connection fosters a sense of responsibility and stewardship towards the environment. Their rituals and ceremonies are often centered around maintaining this harmonious relationship with nature, ensuring the continuity of their knowledge and practices. Preservation of the natural environment is a core aspect of the Garo people's cultural identity. They have developed various sustainable practices to ensure the long-term health and productivity of the land. For instance, they practice shifting cultivation, also known as jhum or slash-and-burn agriculture, which involves rotating cultivation areas to allow for natural regeneration and prevent soil degradation. They have a deep understanding of plant diversity and medicinal herbs, utilizing them for sustenance and healthcare while also ensuring their sustainable management.

The Indigenous Garo people actively engage in community-based conservation efforts. They have established customary laws and regulations to govern resource use, limiting exploitation and promoting sustainable practices. Additionally, they have formed local institutions and organizations to protect their traditional lands and advocate for their rights as custodians of the natural environment. In brief, the Indigenous Garo people's knowledge system of the surrounding natural environment is a testament to their profound understanding, respect, and harmonious relationship with nature. Their role in preserving the environment is vital, as they utilize sustainable practices, draw upon traditional ecological knowledge, and integrate spiritual beliefs to ensure the long-term well-being of the ecosystems they inhabit. Recognizing and valuing their knowledge and contributions is essential for fostering sustainable development and protecting our planet's biodiversity.

REFERENCES

Bal, E. (1999). *Manderangni Jagring: Images of the Garo(s) in Bangladesh*. University Press.

Bal, E. (2007). Becoming the Garos of Bangladesh: Policies of exclusion and the ethnicization of a 'tribal' minority. *South Asia, 30*(3), 439–455. doi:10.1080/00856400701714062

Bal, E. (2007). They ask if we eat frogs: Garo ethnicity in Bangladesh (IIAS/ISEAS series on Asia). Leiden, The Netherlands: Singapore: International Institute for Asian Studies; Institute of Southeast Asian Studies.

Bal, E. (2010). Taking root in Bangladesh: States, minorities and discourses on citizenship. *The Newsletter* (Special issue: Indigenous India), 53, 24–25

Bal, E. W. (2000). *They ask if we eat frogs: social boundaries, ethnic categorisation, and the Garo people of Bangladesh*. Eburon.

Bandyopadhyaya, H. (1966). *Bangiya Sabdakosh*. Sahitya Akademii.

BARCIK (Bangladesh Resource Centre for Indigenous Knowledge). (2006). *Our agriculture, our lives: Shifting agriculture & livelihood struggles of Adivasi Garo in Modhupur* [In Bangla.]. BARCIK.

Biswas, S. K., Majumder, N. M. & Po, L. T. (2015). An ethnographic exploration of the Lyngam ethnic community in Bangladesh. *Sociology and Anthropology 3(3)*, 179-185. Horizon Research Publishing. doi:10.13189/sa.2015.030305

Bleie, T. (2005). *Tribal peoples, nationalism, and the human rights challenge: The Adivasis of Bangladesh*. University Press.

Burling, R. (1963). *Rengsanggri: Family and kinship in a Garo village*. Pennsylvania University Press. doi:10.9783/9781512814972

Burling, R. (1997). *The strong women of Modhupur*. Dhaka University Press.

Burnard, P. (1991). A method of analysing interview transcripts in qualitative research. *Nurse Education Today, 11*(6), 461–466. doi:10.1016/0260-6917(91)90009-Y PMID:1775125

Das, T. K., & Islam, H. Z. (2005). Psycho-social dimensions of ethnicity: The situation of Garo community in Bangladesh. Dhaka. *Asian Affairs, 27*(3), 45–54.

Drong, S. (2004). *Eco-park project threats to evict 25,000 Garos*. Indigenous People's Forum.

FAO. (2012). *Gender and climate change research in agriculture and food security for rural development training guide*. FAO. https://www.fao.org/docrep/013/i2050e/i2050e00.htm

Gain, P. (1989). The History of Mandis. *Dhaka Journal*, (January-February), 19–25.

Gain, P. (Ed.). (1995). *Bangladesh Land Forest and Forest People*. SEHD.

Gain, P. (1998). *Forest and forest people of Bangladesh. Bangladesh: Land Forest and Forest people, Society for Environment and Human Development*. SEHD.

Gain, P. (2011). *Survival on the fringe: Adivasis of Bangladesh*. Society for Environment and Human Development.

Galloway, K. (2010). *Advance guard: climate change impacts, adaptation, mitigation and Indigenous peoples*. UNUIAS.

Islam, M. (2008). *The changing Garo Adivasi culture of Bangladesh: a case study of marriage rituals.* [Unpublished MPhil dissertation, University of Tromso].

Islam, N. (2008). Bangladesh. In B. Roberts & T. Kanaley (Eds.), *Urbanization and Sustainability in Asia.* Asian Development Bank.

Jengcham, S. (1994). *Bangladesher Garo Sampradai.* Bangla Academy. (In Bengali)

Johnston, B. R., Hiwasaki, L., Klaver, I. J., Castillo, A. R., & Strang, V. (Eds.). (2012). *Water, cultural diversity, and global environmental change: Emerging trends, sustainable futures?* (pp. XI–XXI). Springer. doi:10.1007/978-94-007-1774-9

Majumdar, D. N. (1978). *Culture change in two Garo villages (No. 42).* Anthropological Survey of India, Government of India.

Muhammed, N., Chakma, S., Hossain, M. F., Masum, M., Hossain, M., & Oesten, G. (2011). A case study on the Garo ethnic people of the Sal (Shorea robusta) forests in Bangladesh. *International Journal of Social Forestry., 4,* 179–193.

Partha, P. (2018). Indigenous climate calendar: Changes and challenges. *Peoples' Preface, 9.*

Rahman, M. (2006). The Garos: struggling to survive in the valley of death.

Sangma, S. (2010). *Bangladesh indigenous peoples' Forum.* Indigenous People's Forum.

Sangma, U. (1998). *Adibashi Barta.* Tribal Welfare Association, Sunamgonj, Sylhet. (In Bengali)

KEY TERMS AND DEFINITIONS

Ecosystem: It is a community or group of living organisms that live in and interact with each other in a specific environment.

Indigenous Knowledge: It refers to the wisdom, practices, and understandings developed by indigenous peoples over generations, based on their deep connection with the land, nature, and their cultural heritage.

Preservation: It refers to the activity or process of keeping something valued alive, intact, or free from damage or decay.

Traditional Ecological Knowledge: It is the on-going accumulation of knowledge, practice and belief about relationships between living beings in a specific ecosystem.

Traditional Practices: It refers to the actions and knowledge produced by local communities over many generations through which their behavior and autochthonous environment may be better understood.

Chapter 7

Challenges and Opportunities of Preserving African Indigenous Knowledge Using Digital Technologies:
The Case of Bogwera

Kealeboga Aiseng
https://orcid.org/0000-0002-5684-9519
Rhodes University, South Africa

ABSTRACT

Most indigenous knowledge systems, practices, and values disappear due to the influence of technology, human migrations, climate change, globalization, death, memory loss, and civilization. Therefore, indigenous knowledge systems will disappear if they are no longer used. This is because many traditional practices and activities within indigenous knowledge systems that have been used are essential coping and living strategies and are now in danger of disappearing. The chapter investigates how social web technologies, social media platforms, and online video tools can digitize, share, and preserve indigenous knowledge for the current generations that need to be more knowledgeable about these systems and future generations. With the example of bogwera, the chapter studies the role that digital technologies can play in protecting and preserving indigenous knowledge systems in the Taung community in North West, South Africa.

INTRODUCTION

Indigenous knowledge has been part of humanity for centuries. There are many definitions of indigenous knowledge. The description of indigenous knowledge in this chapter will come from two sources. Grey (2014) defines indigenous knowledge as the expressions, practices, beliefs, understanding, insights, and experiences of indigenous groups generated over centuries of profound interaction with a particular

DOI: 10.4018/978-1-6684-7024-4.ch007

Copyright © 2023, IGI Global. Copying or distributing in print or electronic forms without written permission of IGI Global is prohibited.

territory. According to Sraku-Lartey, Acquah, Brefo, and Djagbletey (2017), indigenous knowledge refers to the traditional knowledge of indigenous people, which is oral and usually transmitted from one generation to another and exists mainly in the mind of local people. This knowledge is generally shared through personal communication and demonstration from tutor to pupil or parents to children (Christian cited in Sraku-Lartey et al., 2017). The iterations and mechanisms of what is considered indigenous knowledge are context-based. Communities worldwide have shared indigenous knowledge from generation to generation about farming, architecture, human behaviour, marriage, childbirth, health care, natural disasters, climate, natural resources, and human relationships. Moreover, many people worldwide still rely on indigenous knowledge as part of their lives. Indigenous knowledge is vital, especially for rural communities, as it signifies the technical, cultural, political, and institutional aspects of knowledge and values systems in these communities (Sillitoe & Marzano, 2009). Some people in rural communities conduct their lives relying on indigenous knowledge. It is also considered the social capital of people experiencing poverty; it is their main asset to invest in the struggle for survival, produce food, provide shelter, and achieve control of their own lives (Senanayake, 2006). Sraku-Lartey et al. (2017) explain that traditional knowledge is an integral part of the culture and history of local communities and hence their common asset in their effort to gain control of their lives. However, most indigenous knowledge systems, practices, and values disappear due to the influence of technology, human migrations, climate change, globalization, death, memory loss, and civilization. Senanayake (2006) states that when indigenous knowledge is lost, the tragedy is felt by those that have developed it and made a living through it. Cassidy, Wilk, Kgathi, Bendsen, Ngwenya, and Mosepele (2011) state that indigenous knowledge systems will disappear if they are no longer used. This is because many traditional practices and activities within indigenous knowledge systems that have been used are essential coping and living strategies and are now in danger of disappearing. These arguments call for measures to protect and preserve indigenous knowledge systems. While methods already exist to salvage the little that is remaining, this chapter intends to look at the role of digital technologies in the endeavor to protect and preserve indigenous knowledge. Existing literature on preserving indigenous knowledge is limited to the challenges faced in preserving African indigenous knowledge using digital technologies, specifically in the context of *bogwera*. There is also an insufficient investigation into the unique opportunities digital technologies provide for preserving and disseminating African indigenous knowledge, with a focus on *bogwera*. There is also a limited identification of strategies and best practices for building sustainable repositories and platforms that can effectively safeguard and promote bogwera for future generations.

The chapter aims to fill this gap by investigating how social web technologies, social media platforms, and online video tools can digitize, share, and preserve indigenous knowledge for the current generations that are not knowledgeable about these systems and future generations. With the example of *bogwera*, the chapter studies digital technologies' role in protecting and preserving indigenous knowledge systems in Taung. The aim of the chapter was to determined how digital technologies can facilitate the revitalization and intergenerational transmission of bogwera and identity barriers that need to be addressed to achieve this goal. The following research objectives guided the chapter:

- To determine the critical challenges in preserving indigenous African knowledge through digital technologies, especially in *bogwera*
- To determine the potential opportunities digital technologies offer for preserving and disseminating African indigenous knowledge, with a focus on the *bogwera*

Challenges, Opportunities of Preserving African Indigenous Knowledge

- To determine what cultural and ethical considerations are involved in digitizing and preserving African indigenous knowledge, focusing on *bogwera*
- To determine the implications of digitizing *bogwera* for the communities involved and how their perspectives and needs can be incorporated into the preservation efforts.

CONTEXTUALIZING BOGWERA

In Taung, North West province in South Africa, *bogwera* is one of the remaining indigenous practices the community still practices. *Bogwera* is a cultural practice of the Batswana that marks a rite of passage from boy to manhood. The practice is meant to teach the initiates the traditions and customs of Batswana. This has made *bogwera* one of the reservoirs of knowledge where traditions and customs are preserved and passed on from generation to generation. During the initiation processes, the initiates are also taught about the roles and responsibilities of being a man in the community; they are taught how to face life challenges; initiates also learn about their clans and identities. Education has always been an integral part of Batswana. Even though education was done orally for centuries, Batswana always emphasized the importance of education about life, morals, health, nutrition, respect, and many aspects of humankind. *Bogwera* has always been one of the practices that Batswana used to teach young people the responsibilities of adulthood, respect for elders and royalty, the virtues of obedience, and their rights and obligations in society (Denbow & Thebe, 2006). This initiation process would last for many months. It would promote traditional education where young men would learn their history through praise poems and the teaching of acceptable behaviour through games, riddles, puzzles, and proverbs (Denbow & Thebe, 2006). *Bogwera* goes along with *bojale* (a rite of passage for young girls). During these rites, songs and dances are used as an instructional medium through which young men and women learn the responsibilities of community life. These rites are carried out in isolated locations far from the reach of people, in rural areas, farms, mountains, and highly condensed bushes. However, despite the importance of this practice among the Batswana, early missionaries perceived it as a threat to their authority. They worked hard to ban it because they viewed it as indoctrination of young people "in all that is filthy, in all that is deceitful and unrighteous, and in all that is blasphemous and soul-destroying (Denbow & Thebe, 2006).

Mothoagae (2017) states that *bogwera*, like many cultural practices of Batswana, has its laws, mythology, and superstitions. It is for this reason that the practice is sacred. Information about bogwera is not discussed among those who have not been initiated, and even those who have gone through this process do not discuss its details outside the camp where the practice is held. Everyone who has participated in this rite has sworn to secrecy and does not disclose what occurs during the initiation process (Mothoagae, 2017). The sacred and secret nature of *bogwera* and the exclusion of those who have never undergone initiation point to the challenges that the cultural practice rich with the customs and practices of the Batswana face. This raises concerns about the sustainability and lifespan of this practice if only those that have undergone the initiation are the custodians of the indigenous knowledge sought during the initiation. Hence, the chapter looks to unearth whether digital technologies are possible options to preserve the practice and its wealth of knowledge.

In the case of *bogwera*, the risk of losing the practice and its knowledge comes not through the irrelevance of the practice, the death of elders in the community, memory loss, or the influence of technology like is the case with other indigenous practices, but through the sacred and secret nature of the practice. All people from *bogwera* have vowed not to divulge details of what is happening in the initiation school. However, not everyone who is Motswana in Taung is from the initiation school, which means the knowledge taken from *bogwera* only circulates among those who went through the initiation process. This is a challenge for *bogwera* because recently, the number of initiates from the schools has dropped from the time when I was still a young boy in the early 2000s; some parents do not see the value of taking their children to *bogwera* because they feel like children come back immoral and with no discipline after initiating from bogwera, some children also feel like *bogwera* does not add any value to their lives. These challenges pose a threat to the lifespan and sustainability of *bogwera*. Hence, the study intends to determine if digital tools such as YouTube, Tok-Tok, blogs, social media platforms, and vlogs cannot be used to protect and preserve *bogwera*. The study wants to discover the opportunities and challenges these digital tools can offer to preserve *bogwera*. Digital tools are thus proving to be effective in preserving indigenous knowledge worldwide. However, there remain many challenges to the preservation of indigenous knowledge. However, there are also opportunities that digital tools can provide for those that are interested in preserving indigenous knowledge for the future. These challenges and opportunities can be explored in the case of *bogwera*.

LITERATURE REVIEW

Tjiek (2006) acknowledges that indigenous knowledge systems are still poorly preserved, let alone disseminated by most countries. This means unpreserved indigenous knowledge systems would surely vanish, while the preserved ones would still vanish if not disseminated or replicated elsewhere (Plockey, 2014). By reviewing the literature on the digitalization of indigenous knowledge, the chapter will observe that some challenges affect the preservation and management of indigenous knowledge systems using digital platforms. These include intellectual properties, user needs, cultural and historical values, funding, and national and international context, to name a few (Boamah & Liew, 2017). Krtalic and Hassenay (2012) categorize these challenges into five main clusters: strategic and theoretical, economic and legal, educational, technical, operational, and cultural and social. However, these clusters of factors also offer starting points for improving the preservation and management of indigenous knowledge (Krtalic & Hassenay, 2012). The chapter comes with a theoretical and practical notion that the protection and preservation of *bogwera* must be explored beyond initiates simply going to the school once every year in December. This method can be understood by what Barker (2007) describes as the partial success or failure of projects relating to the preservation of indigenous knowledge. Recognizing the opportunities and challenges presented by new technologies for communities, Boamah and Liew (2017) note digitization as a new cultural tool that provides many benefits to cultural institutions. Sithole (in Plockey (2015) argues that indigenous knowledge is mainly stored in people's minds and passed on through generations by word of mouth rather than in a written form. Therefore, it is vulnerable to rapid change as it is passed from one person to another, one generation to another. However, Plockey (2015) explains that digitizing information often makes preserving, accessing, sharing, and protecting the community's collective memory easier.

Stevens (2008) argues there are benefits of making indigenous knowledge accessible on digital platforms: it makes it more appealing to the youth and others who may see indigenous knowledge as 'old-fashioned.'

Making indigenous knowledge accessible online can also make it easier for government to access it, learn about it, and consider it in policy development and resource management (Plockey, 2014). Plockey (2015) states that while technological advancements are essential to sustainable development, these tools are lacking to protect and preserve indigenous knowledge systems in Africa. Moreover, despite its value, it remains undocumented, and communities risk losing some, if not all, indigenous knowledge. Hence, to avoid this catastrophe, digitization has been applied in many countries to preserve it (Sraku-Lartey et al., 2017). Sraku-Lartey et al. (2017) claim that one modern way to preserve traditional knowledge is documentation in some permanent form and public accessibility using information and communication technologies. In countries such as Australia, efforts have been made to preserve indigenous knowledge systems in accessible forms by recording and documenting the knowledge to assist in its easy retrieval (Nakata & Langton, 2006).

Conway (2010) explains that conservation specialists working in libraries, archives, and museums have explored integrating digitization technologies into indigenous knowledge while also positioning themselves to embrace the challenges of preserving information in digital form. Many agencies worldwide are pursuing the digitalization of indigenous knowledge, yet with different motives and sensitivity toward tensions arising in digitally representing indigenous knowledge and the factors contributing to these tensions (Winschiers-Theophilus, Jensen & Rodil, 2012). Winschiers-Theophilus et al. (2012) claim that in Namibia, as in many parts of the world, the youth have migrated to cities, interrupting the traditional generational knowledge transfer. In these cases, researchers and communities have captured rich multimedia recordings of indigenous practices, which they consider relevant. These measures aimed to create digital platforms where the village elders could represent and share their knowledge meaningfully for future generations and the youth that has migrated to urban areas (Winschiers-Theophilus et al., 2012).

Despite its importance, the role of social media in preserving indigenous knowledge systems in Africa has not been discussed sufficiently. However, as Owiny et al. (2014) argue, social media platforms such as YouTube, Facebook, and Twitter can create, access, and share information or skills within social and geographic African communities and among broader audiences. The advantage of these platforms is that they do not require specialized skills or training, though they require some reading and writing abilities. Hence, they are accessible and user-friendly only to literate individuals and are limited to urban and educated rural populations (Owiny et al., 2014). Considering challenges such as the high illiteracy rate in rural Africa and excluding indigenous knowledge from Western education, it is essential to preserve, manage and share indigenous knowledge (Owiny, Mehta & Maretzki, 2014). Hence, the rapid growth of social media and mobile technologies can create opportunities to form local and international partnerships that can facilitate creating, managing, preserving, and sharing knowledge and skills unique to African communities (Owiny et al., 2014). Most existing research, as sourced in this study, discusses preserving and protecting indigenous knowledge systems using digital technologies. However, they only focus on the use of public libraries and websites. This study is the first to examine how indigenous knowledge systems can be protected, preserved, and spread using digital technologies such as social media platforms. It is essential to consider the importance of these platforms in preserving and spreading indigenous knowledge systems, especially considering their global reach and presence. We live in a world where no one can underestimate the importance of social media platforms. Hence, we need to explore these platforms in the field of indigenous knowledge systems.

METHODOLOGY

This study aims to engage with an initiation school's principal (*Ramophato*[1]), a local Chief from Taung, and graduates of *bogwera* to find out from them the role that digital technologies can play in preserving and protecting *bogwera*. All participants were purposely selected based on their expertise in *bogwera*. Because this was qualitative research, the study used in-depth interviews with the participants mentioned above to understand the role of digital tools in preserving the knowledge, practices, and importance of *bogwera*. The interviews aim to determine whether the participants see the digitalization of *bogwera* as something possible and essential. Data were analyzed thematically.

As this was an exploratory study, the author opted for open-ended questions about using digital tools to preserve and protect bogwera for current and future generations. The research data was obtained through in-depth face-to-face and online interviews with 7 participants from different villages in Taung. Online interviews were vital for this study as data was collected at different times, and it was also vital for participants not at Taung during the data collection period. The participants were a local chief, Ramophato, and five graduates from the initiation schools. The Chief is a 63-year-old male, Ramophato is a 61-year-old male, and the graduates are between 25 and 45. All participants requested that their identities be hidden. Therefore, the study does not use their real names. The interviews were done in a combination of Setswana and codeswitching between English and Setswana. Some participants could explain their arguments better by codeswitching between English and Setswana. The open-ended questions spanned their knowledge of the importance of *bogwera*, preserving culture, their understanding of digital technology devices, and the future of cultural institutions.

Given that the author has not attended the initiation school, it was paramount for him to declare that to the participants first at the beginning of the interviews so that participants knew that they should not divulge "secret" matters of the initiation with the participants. However, this was also a challenge as some participants could not discuss the details of some of their answers because they felt they would say more than they were supposed to. In these instances, the author had to apply caution and allow participants to restrain from speaking further about specific topics that they deemed "sensitive" to discuss with someone who has never been to *bogwera*. The interviews focused on two issues. The first issue was if and how digital technologies can contribute to preserving and protecting *bogwera*. The second issue concerns digital technologies' challenges in preserving and protecting *bogwera*. Both issues were discussed at length by the participants. Some participants felt that digital technologies could be vital in preserving some elements of *bogwera*, but not all of them because of the secret nature of the practice. Other participants were against the involvement of "Western" methods in African cultural practices. However, all the interviewees agreed that indigenous African knowledge systems must be preserved. They differed in the method to protect these indigenous African knowledge systems.

FINDINGS AND DISCUSSIONS

The interviews discovered that *bogwera* is one of the oldest indigenous practices of Batswana. Hence, it needs to be preserved so that it can be passed on from generation to generation. For this reason, the interviewees argued that digital tools could be essential in preserving and protecting this practice. However, it has significant limitations that cannot be ignored. The findings below are divided into two headings, opportunities and challenges. Under the section on opportunities, I will present the findings of the interviewees using three themes: the revolutionary nature of technology, exposure, and memories. These themes show that preserving *bogwera* using digital technologies can help expose the culture to other people and create memories. Under the section on challenges, I present findings of the challenges of using digital technologies to present *bogwera*. Three themes emerged from the interviews with participants in this section: *bogwera* has been commercialized, it is also a secretive cultural practice, and participants suggest that technology should be limited in preserving *bogwera*.

Opportunities of Using Digital Technologies in Preserving Bogwera

- *Technology is revolutionary*

Research shows that measures are being considered worldwide to use digital technologies in preserving cultural institutions, changing the operations of museums, and promoting cultural heritage objects (Kruglikova, 2020). Technology is changing cultural heritage objects, helping communities protect indigenous knowledge systems, and preserving cultural materials for future generations. The interviewees for this study argued that technology is essential for protecting aspects of the Batswana cultures and traditions.

The interviewees expressed an acute awareness of the importance of preserving indigenous knowledge practices and systems. In an interview with a local Chief from Taung, the significance of protecting indigenous knowledge was discussed in detail.

Chief: The loss of culture, indigenous knowledge, practices, and beliefs is a great danger to humanity, not only to us, Batswana. Losing indigenous knowledge systems can cause serious cultural gaps between generations and deny us an opportunity as people to know who we are and where we come from.

Furthermore, Ramophato explains that Batswana have lost their ways of living and adopted "foreign" ways of living.

Ramophato: Batswana have lost their culture. They live foreign lifestyles. Others easily persuade them. However, that does not mean that when we see things work for other cultures, we must not try them in our culture. However, they should not compromise our culture.

Other participants also share this view. Two of the graduates of *bogwera* explained that young people from Taung have lost their culture and find themselves not knowing who and what they are.

Graduate 5: It is sad to see young people in Taung, a rural place, not knowing their history, culture, kings, and traditions. We have become products of White people. It is like we hate being black and Tswana.

Graduate 1: In Taung, once you start speaking about culture, traditions, rituals, and so forth, people think you are mad. They do not even want to hear you. Seeing that people in our villages do not know how to address a Chief is uncomfortable.

These views prompted the author to find different ways to remedy the situation. By bringing up the issue of using technology to preserve cultural practices and traditions, the participants responded positively to technology's role in preserving indigenous cultural systems.

Chief: We must learn from those before us and utilize our elders to learn about ourselves and being as Batswana. Moreover, I believe that if some methods or techniques can be used to protect the elders' knowledge, then it is worth exploring them.

The Chief further noted that technology is integral to our contemporary lives and cannot be ignored.

Chief: Technology has shown us that we need to move with time. We cannot be left behind. It is providing us with opportunities that have never been seen before. Let us explore it.

Ramophato also believes technology can change the Batswana cultural institutions, practices, and values.

Ramophato: I have heard cultural groups use social media platforms to promote their products worldwide. I believe it can also be valuable to us to promote our cultural practices so that others can see how we live our lives as Batswana. However, preserving the wealth of our culture and tradition for the young and future generations can also be helpful. We are losing a vast majority of indigenous knowledge due to the death of the adults who are the custodians of this knowledge. Because we are traditionally people of oral narratives, the majority of the indigenous knowledge that they possess is not written down. However, suppose you start using your new technology to record them while they speak or teach you things. In that case, you will be doing something extraordinary for the future of Batswana.

The interview with the Chief also revealed that there had not been enough work done to explore the role of digital technologies in preserving *bogwera*.

Chief: Scholars and cultural experts worldwide have argued that indigenous knowledge systems are essential for the self-sufficiency and self-determination of the people. Moreover, for us in Taung, practices such as bogwera serve these purposes. Moreover, we are doing everything possible to protect, manage and preserve them. However, the role of digital technologies has not been explored. I have not heard of it.

Other participants expressed their views on the role of digital technologies in preserving *bogwera* but with reservations.

Graduate 5: We have seen what digital technologies can do. It is massive. However, with bogwera, I am not sure. It is a delicate institution. Other parts of our culture, like magadi (lobola negotiations), can be documented to show future generations how it is done today so that they do not do their things in the future and get lost. However, bogwera, that is unchartered territory.

Graduate 3: I am an open-minded person. I am willing to go to the hospital and be by my wife's side as she gives birth. Even though culture does not allow it. I am willing to take a video of that procedure and keep it as a memory of the day my child was born. That I can do because it only affects me as an individual. However, bogwera is a societal practice. I cannot just take a camera and go there to photograph what is happening there. Smartphones are not even allowed there, for your information. To incorporate digital technologies into bogwera, you must convince many generations. Some of those do not even know what you mean by technology. To them, you would be spitting on the culture of their great-grandfathers.

Challenges, Opportunities of Preserving African Indigenous Knowledge

Graduate 1: I believe social media will be vital for access to relevant information to be documented and preserved. However, I do not think the cultural practice should be documented online. Certain things are sacred about the practice and cannot be known by people who have never attended the initiation school. However, other cultural practices can be documented, including wedding ceremonies, traditional medicine, and food. However, sacred ones will not work for us as Batswana.

Participants agreed that digital technologies are essential aspects of our daily lives and should be considered in preserving and protecting aspects of Batswana cultures and traditions. The participants revealed that digital technologies can be used to teach young people about their history, practices, cultures, and beliefs. However, they also had doubts about including digital technologies in *bogwera*. These arguments reveal that cultural practitioners, custodians, and ordinary people are interested in preserving Batswana's indigenous knowledge systems and practices and are willing to explore all possible measures.

- ***Exposure***

Despite the participants having reservations about the employment of digital technologies in preserving *bogwera*, they collectively agreed that digital technologies could play a significant role in some aspects of *bogwera* but not in other aspects considered secretive and sacred. One of the advantages of using digital technologies in preserving some aspects of bogwera that the participants expressed was exposing the culture to other cultural groups.

Graduate 1: What I like about the Zulu people is that their culture is known almost everywhere. They are using these digital technologies to promote their culture. That is something we can consider. We can use social media tools to promote bogwera and show other cultures what we, as Batswana, are made of. There is nothing wrong with that. We can use these technologies to expose our culture to other people.

The Chief also shared his sentiments about exposing the indigenous knowledge systems of Batswana to other cultures using digital technologies.

Chief: We can use any method, including digital technologies, to promote our culture and build pride that we currently lack about our culture as Batswana. Moreover, bogwera is one of the remaining institutions we have to promote using technologies. However, strict limitations must be on documenting what can and cannot be. This is our culture. We cannot surrender everything to manipulation, commercial interests, and death. I guess I am trying to say let us move with time, but we should not lose a sense of who we are in the process.

Ramophato argued that Setswana is rich and should not be allowed to die.
Ramophato: Setswana is a vibrant culture. There is a lot that needs to be explored about our culture. Even I cannot claim to know everything. I am always looking for opportunities to learn from others. However, sometimes those with the information I do not know are far from. Hence, I believe the technology you are talking about can be helpful. I do not have to travel to Rustenburg, Mahikeng, or Botswana to learn about my history or something like that. I can ask my child to find me the information on their phone or computer. As the young ones, you are doing a fantastic job for yourselves and the elders to preserve these indigenous knowledge systems using your technology.

A graduate expressed his views about what can and should be documented digitally about bogwera.

Graduate 2: Using technology to preserve bogwera will be tricky, but I believe certain aspects of bogwera can be protected using technology. The songs (mangae) and praise poems (dithoko) that we perform to entertain people when we graduate from the initiation school can be documented using technology. I would not be against that. However, not what is happening in the initiation school. That is sacred.

Another graduate explained that sharing aspects of *bogwera* with other cultural groups will be necessary.

Graduate 4: Technology will be necessary; it will help us expose bogwera to people unfamiliar with our culture. When I was working in Mpumalanga, people used to ask me about it, but I did not have anything to show them what this tradition looked like. It was just heresy.

The participants expressed their views about using digital technologies to preserve and protect *bogwera*. The participants discussed that digital technologies could be valuable in preserving and protecting *bogwera*. However, the practice has secretive and sacred aspects that cannot be shared with those not attending the initiation school. However, digital technologies can preserve and protect many other aspects of Batswana's bogwera and other cultural practices. These arguments demonstrate that digital technologies can be valuable for future generations when carefully incorporated into indigenous knowledge systems and practices. Through these technologies, future generations will not lose out on the rich knowledge that the current and past generations have about our ways of living.

- *Memories*

The participants also discussed that documenting bogwera events will help keep memories one cherishes for a long time. Creating memories for oneself and future generations was discussed as one of the advantages that using digital technologies in *bogwera* can provide.

Graduate 2: I sometimes look at the pictures of myself when I graduated from bogwera; it is one of the best moments to remember about my life. So, if we approach it from that perspective, it might be worth considering that social media and technology are essential for creating memories.

Another graduate states that seeing videos of bogwera graduations on social media platforms brings back good memories.

Graduate 4: These days, I see videos on YouTube and TikTok about graduation ceremonies from the past, even ten years ago, especially on YouTube. Moreover, I think it is essential to go back in time and enjoy the memories of these beautiful moments.

Another graduate explains that TikTok videos of *bogwera* help connect him with his home; they close the distance between him and home.

Participant 3: Every time I miss home and see the videos of bogwera on TikTok, I feel better; they connect me with home. So, technology can be important in our culture. However, I am worried about exposing the whole culture to technology. We will lose a sense of who we are.

The Chief explains that most of the previous experiences of bogwera are not known because it was only transmitted via word of mouth. However, digital technologies can change that.

Chief: One thing is that bogwera has entirely changed in Taung. For example, the boys and girls no longer go to the King's palace to be named as it was traditionally done. Some of the graduates of bogwera today do not know that. That was a crucial moment in the graduation ceremonies. Those things were not documented. They only hear from other people that it used to happen like that. I remember graduating in 1974; that was a special moment for us to go to the King to be named. However, imagine if technology was there and captured those moments. We would share them with everyone else for generations to come. If we modernize some aspects of our culture and allow room for development and modernization, our cultures will never die.

Challenges of Using Digital Technologies in Preserving Bogwera

While the interviews revealed that digital technologies could be helpful in the preservation of cultural institutions and practices in general, they also revealed that there would be significant challenges for using digital technologies in preserving and protecting *bogwera*. These challenges include the secret nature of *bogwera* and the commercialization of this cultural practice. However, the interview also noted the way forward on how digital technologies can play in preserving and protecting *bogwera*.

- ***Secrecy***

During the interviews, it was discovered that one of the challenges that would be encountered with preserving *bogwera* digitally is the secrecy nature of this tradition. Participants discussed in length how *bogwera* has always been treated and discussed in secret. Hence, it is one of the remaining institutions of Batswana that is still celebrated. Hence, including digital technologies in preserving this tradition would compromise the culture as it is understood and practiced.

Graduate 1: If we start making videos and recordings of what is happening in bogwera and publicizing it, we dilute the culture, losing its significance in society.

Another graduate explains that the secret nature of *bogwera* is one of the elements that make its graduates proud of it, and it gives the culture its beauty and respect.

Graduate 3: Remember that one thing that has kept bogwera alive for such a long time is its secrecy. People hardly question its significance in society because they do not know what is happening there. They have ideas about a few things. However, people do not know about the core things done there. Moreover, that is where our pride comes from. However, if you publicize it, you are losing the beauty of the culture.

It was also narrated that digitizing *bogwera* would kill the culture.

Graduate 2: If we record what is happening in bogwera and make it accessible to everyone, you have killed Setswana.

A graduate indicated that not everything should be done as White people do.

Graduate 1: Not everything must be done according to how White people do them. They have introduced terrible things like recording childbirth, death, and sex. To us, some things are sacred. We do not publicize them.

Another graduate explained that digital technologies could kill cultural practices if not used carefully.

Graduate 4: When introducing technology to a culture, you lose it. There are certain things where technology can be used. However, not to kill the little that we are left.

When asked if it is not possible to use technology to spread *bogwera* and not keep it among the few people that have gone through the initiation practice, participants indicated that those who want to know the culture must go through the traditional process of going to the mountain just like everyone else who has done so.

Graduate 1: If you want to know what is happening in bogwera, you must go to the mountain like all of us. There is no compromise on that.

Another graduate explains that the secret nature of *bogwera* is something they all found, and they will keep it that way.

Graduate 2: We go to bogwera because of the teachings we receive there. Moreover, those teachings cannot be shared with those that have not gone to bogwera. It is a secret. We found it like that.

A graduate also narrates that the teachings in *bogwera* are so sacred that they cannot even be discussed among graduates themselves at home. Hence, digital technologies will compromise everything.

Graduate 3: When you go to bogwera, you take a sacred vow of secrecy. You will never divulge what is happening there outside the camps. Even among us graduates, we cannot just start talking about what is happening at bogwera at home. It is forbidden. We must wait for December when the new cycle of graduates is being initiated, then we start talking about those things. Now, do you see that technology will be an enemy to us?

Another participant explains that Batswana are unlike other cultures that have publicized their initiation schools. The participant explains that Batswana are still conventional in how they approach bogwera.

Challenges, Opportunities of Preserving African Indigenous Knowledge

Graduate 5: Batswana are not like the Xhosas; they do not allow matters of bogwera to be discussed anywhere outside the initiation school. That will make it a massive challenge for us to adopt social media platforms as tools to preserve bogwera.

Ramophato also explains that technology will have limitations in preserving *bogwera*.

Ramophato: If we employ technology to preserve bogwera, the challenge is that there are certain things you are taught in bogwera that should not be discussed with people who have never been there. So, with technology, we will only share or preserve simple things; we cannot go into details because it means you will be initiated digitally. That means you will not know the complete information about bogwera; you will only know a few simple things.

- ### *Commercialization*

The participants were also primarily concerned with how *bogwera* is now being used as a scheme to make a profit. They argued in detail that even if one were to try other methods of preserving bogwera, it would meet resistance from some principals who have commercialized this cultural practice.

Graduate 2: The challenge now is that bogwera has been commercialized. The principals are just concerned about the number of students they have; the more they have, the more profit they make.

A graduate explains that using digital technologies to preserve *bogwera* will interfere with people's businesses.

Graduate 1: It is now just a business. So, incorporating digital technological devices in bogwera will interfere with people's "businesses."

Another graduate clarifies the argument about why using digital technologies to preserve bogwera will be a challenge under the commercialization of this cultural practice.

Graduate 3: The challenge is that when you introduce digital technologies to preserve bogwera, you say fewer people must attend the initiation school and follow the traditional way: going to the mountain for a few weeks and paying. You are now saying the information is accessible online, possibly for free and for everyone. What are you saying about the current school principals and their "business"? Do you now see that you have disrupted their source of income?

It became inevitable during these interviews that the commercialization of *bogwera* is one of the significant concerns among the participants. Moreover, they also note that this will prevent any other measures employed to preserve *bogwera*, especially if those measures interfere with how some people generate income out of *bogwera*. Graduates clarify this issue further in the discussions that follow.

Graduate 1: If the teachings, values, and principles of bogwera become digitalized, then it means there is no need for people to go to bogwera. Moreover, you must understand that some principals use this tradition to make money. They will not agree with you.

Graduate 5: Back in the past, bogwera was not just about numbers; it was about teaching young men the culture of Batswana. That is why it is not a problem to graduate, even five boys. However, these days that would be considered a loss. People want to profit. Moreover, your questions about social media tools will not give people profit. It will take people away from bogwera, meaning taking away food from people's mouths.

Graduate 4: Digital technologies will have their advantages for some people. However, in general, the school principals will not benefit from it. My brother, you must understand that we are no longer producing and promoting culture; we are now selling it. Those people mean business. They will not even entertain that thought.

Another participant explains that technology can be crucial in transmitting information from one generation to another.

Graduate 5: In bogwera, information is transmitted via oral tradition. That has its limitations. However, it is how Batswana have always done it in bogwera. However, I believe technology can play a minor role there, maybe just sharing with people the importance of bogwera in contemporary society using technology, recording, and sharing. But not the teachings of bogwera. That will not be allowed.

Ramophato notes that the commercialization of *bogwera* is a reality and will always prevent changes that seek to prevent money-making mechanisms in the culture.

Ramophato: Unfortunately, most of us are just in this to make money. We no longer see young boys as future leaders who should be groomed into manhood. We only see customers. Any method you implement to bring changes into the culture should not interfere with our potential revenue. That is why we are still behind. Recently, the government suggested improving the nutrition of the initiates during bogwera by supplying us with food. That would mean parents no longer have to provide us with pap and a goat for their child during bogwera. That suggestion was rejected. Why? Because sometimes, we do not finish/cook all the food given to us (which is also wrong) and the remaining ones we sell in the villages when the initiation process is finished. We make more money. Now with the government, that might not be possible. They might want to audit the food and everything. People will get arrested if they do not oblige with the processes.

The Chief's concern is with the commercial nature of digital technologies.

Chief: In as much as ICTs have been proven effective in preserving indigenous knowledge, they have also been accused of turning people into consumers. We need to be careful about selling our culture. We do not want a situation where the owners of cultures are now becoming customers of the same culture that they used to own. That would be reversing the doings of colonialism.

Challenges, Opportunities of Preserving African Indigenous Knowledge

- ***Way forward***

The participants also raised their concerns and solutions regarding the preservation of *bogwera*. Some participants agreed this cultural practice should be preserved and protected, while others disagreed. The latter stated that *bogwera* is no longer applicable today.

Graduate 1: If you were from bogwera, you would understand that it is a useless practice. There is nothing there to preserve and protect. It can die for all that I care. Most young people today are not interested in bogwera.

Another graduate shared the same views as Graduate 1.

Graduate 2: Back in the past, it was necessary. However, these days it is just a money-making scheme for people to get rich. You do not leave there with a certificate proving you are from there. So, I do not see how and why we should worry about its survival.

Graduate 3 indicated there should be methods to preserve *bogwera* from dying, but not with technological devices.

Graduate 3: We can try to protect it, but not with technological devices. Those are not the right way to go about it; they are too White. However, the issue is that bogwera is only relevant in December when we graduate the young boys. Throughout the year, you do not see the significance of this practice. So, I am really on the fence line about this one. However, these digital technologies may make the practice more interesting and relevant.

Another graduate argued that measures to protect and preserve *bogwera* from dying should not mean the culture and its integral parts should be destroyed.

Graduate 4: Some of us still see bogwera as an integral part of our lives. We keep livestock, practice farming, and travel on foot; these aspects of our lives still require specific knowledge you acquire in bogwera. So, if you are not from there, you will struggle a lot with these things. However, it does not mean we should throw away our culture by including Facebook and WhatsApp to encourage people to go there. We would be losing the culture.

This view was also echoed by graduate 5.

Graduate 5: The fact is that not many people still find bogwera interesting. To some, especially the young generations, bogwera is an old-fashioned tradition. That is why I believe that all feasible methods that can be used to protect bogwera should be adopted. However, we should not expose our culture to foreign practices that will kill it further. Technology can work, but it has significant limitations and disadvantages that we should not overlook.

Ramophato argues that technology has its benefits but will be minimal regarding *bogwera*.

137

Ramophato: Regarding bogwera, the technology you are talking about will not be accepted. However, I agree that our indigenous knowledge practices and systems as black people should be protected. Alternatively, we will lose them. However, we need to be careful about how we do that. Culture is compassionate, and we must respect it. If you are hasty in dealing with culture, the ancestors will punish you.

The Chief states that *bogwera* is a cultural institution not yet ready for technological innovations.

Ramophato: Maybe you will be able to include technology in bogwera in the future. I cannot say never because we have already seen Western health methods being introduced in our cultures. There was resistance. However, we agreed with the changes because the world is no longer stuck in the past. So even with technology, I am of the view that we will get there. However, for now, people are not ready. You will expect them to reveal what is happening during the initiation process. They will take offense to that.

CONCLUSION AND RECOMMENDATIONS

The world is currently facing the challenge of losing indigenous knowledge systems. Consequently, measures are being introduced to help protect these systems and practices from disappearance. This chapter focused explicitly on the opportunities and challenges likely to be met by using digital technologies in preserving and protecting *bogwera* as one of Batswana's indigenous knowledge systems and practices. Through interviews with a local Chief, *bogwera* principal, and *bogwera* graduates, the study aimed to demonstrate that *bogwera* is one of Batswana's most crucial indigenous knowledge practices. However, there would be significant challenges in preserving and protecting this cultural practice using digital technologies. Participants in this study narrated that *bogwera* is an important cultural institution in the lives of Batswana and agree that it should be protected. However, some participants are against protecting *bogwera* from extinction because they do not see it as valuable today. Participants indicated that digital technologies are essential for preserving culture and traditions and should be endorsed.

Parcticipants also raised pertinent issues that will stand in the way of digital technologies preserving *bogwera*. In the former, they view digital technologies as necessary for exposing the culture to other people, storing memories for the future, and building pride in one's culture. In the latter, they are concerned about the secret and sacred nature of *bogwera*, the commercialization of culture, and the commercial nature of digital technologies ownership. The study also found that preserving indigenous knowledge through digital tools could lead to issues of ownership and patent. Traditional knowledge is collectively owned by the community and is guided by traditional laws and customs. Hence, digitalizing it could create problems of exclusivity, and private ownership, reducing knowledge and cultural expressions to mere commodities that individuals or corporations can own. This has also been raised by Sraku-Lartey et al. (2017), stating that the ease with which digitized information could be copied and transmitted raises issues about the abilities of the communities to ensure ownership and integrity of their knowledge continuously.

The findings of this chapter suggest that digital tools could prove to be vital in preserving and protecting some aspects of *bogwera* for future generations. However, the sacred features of the practice might be compromised. Hence, digital technologies in preserving and protecting *bogwera* cannot be implemented without limits. These findings reveal that in as much as people and communities are open to using the new technology to preserve indigenous knowledge systems, they still want ownership of the

Challenges, Opportunities of Preserving African Indigenous Knowledge

culture, they still want the protection of the culture, and they do not want the culture to be infiltrated by Western beliefs and practices. The colonial rulers, missionaries, and Eurocentric intellectuals created the impression that indigenous knowledge systems were inferior, primitive, heathen, barbaric, and not worthy of preservation and needed to be turned around (Plockey, 2015). However, as the participants have indicated in this study, digital technologies have the potential to make indigenous knowledge systems more appealing to the masses; digital technology can make people love their culture and their past and integrate it into their daily lives. Ngulube (2004) submits that it is essential to preserve and make indigenous knowledge systems visible in our daily lives so that future generations may learn about it and be proud of their past that was erroneously labeled as primitive by the colonizers.

Therefore, using all means necessary to protect and manage indigenous knowledge systems is essential because, as Plockey (2015) puts it, a vast amount of knowledge and expertise is being lost, leaving humanity in danger of losing its past and perhaps endangering its future. The findings of this study indicated that a vast amount of indigenous knowledge of Batswana is being lost because of the death of the custodians of this knowledge, Western education, and migrations. Hence, the participants argued that measures should be in place to protect the remaining little. The participants discussed that digital technologies can help people learn about their history, chiefs, and ways of living without having to travel to other places to have conversations with the people that know these things. The participants in this study also believed that using digital technologies to preserve and protect *bogwera* would erode and kill the culture. It was clear that, as argued by one participant, they were not ready for that revolution. In a rural community such as Taung, people still respect the sacred nature of *bogwera*. They still believe that its secrecy and sacredness make it unique and powerful. These views resonate with what Lwoga, Ngulube, and Benson (2010) argued, that the documentation and dissemination of indigenous knowledge in Africa are still affected by poor attitudes, knowledge culture, and personal characteristics such as age, gender, status, and wealth. It is still a challenge for people in Taung to see the value of preserving *bogwera* through digital media tools, and this is caused by how they view digital media platforms, their age, social status in society, and their literacy level.

However, Martinez (2011) argues that cultural and rhetorical expression of digital media is necessary for indigenous people to exercise their sovereignty in a digital age. The efforts to digitize indigenous knowledge are common in some African countries. It has proved a viable option for preserving and protecting indigenous knowledge. Christian (cited in Sraku-Lartey et al., 2017) reports that the digitization of traditional medicine in Nigeria is predominantly tacit and embedded in its holders' practices and experiences. This shows positive results when communities use technological tools to preserve indigenous knowledge.

REFERENCES

Barker, S. K. (2007). New opportunities for research libraries in digital information and knowledge management: Challenges for the mid-sized research library. *Journal of Library Administration*, *46*(1), 65–74. doi:10.1300/J111v46n01_05

Boamah, E., & Liew, C. L. (2017). Conceptualizing the digitization and preservation of indigenous knowledge: The importance of attitudes. *Lecture Notes in Computer Science*, *10647*, 65–80. Advance online publication. doi:10.1007/978-3-319-70232-2_6

Cassidy, L., Wilk, J., Kgathi, D. L., Bendsen, H., Ngwenya, B. N., & Mosepele, K. (2011). Indigenous knowledge, livelihoods, and government policy in the Okavango Delta, Botswana. In Kgathi, D.L. Ngwenya, B.N. and Darkoh, M.B.K. (Eds). Rural Livelihoods, Risk and Political Economy of Access to Natural Resources in the Okavango Delta, Botswana. Nova Science Publishers.

Conway, P. (2010). Preservation in the age of Google: Digitalization, digital preservation, and dilemmas. *The Library Quarterly: Information, Community. Policy, 80*(1), 61–79. doi:10.1086/648463

Denbow, J., & Thebe, P. C. (2006). *Culture and Customs of Batswana.* Greenwood Press.

Grey, S. (2014). Indigenous Knowledge. In A. C. Michalos (Ed.), *Encyclopedia of Quality Life and Well-Being Research* (pp. 3229–3233). Springer. doi:10.1007/978-94-007-0753-5_1448

Krtalic, M., & Hassenay, D. (2012). Exploring a framework for comprehensive and successful preservation management in libraries. *The Journal of Documentation, 68*(3), 353–377. doi:10.1108/00220411211225584

Kruglikova, G. A. (2020). Use of information technologies in the preservation and popularizing of cultural heritage. *International Scientific Conference: "Digitalization of Education: History, Trends, and Prospects.* (pp. 446-450). IEEE. 10.2991/assehr.k.200509.081

Lwoga, E. T., Ngulube, P., & Sitwell, C. (2010). Managing indigenous knowledge for sustainable agricultural development in developing countries: Knowledge management approaches in the social context. *The International Information & Library Review, 42*(3), 174–185. doi:10.1080/10572317.2010.10762862

Martinez, C. (2011). Digital Ayayote Rattle: The design of a portable, low-cost digital media system for a mediated Xican Indo Resolana. In Nicola Bidwell and Heike Winschiers-Theophilus (Eds.), *Proceedings of IKT2011: Embracing Indigenous Knowledge Systems in a New Technology Design Paradigm.* Indigenous Knowledge Technology Conference.

Mothoagae, I. D. (2017). The transfusion of bogwera in Luke 2:21 in the 1857 English-Setswana bible. *Theological Studies, 73*(3), 1–9. doi:10.4102/hts.v77i1.6914

Ngulube, P. (2004). Using the SECI knowledge management and other tools to communicate and manage tacit indigenous knowledge. *Innovation, 27*(1), 21–30. doi:10.4314/innovation.v27i1.26484

Owiny, S. A., Mehta, K., & Maretzki, A. N. (2014). The use of social media technologies to create, preserve, and disseminate indigenous knowledge and skills to communities in East Africa. *International Journal of Communication, 8*, 234–247. https://ijoc.org/index.php/ijoc/article/view/1667

Plockey, F. D. D. (2014). The role of Ghana public libraries in the digitization of indigenous knowledge: Issues and Prospects. *The Journal of Pan African Studies, 6*(10), 20–36.

Plockey, F. D. D. (2015). Indigenous knowledge production, digital media, and academic libraries in Ghana. *The Journal of Pan African Studies, 8*(4), 32–44.

Senanayake, S. G. J. N. (2006). Indigenous knowledge as a key to sustainable development. *Journal of Agricultural Sciences, 2*(1), 87–94. doi:10.4038/jas.v2i1.8117

Sillitoe, P., & Marzano, M. (2009). Future of indigenous knowledge research in development. *Futures, 41*(1), 13–23. doi:10.1016/j.futures.2008.07.004

Sraku-Lartey, M., Acquah, S. B., Brefo, S. S., & Djagbletey, G. D. (2017). Digitization of indigenous knowledge on forest foods and medicines. *IFLA Journal, 43*(2), 187–197. doi:10.1177/0340035216681326

Stevens, A. (2008). A different way of knowing: Tools and strategies for managing indigenous knowledge. *Libri, 58*(1), 25–33. doi:10.1515/libr.2008.003

Tjiek, L. T. (2006). Desa informasi: The role of digital libraries in the preserving and dissemination of indigenous knowledge. *The International Information & Library Review, 38*(3), 123–131. doi:10.1080 /10572317.2006.10762713

Winschiers-Theophilus, H., Jensen, K., & Rodil, K. (2012). Locally situated digital representation of indigenous knowledge: Co-constructing a new digital reality in rural Africa. In Strano, M. Hrachovec, H. Sudweeks, F. and Ess, C. (Eds.), Proceedings Cultural Attitudes Towards Technology and Communication 2012, Murdoch University.

KEY TERMS AND DEFINITIONS

Bogwera: It is a cultural practice of the Batswana that marks a rite of passage from boy to manhood.

Digital Preservation: It is a set of processes and activities to ensure that digital information of enduring value remain accessible over a long period of time and usable by future generations.

Digital technologies: refer to digital devices, systems and resources that help create, store, manage and preserve information or knowledge.

Indigenous Knowledge Systems: It is the expressions, practices, beliefs, understanding, insights, and experiences of indigenous groups generated over centuries of profound interaction with a particular territory.

Traditional Knowledge: It is knowledge or practices passed down from generation to generation that form part of the traditions or heritage of indigenous communities.

ENDNOTE

[1]   A title for a principal of an initiation school.

Chapter 8

Efficacy of Acquiring and Transferring Indigenous Medicinal Knowledge Among Its Owners and Practitioners in uMhlathuze in KwaZulu-Natal, South Africa

Nokwanda Charity Khanyile
University of Zululand, South Africa

Petrus Nhlavu Dlamini
University of Zululand, South Africa

Tlou Maggie Masenya
Durban University of Technology, South Africa

ABSTRACT

Most of the population in Africa is still dependent on indigenous medicinal knowledge for treating and managing ailments. However, it is still not yet understood how this valuable knowledge is acquired and transferred from one generation to the next. The aim of this chapter was to assess the process of acquiring and transferring indigenous medicinal knowledge among its owners and practitioners. The study adopted a qualitative research approach. The findings revealed that indigenous medicinal knowledge is acquired in many different ways including visions, dreams and vigorous training and it is transferred to specially chosen children and trainees through vigorous training.

DOI: 10.4018/978-1-6684-7024-4.ch008

Copyright © 2023, IGI Global. Copying or distributing in print or electronic forms without written permission of IGI Global is prohibited.

INTRODUCTION

WHO (2013) defined indigenous medicine as *the sum total of the knowledge, skill, and practices based on the theories, beliefs, and experiences indigenous to different cultures, whether explicable or not, used in the maintenance of health as well as in the prevention, diagnosis, improvement, or treatment of physical and mental illness.* Makhanya (2012) asserted that traditional healing involves a combination of various healing techniques such as spiritualism, divining, and herbalism. The South African government has recognised various types of traditional health practitioners (THPs) who are registered under the Act. These include herbalist (izinyanga or amaxhwele), diviners (izangoma or amagqirha), faith healers (abathandazi) and midwives (abazalisi) (Peltzer, 2008). In addition, some traditional surgeons(ingcibi) perform circumcisions (Peltzer, 2008. The use of the concepts of acquirement and transmission was inspired by the English philosopher John Locke (2001) and Nonaka (1994). Locke (2001) pronounced the birth state of the human mind as "blank slate or tabula rasa" and as noted by Mack and Meadowcroft (2009) people are born knowing nothing and that they acquire knowledge only through experiences. Consequently, knowledge acquisition could be defined as learning through experiences and experiments. It is about grasping, integrating, adapting and confirming knowledge for concept formation, clarification, formulating questions or understanding the problem to be solved or reaching conclusions (Mathew, 1985). However, Sodi et al. (2011) asserted that custodians of indigenous medical knowledge acquire their knowledge through ancestors.

As proposed by Aristotle knowledge acquisition is known to be the method of learning and explained as how it materialised in a knowledge-based system (Bosancic, 2016). This denotes that people acquire knowledge once they are born by learning from their parents and those around them. It means people acquire knowledge from those that are well versed in the subject. Hence, this chapter explored how knowledge is acquired and transferred among indigenous medicinal knowledge owners in uMhlathuze municipality in the province of KwaZulu-Natal South Africa. Concerning transmission of knowledge, Nonaka (1994) opined that knowledge is continuously transmitted from one person (or entity) to another; and that once knowledge has been acquired, it is then shared or transmitted to the intended user. In the context of this study, indigenous knowledge medicine is tacit in nature, it needs to be acquired through learning by doing. Traditional medicinal knowledge owners are considered as custodians of this knowledge and they are the ones who own the rich knowledge, and they are responsible for the transmission of such to the chosen young generation for it to survived (Adekannbi, Olatokun & Ajiferuke, 2014).

There is thus a strong belief that knowledge is valued when it remains to its possessor, however, it becomes valuable when it is shared and used (Kamal, Manjit & Gurvinder, 2007). Hence, the value of indigenous medicinal knowledge is effective when transferred from one chosen generation to the next (Nonaka 1994; Dlamini, 2017). Indigenous medicinal knowledge is primarily transmitted verbally and is held tacitly by its custodians or owners (Yunnus, 2017). Thus, according to Maluleka (2017), indigenous medicinal knowledge is the total of all knowledge and practices, used in diagnosing, preventing, or eliminating a physical, mental, or social disequilibrium, which rely exclusively on experience and observation handed down from generation to generation, verbally or in writing and health practices or approaches. This knowledge is commonly exchanged through personal communication and demonstration and gets transmitted from master to apprentice, from parents to children, from one neighbour to the other and so on (Dlamini, 2016; Ngulube, 2002). Dlamini (2017) opined that knowledge transfer involves being together for some time or living in the same environment, which allows newcomers to understand others' ways of thinking, skills, feelings, and experiences. Hence, Szulanski et al. (2016) articulated that tacit knowledge may be transferred through observations, imitation and practice. A large percentage of traditional medicinal knowledge exists in a verbal form, as it is known by its owners only. Thus, according to Mosoti and Masheka (2010), when an older person dies in an African country, the entire library dies. It can be said that when owners of traditional medicinal knowledge die, they perish with their priceless expertise, causing future generations to suffer (Dlamini & Ocholla, 2018). This is considered a concern in this study since many people living in communities rely on traditional medicinal knowledge for their health, and hence losing this knowledge would be detrimental to them.

Odede (2020) further revealed that the use of traditional medicine is prevalent among most sections of South African's black population, even those who are not from rural or impoverished areas. However, there is a consensus agreement that the reliance on indigenous medicinal knowledge comes from the rural dwellers of various tribes in a country. In KwaZulu-Natal, there are about 25 000 indigenous medicinal practitioners, however, only 7000 of them are registered with the interim professional body of the profession (Zuma et al., 2016). As much as indigenous medicine is appreciated and researched by many scholars, there is a lack of understanding on how the knowledge is acquired and transferred from one generation to another among indigenous medicinal knowledge owners (Truter, 2007). It is, therefore, crucial to uncover how the acquisition and transmission of indigenous medicinal knowledge among indigenous medicinal knowledge owners. Knowledge creation theory by Nonaka (1994) was thus adopted in this study to unveil the process of acquirement and transmission of indigenous medicinal knowledge among traditional medicinal knowledge owners in uMhlathuze municipality in the province of KwaZulu-Natal South.

CONTEXTUAL SETTING

This chapter focuses on the indigenous medicinal knowledge owners who are found in uMhlathuze municipality, in the province of KwaZulu-Natal, South Africa, which are mainly isiZulu and siSwati speaking traditional medicinal knowledge owners or practitioners. The uMhlathuze municipality is located in the northeast of the province of KwaZulu-Natal, and it t is approximately 180 kilometres northeast of Durban. The areas in uMhlathuze municipality where indigenous medicinal knowledge was consulted comprise Richards Bay, Empangeni, Heatville, and Buchanan. uMhlathuze is divided into seven townships: eSkhaleni, eNseleni, Ngwelezana, Felixton, Mandlazini, and uMzingazi. uMhlathuze comprises rural areas, including KwaDlangezwa, Kwabhenjana, Kwamadlebe, Buchanan, Obizo, Somopho, Luwamba, and Fatima, which are all administered by rural authorities (https://www.umhlathuze.gov.za/). As a result, this chapter concentrated on sites inside the uMhlathuze district as illustrated in Figure 1.1.

THE AIM OF THE STUDY

The aim of this study was to assess the process of acquirement and transmission of indigenous medicinal knowledge by traditional medicinal knowledge owners or practitioners in uMhlathuze Municipality, in the province of KwaZulu-Natal, South Africa.

Indigenous Medicinal Knowledge Among Its Owners and Practitioners

Figure 1. Map of uMhlathuze

PROBLEM STATEMENT

Despite the high population of approximately 80% of Africans which heavily rely on indigenous knowledge for medical purposes (Mahomoodally, 2013), this knowledge is still in high danger of getting lost if no proper mechanisms of acquirement, storing and transmission are in place (Dlamini & Ocholla, 2018). Notably, much of indigenous knowledge is preserved in oral traditions such as human memories which are gradually disappearing due to loss of memory and death or other forms of brain drain (Dlamini, 2016; Lwoga & Ngulube, 2009). It is commonly exchanged through personal communication and demonstration and gets transmitted from master to apprentice, from parents to children, from one neighbour to the other, and so on (Dlamini, 2016; Ngulube, 2002). However, Maluleka and Ngulube (2017) lamented that the death of a senior citizen may have devastating implications for a community that depends on the expertise of that particular citizen and more so, if the knowledge was not imparted in any way. Maluleka and Ngoepe (2018) further argued that the danger that has always been associated with indigenous knowledge is that it might be obliterated as a result of several factors such as not being documented or the death of a senior or the most experienced person before such knowledge could be passed on to the next generations. It is regrettable that despite the importance and recognition of indigenous medicinal knowledge globally, the details of acquirement, transmission and documentation of this valuable resource are not known. Therefore, this study intends to unveil the process of acquirement and transmission of indigenous medical knowledge by its owners or practitioners.

CONCEPTUAL FRAMEWORK

This chapter adopted the SECI model, also known as the knowledge creation model, by Nonaka (1994), and the power of this model lies in its efficacy of the interaction between tacit and explicit knowledge. The model uses four modes of interaction which are very effective in the acquirement and transmission of indigenous medicinal knowledge among indigenous medicinal knowledge owners and practitioners, that may facilitate knowledge management, including knowledge transfer among healers. Nonaka and Takeuchi (1995) highlighted four modes of knowledge creation and sharing, namely: socialisation, externalisation, combination and internalisation. Figure 1.2 below demonstrates the acquisition and transmission of tacit and explicit knowledge.

Figure 2. Key elements of the knowledge creation and sharing model.
Source: Nonaka (1994)

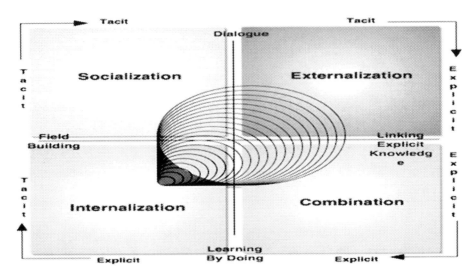

Socialisation

Socialisation is a process that encourages individuals to share their experiences as a manner of learning, allowing for the direct transmission of tacit knowledge (Nonaka, 1994). The primary aspect of socialisation is that tacit information is transmitted between persons by cooperative behaviour such as being together, spending time together and living in the same environment, rather than written form (Hoe, 2006). Socialisation is critical in this study because it enables and supports knowledge sharing between communities and organisations through collaborative actions. It is thus critical for this study to understand how traditional medicinal knowledge holders or owners and notable diviners, acquire, transfer and preserve their knowledge since they get this vital knowledge through ancestral calling (Coleman, 2013).

Externalisation

Essentially, externalisation is the process that entails the transformation of tacit information into explicit information (Nonaka & Konno, 1998; Nonaka & Takeuchi, 1995). Easa (2012) stated that when tacit knowledge is turned to explicit knowledge, it gets "crystallized," allowing it to be shared with other individuals and serve as the foundation for new knowledge such as concepts, visuals, and textual content. Dlamini and Ocholla (2018) asserted that externalisation has the power to bring people from different backgrounds together as it allows people from diverse backgrounds to share their tacit knowledge. In this setting, the purpose of this study was to determine how traditional medicinal knowledge owners acquire and transfer their tacit indigenous medicinal knowledge to their chosen ones in the family or community. For example, externalisation takes place when a person holding tacit knowledge converts it into any secondary form (for example, document or image, or rock painting) where another can retrieve it, even in the absence of a person holding it (Ngulube, 2003; Lwoga, Ngulube & Stilwell, 2010).

Combination

The combination is the process through which explicit knowledge is transferred to other explicit knowledge and as noted by Ngulube (2003) this mode of knowledge creation and sharing involves using the second type of knowledge to generate another secondary form of knowledge.

Internalisation

Easa (2012) describes internalisation as the process in which explicit knowledge is recycled into tacit knowledge, implying that explicit knowledge is absorbed, and this implies that to permanently keep tacit and explicit knowledge in the human mind. Therefore, this means that the acquired indigenous medicinal knowledge through socialisation, externalisation and combination must be internalised and is becomes applicable where it is required.

METHODOLOGY

Sithole (2007) stated that indigenous knowledge is predominantly tacit, embedded in the practices and experiences of its holders commonly exchanged through personal communication and demonstrations from the teacher to the apprentice, from parents to children, from neighbour to neighbour. This chapter investigated the efficacy of acquiring and transferring of indigenous medicinal knowledge among its owners or practitioners in uMhlathuze in KwaZulu-Natal, South Africa. The medicinal knowledge owners in their natural setting was thus explored and tapped into their tacit knowledge in an effort to gain a deeper understanding of how sense of the world and how they construct their everyday lives. According to Pandya (2012), the reality is socially and historically produced by the human mind and is based on the world's experiences. As a result, this study relied on participants' perspectives on the study's subject and their ability to comprehend the structures they have in order to develop fresh interpretations. Interpretivism paradigm which works effectively with a qualitative research approach was thus employed in this study to allow participants to express their personal experiences in their own words and allowing the researchers to grasp the study's topic better. Hence, data was collected through semi-structured interviews and rigorous literature review.

The snowball sampling technique was also used to select the sample for the study because of the nature of the population being investigated. It is important to note that South Africa as a whole has approximately 200 000 traditional practitioners who are practising in 1995 and around 300 000 in 2005 (Aude et al., 2020; Truter 2007). It is thus very complicated to give the precise figure when it comes to practising traditional health practitioners since some are not registered and are not in the database of Traditional Health Practitioners in South Africa (Parliament of South Africa 2005). As already mentioned UMhlathuze municipality is the third-largest municipality in KwaZulu-Natal which is divided into seven townships, as outlined in Figure 1.1. The researchers established contacts in each town as a basis for the snowball. Therefore, snowball sampling allowed the researchers to gain participants from other participants through referrals.

A total number of 15 participants were interviewed and more details of the participants were explained in Table 1 where demographic characteristics of participants were also detailed. The semi-structured interviews were conducted using a voice recorder, supplemented by the notes taken by researchers. The researchers had to take time listening to the recorded notes from the voice recorder while transcribing on

Indigenous Medicinal Knowledge Among Its Owners and Practitioners

Table 1. Demographic profile data of respondents (N=15)

Variables of biographic data		
Variables	**Frequency**	**Percentage %**
Gender		
Male	7	46.6
Female	8	53.3
Total	**15**	**100**
Age		
31-40 yrs.	5	33.3
21-30yrs	4	26.6
41 yrs. and above	6	40
18- 20 yrs.	0	0
Total	**15**	**100**
Level of study		
Primary	7	46.6
Secondary	6	40
Tertiary	2	13.3
Total	**15**	**100**
Location		
Bucanan	1	6.6
Dlangezwa	2	13.3
Ematshani	1	6.6
Kwasokhulu	1	6.6
Madlanzini	1	6.6
Ngwelezane	2	13.3
Enseleni	2	13.3
Ntambanani	1	6.6
Skhawini	4	26.6
Total	**15**	**100**

the paper. The researchers compared the notes that were recorded using a voice recorder with those that were written in the notebook and this was done to ensure that all the required details were noted and to observe if accurate and rich data were collected as well as to make adjustments where it was necessary. The study then organised the collected data according to the themes that emanated from the research objectives.

ETHICAL CONSIDERATIONS

The researchers started by applying for ethical clearance from the University of Zululand and it was granted to the researchers to conduct the study as they intended to. The consent form was used to allow

Indigenous Medicinal Knowledge Among Its Owners and Practitioners

participants to sign if they were agreeing to participate in the study. The researchers had to inform all participants that participation was voluntary and are free not to participate and were also assured that anonymity and confidentiality will be maintained.

Demographic profile of participants

Participants were required to answer structured questions about personal information such as gender, age, degree of education, and geographic place of residence. Specifically, the purpose of these structured questions was to determine the role those demographic parameters played in the acquirement and transmission of traditional medicinal knowledge.

RESULTS AND DISCUSSIONS

The findings of the study were reported by themes derived from the research objectives below.

What Type(s) of Indigenous Medicinal Knowledge Owners or Practitioners Do You Have in uMhlathuze Municipality?

This study believed that it was critical to identify the various kinds of owners or practitioners of traditional medicinal knowledge in their communities to enable the researcher to categorise them according to their roles. This was also to ensure that their arguments were explicitly unequivocally. The participants' comments were classified in Table 2 as follows:

Table 2. Types of indigenous medicinal knowledge owners in uMhlathuze Municipality

Participate	Response
Traditional medicinal knowledge owner 1	*"We have diviners and herbalists in my community."*
Traditional medicinal knowledge owner 2	*"There are others who do the same work like mine, and we also have diviners."*
Traditional medicinal knowledge owner 3	*"There are diviners and herbalists in my community."*
Traditional medicinal knowledge owner 4	*"There are several of them counting diviners, herbalists and faith healers in my community."*
Traditional medicinal knowledge owner 5	*"We have various types such as faith healers or prophets, diviners and herbalists."*
Traditional medicinal knowledge owner 6	*"There are diviners and spiritual healers in my community."*
Traditional medicinal knowledge owner 7	*"We have herbalists and diviners in my community."*
Traditional medicinal knowledge owner 8	*"There are others who perform similar work as mine, which are herbalists and diviners."*
Traditional medicinal knowledge owner 9	*"There are herbalists, diviners and faith healers."*
Traditional medicinal knowledge owner 10	*"We have many like diviners and herbalists."*
Traditional medicinal knowledge owner 11	*"There are diviners and herbalists."*
Traditional medicinal knowledge owner 12	*"We have herbalists, diviners and faith healers."*
Traditional medicinal knowledge owner 13	*Herbalist, and traditional faith healers."*
Traditional medicinal knowledge owner 14	*"Several traditional healers, such as diviners, herbalists, and faith healers, live in our villages."*
Traditional medicinal knowledge owner 15	*"I know of diviners and faith healers."*

The study found that uMhlathuze local municipality had several different types of traditional medicinal knowledge practitioners who are considered traditional practitioners or healers of the community. The study demonstrated that the traditional medicinal knowledge owners were well informed of traditional healers of the community. Thus, the study showed that traditional medicinal knowledge owners in rural communities of uMhlathuze were diviners, herbalists and faith healers. The study's findings concurred with the findings by Bereda (2015), who revealed that diviners are predominantly female who serve as intermediaries between humans and the ancestors and concentrate on discovering mysteries by investigating the reason for unique occasions and explaining the messages of the ancestral spirits. Latiff (2010) referred to herbalist as knowledge of supernatural techniques, including diagnosing illnesses and prescribing correct herbs, preventing calamities in a village, protecting against bewitchment, and bringing wealth into a village. Faith healers or prophets indicate syncretism, a reinterpretation of orthodox Christianity in such a way to be reconcilable with traditional culture (Sebata, 2015). In this light, it can be said that rural communities have different traditional medicinal knowledge healers who use different approaches to diagnose and treat illnesses.

What is Your Role as a Traditional Medicinal Knowledge Owner or Practitioner in the Community?

The study felt it was critical to understand the roles and functions of indigenous medicinal knowledge owners or practitioners in their communities and society at large. It was fascinating to discover that all 15 (100%) participants expressed their views on their roles in their communities as practitioners of traditional medicinal knowledge. The participants' responses were classified in Table 3.

Concerning the roles occupied by indigenous medicinal knowledge owners or practitioners, the study further revealed specialised roles that traditional medicinal knowledge practitioners form part of, and it

Table 3. What is your role as a traditional medicinal knowledge practitioner/owner in the community?

Participate	Response
Traditional medicinal knowledge owner 1	*"I am a herbalist (Inyanga)."*
Traditional medicinal knowledge owner 2	*"I am a faith healer (uMthandazi)."*
Traditional medicinal knowledge owner 3	*"I am a diviner (Isangoma)."*
Traditional medicinal knowledge owner 4	*"I am a diviner (Isangoma)."*
Traditional medicinal knowledge owner 5	*I am a diviner (Isangoma)."*
Traditional medicinal knowledge owner 6	*"I am a faith healer (Umthandazi)."*
Traditional medicinal knowledge owner 7	*"I am the kind that uses traditional medicinal plants to heal people. In short, I am a herbalist (Inyanga)."*
Traditional medicinal knowledge owner 8	*"I am a herbalist (Inyanga)."*
Traditional medicinal knowledge owner 9	*"I am a herbalist (Inyanga)."*
Traditional medicinal knowledge owner 10	*"I am a faith healer (Inyanga)."*
Traditional medicinal knowledge owner 11	*"I am a herbalist (Inyanga)."*
Traditional medicinal knowledge owner 12	*"I am a herbalist (Inyanga)."*
Traditional medicinal knowledge owner 13	*"I am a diviner (Isangoma)."*
Traditional medicinal knowledge owner 14	*"I am a diviner (Isangoma)."*
Traditional medicinal knowledge owner 15	*"I am a diviner (Isangoma)."*

Indigenous Medicinal Knowledge Among Its Owners and Practitioners

was found that a large number of them were considered herbalists and diviners. Moreover, their existence denotes the relevancy of their participation in indigenous medicinal practices. The findings confirm the findings by WHO (2013) that eighty (80) per cent of indigenous people in Africa use indigenous knowledge for medicinal purposes such as maintenance of health and the prevention, diagnosis, improvement, or treatment of physical and mental illnesses.

How Did You Acquire the Knowledge of Traditional Medicine?

It was necessary to ascertain methods of acquiring traditional medicinal knowledge, due to the nature of this knowledge, and the participants were asked about how this knowledge is acquired. The comments on this topic included some truly fascinating narratives in the Table 4.

The study revealed that indigenous medicinal knowledge could be acquired directly or indirectly from the relevant source. The significant ways that participants revealed to acquire their knowledge was through

Table 4. Methods of acquiring the knowledge of traditional medicine

Participate	Response
Traditional medicinal knowledge owner 1	*"The proprietor of the shop where I work demonstrated how things are done and educated me on which medicinal herbs are used to treat and manage specific illnesses."*
Traditional medicinal knowledge owner 2	*"I acquired my knowledge through dreams. I am given instructions through dreams by my ancestors."*
Traditional medicinal knowledge owner 3	*"I was introduced to traditional medicinal knowledge through dreams of which I was later instructed to go to initiation school where I learnt everything I was seeing in dreams."*
Traditional medicinal knowledge owner 4	*"I was on my way to the tuckshop when my ancestors instructed me to alter my route and take a taxi to Kwa Mhlabuyalingana. When I arrived, I was instructed to proceed to a special car where individuals waited to take me to my Master's in Mozambique. I subsequently began the initiation procedure, during which I spent six months in the ocean. I emerged from the ocean with a monstrous snake. For three years, I continued the initiation procedure."*
Traditional medicinal knowledge owner 5	*"At a very young age, it was revealed to me that I had a calling of being a diviner. I, therefore, went to an initiation school in the year 1997 where I spent a year being trained."*
Traditional medicinal knowledge owner 6	*"The traditional medicinal knowledge of healing was a gift given to me by my father. My father left his bags of healing to me so that I can carry on with his duties of healing and treating illnesses."*
Traditional medicinal knowledge owner 7	*"My grandfather used to bring me along when he went to the mountain to collect medicinal plants, and it was there that he began educating me about the numerous medicinal plants and their uses."*
Traditional medicinal knowledge owner 8	*"My ancestors gave this knowledge to me as a gift, and I then went to an initiation school to broaden my skills."*
Traditional medicinal knowledge owner 9	*"My ancestors called me as they revealed everything to me through dreams."*
Traditional medicinal knowledge owner 10	*"It was at a very young age when I received a gift of healing. This gift was given to me through prayer, and with this power, I can glimpse the unknown through my dreams. Through dreams, I was educated about the various medicinal plants and their purposes. For example, while I was seeking work, my ancestor instructed me to blend several traditional medicinal plants and use them to assist people in finding work."*
Traditional medicinal knowledge owner 11	*"I received my knowledge from my mother who used to sell traditional medicine for a living from the age of 7 years. My mother taught me to use various medicinal plants for treating and managing illnesses."*
Traditional medicinal knowledge owner 12	*"I acquired my knowledge through my ancestors."*
Traditional medicinal knowledge owner 13	*"I got it from my ancestors through dreams."*
Traditional medicinal knowledge owner 14	*"I had a dream in which I saw myself walking through a thick forest with an old man holding a stick who gave me the name of a diviner (sangoma). I was then instructed to seek out this particular man who would be my instructor."*
Traditional medicinal knowledge owner 15	*"I used to become sick frequently, to the point where I was forced to drop out of school and attend initiation school. While attending initiation school, I felt as though I was improving since I had accepted my calling."*

ancestral communication in dreams. The study also showed that other traditional medicinal knowledge owners or practitioners acquired their knowledge from their parents or master. Three key informants evidenced that knowledge is passed on from one generation to the next through verbal communication: *"The proprietor of the shop where I work demonstrated how things are done and educated me on which medicinal herbs are used to treat and manage specific illnesses"*, *"I was introduced to traditional medicinal knowledge through dreams of which I was later instructed to go to initiation school where I learnt everything I was seeing in dreams"* and *"My grandfather used to bring me along when he went to the mountain to collect medicinal plants, and it was there that he began educating me about the numerous medicinal plants and their uses"*. Nonaka and Konno (1998) also explained that tacit knowledge that cannot be formally articulated between individuals may be exchanged through joint activities. This may involve being together for some time or living in the same environment, which allows newcomers to understand others' ways of thinking, skills, feelings and experiences. Nonaka (1994) also pointed out that in socialisation, while seniors share their experiences, others are learning in the process. Dlamini (2016) shares similar findings, which pointed out that indigenous knowledge is mainly transferred from one generation to the next by word of mouth through values or norms held by traditional elders. Therefore, it was brought to light that tons of traditional medicinal knowledge exist in its intangible form as its owners tacitly hold it. Although tacit knowledge is difficult to codify, it can be expressed as knowledge and skill when assigned a task or responsibility. This suggests the gap identified in this study, that this knowledge is only shared with the chosen individuals and tacitly held by its owners, remaining undocumented and unpreserved.

How Long Have You Been a Traditional Medicinal Knowledge Owner?

The participants were asked to uncover their time frame as indigenous medicinal knowledge owners or practitioners. Participants answered in a variety of ways, as illustrated by Table 5.

The findings of the study revealed that a large number of indigenous medicinal knowledge owners had vast knowledge of indigenous medicine with only a few less than ten years, indicating that the participants have acquired adequate experience to function in their chosen profession. These findings were in line with Adekannbi, Olatokun and Ajiferuke (2014) who also highlighted that seniors of indigenous medicine are considered legitimate custodians of this knowledge which is handed down to them by their ancestors, and they are in turn expected to pass it on to others for this knowledge to survive.

How Do You Transfer or Share Indigenous Medicinal Knowledge With Your Children and Those You Train?

This question was attended by those indigenous medicinal knowledge owners or practitioners who were very old in the field of indigenous medicine. These are called custodians or seniors because they are full of wisdom in the use of traditional medicine. The study handpicked those who were above 10 years of experience in using traditional medicine and their responses were narrated in Table 6.

The study findings demonstrated that indigenous medicinal knowledge owners or practitioners are fully involved in the transfer or sharing of their knowledge of indigenous medicine. The study further revealed that indigenous medicinal knowledge owners are using several ways of transferring or sharing their knowledge to their blood children and students (trainees). For example, practically demonstrating how to mix plants to treat ailments, identifying plants that are used to join

Indigenous Medicinal Knowledge Among Its Owners and Practitioners

Table 5. Time frame being indigenous medicinal knowledge owner

Participate	Response
Traditional medicinal knowledge owner 1	*"I have been a traditional medicinal knowledge practitioner for three (3) years."*
Traditional medicinal knowledge owner 2	*"It has been five (5) years now."*
Traditional medicinal knowledge owner 3	*"It has been twenty (20) years now."*
Traditional medicinal knowledge owner 4	*"It has not been that long as it is approximately four (4) years so far."*
Traditional medicinal knowledge owner 5	*It has been a while now, and if I am not mistaken, it is twenty-four (24) years."*
Traditional medicinal knowledge owner 6	*"I have been doing this for six (6) years."*
Traditional medicinal knowledge owner 7	*It has been Forty-two (42) years.*
Traditional medicinal knowledge owner 8	*"I have been a herbalist for 15 years."*
Traditional medicinal knowledge owner 9	*"It has been three (3) years."*
Traditional medicinal knowledge owner 10	*"It has been twenty (20) years."*
Traditional medicinal knowledge owner 11	*Eighteen (18) years."*
Traditional medicinal knowledge owner 12	*Seven (7) years."*
Traditional medicinal knowledge owner 13	*"Above ten (10) years."*
Traditional medicinal knowledge owner 14	*"Thirty-five (35) years."*
Traditional medicinal knowledge owner 15	*"Ten (10) years."*

broken bones, showing trainees the amount of water that is mixed with herbs, just to mention a few. These findings suggest that indigenous medicinal knowledge owners or practitioners impart their knowledge to other people for it to survive when they are no more in this world. The findings of the study concurred with Nonaka (1994) that through socialisation, tacit knowledge is passed on through face-to-face communication and experiences in the same environment. Nonaka (1994) further explains that once the knowledge is acquired, it is continuously transmitted from one person (or entity) to another, and emphasised that once knowledge has been acquired, it is then shared or transmitted to the intended user.

What Challenges Are Encountered in Transferring the Indigenous Medicinal Knowledge?

This question was attended by a few indigenous medicinal knowledge owners who were involved in transferring the indigenous medicinal knowledge to other people. Only those with ten years of experience using traditional medicine attended this question. Their responses were narrated in table 7.

The study findings established that indigenous medicinal knowledge owners experience several challenges due to failure to follow instructions by their students. As such, lack of commitment, laziness, failure to attend all classes, and language barrier, to mention a few, are the main challenges. Language is also one of the barriers to the acquisition and transferring of knowledge, as noted by Davis and Ebbe (1995). Hoe (2006) also highlighted that students could not learn if they were not fully committed to their lectures and further indicated that knowledge is tacit and therefore, those who acquire this knowledge must have a strong desire to learn.

153

Table 6. How do you transfer or share indigenous medicinal knowledge with your children and those you train?

Participate	Response
Traditional medicinal knowledge owner 3	*"I have those who come to me for renewal (ukuthwasa). They spend approximately 6 months with me being trained. It is like they are in a class and I am like a teacher to them. All my students are expected to listen attentively and observe the movement of bones as I throw them on the floor. I tell them that each one has a meaning. After each class, they are to do practical to apply what I taught them.*
Traditional medicinal knowledge owner 5	*"I have many students who are learning from me. However, it is not easy to train a student who is not a good listener because the lessons are not easy. I teach them to read the bones because they mean different things. I also tell them how to listen attentively to their ancestors and apply the instructions as they are from their ancestors. I also show them how herbs are mixed to deal with certain ailments"*
Traditional medicinal knowledge owner 7	*"I train my son and other trainees who have a strong desire in the use of herbs to treat and manage ailments. I take my trainees and my son to the mountain to observe how I harvest and mix traditional medicinal plants. I encourage them to write down what I do because it is for their future use as learning is a process. ".*
Traditional medicinal knowledge owner 8	*"I spend most of the time with my students on mountains as I do not want to be disturbed by people when teaching my students. I start by teaching them the different plants and their use. I also demonstrate to my students how to mix the plants for stubborn ailments. I also show them plants that are used to cast evil spirits."*
Traditional medicinal knowledge owner 10	*"I always tell my students (trainees) not to use instructions from any other faith healers (Inyanga) because some are evil. I encourage my trainees to be very attentive to the voice of their ancestors and as they are instructed. I guide them in the use of herbs and not to mix herbs with animal and human parts. I always emphasise that they must never use animal or human parts when treating ailments. I also train my trainees to mix herbs for joining broken bones, treating fever and toothache. I demonstrate to them how to make measurements of herbs and water as this is crucial".*
Traditional medicinal knowledge owner 11	*"I firstly encourage my trainees to stay away from their girlfriends or wives for a period of 6 months if they want to be very powerful healers. You cannot be a strong traditional healer if you spend a lot of time on bad with your wife or girlfriend. You need to fast and listen attentively to your ancestors. I encourage them to always write down all instructions and dreams they receive from their ancestors. I also teach them to use herbs and how to mix them."*
Traditional medicinal knowledge owner 13	*"I teach my students to read bones and how to mix herbs. I also teach them how to listen to their ancestors and note down the instruction given by their ancestors as it is very crucial. Above all, I tell my students to have only one instructor because it is very dangerous to be instructed by many senior diviners (iZangoma)."*
Traditional medicinal knowledge owner 14	*"I teach my daughter and many other trainees who are willing to be diviners (iZangoma". I teach them to use bones to find a solution to a problem that their clients come for. I also teach them to use herbs to treat sicknesses"*
Traditional medicinal knowledge owner 15	*"So far, I have trained my brother whom I have realised that he is called into this office too. I have taught him to always obey the voice of the ancestors and have a notebook to write down all dreams and visions that he is given by the ancestors. I have taught him to read bones as they always give accurate information."*

CONCLUSION AND RECOMMENDATIONS

The chapter quoted Mosoti and Masheka (2010) when saying "when an older person dies in an African country, the entire library dies". Dlamini and Ocholla (2018) also supported Mosoti and Masheka (2010) that when owners of indigenous die, they perish with their priceless expertise and causing future generations to suffer. This study has demonstrated that there is hope for the survival of indigenous medicinal knowledge as the knowledge is still possessed by diviners (iZangoma), herbalists (Inyanga) and faith healers (uMthandazi). The study further established that a large number of indigenous medicinal knowledge owners or practitioners still acquire and transfer their knowledge to trainees and children. The study concluded that the interactions between custodians of indigenous medicinal knowledge and trainees as well as children make it possible for the knowledge to stay longer in these unpredictable times. Additionally, the study established that owners or practitioners of indigenous medicinal knowledge have a willing heart to transfer or share their knowledge during socialisation. It was noted that during socialisation,

Indigenous Medicinal Knowledge Among Its Owners and Practitioners

Table 7. Challenged encountered in transferring the indigenous medicinal knowledge

Participate	Response
Traditional medicinal knowledge owner 3	*"Transferring this knowledge takes much attention and focus from our students. Many of our students are unable to finish the training. They do not want to listen, and they want to take shortcuts. They complain that we must reduce the number of months for training to at least two months. Our students end up being drop-outs because they are not patient ".*
Traditional medicinal knowledge owner 5	*"One of the most challenging issues here is failure to follow instructions, and our students fail to listen and follow the instructions. For example, it is impossible to receive the impartation if you fail to take my instructions while teaching, especially reading bones".*
Traditional medicinal knowledge owner 7	*"Some of our students think we are hard when we say they must take notes when we teach them. Many of my students find it very difficult to mix herbs because they do not write down what I teach them. They think it is the only observation that works, yet for anyone to become a master here, he/she must learn to write down what we teach".*
Traditional medicinal knowledge owner 8	*"Some of our students are not committed to what we teach them. For example, they are unable to abstain from sex for six months. This journey requires a very committed person who is prepared to leave everything behind to gain this knowledge."*
Traditional medicinal knowledge owner 10	*"Some of our students are very lazy to master what we teach them. They do not even have notebooks, and they need to be followed. As a result, I have many drop-outs because of laziness among my students".*
Traditional medicinal knowledge owner 15	*"Training a foreign language student is a huge challenge, and I left training people not from our community because of the language barrier."*

trainees and children are taught theory and practice of the tacit knowledge of which it becomes easier to master the teachings. It is recommended that indigenous medicinal knowledge classes be available to those who are willing to be empowered, as such classes take up to six months to be fully trained and become an indigenous medicinal knowledge owner. The study of this nature should also be conducted in the whole of KwaZulu-Natal province which can lead to the development of a model or framework, demonstrating the process of acquiring and transferring indigenous medicinal knowledge.

REFERENCES

Adekannbi, J., Olatokun, W. M., & Ajiferuke, I. (2014). *Predictors of traditional medical knowledge transmission and acquisition in South-West Nigeria*. Sage. http://idv.sagepub.com/content/ early/2014/12/09/0266666914561534.full.pdf+html

Audet, C. M., Gobbo, E., Sack, D. E., Mlemens, E. M., Ngobeni, S., Mkansi, M., Ailu, M. H., & Wanger, R. G. (2020). Traditional healers use of personal protective equipment: A qualitative study in rural South Africa. *BMC Health Services Research*, *20*(1), 655. doi:10.118612913-020-05515-9 PMID:32669101

Bereda, J. E. (2015). *A model to facilitate the Integration of Indigenous Knowledge Systems in the management of HIV & AIDS within a Primary Health Care context in Limpopo Province, South Africa.* North-West University.

Bosancic, B. (2016). Information in the knowledge acquisition process. *The Journal of Documentation, 72*(5), 930–960. doi:10.1108/JD-10-2015-0122

Bratianu, C., & Orzea, I. (2010). Organizational knowledge creation. *Management & Marketing, 5*(3).

Coleman, A. (2013). Preservation of knowledge in traditional medical practices through information communication technology: A case study in South Africa. *Indilinga, 12*(1), 52–61.

Daves, S., & Ebbe, K. (1995). *Traditional Knowledge and Sustainable Development*. World Bank. https://documents1.worldbank.org/curated/en/517861468766175944/pdf/multi-page.pdf

Dlamini, P., & Ocholla, D. N. (2018). Information and communication technology tools for managing indigenous knowledge in KwaZulu-Natal Province, South Africa. *African Journal of Library Archives and Information Science, 28*(2), 137–153.

Easa, N. F. (2012). *Knowledge management and the SECI model: A study of innovation in the Egyptian banking sector*. University of Striling.

Ebijuwa, A. S., & Mabawonku, I. (2015). Documentation and use of indigenous knowledge by practitioners of alternative healthcare in Oyo State, Nigeria. *African Journal of Library Archives and Information Science, 25*(1).

Faust, B. (2007). Implementation of tacit knowledge preservation and transfer methods: Preservation-and-Transfer-Methods. *Fraser Health*. https://www.fraserhealth.ca/media/Implementation-of-Tacit-Knowledge

Forutnani, S., Nowkarizi, M., Kiani, M. R., & Aski, H. R. M. (2018). The role of rural libraries in preserving the indigenous knowledge of rural residents: The case of South Khorasan Province. *World Journal of Science. Technology and Sustainable Development, 15*(3), 245–256. doi:10.1108/WJSTSD-12-2017-0044

Govender, N., Mudaly, R., & James, A. (2013). Indigenous knowledge of custodians of Zulu culture–Implications for multilogical dialogue in the academy. *Alternation (Durban), 20*(1), 154–177.

Hakim, G., & Chishti, M. (2010). *The traditional healer's handbook: a classic guide to the medicine of Avicenna*. Healing Arts Press.

Hoe, S. L. (2006). Tacit knowledge, Nonaka and Takeuchi SECI model and informal knowledge processes. *International Journal of Organization Theory and Behavior, 9*(4), 490–502. doi:10.1108/IJOTB-09-04-2006-B002

Kamal, K. J., Manjit, S. S., & Gurvinder, K. S. (2007). *Knowledge sharing among academic staff: A case study of Business School in Klang Valley, Malaysia*. USCI. https://www.ucsi.edu.my/cervie/ijasa/volume2/pdf/08A.pdf

Latif, S. S. (2010). *Integration of African traditional health practitioners and medicine into the health care management system in the province of Limpopo*. University of Stellenbosch.

Locke, J. (2001). *An essay concerning human understanding*. Batoche Books.

Lwoga, E. T., & Ngulube, P. (2009). Managing indigenous and exogenous knowledge through information and communication technologies for poverty reduction in Tanzania. *Indilinga, 8*(1), 95–113.

Mack, E., & Meadowcroft, J. (Eds.). (2009). *Major conservative and libertarian thinkers: John Locke*. Continuum.

Mahomoodally, M. F. (2013). Traditional medicines in Africa: An appraisal of ten potent African medicinal plants. *Evidence-Based Complementary and Alternative Medicine, 2013*(1), 14–15. Retrieved October 23, 2019, from https://www.hindawi.com/journals/ecam/2013/617459/. doi:10.1155/2013/617459 PMID:24367388

Makhanya, S. M. (2012). *The traditional healers' and caregivers' views on the role of traditional Zulu medicine on psychosis*. University of Zululand, Maluleka.

Maluleka, J. R., & Ngoepe, M. (2018). Turning mirrors into windows: Knowledge transfer among indigenous healers in Limpopo province of South Africa. *South African Journal of Information Management, 20*(1), a918. doi:10.4102ajim.v20i1.918

Mathew, R. M. (1985). Social analysis of information production and consumption: the new challenges and tasks of Third World Countries. In A. I. Mikhalov (Ed.), *Theoretical problems of informatics: social aspects of modern informatics* (pp. 37–47). All Union Institute for Scientific and Technical Information.

Mokgobi, M. G. (2014). Understanding traditional African healing. *African Journal for Physical Health Education, Recreation and Dance, 20*(sup-2), 24-34.

Mosoti, Z., & Masheka, B. (2010). Knowledge management: The case for Kenya. *The Journal of Language. Technology & Entrepreneurship in Africa, 2*(1), 107–133.

Ngulube, P. (2003). Using the SECI knowledge management model and other tools to communicate and manage tacit indigenous knowledge. *Innovation, 27*(1), 21–30.

Nonaka, I. (1994). A dynamic theory of organizational knowledge creation. *Organization Science, 5*(1), 14–37. doi:10.1287/orsc.5.1.14

Nonaka, I., & Konno, N. (1998). The concept of "Ba": Building a foundation for knowledge creation. *California Management Review, 40*(3), 40–54. doi:10.2307/41165942

Nonaka, I., & Nishiguchi, T. (2001). *Knowledge emergence: Social, technical, and evolutionary dimensions of knowledge creation*. Oxford University Press.

Nonaka, I., & Takeuchi, H. (1995). *The knowledge-creating company: How Japanese companies create the dynamics of innovation*. Oxford university press.

Odede, I. (2020). African traditional medicine research between 1998 and 2018: an informetrics analysis in South Africa. Mousaion: South African Journal of Information Studies, 38(1).

Peltzer, K., Preez, N. F., Ramlagan, S., & Fomundam, H. (2008). Use of traditional complementary and alternative medicine for HIV patients in KwaZulu-Natal, South Africa. *BMC Public Health, 8*(1), 1–14. doi:10.1186/1471-2458-8-255 PMID:18652666

Pretorius, E. (1994). *Traditional healers. South African health review* (5th ed.). Health Systems Trust.

Ramokgopa, G. (2013). *Speech by Deputy Minister Gwen Ramokgopa at the inauguration of the Interim Traditional Health Practitioners Council of South Africa*. Minister Gwen Ramokgopa.

Sebata, T. P. (2015). *The role of traditional healers in the treatment of HIV and AIDS in Tsetse Village: The case of Mahikeng in the North West Province.* [Maters of Arts in indigenous Knowledge system masters thesis, North-West University, Potchefstroom].

Shanhong, T. (2000). *Knowledge management in libraries in the 21st century.* IFLA. https://www.ifla.org/IV/ifla66/papers/057-110e.htm.

Sodi, T., Mudhovozi, P., Mashamba, T., Radzilani-Makatu, M., Takalani, J., & Mabunda, J. (2011). Indigenous healing practices in Limpopo Province of South Africa: A qualitative study. *International Journal of Health Promotion and Education, 49*(3), 101–110. doi:10.1080/14635240.2011.10708216

Szulanski, G., Ringov, D., & Jensen, R. J. (2016). Overcoming stickiness: How the timing of knowledge transfer methods affects transfer difficulty. *Organization Science, 27*(2), 304–322. doi:10.1287/orsc.2016.1049

Truter, I. (2007). African traditional healers: Cultural and religious beliefs intertwined in a holistic way. *South African Pharmaceutical Journal. Suid-Afrikaanse Tydskrif vir Apteekwese, 7*(8), 56–60.

Ukwueze, F. (2012). The role of information and communication technology in the development of indigenous technical/vocational knowledge. *Ikenga International Journal of Institute of African Studies,NN, 12*(2), 233–248.

World Health Organisation (WHO). (2013). *Traditional medicine. Geneva: publication.* WHO. https://www.who.int/mediacentre/ factsheet s/2003/fs134/en/

Yunnus, F. (2017). *Preservation of indigenous knowledge (IK) by public libraries in Westcliff, Chatsworth.* The University of Western Cape.

KEY TERMS AND DEFINITIONS

Indigenous knowledge: It refers to what indigenous people know and do, as well as what they have learned and done for generations through practice that grew through trial and error and proved adaptable to change. It is held by the indigenous proprietors of a particular community.

Knowledge Acquisition: It refers to knowledge activities directed at seeking and obtaining knowledge from the external sources and from the internal environment. Knowledge can be acquired in different ways, for example, through training, conferences, seminars, workshops, buying knowledge resources, learning from experts and many more.

Knowledge Transfer: It refers to the transmission of explicit, implicit and tacit knowledge from a person or organization to one or several people.

Preservation: It is the act of protecting and safeguarding of valuable information or knowledge to ensure long term access by present and future generations.

Traditional medicinal knowledge practitioner: It can be referred to as someone who possesses knowledge that enables them to assist others through traditional medicinal methods.

Traditional medicinal knowledge: It refers to as the use of traditional techniques or health practices that have been adapted to treat and heal ailments. It can also be used in diagnosing, preventing, or eliminating a physical, mental, or social disequilibrium, which rely exclusively on experience and observation handed down from generation to generation, verbally or in writing.

Chapter 9
Agricultural Indigenous Knowledge Systems Practiced in Gutu Rural District of Zimbabwe

Jeffrey Kurebwa

https://orcid.org/0000-0002-8371-8055

Bindura University of Science Education, Zimbabwe

ABSTRACT

This chapter focused on the agricultural Indigenous knowledge systems (AIKS) used in Zimbabwe with specific reference to Gutu rural district. The study relied on qualitative methodology while data was collected using key informant interviews and documentary searches. The study findings indicated that a number of AIKS systems are used in the Gutu rural district. These include pest and disease management, food/grain storage and preservation, soil fertility management, and weather prediction. This study also identified several challenges associated with the documentation of AIKS, and among others include methodology, access, intellectual property rights, and the media and formats in which to preserve knowledge. The chapter concludes that Indigenous knowledge is in danger of disappearing because of global changes, and the capacity and facilities needed to document, evaluate, validate, protect, and disseminate such knowledge are lacking in most developing countries such as Zimbabwe.

INTRODUCTION

Several studies that have been conducted in Africa to prove that rural communities depend on Indigenous Knowledge Systems (IKS) for their agricultural activities (Awuor, 2013; Kamwendo & Kamwendo, 2014; Lwoga et al. 2010). Indigenous knowledge is applied during different farming seasons. Nyota and Mapara (2008) in their study indicated that indigenous knowledge is used during the clearing of land, tilling, selection of seed varieties, planting, harvesting and storage of produce, and identification of weather patterns. Indigenous knowledge used by rural people further includes knowledge of the quality and relationship among crop varieties, soil texture, climate change, pest control, and water management (Smelser & Baltes, 2001). Indigenous knowledge also provides an appreciation of how local communities

DOI: 10.4018/978-1-6684-7024-4.ch009

Copyright © 2023, IGI Global. Copying or distributing in print or electronic forms without written permission of IGI Global is prohibited.

understand their natural environment, organizing folk knowledge of flora and fauna, cultural beliefs, and history to enhance their livelihoods (Gutierrez & Fernandez, 2010). Hall and Midgley (2007) argued that development approaches and interventions that do not consider a community's indigenous knowledge and experiences have proved to be of limited effectiveness in addressing poverty and promoting human development. Human development should encompass building on past practices to ensure sustainability.

Harnessing indigenous knowledge of local communities helps in creating a sense of respect and ownership of interventions designed to address the local communities' problems. This creates positive and sustainable results (Ingram, 2011; Ranganathan, 2004). Interventions that build on local practices enhance communities' decision-making capacity (Kamwendo & Kamwendo, 2014; Awuor, 2013; Ranganathan, 2004). Scholars such as Ghale and Upret (2000) argued that indigenous farming systems that most communities depend on have been replaced by expensive and unsustainable external technologies. This has damaged the natural resource base of rural communities and their production capacity. Indigenous knowledge has gained interest in the academic world, both within the social and natural sciences (Awuor, 2013; Kamwendo & Kamwendo, 2014). Scientists and policymakers are becoming aware of the contribution that indigenous knowledge can make to sustainable development and food security (Kilongozi, et al. 2005). This chapter seeks to document the agricultural indigenous knowledge systems used in the Gutu rural district.

THE CONTEXT OF GUTU DISTRICT

Gutu district is situated in Masvingo province, which is in the southern part of Zimbabwe. The district is divided into five distinct settlement demarcation namely; the old resettlement, newly resettled, small-scale farmers, and communal and urban areas covering 369 744 hectares of land (Agriculture, Technical and Extension Services Department, Gutu, 2011). The district is generally dry; with conditions ranging from arid to semi-arid (Muchineripi, 2011). In terms of climatic regions, the district falls into natural regions 3, 4, and 5, characterized by a rainfall pattern that ranges from normal, to below average per annum. Areas under natural region 3 receive normal rains, enough for productive agriculture, while regions 4 and 5, comprising the greater part of the district, experience droughts, resulting in hunger and poverty due to general food shortages (Agriculture, Technical and Extension Services Department, Gutu, 2011). The district has faced perpetual challenges of droughts over the years and as such, it generated interest in the researcher to try and establish whether the use of indigenous knowledge can help in alleviating food shortages, mainly caused by incessant droughts. Apart from the shortage of food, Gutu district is gradually drifting toward desertification due to ongoing deforestation, siltation of rivers and dams, and limited pastures for grazing animals (Wutete, 2014).

DEFINING INDIGENOUS KNOWLEDGE SYSTEMS

Indigenous Knowledge Systems (IKSs) are a collection of societal systems represented by the totality of products, skills, technologies, processes, and systems developed and adopted by cohesive traditional societies (Odora-Hoppers, 2002:8). Indigenous knowledge refers to the knowledge and know-how unique to a given society or culture that encompasses the cultural traditions, values, beliefs, and worldviews of local people (UNESCO, 2016). Indigenous knowledge is tacit knowledge of the local or indigenous people, which is personal, content-specific, and therefore hard to formalize and communicate. It differs from formal scientific knowledge, which is explicit or "codified" knowledge transmittable in a formal and systematic language. Indigenous knowledge is viewed by rural communities as one of the core components that contribute to sustainable and equitable development (Akullo, 2007; Awuor, 2013; Kamwendo & Kamwendo, 2014; Eyong et al., 2007). In traditional societies, the elders' wisdom combines both ecological and social knowledge and offers solutions to specific societal problems (Awuor, 2013). Indigenous knowledge is informal, interactive, and integrated into people's livelihoods (Claxton, 2010). Indigenous knowledge is a form of knowledge that has originated locally and naturally (Altieri, 1995).

According to Hammersmith (2007), indigenous knowledge is linked to the communities that produce. Hammersmith (2007) argued that natural communities have by complex kinship systems of relationships among people, animals, the earth, and the cosmos, from which knowing emanates. Indigenous knowledge is also known by other names such as traditional knowledge, indigenous technical knowledge, rural knowledge as well as ethnoscience (or people's science) as argued by Altieri (1995). Indigenous knowledge systems manifest themselves through different dimensions. Among these are agriculture, medicine, security, botany, zoology, craft skills, and linguistics (Nyota & Mapara, 2008). Indigenous knowledge has also been referred to as focal ecology, ethnology, indigenous knowledge, customary laws, and knowledge of the land (Kyasiimire, 2010). In the domain of food security, indigenous knowledge refers to knowledge about soil fertility, disease-resistant and quickly growing crops, soil conservation, weather forecasting, pests and disease control, food preservation, processing, and storage as well as water management techniques (Kamwendo & Kamwendo, 2014). Indigenous knowledge is the actual basis for local-level decision-making in the area of seed selection, food storage, and processing (Awuor, 2013). The knowledge is unique to a given culture or society and denotes a deeper understanding of the world around a particular community. Kumar (2010) defines indigenous knowledge as the knowledge that has been developed over time in a community mainly through the accumulation of experiences and intimate understanding of the environment in a given culture. Other terms used to refer to indigenous knowledge include native knowledge, traditional knowledge, cultural knowledge, and civilization knowledge. The indigenous knowledge system, in its broadest sense, encompasses cultural knowledge; social, political, economically, and spiritual; kinship, local politics, and other factors that are tied together and influence one another (Tanyanyiwa et al., 2011), whereas its spiritual nature influences how resources are managed and used by the people of that society (Cobb, 2011). From the above definitions, there seems to be a consensus that indigenous knowledge is unique to a given culture, society, or country.

CONCEPT OF FOOD SECURITY

According to Ingram (2011), food is a primary need basic to all human needs and fundamental human right. Improved food security is critical in alleviating poverty, promoting people's health and labor productivity, contributing to political stability, and ensuring the sustainable development of local communities (FAO, 2011). The Food and Agriculture Organization (FAO) (2014) defines food security as a situation when all people at all times have physical, social and economic access to sufficient, safe, and nutritious food to meet their dietary needs for an active and healthy life. Food and nutrition security is achieved when adequate food is available, accessed, and satisfactorily utilized by all individuals at all times to live a healthy and happy life. This definition implies that nutrition security includes dietary requirements of the consumed food, health care, and sanitation in order for one to live a healthy and active life. Traditionally, nutrition security involves knowledge of the right feeding practices (especially correct infant feeding practices), cooking practices, clean environment, and safe drinking water among others. Nutrition security goes beyond food security by considering adequate access to essential nutrients, not just calories (FAO, 2009). Nutritional security means guaranteed constant adequate dietary intake that helps the body resist and recover from the disease. Food insecurity leads to severe health problems for individuals and society, including malnutrition, obesity, disease, and poverty (Hammond & Dube, 2011). Ending hunger and achieving food and nutrition security is goal number 2 of 17 sustainable development goals. The FAOs definition of food security promotes four key elements: accessibility, availability, utilization, and stability. All four elements of food security cut across areas of food security and involve theories of change that work toward improving food security.

DOCUMENTING AGRICULTURAL INDIGENOUS KNOWLEDGE

It has been widely argued that documentation of the indigenous knowledge system will motivate wide use, application, and easy integration of such knowledge system into other forms of knowledge systems (Msuya, 2007; Shresha et al., 2008), whereas, lack of documentation has been contributing to its decline: elders have been dying without passing on their knowledge system to their grandchildren (Ellis, 2005; Kalanda-Sabola, et al. 2007), threatening its wide use, application and its integration with other forms of knowledge systems (Msuya, 2007). Apparently, documentation of the indigenous knowledge system using signs and codes that are used in the documentation of the scientific knowledge system is not effective (Beckes & Ghimire, 2003), as the former is normally gained and easily understood orally. Such documentation may weaken the social process of teaching and learning (Zazu, 2007). According to Rahman (2000), the amount of indigenous knowledge expressed by indigenous people in words and numbers represents just a fraction of the knowledge, and therefore, its documentation using scientific codes and signs will capture only such a fraction, leading to a further decline of the knowledge system. Furthermore, based on the holistic and interwoven nature of the indigenous knowledge system, which includes taboos, beliefs, sacredness, myths, and indigenous politics, will further complicate the documentation process. Arguably, promotion rather than documentation of the indigenous knowledge system using its indigenous ways of teaching and learning with consideration of both teaching and learning context and process will ensure the sustainability of the knowledge system.

Documentation of agricultural indigenous knowledge has become an inevitable initiative to talk about. This has led to numerous studies and initiatives in the field of knowledge management all over the globe. Many methods were suggested by different authors for the proper documentation of agricultural indigenous knowledge. However, the most unfortunate part is that most of these methods remain on paper as indicated by different studies, especially in the developing world. Latest studies indicate that methods of documenting agricultural indigenous knowledge are more applicable and effective in the developed world. In the developed world such as the USA, for example, Warren et al. (1993) note that agricultural indigenous knowledge studies have been archived in national and international centers in the form of databases. The information in these databases is systematically classified. Warren et al. (1993) further propose that the collection and storage of indigenous knowledge should be supplemented with adequate dissemination and exchange among interested parties using newsletters, journals, and other media.

Agricultural Indigenous Knowledge Systems in Gutu Rural District

As it has been noted, indigenous knowledge has been an important component of development in the developing world. This has been more evident in the agriculture sector. In support of this, Tabuti (2012) observed that farmers' knowledge has been responsible for improving agricultural productivity and ensuring food security for centuries in Tanzania. Many studies recommend the use of Information and Communication Technologies (ICTs) in the documentation and dissemination of agricultural indigenous knowledge. According to Lwoga and Ngulube (2008), ICTs are important tools in enabling the management and integration of indigenous and exogenous knowledge in developing countries. However, Malhan and Gulati (2003) argued differently that the issue of the digital divide hinders the effective use of ICTs in the management of agricultural indigenous knowledge. Malhan and Gulati (2003) indicated that the digital divide continues to grow so wide that many farmers do not have the opportunity to transform into knowledge-driven communities in Africa. The technological, economic, and educational implications of disparities in the distribution of digital technology contribute to this situation (Malhan & Gulati, 2003). Malhan and Gulati (2003) further argued that documenting and disseminating indigenous knowledge through ICTs contributes to the degradation of indigenous cultures and indigenous peoples' loss of intellectual property rights. Malhan and Gulati (2003) also recommended that African governments must improve ICT infrastructures, and develop appropriate Intellectual Property Rights (IPR) and policies that will protect indigenous knowledge for its effective management through knowledge management practices.

Aluma (2010) provided a different argument on agricultural indigenous knowledge documentation, and noted that documentation of indigenous knowledge related to medicinal plants, herbal concoctions, and diseases treated (human and livestock), crop protection, and food preservation has been ongoing but in ad hoc ways. Aluma (2010) further noted that large basic data has been collected "as is" from the practitioner's viewpoint with witness proofs of indigenous knowledge that has worked. However, no funds have been secured to publish these for sharing with others (Aluma, 2010). It is very critical to consider the quality of indigenous knowledge that is managed. Agricultural indigenous knowledge that has already been documented needs to be evaluated to confirm its efficacy and utility. This helps to eliminate any possible doubts about the efficiency of indigenous knowledge. For instance, many potential users of traditional medicine are dissuaded from using it because they are doubtful that it is effective and safe to use. A key challenge to indigenous knowledge development and promotion through documentation and validation is that by reducing indigenous and traditional practices to the knowledge dimension and stripping away their cosmological context (the so-called backward beliefs), we risk losing a major source of indigenous knowledge meaningfulness for the local people and consequently losing indigenous knowledge in the community (Fisher et al. 2001). Lwoga et al. (2010) noted that one of the best modern approaches to the preservation of traditional knowledge is documentation in some permanent form and public accessibility. In addition to the preservation, documentation, and dissemination of agricultural indigenous practices, it provides an effective tool for research and innovation. Perhaps this is a primary role of special libraries. However, Lwoga et al. (2010) observed that research libraries have not been particularly active in documenting agricultural indigenous knowledge. Nakata and Langton (2005) emphasize that libraries must consider indigenous knowledge not simply a part of a historical archive but a contemporary body of relevant knowledge.

CHALLENGES IN DOCUMENTING AGRICULTURAL INDIGENOUS KNOWLEDGE SYSTEMS

There are several challenges associated with the documentation of agricultural indigenous knowledge. Ngulube (2002) argued that the main challenges to the management and preservation of agricultural indigenous knowledge are issues related to methodology, access, intellectual property rights, and the media and formats in which to preserve it. Ngulube (2002) further observed that most of the knowledge management approaches in Africa are inclined toward scientific methods. The prevailing information management approach in Africa, like in many other parts of the world, is based on acquiring and documenting explicit knowledge, which is largely generated by researchers, laboratories, and universities. Such approaches leave little room for indigenous knowledge of the local communities to be integrated into the exogenous knowledge system. Even if some of the indigenous knowledge is preserved in the global, regional, and national repositories, local farmers can only access these databases through an intermediary (that is, a researcher, extension officer, or any agricultural actor) that can afford to access and use these systems. Generally, indigenous knowledge is preserved in people's minds and local practices, which may be eroded by failing memories and death. Indigenous knowledge is shared and communicated orally and through traditions and culture. However, its distribution is always fragmented due to gender dynamics, politics, power, culture, conflicts, resistance, religious beliefs, and government policies (Mudege, 2005). Since indigenous knowledge is essential for agricultural development; it must be managed and preserved in the same systematic way as external knowledge. It is thus pertinent to determine a model for managing agricultural indigenous knowledge before much of it is completely lost.

Furthermore, indigenous knowledge is disappearing because of increasing barriers that affect its transmission among community members. Sighn and Rajoo (1993) observed that one important challenge in documenting agricultural indigenous knowledge is the contradiction between the idea of the transfer of knowledge from one place to another and the need to maintain and develop the cultural diversity of a locality. Moreover, several studies point out that a knowledge system is most often specific to a particular physical, economic, and cultural environment. This view was supported by Karter (1993), who mentioned that indigenous knowledge is rooted in a given socio-cultural environment. From this perspective, this implies that it is difficult to transfer location-specific knowledge from one place to another. Further, it is stressed that questions of property rights and markets are relevant to the transfer of knowledge (Karter, 1993). Karter (1993) provides an example of a blacksmith who may be reluctant to forego the property rights of their knowledge and promote its transfer. Besides, acknowledge that the system is often operational in areas where markets for a particular product exist. Rather, it was argued that institutions such as community-based associations should be promoted to record, preserve, and upgrade a knowledge system within its natural environment (Karter, 1993). Consequently, Karter (1993) highlights the importance of creating awareness among bearers of indigenous knowledge systems.

According to Grenier (1998), there are other specific limitations regarding the applications of indigenous knowledge. However, with scientific knowledge, indigenous knowledge has its limitations. Grenier (1998) further explains that indigenous knowledge is sometimes accepted uncritically because of naive notions that whatever indigenous people do is naturally in harmony with the environment. Grenier (1998) highlighted the idea that there is historical and contemporary evidence that indigenous peoples have also committed environmental 'sins' through over-grazing, overhunting, or over-cultivation of the land. It is misleading to think of indigenous knowledge as always being 'good, 'right', or 'sustainable'. For example, a critical assumption of indigenous knowledge approaches is that local people have a good

Agricultural Indigenous Knowledge Systems in Gutu Rural District

understanding of the natural resource base because they have lived in the same or similar environment for many generations and have accumulated and passed on knowledge of the natural conditions, soils, vegetation, food, and medicinal plants (Grenier, 1998). However, under conditions where the local people are in fact recent migrants from a quite different ecological zone, they may not have much experience with the new environment. In these circumstances, some indigenous knowledge of the people may be helpful or may cause problems (e.g., the use of agricultural systems adapted to other ecological zones).

THEORETICAL FRAMEWORK

This chapter relies on social learning cultural theory or socio-cultural theory. The theory was developed by Russian Psychologist Lev Vygotsky in 1962. The theory stresses the importance of interaction between people and the culture in which they live. Due to the influence of culture, it is believed that parents, caregivers, peers, and culture, in general, are responsible for the development of an individual's higher-order functions. Thus, social learning theory helps in understanding how people learn in social contexts (learn from each other) and informs the construction of active learning in communities. Vygotsky (1962) further explains that learning starts through interactions and communications with other individuals. This means that there is influence from the social environment in which people live. As such, Vygotsky (1962) reiterated that learning occurs through various forms of interactions, for example, when students interact with their peers, teachers, and other experts, learning takes place. Consequently, a teacher creates a learning environment that maximizes the learner's ability to interact with others through discussion, collaboration, and feedback. Moreover, Vygotsky (1962) further illustrates that the culture is the primary determining factor for the knowledge construction. Vygotsky (1962) posits that individuals learn through a cultural lens by interacting with societal members, and they are guided by the rules, skills, and abilities shaped by the culture of that society. Pionke and Browdy (2008) argue that people learn through what begins as an individual's collective ability to experience and interpret the world in a community context. This can be referred to as learning by doing. The social theory of learning thus views the community as a social fabric for learning leading to collective knowledge (Pionke & Browdy, 2008). The theory also looks at the relationships between individuals and how members of society shape their culture. Individuals in society learn from one another more than in isolation. The learning process calls for cooperation among individuals and is based on authentic situations that allow individuals to reflect on how knowledge is applied to everyday situations.

Another important feature of the theory is scaffolding. Under scaffolding, the theory states that when an adult provides support for a child, they will adjust the amount of help they give depending on the child's progress. The help given to the child is a step-by-step procedure until the help is completely withdrawn (Vygotsky, 1978). This progression of different levels of help is called 'scaffolding'. It draws parallels from real scaffolding for buildings that are used as a support for the construction of new material (the skill/information to be learned) and then removed once the building is complete (the skill/information has been learned). The other view of socio-cultural learning theory says that learning occurs through observations by the learners during demonstrations by the teacher (Bandura, 1971:3). Through observations, Bandura (1971) explained that people learn through watching the behaviour of those around them. The behaviour comes in the form of individual performance or as an instruction accompanied by vivid details on how certain activities are done, typical of symbolizing behaviour. Therefore, social learning theory is premised on continuous reciprocal interaction between cognitive, behavioural, and

165

environmental influences. While the theory explains that knowledge is acquired by learners through socialization with knowledgeable members by means such as observation and scaffolding, learners go through step-by-step procedures to acquire the knowledge. However, the same procedures, premised on systematic procedures may not apply to the acquisition of Indigenous Knowledge. Since indigenous knowledge is tacit in nature, it requires the initiative of the one who possesses the knowledge in order for those interested in knowing to benefit. Therefore, the social cultural learning theory works well in the scenario whereby the one possessing indigenous knowledge practices acts as the mentor to the one interested in acquiring the knowledge.

METHODOLOGY

The chapter relied on qualitative methodology while a case study research design of Gutu rural district was used. Data were collected using key informant interviews. The key informants were drawn from traditional leaders and elders (both men and women) in Gutu rural district that were sixty years and above and were identified using the snowballing method, which allowed the identification of the most appropriate participants. It was necessary to target elderly people who had stayed in the district for the past forty (40) years as they had an appreciation of the agricultural indigenous knowledge systems that have been in use. The elders and traditional leaders chosen showed valuable knowledge in different areas of the study such as farming, animal rearing, health care, food preservation, upholding of taboos and conducting of rituals and ceremonies among other indigenous knowledge practices in Gutu district. A total of ten participants were interviewed for the study. Documentary search was also used in the study. Key documents included peer-reviewed journal articles, book chapters, and books related to indigenous knowledge systems. The study sought to understand some of the agricultural indigenous knowledge systems used in the storage and preservation of indigenous seeds, pest and disease management, selection of indigenous seed varieties, and climate change management.

FINDINGS AND DISCUSSION

The findings of the study are based on fieldwork findings. From the study findings, there are mainly four forms of agricultural indigenous knowledge used in the Gutu district. These are indigenous indicators and seasonal forecasting, pest and disease management, food/grain storage and preservation, and soil fertility management. These are discussed below.

Indigenous Indicators and Seasonal Forecasting

Smallholder farmers use wild animals and birds, insects, astronomical, and other independent natural features in seasonal forecasting (Roncoli et al., 2002; Chang'a et al. 2010; Kolawole et al. 2014). Animal behavior is among the important indicators of seasonal forecasting (Kolawole et al. 2014; Chang'a et al. 2010). A traditional leader stated:

Agricultural Indigenous Knowledge Systems in Gutu Rural District

Breeding patterns of certain birds and the sound they produce, for instance, are critical in the field providing short and long-term weather and seasonal information. Singing of southern ground Hornbill (Bucorvus leadbeateri)in this community is associated with imminent rains.

An elder from the district was clear in terms of the type of birds and their meaning in seasonal forecasting. She mentioned:

We have many birds associated with weather forecasting in this area. These include rain cuckoo (haya); ground hornbill (dendera); night jar (dahwa); migratory stock(mafudzamombe); tinker bird (chivangazuva). You can tell that rainfall is imminent when the rain cuckoo is cuckooing during the night. The hornbill hoots early in the season morning. The migratory birds are in large numbers. The singing of the tinker bird and Night jar also signifies the imminence of rainfall.

Both domestic and wild animals were also associated with weather patterns. One traditional leader stated:

Animals such as cattle and sheep can explain the weather prediction through the behavior they exhibit. For example, when cattle sniff the air in the summer with heads raised up, it is a sign that immediate rains are going to fall. When sheep huddle together facing one direction, it is an indication that a dangerous storm is approaching from the direction they are facing.

The traditional leader further stated that wild animals were also used as indicator of imminent rains. He stated:

In this community, when you see the rock duiker (ngururu) continuously singing and jumping around; baboons (makudo) raising their heads toward the direction of the wind; monkeys (shoko) moving in large troops; and goats (mbudzi) bearing a lot of kids then you know we have a good rainfall season.

The instincts in animal behavior were also cited by Svotwa, et al, (2007) in Planet Ark (2004) when they argue that animals can predict disasters as what happened in 2004 when animals escaped the Indian Ocean tsunami, which claimed 24 000 lives. This adds weight to the notion that animals possess a "sixth" sense for predicting seasonal occurrences and impending disasters.

One traditional leader stated:

Usually, when we see fire outbreaks in the Rasa Mountain during the month of October, it is a sign that the rainy season is imminent and therefore people should begin dry planting of grain crops such as finger millet, pearl millet, and sorghum.

Another tradition followed by Gutu communities is rain-making ceremonies (*Mukwerera*). An elder from the community mentioned:

In our area, we usually conduct rain-making ceremonies (mukwerera) during the month of October as a response to the dry weather patterns. The Mukwerera ceremony is conducted at specific locations such as near rivers or at the foot of mountains or under big trees.

An elder in the study also mentioned:

Low breeding patterns by some animals indicate impending uncertainties such as droughts. On the contrary, high breeding patterns of certain animals signify good seasons with enough rain. In other cases, the presence or absence of common or uncommon animals is differently interpreted.

Another elder further supported the above by mentioning that:

The appearance of scarce bee-eaters in October indicates imminent rains. Non-appearance of those animals signifies impending droughts. This information is important in informing decision-making, planning, and adaptation against climate change disasters.

A female elder participant stated:

The profuse flowering and fruiting of trees indicate good farming seasons. Profuse fruiting of trees like muchakata (Parinari curatellifolia) indicates dry seasons with no or below normal rainfall patterns.

A male participant indicated that the community relied on the use of certain tree species in predicting short and long-term weather and seasonal outlook. He posited:

Tree characteristics such as shedding and shooting of leaves, flowering and fruiting are important indicators of seasonal quality. The flowering of indigenous trees indicates imminent rains. For long-term seasonal forecasting, we use the profuse flowering of indigenous trees again as an indicator for a season with normal or above-normal rainfall.

Access to information on imminent rains is integral for farmer planning and preparation for planting. Various studies have indicated that tree phenology is more common than other indicators as an indigenous forecasting indicator (Okonya et al. 2013; Shoko and Shoko, 2013; Roncoli et al. 2002). Some local farmers rely on various insects behavior in seasonal forecasting as a complement to other indigenous indicators (Kijazi et al. 2013). The presence or absence of certain insects provides important forecasting information for short and long-term seasonal outlooks (Okonya et al. 2013; Kijazi et al. 2013). The appearance of termites toward the farming season in Uganda indicates imminent rains (Kijazi et al. 2013). In long-term forecasting, rural farmers in Manicaland of Zimbabwe rely on red ants to predict seasonal quality (Muguti & Maphosa, 2012). The presence of big ants indicates a good season with adequate rainfall. In other cases, the absence or reduced numbers of common insects in Uganda indicates a season with no or inadequate rainfall patterns (Kijazi et al. 2013). Studies conducted across different ecological zones reflect that many local communities also rely on atmospheric indicators, especially for short-term prediction (Zuma-Netshiukhwi et al. 2013; Okonya et al. 2013). Forecasting from atmospheric indicators compliments forecasting information collected from other indigenous indicators. Most local farmers predict weather and seasonal outlook by observing terrestrial movements of clouds, wind type and direction, and moon and stars (Kijazi et al. 2013; Okonya et al. 2013). In rural South Africa, the movement of stars from west to east at night indicates imminent rains (Zuma-Netshiukhwi et al. 2013). Indigenous farmers use short-term predictions for making decisions on activities such as planting crops. The use of rain-making rituals is also practiced by local communities in influencing weather and seasonal

Agricultural Indigenous Knowledge Systems in Gutu Rural District

outlook (Ngara et al. 2014; Roncoli et al. 2002). Execution or non-execution of rain-making rituals has a profound influence on seasonal quality. Consistent and correct conducting of the rain-making rituals guarantees favourable farming seasons (Roncoli et al. 2002). Rain-making ceremonies are common in many parts of Africa such as Burkina Faso (Roncoli et al. 2002), Zimbabwe (Ngara et al. 2014), and Uganda (Okonya et al. 2013). Rain-making rituals are performed for inducing rain or thanking ancestors and gods for good harvests. In some cases, rituals are conducted as a way of ending droughts (Roncoli et al. 2002). Rain-making ceremonies are both a goal and a strategy for avoiding disasters such as droughts.

Pest and Disease Management

The people of Gutu district use indigenous knowledge to control pests and protect their crops. One traditional leader stated:

In our community, we use some methods to control pests and diseases. We slash and burn the infected crops, perform crop rotation and cultivate different varieties of crops to control pest and disease spread.

An elder mentioned:

We have our own local medicines to treat animals and plants when they are attacked by pests and diseases. To control pests and diseases in livestock for instance use a variety of medicinal plants to treat animals. We mix animal urine, animal waste, poisonous plant leaves and ash to treat diseases in their animals such as diarrhea, constipation and stomach and flu in cows and goats.

The people of Gutu district keep livestock such as cattle, sheep, goats, donkeys, pigs and chickens. Livestock is a source of wealth that serves different purposes among those who possess the animals. They provide draught power to farmers, although in traditional times, few individuals would use ox-drawn plowing since ownership of plows is a preserve of a few wealthy individuals.

One elder stated:

We manage the health of animals by using herbs and other natural remedies to treat sick animals. For example, we use soot (chin'ai) mixed with water to treat animals which show signs of constipation, while the maggot tree leaves (muvengahonye) are used to treat animal wounds. Aloe vera (gavakava) is cut into pieces and mixed with drinking water for chickens as a way of treating coccidiosis.

The above findings resonate with previous studies by Aluma (2010) who noted that farmers use indigenous knowledge in the identification, production and/or harvesting of plants, animals and insects and their preparation and preservation for food. He further added that indigenous knowledge is used in the making of drugs for human and animal health, food preservation and crop protection (against pests/diseases); spells, luck, love, business as well as management systems and techniques for crops, livestock, ecosystems conservation and communities. Waziri and Aliero (2005) stated that if pests and diseases cannot be prevented or controlled by cultural and physical means, it may be necessary to use natural pesticides. Many growers have developed ways of making their own sprays from plants such as garlic and hot peppers.

169

Selection, Preservation, and Storage of Indigenous Seed Varieties

When asked about the indigenous seed varieties they used, a female elder mentioned:

We know drought and disease-resistant seeds and therefore we have a drought- coping mechanism. We know which seeds do well in certain types of soils and which do not in certain conditions based on their experiences. We have knowledge about seeds that mature fast and those that are good at responding to drought after long dry spells or other natural disasters.

Another female elder indicated:

In this area, when we anticipate drought, we grow sorghum or rapoko because they are drought-resistant crops. These crops are also not attacked by diseases, unlike maize seed varieties.

To store their crops, one elder stated:

For crops like groundnuts, round nuts, and soya beans, the seeds are stored in pods or sacks so at the time of planting they must be further sorted. Similarly, after harvesting, the grains are also hung in the kitchen or shades in special containers/baskets for them to dry.

The above statement was supported by a traditional leader who mentioned:

For sweet potatoes, we dig a very big hole and put them inside, and cover the hole to protect the sweet potatoes from rotting and insects. We can then eat the sweet potatoes around September and use the remaining during the next season.

A male participant stated:

After harvesting sweet potatoes, we peel and slice them, put them under the sun to dry, and store the dry sweet potatoes. Sweet potatoes can be stored and remain fresh for 2-3 years. However, when pests attack them in the granary, we periodically remove and expose them to direct sunshine and the pests and fleas will die.

Another male participant summarized the preservation of seed by stating:

After harvesting we store our crops using traditional basket granaries, dusting with ash for storage preservation against weevils, winnowing millet to remove thrash, packing cereals in sacks after threshing, sun-drying legumes to dry them fully before storage, and mixing with ash for storage.

One traditional leader stated:

After harvesting crops, people selected well-moulded grains for seed preservation. The grain crops are hung in the huts used for food preparation so that smoke would act as a preserving against the grain borers. As for the rest of the harvested crops, they are adequately dried, thrashed, and stored in grana-

Agricultural Indigenous Knowledge Systems in Gutu Rural District

ries. In preserving grain seeds, the granary walls are smeared with cow dung so that moths are repelled by the dung smell. After storing seeds in the granaries, they are completely sealed such that the grain would last for several years.

During the storage and preservation of agricultural harvest, the farmers noted that they used granaries to store and preserve their farm produce. A female elder remarked that;

After harvesting maize, we dry it and remove it from the corn. After that, we put it in sacks, fix charismas tree leaves and store the maize in a cool dry place. The charismas tree will then dry in the stored maize and the scent will remain in the maize. This scent is very crucial in repelling any potential pest that intends to attach to the stored maize.

Additionally, farmers noted that the use of red pepper to keep and protect their beans from pests is very common. One traditional leader noted:

After harvesting, I dry the beans and remove them from pods by hitting the dry heaps of the beans. I then winnow then, picking out the good seeds mix them with red pepper, put them in the sack, and store them in the kitchen. The beans will never be attacked by the weevils at all.

Thurston (1990) noted that traditional farmers have their own reasons for selecting certain crop production practices, which at times can be pretty strange to scientists. The author further notes that indigenous knowledge has been used in various ways by the local people and has worked for them in areas of agriculture, health, food storage, processing and preservation systems, environmental management, erosion control, and biodiversity conservation. Akullo (2007) stated that the indigenous knowledge of the people is very effective in meeting their food requirements, effective in areas of soil enrichment, land clearing, sowing, harvesting, weeding, and mound/ridge making. She further states that mixed farming mixed cropping, crop rotation, and shifting cultivation help tremendously in their bumper harvest.

Indigenous Soil Identification and Preparation Methods

The study participants indicated that they employ several ways to preserve the soil. One female participant mentioned:

Farmers employ indigenous ways of classifying and characterizing local soil types in fields based on soil characteristics, problems, and suitability for various crops. Farmers also make use of ditches, traditional waterways, stone terraces, vegetative barriers, and contour ploughing to control soil erosion.

A male participant stated:

Given the drought in the area that resulted in the deaths of cattle, some households practice non-tillage farming as a method of soil fertility control whereby the land is cleared by hand or burning and crops raised with minimum disturbance to the soil. Holes for planting are made with hoes. In my experience, there are no significant differences in yield between tillage and non-tillage. Further, there are other

171

benefits such as soil conservation and lower labor inputs compared to mechanized ploughing. Weed infestation is greater with tillage and inputs are also high.

In most literature, there are no specific forms/types of agricultural indigenous knowledge given. Scholars differ in names, but the applicability is the same from community to community. The study findings support Thomas (2008), who noted that agricultural indigenous knowledge is not uniformly distributed and differs between and within communities. These variations, according to (Somnasang & Moreno-Black, 2000), occur because of cultural and geographical diversity. For example, in Uganda, it is estimated that there are more than sixty-five indigenous communities (MGLSD, 2006), each of which is culturally distinct and has unique indigenous knowledge. Even within the same culture, there are variations. For example, for each tribe in Uganda, there exists a diversity of clans, which greatly adds to the diversity in indigenous knowledge (Katende & Kityo, 1996).

Traditionally, some foods, especially cereals like millet, sorghum, and maize and grain such as beans and peas, are stored in granaries. Different granaries are used for different types of grains in most of the rural communities in Gutu district. The granaries are constructed at a raised level to allow the airflow and are smeared with cow dung to prevent grains from being attacked by weevils and pests. As a result, food is stored for quite a long time and thus food security is guaranteed. Harvested grains are first sun-dried to reduce moisture content before putting them in the granary. Specifically, the major purposes of granary storage are fourfold:

(i)   To preserve food for a long time so that it can be consumed in the future in the case of food shortage,
(ii)   To preserve seeds for next season planting,
(iii)   To protect food from pests and weevils and,
(iv)   To protect seeds from destruction by rainwater.

Although the granary system is primarily used for food storage, it has also served other purposes. It is a means of encouraging people to work hard so that they own granaries. Study findings showed that farmers with many granaries would boast of being food secure, which is prestigious in the community.

The study findings indicated that smoking was one of the trusted traditional methods of preserving food in most communities in the Gutu district. Local people have precise knowledge of smoking food items such as meat, fish, and maize. One female participant mentioned:

The common practice is that racks are built in the kitchen on top of cooking fire, and meat or any other given food is placed on the rack and smoked until it is thoroughly dried. The purpose is to prolong its shelf life and preserve it from contamination. This process is very important not only as a means of food preservation but also as a health-promoting practice. Smoked meat is prepared whenever there is an emergency or in a time of food shortage. Traditionally, smoking meat is performed as a means of preserving it because smoke itself acts like an acidic coating on the surface of meat hence preventing the growth of bacteria.

Indigenous knowledge is gaining attention in climate management and adaptation (Roncoli, et al. 2002). It is hailed for providing grassroots and sustainable solutions to problems affecting smallholder agriculture (Chang'a et al. 2010). Integrating indigenous knowledge and biophysical knowledge is important in seasonal forecasting and adaptation to climate change impacts (Alexander, 2011). Neverthe-

Agricultural Indigenous Knowledge Systems in Gutu Rural District

less, biophysical overlooked the role of indigenous knowledge in seasonal prediction and climate change adaptation. Sympathizers of indigenous knowledge express that it can work well if supported by good policies (Pasteur, 2011).

Indigenous knowledge information on seasonal forecasting emerges from various natural features (Kolawole et al. 2014, Chang'a et al. 2010). Multiple indigenous indicators provide forecasting information for short and long-term seasonal outlooks. Local farmers obtain seasonal information through the interpretation of behaviors and events from indicators such as domestic and wild animals, trees, insects, birds, and terrestrial indicators (Roncoli et al. 2002). Indigenous indicators play an equal role in forecasting, just like scientific forecasting. In some cases, the two forecasting sources are complementary by local farmers (Chang'a et al. 2010). Sympathizers of indigenous knowledge encourage its preservation and use in smallholder farming (Alexander, 2011; Kolawole et al. 2014). They regard it as the sustainable bedrock for detecting and coping with climate change risk at the local level. Indigenous knowledge is highly ranked because it emanates from interpretations of the natural environment (Gundlanga & Makaudze, 2012). Relying on readily available and locally engineered knowledge fast-track adaptation regimes and planning models (Roncoli et al. 2002; Gundlanga & Makaudze, 2012). Local solutions reduce protracted vulnerability to disasters while improving resilience and adaptive capacity.

FUTURE RESEARCH DIRECTIONS

This chapter has documented some agricultural indigenous knowledge systems practiced in Gutu Rural District. Future research should also focus on investigating the central role of women in the conservation and preservation of agricultural indigenous knowledge systems.

CONCLUSION AND RECOMMENDATIONS

This chapter concludes that indigenous knowledge is in danger of disappearing not only because of the influence of global processes of rapid change but also because the capacity and facilities needed to document, evaluate, validate, protect, and disseminate such knowledge are lacking in most developing countries, as observed by Nwokoma (2012). Notwithstanding this, there are many grounds for believing that indigenous knowledge is vital for rural communities' food and nutrition security, hence the need for preserving it (FAO, 2014; Awuor, 2013). It is therefore essential to collect indigenous knowledge and document it in a coherent and systematic fashion so that it can be archived in the form of a database. This can make it easily shared among the interested parties, particularly the farming communities, agricultural extension workers, and policymakers for the promotion of household food and nutrition security (Agrawal, 1995). Indigenous knowledge, apart from being vital for communities with low income where poverty, malnutrition, and hunger are common, would also form the bottom line for sustainable food and nutrition security (FAO, 2014). It is therefore important to encourage rural farmers to preserve and share indigenous knowledge for sustainable food security. Among others, equal valuation of indigenous knowledge will increase its wide use and application and, thereof, its integration into other forms of knowledge systems: as stigmatization has been significantly influencing its decline (Cobb, 2011). Similarly, the lack of integration of the indigenous knowledge system has been a result of the indigenous people themselves not accepting the use of their own knowledge system because of their knowledge being labeled valueless by the colonial system (Zazu, 2007). Equal valuing of the indigenous knowledge system as a complete body of knowledge system, therefore, will stimulate its wide use, application, and integration with the scientific knowledge system.

REFERENCES

Akullo, D., Kanzikwera, R., Birungi, P., Alum, W., Aliguma, L., & Barwogeza, M. (2007). *Indigenous Knowledge in Agriculture: a case study of the challenges in sharing knowledge of past generations in a globalized context in Uganda.* IFLA.

Alexander, C. (2011). *Linking Indigenous and Scientific Knowledge of Climate Change.* America Institute of Biological Sciences: University of California Press. doi:10.1525/bio.2011.61.6.10

Aluma, J. R. (2010). Integration of indigenous knowledge (IK) agriculture and health development processes in Uganda. *Journal of Sustainable Development in Africa, 10*(3), 12–26.

Awuor, P. (2013). Integrating Indigenous Knowledge for Food Security: Perspectives from Millennium Village Project at Bar-Sauri in Nyanza Province in Kenya. *Paper presented to the African Research and Resource Forum (ARRF) held in Kampala Uganda, on 16 – 17 November 2011.*

Bandura, A. (1977). *Social Learning Theory.* General Learning Press.

Chang'a, L. B., Yanda, P. Z., & Ngana, J. (2010). Indigenous Knowledge in Seasonal Rainfall Prediction in Tanzania. *Journal of Geography and Regional Planning, 3*(4), 20–34.

Claxton, M. (2010). Indigenous Knowledge and Sustainable Development. A lecture on Cropper Foundation, UWI, St Augustine, Trinidad, Tobago, September, 2010.

Cobb, A. (2011). *Incorporating indigenous knowledge systems into climate change discourse.* Colorado conference on earth system Governance: Crossing boundaries and Building Bridges.

FAO. (2014). *Second International Conference on Nutrition; Better Nutrition-better lives.* FAO.

Gundhlanga, E. S., & Makaudze, G. (2012). Indigenous Knowledge Systems: Confirming Legacy of Civilization and Culture on the African Continent. [PJSS]. *Prime Journal of Social Science, 1*(4), 72–77.

Hammersmith, J. A. (2007). *Converging Indigenous and Western Knowledge Systems: Implications for Tertiary Education.* [Unpublished Doctoral Thesis. University of Pretoria: South Africa].

Ingram Irving, S. J. (2011). *From Food Production to Food Security: Developing Interdisciplinary, Regional Level Research.* [Doctoral Thesis, Wageningen University: The Netherlands].

Kamwendo, G., & Kamwendo, J. (2014). Indigenous Knowledge Systems and Food Security: Some examples from Malawi. *Journal of Human Ecology (Delhi, India), 48*(1), 97–101. doi:10.1080/09709 274.2014.11906778

Kijazi, A. L., Chang'a, L. B., Liwenga, E. T., Kanemba, A., & Nindi, S. J. (2013). The use of indigenous knowledge in weather and climate prediction in Mahenge and Ismani Wards, Tanzania. Proceedings of the first *Climate Change Impacts, Mitigation and Adaptation Programme Scientific Conference.*

Kolawole, O. D. P., Wolski, B., Ngwenya, B., & Mmopelwa, G. (2014). Ethno-meteorology and scientific weather forecasting: Small farmers and scientists' perspectives on climate variability in the Okavango Delta. *Climate Risk Management, 4*(5), 43–58. doi:10.1016/j.crm.2014.08.002

Kumar, K. A. (2010). Local Knowledge and Agricultural Sustainability: A Case Study of Pradhan Tribe in Adilabad District. *Centre for Economic and Social Studies, 15*(6), 1–38.

Kyarisimire, S. (2010). The role of indigenous knowledge in conservation of Uganda's National Parks (Bwindi). Kampala: Royal Geographical Society London: IT Publications.

Lwoga, E. T., Ngulube, P., & Stilwell, C. (2010). Understanding indigenous knowledge: Bridging the knowledge gap through a knowledge creation model for agricultural development. *South African Journal of Information Management, 12*(1), 8–16. doi:10.4102ajim.v12i1.436

Muchineripi, P. C. (2008). *Feeding Five Thousand: The case for indigenous crops in Zimbabwe.* African Research Institute.

Muguti, T., & Maposa, S. R. (2012). Indigenous Weather Forecasting: A phenological study engaging the Shona of Zimbabwe. *Journal of African Studies, 4*(2), 102–112.

Ngara, R., Rutsate, J., & Mangizvo, R. V. (2014). Shangwe Indigenous Knowledge Systems: An Ethno metrological and Ethno musicological Explication. *International Journal of Asian Social Sciences, 4*(1), 81–88.

Nwokoma, A. (2012). Nigeria Indigenous Knowledge Application in ICT Development, School of Information Communication; American University of Nigeria, Yola, Adamawa state, Nigeria. *Journal of Education and Social Research, 2*(7).

Nyota, S., & Mapara, J. (2008). Shona Traditional children's games and play songs as indigenous ways of knowing. *The Journal of Pan African Studies, 2*(4), 184–202.

O'Dora-Hoppers, C. (Ed.). (2002). *Indigenous Knowledge and the Integration of Knowledge Systems: Towards a Conceptual and Methodological Framework.* New Africa Books.

Okonya, J. S., & Kroschel, J. (2013). Indigenous Knowledge of Seasonal Weather Forecasting: A Case Study in Six Regions of Uganda. *Agricultural Sciences, 4*(12), 641–648. doi:10.4236/as.2013.412086

Pasteur, K. (2011). *From Vulnerability to Resilience: A Framework for Analysis and Action to build Community Resilience.* Practical Action Publishing. doi:10.3362/9781780440583

Pionke, L., & Browdy, T. (2008). Communities of practice in action-the implementation and use of an enterprise-wide information system, *Proceedings of the 5th International conference on intellectual capital and knowledge management,* New York: Institute of Technology.

Planet Ark. (2004). *Where Are All The Dead Animals? Sri Lanka Asks.* Reuters Limited. www.planetark.com

Shoko, K., & Shoko, N. (2013). Indigenous Weather Forecasting Systems: A case study of biotic weather forecasting indicators for ward 12 and 13 in Mberengwa District, Zimbabwe. *Asian Social Science, 9*(3), 285–297. doi:10.5539/ass.v9n5p285

Svotwa, E. J., Manyanhaire, I. O., & Makanyire, J. (2007). Integrating Traditional Knowledge Systems with Agriculture and Disaster Management: A Case for Chitora Communal Lands. *Journal of Sustainable Development in Africa, 9*(3), 59–60.

Tanyanyiwa, I. V., & Chikwanha, M. (2011). The role of indigenous knowledge systems in themanagement of forest resources in Mugabe area, Masvingo, Zimbabwe. *Journal of Sustainable Development in Africa, 13*(3), 132–149.

UNESCO. (2016). *Global Education Monitoring report. Indigenous knowledge and implications for sustainable development agenda.* UNSECO.

Vygotsky, L. S. (1962). *Thought and Language.* MIT Press. doi:10.1037/11193-000

Vygotsky, L. S. (1978). *Mind in Society: The development of higher psychological processes.* Harvard University Press.

Wutete, O. (2014). *The Role of Indigenous Knowledge in Agriculture and Environmental Conservation: The Case of Gutu District, Zimbabwe.* [Unpublished Doctoral Thesis, Fort Hare University: South Africa].

Zuma-Netshiukhwi, G., Stigter, K., & Walker, S. (2013). Use of Traditional Weather/Climate Knowledge by farmers in the South-Western Free State of South Africa: Agro metrological Learning by Scientists. *Atmosphere (Basel), 4*(4), 383–410. doi:10.3390/atmos4040383

ADDITIONAL READINGS

Agrawal, A. (1995). Indigenous and scientific knowledge: Some critical comments. *Development and Change, 26*(3), 413–439. doi:10.1111/j.1467-7660.1995.tb00560.x

Drouin-Gagne, M. (2014). Western and indigenous sciences: Colonial heritage, epistemological status, and contribution of a cross-cultural dialogue. *Ideas in Ecology and Evolution, 7,* 56–61. doi:10.4033/iee.2014.7.12.c

Ellis, F. (2000). *Rural Livelihoods and Diversity in Developing Countries.* Oxford University Press.

Hart, T., & Mouton, J. (2007). Indigenous knowledge and its relevance for agriculture: A case study in Uganda. *Indilinga, 4*(1), 249–260.

Nakata, M. (2005). Indigenous knowledge and the cultural interface: Underlying issues at the intersection of knowledge and information systems. *IFLA Journal, 28*(5/6), 281–291.

Nonaka, I., & Toyama, R. (2003). The knowledge-creating theory revisited: Knowledge creation as a synthesizing process. *Knowledge Management Research and Practice, 1*(1), 2–10. doi:10.1057/palgrave.kmrp.8500001

Tabuti, J. R., & Van Damme, P. (2012). Review of indigenous knowledge in Uganda: Implications for its promotion. *Afrika Focus, 25*(1), 29–38. doi:10.1163/2031356X-02501004

Taylor, S. (2003). State Library of Queensland indigenous library services: Overcoming barriers and building bridges. *Australian Academic and Research Libraries, 34*(2), 278–287. doi:10.1080/0004862 3.2003.10755248

KEY TERMS AND DEFINITIONS

A Farming System: This can be defined as a unique and reasonable stable arrangement of farming enterprises that the house hold manages according to well defined practices in response to physical, biological and socio- economic conditions and with accordance to household's goals, preferences and available resources.

Decision-Making: This is a cognitive or social process of selecting a course of action from among several alternative possibilities on the values and preferences of the decision maker(s).

Food Security: This is a situation when all people at all times have physical, social and economic access to sufficient, safe and nutritious food to meet their dietary needs for an active and healthy life.

Indigenous Knowledge (IK): This can be described as the knowledge that has been developed over time in a community mainly through accumulation of experiences and intimate understanding of the environment in a given culture.

Knowledge Management (KM): This is the process of gathering, managing and sharing employees' knowledge capital throughout the organisation.

Chapter 10

Enhancing African Indigenous Knowledge Collection Management in Ugandan Public University Libraries:
Lived Experiences of Senior Library Staff

Nina Olivia Rugambwa
Kyambogo University, Uganda

Francis Adyanga Akena
Kabale University, Uganda

Claire Clement Lutaaya Nabutto
Makerere University, Uganda

Grace Kamulegeya Bugembe
Makerere University, Uganda

ABSTRACT

Various studies in library and information science have emphasized that indigenous knowledge management is still a neglected area and a challenge in the discipline of information management. However, the rationale for this neglect and driving challenges in university libraries has not been documented from the practitioner's perspective. This chapter shares lived experiences from experienced senior staff of public University libraries in Uganda regarding the management of African Indigenous knowledge collections. The study uses the theoretical lens of Wilson's information behavior model interpolated with participants' views to gain insight into the perspectives of the practitioners. The findings revealed challenges in lack of appropriate metadata descriptors to accommodate this knowledge, biased knowledge organization tools that are incompatible with African indigenous knowledge metadata characteristics, and limited funding in university libraries for research and indigenous knowledge collection development.

DOI: 10.4018/978-1-6684-7024-4.ch010

Copyright © 2023, IGI Global. Copying or distributing in print or electronic forms without written permission of IGI Global is prohibited.

INTRODUCTION

Indigenous Knowledge (IK) refers to the knowledge, innovation, and practices of indigenous and local communities around the world, developed from experience over centuries (Grienier, 1998; Broadhead & Howard, 2011). Indigenous knowledge is adapted to the local culture and environment and transmitted orally from generation to generation (Nakata & Langton, 2005). Indigenous knowledge is critical for the survival of under privileged communities because it informs decision - making and sustainable development (Grienier, 1998; Kiggundu, 2007). Indigenous knowledge is a pillar for creativity, growth, and advancement in nations across the globe (Ezeanya-Esiobu, 2019). Indigenous knowledge systems are vast including knowledge of ecology, hunting, food preservation and aesthetics (Gateway Development Tanzania, 2011; Grenier, 1998). It also entails learning systems, local organization, controls and enforcement, local classification, and quantification systems (Lwoga, Ngulube, & Stilwell, 2011). Other components include human health, animals and animal diseases, traditional water management, soil conservation practices, agroforestry, conflict resolution and agriculture (Abdulla, 2016; Mawere, 2015; Kovach, 2015). Indigenous knowledge is on the verge of extinction globally (IFLA, 2002; Cámara-Leret, & Bascompte, 2021). A recent study (Cámara-Leret, & Bascompte, 2021) revealed that language extinction triggers the loss of indigenous medicinal knowledge. The United Nations proclamation of 2022–2032 as the International Decade of Indigenous languages seeks to raise more awareness globally on the need to preserve indigenous languages as a means for safeguarding heritage and sustainable development. The proclamation also raises awareness on the impeding danger of loss of massive indigenous knowledge if nations do not develop strategies to preserve it. Language was also identified as a tool through which indigenous knowledge is transferred from one generation to another.

A study conducted in Uganda, revealed that loss of Indigenous knowledge is still a threat in Uganda due to its oral nature, inadequate documentation, acculturation, colonization, and globalization, yet it is important for the survival of local communities and sustainable development (Tabuti & Van Damme, 2012). Various studies have emphasized the need for deliberate efforts by countries globally to preserve indigenous knowledge for enhancing sustainable development (Abdulla, 2016; Gateway Development Tanzania, 2011; Lwoga, Ngulube, & Stilwell, 2011; Mawere, 2015; WSIS, 2013). Indigenous knowledge forms the foundation of knowledge for much of Africa's population, nonetheless, this knowledge is neglected (Ezeanya-Esiobu, 2019). Libraries and information scientists play a fundamental role in promoting access to indigenous knowledge and preserving the indigenous heritage of a nation (IFLA, 2008; IFLA, 2023). IFLA (2008) highlights the different roles that libraries should play in the context of indigenous knowledge management including, identifying, collecting, preserving, and disseminating indigenous knowledge by publicizing the value, contribution, and importance of indigenous knowledge to both non-indigenous and indigenous people as well as protecting intellectual property rights of the communities.

However, a study in Uganda on the role of community libraries in the preservation of endangered indigenous knowledge (Kacunguzi, 2019) revealed that there is more effort required by community libraries to identify, collect, and preserve IK collection from their communities in the libraries. A related study (Okarafor, 2010) noted that there are few qualified and competent documentarists in the management of indigenous knowledge which has continued to affect the preservation of Indigenous Knowledge in Libraries in Africa. Boosting the utilization of indigenous knowledge collections by academicians in higher institutions of learning is paramount for stimulating learning, research, and innovations among researchers (Sekiwu, Akena & Rugambwa, 2022). Recognition of African indigenous knowledge requires the revitalization of its collection development processes for their preservation. To build a strong African Indigenous knowledge base for sustainable development in the information age, deliberate efforts towards strengthening the collection development and management of this rare Knowledge is critical (Ezeanya-Esiobu, 2019; Cámara-Leret, & Bascompte, 2021; Sekiwu, Akena & Rugambwa, 2022).

PROBLEM STATEMENT

It is well documented that indigenous knowledge is minimally used despite its immense value in various disciplines of knowledge (Griener, 1998; Dube, Akena, 2012; Ngulube & Mhlongo, 2015; Magara, 2015; Dei, Hall & Rosenberg, 2000; Akena, 2022). This gap was also recognized among information science practitioners involved in library service provision in academic libraries in Uganda (Tumuhairwe, 2013). Academicians in Library and Information science Schools indicated that there is still limited course content in Library and Information Science curriculum related to indigenous knowledge systems (Chinaka *et al.*, 2015; Magara, 2015). Recent studies have added that the challenge still exists, and that indigenous knowledge is still marginalized for teaching and research in higher institutions of learning in Africa (Adyanga & Romm, 2016; Ezeanya-Esiobu, 2019; Sekiwu, Akena & Rugambwa, 2022). Heritage institutions such as, National library, public libraries, museums are mandated by the Ugandan constitution to preserve documented indigenous knowledge as national heritage (Museum and Monuments Act, 2023; National Library Act, 2003; National Records and Archives Act, 2001; Deposit Library and Documentation center Act, 1969; Makerere University College Deposit Library Act, 1964). However, little is known from the library practitioners' perspective about why IK collections are underutilized in Ugandan public university libraries as well as the strategies to improve access and use of the knowledge collections by academicians to boost research and innovation. The focus of this chapter is to highlight views of experienced library practitioners on the reasons why indigenous knowledge collections in public university libraries in Uganda are underutilized and their proposals for improving access and use of the knowledge collections in public universities. The purpose of the chapter is to discuss strategies for enhancing African indigenous knowledge collections and management in public university libraries in Uganda. The chapter was guided by the following key research questions:

- Why are Indigenous Knowledge collections underutilized in Uganda's public universities?
- How can African Indigenous Knowledge collections be made more accessible and usable by information scientists in Uganda public university libraries?

THEORETICAL FRAMEWORK

Wilson's (1999) information behavior model (IBM) has been adopted as the theoretical lenses of this study. The model highlights the following constructs: context of information need, person in context, activating mechanism, information search behaviors and information processing and use. The model explains the reasons why some information seekers are successful seekers of information and others not. Wilson (1999) provides justification for why a specific information source may be sought after and argues that information needs are secondary needs that arise from contexts unique to persons, and explained this in reference to the constructs of person in context and context of information need. Wilson (1999) also

Enhancing African Indigenous Knowledge Collection in Public Libraries

adds that individual unique contexts such as; one's occupation and job description, environment in terms of existing technology, political and economic environments, physiological, cognitive, and emotional needs may impact the specific information sought for by information seekers.

Wilson (1999) further observes that not all information needs result in information seeking, rather there are factors that may compel or hinder people to seek for information. These factors act as the activating mechanism and provides examples, the need to cope with a stressful situation or anxiety, demographics, source characteristics, risks associated with not seeking for the information or rewards accruing and self-efficacy entailing abilities and skills that support seeking for information (Wilson, 1999). Thus, those with information skills are better information seekers and vice versa. Equally the model explains that information seekers may seek for information passively or actively. Passive seekers are those who accidentally access relevant information while active information seekers invest a lot of time and effort is ensuring that they exploit all avenues to acquire useful information from information sources. The last constructs information processing and use, highlight the fact that information does not exist on its own and must be identified, processed for it to be utilized. Thus, information should be repackaged in an acceptable format to make it usable and relevant to the users' information needs. Therefore, the application of IBM was instrumental in articulating the low utilization of indigenous knowledge in public universities libraries by unearthing some of the salient challenges. This allowed for making tailored recommendations for improving the Knowledge access, retrieval, utilization, and expansion.

METHODOLOGY

This chapter adopted a qualitative research approach to capture context-specific information from senior librarians and information science specialists with expertise in knowledge organization such as classification, cataloguing, and indexing in a university library setting. A phenomenological research design was employed to explore the lived experiences of senior information science practitioners in managing African indigenous knowledge collections in public university libraries in Uganda. These include practitioners from Kyambogo central library, Makerere university library, Mbarara central library and Kabale Mukombe university library.

Participants' Selection

A total number of 13 participants comprising, 3 university librarians, 2 senior librarians and 8 cataloguers from four public universities in Uganda were recruited for the study, using purposive sampling. Purposive sampling was used to identify participants who are directly involved in the management of university libraries, and engaged in the acquisition, processing, and preservation of African indigenous collections. Specifically, using this sampling method, participants were selected based on the following characteristics: those in position of university librarians, deputy university librarians and cataloguers working in the technical departments of the library, years of experience in the library and academic qualifications. All university librarians interviewed were PhD holders with more than eight years of experience at senior management level. While deputy university librarians and senior technical staff held master's degree in library and information science. The principle of saturation (Glaser & Strauss, 1967; Glasier, 2017) guided the study on the sample size. When the same responses were registered in the study from several participants, it was understood that saturation had been attained. As a result, the recruitment of participants, and data collection stopped. Data was collected through in-depth key informant interviews to allow the participants to share their experiences extensively.

Ethical Considerations

Ethical research standards were followed. These included voluntary participation which was well explained to them. Participants consented to participate in the study and were briefed about the purpose of the study and its benefits. The identity of all participants was concealed through assigning them pseudo names inform of labels (such as, L1, L2) to protect their privacy and confidentiality in any report to be produced from the study.

Data Presentation and Analysis

Data collected was transcribed verbatim and coded in three phases, involving descriptive coding, concept, and pattern coding (Saldana, 2021). Content and thematic analysis was used to analyze the data and Wilson (1999) 's information behavior model provided the theoretical lens to interpretation and discussion of data.

Limitation of the Study

The study findings are based on the views and lived experiences of information managers interviewed in four public university libraries in Uganda. The perspectives of academic staff and learners were not captured. A survey will be conducted to capture more comprehensive information about the study in future studies.

FINDINGS OF THE STUDY

Finding One

This section presents results from the lived experiences of senior library staff, documented through interviews with participants consisting of university librarians, cataloguers, and indexers from the four public university libraries in Uganda. Results on the first research question *"Why indigenous collections are minimally utilized by patrons in their libraries?"* are thematically presented.

- **Absence of compatible standard knowledge classification tools**

In response to the research question, participants argued that African indigenous knowledge collections were underutilized in their libraries because they are not well processed to facilitate access and use. The participants indicated that it was difficult to assign appropriate metadata descriptors to indigenous knowledge collections because the existing knowledge classification systems were designed for processing western knowledge in libraries.

Enhancing African Indigenous Knowledge Collection in Public Libraries

One of the cataloguers stated that:

Indigenous knowledge collections in the library are minimally utilized because they are not compatible with Western knowledge systems and descriptors used for metadata generation. Information capture processes and resources in the library follow Western knowledge systems like the library of congress, Dewey classification schemes, Sears lists, and Thesaurus, and these do not have provisions for indigenous knowledge capture (Cataloguer 2, Kyambogo University, 2021).

Another cataloguer said:

"In our library indigenous collections are classified using natural language and for sure it is hard to organize such collections making their use difficult because they are not accessible on western driven global information systems." (Cataloguer 1, Main Library Makerere University, 2021).

Both participants agreed that classification systems used in their libraries were biased toward Western based knowledge and were unable to effectively classify African indigenous collections housed in the libraries.

- **Acquisition of information resources biased toward Western publishers**

There was a general view among librarians in the universities that limited funds are dedicated to purchasing books that are published by local authors in Uganda resulting in limited awareness about the rich indigenous knowledge and heritage of over sixty- five ethnic groups. They argued that there was more preference for Western books and journals which has made it difficult to accumulate African indigenous knowledge collections. One of the librarians also highlighted that the lists of reading materials used in the university curriculum have been dominated by Western authors who share their experiences in writing and are widening the Western knowledge system at the expense of African indigenous knowledge.

- **Limited Funding for Research in university libraries and Indigenous Knowledge collection development**

There was a concern by senior practitioners that Universities have neglected research funding for libraries and funding of research themes associated with indigenous knowledge management. As a result, it was noted that while libraries have a mandate of preserving community heritage, they are unable to reach out to the local communities to identify, collect, process, store and preserve valuable indigenous knowledge. They also argued that a lot of indigenous knowledge is still undocumented and not known to the global world, but also, at the verge of extinction if it is not preserved because it is stored in the minds of knowledge custodians. The participants emphasized that academic libraries play an instrumental role in promoting and preserving national heritage. However, their services are only pronounced in the university community.

A participant stated that:

"There is also less effort to collect this information from the communities. Hmmm, you know indigenous knowledge is the minds of people and orally transmitted. Limited resources have been put ... to document the birds, farming systems, and food preservation systems leaving a lot of knowledge untapped..." (L1 university librarian, 2021).

Finding Two

This section presents results from the second research question "How can African Indigenous Knowledge collections be made more accessible and usable to academicians in Uganda's public university libraries? The results are thematically presented in the subsequent paragraphs.

- **Dedicating more research funds to university libraries for indigenous knowledge management and outreach services to local communities**

In response to the research question, some senior library staff emphasized that the government of Uganda and university management should prioritize research funds for university libraries to improve on indigenous knowledge collection management. Other participants added that outreach services are important activities of the university and libraries are mandated to document and preserve the heritage of communities they serve but are poorly facilitated and have greatly neglected engagement with the local community. They argued out that if this were improved library staff would start engaging with local communities to identify and document valuable indigenous knowledge, process it for use by academicians in their libraries.

- **Promotion of local publishers and scholarly work in Libraries**

The participants argued that local publishers and scholars should be promoted by university librarians and Heads of Department when reading lists and author bibliographies are being compiled for the acquisition of information materials. This they argued would change the attitude of scholars, and the university community to believe that only information resources from the Western world should be read and contain valuable information. One of the cataloguers added that these are the simple steps to promoting locally generated materials for libraries.

- **Deliberately Integrate Indigenous knowledge systems in university curriculum and Management of indigenous knowledge in library and Information Science Schools in Uganda**

The participants also agreed that the first step to promoting the use of indigenous knowledge by scholars in universities is through integrating course content on indigenous knowledge systems. They also highlighted that Library and Information Science schools should train information scientists in the management of indigenous knowledge systems and collections because this is the skill and knowledge

Enhancing African Indigenous Knowledge Collection in Public Libraries

gap that has been identified among their current practitioners who are more proficient with management of Western knowledge systems but not their own. One of the senior library staff emphasized that this explains why the few existing collections are not accessible to researchers because the knowledge is not systematically processed for use.

- **Develop innovative customized classification schemes and metadata descriptors to accommodate indigenous knowledge collections**

Some participants emphasized that besides equipping information scientists with the knowledge and skills to document indigenous knowledge in Library and Information Science schools, the students should be challenged to come up with projects to develop customized indigenous knowledge classification schemes, metadata descriptors and knowledge repositories for the vast indigenous knowledge systems. This they agreed would ensure that indigenous knowledge is systematically processed and can be used by academicians to develop inventions and innovations for sustainable development in Uganda. Other participants added that this strategy would also ensure that African indigenous knowledge systems are not confined to local libraries through customized local reference sources but are accessible and usable in global information systems.

The next section presents a discussion of findings concerning results, and the works of other scholars. This is buttressed with the theoretical lens of Wilson's Information Behavior model and its relevance in enhancing the collection management of African indigenous collections in academic libraries in Uganda.

DISCUSSION OF FINDINGS

Finding One

- **Incompatibility with western knowledge organization tools and systems**

The view that African indigenous knowledge collections are minimally accessed and used by patrons in the libraries was attributed to its unique features in terms of metadata descriptors that are not compatible with international subject headings and library nomenclature used in the classification of information in global Western knowledge organization systems. This finding is affirmed by Cherry and Mukunda (2015) and Sandy and Bossaller (2017) in their studies that explored ways of enhancing access and use of indigenous knowledge through knowledge organization systems. With this, the classification of indigenous knowledge using conventional knowledge organization systems used in Library Science has become a challenge. This is because the classification process follows Western-based approaches that are unable to capture metadata for indigenous knowledge that is context- dependent. Previously, Agrawal (2002) raised similar concerns with the postulation that some minimal databases and catalogues are dynamically designed to appropriately capture and represent context-dependent African indigenous knowledge. This paper echoes that biased classification schemes are a barrier to access to useful African indigenous knowledge and information resources in University libraries in Uganda. Therefore, there is a need to advocate for inclusive and improved subject headings in both the Library of Congress and Dewey decimal classification schemes to enhance the universality of subject headings to boost knowledge generation of knowledge among scholars and innovation in various disciplines of learning. The findings highlight the relevance of the construct person in context as it affirms that organizing indigenous knowledge will be possible when the technology and knowledge organization tools used are customized to the nature and context of indigenous knowledge metadata characteristics. Then, the information expert will be able to process it and make it usable by patrons in the library.

Further, Akena (2022) states that the failure by Africans to institutionalize and document the ancient history, civilization and knowledge is costly and calls on scholars to reverse this mistake by treading with caution to avoid the danger of losing valuable indigenous knwoledge, indigenous cultures, and customs. Earlier, Dei (2008) warned against irresponsible documentation, thus.

It is also important to understand what happens when Indigenous Knowledge is documented in ways that disembody it from the people who are its agents, when the knowers of that knowledge are separated out from what comes to be known, in ways that dislocate it from its locale, and separates it from the social institutions that uphold and reinforce its efficacy (p. 08).

Although the cataloguing of indigenous knowledge is championed in this manuscript as a strategy to increase its availability, accessibility, and utilization in universities, caution ought to be taken to mitigate the unintended outcomes such as disembodiment raised by scholars in as far as documentation pertains. Elsewhere, Adyanga and Romm (2016) emphasized that the integration (and cataloguing) of indigenous knowledge in formal education could involve the elders who are the custodian of such knowledge.

- **Limited Funding for Research in university libraries and Indigenous Knowledge collection development**

The findings revealed that indigenous knowledge collection development especially the acquisition of information materials was biased towards Western publishers, and this affected the stock of indigenous knowledge in the libraries. Information science practitioners also reiterated that there was neglect of funding on research and outreach services related to indigenous knowledge in their Libraries resulting in limited collections in the libraries and undocumented knowledge untapped from the communities. This concern was highlighted by Stevens (2008) who emphasized that libraries need to collaborate with indigenous communities to acquire, store, and make indigenous knowledge accessible. Consequently, documentation is important to preserve indigenous knowledge and make it accessible to future generations. The views expressed by the participants feed into the concerns raised by an indigenous scholar in recent work, Akena (2022) who raised an alarm over the danger of dwindling resource allocation to the study of indigenous knowledge post- Covid-19 due to purported outdated traditionalism. This is further reinforced by Keane, Khupe and Seehawer (2017) who argued that much IK research tries to align with the constraints and dictates of Western gatekeeping. Unfortunately, this has contributed to attaining dominant knowledge credibility and thereby subjecting IK only to the gate of mere recognition.

The finding is in line with Wilson's construct of activating mechanism that emphasizes that users will seek information because of specific characteristics such as format or due to psychological factors. In the context of the study findings, indigenous knowledge collections have limited access to public university library shelves because there is a negative attitude towards locally published content. More preference is given to information resources published by publishers from the Western world. Consequently, the patrons will have more access and exposure to Western based knowledge than local content that contains indigenous knowledge. The findings suggest a gap and need for attitude change among information

Enhancing African Indigenous Knowledge Collection in Public Libraries

scientists and managers in academic institutions to contribute towards the process of acquiring and facilitating use of indigenous knowledge collections. These views are still reiterated by another study on integrating indigenous knowledge in Higher education in Uganda (Sekiwu, Akena, & Rugambwa, 2022) where scholars have emphasized that there is a need for deliberate efforts to integrate IK systems into the formal curriculum in Higher learning institutions to preserve African identity, decolonize the pedagogy and boost sustainable development through innovation.

Scholars in the discipline of Library and Information science (Chinaka *et al.*, 2015; Magara, 2015; Tumuhairwe, 2013) had earlier raised concerns that Library and Information Science curriculums in African universities still had limited course content on indigenous knowledge systems. Yet, information scientists by training are the custodians of community knowledge and they must have competencies not only in managing Western knowledge but also their African indigenous knowledge. Thus, Library and Information Science Schools in Uganda have the mandate and platform to spearhead deliberate efforts in prioritizing indigenous knowledge management in their curriculums. We argue that indigenous knowledge is a distinct system of knowledge requiring specialized knowledge and competencies to manage and preserve national indigenous heritage.

Otherwise, neglecting this important mandate is a dis-service to the scholars, as well as the nation because the practitioners would be incompetent in managing their indigenous knowledge but competent in organizing Western knowledge. As a result, education in higher institutions of learning would continually be dominated by Western knowledge management approaches and ideologies. Nelson (2015) adds to this view by arguing that if indigenous knowledge is not properly documented and distributed, even the little that is in circulation is notably underrated in favor of Western dominant knowledge. Okarafor (2010) emphasized that there are few qualified and competent documentalists in the management of indigenous knowledge which has continued to affect the preservation of indigenous knowledge in Libraries in Africa. This emphasizes the importance of addressing this knowledge gap in all Library and Information Science schools in Africa in order to strengthen the management of both documented and undocumented indigenous knowledge as well as increased awareness on the need to preserve African heritage for future generations.

With the above submission, we also argue that funders of Higher education institutions are seemingly less interested in allocating resources towards indigenous knowledge research, dissemination, and archival preservation. This deliberate discrimination aligns the challenging history of research practices and research dissemination with, for, and on Indigenous peoples in diverse academic disciplines (Quayle & Sonn, 2019). Attitude change is, therefore, critical in improving the development of African indigenous collections and enhancing their use in university libraries in Uganda.

- **Strategies to improve utilization of this information in Uganda Public University Libraries**

To address the challenges identified by the participants Wilson's Information Behavior (WIB) model (1997) and literature has been used in the study to understand how library practitioners can make indigenous knowledge collections in public universities more accessible and usable. Responses from the participants have been interpolated with the model to highlight critical concerns that must be considered to improve access and use of the collections in the libraries. The strategies that were identified by participants are presented as follows.

- **Engaging with Indigenous knowledge sources, and funding documentation of Indigenous Knowledge**

Participants raised concerns that they have neglected one of the core mandates of libraries by not dedicating more time to conduct outreach services. Other participants highlighted that their libraries did not have budgets to support outreach programs that would enable them to identify, collect and document indigenous knowledge in their communities. They identified indigenous knowledge custodians to include, the elders, herbalists, museum curators, heritage centers, libraries, custodians of ancestral homes, and marginalized communities. They argued that key stakeholders must be continually engaged to promote awareness of the importance of indigenous knowledge, to preserve it and identify information needs of all the patrons for effective selective information dissemination. They also identified beneficiaries of indigenous knowledge information systems to include university academic and administrative staff, student body, researchers, and the surrounding university community who benefit from indigenous knowledge. Thus, they proposed that they need to advocate for more funding from the government and agencies like UNESCO to support them in mapping out indigenous knowledge sources and to preserve the valuable knowledge which is at the verse of extinction if no intentional interventions are made. The finding is in line with studies that have indicated that effective management of indigenous knowledge involves acknowledging the involvement of indigenous people and their institutions (Lwoga, 2011; Masalu et al., 2010). Thus, continuous engagement with the local communities is critical in ensuring that indigenous knowledge can be captured and processed so that it is made available for use in university libraries.

- **Identification of Indigenous knowledge systems**

Participants also echoed the importance of processing indigenous knowledge starting with identifying the existing indigenous knowledge systems that are so vast. Various examples were cited such as, categorization of unique indigenous knowledge heritage of bird families existing in Kabale district, indigenous knowledge on food preservation techniques, indigenous mummification for the dead, indigenous Knowledge practices for environmental conservation, Totems and biodiversity, Traditional African medicine, traditional waste management systems, traditional architectural systems, learning systems, ethno-medicinal and valuable indigenous knowledge on wild fruits. The participants emphasised that the identified knowledge systems were still underexploited and needed to be documented before their custodians pass away with a wealth of knowledge. They also emphasised that such knowledge will be accessible and known to the global world when it is processed by information managers.

Developing Classification Schemes and Metadata Descriptors Customized to Indigenous Knowledge Collections of Uganda

Findings revealed that indigenous knowledge collections lacked clear metadata descriptors and that some labels assigned were generic in nature contributing to limited access. They also emphasized that indigenous knowledge is context specific and unique to specific communities. The practitioners emphasized that the process would entail developing knowledge organization tools customized to accommodate the native nomenclature for describing various indigenous knowledge systems through assigning suitable metadata descriptors and developing customized classification schemes for such unique knowledge. They also emphasized that indigenous knowledge is context specific and unique to specific communities. Thus, the participants proposed that developing customized metadata descriptors, subject headings and classification schemes would contribute to better indigenous knowledge management in university libraries.

Some participants emphasized that the academic community especially in the field of biological sciences would gain a lot of information and come up with new innovations by tapping indigenous knowledge about, categorization of bird families in their native nomenclature and their meanings if such information is made accessible. Adopting context based Indigenous Knowledge organization systems they emphasized would entail developing indigenous metadata descriptors for each unique indigenous knowledge system. They added that striving to have inclusive subject headings, and indexes developed would contribute to having universality of subject headings for inclusiveness of African indigenous knowledge knowledge collections in libraries. In reference to Wilson (1999) concept of information processing and use, by identifying, processing and documenting indigenous knowledge this strategy would transform indigenous knowledge which is in tacit form to be more usable and accessible on global information systems in libraries.

This finding is also in line with Wilson's concept of person in context which emphasizes that for information to be effectively used, the information systems developed must prioritize user characteristics and their information needs. In the context of the findings, providing customized indigenous knowledge organization tools would contribute to more access and utilization of indigenous knowledge collections in public libraries in Uganda. This also feeds into the information processing construct in Wilson's information behavior model that describes the information lifecycle with different stages of information capture, up to use. Thus, emphasizes that information cannot exist on its own. But it must be deliberately collected (created), captured in different formats and processed based on user information needed to make it usable.

This finding is in line with a related study that was conducted in Canada (Doyle, Lawson & Duports, 2015) that supports the view that effective knowledge capture of indigenous knowledge collections requires customized indigenous classification schemes and subject headings to aid knowledge capture, retention, and access to indigenous knowledge. Previous studies also continue to emphasize a gap that needs to be improved so that collection management of indigenous knowledge is improved in libraries. The findings echo earlier studies that have emphasized that indigenous knowledge management has been neglected as a course content in higher institutions of learning (Ezeanya-Esiobu,2019) and especially in the field of library and Information Science (Magara, 2015; Tumuhairwe, 2013; Kacunguzi, 2019) where there are still few documentalists with expertise in the management of indigenous knowledge (Okarafor, 2010).

Clearly, the opportunities for using dual knowledge (indigenous and dominant) system are insurmountable. According to Durie (2005) the duality of knowledge integration can be realized, and indigenous worldviews can be matched with contemporary realities. Additionally, Cajete (2000) makes a succinct case for valuing indigenous knowledge. He argued that the cosmology of many indigenous cultures is unique and inseparable from the physical surrounding and as a result, students raised within an indigenous culture have a unique comparative advantage over their colleagues from the colonizing culture when it comes to practical science education. The critical question and discussion linger on the colonial mentality and need for attitude change and re-examination by African information scientists to ask key questions, in the information age where knowledge is power:

a. Who is managing our indigenous knowledge collections in information repositories when we have not developed classification schemes for organizing our knowledge and have not prioritized management of indigenous knowledge systems in our curriculum?

b. Why are we prioritizing management of Western knowledge systems at the expense of our indigenous knowledge in training professionals in the Library and Information Science schools?

Yet, the expected skills of an information science graduate in this information age should be one with the knowledge and skills to manage all forms of knowledge. The reality as confirmed by literature (Okarafor, 2010) is contrary, our graduates lack expertise in documenting indigenous knowledge but have been trained to be experts of western knowledge systems where this information is very accessible. The implication is that indigenous knowledge will be extinct soon if this call is not responded to by leaders. This observation is supported by an earlier study (Adyanga, 2012; Adyanga, 2014; Kaya, 2014) that affirms that neglect of indigenous knowledge by Africans hinders their development and kills innovation among the young generation.

CONCLUSION AND RECOMMENDATIONS

The discussions in this manuscript call for deliberate effort to be made in ensuring that local cultures, knowledge, customs, and archival system are engendered and respected by the gatekeepers of education institutional libraries. In the view of Riggs (2005), this can be done without imposing personal sentiment and/or unnecessary demands on knowledge marked for sharing. Further, in this article, we have advocated for more efforts to be made towards building African Indigenous collection development in university libraries. In this way, enhancement of access and utilization of African indigenous knowledge collection will improve, and knowledge can be used for sustainable development in various academic disciplines and courses offered in universities. More efforts by academicians in Information science schools should be put into developing curriculums with African Indigenous Knowledge systems as the starting point to popularizing importance of preserving indigenous knowledge and equipping the learners with the skills to manage their own knowledge given that most graduates are knowledgeable in classifying, cataloguing, indexing, storing and retrieving Western knowledge. This is a gap that needs to be addressed in the schools to ensure that our own knowledge systems and bases are not excluded but are preserved and developed. The elevation of African indigenous knowledge should be noticeable in Library and Information Science curriculums, university library collections and research for more vibrant African universities.

Lastly, in education planning, the need to reinvigorate the profound contribution of elders in knowledge production needs to be accommodated (Adyanga & Romm, 2016). Elders' participation strengthens the preferment of orality, a fundamental process for cultural and indigenous knowledge survival. Orality as a method of knowledge generation, validation, transmission and archival is significant for disrupting systemic power relations that have permeated the supremacy of Western mode of knowledge generation and archiving in education institutions (Adyanga, 2012; Akena, 2022). We also argue that higher institution libraries should harmonize their IK archival effort with researchers, the government, and other stakeholders (Okorafor, 2010) in tackling the challenges associated with the documentation of this generational knowledge for future survival.

Recommendations

Using the theoretical lens of Wilson's information behavior model interpolated with participants' views, the main recommendations from the study are presented below.

- Given the negative attitude towards publishers of local content and preference accorded to acquisition of information resources from Western publishers, more advocacies should be done in higher education on the importance of preserving African heritage.
- To make this knowledge useful to a wider population and future generations, we recommend that African indigenous knowledge is promoted as alternative knowledge in Library and information science curriculum and learners equipped with relevant skills to manage it. This also calls for the embracement of an indigenous paradigm within higher education research and teaching spaces alongside the big four paradigms (post positivism, critical theory, and constructivism) as advocated by Adyanga and Romm (2022).
- Recognizing the limited funding often allocated to research involving indigenous knowledge sources, collection, and its preservation; we recommend that funding for research geared towards indigenous knowledge collection development be prioritized to make the knowledge accessible and usable to boost innovations and sustainable development. This is because African indigenous knowledge defines the culture, identity, and the heritage of the people in Uganda.

The implementation of these recommendations will lay the foundation for opening access to massive valuable knowledge hidden in undocumented indigenous knowledge systems for utilization by researchers and academicians in the global information systems of the world.

REFERENCES

Adyanga, F. A. (2014). *African Indigenous Science in Higher Education in Uganda*. [Unpublished PhD Thesis, Ontario Institute for Studies in Education, University of Toronto]

Adyanga, F. A., & Romm, N. R. (2022). Reflections Upon our Way of Invoking an Indigenous Paradigm to Co-Explore Community Mobilization against Irresponsible Practices of Foreign-Owned Companies in Nwoya District, Uganda. *Qualitative Report, 27*(7). Advance online publication. doi:10.46743/2160-3715/2022.5147

Adyanga, F. A., & Romm, N. R. A. (2016). Researching Indigenous science knowledge integration in formal education: Interpreting some perspectives from the field. *International Journal of Educational Development, 3*(1), 1–14.

Agrawal, A. (2002). Indigenous knowledge and the politics of classification. *International Social Science Journal, 54*(173), 287–297. doi:10.1111/1468-2451.00382

Akena, F. A. (2012). Critical Analysis of the Production of Western Knowledge and Its Implications for Indigenous Knowledge and Decolonization. *Journal of Black Studies, 43*(6), 599–619. doi:10.1177/0021934712440448

Akena, F. A. (2022 in press). Education transformation post Covid-19 in Uganda, implications for Indigenous Knowledge Systems: The conversational approach. In *A. Fymat, N. R.A. Romm & Kapalanga J. (2022). Covid-19 pandemic: Perspectives across Africa*. Tellwell publishing.

Broadhead, L. A., & Howard, S. (2011). Deepening the debate over 'sustainable science': Indigenous perspectives as a guide on the journey. *Sustainable Development (Bradford), 19*(5), 301–311. doi:10.1002d.421

Cajete, G. (2000). *Native science: Natural laws of interdependence*. Clear Light Publishers.

Cámara-Leret, R., & Bascompte, J. (2021). Language extinction triggers the loss of unique medicinal knowledge. *Proceedings of the National Academy of Sciences of the United States of America, 118*(24), e2103683118. doi:10.1073/pnas.2103683118 PMID:34103398

Cherry, A. &Mukunda, K. (2015). A case Study in Indigenous Classification: Revising and Reviving the Brian Deer Scheme, *Catalouging and Classification Quartely, 53*(5-6), 548-567.

Cherry, A., & Mukunda, K. (2015). A case study in indigenous classification: Revisiting and reviving the Brian Deer scheme. *Cataloging & Classification Quarterly, 53*(5-6), 548–567. doi:10.1080/01639 374.2015.1008717

Dei, G. J. S. (2008). Indigenous knowledge studies and the next generation: Pedagogical possibilites for anti-colonial education. *Australian Journal of Indigenous Education, 37*(S1), 5–13. doi:10.1375/ S1326011100000326

Dei, G. J. S., & Hall, L. B. L., & Rosenberg, D. G (2000). Indigenous knowledge in global contexts: multiple readings of our world. Toronto Canada: University of Toronto Press.

Doyle, A. M., Lawson, K., & Dupont, S. (2015). *Indigenization of knowledge organization at the Xwi7xwa Library*. University of British Columbia.

Doyle, M. A., Lawson, K., & Dupont, S. (2015). *Journal of Library and Information Studies, 13*(2), 107–134.

Dube, L., Ngulube, P., & Mhlongo, M. (2015). Towards a cartography of indigenous knowledge systems in library and information science training and education in Anglophone eastern and southern Africa. *Indilinga, 14*(2), 145–168.

Durie, M. (2005). Indigenous knowledge within a global knowledge system. *Higher Education Policy, 18*(3), 301–312. doi:10.1057/palgrave.hep.8300092

Ezeanya-Esiobu, C. (2019), Indigenous Knowledge and Education in Africa. *Frontiers in African Business Research.*

Glaser, B. G., & Strauss, A. L. (1967). *The discovery of grounded theory: Strategies for qualitative research*. Aldine De Gruyter.

Glaser, B. G., & Strauss, A. L. (2017). *The discovery of grounded theory: Strategies for qualitative research*. Routledge. doi:10.4324/9780203793206

Government of Uganda. (2003) The National Library Act, 2003, Kampala Uganda Government of Uganda (2023) Museum and Monument Act,2023, Kampala Uganda

Grande, S., San Pedro, T., & Windchief, S. (2015). Indigenous peoples and identity in the 21st century: Remembering, reclaiming, and regenerating. *Multicultural perspectives on race, ethnicity, and identity*, 105-122.

Grenier, L. (1998). *Working with indigenous knowledge: A guide for researchers*. IDRC.

IFLA. (2023)IFLA statement on Indigenous Traditional Knowledge. IFLA. https://www.ifla.org/publications/ifla-statement-on-indigenous-traditional-knowledge

International Federation of Library Associations and Institutions. (2002). IFLA Statement on Indigenous Traditional Knowledge. IFLA. http://ifla.queenslibrary.org/III/eb/sitk03.html

Johnson, P. (2018). *Fundamentals of collection development and management*. American Library Association.

Kacunguzi, D. T. (2019). Preservation of Endangered Indigenous Knowledge: The Role of Community Libraries in Kampala –Uganda. [QQML]. *Qualitative and Quantitative Methods in Libraries, 8*, 61–72.

Kaya, H. O. (2014). Revitalizing African indigenous ways of knowing and knowledge production. *Restoring Indigenous Self-Determination*, 105.

Keane, M., Khupe, C., & Seehawer, M. (2017). Decolonising methodology: Who benefits from indigenous knowledge research? *Educational Research for social change, 6*(1), 12-24.

Kiggundu, J. (2007). Intellectual property law and the protection of indigenous knowledge. In I. Mazonde & P. Thomas (Eds.), *Indigenous knowledge systems and intellectual property in the twenty-first century; perspectives from Southern Africa* (pp. 26–47). Dakar Codesria.

Lwoga, E. T., Ngulube, P., & Stilwell, C. (2020). Indigenous knowledge management practices in indigenous organizations in South Africa and Tanzania. In Indigenous Studies: Breakthroughs in Research and Practice (pp. 37-57). IGI Global. doi:10.4018/978-1-7998-0423-9.ch003

Magara, E. (2015). Integration of indigenous knowledge management into the university curriculum: A case for makerere university. *Indilinga, 14*(1), 25–41.

Mawere, M. (2015). Indigenous knowledge and public education in sub-Saharan Africa. *Africa Spectrum, 50*(2), 57–71. doi:10.1177/000203971505000203

Mohanty, C. T. (2003). *Feminism without borders: Decolonizing theory, practicing solidarity*. Duke University Press.

Nakata, M., & Langton, M. (2005). Australian indigenous knowledge and libraries (p. 188). UTS ePRESS.

Nelson, H. E., & NO, R. (2015). *Challenges of documenting and disseminating agricultural indigenous knowledge for sustainable food security in Soroti District*. Kampala: Makerere University.

Ntuli, P. (1999). The missing link between culture and education: are we still chasing Gods that are not our own? In M. W. Makgoba (Ed.), *African renaissance*. Mafube-Tafelberg.

Odora-Hoppers, C. A. (Ed.). (2002). *Indigenous knowledge and the integration of knowledge systems: towards a philosophy of articulation*. New Africa Books.

Okorafor, C. N. (2010). Challenges confronting libraries in documentation and communication of indigenous knowledge in Nigeria. *The International Information & Library Review*, *42*(1), 8–13. doi:10.1080/10572317.2010.10762837

Quayle, A. F., & Sonn, C. C. (2019). Amplifying the voices of indigenous elders through community arts and narrative inquiry: Stories of oppression, psychosocial suffering, and survival. *American Journal of Community Psychology*, *64*(1-2), 46–58. doi:10.1002/ajcp.12367 PMID:31365131

Riggs, E. M. (2005). Field-based education and indigenous knowledge: Essential components of geoscience education for Native American communities. *Science Education*, *89*(2), 296–313. doi:10.1002ce.20032

Saldaña, J. (2021). The coding manual for qualitative researchers. *Sage (Atlanta, Ga.).*

Sekiwu, D., Akena, F. A., & Rugambwa, N. O. (2022). Decolonizing the African University Pedagogy Through Integrating African Indigenous Knowledge and Information Systems. In *Handbook of Research on Transformative and Innovative Pedagogies in Education* (pp. 171–188). IGI Global. doi:10.4018/978-1-7998-9561-9.ch010

Sithole, J. (2007). The challenges faced by African libraries and information centres in documenting and preserving indigenous knowledge. *IFLA Journal*, *33*(2), 117–123. doi:10.1177/0340035207080304

Tabuti, J. R. S., & Van Damme, P. (2012). Review of indigenous knowledge in Uganda: Implications for its promotion. *AFRICA FOCUS*, *25*(1), 29–38. doi:10.1163/2031356X-02501004

Tella, R. D. (2007). Towards promotion and dissemination of indigenous knowledge: A case of NIRD. *The International Information & Library Review*, *39*(3-4), 185–193. doi:10.1080/10572317.2007.10762748

Tumuhairwe, G. K. (2013). *Analysis of library and information science/studies (lis) education today: The inclusion of indigenous knowledge and multicultural issues in lis curriculum.* IFLA.

Uganda. (2006). *The Uganda National Culture Policy: A Culturally vibrant, cohesive and Progressive Nation.* Ministry of Gender, Labour & Social Development.

Wilson, T. D. (1999, August 1). Models in information behaviour research. *The Journal of Documentation*, *55*(3), 249–270. doi:10.1108/EUM0000000007145

Wilson, T. D., & Walsh, C. (1996). *Information behaviour: An interdisciplinary perspective.* Sheffield: University of Sheffield department of information studies.

WSIS (World Summit on the Information Society). (2013). *WSIS Forum 2013 13-17 May, Geneva.* WSIS. https://www.itu.int/net/wsis/implementation/2013/forum/

KEY TERMS AND DEFINITIONS

African Indigenous Knowledge: This refers to the Knowledge, innovation, and indigenous practices of local communities in Africa developed from experience over centuries and transmitted by the word of mouth from generation to generation.

Collection Development and Collection Management: Collection development refers to the thoughtful process of developing or building a library collection in response to institutional priorities and community or user needs and interests, and collection management is the equally thoughtful process of deciding what to do after the collection is developed.

Indigenous Knowledge Collection Development: The process of developing indigenous knowledge collection in response to institutional priorities and user nee

Indigenous Knowledge: In this study Indigenous Knowledge (IK) refers to the knowledge, innovation, and practices of indigenous and local communities around the world, developed from experience over centuries. This knowledge is adapted to the local culture and environment and transmitted orally from generation to generation.

Chapter 11

Turbulences in Repackaging Traditional Knowledge in an Era of Sovereignty:
Case of Uganda and Zimbabwe

Collence Takaingenhamo Chisita
https://orcid.org/0000-0002-7375-8627
Durban University of Technology, South Africa

Sarah Kaddu
Makerere University, Uganda

ABSTRACT

Traditional or Indigenous systems have always been the bedrock of Africans' socioeconomic and political livelihoods before the dawn of colonialism in developing countries like Uganda and Zimbabwe. Indigenous practices are important to people's daily lives. This chapter looks to strengthen classical African systems and methods for decoloniality. The study explored traditional knowledge with a focus on its meanings and critical features, reviewed the laws protecting traditional knowledge in Uganda and Zimbabwe, and how libraries can contribute to preserving such classical knowledge in Zimbabwe and Uganda. It explored the factors that affect the preservation of traditional and proposed strategies to enhance conventional conservation by libraries in Zimbabwe and Uganda. An Afrocentric paradigm underpins the chapter, and data were collected from the literature review and the researchers' personal experiences as members of indigenous communities.

INTRODUCTION AND BACKGROUND

Traditional or Indigenous knowledge systems have always been the bedrock of Africans' socioeconomic and political livelihoods before the dawn of colonialism. Traditional knowledge is the primary element millions depend on in developing countries (Carrea, 2001). Indigenous knowledge and practices are

DOI: 10.4018/978-1-6684-7024-4.ch011

Copyright © 2023, IGI Global. Copying or distributing in print or electronic forms without written permission of IGI Global is prohibited.

verbally transmitted to succeeding generations and firmly and broadly anchored in the intergenerational experience of the environment (Kamau & Winter, 2009). Different nomenclatures are under several names in indigenous systems, including indigenous and traditional knowledge of the environment, traditional ecological knowledge, and Native Science (Bucket, 2013). The protection of indigenous cultural heritage can be realised by empowering them to reclaim their sovereign space among other social groups. As stated by Latulippe and Klenk (2020), a two-pronged solid conceptual framework for indigenous sovereignty is concerned with enhancing indigenous systems, ensuring their transfer within indigenous governance structures, and reducing external obstacles to indigenous expression on the land. The United Nations (2008) states that worldwide, indigenous peoples have the right to their natural resources and grounds, to consciousness, and to make accessible, prior, and informed decisions in all indigenous territories and to practice their legal systems, political systems, and intellectual traditions (Pillay, 2013). Additionally, sovereignty is not contingent on other people's acceptance of indigenous systems, the generous funding of short-term programs, or the encouragement of equity among various communities. It is a right derived from indigenous sovereignty, title, and ownership (Latulippe & Klenk, 2020). Indigenous sovereignty is the basis of sovereignty in indigenous peoples and their culture. The notion of indigenous sovereignty rests on the idea that the indigenous people are of sovereign descent, as their Deoxyribonucleic acid (DNA) covers the challenges and day-to-day activities that they face when fighting for survival (Birch, 2007). The concept of sovereignty is distinctly stated in the United Nations' (UN) Declaration on the Rights of Indigenous Peoples (2008), in which the sovereign rights of such groups to self-determination are explicitly stated by Article 31,1. Indigenous peoples have the right to protect, administer, and enhance their knowledge, cultural practices, and scientific, technological, and cultural manifestations, including seeds, medicines, and human and genetic resources. Flora and wildlife traits, oral traditions, literary genres, designs, sports, traditional games, and the visual and performing arts are essential to Africa's epistemic revolution. Additionally, they are entitled to maintain, control, safeguard, and further their Intellectual Property (IP) rights concerning cultural heritage, knowledge, and conventional cultural representations. There are numerous cases whereby indigenous groups have lost their sovereignty over their natural resources due to biopiracy as will be highlighted in the subsequent paragraphs.

Fredriksson (2022) analyzed *Curcuma Longa's* case and a plant patented by the University of Mississippi through the United States Patent and Trademark Office and then revoked. The patent mentioned above was withdrawn due to pressure from India on the grounds of uniqueness, which marked great success in countering biopiracy by a third-world country. Fredriksson (2022) reported that the Indian government's Council of Scientific and Industrial Research challenged the patent for its use of traditional Indian practices. Hasfera (2017) conducted a study investigating the reprocessing and preservation of Minangkabau folklore from Indonesia's West Sumatra province. The growing disinterest of young people triggered the investigation into reading indigenous folklore, which posed a challenge for librarians. The Nagari Library began a mission to repackage Minangkabau folklore and upload the content to the institutional repository. The oral legend was converted into multimedia and shared with the community (Hasfera, 2017). Similarly, Sithole (2007) explains that documentation of indigenous knowledge is a necessary and legitimate method to validate it and ensure its defence against biopiracy and other abuse. The court dispute over the patenting of the hoodia plant used for medicinal purposes demonstrated the need for paperwork. Sources of the plant were the Kalahari people, who generously disseminated it worldwide; however, it was patented without informing and compensating the original owners (Yunnus, 2017).

The Hoodia *Gordonii* case from South Africa has exposed the vulnerabilities of traditional knowledge in an era of greedy consumerism, as stated below:

Case of Hoodia Gordonii, a succulent plant researched in the early 1960s by the South African government-funded Council for Scientific and Industrial Research (CSIR) for its appetite and thirst-quenching properties, represents the most iconic cases of biopiracy in all of Southern Africa and worldwide"(Wynberg, 2023). As noted by Wynberg (2023), the benefit of sharing with the indigenous peoples was demonstrated in the Hoodia case, which set a significant precedent.

A classic example of biopiracy in South Africa is a pharmaceutical company's operation with the Hoodia plant. Robinson (2010) described biopiracy as a process whereby companies or researchers appropriate the genetic resources, knowledge, and customs of various nations, indigenous peoples, and local communities (usually from the Global South) without their consent and then patent this information to secure the ability to resell it for profit. Zimu-Biyela, (2021), citing Tsekea (2016) noted that the Amendment of Intellectual Property (IP) Laws, No. 28 of 2013 guaranteed proper IP protection measures for indigenous knowledge as IP. The Intellectual Property Laws Amendment Act 38 of 199 (IPLAA) (2013) recognizes indigenous systems as forms of IP, and among other things, the law aims to conserve geographical indicators and forbids the recording of indigenous knowledge without the agreement of the indigenous people. As an illustration of patenting, consider the Hoodia cactus, an indigenous plant with appetite-suppressing properties that the Khoisan people discovered in the 19th century, for who Pfizer was obliged to compensate (Tsekea 2016: 213). Wynberg (2023) highlighted that the Hoodia Case was primarily the development of the agreement that promoted the ability of the South African San Council to facilitate benefits through negotiations with industry. Representatives of indigenous San and more recently, Khoi organizations are leading numerous business transactions concerning South Africa's biodiversity, including claims to knowledge. The cases of *Curcuma longa* (India), *Minangkabau folklore* (Malaysia), and *Hoodia Gordonii* (South Africa) illustrate the importance of IP rights in repackaging and patenting indigenous knowledge. Cases of revocation of the culturally appropriated patent confirm that protecting indigenous systems is threatened by greedy corporate organizations seeking to profit from such resources. The above reasons justify enacting laws to safeguard indigenous knowledge in the Global South and Zimbabwe and Uganda is no exception.

STATEMENT OF THE PROBLEM

Indigenous knowledge plays a critical role in the lives of African people, even though it has been disparaged because of the colonial and imperial onslaught. Chisita, Rusero and Shoko (2016) argued that the dawn of colonialism marked the genesis of a systematic strategy to denigrate anything indigenous in an attempt to establish colonial rule. According to the authors, the colonial settlers' grand design was to wipe out any traits of indigeneity and create a culturally confused mass that would sheepishly embrace the new colonial and imperial order. Even though Africans had always relied on indigenous knowledge before colonialism to sustain their livelihood in all aspects, the new colonial doctrine underpinned by the imperial mission of "Commerce, Christianity and Civilisation," commonly abbreviated as the 3Cs resulted in Africans succumbed to neo-colonial epistemic values. However, Uganda and Zimbabwe cannot continue to celebrate epistemic injustice when globally, there are growing calls to reassert and reaffirm the importance of indigenous culture, including its systems through praxis-oriented combative decoloniality. The founders' ideals of Africa's struggles against colonialism drew inspiration from Pan-Africanism, an ideology that upholds the sovereign independence of Africans, including the right to self-determination. Indigenous knowledge has become a victim of the machinations of colonial and neo-colonial institutions as it has been peripherised yet it holds solutions to the current problems humanity is experiencing. The failure to preserve indigenous knowledge will rob Uganda, Zimbabwe, and Africa of their critical cultural and epistemic capital. The clarion call to protect and maintain indigenous knowledge has always been the rallying point of the struggle against colonialism and neo-colonialism in the context of combative decoloniality discourse and praxis as highlighted by Torres & Medina (2021). The advent of globalization has facilitated covert and overt ways of pillaging indigenous knowledge in the guise of tourism and international trade. Biopiracy has become a strategic instrument of greedy capitalism to dispossess the already disposed of people of Uganda, Zimbabwe, and Africans' key stronghold for indigenous knowledge. This chapter seeks to contribute to the discourse on preserving Indigenous Knowledge, including knowledge to protect the sustainability of Africa in the face of globalization. The objectives of the chapter aimed to:

- Establish the traditional knowledge in Uganda and Zimbabwe
- Analyze the key features of traditional knowledge
- Review the laws that protect traditional knowledge in Zimbabwe and Uganda
- Identify the roles of libraries in the process of knowledge repackaging
- Suggest ways to enhance the conservation of traditional knowledge in Zimbabwe and Uganda

METHODOLOGY

There are a variety of research paradigms, even though the dominant paradigms in the world are influenced by "Euro-Western" thought including positivism, post positivism, interpretivism, transformational, and indigenous paradigms based on their ontology, epistemology, axiology, and methodology (Chilisa, 2012). This chapter is premised on an Afrocentric paradigm as enunciated by (Asante, 1991a). The proponent of Afrocentrism (Asante, 2005b) argued and emphasized the need to x-ray issues concerning Africans using an Afrocentric lens to reconstruct African experiences using an Afronographic methodology while keeping Africans' attention at heart when seeking to answer epistemological and axiological questions (Rodgers, 2022). Asante (2005) describes Afronography as a method of recording and writing the African experience from an Afrocentric perspective (Asante, 2005b). Chilisa, (2012) identified Afrocentrism as a worldview that embodies African ways of perceiving reality, knowledge, values, and methodology in research. Afrocentrism encapsulates the ethos of combative decoloniality as a special vehicle to reclaim indigenous sovereignty.

LITERATURE REVIEW

There are various definitions of traditional knowledge, ranging from those that are explicit and those implicit. World Intellectual Property Organisation (WIPO) (2020) defines traditional knowledge as a community's knowledge, know-how, skills, and traditions that are created, maintained, and passed down from generation to generation; frequently, these elements contribute to the community's cultural or spiritual identity. As noted by WIPO (2003), traditional knowledge and Cultural Expressions (TCEs) have intrinsic social, cultural, spiritual, economic, scientific, intellectual, and educational value. Cultures and systems representing traditional knowledge are living plans subject to constant innovation and creativity. Traditional knowledge has wide and narrow definitions. Shabalala (2017), using a *lato sensu* perspective, describes traditional knowledge as an epistemological framework embracing the traditions, customs, and bases of local communities and indigenous peoples. In a narrow sense (*stricto sensu*), Shabalala (2017) describes traditional knowledge as produced by intellectual endeavour in a traditional setting and includes know-how, practices, skills and innovations. Ranjan and Singh (2020) described traditional knowledge as passed from one person to another via practice and employment as evolving following nature. Traditional knowledge exists in varied contexts ranging from agriculture, science, technology, ecology, and medicine, including related treatments, remedies, and biodiversity-related (Shabalala, 2017).

Indigenous Knowledge Systems

Indigenous knowledge encompasses systems of traditional knowledge based on place and specific to an area or state's original inhabitants (Moichela, 2017). Abebe et al. (2021) and Seroto (2011) argued that philosophical practices among indigenous peoples took the form of oral traditions in pre-colonial Africa. Abebe et al. (2021), citing Okot p'Bitek (1975), assert that oral procedures are prompter and more effective. Indigenous knowledge in the form of the classical art of African conversation is common throughout all Indigenous communities, and they help to distinguish one community from another. As Jasmine, Singh, Onial, et al. (2016) explain, indigenous knowledge can refer to a wide range of abilities, innovations, or practices originating from indigenous people. Many communities depend on their traditions to survive. For instance, Uganda has an investigation into that culture's unique characteristics and the circumstances under which it exists (Mugabe, Kameri-Mbote & Mutta, 2001). WIPO (2003) articulates the oral-shaped nature of traditional knowledge such as folklore as an inter-generational and collaborative creative process that reflects and identifies a community's history, cultural and social identity, and values. The oral-shaped culture of Africa includes verbal expressions, such as folktales, folk poetry, riddles, signs, words, symbols, and indications; musical terms, such as folk songs and instrumental music; and actions, such as folk dances and plays (WIPO, 2003). Several indigenous knowledge systems generate, manage, and disseminate this body of knowledge, including informal education, apprenticeships, internships, and mentoring based on traditional beliefs and practices (Afful-Arthur et al., 2022). However, the critical question is, "Do indigenous people have sovereignty over their data and knowledge?"

On the other hand, indigenous knowledge sovereignty refers to practices that support indigenous knowledge systems, ensure their transmission occurs according to indigenous governance structures, and remove external barriers to their expression on the land (Whyte, 2018). Indigenous people have been left by their government vulnerable to capitalism and neo-colonialism, as evidenced by the unwarranted pillaging of their cultural heritage and their use as objects of unfair research practices. Foxworth and Ellenwood (2023) noted that as a complement to the mainstream research principles of Findability, Accessibility, Interoperability and Reusability (FAIR), Indigenous leaders have developed CARE principles to protect and advocate for Indigenous data governance rights. In CARE, Collective Benefit, Authority to Control, Responsibility, and Ethics are emphasized (Foxworth & Ellenwood, 2023). Data is vital in advancing Indigenous development and self-determination so they can benefit from research according to the CARE principles (Carrol et al., 2022).

Traditional Knowledge in Africa

Sindiga, Nyaigotti-Chacha and Kanunah (1995) argued that in Africa, traditional knowledge exists as an unwritten science; for instance, in the field of medicine, the majority regarding the qualities of medicinal plants has remained unstudied and even a closely-kept secret among mystics and conventional physicians. For decades, traditional knowledge has been transmitted verbally from one person to another. Traditional knowledge, including songs, rituals, traditions, folklore, and unwritten laws, can be articulated differently. Other forms can be communicated through artefacts, drawings, and other documents of art and technology, as supported by Singh et al. (2023) when they noted that:

Traditional is rarely fully documented because it is mostly transmitted through stories, songs, customary ceremonies, traditional laws, and farming practices (Singh et al., 2023).

Traditional and indigenous knowledge eventually become a part of the community's distinctive spirituality and culture. A significant component of human existence has always been and will continue to be indigenous (Magni, 2017). Indigenous knowledge refers to the systems of traditional knowledge based on place and specific to an area or state's original inhabitants (Moichela,2017). Abebe et al. (2021) and Seroto (2011) argued that in pre-colonial Africa, philosophical practices among indigenous peoples took the form of oral traditions. Abebe et al. (2021), citing Okot p'Bitek (1975), contend that oral procedures are quick and decisive. WIPO (2003) articulates the oral-shaped nature of traditional knowledge as folklore which includes, verbal expressions, such as folktales, folk poetry, riddles, signs, words, symbols, and indications; musical terms, such as folk songs and instrumental music; and actions, such as folk dances and plays. The revitalization of indigenous knowledge resonates with the philosophy of the African Renaissance (2009). The intelligentsia should be at the forefront of such struggles. Mbeki (2009) highlighted that the success of an African Renaissance is not only in the interest of African nations and people but also the entire globe. Cossa (2009) cites Mbeki's (2009) statement concerning the African Renaissance:

I am convinced that a significant burden rests on the shoulders of Africa's intelligentsia to help us to achieve these objectives... we have arrived at the point where the enormous brain power which our continent possesses must become a vital instrument in helping us to secure our equitable space within a world affected by a rapid process of globalization and from which we cannot escape (Cossa, 2009).

Van Wyk and Higgs (2004) argued that to address the colonial damage in South Africa, a uniquely African system would strive to rediscover the humanistic and ethical principles entrenched in African philosophy, particularly in communality and Ubuntu.

Repackaging Traditional Knowledge in Uganda and Zimbabwe

Like any other indigenous community in Zimbabwe, indigenous knowledge systems appear in various fields including linguistics, botany, zoology, security, agriculture, medicine, and other areas (Mapara, 2009). However, there are concerns that if indigenous knowledge is not rapidly investigated and preserved, it will disappear with subsequent generations. (Hostettmann, Marston, Ndjoko & Wolfender, 2000). Mposhi, Manyeruke and Hamauswa (2013) argued that indigenous knowledge systems offer cheaper answers to most of Zimbabwe's and Africa's healthcare issues. The traditional medicine has thus become the most effective healthcare option for modern medical procedures for treating various diseases. Maroyi (2013) cited *Albizia antunesiana* (Muriranyenze), *Annona stenophylla* (Muroro), *Cassia abbreviate* (Muremberembe), *Albizia antunesiana* (Muriranyenze), *Strychnos cocculoides* (Mutamba muzhinyu) considered valuable medicinal plants with at least six different therapeutic uses across the majority of Zimbabwe's areas. Albizia antunesiana roots have been used in tropical Africa for various conditions and it helps treat numerous ailments such as abdominal pains, cuts, depressed fontanelles, sexually transmitted diseases, infertility, oedema, pneumonia, preventing abortions, tonsillitis, tuberculosis, ulceration and constipation (Maroyi, 2013).

Mujere, Chanza, Muromo, et al. (2023) argued that indigenous cultures employ various techniques to predict and gauge the scope and severity of drought. The above methods include spirituality, weather-related research, witnessing natural fires, and analysing plant- and animal-species behaviour. As stated by Kaddu, Nakaziba and Juma (2021), indigenous medicine was incorporated into treatment procedures in emerging nations, for example, in sub-Saharan Africa, indigenous medicine has proved essential to healthcare mainly because of its accessibility and affordability (Segun, Ogbole & Ajaiyeoba, 2018). The leaves and bark extracted from African Cherry (*Prunus Africana*) (Entaseesa or Ngwabuzito in Luganda) and (Muchambati in the Shona language) has proved to be a wonder anti-cancer tree. Cancer patients are given cooked water from its leaves (Kaddu, Nakaziba & Juma, 2021). The study highlighted above disclosed the use of marijuana (*Enjaga* in Luganda) and (*mbanje* in the Shona language) in treating cancer. Uganda and Zimbabwe have outlawed the growing, use, and sale of marijuana, although its use is widespread. Kaddu, Nakaziba and Juma's (2021) study on Cancer Indigenous (CIK) highlighted the widespread use of Aloe vera leaves (*Ekigagi* in Luganda and *Gavakava* in Shona). The above-mentioned herbal plant's leaves are blended with juices or boiled and served as a drink. Rajeswari et al. (2012), in concurrence with (Kaddu, Nakaziba & Juma 2021), stated that fluids from Aloe vera leave sustains normal human cell regeneration, reduce pain and inflammation, and enhance healing in the wounded cell monolayers. Because of its bioactive compounds, *aloe vera* has shown efficacy in treating allergies, burns, ulcers, diabetes, rheumatoid arthritis, diarrhoea, acid reflux, skin conditions, dysentery, and digestive system inflammation and piles (Sharma et al. 2014). The uses of Aloe *Vera* in Sub -Saharan Africa are the same among indigenous communities as highlighted above.

THEORETICAL FRAMEWORK

This chapter analyses how decoloniality resonates with the aspirations of those seeking to reverse the devastating effects of epistemic injustice coupled with cultural appropriation. It employs the cultural appropriation theory as a basis for investigation. Arya (2021) contends that naming cultural appropriation and acting upon it implies understanding the histories of colonialism and imperialism and their legitimization of the act. Commodification underpins the practice of cultural appropriation because it provides the means through which cultural goods or ideas are converted into commodities or objects of trade. From a Marxist perspective, the exchange value, essentially its commercial worth- the cultural significance of owning the thing (Marx, 1986), replaces an object's use value (the cost of making). Arya (2021) contends that cultural appropriation is significant and allures one to the fact that cultural exchange can be a zero-sum game, hence interrogations of the ethics of a dominant culture taken from a marginalized culture. Ziff and Rao (1997) stated that cultural appropriation was the taking, from another culture, of IP, cultural expressions or artefacts, history and ways of knowing. It causes offences, including sacredness desecration and the authentic culture's wrong reproduction (Young, 2010).

Similarly, Young (2010) and Lalonde (2021) described non-recognition within cultural appropriation as a phenomenon encapsulated in voicelessness and invisibility. McConkey (2004) argued that Epistemic injustice results from voicelessness in non-recognition since cultural members disregard epistemic contributions about their culture and cultural property. The denial of cultural appropriation refers to denied cultural property ownership claims. Taylor (1992) argues that Misrecognition or non-recognition can cause harm, enslave, or imprison someone in a distorted, reduced state of being. By asserting and reaffirming their right to self-determination, Eason, Brady and Fryberg (2018) call on indigenous communities to resist non-recognition, misrecognition, and exploitation. Traditional knowledge is rarely coded to its fullest extent since it is transmitted through stories, songs, customary rituals, ceremonial laws, and agricultural practices (Singh et al., 2023). A significant component of human existence has always been and will continue to be indigenously grounded in indigenous epistemologies and axiologies (Magni, 2017).

FINDINGS AND DISCUSSIONS

This section presents the study findings in sync with the guidance of the research objectives highlighted above.

- **Establish traditional Knowledge in Uganda and Zimbabwe**

Traditional knowledge diffuses every aspect of life in Uganda and Zimbabwe, for example, totemism, food sovereignty, farming, medicine, health, conflict resolution, weather prediction, education, wildlife management, and spiritual healing, among many other uses. The proceeding section analyzed selected cases concerning traditional knowledge. Mapira and Mazambara (2013) cited totemism as a common tradition among Zimbabwe's indigenous groups. Totemism refers to the indigenous practice of symbolically creating a synergy between human beings and non-human objects, including plants and animals (Mapira & Mazambara, 2013). Totemism involves people claiming an animal as a mythological ancestor (Jary & Jary, 1995). There is a systematic association between groups of people and animals (occasionally plants or inanimate objects) associated with particular elements of social organization (Tarugarira, 2017). In the author's opinion, focusing on the totem and its accessories increases our understanding of aspects of clan cultural heritage. It provides insight into traditional knowledge systems used in environmental management (Tarugarira, 2017). The concept of totemism is significant among the indigenous people of Zimbabwe because it bonds the living and the ancestors in protecting the environment. Totemism is buttressed by taboos because eating one's totem can result in fatal consequences, for example, misfortunes, illness, death, falling away of a victim's teeth, and abject poverty (Kasere,2010). For clan members in Uganda, killing certain animal species is forbidden to avoid bringing a bad omen on themselves (Ochieng, Koh, & Koot, 2022).

Ruhinirwa et al. (2019) argued that in Uganda, each clan in the region of Buganda identifies with a totem which may be an animal or plant. It is forbidden to eat your totem, and clan members are obliged to protect them from harm or destruction. This practice has enhanced the sustainable use of natural resources over generations. The findings on totemism and its significance in Zimbabwe by Tarugarira (2017) resonate with Ruhinirwa et al. (2019) regarding eating one's totem and the consequences that one might face. However, the effects of modernization threaten totemism because the bible teaches its adherents that the practice is satanic, and people converted to Christianity proudly proclaim Jesus as their totem. As of 2016, agriculture is responsible for approximately 24% of the Ugandan GDP, nearly 48% of export earnings, and 80% of the household's livelihoods (Kansiime et al., 2016). In food and agricultural debates, 'food sovereignty' empowers nations and peoples to control their food systems, including their markets, production modes, food cultures, and environment (Wittman, Desmarais & Wiebe, 2010).

Martiniello (2015) argued that introducing genetically modified sorghum and finger millet varieties in an open environment will most likely engender the pollination of all other indigenous types. The effect would presumably be a reduction in the bio-diverse patrimony and standardization of the different sorghum and millet grown for millennia by eastern African peasants (Martiniello, 2015). Food sovereignty in Uganda is achievable by controlling access to land, mobilizing labour, and reproducing indigenous seeds, all of which are integral to food sovereignty's social, economic, and political ideals (Martiniello, 2015). Similarly, Mandisvika, Chirisa and Bandauko's (2015) study on Zimbabwe emphasizes that local people should secure control over natural productive resources, possess a right to land, and utilize and protect their indigenous knowledge and cultural identity. Chirisa, & Bandauko's (2015) argued that millet and sorghum are the best crop alternatives, as they can withstand the low rainfall and high temperatures indigenous to this region agro-ecological region 5 in Zimbabwe, such as Masvingo and Chiredzi. In Uganda, much indigenous knowledge helps manage soil and water, grow crops, livestock care, and process and store food (Tabuti, 2003). Haumba and Kaddu (2017) explain that to treat animals and plants when pests and diseases attack them, for instance, the farmers in Soroti employ indigenous medicine. Farmers use a variety of locally made medicinal plants to treat the animals. For example, to prevent the spread of pests and illnesses, farmers burn the infected crops, practice crop rotation, and grow various crops (Haumba & Kaddu (2017). This finding further supports Waziri and Aliero's (2005) assertion that growing the same crops in the same garden year after year might stimulate the development of pests and illnesses in the soil. These destructive agents keep on spreading from one crop to the next. Jiri, Mafongoya and Chivenge (2015) highlighted that the significant role of traditional knowledge in smallholder agriculture should not be underestimated. Our research has shown that most traditional leaders and older people fully understand the use of indigenous knowledge in forecasting seasonal characteristics. However, even they have noticed the erosion of local knowledge. Despite this result, farmers still use indigenous knowledge to make certain coping and adaptation decisions. Climate change may bring about new weather patterns and extreme events that are well beyond what the local communities can handle.

IP protection of indigenous knowledge is crucial. Hence, indigenous peoples, local communities, and governments seek its protection (WIPO, 2003). The world of traditional knowledge is rapidly depleting its natural resource base. It is in danger of becoming extinct due to the swiftly transforming global environment and economic, political, and cultural developments. As noted by Horsthemke (2021), it is relatively straightforward to justify focusing on indigenous African Knowledge, science, and technology, especially considering colonialism's destruction, suppression, and exploitation of traditional systems. Isife (2023) argued that African science/technology has never followed the Western scientific method yet has a functional basis and uses. Understanding the depth of African ontology and the metaphysical framework on which African scientific epistemology is essential to appreciate the African approach to scientific methodology (Isife, 2023). Cosmology is a branch of science that deals with the universe and what exists in it. How the Africans know and relate to this world or environment can pass the methodology, and how Africans know and connect the universe and its surroundings pass the test of a scientific method (Isife, 2023).

Turbulences in Repackaging Traditional Knowledge in an Era of Sovereignty

As Isife (2023) explained, through extractive biocolonialism, indigenous peoples' valuable genetic resources and associated agricultural and medicinal are sought, legally converted into IP, transformed into commodities, and sold on genetic markets. As Onayade, Onayade and Sowofora (1996) noted, traditional African medicine relies on plants as herbal remedies to heal wounds, extract pus, and treat infected and festering wounds. Onayade et al. (2009) and Kazembe and Mashoko (2008) concurred that traditional herbal medicines helped treat snakebites, stomach aches, and reproductive disorders. Over (75%) of modern medicine is plant-based. In contrast, (25%) is derived from synthetic materials, which proves the need to develop sustainable environmental management strategies to protect indigenous plants. In Zimbabwe, the Ministry of Environment and Tourism and other quasigovernmental organizations like the Environmental Management Agency (EMA), Forestry Commission of Zimbabwe, and the non-governmental Southern African Foundation for Indigenous Resources (SAFIRE), have contributed towards the promotion and protection of biological species.

Ray (2023) argues that the perception of traditional knowledge through contemporary scientific concepts and philosophies will authenticate it for broader adoption as a tried and true type of science in society to create a solid future-oriented foundation for research and innovation. Sindiga et al. (1995) criticized colonialism and the Christian crusades for failing to accept traditional systems by establishing control over the conquered people and acculturating them in the name of Christianity, Commerce, and Civilisation (3Cs). Traditional medicine and techniques are very much alive in Uganda and Zimbabwe, even though Africans disparage traditional methods in public but surreptitiously seek them out when they think no one is watching them (Chisita & Kaddu, 2009).

Critical Features of Traditional Knowledge

Sharma et al. (2020) analyzed the characteristics of traditional knowledge in various ways as follows:

- generated within communities, location, and culture-specific;
- decision-making and survival strategies;
- not systematically documented;
- concerns critical issues of human and animal life; and,
- dynamic and based on innovation, adaptation, and experimentation, oral and rural.

Traditional knowledge saturates every facet of the indigenous people's ways of life, as illustrated in Figure 1. Sharma et al. (2020) raise important issues concerning the nature of traditional knowledge and its place among other knowledge systems. While Western science rests on analytical and reductionist paradigms, traditional has a more intuitive and holistic view of reality (Mazzocchi, 2006). Traditional knowledge is transmitted orally from generation to generation (Sharma et al., 2020). Furthermore, as highlighted above, traditional knowledge depends on its context and particular local conditions (Nakashima & Roué, 2002). Traditional knowledge recognizes the robust correlation between humans and nature because of its spiritual thrust, unlike Western empirical science, which is more quantitative (Mazzocchi, 2006). The common denominator between Western and traditional Knowledge is that both rely on observation, experimentation, pattern recognition, skepticism of second and third-hand sources, creativity and intuition. The two knowledge systems are complex and dynamic (Sharma et al., 2020). Traditional knowledge develops in a communal setting where social actors play various roles in its

Figure 1. Characteristics of traditional knowledge
(Adapted from: Sharma et al., 2020).

invention, use, and gradual alteration in response to the requirements and conditions of the community through time (Muzah, 2016).

- **Analyze the key features of traditional knowledge**

Protecting traditional knowledge involves prohibiting unauthorized parties from unfairly acquiring Intellectual rights to indigenous peoples' knowledge, innovations, and customs. Zimbabwe and Uganda are members of the Intergovernmental Committee on IP and Genetic Resources, Knowledge, and Folklore (Session, 2022). Membership to such an august committee is beneficial for African countries to contribute to realizing an international IP law protecting knowledge. There are a variety of international conventions meant to protect indigenous knowledge. The World Health Organisation (WHO) (1978) Declaration of Alma Ata International conference on primary health care, Alma-Ata recognized the contributions of traditional healers in the primary health care sector. The International Treaty on Plant Genetic Resources for Food and Agriculture (ITPGRFA, 92019) recognizes farmers' rights and protects traditional plant genetic resources for food and agriculture. The UNESCO Convention on Safeguarding Intangible Cultural Heritage also covers and preserves traditional knowledge. IP protection in the West was built following the expectations of technologically advanced societies during industrialization, according to WIPO (2012). The growing awareness of indigenous communities and governments from developing countries has led to demands for epistemic justice and sovereignty for knowledge. African Regional IP Organization (ARIPO) developed the Swakopmund Protocol (2019) to protect the region's knowledge, genetic resources, and folklore. Zimbabwe and Uganda are signatories to the Swakopmund Protocol.

The Constitution of Zimbabwe (2013) supports and protects cultural norms and values that advance Zimbabweans' equality, well-being, and dignity. The Stare and its institutions and agencies of government are obliged to respect traditional institutions that embody the country's cultural values (Constitution of Zimbabwe,2013). According to the Zimbabwean Constitution, conventional protection will be realized through the Legal status of treaties, international law, and treaty ratification, as highlighted in previous study sections. Zimbabwe has other valuable legislation protecting knowledge, such as the Patents Act (Chapter 26:03) and the Copyrights and Neighbouring Rights Act as an additional IP legal instrument.

Review the Laws That Protect Traditional Knowledge in Zimbabwe and Uganda

Uganda and Zimbabwe have robust legal frameworks that protect traditional knowledge. The proceeding section briefly discuss some of these laws.

- *The National Intellectual Property Policy (NIPP)*

The implementation of copyright and other IP rights in Uganda is majorly affected by the lack of an integrated IP policy, as noted by Ssuuna (2017). However, this was resolved by a cabinet approval of the National IP Policy in May 2019 and its subsequent launch by the President of the Republic of Uganda on 23 September 2020 (Uganda Registration Services Bureau-URSB, 2020). NIIP (2019) explicitly supports the development of a framework to protect traditional knowledge and Traditional Cultural Expressions and create a digital database of traditional knowledge and Traditional Cultural Expressions to preserve cultural heritage from unauthorized exploitation in Uganda. The Zimbabwe National Intellectual Property Policy (2018-2022) recognizes the value of indigenous knowledge systems (IKS) as critical activities for protecting and leveraging the knowledge and intellectual traditions of the indigenous peoples of Zimbabwe. In defending the National Intellectual Property Policy (2018-2022), Shonge (2018) argued that the policy must balance IP creation, IP protection, and IP commercialization, focusing on creating a system for protecting traditional knowledge and preventing misappropriation and exploitation to provide a basis for decolonial combativeness among the indigenes.

- *Copyright and Neighbouring Rights Act, 2006, and the Copyright and Neighbouring Rights Regulations, 2010*

The primary law protecting against piracy is the Copyright and Neighbouring Rights Act, 2006 (C&NRA, 2006) and the Copyright and Neighbouring Rights Regulations, 2010. Kawooya, Kakungulu and Akubu (2010) highlighted that Section 5 of the (C&NRA 2006) clarifies the peculiar types of protected works in Uganda, for example, literary, scientific, and artistic works (including computer programs, illustrations, and traditional folklore and knowledge, as well as derivative works such as translations, transformations, and collections. However, the (C&NRA, 2006) does not provide a mechanism for reproducing traditional knowledge.

- *The Copyright and Neighbouring Rights Regulations 2010*

The government legislated the Copyright and Neighbouring Rights Act, 2006 (C&NRA, 2006) and the Copyright and Neighbouring Rights Regulations, 2010. The regulations are broad and cover all the key provisions of the international and regional conventions, including the Berne Convention, as revised in Stockholm in 1979. The above legislation consists of nine parts, with seven details relating directly to copyright protection, contracts about the exploitation of authors' rights, general administration of copyright, collecting societies, general provisions, and repeal of the then-existing copyright act. The regulation also provides for the different forms used in applying and granting various privileges. Zimbabwe's Copyright and Neighbouring Rights Act (2004) acknowledges and protects traditional knowledge embodied in

Table 1. Selected riddles in the Shona language

Shona riddle	Answer in English /Shona
Pota neko tisangane	The two ends of a belt will meet when it encircles something.
Rakazvirova rikazhamba	The rooster flaps its wings when it crows.
Chidembo tambatamba muswe ndakabata	Hoe (Badza)
Amai vari papa kutsvuka kutsvuka havo asi kuroya havabvire	Chillies (Mhiripiri)
Mombe yababa vangu inomwa mvura yakabatwa muswe	Cup
Jira rababa vangu risingapere kupetwa	Sky (Denga)
Imba yekwedu isina musuowo	An egg (Zai)
Imba yamai vangu inomira nedziro rimwe	Mushroom (hwohwa)
Danda radonha vanavakati kumatsotso	Sunrise

the traditions peculiar to one or more communities in Zimbabwe, including folk tales, folk poetry, and traditional riddles; and folk songs and instrumental folk music; folk dances, plays, and artistic forms of ritual; and productions of folk art, in particular drawings, paintings, sculptures, pottery, woodwork, metalwork, jewellery, baskets, and costumes. Another unique African Art of conversation relates to the everyday use of riddles. Bhebhe (2018) interpreted riddles as games of wits and intellect that require a higher level of display of philosophical wisdom. Riddles are a form of traditional African literature, commonly called oral literature, that serves numerous functions, including socialization, communication, instilling discipline among the youths, preserving history and culture, carrier of language, and an index to the identity of unique traditional cultural groups in Africa (Chauke, 2022). Shona riddles are the analogy argument that Horner and Westacott (2000) define as a resemblance between two things or situations. The following table provides selected examples of riddles in the Shona language:

Friday and Oghenerioborue (2023) contend that Riddles call for critically examining the surrounding environment, human civilization, its composition, society's operations, and how animals and other living organisms behave. Besides imparting knowledge, riddles also enhance one's memory and intellect. The observation is consistent with Gelfand (1979), who, while discussing the role of riddles among children, highlighted how they empower children with skills and knowledge to comprehend, apprehend and analyse societal values and provide yardsticks for evaluating them by educating them on their existence. Bhebhe (2018) highlighted that children should deduce deeper meanings from riddles and extrapolate such purposes from the implications society attaches to them. Proverbs, riddles, folktales, songs, stories, and myths selected examples of pedagogical methods the indigenous people of Africa used to educate their children. Riddles were also utilized to encourage children's critical thinking skills. Riddles have proven that traditional knowledge is a dynamic kind of education, entertainment, or edutainment, as some people now refer to blending education and joy (Mapara, 2009). Mapara (2009) highlighted that Zimbabweans, like any other indigenous Africans, have maintained the tradition of teaching youngsters through the classical African art of conversation, for example, proverbs, riddles, folktales, songs, legends, and myths. Such words usually prefix the Shona people's teachings to the young as *"Vakuru vedu vanoti ...or Vakuru vedu vaiti ..."* (Mapara, 2009). Translated in English to mean "Our elders used to say ..." or "Our elders say ...."

The Role of Libraries in the Process of Information/Knowledge Repackaging

Dogara, Yashim and Peter (2022) observe that "information repackaging" refers to repackaging information again or in a more attractive format to effectively meet library users' information needs. The librarian in the age of combative decoloniality should be the vanguard for social change in reaffirming indigenous peoples sovereignty over their culture including indigenous knowledge. According to the authors above, repackaging involves converting data into a convenient, easily understandable format. Information Repackaging involves packaging information into a user-friendly design and arranging all these materials appropriate for the user, thus combining two fundamental concepts inherent in reprocessing and repackaging. Paul (2022) described repackaging as selecting, analyzing, processing, and translating information to communicate a message effectively and conveniently to a defined audience. Paul (2022) noted that well -repackaged information can potentially share the intended message with the target audience.

Oyadonghan, Eke and Fyneman (2016) refer to repackaging information as repackaging information in a more appealing way to serve library patrons' information needs better is known as "information repackaging. Repackaging the information in a way that can be handy and readily understood; packaging information and arranging all these materials in a way that is appropriate to the user, thus combining two essential concepts inherent in the term repackaging, that is, reprocessing and repackaging. Information repackaging refers to promoting quick and meaningful decision-making for outcome-based effect by giving information to various groups of users in an encapsulated form based on needs analysis (Ugwuogu, 2015). Similarly, Chisita (2011) and Mole, Ekwelem and Din (2018) used information repackaging to refer to how information centres and services select materials and repackage the materials according to user specifications. Repackaging can take various forms, for example, through celebrity theatre, drama, storytelling, dance and songs.

Libraries are also vital to preserving indigenous knowledge because they play a critical role in providing answers to users' epistemological needs through information provision. Librarians should collaborate with the host communities to appropriately use, document, maintain and disseminate indigenous knowledge. They should be a resource for locating, identifying, and preserving indigenous knowledge sources in their communities (Ngozi, Ihekwoaba & Ugwuanyi, 2014). Professional ethics, local and international legal frameworks, beliefs, aspirations, and values of the communities should guide the roles of libraries in repackaging information/ knowledge. Various activities should be undertaken, such as documenting and preserving knowledge, indexing and abstracting traditional knowledge, advocating, raising awareness through education, incorporating Intellectual Property into meta-literacy programs, and forging strategic partnerships with other memory institutions involved in preserving indigenous knowledge. Maundu (1995) suggests that before any collection of indigenous knowledge can take place, there is a need to formulate a plan the following: the purposes, aims, and goals; profile the community; develop data-gathering strategies; identify community leaders and key informants, including the community leaders; communicate the program to the community; and formulate the action plan, and mobilize the necessary resources. Libraries and related institutions should partner with the government, communities, lawyers, and development partners to map a feasible strategy for preserving indigenous knowledge. Advice from the stakeholders mentioned above is critical because government policies and laws and the interests of the communities should inform a plan to protect indigenous knowledge. Libraries as citadels of combative decoloniality ought to cooperate and work closely with indigenous knowledge practitioners who are custodians of unpublished records and within the purview of Library and Information Science of unwritten information to close the gap between the practice of information management by non-professionals who had concentrated mainly on unpublished information resources (Sarah, 2015). Shiri, Howard and Farnell (2022) highlighted the importance of embarking on Indigenous digital projects that have become so popular among Indigenous communities worldwide. Additionally, continuously repurposing and reselling technology solutions and disseminating out-of-context solutions that increase reliance on Global North resources allow them to preserve their asymmetrical power relations (Abede et al., 2021). Udensi (2010) discussed the forms of information repackaging and highlighted the following points, which include, but are not limited to reformatting and synthesizing basic information, combining expertise or consulting on a subject with access to relevant information sources, providing training or assistance to a user in accessing an information product, drama, song, dance, storytelling, audiovisual materials, translation, oral transmission, group discussions, poetry, and technological tools including digital storytelling. However, the librarian should be conversant with the laws affecting *sui generis* works (collectively owned) of collective, such as indigenous knowledge).

CONCLUSION AND RECOMMENDATIONS

African countries are central to cultural and social transformation as traditional knowledge intersects with research and teaching in educational settings. The weak laws that protect traditional Knowledge in Zimbabwe and Uganda should be revisited and strengthened through further consultation with key stakeholders. The roles of libraries in repackaging conventional knowledge should be explicitly clarified. Governments in Uganda and Zimbabwe must emphasize preserving and conserving ancestral through memory institutions, including the communities, libraries, archives, galleries, and museums through praxis-oriented approaches that resonate with the aspirations of indigenous communities as a collective. Additionally, librarians should help promote conversations concerning converting indigenous knowledge into tangible through technology and applying management principles. There is a need for Africa, Uganda, and Zimbabwe to prioritize inter-disciplinary and inter-institutional research in traditional as it is part of the production. There is a need for African scholars to research indigenous Knowledge in Africa. This chapter should not be misinterpreted as a blind romanticization of the African past. The article serves as an escallier to the brighter world of an equipoised knowledge system. The chapter builds on the strength of classical African knowledge systems and methods to contribute towards decoloniality as espoused by (Ndlovu-Gatsheni, 2015). Finally, the researchers make the following recommendations:

- Governments and indigenous groups should continue advocating for an international legal framework that protects traditional or indigenous knowledge and such an instrument should consider technological shifts in generation and transmission. A preservation and conservation law should be comprehensive enough to cover the administrative costs of legislating and maintaining the law and take cognizance of the interests of diverse groups;
- Advocating for libraries as critical role-players in preserving traditional knowledge is necessary;
- Higher Educations institutions, including libraries, should invest more resources towards research on traditional knowledge concerning its inclusion into the curriculum at all levels, repackaging, IP rights and preservation;
- Libraries should advocate to be key role-players in traditional knowledge.

- Libraries should adapt combative decoloniality and be on the forefront in raising awareness of the value of for indigenous knowledge sovereignty;
- Indigenous knowledge has collective ownership, and ensuring adequate protection under current copyright regimes that have set rigorous registration standards requiring proof of protected ownership is challenging; and
- Librarians provide for people's epistemological needs and should seize the opportunity to play a critical role in protecting traditional knowledge to reposition themselves as indispensable professionals in an era of epistemic injustice and as a result they should assume the role of decolonial combatants whereby they energise and weaponise people towards total liberation and sovereignty.

REFERENCES

Abebe, R., Aruleba, K., Birhane, A., Kingsley, S., Obaido, G., Remy, S. L., & Sadagopan, S. (2021, March). Narratives and counternarratives on data sharing in Africa. In *Proceedings of the 2021 ACM conference on fairness, accountability, and transparency* (pp. 329-341). ACM. 10.1145/3442188.3445897

Afful-Arthur, P., Kwafoa, P. N. Y., Ampah-Johnston, M., & Mensah, V. (2022). Managing and accessing Indigenous for national development: The role of academic libraries in Ghana. *Information Development*, *38*(4), 535–548. doi:10.1177/02666669211009916

African Regional Intellectual Property Organization. (2019). *Swakopmund Protocol on the Protection of Traditional & Expressions of Folklore*. ARIPO. https://www.aripo.org/wp-content/uploads/2019/06/Swakopmund-Protocol-on-the-Protection-of-Traditional knowledge -and-Expressions-of-Folklore-2019.pdf Accessed 12 March 2023.

Andrews, D. H., & Goodson, L. A. (1980). A comparative analysis of models of instructional design. *Journal of instructional development, 3*(4), 2-16.

Arya, R. (2021). Cultural appropriation: What it is and why it matters? *Sociology Compass*, *15*(10), e12923. doi:10.1111oc4.12923

Asante, M. K. (1991a). The Afrocentric idea in education. *The Journal of Negro Education*, *60*(2), 170–180. doi:10.2307/2295608

Asante, M. K. (2005b). Afronography. Encyclopedia of black studies, 76-77.

Asante, M. K. (2007c). An Afrocentric Manifesto: Toward an African Renaissance. *Polity*.

Asante, M.K. (2013d). *The African American people: A global history*. Routledge. doi:10.4324/9780203145807

Bhebhe, S. (2018). Interrogating myths surrounding sex education in Zimbabwean schools: Lessons to be learned from Ndebele traditional literature/oral traditions. *Oral History Journal of South Africa, 6*(1), 18. doi:10.25159/2309-5792/3322

Birch, T. (2020). 'The invisible fire': Indigenous sovereignty, history and responsibility. In *Sovereign Subjects* (pp. 105–117). Routledge. doi:10.4324/9781003117353-11

Carroll, S. R., Garba, I., Plevel, R., Small-Rodriguez, D., Hiratsuka, V. Y., Hudson, M., & Garrison, N. A. (2022). Using indigenous standards to implement the CARE principles: Setting expectations through tribal research codes. *Frontiers in Genetics*, *13*, 823309. doi:10.3389/fgene.2022.823309 PMID:35386282

Chauke, O. R. (2022). ORATURE IN AN AFRICAN CONTEXT: VATSONGA AS A CASE IN POINT. *Journal of Positive Psychology and Well-being*, 67-74.

Chilisa, B. (2012). *Indigenous research methodologies*. Sage.

Chisita, C. T. (2011). Role of libraries in promoting the dissemination and documentation of indigenous agricultural information: Case study of Zimbabwe. *IFLA WLIC. San Juan, Puerto Rico*, 10-11. In *Paper Of World Library And Information Congress: 77th IFLA General Conference And Assembly*. IFLA. https://www.ifla.org/past-wlic/2011/78-chisita-en.pdf Accessed 23 February 2023.

Chisita, C. T., Rusero, A. M., & Shoko, M. (2016). 18 Leveraging Memory Institutions to Preserve Indigenous Knowledge in the Knowledge Age. Indigenous Notions of Ownership and Libraries. *Archives and Museums*, *166*, 273.

Copyright and Neighbouring Rights Act Chapter 26:05 (2004) Available https://media.zimlii.org/files/legislation/akn-zw-act-2000-11-eng-2004-09-10.pdf Accessed 13 July 2023

Copyrights and Neighbouring Rights Act, 2018. Act No. 4. https://wipolex-res.wipo.int/edocs/lexdocs/laws/en/sz/sz017en.pdf

Correa, C. M. (2001). Traditional and intellectual property. Geneva: The Quaker United Nations Office (QUNO), 17.

Cossa, J. A. (2009). African Renaissance and globalization: A conceptual analysis. *Ufahamu. Journal of African Studies*, *36*(1).

Cuaton, G. P., & Su, Y. (2020). Local-indigenous knowledge on disaster risk reduction: Insights from the Mamanwa indigenous peoples in Basey, Samar after Typhoon Haiyan in the Philippines. *International Journal of Disaster Risk Reduction*, *48*, 101596. doi:10.1016/j.ijdrr.2020.101596

Dogara, P. D., Yashim, A. B., & Peter, Y. L. (2022). Enhancing Information Service Delivery through Effective Information Repackaging in Colleges of Education Libraries. *Niger Delta Journal of Library and Information Science, 3*(1).

Fredriksson, M. (2022). Balancing community rights and national interests in international protection of knowledge: A study of India's Traditional Digital Library. *Third World Quarterly*, *43*(2), 352–370. doi:10.1080/01436597.2021.2019009

Friday, A., & Oghenerioborue, U. P. (2023). Cultural Riddles and Performance in Modern African Societies. *Randwick International of Social Science Journal*, *4*(1), 118–131. doi:10.47175/rissj.v4i1.633

Gelfand, M. (1979). *Growing up in Shona society: from birth to marriage*. Mambo Publishers.

Gladman Chibememe, G, Dhliwayo, M, Gandiwa, E, Mtisi, S, Muboko, N, & Kupika, O.L (2014). *Review of National Laws & policies that support or undermine Indigenous peoples and Local Communities*. Natural Justice. naturaljustice.org/wp-content/uploads/2015/09/Zimbabwe-Legal-Review.pdf .

Goldman, M.J., Turner, M.D. & Daly, M. (2018). A critical political ecology of human dimensions of climate change: Epistemology, ontology, and ethics. *Wiley Interdisciplinary Reviews: Climate Change, 9*(4), p.e526.

Haumba, E. N., & Kaddu, S. (2017). Documenting and disseminating agricultural indigenous for sustainable food security in Uganda. *University of Dar es Salaam. Library Journal, 12*(1), 66–86.

Horsthemke, K. (2017). Indigenous (African) Systems, Science, and Technology. In A. Afolayan & T. Falola (Eds.), *The Palgrave Handbook of African Philosophy.*, doi:10.1057/978-1-137-59291-0_38

Hostettmann, K., Marston, A., Ndjoko, K., & Wolfender, J. L. (2000). The potential of African plants as a source of drugs. *Current Organic Chemistry, 4*(10), 973–1010. doi:10.2174/1385272003375923

Intellectual Property Laws Amendment Act, No. 28. https://www.gov.za/sites/default/files/gcis_document/201409/37148gon996act28-2013.pdf

Isife, E.E. (2023). African environmental ethics and the challenge of decolonizing science and technology for Africa's growth and development. *AKU: An African Journal of Contemporary Research, 4*(1).

Jasmine, B., Singh, Y., Onial, M., & Mathur, V. B. (2016). Traditional systems in India for biodiversity conservation. *Indian Journal of Knowledge, 15*(2), 304–312.

Jiri, O., Mafongoya, P. L., & Chivenge, P. (2015). Indigenous knowledge systems, seasonal 'quality and climate change adaptation in Zimbabwe. *Climate Research, 66*(2), 103–111. doi:10.3354/cr01334

Kaddu, S., & Chisita, C. (2009). *The Challenges of Repackaging Traditional in the Context of Intellectual Property Rights: Case of Zimbabwe and Uganda.* Uganda Christian University.

Kamau, E. C., & Winter, G. (2009). Protecting TK amid disseminated Knowledge–A new task for ABS regimes? A Kenyan legal view. In Genetic Resources, Traditional Knowledge and the Law (pp. 177-204). Routledge.

Kansiime, M., Mulema, J., Karanja, D., Romney, D., & Day, R. (2016). *Crop pests and disease management in Uganda: Status and investment needs. Final report.* CAB International, Wallingford, UK.

Kasere, S. (2010). *CAMPFIRE: Zimbabwe's Tradition of Caring.* UN System. https://www.unsystem.org/ngls/documents/publications.en/voices.africa/number6/vfa6.08.htm

Kawooya, D., Kakungulu, R., & Akubu, J. (2010). Uganda. *Access to Knowledge in Africa: The role of copyright*, 281-316.

Kazembe, T., & Mashoko, D. (2008). Should traditional medicine practised in Chivi, Zimbabwe, be included in school curricula? *Zimbabwe Journal of Educational Research, 20*(1), 49–69.

Lalonde, D. (2021). Does cultural appropriation cause harm? *Politics, Groups & Identities, 9*(2), 329–346. doi:10.1080/21565503.2019.1674160

Latulippe, N., & Klenk, N. (2020). Making Room and moving over: Co-production, Indigenous Sovereignty and the Politics of global environmental change decision-making. *Current Opinion in Environmental Sustainability, 42*, 7–14. doi:10.1016/j.cosust.2019.10.010

Magni, G. (2017). Indigenous and Implications for the sustainable development agenda. *European Journal of Education*, *52*(4), 437–447. doi:10.1111/ejed.12238

Mandisvika, G., Chirisa, I., & Bandauko, E. (2015). Post-harvest issues: Rethinking technology for value-addition in food security and food sovereignty in Zimbabwe. *Advances In Food Technology and Nutrifional Sciences–Open Journal*, *1*(1), S29–S37. doi:10.17140/AFTNSOJ-SE-1-105

Mapara, J. (2009). Indigenous systems in Zimbabwe: Juxtaposing postcolonial theory. *The Journal of Pan African Studies*, *3*(1), 139–156.

Maroyi, A. (2018). *Ethnomedicinal uses of exotic plant species in south-central Zimbabwe*. Research Gate. https://www.researchgate.net/publication/236636386_Traditional_use_of_medicinal_plants_in_south-central_Zimbabwe_Review_and_perspectives

Martiniello, G. (2015). Food sovereignty as praxis: Rethinking the food question in Uganda. *Third World Quarterly*, *36*(3), 508–525. doi:10.1080/01436597.2015.1029233

Marx, K. (1986). *Karl Marx: The Essential Writings*. Westview Press.

Maundu, P. (1995). Methodology for collecting and sharing indigenous knowledge WLEDGE: A case study. *Indigenous and Development Monitor*, *3*(2), 3–5.

Mazzocchi, F. (2006). Western science and Knowledge: Despite their variations, different forms can learn from each other. *EMBO Reports*, *7*(5), 463–466. doi:10.1038j.embor.7400693 PMID:16670675

Mazzocchi, F. (2006). Western science and Knowledge: Despite their variations, different forms can learn from each other. *EMBO Reports*, *7*(5), 463–466. doi:10.1038j.embor.7400693 PMID:16670675

Mbeki, T. (1998). *Africa, the time has come*. Tafelberg.

Mbeki, T. (2005). Goals of higher education in Africa. *USA/Africa Dialogue, 588.*

Moichela, K. Z. 2017. *Integration of indigenous systems in the curriculum for basic education: possible experiences of Canada* [Doctoral dissertation, University of South Africa]. https://core.ac.uk/download/pdf/162048463.pdf

Mposhi, A., Manyeruke, C., & Hamauswa, S. (2013). The importance of patenting traditional medicines in Africa: The case of Zimbabwe. *International Journal of Humanities and Social Science*, *3*(2), 236–246.

Mugabe, J., Kameri-Mbote, P., & Mutta, D. (2001). *Knowledge, genetic resources, and intellectual property protection: towards a new international regime*. International Environmental Law Research Centre. https://www.ielrc.org/content/w0105.pdf.

Mujere, N., Chanza, N., Muromo, T., Guurwa, R., Kutseza, N., & Mutiringindi, E. (2023). Indigenous Ways of Predicting Agricultural Droughts in Zimbabwe. In *Socio-Ecological Systems and Decoloniality: Convergence of Indigenous and Western* (pp. 51–72). Springer International Publishing.

Muzah, G. (2016). *Legal protection of Knowledge*. Lessons from Southern Africa. In WIPO-WTO COLLOQUIUM PAPERS.

Nakashima, D., & Roué, M. (2002). Indigenous KNOWLEDGE, peoples, and sustainable practice. Encyclopedia of global environmental change, 5, 314-324.

Ndlovu-Gatsheni, S. J. (2015). Decoloniality as the future of Africa. *History Compass, 13*(10), 485–496. doi:10.1111/hic3.12264

Ngozi, O. R., Ihekwoaba, E. C., & Ugwuanyi, F. C. (2014). Strategies for Enhancing Information Access to Traditional Medical Practitioners to Aid Health Care Delivery in Nigeria. *Library Philosophy and Practice*, 0_1.

Ochieng, A., Koh, N. S., & Koot, S. (2023). Compatible with Conviviality? Exploring African Ecotourism and Sport Hunting for Transformative Conservation. *Conservation & Society, 21*(1), 38–47. doi:10.4103/cs.cs_42_21

Onayade, O.A., Onayade, O.A. and Sowofora, A.(1996). Wound Healing with Plants: The African perspective in IOCD Chemistry. *Biology and Pharmacologic properties of African medicinal plants.*

Oyadonghan, J. C., Eke, F. M., & Fyneman, B. (2016). Information repackaging and its application in academic libraries. *International Journal of Computer Science and Information Technology Research, 4*(2), 217–222.

p'Bitek, O. (1964). Fr. Tempels' Bantu Philosophy. *Transition*, (13), 15–17. doi:10.2307/2934418

Paul, C. (2022). MANAGEMENT PRACTICES IN AGRIBUSINESS FIRMS. *European Journal of Information and Management, 1*(1), 11–20.

Pillay, N. (2013). Free, prior and informed consent of indigenous peoples. Foreword to the Manual for National Human Rights Institutions, 1-2.

Rajeswari, R., Umadevi, M., Rahale, C. S., Pushpa, R., Selvavenkadesh, S., Kumar, K. S., & Bhowmik, D. (2012). Aloe vera: The miracle plant and its medicinal and traditional uses in India. *Journal of Pharmacognosy and Phytochemistry, 1*(4), 118–124.

Ranjan, P., & Singh, B. K. (2020). Conservation of Traditional Knowledge in India and Need of Knowledge Networks. In *First International Conference on Bridging Traditional Knowledge to Modern Science–2020.* Research Gate.

Ray, S. (2023). Weaving the links: Traditional Knowledge into modern science. *Futures, 145*, 103081. doi:10.1016/j.futures.2022.103081

Robinson, D. (2010). *Confronting biopiracy: challenges, cases, and international debates.* Routledge. doi:10.4324/9781849774710

Ruhinirwa, F. W., Katabulawo, P., Atukwase, R. B., Otiti, R., & Musingo, D. (2019). *Using indigenoUs knowledge to connect FaMilies with natUre For conservation in Uganda.* IZE JOURNAL.

Sarah, E. A. (2015). The Role of Libraries in Preserving indigenous knowledge in primary healthcare in Nigeria. *International Journal of digital library services, 5*(2), 43-54.

Seroto, J. (2011). Indigenous education during the pre-colonial period in southern Africa. *Indilinga African Journal of Indigenous Systems, 10*(1), 77–88.

Session, F. T. (2022). Intergovernmental Committee on Intellectual Property and Genetic Resources. *Traditional Knowledge and Folklore*. ABS. https://abs.igc.by/wp-content/uploads/2022/07/Glossary-of-key-terms-wipo_grtkf_ic_43_inf_7.pdf

Shabalala, D. B. (2017). Intellectual Property, Knowledge, and Traditional Cultural Expressions in Native American Tribal Codes. *Akron Law Review, 51*, 1125.

Sharma, I. P., Kanta, C., Dwivedi, T., & Rani, R. (2020). Indigenous agricultural practices: A supreme key to maintaining biodiversity. *Microbiological Advancements for Higher Altitude Agro-Ecosystems & Sustainability*, 91-112.

Sharma, P., Kharkwal, A. C., Kharkwal, H., Abdin, M. Z., & Varma, A. (2014). A review on pharmacological properties of Aloe vera. *International Journal of Pharmaceutical Sciences Review and Research, 29*(2), 31–37.

Shiri, A., Howard, D., & Farnel, S. (2022). Indigenous digital storytelling: Digital interfaces supporting cultural heritage preservation and access. *The International Information & Library Review, 54*(2), 93–114. doi:10.1080/10572317.2021.1946748

Shonge, R. (2018). An Analysis of the Zimbabwe National Intellectual Property Policy and Implementation Strategy (2018-2022). *African Journal of Intellectual Property, 3*(1), 45–60.

Sindiga, I., Nyaigotti-Chacha, C., & Kanunah, M. P. (Eds.). (1995). *Traditional medicine in Africa*. East African Publishers.

Singh, H. B., Yaipharembi, N., Huidrom, E., & Devi, C. A. (2023). Knowledge, Beliefs, and Practices Associated with Ethnic People of Manipur, North East India in Conservation of Biodiversity. In *Traditional Ecological of Resource Management in Asia* (pp. 61–75). Springer International Publishing.

Tabuti, J. R. S. (2004). *Locally used plants in Bulamogi County, Uganda: Diversity and modes of utilization. Medicinal, edible, fodder, and firewood species*. Semantic Scholar.

Tarugarira, G. (2017). Dimensions of totemic history and its related accessories among the Gumbo-Madyirapazhe clan of Gutu, Zimbabwe. *DANDE Journal of Social Sciences and Communication, 2*(1).

Taylor, C. (1992). Modernity and the rise of the public sphere. The Tanner Lectures on Human Values. *Delivered at Stanford University, 25*(February), 1992.

The Constitution of Zimbabwe. Amendment (N0.20) 2013.

The Copyright and Neighbouring Rights Act, 2006. https://www.aripo.org/wp-content/uploads/2018/12/Uganda-Copyright-Act.pdf

Torres, F. L., & Medina, C. L. (2021). Cuentos Combativos: Decolonialities in Puerto Rican Books About María. *Journal of Literacy Research, 53*(2), 242–264.

Udensi, J. (2010). Information repackaging-a necessity in Nigerian Libraries. Modern Library and information science for information professionals in Africa. Ibadan. Textlinks Publishers.

Ugwuogu, U. O. (2015). Expectations and challenges of information repackaging in Nigerian Academic Libraries. *International Journal of Learning and Development, 5*(2), 56–64.

UNESCO. I. (2020). *Basic texts of the 2003 Convention for the Safeguarding of the intangible cultural heritage*. UNESCO. https://ich.unesco.org/doc/src/2003_Convention_Basic_Texts-_2022_version-EN_.pdf Accessed 11 March 2023.

United Nations. (2008). United Nations Declaration on the Rights of Indigenous Peoples. UN. https://www.un.org/esa/socdev/unpfii/documents/DRIPS_en.pdf Accessed 18 February 2023.

Van Wyk, B., & Higgs, P. (2004). Towards an African philosophy of higher education: Perspectives on higher education. *South African Journal of Higher Education, 18*(3), 196–210.

Waziri, A. F., & Aliero, B. L. (2004). Soil physicochemical properties under two different species of range land grasses at Gangam rangeland, Shagari local government area, Sokoto State. [SAN]. *Bulletin of Science Association of Nigeria, 26*, 274–281.

WHO. (1978). *Declaration of Alma Ata. International conference on primary health care, Alma-Ata, USSR, 6-12 September 1978*. Geneva: WHO. https://cdn.who.int/media/docs/default-source/documents/almaata-declaration-en.pdf?sfvrsn=7b3c2167_2 Accessed 12 March, 2023.

Whyte, K. (2017). What do indigenous knowledges do for indigenous peoples? M. Nelson and D. Shilling (eds) Keepers of the Green World: Traditional Ecological Knowledge and Sustainability. Cambridge University Press.

WIPO. (2017). *Protect and Promote Your Culture: A practical guide to intellectual property for Indigenous Peoples and local communities*. World Intellectual Property. https://www.wipo.int/edocs/pubdocs/en/wipo_pub_1048.pdf

WIPO. (2018). *Glossary: Key Terms Related to Genetic Resources, Knowledge, and Traditional Cultural Expressions*. WHO. https://www.wipo.int/meetings/en/doc_details.jsp?doc_id=410022,

Wittman, H., Desmarais, A., & Wiebe, N. (2010). The origins and potential of food sovereignty. *Food sovereignty: Reconnecting food, nature and community*, 1-14.

World Intellectual Property Organisation (WIPO). (2012). Traditional and Intellectual Property – Background Brief. WHO. https://www.wipo.int/pressroom/en/briefs/traditional_ip.html

World Intellectual Property Organization. (2003). *Intellectual property and traditional cultural expressions/folklore* (Vol. 913). WIPO.

Wynberg, R. (2023). Biopiracy: Crying wolf or a lever for equity and conservation? *Research Policy, 52*(2), 104674. doi:10.1016/j.respol.2022.104674

Yanou, M. P., Ros-Tonen, M., Reed, J., & Sunderland, T. (2023). Local and practices among Tonga people in Zambia and Zimbabwe: A review. *Environmental Science & Policy, 142*, 68–78. doi:10.1016/j.envsci.2023.02.002

Young, J. O. (2005). Profound offence and cultural appropriation. *The Journal of Aesthetics and Art Criticism, 63*(2), 135–146. doi:10.1111/j.0021-8529.2005.00190.x

Young, J. O. (2010). *Cultural appropriation and the arts*. John Wiley & Sons.

Ziff, B. H., & Rao, P. V. (Eds.). (1997). *Borrowed power: Essays on cultural appropriation*. Rutgers University Press.

Zimu-Biyela, A. A. N. (2021). What is the role of libraries in disseminating about South African intellectual property laws in rural communities? *South African Journal of Library and Information Science*, *87*(2), 21–29. doi:10.7553/87-2-1956

KEY TERMS AND DEFINITIONS

Afrocentricity: Aa conceptual framework that argues that African culture and assumptions of human behaviour are pivotal to any scrutiny involving the study of African experiences.

Indigenous Knowledge: This refers to a corpus of dissimilar knowledge and practices of societies accumulated through a serial interface with their natural milieu.

Knowledge: The familiarity, awareness, or understanding of someone, something, or phenomena, such as facts, information, descriptions, or skills, derived from experience or education.

Repackaging Indigenous Knowledge Refers: The process of repackaging IK to become more understandable, readable, acceptable, and usable, including its adaptation to the needs and characteristics of the individual or user group and matching it with the information provided, thereby facilitating the diffusion of knowledge.

Traditional Knowledge: This constitutes a community's knowledge, know-how, skills, and traditions created, maintained, and passed down from generation to generation.

Chapter 12
African Indigenous Knowledge on the Cloud:
The Role of Libraries, Archives, and Museums

Madireng Monyela
University of Limpopo, South Africa

ABSTRACT

Indigenous knowledge is knowledge that people have of their local environment acquired through the accumulation of experiences, informal experiments, and observation rooted in particular places and practised as culture. This kind of knowledge is not documented as it is tacit and transferred though oral tradition. Being largely uncodified, it is constantly changing and forgotten as people adapt to changing circumstances due to beliefs, intercultural settings, and colonisation. Therefore, it faces a danger of fading. Libraries, archives, and museums (LAM) should be proactive in their approach and should ensure that indigenous knowledge, although based on orality and oral traditions, should be managed and preserved just like other documentary materials that are grounded in western codified knowledge schemes and create sustainable strategies to preserve it for future use.

INTRODUCTION

Indigenous knowledge (IK) is described as knowledge that ordinary people have of their local environment acquired through the accumulation of experiences, informal experiments and observations, rooted in particular places and practised as culture (Morris, 2010; Rajasekaran, 1993; Masango, 2010). This knowledge is informal and it is not codified and is transmitted orally in an informal manner, outside the ritual context, and much of it is experiential knowledge based on personal experiences. Being largely uncodified it is constantly forgotten and changing, as people adapt to changing circumstances (Morris, 2010). Therefore, LAM as the custodians of knowledge should preserve and disseminate this IK on the cloud using available technologies such as blogs, social networking websites, e-commerce, wikis, social

DOI: 10.4018/978-1-6684-7024-4.ch012

Copyright © 2023, IGI Global. Copying or distributing in print or electronic forms without written permission of IGI Global is prohibited.

cataloguing, streaming videos and e-libraries to name but a few for future use. According to Fernandez (1994) indigenous knowledge is greatly affected by gender stratification as viewed by the society. Women have much more knowledge of soil classification for cultivation, hut construction and pottery, while men have more knowledge on livestock management. According to Maluleka (2017) Africans has indigenous institutions to deal with social, spiritual, education, political, legal, and psychological and health problems. Legal institutions dealt with disputes that arose in any family or society. Ayittey (2006) indicated three branches within the legal institutions as natural, contractual, statutory, and customary laws. Natural law constitutes the body of rules people of a particular society must follow in order to live and work in peace. First, they must avoid physical harm or damage to another's work or property such as land, houses, livestock and other belongings. Second, they must honour their obligations or contracts with others, and, third, they should compensate those on whom they inflict harm and whose property they damage. Contractual law on the other hand deals with agreements, informal or formal, mostly in the presence of a witness or none. For example, the parent may owe another parent and agree that they may marry their daughter as a form of payment. Statutory laws are instigated by the kings and chiefs and enforced by the guards of the kings. Those guards typically have a monopoly over the use of force or the weapons required for redressing injustices. Customary laws are not commands or legislated rules. They are conventions and enforceable rules that have emerged and are respected spontaneously, without formal agreement, among people as they go about their daily business and try to solve the problems that occasionally arise in it without upsetting the patterns (Ayittey, 2006).

One common customary law that still exists among tribes and ethnic groups is customary marriage. Most customary marriages go through a number of stages, and this varies from community to community. In all of them, there must be the introduction stage or declaration of intention to marry the bride by the intending groom where specific family members like aunts and uncles are sent to the prospective bride's home. After this generally, a bride price is paid in cows and provision of gifts and drinks are made, as soon as confirmation has been done. Then, the ceremonial and public celebration is done they then slaughter a cow and goat at the bride's home and make a traditional beer and perform rituals to join the two families. This involves the invitation of friends, extended families and people from the community and neighbouring villages to eat, drink and to wish luck to the newly married couple. Each stage in the customary marriage involves the presentation of drinks, and gift items to the bride's and groom's people. However in other traditions the gifts are presented only to the bride's family. A customary marriage celebration terminates here and goes no further. It is potentially polygamous and the man is allowed to marry as many wives as he desires by custom. However the first wife must be consulted before polygamy takes place. Here, the rights, liabilities and obligations of the spouses are determined by customary law with the attendant submission of the female.

In the African traditional setting the supremacy of the male is not negotiable. He is therefore the head of his household, and deals with it as he deems fit. Any offspring from the marriage primarily belongs to the man who mainly takes decisions concerning the upbringing of the children. The marriage is not registered in any form and is potentially polygamous with protection, rights and obligations provided for the parties only by customary law which is the legal regime under which it is celebrated (Anyogu & Ibekwe, 2020; Moore, 2015). Political institutions were governed by kingdoms existed as independent entities which resulted from conquests or voluntary submissions (Ayittey, 1991). The organizational structure and objective of indigenous political systems were generally based upon kinship, ancestry, and survival in much the same way as social organizations were. Each ethnic group devised its own system of government, although there was much cross-ethnic pollination. There were no written constitutions

African Indigenous Knowledge on the Cloud

and the procedures for government were established by custom and tradition. The potential for diversity was extant in indigenous political systems, but there were many commonalities (Ayittey, 2006). Recognition of the principles found expression in the constitution of the council, variously called Imbizo, or Pitso or Kgotla, which governs the affairs of the tribe. The council (of elders) was so completely democratic in the indigenous political institution that all members of the ethnic group could participate in its deliberations. Chief and subject, warriors and traditional healers all took part and endeavoured to influence the decisions (Ayittey, 2006).

Education institutions well-known ones are initiation schools for boys and girls. These initiations differs from tribe to tribe. However, they are organised more as single-sex schools boys and girl's initiation happened separately among many if not all African tribes. Among the Basotho tribe for instance, *lebollo* is regarded as a systematic form of knowledge production and transfer, which was animated/instituted to ensure that the sustainability of nations was not left to chance. This situation probably served to entrench the distinctive caricatures of masculine and feminine virtues that are indispensable to cherished social goals, but was rather a well-orchestrated symphony of principles (Maharasoa & Maharaswa, 2004). Men initiation span a minimum period of six months on a mountain away from the disturbances of village life for maximum concentration and increased chances of attaining training objectives. During this period, the initiates are forbidden to visit their homes, their only contact with family is through visits paid to the school by men who have themselves undergone initiation. The prime purpose of initiation *lebollo* as per Basotho tradition was to prepare boys and girls for adulthood including marriage, counselling, sexuality education, herbology, as well as law and democracy. In that way it is believed that the graduates will be effective role players in the sustainable and continued existence of their societies. *Lebollo* was regarded the highest band of the education of youngsters; it was actually the pinnacle of the socialisation process. It thus became a high-profile endeavour that attracted the participation of most citizens within a given society as a form of educating and instilling knowledge and societal principles in young girls and boys (Maharasoa & Maharaswa, 2004). Spiritual institutions on the other hand, includes ancestral worship, rain making etc. For example the different tribes in Zimbabwe claims that spirit mediums (mhondoro/svikiro/homwe) used to conduct rain making prayers (mukwerera/mukweverera/mutoro/ makoto!bira). The mhondoro conveys information and requests to God (Mwari/ Musikavanhu/Marure) via the ancestors (Gelfand, 1984).Other tribes in Africa also has their ways of practising rain making. Health institutions involved traditional healing and use of herbs.

Traditional healing is referred to as the sum total of all knowledge and practices, whether explicable or not, used in diagnosing, preventing or eliminating a physical, mental or social imbalance and which rely exclusively on past experience and observation handed down from generation to generation, verbally or in writing and health practices, approaches, knowledge, and beliefs incorporating plant, animal and mineral based medicines, spiritual therapies, manual techniques and exercise, applied singular or in combination, to treat, diagnose and prevent illnesses or maintain well-being (WHO, 1976). Therefore to preserve this knowledge, Libraries, Archives and Museums (LAM) should be proactive in their approach and should ensure that indigenous knowledge, although based on orality and oral traditions, should be managed and preserved just like other documentary materials that are grounded in western codified knowledge schemes (Ngulube, 2002).These includes traditional artefacts.The museums should register every artefact as fully as possible. For instance, Motsamai (2019) opined that Museum collections should be documented according to accepted professional standards. Such documentation should include a full identification and description of each item, its associations, provenance, condition, treatment and present location. Such data should be kept on the cloud using Resource Description Framework (RDF) and be supported by retrieval systems providing access to the information by the museum. Furthermore, the summary of the artefact should indicate its purpose, use and benefits.

Problem Statement

African countries that were colonised mainly because of apartheid laws and the missionaries such as Congregational, Methodist, Anglican, Lutheran and Catholic were aggressively opposed to traditional African knowledge, beliefs and practices, such as ancestral worship, traditional healing, initiation etcetera because, according to them, these were barbaric, inferior, primitive, heathen and simply not worthy of preserving and based on superstitions (Plockey, 2015). Even with the proliferation of African Independent, churches remained the same (Maluleka, 2017). Moreover, in recent years, the initiation practice has been characterized by an increasing number of fatalities and criminal activities among the initiates in other parts of Africa. Something that was rare in the past (Myemana, 2004; Meissner and Buso, 2007) that leads to slow "death" of African indigenous knowledge. Consequently, churches and other leaders are calling for the practice to be abolished (Ntombana, 2011). Moreover, the actual activities that happens during the initiation are culturally remain the preserve of those who have graduated and are not shared by any form as it is regarded as taboo (Maharasoa & Maharaswa, 2004).

Maluleka (2017) opined that IK is in the danger of being forgotten due to factors, such as the lack of interest from younger generations, low life expectancy where people die before transferring it to the next generation and not being documented. Due to the fact that IK is not documented and or codified it is constantly changing and lost within the society, for instance in Sepedi culture found among South African habitants, customary marriage is practised differently and no one is able to identify the correct way of practising it. For example when the people from the intended groom are sent to the prospective bride to ask for the bride there are discrepancies and how they present themselves among one community that should have practise the same principle some hold a calabash, some a cup, some a broom. According to traditional practices, those gifts mean something and are connecting the ancestors. An anecdotal study revealed that whatever is presented on the day of asking for the bride, the bride must take it with to the groom's house on the day of the wedding. Failure to do that there could be some consequences. There are some traditional principles again when coming to which part of the cow should the bride eat on the day on the wedding.

People has been practising it differently and faced some consequences. This is due to the fact that IK, by its very nature, is generally known to have been passed on from generation to generation through oral tradition. Considering the fact that climate change causes water and food insecurity, it shows that Africans themselves have failed to pay enough attention to understand how their ancestors managed to counter the effects of climate change using their own rain making science. Therefore, there is a need for LAM to collect, document and preserve knowledge on how indigenous people practised their rituals for rain making and keeping other indigenous institutions a success and beneficial to them for cultural, educational and future utility purposes. Moreover, the National Recordal System (NRS) initiative was first raised in the Indigenous Knowledge Systems (IKS) Policy where it is stated that, in order to secure the rights to knowledge, a recordal system needs to be put in place where communities, guilds and other IK holders can record their knowledge holdings in order to assist their interest in future economic benefits and social good, based on IK. The LAM should assist the indigenous people thereof (Khalala, Botha, & Makitla, 2016). The World Bank also added to the warning that IK faces extinction unless it is properly documented, analysed and disseminated, the knowledge could be lost forever (Sithole, 2007). The chapter was guided by the following objectives:

- To explore the role of LAM on preserving African indigenous knowledge
- To recommend sustainable strategies to collect African indigenous knowledge
- To determine strategies to document and catalogue African indigenous knowledge
- To identify methods to digitize African indigenous knowledge
- To establish the intellectual property rights of indigenous people

Methodology

This chapter exploited existing literature from published research, journals, conference proceedings, databases, theses, books and internet with the aim of understanding sustainable methods of preserving indigenous knowledge in LAM among others. Various databases such as Emerald, Ebscohost, Science direct, Google scholar, ProQuest and SABINET were used. The choice of the databases were influenced by their content and coverage on IK research. The keywords used to search information were indigenous knowledge, indigenous knowledge systems, digitization of indigenous knowledge, and preservation of indigenous knowledge, catalogues and documentation of indigenous knowledge.

The search strategies used were Boolean to include binary words, proximity search such as truncation and wild card to include words with the same stem in one search, faceted search to refine the documents by format and or information source, however the publication date were not refined because IK should not lose its value nor considered outdated. Building blocks and pearl growing search strategies were also used to retrieve the documents on indigenous knowledge. The search excluded the results from other countries unless used as a reference point and included Southern African Development Community (SADC) countries and few elements of sub Saharan Africa because it is the focus of the paper. The findings were critically analysed and presented in the literature to meet the objectives of the study.

Scope of the Study

Although sub-Saharan Africa was included to a minimal extent, the paper focused more on the literature from the SADC countries since they were mainly affected by colonialism and apartheid regime and lost their power in the running of their countries systems such as educational, economic, language, etcetera. In fulfilling their mission to promote sustainable and equitable economic growth and socio-economic development through efficient, productive systems, deeper cooperation and integration, good governance and durable peace and security, SADC countries should also use the IK in conjunction with other knowledge so that the region emerges as a competitive and effective player in international relations and the world economy. For example, Africans also had their ways of producing and preserving food to boost food security. Besides the fact that preserving food using the old methods may be cheaper, many of the traditional African food may lose their taste if they are not treated with the old methods. Some cuisines will only produce their defining aroma when preserved in certain ways. Therefore, the food that is made with the traditional methods remain special and can be used to attract tourism, eradicate poverty and boost the economy (Glasson, Mhango, Phiri & Lanier, 2010; Achi & Ukwuru, 2015).

LITERATURE REVIEW

The literature review were derived from the objectives of the chapter and covered the role of LAM on preserving African indigenous knowledge; sustainable strategies to collect African indigenous knowledge; strategies to document and catalogue African indigenous knowledge ; methods to digitise African indigenous knowledge as well as intellectual property rights of indigenous people.

The Role of Libraries, Archives, and Museums on Preserving Indigenous Knowledge

Greyling (2010) opined that, whilst libraries elsewhere in the world have been preserving indigenous knowledge for many years (e.g. Library of Congress, Smithsonian Institution's Center for Folklife and Cultural Heritage; New York Public Library's Schomburg Center for research in Black Culture, the situation has been different with African libraries. Libraries in Africa were originally designed to serve colonial interests, stocking books of primarily foreign content which comes down to local branches from the formal publishing and bookselling sectors via library system headquarters (Omole, 2002). With the coming of independence to many African states, transformation did not reach the libraries (Sithole, 2006). Although, the library and information professionals have either to concentrate mainly on managing published information resources, the onus falls on them to also preserve unpublished records within the purview of Library and Information Science (LIS) of unwritten information. Libraries theories and systems are geared mainly to dealing with published documents and are generally more comfortable dealing with publications than with unrecorded and unpublished knowledge. Librarians in Africa are specialized in dealing with artefacts such as books, videos, computer diskettes, files and folders that are already published in all formats (print, electronic and audio-visuals) (Lor, 2004).

However, progressive librarians recognize that the community itself has many untapped resources, including community leaders and elders who are custodians of traditional culture and indigenous knowledge. In some public libraries, databases of community information and registers of local expertise are maintained so that these resources can be mobilized (Lor, 2004). Lor (2004) is of the view that community orientated public libraries should be able to serve as antennae for identifying and locating IK resources in communities as they are in a good position to gain the confidence of indigenous knowledge holders and to enter into partnerships with indigenous knowledge researchers, assisting them in liaising with the community and thus in the recording of indigenous knowledge since they are already part of the community. Raseroka (2002) recommended that professionals such as librarians could empower local communities by giving the indigenous knowledge systems a voice and by facilitating interactive activities that bring communities on board as equal partners in knowledge creation, sharing and use. In that way indigenous knowledge holders will value themselves and their knowledge. Therefore knowledge sharing will be improved. Other methods that may be used to create awareness and sharing of IK according to Waungana (1984) is through story-telling sessions in the children's library during which older members of the community can enthral their young audience with folktale. Exhibitions of books about indigenous knowledge, can also be considered. Such events should be interactive. Elders could be invited to participate and contribute their versions of stories and their understanding of indigenous knowledge as they have learned and used it in their families and neighbourhoods. Such events should be recorded and documented by librarians. These will require some shifts in attitudes and modification of collection development policies. On the other hand the national library of the country pledge to adhere

African Indigenous Knowledge on the Cloud

to the responsibility of collecting, organizing, preserving and making available the country's recorded heritage, with special emphasis on the published portion thereof (Lor,1997).

Strategies and policies should be identified and modified to include indigenous knowledge in their collection as part of the country heritage acknowledging that the documentation of traditional Indigenous knowledge is not confined to remote areas where traditional structures or practice are still evident. In urban and regional areas, there is an increasing trend to document the knowledge of people and place belonging to groups whose traditional connections have been severely disrupted by colonial intervention and government policies and which are now literally overlaid by the urban and regional sprawl of the modern nation (Nakata et al., 2013). However, Lor (2004) opine that, the holders of indigenous knowledge and other stakeholders in the field would need to be consulted before the strategies and policies are established because IK is owned by a particular society therefore their rights and intellectual property should be respected. United Nations Educational, Scientific and Cultural Organization (UNESCO) and the World Intellectual Property Organization (WIPO) encourage institutions to engage with scholars and Indigenous peoples to create policies and procedures that would not just protect and preserve cultural heritage materials, but also, at the same time, promote the dynamism and ongoing creation of cultural traditions (Christen, 2015).

Strategies to Collect, Document, and Catalogue Indigenous Knowledge

The documentation of indigenous knowledge is important and provides an acceptable way to validate it and grant it protection from theft and other forms of abuse. In the world of globalization and knowledge societies, indigenous knowledge has to be recognized and paid for. Documentation provides evidence that local communities are the owners of a complex and highly developed knowledge system. The processes of documentation are necessary to establish the claims of local communities to share profits obtained from the commercialization of products derived from their knowledge (Sithole, 2007). However, the authentication of IK during documentation is a challenge to many institutions and individuals. Magara (2002) noted from a SWOT (Strengths, Weakness, Opportunities and Threats) analysis that it is not easy to ascertain the authenticity of oral sources that are often forgotten. The challenge therefore, is on how to document this unrecorded knowledge without validation and still be able to claim that it works. An example is the discourse on treating HIV and AIDS through traditional medicine as opposed to addressing the opportunistic infections (Sithole, 2007). In India, Phillipine and Uganda, Kenya, South Africa and other parts of the world to name but a few, validation of indigenous knowledge primary health care systems is done through ethnobotanical studies (Savithramma, et al., 2014; Dapar and Alejandro, 2020).

Indigenous knowledge should thus be catalogued to improve accessibility and use. Motsamai (2019) suggested contemporary cataloguing model for Difala vessels includes both historical and contemporary information about material objects and their environment and clarifies what happens to these objects once they become part of a museum collection. In that way there will be a paper trail on how knowledge was acquired and most importantly how can it be used to benefit the society. The same can be done to other indigenous knowledge systems. This should also include social cataloguing and tagging where users could be able to add keywords on the catalogue, review the document and share. A social cataloguing application is a web application that helps users to catalogue various items such as books, journals, CDs, etc. The social cataloguing is only few years old concept but has already reached a high level in present day environment. Users can catalogue various items by their own vocabulary or metadata or tags, which may be more acceptable to the other users. This will afford indigenous knowledge owners

225

to contribute to the metadata of their knowledge (Sarkar & Bhattachrya, 2019). Social cataloguing sites exists for a variety of media such as books and DVD. Users in social cataloguing services use tags for the purpose of facilitating retrieval of items and for sharing their opinions and communicating with other users (Ames & Naaman, 2007).

Social cataloguers classify tags into five categories: content based tags which describe the content or categories of an object or knowledge (e.g sefala vessel); context-based tags which represent time or location that object was created (Botwana 1810-10-19); attribute tags which show the properties of an object (e.g cow dung, clay) subjective tags which explain user's opinion or emotion (e.g., funny, cool). Zhang and Liu (2012) suggested a diffusion-based hybrid recommendation algorithm considering the roles of the tags that organizes items and connects between user and item. They show that the role of tags is more helpful to recommend items, and the hybrid approach shows the best results. LAM may introduce social tagging to promote IK and involve its users and owners to contribute on its catalogue since it would be available on the cloud by the use of social tagging application. Balogun and Kalusopa (2022) also suggested that the descriptive metadata proposed by OCLC's Research Library Partnership Web Archiving Metadata Working Group should be adopted in the archival of indigenous knowledge. The Dublin Core metadata has 15 core elements split into three (3) main groups which are the Content, Intellectual Property, and Instantiation. The Content part of the metadata includes title, description and, subject (keywords), type, relations, source, and coverage. The Intellectual Property part covers the creator, contributor, publisher, and rights. Instantiation on the other hand covers areas like date, format, identifier, and language. However when recoding the creators names of indigenous people, the authority file should be created in order to record the proper form of the name since the international cataloguing standards do not adequately meet the needs for cataloguing of non-roman names (Monyela, 2021).

The diversity and linguistic syntax of non-Roman languages such as African languages cannot use the umbrella standard form as prescribed by the international standards because they are not modelled on an alphabetical system and Roman numbering or scripting system. For example, Mutula and Tsvakai (2002) found that African names suffers from a lack of bibliographic tools that could help standardize their diversity. Other problems that make standardization of names important but difficult are the fact that African naming schemes are so complex. "African personal names," according to Bein (1993, 97), are as profuse, rich and varied as African languages. For example, a first name in certain ethnic groups may be a surname in another. The problems of classification and cataloguing African materials are intensified by the fact that some names have certain meanings attached to them relating to events, people, spirits, or places; and providing an equivalent English word would be difficult. In Setswana, Sepedi, IsiZulu for example, one English word may require a phrase or even a sentence when translated. The direct interpretation of a given word in any language may result in inaccuracies leading to difficulties in accessing the information needed. Cataloguing and classifying African materials suffer from the lack of name and subject authority tools, especially considering the fact that many names in Africa can be very common with variant forms (Mutula and Tsvakai, 2002). There is also great variation in names of people from one country to another or even within the same country. In Kenya, South Africa and other parts of Africa for example, names like Tina, Daina, Dina and Diana are variants of the name Dinah. Another example could be the name of the late Kenyan former president, Daniel Arap Moi. This name have variant forms and meanings depending on the part of Kenya one comes from. In Western Kenya this name would be Daniel Moi while in Central Province the name is Daniel Wa Moi.

In Nyanza Province he was called Daniel K'Moi (Mutula and Tsvakai. 2002). These variations of the same name causes headaches for even the most experienced and professional cataloguers. Filing such

African Indigenous Knowledge on the Cloud

variations in names can be varied, should the surname of the late former Kenyan President Moi be filed as Moi or Arap Moi (Arap means son of) or Wa Moi or K'Moi since there are no standards on how to file such names. In the LC Name Authority File (LCNAF) the preferred form of the name is (Moi, Daniel Arap, 1924-) and the variants are: Moi, D. T. Arap, 1924-; Moi, D. T. Arap (Daniel Torotich Arap), 1924-; Moi, Daniel Torotich Arap, 1924-; Moi, Daniel, 1924-; Moi, Daniel Arap (Daniel Torotich Arap), 1924-.The sources consulted when recording the name were his statement on application of the new Immigration act inrelation.1968.;Int.yrbk. &statesmen'sWWW, 1981etc. (LCNAF) It looks like he, his family or his country of origin was never consulted to interpret his name because none was indicated on the sources. He died on 4 February 2020, however the date of death is not indicated (Monyela, 2021). When cataloguing the names of the indigenous people, they should be consulted to give the proper form of their names as preferred by them. The social cataloguing app could be useful in this regard.

Strategies to Digitise and Preserve Indigenous Knowledge

In the 21st century, when more and more content and data is born digital or converted to digital to enhance access, LAM, researchers and other resource centres are grappling with providing effective digital preservation so that this indigenous knowledge is not just accessible now, but well into the future (Noonan, 2014). Nevertheless, at the same time digital contents are more vulnerable to loss due to several reasons like hardware failure, technological obsolescence, natural disasters, human errors, and malware attacks (Adu, 2016; Pendergrass et al., 2019; Srirahayu et al., 2020). There is a need for digital preservation policies to digitise indigenous knowledge. The establishment of the policy should also involve indigenous knowledge owners and stakeholders. Digital preservation according to Noonan (2014) can be defined as the combination of policies, strategies and actions to ensure access to and accurate rendering of authenticated reformatted and born digital content over time regardless of the challenges of media failure and technological change. Madsen and Hurst (2019) are of the view that, availability of the policy is one of the most important requirements for a digital preservation program. Such policy provides guidelines to the organizations for complete course of action during the life cycle of digital contents (Bieman, 2021).

Digital preservation policies also provide a path to the organizations about acquisition of digital contents, ingestions, metadata, storage security, normalization, migration, media refreshing and encapsulation. The availability of digital preservation policies enables the staff member of organizations to take appropriate actions as and when required in adherence to the path laid down in the policy especially because indigenous knowledge is owned by a particular society and the owners wishes should be adhered to. Developing policies for digital preservation of indigenous knowledge can help out in setting paths and improving the collection and access (Hedstrom & Montgomery, 1998). However, the lack of these policies can create troubles for staff members in deciding the course of action required. The survey of Masenya and Ngulube (2019) revealed availability of digital preservation policy in most (77.3%) of the 22 libraries in South Africa. Many (58.3%) of the 24 university libraries in Africa (having IRs) also affirmed availability of digital preservation policy (Anyaoku et al., 2019).

These libraries should extend the policy to cover indigenous knowledge and assist the Indigenous Knowledge Documentation Centres (IKDCs) in establishing the digital preservation policy. Balogun and Kalusopa (2022) found lack of digital preservation policy at the IKDCs in South Africa and suggested web archiving framework which is recommended as a part of the digital preservation policy in the IKS repositories in South Africa. However, South Africa has instituted the web-based portal of the national heritage resources known as 'National Heritage Repository'. It is hosted by NRF and can be accessed on http://digi.nrf.ac.za (Biyela, Oyelude & Haumba, 2016) Biyela, Oyelude & Haumba (2016)further observed that in 2010 the Department of Arts & Culture (DAC) in South Africa promulgated the National Policy on Digitization of Heritage Resources. The National Heritage Repository has helped in incorporating heritage resources of various kinds such as photographs; history papers and formats in one portal.

However Linked Data (LD) should be used in such projects to enhance visibility of indigenous knowledge from the silos such as the particular library, archive or museum that holds it and release it to the web. The LD technology includes a set of good practices and rules for interlinking machine-readable data sets using Uniform Resource Identifiers (URIs) and the Resource Description Framework (RDF) metadata schema to display, disseminate and merge data in a web environment (Nahotko, 2020).This technology was created for all information-processing applications as long as structural data elements such as the creator, publisher, title, the date of information sources are recorded accordingly. The LD technologies hold the potential to evolve the current web of documents such as HTML, SGML, XML, JSON, XUL, SVG files into the Web of Data. The Web of Data consists of structured data located in servers through the existence of links. This data is also called LD because it is data connected through links. In the hypertext web, HTML documents are connected to each other using untyped hyperlinks, whereas LD depends on the documents having RDF formats to create typed links that connect things globally, forming the Web of Data (Jacksi, Zeebaree & Dimililer, 2018). Moreover the main purpose of collecting, digitising and preserving IK is for people to access such knowledge, learn about it, create theories and frameworks for research, and most importantly use it for societal development and survival. Therefore, exposure of indigenous knowledge in the semantic web and the internet will lead to more accessibility and, ultimately, more usage and better services to users. Alemu, Stevens, Ross and Chandler (2012) are of the view that the adoption of LD can provide an open interactive system, with external links and the ability to make information easily accessible and re-usable, and with the possibility to discover other related resources. Gonzales (2014) and Warraich and Rorissa (2018) further opine that since the internet is often the first place users turn to for information, LAM and other IKSDs should take advantage of the concepts behind LD to put their resources out on the web where they can be found by users and, in turn, bring those users back to the holders through the lure of authoritative, high-quality resources. Furthermore. Warraich and Rorissa (2018) state that, in this digital environment, information seekers and users have high expectations, and information professionals design different strategies to make relevant information readily available. LD is a potential technology to be used in to provide better accessibility for researchers of all backgrounds (Monyela, 2022).

Moreover, Owiny et al. (2014) suggested the use of social media, Web 2.0 media such as radio, television to preserve IK. Owiny et al further opined that, LAM could also post audio feeds or videos of indigenous knowledge to the social media and communication technologies available in a particular community. For example, most rural residents have radios, so recorded or live information on how to grow and market local indigenous vegetables might be featured on a radio program using the indigenous knowledge of the areas. Moreover, several preservation initiatives in Africa use the Web 2.0 technologies. The Ulwazi Programme (http://www.ulwazi.org) is an initiative of the eThekwini Municipal Library to preserve the indigenous knowledge and local histories of communities in the greater Durban area, South Africa. It is based on a model whereby online indigenous knowledge resources are established as an integral part of local public library and information services. The Ara Irititja project (http://www.irititja.com), supported by the South Australian Museum, partners with local Aboriginal organizations to collect and preserve both traditional and current Anangu material and stories. Through an interactive multimedia archive database, the materials are then given back to the community. (Owiny et al., 2014)

African Indigenous Knowledge on the Cloud

WEB PRESERVATION FRAMEWORK

Khan and Rahman (2019) opined that, there are different aspects of the preservation process and web archiving such as digital objects' ingestion to the archive during preservation process, digital object's format and storage, archival management, administrative issues, access and security to the archive, and preservation planning. These aspects need to be understood for effective web preservation and will help in addressing the challenges that occur during the preservation process. The first step is to select the website to define the scope. The website could be the site centric archive that focuses on a particular website for preservation or topic centred archive that focuses on preserving information on a particular topic such as customary marriage, initiation school and cuisine to name but a few classifications of indigenous knowledge. These topics should be published on the web for future use. The other approach could be a domain centric archive that covers websites published with a specific domain name DNS, using either a top-level domain (TLD), e.g., .com, .edu, or .org, or a second-level domain (SLD), e.g., .edu.pk or .edu.fr. (Orduña-Malea, 2021). An advantage of domain-centric archiving is that it can be created by automatically detecting specific websites (Khan & Rahman, 2019).

The second step is to understand the web structure provided by the selected domain and how the information has been presented using various protocols such as HTTP. HTTPs, FTP etc. in order for the users to access the information. The other step is to identify the web resources such as blogs, websites, social networking sites, newspaper websites, etc. depending on the information seeking behaviour of the users. The web content such as textual, visual and multimedia should also be considered at this stage. The other step is to identify the designated community by learning the information need and information seeking behaviour of different information users. Then there should be policies governing all the preservation process. The preservation team should understand such parameters as the technical issues, the future technologies, and the expected inclusion of other related content (Khan and Rahman, 2019).

Intellectual Property Rights of Indigenous People

UNESCO's 2003 Convention for the Safeguarding of the Intangible Cultural Heritage that recognizes the ''deep-seated interdependence between the intangible cultural heritage and the tangible cultural and natural heritage'' of local, traditional, and Indigenous peoples, and the WIPO Intergovernmental Committee on Intellectual Property and Genetic Resources, Traditional Knowledge and Folklore (IGC) have sought to develop an international legal instrument that would give traditional knowledge, genetic resources, and traditional cultural expressions protection. Although they have yet to formalize or ratify any set of positions, their definitions stress the dynamism of tradition and the varied modalities and localities of and for traditional knowledge (Aikawa, 2004) Lazaro and Jimenez (2022) opined that the process for recognition of the existence of intangible cultural heritage (ICH) has been both slow and controversial. UNESCO established the basis for this recognition under its Convention for the Safeguarding of the Intangible Cultural Heritage adopted by the General Conference of UNESCO at its 32nd session in October 2003. Nonetheless, the precursor to this Convention was UNESCO's Convention. Concerning the Protection of World Cultural and Natural Heritage of 1972 and the associated World Heritage List. It was precisely the criticism regarding the shortcomings of this List which led to the growing acceptance of the idea of intangible heritage (Ahmad 2006). The assets recognised as 'heritage of humanity' were limited solely to material objects, without application of a comprehensive and holistic approach (Bouchenaki, 2007).

229

This concept of heritage was based on historical and aesthetic arguments, with an emphasis on monumentally grand and aesthetic sites and places, archaeological remains and, in terms of natural heritage, features or sites of outstanding universal value. Critics of the Convention and the World Heritage List questioned the very definition of 'heritage' provided and the difficulty of its interpretation (Blake, 2000) given that it is founded on a Eurocentric perspective, even in terms of the meanings given to the term (Craith, 2008). After the years that have passed, almost two decades, it is considered important to demonstrate whether the objectives that UNESCO intended to achieve with the Convention and the recognition of the existence of Intangible Cultural Heritage have been achieved. However it was concluded that only states can ratify the Convention, when this gives rise to rights and duties at both a national and international level' (Duvelle, 2017).

As also stated by Kurin (2004) the Convention is clearly a work in progress by experts and community members, indigenous people, legislators and academics to seek to determine how to safeguard culture in the coming years' (Kurin, 2004). Lazaro and Jimenez (2002) further emphasise that individuals and their communities are the true bearers of ICH and their active participation is necessary in safeguarding processes. However it should be mentioned that there are communities in which heritage protagonists are unaware of the legal strategies for initiating a UNESCO nomination process and do not have the financial means to meet the criteria for inscription on the ICH lists. Greater attention to the list of ICH in need of urgent safeguarding would avoid some of the inequalities in the elements of the different inscribed countries, since these urgent heritages are mainly found in the countries that have the least possibilities of taking measures to protect them. The network of facilitators proposed by UNESCO can become an appropriate tool to address these imbalances between countries. Facilitators are familiar with UNESCO tools and training materials, which they adapt to the local context and use to provide training and capacity building services, such as needs assessments, technical assistance and policy advice, at the national level. This network should be further enhanced to accommodate all countries (Lazaro & Jimenez, 2002).

FUTURE RESEARCH DIRECTIONS

The findings from this study has the potential to be used as a reference to empirical studies on collection, documentation, catalogues and preservation of IK in LAM. The data could be used to formulate policies and guidelines on sustainable methods to preserve IK in LAM in SADEC and other countries that were colonised and lost their identity and power.

CONCLUSION AND RECOMMENDATIONS

Living in the modern democratic society, the researcher is of the view that LAM should take up responsibility and use their skills as information providers to collect, document, catalogue and preserve indigenous knowledge for the coming generation and give them the opportunity to know about their culture. This knowledge is a hallmark of African identity, it is by looking at the past that we can remember who we are and that we can have a sense of pride to pass down to future generations. SADC countries should consider the IK to grow their economy (Glasson, Mhango, Phiri & Lanier, 2010; Achi & Ukwuru, 2015). Such knowledge should be available on the cloud through the use of advanced technology. The chapter therefore recommends the following:

African Indigenous Knowledge on the Cloud

- The establishment of policies to include collection, documentation and preservation of indigenous knowledge in LAM, using available technologies.
- The establishment of local descriptive standards to catalogue indigenous knowledge for easy retrieval.
- Web preservation framework to guide the LAM in preserving indigenous knowledge on the cloud for future use.
- Available technologies such as social media platforms, wikis, social cataloguing applications and others can also be used to preserve indigenous knowledge IK on the cloud for future use

REFERENCES

Achi, O. M., & Ukwuru, M. (2015). Cereal-Based Fermented Foods of Africa as Functional Foods. *International Journal of Microbiology and Application.*, *2*(4), 71–83.

Adu, K. K. (2016). *Framework for digital preservation or electronic government in Ghana* [Doctoral thesis, University of South Africa, UNISA, South Africa]

Aikawa, N. (2004). An historical overview of the preparation of the UNESCO International Convention for the Safeguarding of the Intangible Cultural Heritage. *Museum International*, *56*(1-2), 137–149. doi:10.1111/j.1350-0775.2004.00468.x

Alemu, G., Stevens, B., Ross, P., & Chandler, J. (2012). Linked data for libraries: Benefits of a conceptual shift from library-specific record structures to RDF-based data models. *New Library World*, *113*(11/12), 549–570. doi:10.1108/03074801211282920

Anyaoku, E. N., Nwafor-Orizu, O. E., & Eneh, E. A. (2015). Collection and preservation of traditional medical knowledge: Roles for medical libraries in Nigeria. *Journal of Library and Information Science*, *3*(1), 33–43. doi:10.15640/jlis.v3n1a2

Anyogu, F., & Ibekwe, C. S. (2020). A Comparative Exposition of Customary Law Marriage in Nigeria and South Africa. *[IJOCLLEP]. International Journal of Comparative Law and Legal Philosophy*, *2*(2), 60–74.

Ayittey, G. (2006). *Indigenous African Institutions*. Transnational Publishers Inc. doi:10.1163/ej.9781571053374.i-586

Balogun, T., & Kalusopa, T. (2022). Web archiving of indigenous knowledge systems in South Africa. *Information Development*, *38*(4), 658–671. doi:10.1177/02666669211005522

Bein, A. (1993). Cataloging of materials in African languages. *Cataloging & Classification Quarterly*, *17*(1-2), 97–114. doi:10.1300/J104v17n01_07

Biyela, N., Oyelude, A., & Haumba, E. (2016). Digital preservation of Indigenous Knowledge (IK) by cultural heritage institutions: a comparative study of Nigeria, South Africa and Uganda. HDL. http://hdl.han dle.net/20.500.11910/10196

Blake, J. (2000). On Defining the Cultural Heritage. *The International and Comparative Law Quarterly, 49*(1), 61–85. doi:10.1017/S002058930006396X

Bouchenaki, M. (2007). A Major Advance Towards A Holistic Approach to Heritage Conservation the 2003 Intangible Heritage Convention. *International Journal of Intangible Heritage, 2*(105–109), 51–78.

Christen, K. (2015). Tribal archives, traditional knowledge, and local contexts: Why the "s" matters. *Journal of western archives, 6*(1), 1-21

Craith, M. N. (2008). Intangible Cultural Heritages. *Anthropological Journal on European Cultures, 17*(1), 54–73. doi:10.3167/ajec.2008.01701004

Dapar, M. L. G., Alejandro, G. J. D., Meve, U., & Liede-Schumann, S. (2020). Quantitative ethnopharmacological documentation and molecular confirmation of medicinal plants used by the Manobo tribe of Agusan del Sur, Philippines. *Journal of Ethnobiology and Ethnomedicine, 16*(1), 1–60. doi:10.118613002-020-00363-7 PMID:32138749

Duvelle, C. (2017). Aventuras y desventuras de una hermosa Convención Internacional. *Revista Andaluza de Antropología, 12*(12), 31–47. doi:10.12795/RAA.2017.12.02

Fernandez, M.E. (1994). Gender and indigenous knowledge. *Indigenous knowledge and development monitor, 2*(3), 6-7.

Gelfand, J. A. (1984). Infections in burn patients: A paradigm for cutaneous infection in the patient at risk. *The American Journal of Medicine, 76*(5, 5A), 158–165. doi:10.1016/0002-9343(84)90259-6 PMID:6372465

Glasson, G. E., Mhango, N., Phiri, A., & Lanier, M. (2010). Sustainability science education in Africa: Negotiating indigenous ways of living with nature in the third space. *International Journal of Science Education, 32*(1), 125–141. doi:10.1080/09500690902981269

Greyling, E., & Zulu, S. (2010). Content development in an indigenous digital library: A case study in community participation. *IFLA Journal, 36*(1), 30–39. doi:10.1177/0340035209359570

Hedstrom, M. L., & Montgomery, S. (1998). *Digital preservation needs and requirements in RLG member institutions.* Research Libraries Group.

Jacksi, K., Zeebaree, S. R., & Dimililer, N. (2018). LOD explorer: Presenting the web of data. (IJACSA). *International Journal of Advanced Computer Science and Applications, 9*(1), 45–51. doi:10.14569/IJACSA.2018.090107

Khalala, G., Botha, A., & Makitla, I. (2016). *Process as an element of UX in collecting Indigenous Knowledge: A case study in South Africa. In 2016 IST-Africa Week Conference.* IEEE.

Khan, M., & Rahman, A. U. (2019). A systematic approach towards web preservation. *Information Technology and Libraries, 38*(1), 71–90. doi:10.6017/ital.v38i1.10181

Kurin, R. (2004). Safeguarding Intangible Cultural Heritage in the 2003 UNESCO Convention: A Critical Appraisal. *Museum International, 56*(1-2), 66–77. doi:10.1111/j.1350-0775.2004.00459.x

Lazaro Ortiz, S., & Jimenez de Madariaga, C. (2022). The UNESCO convention for the safeguarding of the intangible cultural heritage: A critical analysis. *International Journal of Cultural Policy*, *28*(3), 327–341. doi:10.1080/10286632.2021.1941914

Lor, P. (2004). Storehouses of knowledge? The role of libraries in preserving and promoting indigenous knowledge. *Indilinga*, *3*(1), 45–56.

Lor, P. J. (1997). *Guidelines for Legislation for National Library Services (CII-97/WS/7)*. United Nations Educational, Scientific and Cultural Organization.

Madsen, C., & Hurst, M. (2019). Digital preservation policy and strategy: where do I start? In J. Myntti & J. Zoom (Eds.), *Digital preservation in libraries: preparing for a sustainable future* (pp. 37–48). ALA.

Magara, E. (2002) *Community based indigenous knowledge: strategy for Uganda*. In Proceedings of the 15th Standing Conference of Eastern, Central and South African Library and Infor-mation Professionals, Johannesburg.

Maharasoa, M. M. A., & Maharaswa, M. B. (2004). Men's initiation schools as a form of higher education within the Basotho indigenous knowledge systems: Perspectives on higher education. *South African Journal of Higher Education*, *18*(3), 106–114.

Maluleka, J. R. (2017). *Acquisition, transfer and preservation of indigenous knowledge by traditional healers in the Limpopo province of South Africa*. [Doctoral thesis, University of South Africa, South Africa].

Masango, C. A. (2010). Indigenous traditional knowledge protection: Prospects in South Africa's intellectual property framework? *South African Journal of Library and Information Science*, *76*(1), 74–80. doi:10.7553/76-1-88

Meissner, O., & Buso, D. L. (2007). Traditional male circumcision in the Eastern Cape-scourge or blessing? *South African Medical Journal*, *97*(5), 71–373. PMID:17599221

Monyela, M. (2021). Call Us by Our Names: The Need to Establish Authority Control Standards for Non-Roman Names. *Library Philosophy and Practice*, *1*(1), 1–10.

Monyela, M. (2022). Knowledge organisation in academic libraries: The Linked Data approach. In T. M. Masenya (Ed.), *Innovative Technologies for Enhancing Knowledge Access in Academic Libraries* (pp. 71–88). IGI Global. doi:10.4018/978-1-6684-3364-5.ch005

Morris, B. (2010). Indigenous knowledge. *The Society of Malawi Journal*, *63*(1), 1–9.

Motsamayi, M. F. (2019). *Sotho-Tswana'Difala vessels in selected South African museums: challenges in descriptions and catalogues* [Doctoral dissertation, University of Kwa Zulu Natal, Durban. South Africa]

Mutula, S. M., & Tsvakai, M. (2002). Historical perspectives of cataloguing and classification in Africa. *Cataloging & Classification Quarterly*, *35*(1-2), 61–77. doi:10.1300/J104v35n01_05

Myemana A. (2004). *Should Christians undergo the Circumcision Rite?* East London: 3 Eden Ministries.

Nahotko, M. (2020). OPAC development as the genre transition process, PART 1: OPAC generations historical development. *Annals of Library and Information Studies*, *67*(2), 107–117.

Nakata, M. (2013). The rights and blights of the politics in Indigenous higher education. [). Routledge.]. *Anthropological Forum*, *23*(3), 289–303. doi:10.1080/00664677.2013.803457

Ngulube, P. (2002). Managing and preserving indigenous knowledge in the knowledge management era: Challenges and opportunities for information professionals. *Information Development*, *18*(2), 95–102. doi:10.1177/026666602400842486

Noonan, J. (2014). Radical Philosophy and Social Criticism. *International Critical Thought*, *4*(1), 10–20. doi:10.1080/21598282.2014.878143

Ntombana, L. (2011). Should Xhosa male initiation be abolished? *International Journal of Cultural Studies*, *14*(6), 631–640. doi:10.1177/1367877911405755

Orduña-Malea, E. (2021). Dot-science top level domain: Academic websites or dumpsites? *Scientometrics*, *126*(4), 3565–3591. doi:10.100711192-020-03832-8

Owiny, S. A., Mehta, K., & Maretzki, A. N. (2014). The use of social media technologies to create, preserve, and disseminate indigenous knowledge and skills to communities in East Africa. *International Journal of Communication*, *8*, 234–247.

Pendergrass, K. L., Sampson, W., Walsh, T., & Alagna, L. (2019). Toward environmentally sustainable digital preservation. *The American Archivist*, *82*(1), 165–206. doi:10.17723/0360-9081-82.1.165

Rajasekaran, B. (1993). *A framework for incorporating indigenous knowledge systems into agricultural research and extension organizations for sustainable agricultural development in India. Iowa State University.* [Doctoral thesis, Lowa State University, Lowa. United States]

Raseroka, H. K. (2002). From Africa to the world – the globalisation of indigenous knowledge systems: setting the scene. In From Africa to the World – the Globalisation of Indigenous Knowledge Systems. *Proceedings of the 15th Standing Conference of Eastern, Central and Southern African Library and Information Associations.* Library and Information Association of South Africa.

Savithramma, N., Yugandhar, P., & Lingarao, M. (2014). Ethnobotanical studies on Japali Hanuman theertham-a sacred grove of Tirumala hills, Andhra Pradesh, India. *J Pharm Sci Res*, *6*, 83–88.

Sithole, J. (2007). The challenges faced by African libraries and information centres in documenting and preserving indigenous knowledge. *IFLA Journal*, *33*(2), 117–123. doi:10.1177/0340035207080304

Warraich, N. F., & Rorissa, A. (2018). Adoption of linked data technologies among university librarians in Pakistan: Challenges and prospects. *Malaysian Journal of Library and Information Science*, *23*(3), 1–13. doi:10.22452/mjlis.vol23no3.1

Waungana, E. (1984). Children's story telling and reading activities in Zimbabwe, Library Work for Children and Young Adults in the Developing Countries. *Proceedings of the IFLA/UNESCO Pre-Session Seminar in Leipzig, GDR*, München .

ADDITIONAL READINGS

Agyemang, B. K., Ngulube, P., & Dube, L. (2019). Utilising knowledge management methods to manage beads-making indigenous knowledge among the Krobo communities in Ghana. *South African Journal of Information Management*, *21*(1), 1–9. doi:10.4102ajim.v21i1.1008

Anwar, M. A. (2010). Role of information management in the preservation of indigenous knowledge. *Pakistan Journal of Information Management and Libraries*, *11*(1), 1–10. doi:10.47657/201011792

Chepchirchir, S., Kwanya, T., & Kamau, A. (2019). Maximising the socioeconomic value of indigenous knowledge through policies and legislation in Kenya. Global Knowledge. *Memory and Communication*, *68*(1/2), 60–75.

Chikonzo, A. (2006). The potential of information and communication technologies in collecting, preserving and disseminating indigenous knowledge in Africa. *The International Information & Library Review*, *38*(3), 132–138. doi:10.1080/10572317.2006.10762714

Kuyu, C. G., & Bereka, T. Y. (2020). Review on contribution of indigenous food preparation and preservation techniques to attainment of food security in Ethiopian. *Food Science & Nutrition*, *8*(1), 3–15. doi:10.1002/fsn3.1274 PMID:31993127

Masekoameng, M. R., & Molotja, M. C. (2019). The role of indigenous foods and indigenous knowledge systems for rural households' Food Security in Sekhukhune District, Limpopo Province, South Africa. *Journal of Consumer Sciences*, *4*(1), 34–48.

Muthee, D. W., Gwademba, G. K., & Masinde, J. M. (2019). The role of indigenous knowledge systems in enhancing agricultural productivity in Kenya. [EAJCR]. *Eastern African Journal of Contemporary Research*, *1*(1), 34–45.

Owusu-Ansah, F. E., & Mji, G. (2013). African indigenous knowledge and research. *African Journal of Disability*, *2*(1), 1–5. doi:10.4102/ajod.v2i1.30 PMID:28729984

KEY TERMS AND DEFINITIONS

Cataloguing: The process of creating metadata representing information resources, such as books, sound recordings, moving image etc.

Documentation: The process of classifying and annotating texts, photographs, etc.

Indigenous Knowledge: Traditional knowledge, indigenous knowledge and local knowledge generally refer to knowledge systems embedded in the cultural traditions of regional, indigenous, or local communities.

Linked Data: A set of techniques that represents and connects structured data such as metadata or catalogue data using links that connects on the web.

Preservation: The process of working to protect something valuable so that it is not damaged or destroyed.

Resource Description Framework: A standard model for data interchange on the web, using simple Subject-Predicate-Object (also called triple) statements.

Chapter 13

Electronic Documentation of Nigerian Indigenous Arts and Crafts for Historical Research Engagements and Tourism

Valentine Joseph Owan
University of Calabar, Nigeria & Ultimate Research Network, Nigeria

David Adie Alawa
University of Calabar, Nigeria

Kinsley Bekom Abang
University of Calabar, Nigeria

Mercy Valentine Owan
University of Calabar, Nigeria & Ultimate Research Network, Nigeria

Felicia Agbor-obun Dan
University of Calabar, Nigeria

Delight Omoji Idika
University of Calabar, Nigeria

Daniel Clement Agurokpon
University of Cross River State, Nigeria

ABSTRACT

Indigenous arts, crafts, and culture are critical components of the world's diverse cultural heritage. Unfortunately, preserving this rich heritage remains challenging for most developing countries, especially with the increasing use of electronic media and the marginalisation of indigenous communities. This chapter discussed digital documentation strategies for Nigerian indigenous arts, crafts, and cultures to support future historical research engagements and tourism. It begins by examining indigenous arts, crafts, and cultures, such as stone carving, bronze and brass, weaving, pottery, etc. It tackled the importance and challenges of electronic documentation of these indigenous arts for historical research and tourism. Some case studies of successful electronic documentation of indigenous arts, crafts, and cultures in other societies were reviewed. Lessons were drawn from such previous efforts to shape future initiatives. It was concluded that documenting and preserving indigenous arts, crafts, and cultures is crucial for promoting and preserving cultural heritage.

DOI: 10.4018/978-1-6684-7024-4.ch013

Copyright © 2023, IGI Global. Copying or distributing in print or electronic forms without written permission of IGI Global is prohibited.

INTRODUCTION

Nigeria is home to a rich and diverse range of indigenous arts and crafts, reflecting the country's vibrant history and diverse ethnic groups. These art forms include traditional sculptures, textiles, pottery, basketry, beadwork, metalwork, and woodcarving, among others. Nigerian indigenous arts and crafts are often imbued with cultural and spiritual significance, telling the stories and histories of the people who create them. According to Osasona (2007), Nigeria's arts are also reflected in the indigenous design and architecture of its buildings across the northern, eastern, and southern parts of the country. Nigerian indigenous arts are significant to Nigeria's cultural heritage and are globally relevant. These art forms are an essential part of African cultural history and testify to the creativity and ingenuity of African artisans.

Nigerian crafts are intertwined with the country's spiritual philosophies and serve as valuable tools for promoting and preserving tourism. Nigeria's handicrafts encompass a variety of categories, including fabrics, ceramics, bronze, brass and iron works, fibres, handicrafts, ivory, jewellery, leatherwork, tie and dye, woodwork, pumpkin decorations, and more (Akintonde, 2013). Many of Nigeria's artistic works are displayed in museums worldwide. The utilisation of arts and crafts can catalyse sustainable development and industrial growth in an economy, as many people are not cognizant of the value, potential, and importance of Crafts in their daily lives (Irivwieri, 2009).

Despite the importance of Nigerian indigenous Arts and Crafts, there is a significant gap in the documentation and preservation of these art forms. Many of these art forms are at risk of being lost due to urbanisation, globalisation, and neglect (Kashim et al., 2013). Therefore, there is an urgent need for effective documentation strategies to preserve and promote Nigerian indigenous Arts and Crafts for future generations. The traditional practices of Nigeria are a valuable art historical resource that, if not studied in the present, may become inaccessible in the future due to the constantly changing nature of these practices. For Indigenous Knowledge (IK) to significantly promote sustainable development in African communities, it needs to be recorded, formalised, made available, exchanged, and spread widely (Tapfuma & Hoskin 2016). This is evidenced by many sculptures being lost, removed, or replaced while new ones are regularly created (Akintonde, 2013). The documentation and preservation of Nigerian indigenous arts are crucial in ensuring the continuity of these art forms and their cultural significance. The documentation of Nigerian indigenous arts and crafts allows for creation of an archive that can be used for future research and education. Researchers can study these arts to understand the historical, cultural, and artistic significance of these art forms. Preserving these arts ensures the longevity of the art forms and promotes cultural tourism, which can boost the economy of Nigeria and the African continent (Ezenagu, 2020). The exportation of Nigerian indigenous arts has the potential to foster cultural exchange and understanding between Nigeria and other countries.

Based on the available literature, the responsibility for preserving IK in Nigeria has been primarily handed over to the National Museum. Areo and Kalilu (2013) note that several Nigerian museums nationwide have established skill acquisition centres for tie and dye (Adire) production. This initiative, led by the national museums, has not only contributed to the growth of the textile industry but has also empowered numerous women and youth by providing them with employment opportunities. However, scholars have advocated for a shift in the preservation of IK by the realities of the 21st century, emphasising the use of Information and Communication Technologies (ICTs) (Demssie et al., 2020). The rationale behind this perspective is that ICTs facilitate easy information retrieval, ensuring enhanced accessibility to stored knowledge. Nevertheless, the literature suggests an evidence gap since there seem to be three schools of thought conceiving how IK should be preserved.

The first school advocates for using traditional methods to preserve indigenous knowledge (Okoye & Oni, 2017). The second school supports the application of modern approaches such as libraries and ICTs (Mdhluli et al., 2021). The ongoing debate between the two schools is such that neither of these methods has fully addressed the existing challenges in knowledge management (Zimu-Biyela, 2016). Given the complexity of IK preservation, the third school emerged, where authors have argued that a combination of both traditional and modern methods should be employed (Masenya, 2022; Mbilinyi & Mwabungulu, 2020; McGinnis et al., 2020). In line with this argument, this chapter proposes electronic documentation strategies for Nigerian indigenous arts and crafts that address the challenges of documenting these cultural resources. The chapter presents some case studies to demonstrate the effectiveness of the proposed approach. It highlights the importance of electronic documentation in preserving and promoting Nigerian indigenous arts and crafts. The chapter emphasises the potential impact of electronic documentation on historical research and tourism, contributing to the economic development of Nigeria.

CONCEPT OF ELECTRONIC DOCUMENTATION

Electronic documentation refers to recording and storing information, data, or documentation in electronic format. It uses digital technologies and tools to create, organise, store, retrieve, and manage documents and records. Electronic documentation can include various types of files, such as text documents, spreadsheets, presentations, images, videos, audio recordings, and more (Gilmore et al., 2018). Electronic documentation offers several advantages over traditional paper-based documentation, including easier storage, accessibility, searchability, and sharing of information (Gilmore et al., 2018). It allows for efficient organisation and retrieval of documents, enables collaborative work and remote access, reduces physical storage requirements, and supports the integration of multimedia elements into documentation. Examples of electronic documentation include word-processing documents, PDF files, email communications, databases, content management systems, and knowledge bases (Jordan et al., 2022). Electronic documentation plays a crucial role in various fields, such as business, healthcare, education, research, and government, facilitating the efficient management and preservation of information (Mukred et al., 2019).

In this chapter, the concept of electronic documentation involves digitising and preserving traditional knowledge and practices of indigenous communities using electronic tools and technologies. It aims to capture, record, and store indigenous knowledge in a digital format, making it accessible, searchable, and shareable. It involves using digital platforms, databases, multimedia tools, and other electronic means to record and document various aspects of indigenous knowledge, including language, folklore, medicinal practices, agricultural techniques, cultural traditions, and ecological wisdom. By digitising indigenous knowledge, electronic documentation helps overcome the challenges of oral transmission and the potential loss or degradation of traditional knowledge due to various factors like globalisation, urbanisation, and environmental changes (Carr et al., 2016; Eichler, 2021; Fernández-Llamazares & Cabeza, 2018). Electronic documentation of indigenous knowledge also facilitates knowledge exchange, collaboration, and engagement between indigenous communities, researchers, scholars, and policymakers (Fernández-Llamazares & Cabeza, 2018).

NIGERIAN INDIGENOUS ARTS AND CRAFTS THAT ARE ELECTRONICALLY DOCUMENTABLE

This section discusses Nigeria's indigenous arts and crafts that can be electronically documented. These include the following:

Stone Carving/Sculpture

Stone carving has a long history in Nigeria, with evidence of early stone tools dating back thousands of years. The Nok people are renowned for their sophisticated stone sculptures, which often depict human and animal figures with intricate details and stylised features (Breunig et al., 2008). In particular, the southern regions of Nigeria are known for using stone in creating tall monoliths, narrow stone pillars typically featuring elaborate carvings and inscriptions. One notable example is the *Lechor Olikplikpo* in the Yala-Obubra community, Cross River State, Nigeria. *Lechor Olikplikpo* is a mysterious stone monolith that physically measures just an arm's length but comparatively longer than anyone that dares to measure his or her height with it; hence the submission that most Nigerian crafts and arts have spiritual significance. Many other stone monoliths in the Yala-Obubra community are yet to be documented electronically, such as the Ukpochi Playground monolith and the Omindom playground monolith, amongst others inside the river, seashores, in the community and forest of the area.

Another example is the Alok Ikom stone monoliths, which are believed to date back to the 17th century and are made from a local basalt known as *"akwasnshi/Atal"* (Nwankwo et al., 2018; Okwoche et al., 2021). They feature intricate carvings of human and animal figures and geometric designs. While they have some similarities, each stone is distinctive in its design and execution, much like a human fingerprint (Stout et al., 2008). Another example of stone carving in Nigeria is the Oshun Grove, a sacred site in Osogbo in southwestern Nigeria (Ijisakin, 2021; Shipley, 2017). The grove is home to intricately carved stone sculptures representing various deities and spiritual forces in the Yoruba religion. Examples of stone monoliths can be seen in Figure 1.

Figure 1. Stone monoliths

Bronze and Brass Craft

Bronze and brass crafting is a traditional art form still widely practised in Nigeria today. Various regions, such as Benin, Bida, and the southwest, are well-known for their skilled artisans. Although these indigenous works have been a part of Nigeria's artistic heritage for centuries, they gained international recognition when the Ife and Benin bronzes were discovered. Alongside these famous pieces, the Igbo-Ukwu archaeological finds have revealed an impressive collection of ancient and highly sophisticated works of art (McIntosh, 2022). The Igbo-Ukwu bronzes stand out for their elaborate and intricate designs, demonstrating remarkable symmetry and rivalling even the celebrated Ife works. These discoveries have greatly contributed to the appreciation and understanding of Nigeria's rich artistic heritage, attracting the attention of art enthusiasts worldwide. Examples of bronze and brass art are provided in Figure 2.

Wood Carving

Wood carving has been a prominent art form in Nigeria for centuries, with artisans producing various objects for various purposes (Sobowale et al., 2020). While places like Osogbo, Benin, Oyo, and Awka are often regarded as the centres of wood carving, skilled carvers have thrived throughout southern Nigeria (Sunday et al., 2022), creating figures for shrines, masks, portraits, representations of spirits, country, sky, sea, land, forest, fire, and thunder, as well as tools and ornaments that are still used today. Many of these intricate and exquisite works of art can be found in museums worldwide (Duncan & Wallach, 2019).

Figure 2. Bronze and brass craft

Electronic Documentation of Nigerian Indigenous Arts and Crafts

Over time, the art of wood carving in Nigeria has evolved (Ijisakin, 2019). Today, it is used for traditional and commercial purposes, such as producing furniture, bowls, doors, panels, and boxes, which are in high demand locally and internationally. The contemporary production of wooden furniture and other items in Nigeria reflects a blend of traditional techniques and modern design concepts. The demand for Nigerian wooden furniture has grown in recent years as consumers appreciate the beauty and durability of handmade items. From producing objects for traditional shrines to creating contemporary furniture, Nigerian wood carvers have demonstrated their exceptional skills and creativity in carving. Today, their works continue to be appreciated and admired by art enthusiasts worldwide. Figure 3 provides a pictorial depiction of some Nigerian arts made from wood carvings.

Ivory Carving

Ivory carving is a traditional art form in various parts of Nigeria, including Benin, Owo, Oyo, and traditional rulers' palaces. Ivory, derived from the tusks of elephants, has long been a precious material in Nigerian art and culture (Hornbeck, 2015). Ivory carvers in Nigeria create various intricate and decorative pieces, including necklaces, bracelets, hats, paper knives, cigar boxes, and other decorative items. In addition to their aesthetic value, ivory carvings have significant cultural and historical importance in Nigeria. These carvings are associated with traditional religious practices and rituals, serving as important spiritual and cultural heritage symbols. Ivory carvings are also often used as symbols of status and power, particularly in the palaces of traditional rulers. However, the practice of ivory carving in Nigeria has faced significant challenges in recent years due to international regulations on the trade of ivory (Aryal et al., 2018). Many countries have banned the trade of ivory to combat the illegal poaching of elephants and to protect endangered species. As a result, ivory carving in Nigeria has become increasingly rare, and many traditional carvers have had to find new materials to work with. Despite these challenges, the art of ivory carving in Nigeria remains an important part of the country's cultural heritage. An example of arts made through ivory carvings is represented in Figure 4.

Figure 3. Examples of wood carvings art

Figure 4. Ivory carvings

Weaving Craft

Weaving is an important craft in Nigeria with a rich history that dates back thousands of years. Some of Nigeria's most famous weaving traditions include the Aso-oke, Akwete, and Adire (Ojo, 2007; Seidu et al., 2022). Aso-oke is a handwoven cloth made by the Yoruba people, primarily for special occasions such as weddings, festivals, and funerals. The fabric is made from locally grown cotton and comes in various colours and designs. It is characterised by its stiffness and durability, making it a popular material for clothing, bags, and hats. The Akwete cloth, on the other hand, is woven by the Igbo people using a traditional horizontal loom. Made from locally grown cotton, it features intricate patterns and designs unique to the region. The Akwete cloth is often used for clothing, wrappers, and ceremonial purposes. Another popular weaving tradition in Nigeria is Adire, a resist-dyed cloth made by the Yoruba people (Areo & Kalilu, 2013; Renne, 2020). The cloth is made by tying, stitching, or folding the fabric before applying the dye, resulting in a unique pattern. Examples of wrappers produced from the adire cloth are shown in Figure 5.

In addition to these weaving traditions, many other weaving styles and techniques are practised across Nigeria, including raffia, straw, and other natural fibres. For instance, the Ndam and Esighi materials are specially produced by the Efik people in Cross River State, from Palm trees to weave beautiful and colourful attires worn by different *Ekpe* and masquerades. Similarly, the Yala-Obubra community in Cross River State has a special plant called "*Akwubleh*", which looks like the sugar cane plant but grows taller and inedible. The leaves of this plant are harvested, and sleeping mats are weaved from it. Similarly, the

Figure 5. Examples of Adire wrappers

stems of the *Akwubleh* plant are cut and smashed or pounded into tiny strips, which can be used to weave clothes, usually worn by masquerades. Cane weaving is another traditional craft in Nigeria, with a long history of producing functional and decorative items (Okonkwo et al., 2016). The craft involves weaving dried cane or bamboo strips into baskets, mats, furniture, and other household items. Cane weaving is still practised in many parts of Nigeria, and some artisans have adapted the craft to create contemporary designs for a global market. Figure 6 is a pictorial representation of craftwork made from cane weaving. A sample of products made from bead weaving in Nigeria is displayed in Figure 7.

Pottery

Pottery-making in Nigeria is a traditional practice predominantly carried out by women (Peters, 2021). Nigerian potters create both functional and decorative pieces using various techniques and materials. The most common types of pottery in Nigeria are earthenware (Matshameko et al., 2022) and stoneware (Uriah et al., 2014). Earthenware is made by forming clay into a desired shape, drying it in the sun, and then firing it in a kiln. Earthenware pottery is known for its rough texture and is often used for cooking and storage. It is commonly found in the northern part of Nigeria. On the other hand, stoneware is made by adding sand or other materials to the clay, making it more durable and heat-resistant. Stoneware pottery is smoother and more refined than earthenware and is often used for decorative purposes. It is commonly found in the southern part of Nigeria. Nigerian pottery is known for its intricate designs and patterns, often inspired by nature, traditional symbols, and cultural heritage. Some potters also incorporate other materials, such as cowrie shells, beads, and metal, into their designs. Pottery-making is often a family tradition passed down from generation to generation. In some communities, pottery-making is considered sacred art to create ritual objects and vessels for traditional ceremonies. Today, Nigerian

Figure 6. Products of cane weaving in Nigeria

Figure 7. Products made from beads in Nigeria

pottery is sold in markets throughout the country and exported to other parts of the world. Samples of clay products in Nigeria are displayed in Figure 8.

Hides, Skins, and Leatherwork

Hides, skins, and leatherwork have long been important to Nigerian art and culture (Oladejo, 2019; Siyanbola et al., 2012). The production of leather goods has traditionally been male-dominated, with many

Figure 8. Clay pots made in Nigeria

artisans passing their skills down through generations. The leather is often sourced from domesticated animals, such as cows and goats, and is carefully treated and processed to create a durable material. In northern Nigeria, the Hausa people are particularly renowned for their leatherwork (Noah & Çağnan, 2021). They use traditional techniques to create various items, including bags, belts, sandals, and armour. The leather is often dyed using natural pigments, such as indigo and henna, and is then embellished with intricate designs and patterns. In addition to leatherwork, hides and skins are also used to produce textiles. The Fulani people of Nigeria are also known for using hides and skins in their artwork (Abubakar, 2021). They create intricate carvings and relief sculptures using a combination of leather and wood, often depicting scenes from everyday life or religious and cultural symbols. Overall, hides, skins, and leatherwork are an important part of Nigeria's rich artistic heritage, with artisans continuing to produce high-quality pieces using traditional techniques and materials. Figure 9 shows some artwork produced from skins, hides and leather.

Tie and Dye

Tie-dye is a traditional fabric art in Nigeria that involves tying, folding, twisting, or pleating fabric and then applying dye to create patterns and designs. This technique is widely used in traditional Nigerian clothing, such as the Buba and the Gele. It has also been adopted by contemporary fashion designers who use it to create vibrant and unique clothing designs. This technique is called Adire, a Yoruba word meaning "tie and dye." Adire is a popular textile craft in southwestern Nigeria, particularly in Abeokuta in Ogun State. Traditionally, tie-dye was done using indigo dyes (Maiwada et al., 2012) made from indigo plants grown in Nigeria. The indigo dye was mixed with cassava paste, which acted as a resist and prevented the dye from spreading to certain areas of the fabric. This allowed the artist to create intricate patterns and designs on the fabric. Today, tie and dye artists in Nigeria use a variety of dyes, including synthetic dyes, to create vibrant and colourful fabrics. They also use a range of local materials, such as Adire Eleko (Areo & Kalilu, 2013; Renne, 2020), a type of cassava starch), cowries (a type of shell), and local leaves such as moringa (Adesina et al., 2021), to create unique patterns and designs. Tie-dye

Figure 9. Bags and shoes produced using animal skins and leather

creates various fabrics, including clothing, bedspreads, tablecloths, and wall hangings. It is a popular art form celebrated in Nigeria and worldwide for its vibrant colours, intricate designs, and cultural significance. In recent years, there has been a resurgence of interest in traditional tie and dye techniques, with many young artists incorporating these techniques into their work and experimenting with new materials and designs.

IMPORTANCE OF ELECTRONIC DOCUMENTATION OF INDIGENOUS ARTS AND CRAFTS FOR HISTORICAL RESEARCH AND TOURISM

This section articulates the vital role of electronic documentation in preserving and promoting indigenous Arts and Crafts for historical research and tourism. By capturing and sharing these cultural expressions, electronic platforms ensure their longevity, accessibility, and appreciation, fostering cross-cultural understanding, supporting cultural revitalisation, and promoting responsible tourism practices. The following are some importance of electronically documenting indigenous Arts and Crafts:

Increased Information

Electronic documentation provides historians access to a wealth of information that may not have been available. The internet, for example, has made it possible to access a vast amount of historical material from around the world, making it easier for researchers to conduct comprehensive and interdisciplinary studies. Online databases, digital libraries, and archives provide researchers with access to rare or out-of-print books, manuscripts, and primary sources that they may not have been able to access previously. This is important for historical research as it allows researchers to understand the past better, leading to more accurate and insightful interpretations. For tourism, increased access to historical information can

Electronic Documentation of Nigerian Indigenous Arts and Crafts

enhance the visitor experience by providing more detailed and accurate information about historical sites and landmarks. For example, imaging technology can be used to create virtual tours or exhibits, providing visitors with access to historical information that they may not have been able to access otherwise.

Preservation

Preservation is one of the most important benefits of electronic historical artefact documentation. With digital technology, it is possible to create high-quality digital copies of artefacts, which can be stored in a secure digital archive. This allows the original artefacts to be preserved and protected from wear and tear caused by handling or exposure to the elements. In addition, electronic documentation provides an efficient way to monitor the condition of artefacts over time. It allows researchers to compare digital copies created at different times to detect changes in condition or deterioration. For tourism, preserving historical artefacts through electronic documentation enables the creation of virtual exhibits or displays. This can be especially useful for tourists who may not have the opportunity to visit physical museums or historical sites. From a historical research perspective, preserving artefacts through electronic documentation is crucial for ensuring they remain available for future generations to study and learn from. This is especially important given the limited lifespan of many artefacts, which can deteriorate or become lost or damaged due to natural disasters or human conflict. With electronic documentation, historians can be assured that important historical artefacts are preserved for future research and understanding.

Accessibility

Electronic documentation provides unprecedented access to historical information, making it easier for people to research and learn about historical sites and landmarks. With the vast amount of historical material available online, historians can access a wealth of information that may not have been available, enabling them to conduct more thorough and detailed analyses of historical events and phenomena. For tourism, this means that potential visitors can research and plan their trips from anywhere in the world, even if they cannot visit the location physically. This enables them to learn about the historical significance of the site or landmark, which can increase their interest in visiting and promote tourism. This, in turn, can have significant economic benefits for the surrounding community. For historical research, electronic documentation enables scholars to access historical information from anywhere in the world, removing the physical barriers that may have hindered research in the past. This allows historians to research and collaborate with colleagues regardless of location, leading to more comprehensive and interdisciplinary studies. Furthermore, the results of studies can be disseminated more widely, reaching a broader audience and facilitating a greater understanding and appreciation of historical events and phenomena.

Organisation

Electronic documentation enables historical information to be organised in a way that may not have been possible with physical records. This organisation can help make historical information more accessible to both tourists and historians. For tourism, organised information enables visitors to find information quickly and easily about historical sites and artefacts, enhancing their experience and allowing them to make the most of their visit. This can increase interest in historical sites and landmarks, promoting tourism and benefiting the surrounding community. Organised historical information can help researchers quickly find and analyse information, leading to more efficient and effective research. This is particularly important for large-scale studies, where the sheer volume of information can be overwhelming.

Collaboration

Electronic documentation can efficiently allow researchers and institutions to collaborate on historical research projects. Researchers can easily share resources using electronic communication tools, including data, images, and manuscripts. This facilitates interdisciplinary research, allowing researchers from different fields to contribute their expertise and perspectives to a project. Collaboration can lead to new insights into history and culture, as well as new research methods that are more efficient and effective. Collaborative research can also help identify new areas of interest, leading to the development of new tourism opportunities. For example, collaborative research on the history of a particular region might reveal a previously unknown cultural practice that can be incorporated into a tourism package. For tourism, collaborative research can lead to more accurate and interesting information about historical sites and artefacts. This can enhance the visitor experience by providing a more comprehensive understanding of the history and culture of a particular location. Furthermore, collaboration can foster partnerships between researchers and tourism stakeholders, such as museums, heritage sites, and local communities (Owan et al., 2023). This can lead to the development of joint projects and initiatives that benefit both the tourism industry and historical research.

Tourism Promotion

Electronic documentation can provide a platform for promoting tourism by showcasing historical sites and landmarks. Digital media and online platforms such as social media, blogs, and websites can attract potential visitors to historical sites and landmarks by providing detailed information and visuals about the sites. This can create interest and generate buzz around the sites, increasing tourism and economic benefits for the surrounding community. For example, electronic documentation can be used to create virtual tours and exhibits of historical sites, providing visitors with an immersive and interactive experience that can enhance their understanding and appreciation of the history and culture of the location. This can be especially important for visitors who cannot physically visit the location due to physical or financial constraints. Promoting tourism for historical research can increase funding and support for preservation and research projects, which can benefit researchers and the wider community. By generating interest and awareness about historical sites and artefacts, researchers can attract the attention of potential donors, sponsors, and supporters interested in preserving and promoting cultural heritage.

FACTORS THAT IMPEDE THE ELECTRONIC DOCUMENTATION OF NIGERIAN INDIGENOUS ARTS AND CRAFTS

The following are the factors that affect the documentation of Nigerian indigenous arts and crafts in electronic databases.

Electronic Documentation of Nigerian Indigenous Arts and Crafts

Historical Factors

The documentation of Nigerian indigenous Arts and Crafts faces several historical factors that impede its progress. One of the main factors is the oral nature of many of these cultures, where traditions and knowledge are passed down from generation to generation through storytelling, dance, and music. This means that much of these communities' history and cultural knowledge may not have been documented in written form and can be lost over time. Additionally, colonialism and the slave trade have significantly impacted the documentation of Nigerian indigenous Arts and Crafts. Many cultural artefacts were taken away during the slave trade, while colonialism disrupted traditional social structures and cultural practices. This led to a loss of cultural heritage and knowledge, making it more difficult to document and understand these cultures.

Another factor is the lack of resources and infrastructure to document and preserve these cultural artefacts. Many communities lack access to modern technology or trained personnel to properly document their culture and artefacts (Istvandity, 2021; Rakemane & Mosweu, 2021). This can lead to poor documentation, inaccurate preservation, and even loss of cultural heritage. Moreover, political instability and conflicts have also impeded indigenous arts, crafts, and culture documentation. Nigeria has experienced various forms of political unrest, including civil wars and insurgencies, which have destroyed cultural artefacts and displacement of communities. Lastly, the globalisation of culture and the dominance of Western culture have also impacted the documentation of indigenous Arts and Crafts. Many communities are pressured to conform to Western standards and abandon their traditional practices, leading to a loss of cultural heritage and knowledge.

Technological and Logistical Factors

Technology and logistics have also impeded Nigerian indigenous arts, crafts, and culture documentation. One of the major technological challenges is the lack of access to modern recording equipment and software. Many remote communities where these arts and crafts are practised lack the necessary infrastructure to support the use of technology, making it difficult to document their practices. Additionally, the cost of such equipment is often prohibitive, making it difficult for researchers to access them. Logistical challenges also play a significant role in impeding the documentation of indigenous arts and cultures. Nigeria is a vast and diverse country with many ethnic groups and languages. Researchers often face difficulty accessing remote locations due to poor transportation networks, rugged terrain, and lack of infrastructure. This makes it difficult to document the cultural practices of these communities, which are often only passed down orally and through practical demonstrations.

Another logistical challenge is the language barrier. Nigeria has over 500 languages, making it difficult for researchers to communicate with members of these communities. This is particularly problematic when attempting to document cultural practices only passed down through oral traditions. Valuable cultural knowledge may be lost or misrepresented without proper translation and interpretation. Furthermore, cultural and religious sensitivities often exist around the documentation of indigenous arts and cultures. Some communities may view the documentation of their practices as a violation of their cultural heritage, leading to resistance or reluctance to share their knowledge with outsiders. This can make it difficult for researchers to gain the trust of these communities and access the information they need.

Socio-Cultural Factors

Socio-cultural factors can also impede the documentation of indigenous Arts and Crafts in Nigeria. The first factor is the lack of interest and appreciation for indigenous arts and crafts. Many people value Western art and crafts over traditional ones, leading to a lack of demand for indigenous artworks. As a result, there is a limited market for indigenous arts, and artists may not see the need to document their work or its cultural significance. Secondly, some cultural beliefs and practices restrict the documentation of certain artworks and cultural practices. For instance, some Nigerian cultures believe certain artistic works and practices are sacred and should not be shared or documented with outsiders. This can make it difficult for researchers to access certain cultural artefacts and practices, hindering documentation.

Thirdly, the social status of indigenous artisans can also be a factor. Many indigenous artisans in Nigeria are from lower socioeconomic backgrounds, and their work is not always valued or recognised. This can lead to a lack of resources and infrastructure for documenting their work and limited access to technology and training in documentation techniques. Lastly, the lack of institutional support and funding for documenting indigenous arts and crafts poses a challenge. Many institutions and organisations may prioritise Western art and culture over indigenous ones, leading to a lack of funding and support for documenting indigenous cultural practices. This can hinder the efforts of researchers and indigenous artisans in documenting their work and culture.

Economic Factors

Economic factors can also impede the documentation of indigenous Arts and Crafts. Many indigenous communities often live in poverty and lack the resources to invest in documenting their cultural practices. As a result, documenting their cultural heritage may not be a priority, and they may lack the funds to purchase equipment or pay for the services of professional documentarians. Furthermore, there may be limited economic opportunities for commercialising indigenous arts and crafts, which may discourage the investment of resources in their documentation. The lack of economic incentives for documenting indigenous arts and crafts can also lead to a lack of interest from private companies and government agencies in funding documentation efforts. Additionally, economic factors can contribute to exploiting indigenous cultures and resources. In some cases, individuals or companies may seek to profit from commercialising indigenous cultural practices without the consent or benefit of the communities in question. This can lead to a reluctance among indigenous communities to share their cultural practices and knowledge, as they may fear exploitation or cultural appropriation.

Political Factors

Political factors can also impede the documentation of indigenous Arts and Crafts in Nigeria. One major factor is government policy, which can hinder documentation efforts. Government policies may not prioritise the documentation of indigenous arts and cultures, leading to a lack of resources and funding for documentation efforts. Additionally, political instability and conflict in certain regions of Nigeria can make it difficult for researchers to access and document indigenous cultures. Another political factor is censorship and control of information. In some cases, governments may limit or control the documentation of indigenous cultures due to cultural or political sensitivities. This can result in a lack

Electronic Documentation of Nigerian Indigenous Arts and Crafts

of information available to researchers and the wider public, hindering efforts to document and preserve indigenous cultures. Furthermore, the lack of government recognition and support for traditional art forms and cultural practices can lead to declining interest and investment in documenting indigenous arts and cultures. This can result in a lack of resources and infrastructure to support documentation efforts, making it difficult for researchers to collect and preserve information.

Religious Factors

Religion can also be a factor that impedes the documentation of indigenous Arts and Crafts in Nigeria. Some indigenous cultures and art forms are closely tied to religious practices and beliefs. These cultures and art forms may not be readily shared with outsiders, as they are considered sacred and restricted to members of a particular religious group. In some cases, religious beliefs may also destroy or alter indigenous art and cultural artefacts. Certain religious groups may view certain art forms or practices as pagan or idolatrous and seek to eliminate or modify them. For instance, the penetration of Christianity into Africa and Nigeria, in particular, has altered various traditional practices. In some cases, pastors and church ministers are observed burning indigenous arts and crafts, and abolishing certain cultural practices, terming them "fetish" or "unholy". As a result, some indigenous people have stopped practising or teaching traditional arts and crafts, leading to a decline in the transmission of knowledge about these practices, affecting documentation efforts.

Furthermore, Christian missions and missionaries often prioritise the documentation and preservation of Christian arts and artefacts over indigenous ones, which can further marginalise indigenous cultures and contribute to the loss of traditional knowledge. Religious conflicts and tensions complicate documenting and preserving indigenous arts and cultures. Nigeria has experienced several religious conflicts, with some destroying cultural artefacts. This can make it difficult for historians and researchers to access and study these artefacts, as they may have been destroyed or lost.

STRATEGIES FOR ELECTRONIC DOCUMENTATION OF NIGERIAN INDIGENOUS ARTS AND CRAFTS

This section discusses the strategies for electronically documenting Nigerian indigenous Arts and Crafts.

Creation of a Digital Repository

Creating a digital repository for Nigerian indigenous Arts and Crafts is an essential strategy for electronic documentation. This repository can be a central hub for storing and sharing digital copies of artefacts, photographs, audio recordings, and other relevant materials. For instance, the Igbo-Ukwu bronze artefacts, a collection of brass objects discovered in Igbo-Ukwu, can be preserved and accessible to scholars and the general public through this strategy.

Digitisation of Physical Archives and Manuscripts

The digitisation of physical archives and manuscripts is another key strategy for electronic documentation. This will help to preserve these materials and make them more accessible to researchers, scholars, and the public. For example, digitising manuscripts and archives related to the Nok Terracotta can aid in preserving and sharing information about the culture and art of the Nok people.

Development of Multimedia Resources

The development of multimedia resources, such as videos, podcasts, and interactive exhibits, can help to engage a wider audience and promote interest in Nigerian indigenous Arts and Crafts. These resources, including social media and the digital repository, can be shared online. For example, a video showcasing the weaving process of the Akwete cloth of the Igbo people can be developed to help promote the art and craft to a wider audience.

Collaboration With Local Communities

Collaboration with local communities is crucial for the successful electronic documentation of Nigerian indigenous Arts and Crafts. This collaboration can help ensure that cultural practices and traditions are accurately represented, and that the community has a stake in preserving and promoting its heritage. For example, collaborations with the Efik or Ibibio communities can aid in preserving the Ekpe Masquerade, a prominent cultural practice in the region.

Training of Local Experts

The training of local experts in electronic documentation techniques and technologies can help to build capacity and ensure the sustainability of the documentation efforts. This can involve training in digital photography, audio recording, metadata management, and other relevant skills. For instance, training in digital photography, audio recording, metadata management, and other relevant skills can be provided to the community members with traditional knowledge of stone carving/ sculpturing in Cross River State.

Promotion of Electronic Documentation Efforts

Promoting electronic documentation through targeted marketing campaigns can raise awareness and generate interest among potential stakeholders, including tourists, scholars, and funding agencies. This can involve the development of a website or social media presence for the digital repository, as well as outreach to relevant organisations and institutions.

Integration With Education

Integration of electronic documentation efforts with education can ensure that future generations are aware of and engaged with Nigerian indigenous Arts and Crafts. This can involve the development of educational materials and resources, such as online courses, workshops, and classroom materials, that incorporate the digital repository and multimedia resources. For instance, this strategy can teach the Yoruba people's history and traditional use of Aso Oke cloth in Nigerian schools.

CASE STUDIES OF SUCCESSFUL ELECTRONIC DOCUMENTATION OF INDIGENOUS ARTS AND CRAFTS

This section reviews successful projects documenting indigenous arts, crafts or cultures in different parts of the world. The first case study is the Museum of Anthropology at the University of British Columbia (MOA) has a digital collection of Northwest Coast Indigenous art that includes over 12,000 objects, photographs, and archival documents (Kramer, 2013). The strengths of this project include the extensive scope of the collection, the quality of the digital images, and the user-friendly online platform. The digital collection provides access to artefacts that may be difficult for researchers and community members to access in person due to geographic and cultural barriers.

The Smithsonian Institution's National Museum of the American Indian (NMAI) in the United States is another example of successful electronic documentation of indigenous Arts and Crafts. The NMAI has created an extensive digital repository of materials related to the Native peoples of the Americas, including images, audio recordings, and videos (Drumheller & Kaminitz, 1994; Rosoff, 2005). One strength of the NMAI's digital repository is its focus on community engagement and collaboration. The museum has worked closely with Native communities to ensure that their cultural traditions and practices are accurately represented in the digital collection. The NMAI has also provided training to Native community members on using the digital tools and technologies needed for documentation and preservation. Another strength of the NMAI's electronic documentation efforts is the development of multimedia resources. The museum has produced various videos, podcasts, and interactive exhibits that help engage a wider audience and promote interest in Native American cultures. These resources are available on the museum's website, as well as on social media platforms.

One notable example of a successful electronic documentation project for indigenous Arts and Crafts is the "Digital Library of the National Museum of Anthropology" in Mexico City. The National Museum of Anthropology is one of the world's most important museums dedicated to Mexico's history and anthropology. It contains many artefacts, including many examples of indigenous art and craftwork (Lau, 2009). One of the strengths of this project is the high-quality digital reproductions of the artefacts, which allow users to examine the items in detail and appreciate their intricate details. The digital library also includes detailed descriptions and contextual information about each item, providing users with important cultural and historical context. Another strength of the project is its accessibility, with the digital library available online for free to anyone with an internet connection. This has helped promote interest in Mexican indigenous Arts and Crafts locally and internationally.

The British Museum in London, United Kingdom, has implemented electronic documentation strategies to preserve and promote the cultural heritage of indigenous communities across the world (Ballard et al., 2017; Harris, 2015). They have a digital repository that includes thousands of photographs, videos, and other digital resources, as well as multimedia exhibits and educational materials. The British Museum's electronic documentation strategies have several strengths. First, their digital repository contains many materials, making it a valuable resource for researchers, scholars, and the general public. Second, the multimedia exhibits and educational materials help to engage a wider audience and promote interest in indigenous cultures (Taylor & Gibson, 2017). Third, the collaboration with local communities, as evidenced by the inclusion of contemporary voices and perspectives in the materials, ensures that the cultural heritage is accurately represented and respects the community's stake in their heritage (Srinivasan et al., 2009).

The National Museum of Mali has implemented electronic documentation strategies to preserve and promote the cultural heritage of indigenous communities in Mali. Their digital repository includes photographs, videos, other resources, multimedia exhibits, and educational materials. The National Museum of Mali's implementation of electronic documentation strategies is a strength because it allows for preserving and promoting indigenous cultures in Mali. The digital repository allows for wider access to cultural resources, which can help increase awareness and understanding of these communities (Arnoldi et al., 2021; Konaré, 1981). The multimedia exhibits and educational materials can also help engage a wider audience and promote interest in Mali's indigenous cultures. One potential weakness of the project may be the accessibility of the digital resources to the local communities themselves (Arnoldi, 2006). While it is important to have a wider reach, it is also crucial that local communities have access to their cultural heritage.

LESSONS LEARNED FROM PREVIOUS ELECTRONIC DOCUMENTATION EFFORTS OF INDIGENOUS ARTS AND CRAFTS

Based on the weaknesses identified in earlier attempts to document indigenous Arts and Crafts electronically, this chapter can derive the following lessons learned and recommendations for future efforts in Nigeria:

Community Involvement

Many past initiatives lacked the involvement of Indigenous communities in creating and managing digital collections, resulting in a lack of cultural sensitivity and inclusivity. This lack of community involvement meant cultural materials were often collected without proper consultation or permission, leading to distrust and frustration among Indigenous communities. Future initiatives should prioritise community involvement in creating and managing digital collections, ensuring that Indigenous communities are consulted and involved in all aspects of the collection process. This can be achieved by establishing partnerships with local organisations and community leaders and involving community members in training and capacity-building activities.

Cultural Sensitivity

Some past efforts neglected indigenous communities' cultural practices and beliefs, leading to incomplete or inaccurate documentation of cultural objects. This resulted in misrepresentations of cultural materials, which indigenous communities viewed as offensive or disrespectful. As a result, many indigenous communities hesitated to participate in future initiatives. Future efforts should prioritise cultural sensitivity in the documentation process to respect Indigenous communities' cultural practices and beliefs. This can be achieved by involving Indigenous communities in the documentation process, providing adequate training and support to researchers and project teams, and creating culturally-sensitive metadata and descriptive information.

Accessibility

Previous initiatives often faced challenges in accessibility, with collections being available only in certain languages or through limited platforms. This limited access made it difficult for Indigenous

Electronic Documentation of Nigerian Indigenous Arts and Crafts

communities to access and use digital collections, reducing the potential impact of the collections. To ensure digital collections are accessible to all, future initiatives should prioritise accessibility by making collections available in various Nigerian languages and accessible through multiple platforms, including mobile phones. This can be achieved by partnering with local technology companies and telecommunication providers and providing training and resources to community members on how to access and use digital collections.

Sustainability

Many earlier initiatives were not sustainable, resulting in outdated or inaccessible collections due to insufficient funding or resources. Digital collections became obsolete over time, with limited capacity for future updates or maintenance. This undermined the potential long-term impact of digital collections. To ensure the long-term viability of digital collections, subsequent attempts should prioritise sustainability by establishing partnerships with local universities and research institutions and securing adequate funding for the ongoing maintenance and development of digital collections.

Capacity Building

Previous initiatives often failed to build capacity within Indigenous communities to manage and curate digital collections, leading to a lack of ownership and control over cultural materials. This lack of ownership and control meant that Indigenous communities often felt excluded from the digital collection process, reducing the potential impact of digital collections on these communities. Therefore, future initiatives should prioritise capacity building by providing training and resources tailored to the needs and context of different communities to ensure Indigenous communities are equipped to manage and curate digital collections. This can be achieved by establishing partnerships with local organisations and community leaders.

Digital Preservation

Past initiatives lacked comprehensive digital preservation policies, leading to the loss or degradation of digital collections over time. This meant that many collections were lost or damaged due to insufficient backup or storage mechanisms, undermining the potential impact of digital collections on future generations. Thus, subsequent attempts to document indigenous Arts and Crafts by nations such as Nigeria should prioritise comprehensive digital preservation policies by adopting established digital preservation standards and best practices and partnering with local technology companies and research institutions to prevent the loss or degradation of digital collections and ensure that digital collections are properly maintained and preserved.

Evaluation and Assessment

Many past efforts failed to evaluate the impact of digital collections on Indigenous communities and broader audiences. This lack of evaluation made it difficult to determine the effectiveness of digital collections and identify areas for improvement. As a result, many digital collections failed to meet their intended objectives or have the desired impact on their intended audiences. To regularly assess and monitor the impact of digital collections, future efforts should prioritise evaluation and assessment by developing frameworks tailored to the needs and context of different communities and partnering with local organisations and research institutions to collect and analyse data on the impact of digital collections.

CONCLUSION AND RECOMMENDATIONS

In conclusion, documenting and preserving indigenous Arts and Crafts is crucial for promoting and preserving cultural heritage. Electronic documentation offers immense potential to achieve this objective but requires careful planning and implementation. The lessons learned from previous electronic documentation efforts of indigenous Arts and Crafts provide useful insights and recommendations for future initiatives in Nigeria and other nations. Community involvement, cultural sensitivity, accessibility, sustainability, funding, capacity building, digital preservation, and evaluation and assessment are all critical factors to consider in future efforts. By prioritising these factors, we can ensure that digital collections of indigenous Arts and Crafts are comprehensive, accessible, and sustainable, positively impacting Indigenous communities and broader audiences for years to come. Moreover, these initiatives can foster trust, collaboration, and co-creation with Indigenous communities, ultimately promoting cultural preservation, revitalisation, and empowerment. The digital collections resulting from these initiatives can be used for research, education, and cultural promotion, benefiting not only Indigenous communities but also broader audiences interested in learning about the diverse cultural heritage of Nigeria.

REFERENCES

Abubakar, S. (2021). Youth empowerment as a tool for socio-economic changes in Nigeria. *International Journal of Youth Economy*, *5*(1), 19–27. doi:10.18576/ijye/050103

Adesina, O. A., Taiwo, A. E., Akindele, O., & Igbafe, A. (2021). Process parametric studies for decolouration of dye from local 'tie and dye industrial effluent using moringa oleifera seed. *South African Journal of Chemical Engineering*, *37*, 23–30. doi:10.1016/j.sajce.2021.03.005

Akintonde, M. A. (2013). Typology and geography of outdoor sculpture in southwestern Nigeria. *Research on Humanities and Social Sciences, 3*(10), 120-129. https://core.ac.uk/download/pdf/234673566.pdf

Areo, M. O., & Kalilu, R. O. R. (2013). Adire in southwestern Nigeria: Geography of the centres. *African Research Review*, *7*(2), 350–370. doi:10.4314/afrrev.v7i2.22

Arnoldi, M. J. (2006). Youth festivals and museums: The cultural politics of public memory in postcolonial Mali. *Africa Today*, *52*(4), 55–76. doi:10.1353/at.2006.0037

Arnoldi, M. J., Kéita, D., & Sidibé, S. (2021). The national museum of Mali, 1960–present: Protecting and promoting the national cultural heritage. In R. Silverman, G. Abungu, & P. Probst (Eds.), *National museums in Africa* (pp. 139–158). Routledge., doi:10.4324/9781003013693-8

Aryal, A., Morley, C. G., & McLean, I. G. (2018). Conserving elephants depend on a total ban of ivory trade globally. *Biodiversity and Conservation*, *27*(10), 2767–2775. doi:10.100710531-018-1534-x

Electronic Documentation of Nigerian Indigenous Arts and Crafts

Ballard, H. L., Robinson, L. D., Young, A. N., Pauly, G. B., Higgins, L. M., Johnson, R. F., & Tweddle, J. C. (2017). Contributions to conservation outcomes by natural history museum-led citizen science: Examining evidence and next steps. *Biological Conservation, 208,* 87–97. doi:10.1016/j.biocon.2016.08.040

Breunig, P., Franke, G., & Nüsse, M. (2008). Early sculptural traditions in West Africa: New evidence from the Chad Basin of north-eastern Nigeria. *Antiquity, 82*(316), 423–437. doi:10.1017/S0003598X00096915

Carr, A., Ruhanen, L., & Whitford, M. (2016). Indigenous peoples and tourism: The challenges and opportunities for sustainable tourism. *Journal of Sustainable Tourism, 24*(8-9), 1067–1079. doi:10.10 80/09669582.2016.1206112

De Sutter, E., Borry, P., Geerts, D., & Huys, I. (2021). Personalized and long-term electronic informed consent in clinical research: Stakeholder views. *BMC Medical Ethics, 22*(1), 1–12. doi:10.118612910-021-00675-7 PMID:34332572

Demssie, Y. N., Biemans, H. J., Wesselink, R., & Mulder, M. (2020). Combining indigenous knowledge and modern education to foster sustainability competencies: Towards a set of learning design principles. *Sustainability (Basel), 12*(17), 6823. doi:10.3390u12176823

Drumheller, A., & Kaminitz, M. (1994). Traditional care and conservation, the merging of two disciplines at the national museum of the American Indian. *Studies in Conservation, 39*(2), 58–60. doi:10.1179ic.1994.39.Supplement-2.58

Duncan, C., & Wallach, A. (2019). The Museum of Modern Art as Late Capitalist Ritual: An Iconographie Analysis. In D. Preziosi & C. Farago (Eds.), *Grasping the World* (pp. 483–499). Routledge. doi:10.4324/9780429399671-31

Eichler, J. (2021). Intangible cultural heritage, inequalities and participation: Who decides on heritage? *International Journal of Human Rights, 25*(5), 793–814. doi:10.1080/13642987.2020.1822821

Ezenagu, N. (2020). Heritage resources as a driver for cultural tourism in Nigeria. *Cogent Arts & Humanities, 7*(1), 1734331. doi:10.1080/23311983.2020.1734331

Fernández-Llamazares, Á., & Cabeza, M. (2018). *Rediscovering the potential of indigenous storytelling.* Wiley.

Gilmore, R. O., Kennedy, J. L., & Adolph, K. E. (2018). Practical solutions for sharing data and materials from psychological research. *Advances in Methods and Practices in Psychological Science, 1*(1), 121–130. doi:10.1177/2515245917746500 PMID:31157320

Harris, F. (2015). Understanding human remains repatriation: Practice procedures at the British Museum and the natural history museum. *Museum Management and Curatorship, 30*(2), 138–153. doi:10.1080 /09647775.2015.1022904

Hornbeck, S. E. (2015). Elephant ivory: An overview of changes to its stringent regulation and considerations for its identification. *Objects Spec. Group Postprints AIC, 22,* 101–121.

Ijisakin, E. T. (2019). Printmaking in Nigeria: Its evolution and developmental history. *Academic Journal of Interdisciplinary Studies, 8*(2), 247–260. doi:10.2478/ajis-2019-0036

Ijisakin, E. T. (2021). Printmaking and cultural imagination in contemporary Nigerian art. *Critical Arts, 35*(1), 1–16. doi:10.1080/02560046.2020.1856900

Irivwieri, G. O. (2009). Arts and crafts as a springboard for sustainable development and industrialisation in Nigeria. *International Journal of Creativity and Technical Development, 1*(1-3), 1–18. https://www.academia.edu/8151930/Arts_and_crafts

Istvandity, L. (2021). How does music heritage get lost? Examining cultural heritage loss in community and authorised music archives. *International Journal of Heritage Studies, 27*(4), 331–343. doi:10.1080/13527258.2020.1795904

Jordan, S., Zabukovšek, S. S., & Klančnik, I. Š. (2022). Document Management System–A Way to Digital Transformation. *Naše gospodarstvo/Our economy, 68*(2), 43-54. doi:10.2478/ngoe-2022-0010

Kashim, I. B., Adelabu, O. S., Fatuyi, S. A., & Fadairo, O. O. (2013). Bridging the Gap: Artistry of Felicia Adepelu, Potter of Igbara-Odo, Ekiti State, Nigeria. *Critical Interventions, 7*(1), 50–64. doi:10.1080/19301944.2013.10781426

Konaré, A. O. (1981). Birth of a museum at Bamako, Mali. *Museum International, 33*(1), 4–8. doi:10.1111/j.1468-0033.1981.tb01936.x

Kramer, J. (2013). Möbius museology: Curating and critiquing the multiversity galleries at the museum of anthropology at the University of British Columbia. *The International Handbooks of Museum Studies*, 489-510. doi:10.1002/9781118829059.wbihms421

Lau, J. (2009). Mexican libraries, archives and museums: a snapshot. In P. Elis (Ed.), *Encyclopedia of Library and Information Science* (3rd ed., pp. 1–40). Taylor & Francis. https://core.ac.uk/download/pdf/16292208.pdf

Maiwada, S., Dutsenwai, S. A., & Waziri, M. Y. (2012). Cultural industries and wealth creation: The case of the traditional textile industry in Nigeria. *American International Journal of Contemporary Research, 2*(5), 159–165. http://www.aijcrnet.com/journals/Vol_2_No_5_May_2012/17.pdf

Masenya, T. M. (2022). Digital Preservation of Indigenous Knowledge in South African Rural Communities. In R. Tshifhumulo & T. Makhanikhe (Eds.), *Handbook of Research on Protecting and Managing Global Indigenous Knowledge Systems* (pp. 317–340). IGI Global. doi:10.4018/978-1-7998-7492-8.ch017

Matshameko, Y., Kebonye, N. M., & Eze, P. N. (2022). Ethnopedological knowledge and scientific assessment of earthenware pottery-making soils of southern Botswana for natural resource management. *Geoderma Regional, 31*, e00580. doi:10.1016/j.geodrs.2022.e00580

Mbilinyi, D., & Mwabungulu, E. M. (2020). The fate of indigenous knowledge: The role played by libraries in Tanzania. *Information Development, 36*(4), 489–502. doi:10.1177/0266666919871088

McGinnis, G., Harvey, M., & Young, T. (2020). Indigenous knowledge sharing in Northern Australia: Engaging digital technology for cultural interpretation. *Tourism Planning & Development, 17*(1), 96–125. doi:10.1080/21568316.2019.1704855

McIntosh, S. K. (2022). Igbo-Ukwu at 50: A symposium on recent archaeological research and analysis. *African Archaeological Review, 39*(4), 369–385. doi:10.100710437-022-09495-5 PMID:36405395

Mdhluli, T. D., Mokgoatšana, S., Kugara, S. L., & Vuma, L. (2021). Knowledge management: Preserving, managing and sharing indigenous knowledge through digital library. *Hervormde Teologiese Studies*, *77*(2), 1–7. doi:10.4102/hts.v77i2.6795

Mukred, M., Yusof, Z. M., Alotaibi, F. M., Asma'Mokhtar, U., & Fauzi, F. (2019). The key factors in adopting an electronic records management system (ERMS) in the educational sector: A UTAUT-based framework. *IEEE Access : Practical Innovations, Open Solutions*, *7*, 35963–35980. doi:10.1109/ACCESS.2019.2904617

Noah, E. A., & Çağnan, Ç. (2021). A Study of Vernacular Architecture In Relation To Sustainability; the Case of Northern Nigeria. *YDÜ Mimarlık Fakültesi Dergisi*, *3*(1), 21–35.

Nwankwo, E., Oguamanam, C., & Obieluem, U. (2018). Sustainable safety and preservation mechanisms for cross river monoliths. *Journal of Tourism and Heritage Studies*, *7*(2), 52–62. doi:10.33281/JTHS20129.2017.2.5

Okonkwo, E. E., Ukaegbu, M. O., & Eyisi, A. P. (2016). A documentation of some traditional aspects of wood consumption in Anaocha, Nigeria. *SAGE Open*, *6*(2), 2158244016649417. doi:10.1177/2158244016649417

Okoye, J., & Oni, K. (2017). Promotion of indigenous food preservation and processing knowledge and the challenge of food security in Africa. *Journal of Food Security*, *5*(3), 75–87.

Okwoche, A. S., Okonkwo, E. E., & Oyong, T. A. (2021). Ethnographic studies of Bakor stone monolith and their implication to tourism development. *Lakhomi Journal Scientific Journal of Culture*, *2*(4), 171–187. doi:10.33258/lakhomi.v2i4.556

Oladejo, M. T. (2019). Challenges of technical and vocational education and training in Nigerian history. *Makerere Journal of Higher Education*, *11*(1), 67–81. doi:10.4314/majohe.v11i1.6

Osasona, C. O. (2007). Indigenous art and Nigerian contemporary residential architecture. *WIT Transactions on the Built Environment*, *95*, 129–139. doi:10.2495/STR070131

Owan, V. J., Ameh, E., & Anam, E. G. (2023). Collaboration and institutional culture as mediators linking mentorship and institutional support to academics' research productivity. *Educational Research for Policy and Practice*, *22*(2), 1–26. doi:10.100710671-023-09354-3

Peters, E. E. (2021). Implication of early pottery practice by women in Nigeria: A focus on women pottery practice in Akwa Ibom state. *Academicia: An International Multidisciplinary Research Journal*, *11*(1), 474–481. doi:10.5958/2249-7137.2021.00067.7

Rakemane, D., & Mosweu, O. (2021). Challenges of managing and preserving audio-visual archives in archival institutions in Sub Saharan Africa: A literature review. *Collection and Curation*, *40*(2), 42–50. doi:10.1108/CC-04-2020-0011

Renne, E. P. (2020). Reinterpreting Adire cloth in northern Nigeria. *Textile History*, *51*(1), 60–85. doi:10.1080/00404969.2020.1747372

Rosoff, N. B. (2005). Integrating native views into museum procedures: Hope and practice at the national museum of the American Indian. In N. B. Rosoff (Ed.), *Museums and source communities* (pp. 83–90). Routledge. doi:10.4324/9780203987834-14

Seidu, R. K., Howard, E. K., Apau, E., & Eghan, B. (2022). Symbolism and conservation of indigenous African textiles for museums. Handbook of Museum Textiles, 1, 239-265. doi:10.1002/9781119983903.ch13

Shipley, J. W. (2017). From primitivism to Pan-Africanism: Remaking modernist aesthetics in postcolonial Nigeria. *Ghana Studies*, *20*(1), 140–174. doi:10.3368/gs.20.1.140

Siyanbola, W. O., Egbetokun, A. A., Oluseyi, I., Olamade, O. O., Aderemi, H. O., & Sanni, M. (2012). Indigenous technologies and innovation in Nigeria: Opportunities for SMEs. *American Journal of Industrial and Business Management*, *2*(2), 18846. doi:10.4236/ajibm.2012.22009

Sobowale, T. O., Olarinde, O. J., Uzzi, F. O., & Sunday, O. S. (2020). Creative Welded Metal Art: A Means to Financial Sustainability. *KIU Journal of Humanities*, *5*(1), 77–86.

Srinivasan, R., Boast, R., Furner, J., & Becvar, K. M. (2009). Digital museums and diverse cultural knowledge: Moving past the traditional catalogue. *The Information Society*, *25*(4), 265–278. doi:10.1080/01972240903028714

Stout, D., Toth, N., Schick, K., & Chaminade, T. (2008). Neural correlates of early stone age toolmaking: Technology, language and cognition in human evolution. *Philosophical Transactions of the Royal Society of London. Series B, Biological Sciences*, *363*(1499), 1939–1949. doi:10.1098/rstb.2008.0001 PMID:18292067

Sunday, O. O., Oyeniran, G., & Akeju, A. A. (2022). Community Participation in Conservation and Management of Cultural Heritage Resources in Yoruba Ethnic Group of South Western Nigeria. *SAGE Open*, *12*(4), 21582440221130987. doi:10.1177/21582440221130987

Tapfuma, M., & Hoskins, R. (2016). Visibility and accessibility of indigenous knowledge on open access institutional repositories at universities in Africa. In P. Ngulube (Ed.), *Handbook of Research on Theoretical Perspectives on Indigenous Knowledge Systems in Developing Countries* (pp. 248–266). IGI Global. doi:10.4018/978-1-5225-0833-5.ch011

Taylor, J., & Gibson, L. K. (2017). Digitisation, digital interaction and social media: Embedded barriers to democratic heritage. *International Journal of Heritage Studies*, *23*(5), 408–420. doi:10.1080/13527258.2016.1171245

Uriah, L., Dungrit, C., & Rhoda, G. (2014). Locally made utensils as potential sources of heavy metals contamination of water: A case study of some pots made in Nigeria. *American Journal of Environmental Protection, 3*(6-2), 35-41. doi:10.11648/j.ajep.s.2014030602.16

Zimu-Biyela, A. N. (2016). *The management and preservation of indigenous knowledge in Dlangubo village in Kwazulu-Natal, South Africa.* [Doctoral Dissertation, University of South Africa, Pretoria]. http://hdl.handle.net/10500/22968

ADDITIONAL READING

Edeoja, J. A., Fouseki, K., & Albuerne, A. (2022). Heritage values and heritage management frameworks in Nigeria. In K. Fouseki, M. Cassar, G. Dreyfuss, & K. A. K. Eng (Eds), Routledge handbook of sustainable heritage (pp. 58-71). Routledge. https://doi.org/ doi:10.4324/9781003038955-6

Madandola, M., & Boussaa, D. (2023). Cultural heritage tourism as a catalyst for sustainable development; the case of old Oyo town in Nigeria. *International Journal of Heritage Studies*, *29*(1-2), 1–18. doi:10.1080/13527258.2023.2169332

Novelli, M. (2015). *Tourism and development in Sub-Saharan Africa: Current issues and local realities.* Routledge. doi:10.4324/9780203069325

Osuchukwu, N. P., & Udeze, N. S. (2021). Enabling cultural heritage spaces in Nigerian public libraries: A case study of the Anambra State Library Board. *IFLA Journal*, *47*(3), 398–405. doi:10.1177/03400352211024673

KEY TERMS AND DEFINITIONS

Cultural Heritage: The tangible and intangible products of a community's cultural and artistic traditions inherited from previous generations and transmitted to future generations.

Digital Preservation: The process of ensuring that digital content is stored, maintained, and usable over time, often involving measures to prevent data loss or degradation.

Indigenous Knowledge: Knowledge and practices unique to a particular culture or community often passed down through generations, reflecting a deep understanding of the natural environment and its resources.

Metadata Management Software: Software designed to facilitate the creation, management, and retrieval of metadata for digital objects.

Open Access: The practice of making digital resources freely available to the public, often through online platforms, without restrictions on use or reuse.

Chapter 14

Indigenous Livestreaming in Brazil:
A Methodological Case for Reflective Distant Witnessing

Tom Kissock-Mamede

(iD) https://orcid.org/0000-0002-7482-8818

University of Cambridge, UK

ABSTRACT

This chapter explores how livestreaming is a means to advocate for Indigenous rights and seeks to understand how Indigenous communal organizing is disseminated to distant others, focusing on researchers. Using video data analysis (VDA), it empirically explores a livestream on Instagram by the Huni Kuin showing a food distribution program. The key findings show that livestreams have both epistemological insights and rifts regarding the information that can be gained from distant witnessing. It argues that indigenous streaming is a positive, however, it's vital to remain reflexive as researchers when examining Indigenous livestreams. It postulates that we should understand streams as a form of witnessing rather than observation and sets out best practices for conducting empirical research on them. It conceptualizes a methodology for cataloguing livestreams by expanding on VDA and amalgamating it with critical auto-ethnographic reflections as a distant researcher. It concludes we should be sharing spaces as solidarity witnesses, and provision testimony in a form of knowledge transfers.

INTRODUCTION

We may think of a Zoom or Teams meeting as a Livestream; however, livestreams are public-facing and not always a webinar held on conferencing software unless the meeting is simultaneously being broadcasted on a social media platform. Yet, there's many similarities considering that the video is transmitted in real-time between participants synchronically. Therefore, livestreams have a range of definitions in the literature, and many organizations who use livestreaming, often internally disagree on

DOI: 10.4018/978-1-6684-7024-4.ch014

Copyright © 2023, IGI Global. Copying or distributing in print or electronic forms without written permission of IGI Global is prohibited.

Indigenous Livestreaming in Brazil

what constitutes a Livestream (Faklaris *et al.*, 2016). This chapter defines a livestream as a transmission of audio and video across a network in real-time and explores how indigenous communities in Brazil use livestreaming on Instagram as a form of narrowcasting where videos are intended for a specific public, like the channel's followers, whom may not be from the same community as the indigenous streamer. It subsequently sheds light on how distant researchers should be witnessing livestreams. With the increased availability of internet connectivity in the Brazilian Amazon (Gabrys, 2022), Indigenous activists are using information communication technologies (ICTs) to discuss Citizenship and environmental rights (Salzar, 2006; Kissock, 2020b). Livestreaming is a relatively new method of capturing video evidence, asserting liberties, or affirming belonging to a community (Kissock, 2020c). The technology's lineage can be traced back to the 1980s, when researchers from Stanford University pioneering IP Multicasting to facilitate the transmission of video and audio data packets simultaneously to multiple destinations across a network. Initially, they wanted to create a new conferencing system for sharing scholarly research (Robinson, 2020). Then the 1990s saw the first commercial uses for Livestreaming when in 1993, the band Severe Tire Damage performed a livestream on the platform MBone (Alfred, 2009). In the 2000s, the invention of the mp4 video protocol theoretically gave almost everyone the capability to stream video content from their mobile phones. Until recently, this was limited to individuals who lived in urban environments and were within reach of mobile cell towers, however during the 2010's multiple societies saw a rapid expansion of telecoms companies extending their networks into rural areas. Hence, communities like some Indigenous Brazilians are better connected to the internet and are active on platforms like Instagram, TikTok, and Kwai, and film events and advocacy campaigns in real-time (Whitson, 2021).

Livestreaming across indigenous communities in Brazil has thus become a pastime, with the practice and its importance for cultural preservation being mentioned by the Head Brazils new Ministry for Indigenous Peoples Sonia Guajajara at the COP27 Brazil Climate Hub in Egypt. Minister Guajajara's comments can be placed within a contextual global push for the preservation of indigenous knowledges, for example UNESCO have declared 2022-2023 as the decade of Indigenous Languages (UNESCO, 2021). Thus, livestreaming as a cultural phenomenon coupled with the Covid-19 pandemic meant researchers had to address livestreams as cultural artefacts, the pandemic also afforded distant witnesses like myself the ability to glimpse into these digital spaces in real-time. This then raises some important questions such as: How should we be researching livestreams of distant communities and how reliable or robust is the empirical data we can gain from them?

Historicising Land Conflict and Indigenous Techno Activism in Brazil

The situation of Brazilian Indigenous land rights reached a low point with President Jair Bolsonaro in office (Menton *et al.*, 2021; Mantelli, Neiva and Ingrams, 2022), with his government implementing or attempting to implement neo-colonial policies (Urt, 2016). An example of this is the Marco Temporal thesis which is a collection of bill proposals designed to delimit indigenous rights (Leal de Oliveira, Ruy Bragatto and Montenegro de Souza Lima, 2023). One such bill is PL490, which was approved by the Brazilian Congress on the 30th of May 2023 (by an Agri-business and Pro-Bolsonaro lobby) and means that Indigenous communities who can't prove they occupied their ancestral land as of the 1988 constitution wouldn't be entitled to have that land demarcated, which brings forth numerous problems such as ignoring the vast numbers of displaced indigenous peoples in Brazil as just one example (FUNAI, 2023). Much of the scholarship arrives at the consensus that this leads to adverse outcomes for Indigenous peoples, where the only divergence within the current literature is found in framings, for

263

example where some scholars also focus on small holders' rights and rural Brazilians' ability to own and cultivate land sustainably (Hoelle, 2017; Rojas, de Azevedo Olival and Alves Spexoto Olival, 2021). This analysis belongs to a pattern of empirical trends over the past four decades that has highlighted numerous examples of how Brazil's political economy is dependent on the pressures of globalization (Garrett *et al.*, 2021) and has thus led to undesirable rights violations occurring against Indigenous populations and consequently disregarding Indigenous people voices in Brazil's Congress (Ribeiro, 1975, 1977; Davis, 1977; Vidal, 1986; Carneiro da Cunha, 1992; Ramos, 1998; Carvalho, 2000; Liverman and Vilas, 2006; Chisita, Rusero and Shoko, 2016; Villén-Pérez *et al.*, 2021).

Bolsonaro's Kakistocratic Government (Marques, 2022) has followed this trend by encouraging criminals to perpetuate paternalistic violence against Indigenous peoples. This has led organisations such as The Articulation for Indigenous Peoples (APIB) to bring a case of genocide against him to the International Criminal Court (Freeman and Vazquez Llorente, 2021). Bolsonaro's government's lack of protection policies was a planned policy of destructive neoliberal development he's pushed through discourse and defunding. This has constructed an aura of impunity for wildcat miners, illegal loggers, cattle ranchers, illegal fishermen, evangelical and neo-Pentecostal missionaries, and organised criminal gangs. Some of these criminal organisations include the PCC (Third Capital Command) and CV (Red Command), which have taken control of drug trafficking routes and, in some cases, caused complications with FUNAI (the Government Ministry in charge of Indigenous legal affairs in Brazil) going into indigenous territories. The compounding culmination of these issues came to a head in 2022 when a ten-day Indigenous demonstration in the capital Brasilia was organised. It was known as the ATL Land Camp and saw over 7,000 Indigenous people protesting and livestreaming against these issues and a specific government Bill the PL191. Brazil's Congress fast-tracked Bill Pl191 to extract fertilizer from Indigenous lands, citing supply shortages because of the Russian invasion of Ukraine (Boadle, 2022) even though this is unconstitutional under Article 231 of the 1988 constitution (Art. 231 Da Constituição Federal de 1988; Langlois, 2022). Article 231 states that the Brazilian government is responsible for protecting demarcated Indigenous territories, which to date hasn't happened. The bill threatens at most minuscule 43 Indigenous groups across 25 demarcated Indigenous reserves and potentially even isolated groups (Villén-Pérez et al., 2021). Some of these communities are in remote areas like the Javari Valley in the westernmost part of the Brazilian Amazon, where British Journalist Dom Philips and his guide and Indigenous expert Bruno Perriera were assassinated in the summer of 2022. Assassinations of land defenders and territorial invasions of Indigenous and Quilombo communities under Bolsonaro increased year on year (Roy, 2022), with Brazil becoming increasingly dangerous for forest defenders. The Brazilian governments push to pass these kinds of policies showed a troubling trend, with 2022 having the highest rate of deforestation since 2008, and many scientists believing the forests are at tipping point (Lovejoy & Nobre, 2018). Some scientists even argue that the forest has already reached the tipping point, and the process of aridification, survannarization and unpredictable weather conditions has already begun in parts of the Amazon (Quintanilla, Guzmán León and Josse, 2022).

2022: Contextualising Brazilian Indigenous Streaming and Activism

However, Indigenous communities now use social media as a weapon to amplify their struggles, discuss the environment, and highlight charitable and community initiatives (Hisayasu, 2019). Over the last decade, a surge of Indigenous video activism has enabled communities in Brazil to mobilize to varying degrees, to protest mining projects, congressional bills, and agrobusiness lobbies (Hanna,

Indigenous Livestreaming in Brazil

Langdon and Vanclay, 2016). This has crossed over into Brazil's national politics, with 2022 having Indigenous political candidates being front and centre and a preferred communication method being livestreaming. In 2022, Brazil saw the most significant number of appointments of indigenous candidates in its history. Sonia Guajajara and Celia Xakribaba were elected as Federal State Deputies, utilizing livestreaming to reach wider audiences. Other Indigenous political candidates used livestreaming to build campaigns, like Vanda Witoto from Manaus. Indigenous politicians adopting technologies to amplify their voices isn't a recent phenomenon, the first indigenous Brazilian to be voted into Congress Mário Juruna, famously used a tape deck to record other politicians' racist discussions about indigenous Brazilians (Bradford, 2002).

Due to the urgency and the backdrop to the ATL Land Camp, on April 12, the newly appointed President Lula da Silva spoke on stage, which at the time was part of his political campaign. Lula promised that if re-elected, he would repair all the damages the Bolsonaro government has done to Brazil's Indigenous Peoples and create a new Indigenous Ministry. One of these promises would encapsulate reducing land invasions and deforestation. When he first served as President between 2003 and 2010, he reduced deforestation in the Brazilian Amazon by up to 70% (Chaves, 2022). However, in 2022 after a global pandemic, in addition to not being able to leverage excess capital from a commodities boom (which was the case under Lula's previous government) as well as having to contend with an environmental ministry that has been gutted by Bolsonaro's government this is a huge promise to keep. Interesting, his campaign speech was livestreamed across multiple Indigenous social media channels and Journalists from Folha de São Paulo and Reuters subsequently picked it up. This process tracing suggests the communicative power of Indigenous livestreaming to disseminate political messaging.

Even if we argue that there could have been backchannels of communication between the demonstration organisers and the Journalists, it's still significant to note that there was a backchannel focusing on Indigenous voices and struggles. It's this kind of political affordance that livestreaming provides that also emboldened Bolsonaro to adopt Facebook Live, yet his livestreams were produced to avoid Journalists being able to hold him accountable (Kissock, 2020a; Piauí, 2022). With demonstrations and protests becoming common in Brazil, it's important to emphasize the use of video as evidence and revitalize the research into the effects of livestreaming and how it can be critically understood when thinking about Indigeneity, Citizenship, civic participation, territorial sovereignty, and community, be it physical, digital, near or far. Human and environmental rights violations have coincided with the rise of video technology being able to provide evidence of them. This is seen in livestreams from 2022, where an Indigenous women's advocacy headquarters was burned down on the Tapajos River, where the Policia Militar violently invaded Indigenous homes, or state forces shot at Indigenous people from a helicopter (Camara, 2022). Unfortunately, the criminalisation of indigenous groups is part of an ongoing trend in Brazil. However, as video is a dual-functional tool, livestreaming can also be empowering. For example, the Artist and Activist Y (synonymized to protect her identity) streamed her local community food distribution programme '*SOS Povo Huni Kuin*' on her Instagram. The material portrayed her holding up a mirror to shine a light on Bolsonaro's Government's failings to provide adequate services in the Brazilian state of Acre during the COVID-19 pandemic. Yet importantly it displayed how livestreams can challenge the notions of Brazilian Citizenship by showing how communities can independently organise distribution programs and market them via livestreams. Or so as a distant researcher I originally thought.

The Ephemeral Huni Kuin Livestream

Individuals participating in livestream activism, helps inform their understanding of Citizenship and Indignity. Furthermore, distant others can interpret their knowledge, cultural, and/or environmental struggles as second order witnesses. Yet, the wider literature on the provision testimony in the context of rights and video activism has seldom explored linkages between technological affordances, Citizenship, and ritual, of which I use Turner's definition of rituals as processes of social events containing "*units of aharmonic and disharmonic process*" that arise from conflict situations seen within Indigenous activism (Turner, 1980, 1994; Hanna de Almeida Oliveira, 2012), when examining video witnessing between Indigenous activists. Hence, this chapter aims to conceptualise how distant others interpret ephemeral activist interactions and video language to acquire socio-political knowledge of regional environmental struggles. The case of the Huni Kuin is an excellent example to explore.

The name Huni Kuin (as part of the Pano linguist family) translate to 'genuine' or 'true' people. They reside in the western Brazilian Amazon in the state of Acre on the Peruvian border in the Kaxinawá region. Yet, their distance from cities and municipalities has not meant that as a community they haven't been shaped by the outcomes of colonialism. First by the Portuguese, then by Bandeirantes (explorers who were second generation Brazilians onwards), through to neo-colonialist missionaries and the horrors of land grabbing and expansions throughout the 20th century. During this period, Brazil was subject to numerous dictatorships which encouraged infrastructure projects throughout the Amazon. A well cited case is the 1964-1985 military dictatorship, which was responsible for commissioning and constructing the Trans-Amazonian highway, that cut directly through Indigenous Lands. Projects like this led to further abuses and violations taking place against Indigenous populations, and upon Brazil's return to democracy in 1985, these cases would be contributing factors to creating the demarcation of Indigenous reserves. Subsequently, the 1988 constitution was born out of a multi-pronged disapproval of the military dictatorships handling of almost all aspects of socioeconomic life in Brazil. The document focused on building democratic institutions that could withstand future crisis's and ensure the rights of all Brazilian citizens, hence it was termed the 'Citizens' Constitution (M. Schwarcz and M. Starling, 2019). Though it's important to mentioned the democratization of Brazil has not always seen a solidarity or progressive approach to indigenous rights (Guadalupe Moog Rodrigues, 2002). Bolsonaro's brand of conquest, bootstrap capitalism, was just the latest extension of elitist ideology symbolical of violent extractivism that encouraged criminals to illegally expand their activities into Indigenous reserves, which means for many indigenous groups colonialism is very much a lived experience (Samson and Gigoux, 2016). It's these Indigenous communities that are at the heart of the conversation taking place on social media with a strong use of livestreaming.

The remoteness of some Huni Kuin villages can sometimes mean they're more susceptible to mother nature. Perhaps due to the increasingly unpredictable weather changes in the Amazon due to illegal deforestation, the Huni Kuin previously experienced intense flooding, that made it extremely difficult to receive outside services such as food and medical supplies (Pontes, 2022). Therefore, Y and her friend decided to livestream about the situation and show their social media audience the damage and destruction that had taken place along the River Jordão; Y's friend shows us a house, almost completely submerged in the flood water. Throughout the video we see members of the community (the majority being women and children) queuing outside a home with a veranda, where there are three men distributing flour and rice and ticking names off a list. During the livestream we witness another boy filming the

Indigenous Livestreaming in Brazil

distribution program from the other side of the veranda. Y narrates over the livestream explaining what was happening with the SOS Povo Huni Kuin project and how as a community, they organise the food distribution for some of the vulnerable members. Contextually, the video portrayed how Bolsonaro's government failed to provide services because he had spent three and a half years in office by the time the livestream took place, systematically defunding Institutions like FUNAI and IBAMA, the environmental law enforcement agency.

Though the livestream took place in the Kaxinawá region, this wasn't the only area in the Huni Kuin territory affected by the floods. We also see online campaigns asking the public to donate via PIX (a very popular instant payment system created by Brazil's central bank) for other regions where the Huni Kuin live such as the Rio Alto Purus, which is approximately 140 miles away from where the livestream was filmed. The commonality with these campaigns is that individuals are asking for a *cesta básica* (similar to a care package) for each family and for their voices to be heard by the outside world (Flavia Costa Netto, 2022). Fortunately, platforms like Instagram and Kwai are yielding evidence that Indigenous voices are being heard. For example, the Indigenous streamer *'Da Aleida'* has at least 400 thousand followers on his Kwai, and Y's livestream of the distribution program has over 14 thousand views, even though the livestream was originally meant as a local community narrowcast, rather than a broadcast. In the case of the Huni Kuin, many of those viewers could have been individuals who were close enough to the site and were able to collect *cesta básicas*. Yet, this regional narrowcasting phenomenon for individuals within a close proximity poses a question: where did I sit as a distant researcher?

Witnessing Indigeneity and Citizenship at a Mediated Distance

When examining how livestreamed video activism leads to knowledge production, there's an identifiable gap in the literature that simplifies theories of Citizenship, its definition, and how it interacts with the practice of witnessing and Indigeneity. Dougherty (2011) defines Citizenship in the context of citizen journalism from the Oxford Dictionary. Zhang & Luther (2020) speak of the citizenry in 4th century Greece and the cosmopolitanism of *'Citizen Journalism.'* Likewise, Chouliaraki (2006) discusses global cosmopolitan citizens, and Peters (2009) only quotes Nietzsche's statement, *'citizens must inform the day's events,'* but doesn't extrapolate further. Kozol (2015) does discuss the intersectionality of witnessing and Citizenship within the context of gender, war, and trauma. Her book, *Distant Wars*, is conceptualized around empirical examples of Citizenship that link to Land, space, and belonging. Yet she spends substantial time discussing Western-centric hegemonic Citizenship and doesn't explore linkages to Indigeneity. Many authors, except for Ong (2015), subscribe to notions of Citizenship that assume Western centricities and consider their readers' understanding of citizenry as a virtue, regardless of many stating they're adopting critical or postcolonial frameworks (Höijer, 2004; Ibrahim, 2010; Mortensen, 2015; Ristovska, 2016; Thorburn, 2017; Martini, 2018; Huiberts and Joye, 2019). Thus, they inadequately explore or attempt to define the term, especially in an Indigenous context.

Citizenship is intrinsically linked to the nation-state, and nation-states are built around representations and interpreted ideals that shape collective perceptions and laws (Anderson, 2011). Weber examines the constructionist linkages between the state and Citizenship (Weber, 1992; Scaff, 2021). However, Verderys (1999) emphasized 'collective memory and kinship,' arguing that rational choice theory led to specific interpretations of *'citizen-making'* becoming *'flat, narrow, and constructionist.'* Brazilian Anthropologist Eduardo Viveiros de Castro mirrors this, arguing that Brazilian indigenous groups are founded on kinship or co-residence relations between members who maintain historical-cultural ties.[1]

And it's these notions that make Brazil a critical case, as both perspectives have theoretical merits. For example, Y's livestream on Instagram about the collection points appears to bypass State or Federal distribution programs and can be theorized as collective kinship, mirroring Verderys' and Castros arguments. These livestreams about distribution programs can be theorized as collective kinship and citizenship affirmation within a community separate from a nation state (Ginsburg, 1992; Andermann, 2010) and allude to the idea of affirming Indigeneity. This is because what it means to be a Brazilian Citizen is heterogenous, highly contested, and shouldn't ascribe to the myth of Brazil as a racial democracy (Cicalo, 2018; M. Schwarcz and M. Starling, 2019). Much of the scholarship on video activism and witnessing tends to take the readers understanding of Citizenship and Indigeneity as a virtue, witnessing as somewhat empirically quantifiable; and sometimes frames citizen journalism as a contestation to the norms of traditional journalism, which can undermine individual agency to record and distribute journalist content such as Y did. This contestation is apparent in other videos with the SOS Povo Huni Kuin, where the group mobilizes across social media to tell stories affecting their community. The human rights scholarship terms this as '*citizen witnessing*', however contestations arise when a Deleuzian sign/signifier dynamic is created between the Individual as the sign and the State as the signifier, where the former is often demonstrating against the latter. This can also be seen in the multiple livestreams cases from the Indigenous protests in Brasilia in 2021 (Kissock, 2021), and the recent livestreams of the land camp protests against Bill PL191 (Langlois, 2022). To navigate the Individual/State binary, we can turn to Holston's (2008) theory of differentiated Citizenship as a concept of critically examining historical and contextual notions of who is excluded as a citizen. Though much of Holston's theory centres around marginalised urban Brazilians, it can be translated to understand constraints that are also felt by rural and Indigenous Brazilians. Holston argued Brazilians were generally excluded for attaining statuses of Citizenship, defined by socio-political participation, up until the 1980s due to the illiteracy rates. Anderson (2006), also argued that macro levels of the nation state's relation to Citizenship were born from this idea of bureaucracies leveraging the power of the printing press and starting to publish work to either include or exclude individuals. Therefore, livestream activism sits in a unique position where the practice and technology can bypass literacy levels and include individuals as witnesses, akin to democratising a '*disruptive*' Insurgent Citizenship (Holston, 2008). Thus, streaming is also a preservative tool for communicating in Indigenous languages, and disseminating ancestral knowledges (UNESCO, 2021). It also provides distant researchers a unique technological affordance and positionality to marry and design methodologies when exploring indigenous issues.

Amalgamating Methods: Video Data Analysis and Auto-Ethnography

The investigation into how knowledge is transferred through livestreamed videos with video data analysis and auto-ethnography shouldn't constrain itself to notions of virtual, online, or digital ethnography. In many cases, ethnography encircles both digital and physical field sites with a rapid expansion to young networked publics (Boyd, 2007). The COVID-19 pandemic also pushed researchers to discover and explore innovative methods for conducting studies, leading to custom-made and ready-made video livestream research (Rahat *et al.*, 2022). Here custom-made video refers to video made for research purposes and ready-made video refers to videos that are not a by-product of scholarly research and/or experiments (Nassauer and M. Legewie, 2022). The pandemic also made it visible to wider publics that indigenous people have more access than ever to online devices and tools (Goodwin Gómez, 2006). The empirical research topic legitimates this claim by researching connected Indigenous communities in Brazil who,

Indigenous Livestreaming in Brazil

in some circumstances, draw large audiences with their videos (McCoy, 2021). Qualitative auto-ethnography is also a suitable methodology to examine livestreams as digital artefacts (Drinot, 2011) because critical self-reflective conclusions can be drawn from online interactions and allow researchers space to contemplate what knowledge was disseminated during the act of witnessing. Qualitative approaches are robust when exploring knowledge constructions because it allows researchers to follow the streamers content when they're expressing their own interpretations of knowledge. It affords researchers space to reflect on the video content that was analysed. Yet, ethnography isn't reinventing the wheel, as it has been used extensively in the research on video activism. Some of the most cited authors have applied similar research designs like Kavada et al. (2019) and Ristovska (2016).

However, this chapter seeks venture beyond their empirical parameters, where they may have been somewhat constrained by theoretical frameworks, to attribute a more rounded understanding of how witnessing can lead to knowledge via livestreaming. Thus, it's important to incorporate critical auto-ethnography of online witnessing to refer to how we should be reflective researchers from an ontologically different environment (for example, a western male from an urban setting, rather than an Indigenous female activist from the Brazilian Amazon). It's vital for the purpose of decolonizing solidarity when researching indigenous causes to *'Turn the lens onto ourselves'* as Clare Land discussed at length in her book *Decolonializing Solidarity*. She argues that non-Indigenous activists and researchers such as herself must participate in Indigenous solidarity, ethnography, and research, by approaching projects with long-term commitments in mind and from a self-critical stance (Land, 2015). This will sometimes be uncomfortable and difficult, but it is necessary for decolonizing indigenous research and solidarity, especially as an auto-ethnographer who isn't on the ground with the research participants. Though ethnographic fieldwork is becoming totalising when considering digital environments (Custódio, 2017), it can still lead to epistemological conundrums such as *'being there'* (Hunter, 2019). Therefore, autoethnographic live reflection and note taking allow a non-indigenous researcher to critically reflect and engage from a distance surrounding introspective questions such as, where did I witness the Livestream? What was I doing before the livestream? How did it make me feel? We can only learn through the act of reflection because reflection and introspection give us time to think and process these thoughts. Once we have the space to process our thoughts, we can only share them as shows of solidarity.

Innovating and Indigenizing *'Livestream'* Video Data Analysis

The literature on livestreaming focuses on the analysis of livestreams on platforms where the On Demand (OD) or Digital Video Recorder (DVR) setting has been turned on. This means that the videos have been saved directly to the individual's social media profile or locally to a device and then reuploaded later. This affords the researcher the luxury of returning to watch the video again and again to reflect on its contents. The video can then be studied with video data analysis methods such as rundown analysis, count quantification, coding, sequence analysis, or process tracing to triangulate the video with other sources. Yet, even if the video has been recorded, livestreamed and reuploaded later, it can still cause issues because in some circumstances it can output false metadata about the time a video was filmed and therefore its content. For example, YouTube calculates the time a video was uploaded by defaulting to the time zone to where their servers are, in San Jose California. This enabled the Russian government to try and denial the authenticity of a video that was uploaded to YouTube showing a chemical weapons attack in Syria perpetrated by Russian aircraft. Russia argued that the video was staged because of the time and date on the video, which had in fact defaulted to California, which was 10 hours in front of the Syrian time zone. Therefore, it may be logical for a video maker to simply livestream in order to capture an event instead of filming it and reuploading it later. This would then pose an uncomfortable question, what if the DVR or OD settings are just turned off, for example, only making the video available to viewers in real-time? Some would argue that there's little that can be done, however there are two methods of conducting livestream research which lend themselves to specifically witnessing Indigenous Live streamers.

Methods of Conducting Livestream Research

The first step, via an iterative research process, is to identify the accounts you wish to engage with to build a research case (Nassauer and M. Legewie, 2022). This is an important procedure before starting to thematically code any videos because it allows a distant researcher time to engage and show solidarity with a community from a distance. Thus, it's also considered good practice to create a separate social media account only for research purposes (McPherson, 2018). Yet, In the case of this research surrounding the Huni Kuin, I decided that, as I'm researching Indigenous communities who can sometime be untrusting of outsiders (for good reason), it would be more appropriate to use my personal Instagram account. Then for conducting Live VDA, it's important to set notifications on applications like Instagram, TikTok, Twitch, YouTube, and Kwai for when each of the streamers go live. This helps the researcher build a pattern of who, how, and when each indigenous activists in a network '*tend*' to stream. For example, Brazil is three to four hours behind the United Kingdom, and generally activism and academic livestreams happen after business hours i.e., the times when they can be witnessed.

There are two methods of conducting this research; first it's possible to maintain specific research hours for when a livestream might start in a comfortable workspace. This is achieved by constructing a workspace with a computer or phone ready to observe and research any livestream, safe in the knowledge that the researcher is prepared to capture it via a screen recorder with prior consent from the participant and then take notes. This is a practical approach depending on the research question the researcher is attempting to answer, however for explorative indigenous research conducted by a non-indigenous person this method can set out an asymmetrical power dynamic between the researcher and participant. This is because the researcher is making a value judgement by predetermining the parameters of when said research will take place without necessarily consulting the content creators. Therefore, it's recommended and should be the duty of a non-indigenous researcher to take an all-encompassing stance to the research and witness livestreams as soon as they go live regardless of the distance and physical settings. By enacting this procedure, it equilibrized the terms of witnessing and research engagement towards indigenous people and communities. Subsequently, it allows for further exploration and places the power solely in the streamers hands and allowing them to decide upon the research terms of engagement and thus situates the researcher as secondary. Too often in the fields of anthropology and sociology researchers have tried to dictate the terms of engagement with research participants, yet the study of livestreaming if implemented like so can turn this power dynamic on its head, because of the technology's spontaneity and ephemerality. However, there are also downsides to the second method, one of which is that the researcher needs to keep their mental health in check by making sure there are hours when they're not working. Yet, they must not offset those non-working hours by making value judgements or discriminating against livestreams and/or streamers that they feel may not be relevant to the proposed research question. It can also be difficult reflecting on what is seen if the researcher in public or with company, yet this can be incorporated into self-critical autoethnographic fieldnotes. This also speaks more broadly to Land's

Indigenous Livestreaming in Brazil

(2015) argument surrounding the practice of decolonizing solidarity and the comfortable privilege that some researchers experience when being able to reflect upon how indigenous data is transmitted.

However, there are practices researchers can apply to make the exercise of reflection more accomplishable. This involves wearing headphones to isolate the audio and not disturb others in public spaces, knowing the technical procedural process of recording a live video to make the practice efficient on a mobile device, having a screen recorder installed, taking screengrabs, and saving the video to a secure location in the cloud. This affords the researcher time reflect via the means of performing a practical operation on a mobile device and thus rotates the notion of ephemerality on its head by preserving the video. Yet, much the same way as not knowing the contents of a video and when the video will start, there's also no way of knowing when the video might end. If researching influencers, sometimes the amount of likes they receive during a livestream incentivizes them to stay live for longer. For the research, its best to keep recording in case something is missed which cannot be reflected or learnt from later. Therefore, the researcher needs adequate local storage space for videos and pictures on a mobile device.

Building 'credibility': It's important to provide some reflection on how a researcher conducts research on the indigenous Instagram networks and becomes a recognisable account within the online community. I wished to create trust and mentioned in my bio that I was PhD researcher, my institution, and that I was studying Indigenous video activism in Brazil. This meant all my previous posts with my friends, activities, and political leanings were visible; rather than a clinical empty account, where there could have been scepticism about who I was and what my intentions could be. As I wasn't part of this community, it was important to establish that I was a real person, and interested in Brazilian indigenous advocacy and land rights, most of my Instagram stories are reshares from those same indigenous accounts. It was therefore also important, that I also engaged in practical activism such as organising, demonstrating, or donating to those same causes. In the case of the Huni Kuin, I would usually donate to the causes and send clapping emoji's during their livestreams on Instagram as a show of support for the content that was being discussed. This helped some of the activists in the network ascertain that I wasn't a Bot and they could see various aspects of my life. My cultural capital was also raised when I happened to meet Txai Surui, who is one the most important Brazilian indigenous activists on the global stage at the screening of her film 'The Territory'. I spoke with Txai and the protagonist of the documentary Bitate, and subsequently they followed me on Instagram. This acted as a *'credential,'* and other activists I engaged with online were able to see I was followed by important people who reflect their situation and struggles. One might argue that this was an uncomfortable neo-liberal approach reducing Instagram followers to commodities, or physical 'trust credentials', and is reflective of Bourdieu's postulations surrounding entitlements (be it online) as modules of various social, cultural, and political capitals (Sallaz, 2018). In other words, because I had important Activists following me on social media, I was then considered someone with online social capital, and therefore trustworthy. Pragmatically this may have acted as putting some minds at ease that I was someone worth following or would not be a potential threat if I was to follow someone.

Nonetheless, this method did have drawbacks, for example, Instagram's algorithm can inundate newsfeeds with stories only relating to research topics. This isn't an issue if a researcher is only using the platform for empirical research from a separate account, but if not, it will phase out stories and pictures relating to your friends and social life. This is the results of an amalgamation of Damgaard's 'informational cascades' (2018) and Lazer et al.'s (2014) reminder of 'algorithmic drift', where algorithms aren't stable entities and tend to drift overtime. This is because a deluge of different information (in the form of content) becomes available on a platform and is then fed to individual users, when those users subsequently interact with the content (watching videos, clicking on pop ups), the algorithm will recalibrate to provide similar content and therefore thematically drifts as a result. An illustrative example of this was when I witnessed an indigenous influencer showing off some fashion accessories, and then on the same newsfeed one post later, a video showing the evidence of another indigenous group being shot at from a helicopter. One event was in from Amazonas and the other from Mato Grosso, which is also demonstrative gives testament of how the heterogeneous Brazilian Indignity is.

Data Collection

Instagram does have a practical tool built in for research and archival purposes which can code and save posts in your account on Instagram, by making folders with different sub-headings. Then to empirically explore the case of witnessing Indigenous video activism from afar via Instagram, this researcher adopted the second method of examining the livestreamed 'SOS Povo Huni Kuin' video via synchronic distant witnessing and then implementing video data analysis, specifically situational dynamic sequencing and content analysis. Once this was completed, the video was then triangulated with OSInt discovery methods to explore other social media platforms like YouTube, Facebook, Twitch, Twitter, Kwai, and TikTok and other posts on Instagram to extrapolate secondary resources, in this case this method was utilized to cross correlate Y's and the Huni Kuin case. Yet, it's also important to remember that these digital environments are used by activists to output their own news (Zhao, 2020), but also appear to have baked-in algorithms that censor activism (Sage Rauchberg, 2022) or cannot distinguish between video evidence of human rights violators and the victims (Gregory, 2022). This has been seen in the case of Meta (who own Instagram) and therefore these instances are crucial because platforms like Kwai, which was the third most downloaded Brazilian application in 2021 sporting 45 million monthly users (Deck and Marasciulo, 2022), may also have these complications. Scholarly research is still at the early stages of examining advocacy on this streaming platform and thus it could be interesting to explore Indigenous activism and technological affordances and constraints on these new environments.

Data Analysis

Once the collection phase encompassed sufficient data and artefacts the procedure of thematically coding the video and conducting a rundown analysis of both transcripts and frequencies surrounding content analysis can be performed. In the case of the Huni Kuin Livestream, the empirical output was then added to an excel spreadsheet with various columns each containing empirical datapoints about the contents of the Huni Kuin video. The DVR version of the video was then stored in a folder on Instagram and watched multiple times, it was explored for themes and comments, and then reflected upon autoethnographically as a 'prosumer' (Ibrahim, 2020). Operationally, the research process then requires analysis of the vast amount of secondary data that was collected to distinguish thematic patterns in the video surrounding contestation or reaffirmation of Indigeneity. Then it was possible to triangulate the video via processing tracing the SOS Huni Kuin campaign online. NVivo software was then utilized to manage the amount of thematic secondary data using Gibbons et al.'s (1986) ethnographic funnel structure method to sift the secondary data to what was deemed most relevant to contextualise the empirical case of analysis in the livestreams content.

Indigenous Livestreaming in Brazil

On Demand Huni Kuin Livestream: The Corrected Case

Considering, the discussion about livestream research, it's important to mention distant witnessing and how this can throw us off track as researchers. This is because all the information comes out from what we initially see in livestreams, fortunately in this case Y had turned on the On Demand settings for her livestream and I was thus able to revisit and reflect on the content. This is because when the On-Demand settings are turned on there's the option to upload the local file that has been recorded during the livestream i.e. the video that was saved on the phone rather than outputted over the internet. Initially when watching the stream in real time I theorized my empirical parameters as the Huni Kuin contesting their Citizenship; however, this wasn't the case. When Y panned the camera around on the initial stream, the video dropped out for a matter of seconds. This camera pan turned out to be very important because it showed a banner advertising the Fundação Brasileiros Pelo Brasil Program. In short, it's a program committed to distributing food and goods to rural Brazilians (Veloso Ferreira, 2022) and was set up by the Bank of Brasil, which is controlled by the Brazilian government and has multiple corporate social responsibility funding programs. This wasn't mentioned again during the livestream. What was mentioned was the SOS Povo Huni Kuin Program with the PIX number for people to donate to. The SOS Povo Huni Kuin program is a charity organisation with nothing to do with the Brazilian state, leading me to ascertain that it was solely a self-funded program and therefore could be understood as the Huni Kuin contesting their Citizenship against the Brazilian state, and instead asserting their cultural identity as Huni Kuin. Whilst synchronically watching the video I assumed it showed how Bolsonaro systematically defunded agencies to the point of inoperancy and/or appointed unqualified individuals to run, which is true, but after observing the Fundação sign in the on-demand video, no longer makes sense within the context of this livestream. However, it's important to highlight that Acre, where the Huni Kuin reside, is the least prioritised Brazilian state in the Fundação program, having minimal resources being distributed to it.[2] Ultimately, this poses questions about how we should be witnessing livestreams and the information that can be disseminated by them when it comes to understanding modes of citizenry and Indigeneity. It also raises important ethical research questions about researcher biases and the kind of sources we decide to triangulate videos with, especially when researching distant indigenous contexts through mediated technology.

Globally internet connectivity is improving, yet livestreams are still susceptible to data packet loss with video and audio drop off, and therefore can fragment important information. This is true both on the side of an Indigenous first order streamer in a remote location, and a second order witness in a city where WIFI can also drop or 4G and 5G signals can temporality be disrupted. Livestreaming is a relatively new public tool, and this could ultimately happen to any researcher running thematic content analysis any location. If research participants have allowed their DVR or OD settings to be turned on at their account level, videos stay available but on some platforms function like an output capture and not a local recording i.e recording any loss of bandwidth. It was only on a second observation I saw the Fundação Sign (for around 4 or 5 frames) and then I was able to re-evaluate my initial empirical parameters. This example could have been a huge issue if it was evidence of a land invasion or war crime (which we are seeing in the case of the Ukraine with livestreaming over TikTok).

There's also an inherent difference between the ATL Land Camp and the '*SOS Povo Huni Kuin*' examples regarding the feasibility of research triangulation. In many respects we can triangulate the case of the ATL Land camp as it was a large Indigenous demonstration with multiple camera phones covering the events and Journalists who could have been present at Lula's speech or at least could have had a backchannel communication open with people on the ground. This means as a researcher the event is more likely to have been separately recorded and can be triangulated on by analysing other videos and secondary research artefacts such as newspaper articles and other social media. However, in the case of the 'SOS Povo Huni Kuin' this becomes almost impossible to triangulate as it was best understood as a local community 'narrowcast' rather than a 'traditional' broadcast, and one can only use the online donation pages, and social media posts. The only way we might be able to triangulate the video is to reach out to the streamer and request to interview them. The humanities and social sciences have ubiquity of digitally mediated tools that can be utilized for research purposes, this means that future researchers need to place much more emphasis on the triangulation of empirical data. Especially when also considering modern research trends, topics and threat vectors such as generative AI, mis/disinformation, and the climate change; all of which are of paramount importance because these issues don't just impact the preservation of Indigenous knowledge, but the preservation of all knowledge. Thus, there needs to be more researcher ownership when our empirical data, is or may be flawed.

CONCLUSION AND RECOMMENDATIONS

Therefore, researchers need to think about broader norms of researching online participants and how livestreams can yield evidence especially surrounding rights and Indigeneity. Ruberg & Brewer (2022) discussed new methodologies for witnessing livestreaming surrounding gender; we should implement similar methodologies when researching livestreams within indigenous and rights-based contexts. It's our responsibility as researchers to keep building on new technological advances as they happen. We should also borrow from the literature on distant witnessing to translate our own epistemology as researchers and make sure we use relevant terminology to describe our research, for example, witnessing rather than observation. Our research in an Indigenous rights context should be understood as witnessing as this allows us as praxis researchers to provide testimony as a form of solidarity. To provide testimony that is fair and honest, a recommendation for researchers is to always remain reflexive when exploring distance communities via or through technological devices, which may function to mediate empiricisms. It's an ethical responsibility to also articulate that as researchers, we are sharing space (be it digital or physical) with Indigenous causes like that of the Huni Kuin's and showing solidarity by researching their territorial struggles. In some instances, all our impact could be is transferring knowledge within academic circles (Smith, 2021). We all have the responsibility when indigenous rights are at stake to provide testimony in some capacity as a knowledge transfer, whether in the format of a policy report, paper, conference, lecture, or book chapter such as this. However, we should always be careful when providing these knowledge transfers in the form of livestreams, because the information may be misinterpreted if our connection drops.

REFERENCES

Alfred, R. (2009). June 24, 1993: Concert Goes Live on Net. *Wired*. https://www.wired.com/2009/06/dayintech-0624/ (Accessed: 14 December 2022).

Andermann, J. (2010). State Formation, Visual Technology and Spectatorship: Visions of Modernity in Brazil and Argentina. *Theory, Culture & Society*, *27*(7), 161–183. doi:10.1177/0263276410384749

Indigenous Livestreaming in Brazil

Anderson, B. (2006). *Imagined Communities: Reflections on the Origin and Spread of Nationalism* (2nd ed.). Verso.

Art. 231 da Constituição Federal de 88 (1988) *Constituição Federal de 1988.* Brazil: Brazilian Goverment. https://www.jusbrasil.com.br/topicos/10643688/artigo-231-da-constituicao-federal-de-1988

Boadle, A. (2022) *Indigenous protest camp erected in Brazilian capital to press land rights.* Reuters. https://www.reuters.com/world/americas/indigenous-protest-camp-erected-brazilian-capital-press-land-rights-2022-04-05/

Boyd, D. (2007). Why Youth Heart Social Network Sites: The Role of Networked Publics in Teenage Social Life. *Berkman Center for Internet and Society at Harvard University, 7641*(2007–16). doi:10.31219/doi:osf.io/22hq2

Bradford, S. (2002). Mário Juruna. *The Guardian.* https://www.theguardian.com/news/2002/aug/03/guardianobituaries1

Camara, J. (2022) *Entenda os motivos para o conflito entre indígenas guarani kaiowá e polícia em Amambai (MS).* Mato Grosso do Sul, G1. https://g1.globo.com/ms/mato-grosso-do-sul/noticia/2022/06/26/entenda-os-motivos-para-o-conflito-entre-indigenas-guarani-kaiowa-e-policia-em-amambai-ms.ghtml

Carneiro da Cunha, M. (1992). *'Legislação indigenista no século XIX', Uma compilação (1808-1889).* CPI-SP/Edusp.

Carvalho, G. O. (2000). The politics of indigenous land rights in Brazil. *Bulletin of Latin American Research, 19*(4), 461–478. doi:10.1016/S0261-3050(00)00032-2

Chaves, L. (2022) *The challenges Lula will face to eradicate illegal deforestation in Amazonia by 2028.* InfoAmazonia. https://infoamazonia.org/en/2022/11/11/the-challenges-lula-will-face-to-eradicate-illegal-deforestation-in-amazonia-by-2028/ (Accessed: 14 December 2022).

Chisita, C. T., Rusero, A. M., & Shoko, M. (2016). Leveraging Memory Institutions to Preserve Indigenous Knowledge inthe Knowledge Age. In *Indigenous Notions of Ownership and Libraries* (p. 273). Archives and Museums. doi:10.1515/9783110363234-021

Chouliaraki, L. (2006) The Spectatorship of the Suffering. SAGE Publications Ltd. doi:10.4135/9781446220658

Cicalo, A. (2018). Goodbye "Racial Democracy"? Brazilian Identity, Official Discourse and the Making of a "Black" Heritage Site in Rio de Janeiro. *Bulletin of Latin American Research, 37*(1), 73–86. doi:10.1111/blar.12636

Custódio, L. (2017). *Favela Media Activism Counterpublics for Human Rights in Brazil* (1st ed.). Lexington Books.

Damgaard, M. (2018). 'Cascading corruption news : Explaining the bias of media attention to Brazil ' s political scandals'. *Opinião Pública, 24*(1), 114–143. http://dx.doi./10.1590/1807-01912018241114. doi:10.1590/1807-01912018241114

Davis, S. H. (1977). *Victims of the miracle : development and the Indians of Brazil* (1st ed.). Cambridge University Press.

Deck, A., & Marasciulo, M. (2022) TikTok's biggest Chinese competitor bets big on Brazil. Rest of World. https://restofworld.org/2022/tiktok-competitor-kwai-brazil/ (Accessed: 27 March 2022).

Dougherty, A. (2011). Live-streaming mobile video: Production as civic engagement. *Mobile HCI 2011 - 13th International Conference on Human-Computer Interaction with Mobile Devices and Services*, (pp. 425–434). IEEE. 10.1145/2037373.2037437

Drinot, P. (2011). Website of memory: The war of the Pacific (1879-84) in the global age of YouTube. *Memory Studies, 4*(4), 370–385. doi:10.1177/1750698011409290

Faklaris, C. (2016). Legal and Ethical Implications of Mobile Live-Streaming Video Apps. In *Proceedings of the 18th International Conference on Human-Computer Interaction with Mobile Devices and Services Adjunct*. New York City: ACM. 10.1145/2957265.2961845

Flavia Costa Netto, A. (2022) *SOS POVO HUNI KUIN DO ALTO RIO PURUS – ACRE*. Vakinha. https://www.vakinha.com.br/vaquinha/sos-povo-huni-kuin-no-acre

Freeman, L., & Vazquez Llorente, R. (2021). Finding the Signal in the Noise. *Journal of International Criminal Justice, 19*(1), 163–188. doi:10.1093/jicj/mqab023

FUNAI. (2023). *PL 490/07 e marco temporal colocam em risco os direitos dos povos indígenas.* Fundação Nacional dos Povos Indígenas. https://www.gov.br/funai/pt-br/assuntos/noticias/2023/201cpl-490-07-e-marco-temporal-colocam-em-risco-os-direitos-dos-povos-indigenas201d-alerta-presidenta-da-funai (Accessed: 29 May 2023).

Gabrys, J. (2022). *Instrumental Citizens: How to Retool Action.* University of Minnesota Press. https://manifold.umn.edu/projects/citizens-of-worlds

Garrett, R. D., Cammelli, F., Ferreira, J., Levy, S. A., Valentim, J., & Vieira, I. (2021). Forests and Sustainable Development in the Brazilian Amazon: History, Trends, and Future Prospects. *Annual Review of Environment and Resources, 46*(1), 625–652. doi:10.1146/annurev-environ-012220-010228

Gibbons, J. A., Hammersley, M., & Atkinson, P. (1986). Ethnography: Principles in Practice. *Contemporary Sociology, 15*(3), 451. Advance online publication. doi:10.2307/2070079

Ginsburg, F. (1992). Indigenous Media: Faustian Contract or Global Village? In G. E. Marcus (Ed.), Rereading Cultural Anthropology. Duke University Press., Available at http://read.dukeupress.edu/books/book/chapter-pdf/664756/9780822397861-019.pdf, Retrieved May 2, 2022, from.

Goodwin Gómez, G. (2006). Computer Technology and Native Literacy in the Amazon Rain Forrest. In L. Everlyn Dyson, M. Hendriks, & S. Grant (Eds.), *Information Technology and Indigenous People* (1st ed., pp. 17–20). Information Science Publishing., doi:10.4018/978-1-59904-298-5.ch013

Gregory, S. (2015). *Ubiquitous witnesses : who creates the evidence and the live (d) experience of human rights violations ?* Taylor and Francis. . doi:10.1080/1369118X.2015.1070891

Gregory, S. (2022) *TikTok Must Not Fail Ukrainians.* WIRED. https://www.wired.com/story/tiktok-must-not-fail-ukrainians/

Guadalupe, M. R. (2002). Indigenous Rights in Democratic Brazil. *Human Rights Quarterly, 24*(2), 487–512. https://www.jstor.org/stable/20069611. doi:10.1353/hrq.2002.0028

Hanna, P., Langdon, E. J., & Vanclay, F. (2016). Indigenous rights, performativity and protest. *Land Use Policy, 50*, 490–506. doi:10.1016/j.landusepol.2015.06.034

Hanna de Almeida Oliveira, P. (2012). *The social impacts of large projects on Indigenous Peoples, University of Groningen.* University of Groningen., doi:10.1016/B978-0-12-373932-2.00298-2

Hisayasu, L. (2019). *Mediated Memory and the Internet : Indigenous Protagonism in Brazil.* Danube University.

Hoelle, J. (2017). Jungle beef: Consumption, production and destruction, and the development process in the Brazilian Amazon. *Journal of Political Ecology, 24*(1), 743. doi:10.2458/v24i1.20964

Höijer, B. (2004). The discourse of global compassion: The audience and media reporting of human suffering. *Media Culture & Society, 26*(4), 513–531. doi:10.1177/0163443704044215

Holston, J. (2008). *Insurgent Citizenship: Disjunctons of Democracy and Modernity in Brazil.* Princton University Press.

Huiberts, E., & Joye, S. (2019). Who cares for the suffering other? A survey-based study into reactions toward images of distant suffering. *The International Communication Gazette, 81*(6–8), 562–579. doi:10.1177/1748048518825324

Hunter, L. B. (2019). Live streaming and the perils of proximity. *International Journal of Performance Arts and Digital Media, 15*(3), 283–294. doi:10.1080/14794713.2019.1671697

Ibrahim, Y. (2010). Distant Suffering and Postmodern Subjectivity: The Communal Politics of Pity. *Nebula, 7*(1/2), 122–135. http://content.ebscohost.com/ContentServer.asp?T=P&P=AN&K=51594697&S=R&D=hlh&EbscoContent=dGJyMNHX8kSeqLE4y9fwOLCmr0ueprRSsa64TbWWxWXS&ContentCustomer=dGJyMPPZ8oTn2LmF39/sU+Pe7Yvy%5Cnhttp://search.ebscohost.com/login.aspx?direct=true&db=hlh&AN=51594697&si

Ibrahim, Y. (2020). *Technologies of Trauma: Flesh Witnessing to Livestreaming Online.* Human Arenas. doi:10.100742087-020-00120-y

Kavada, A., Treré, E., & Kavada, A. (2019). Live democracy and its tensions : Making sense of livestreaming in the 15M and Occupy livestreaming in the 15M and Occupy. *Information Communication and Society, 0*(0), 1–18. doi:10.1080/1369118X.2019.1637448

Kissock, T. (2020a). Bolsonaro's Congressional Cheerleaders in the Global Post-Truth Era: Demagoguery as communication, and YouTube as the tool. UCL: University College London. doi:10.13140/RG.2.2.27059.96800/1

Kissock, T. (2020b). *Jungle Drones: Can Indigenous drone projects in Latin America and the Caribbean be more sustainable?* Tom Kissock. https://www.tomkissock.com/post/jungle-drones-indigenous-drone-projects

Kissock, T. (2020c). Live Streaming: A confirmation of community and exercise of citizenship. I by Tom Kissock-Mamede. *Medium.* https://medium.com/@tomkissock-mamede/live-streaming-a-confirmation-of-community-and-exercise-of-citizenship-d615f71e1244

Kissock, T. (2021). *Why the English-speaking world should take notice of Brazil's #3JForaBolsonaro Movement.* LatAMDialogue. https://www.latamdialogue.org/post/why-the-english-speaking-world-should-take-notice-of-brazil-s-3jforabolsonaro-movement (Accessed: 25 March 2022).

Kozol, W. (2015). *Distant Wars Visible* (1st ed.). University of Minnasota Press. doi:10.5749/minnesota/9780816681297.001.0001

Land, C. (2015). *Decolonizing solidarity: dilemmas and directions for supporters of indigenous struggles.* Zed Books.

Langlois, J. (2022) For the Kayapó, a Long Battle to Save Their Amazon Homeland. *Yale Enviroment 360.* https://e360.yale.edu/features/for-the-kayapo-a-long-battle-to-save-their-amazon-homeland.

Lazer, D., Kennedy, R., King, G., & Vespignani, A. (2014). The Parable of Google Flu: Traps in Big Data Analysis. *Science, 343*(6176), 1203–1205. doi:10.1126cience.1248506 PMID:24626916

Leal de Oliveira, A., Ruy Bragatto, J., & Montenegro de Souza Lima, M. (2023). *A Inconstitucionalidade Do Marco Temporal: Riscos E Ameaças À Tutela Dos Povos Indígenas Originários Do Brasil, Revista Direitos Sociais e Políticas Públicas.* UNIFAFIBE. doi:10.25245/rdspp.v10i3.1349

Liverman, D. M., & Vilas, S. (2006). Neoliberalism and the Environment in Latin America. *Annual Review of Environment and Resources, 31*(1), 327–363. doi:10.1146/annurev.energy.29.102403.140729

Mantelli, G., Neiva, J. M. and Ingrams, M. (2022). Deforestation And Climate Change In Brazil. *Legal and policy gaps.*

Marques, J. (2022) *Mendonça trava julgamento do STF sobre desmatamento na Amazônia - 06/04/2022 Ambiente.* Folha. https://www1.folha.uol.com.br/ambiente/2022/04/mendonca-indicado-de-bolsonaro-trava-julgamento-do-stf-sobre-desmatamento-na-amazonia.shtml (Accessed: 8 April 2022).

Martini, M. (2018). *Online distant witnessing and live-streaming activism : Emerging differences in the activation of networked publics.* Sage. . doi:10.1177/1461444818766703

McCoy, T. (2021). Cunhaporanga Tatuyo became a TikTok star by sharing glimpses of her life in a remote indigenous community in the Amazon. *The Washington Post.* https://www.washingtonpost.com/world/interactive/2021/brazil-indigenous-tik-tok-star/

McPherson, E. (2018). Risk and the Pluralism of Digital Human Rights Fact-Finding and Advocacy. In K. Land, M. and D. Aronson, J. (eds) Human Rights New Technologies for Human Rights Law and Practice. Cambridge University Press. doi:10.1017/9781316838952.009

Indigenous Livestreaming in Brazil

Menton, M., Milanez, F., Souza, J. M. A., & Cruz, F. S. M. (2021). The COVID-19 pandemic intensified resource conflicts and indigenous resistance in Brazil. *World Development, 138*, 105222. doi:10.1016/j. worlddev.2020.105222

Mortensen, M. (2015). Connective witnessing: Reconfiguring the relationship between the individual and the collective. *Information Communication and Society, 18*(11), 1393–1406. doi:10.1080/136911 8X.2015.1061574

Nassauer, A., & Legewie, M. N. (2022) Video Data Analysis: How to use 21st century video in the social sciences. Sage Publishing.

Ong, J. C. (2015). Witnessing distant and proximal suffering within a zone of danger: Lay moralities of media audiences in the Philippines. *The International Communication Gazette, 77*(7), 607–621. doi:10.1177/1748048515601555

Peters, J. D. (2009). Witnessing. In P. Frosh & A. Pinchevski (Eds.), *Media Witnessing* (1st ed., pp. 23–42)., doi:10.1057/9780230235762_2

Piauí, R. (2022). *Revista piauí on Twitter: "In Brazil, the coup will be live-streamed. Piauí analyzed 181 of Jair Bolsonaro's live streams and can now show, in video, how the president has prepared his supporters to discredit tomorrow's election. A crash course on coup-mo, Revista Piauí.* Twitter. https:// twitter.com/revistapiaui/status/1576199768031756288

Pontes, F. (2022). *Após descida do rio, indígenas recolhem produtos descartados por comerciantes - Amazônia Real, Amazonia Real.* Amazon IA Real. https://amazoniareal.com.br/apos-descida-do-rio-indigenas-recolhem-produtos-descartados-por-comerciantes/ (Accessed: 15 April 2022).

Quintanilla, M., Guzmán León, A., & Josse, C. (2022) *Amazonia Against the Clock, A Regional Assessment on where and how to protect 80% by 2025.* Amazonia.

Rahat, M. (2022). *Problematic video-streaming: a short review.* Science Direct. . doi:10.1016/j.cobeha.2022.101232

Ramos, A. R. (1998). *Indigenism: ethnic politics in Brazil* (1st ed.). University of Wisconsin Press.

Ribeiro, D. (1975). *Configurações histórico-culturais dos povos americanos.* Global Editora e Distribuidora Ltda.

Ribeiro, D. (1977). *Os índios e a civilização.* Editora Vozes.

Ristovska, S. (2016). Strategic witnessing in an age of video activism. *Media Culture & Society, 38*(7), 1034–1047. doi:10.1177/0163443716635866

Robinson, D. (2020). T202. Multicast: Has Its Time Finally Arrived? [Video] YouTube. *Streaming Media West.* https://www.youtube.com/watch?v=KG-ecsdmodI&list=PL_tg9vfNLui1vnqdPEHFd-M3S_b8zc3RW1&index=14

Rojas, D., de Azevedo Olival, A., & Alves Spexoto Olival, A. (2021). Despairing Hopes (and Hopeful Despair) in Amazonia. In B. Junge, (Ed.), *Precarious Democracy* (1st ed., pp. 129–141). Rutgers University Press., doi:10.36019/9781978825697-012

Ruberg, B., & Brewer, J. (2022). Digital Intimacy in Real Time : Live Streaming Gender and Sexuality. *Television & New Media*, *00*(0), 1–8. doi:10.1177/15274764221084071

Sage Rauchberg, J. (2022). '#Shadowbanned. In P. Paromita (Ed.), *LGBTQ Digital Cultures* (1st ed., p. 196). Routledge. doi:10.4324/9781003196457-15

Sallaz, J. J. (2018). Is a Bourdieusian Ethnography Possible? In T. Medvetz & J. J. Sallaz (Eds.), *The Oxford Handbook of Pierre Bourdieu* (pp. 1–24). Oxford University Press. doi:10.1093/oxfordhb/9780199357192.013.21

Salzar, J. F. (2006). Indigenous Peoples and the Cultural Construction of Information and Communication Technology (ICT) in Latin America. In L. Everlyn Dyson, M. Hendriks, & S. Grant (Eds.), *Information Technology and Indigenous People* (1st ed., pp. 14–27). Information Science Publishing. doi:10.4018/978-1-59904-298-5.ch002

Samson, C., & Gigoux, C. (2016). *Indigenous Peoples and Colonialism: Global Perspectives* (1st ed.). Polity Press.

Scaff, L. A. (2021). Max Weber. In P. Kivisto (Ed.), *The Cambridge Handbook of Social Theory* (pp. 124–144). Cambridge Univeristy Press.

Schwarcz, M. L. & Starling, H. (2019) Brazil a biography. First. Farrar, Straus and Giroux.

Smith, L. T. (2021) Decolonizing Methodologies: Research and Indigenous Peoples was Third. Zed Books. doi:10.5040/9781350225282

Thorburn, E. D. (2017). Social reproduction in the live stream. *TripleC*, *15*(2), 425–440. doi:10.31269/triplec.v15i2.774

Turner, S. (1994). *The Social Theory of Practices: Tradition, Tacit Knowledge, and Presuppositions* (1st ed.). Polity Press.

Turner, V. (1980). Social Dramas and Stories about Them. *Critical Inquiry*, *7*(1), 141–168. https://www-jstor-org.ezp.lib.cam.ac.uk/stable/1343180?seq=1. doi:10.1086/448092

UNESCO (2021) *GLOBAL ACTION PLAN OF THE INTERNATIONAL DECADE OF INDIGENOUS LANGUAGES (IDIL2022-2032)*. UNESCO.

Urt, J. N. (2016). How Western Sovereignty Occludes Indigenous Governance: The Guarani and Kaiowa Peoples in Brazil. *Contexto Internacional*, *38*(3), 865–886. doi:10.15900102-8529.2016380300007

Veloso Ferreira, L. (2022). *Brasileiros pelo Brasil completa 3 meses com mais de 900 mil pessoas atendidas*, Fundação Banco do Brasil. https://fbb.org.br/pt-br/component/k2/conteudo/brasileiros-pelo-brasil-completa-3-meses-com-mais-de-900-mil-pessoas-atendidas

Verdery, K. (1999). *The Political Lives of Dead Bodies: Reburial and Post socialist Cahange* (1st ed.). Colombia University Press.

Vidal, L. B. (1986) 'A questão indígena', Carajás: desafio político, ecologia e desenvolvimento, p. 222.

Villén-Pérez, S., Anaya-Valenzuela, L., Conrado da Cruz, D., & Fearnside, P. M. (2021). Mining threatens isolated indigenous peoples in the Brazilian Amazon. *Global Environmental Change, 72*, 102398. doi:10.1016/j.gloenvcha.2021.102398

Weber, M. (1992). The Protestant Ethic and the Spirit of Capitalism. Journal of Geophysical Research. Routledge.

Whitson, J. (2021). Indigenizing instagram: Challenging settler colonialism in the outdoor industry. *American Quarterly, 73*(2), 311–334. doi:10.1353/aq.2021.0029

Zhang, X., & Luther, C. A. (2020). Transnational news media coverage of distant suffering in the Syrian civil war: An analysis of CNN, Al-Jazeera English and Sputnik online news. *Media, War & Conflict, 13*(4), 399–424. doi:10.1177/1750635219846029

Zhao, Y. (2020) Analysis of TikTok's Success Based on Its Algorithm Mechanism. *Proceedings - 2020 International Conference on Big Data and Social Sciences, ICBDSS 2020*, (pp. 19–23). IEEE. 10.1109/ICBDSS51270.2020.00012

KEY TERMS AND DEFINITIONS

Ephemeral: Moment in a short window of time.
Indigenous: People originating from a territory.
Livestreaming: Transmission of audio and video across a network in real-time.
Reflection: An introspective action to engage in a process of continuous learning.
Witnessing: Observations contingent on the provision of testimony.

ENDNOTES

[1]   This description can be found on the PIB website: https://pib.socioambiental.org/en/Who_are_they%3F

[2]   This could be seen as an interactive Map on the program's webpage which has now been taken down: https://brasileirospelobrasil.fbb.org.br/mapa

Chapter 15

Decolonising and Humanising Pedagogies in South African Postgraduate Education:
Lessons From Indigenous Knowledge Systems

Mothusiotsile Edwin Maditsi
North-West University, South Africa

Monicca Thulisile Bhuda
University of Mpumalanga, South Africa

ABSTRACT

Indigenous knowledge systems (IKS) have been marginalized in higher education institutions that have mostly followed Western paradigms of teaching, learning, and research. The prevalence of western pedagogies and worldviews has prompted certain stakeholders, such as the #FeesMustFall movement, to ask for the decolonization and humanization of South African higher education institutions' curricula. This chapter employed a qualitative document analysis (QDA) method to investigate how IKS could be used as a foundation for decolonizing and humanizing pedagogies at South African universities. It used Ubuntu's indigenous philosophy to elicit meaning, understanding, and case studies in which Ubuntu enshrines norms and values commensurate with African worldviews and epistemologies in order to humanize pedagogies. The study concludes that IKS is a social capital that can change the way universities design and apply pedagogies for teaching, learning, and research. The indigenous pedagogical praxis is the link between decolonization and humanization of higher education.

DOI: 10.4018/978-1-6684-7024-4.ch015

Copyright © 2023, IGI Global. Copying or distributing in print or electronic forms without written permission of IGI Global is prohibited.

INTRODUCTION

In recent years, there have been talks around the decolonizing of knowledge at South African universities. Many scholars view this widespread call for decolonization as overdue in the South African higher education sphere. Scholars such as Heleta (2018) have headed the calls to dismantle the Eurocentric hegemony within the HEIs in South Africa. Reference is made to the establishment of a movement *#feesmustfall* to decolonize higher education by students in 2015. Students across South African universities had reached a consensus that what the former president, Tata Nelson Rolihlahla Mandela and his generation negotiated at the Convention for a Democratic South Africa (CODESA) has failed to break the paradigm of difference whereby ethnic communities remain marginalized in the knowledge economy (Ndlovu-Gatsheni, 2018). Inevitably, students demanded immediate decolonization of universities. Increasing efforts as noted by Zembylas (2018) have been explored to pinpoint what decolonization in university curricula entails. However, less theorization has been made to underpin what decolonization implies for higher education pedagogy and praxis (Heleta, 2018; Le Grange, 2016).

The colonial era, or apartheid in the case of South Africa repressed indigenous knowledge as well as indigenous epistemologies and worldviews. It is noteworthy to realize that South African universities' curricular remains endowed in the Eurocentric knowledge domain and worldviews and this has seen other forms of knowledge such as indigenous knowledge systems being left in the periphery of the knowledge economy. This marginalization of indigenous knowledge system has left the knowledge being produced at the postgraduate level to remain Eurocentric thus devaluing and ignoring other alternative knowledge systems. There is therefore a need to drive a decolonial agenda at the postgraduate level, thereby aiding the humanizing aspect of knowledge. Decolonization of knowledge implies the end of reliance on imposed knowledge, theories and interpretations and theorizing based on one's own past and present experiences and interpretation of the world (Zembylas, 2018).

Shahjahan et al (2022) note that curriculum and pedagogy is deeply implicated in grounding, validating, and/or marginalizing systems of knowledge production. Therefore, there is a need to transform Higher Education Institutions (HEIs) and this can be achieved by various scholars, including indigenous scholars who can stand steadfast and counter the non-transformation that seems to bring the HEIs of South Africa to stagnation. Nonetheless, some questions remain as many ask themselves, to what extent the changes in HEIs, including pedagogies and curriculum, have "decolonized" higher education, and whether full decolonization is even possible.

The Afrocentric theoretical perspective that has been brought forth by Molefi Asante is realized by South African universities as a leeway to foster Africanization within this institution (Sebola & Magoboya, 2020). Afrocentricity, according to Asante (1999), is a critical corrective to a displaced agency among Africans by re-centring African minds. Afrocentricity may also be viewed as a paradigm based on the idea that African people should re-assert a sense of agency in thought and practice within the livelihood of Africans, their societal institutions, and processes in order to achieve sanity. This theoretical perspective provides an indigenized lens which can be understood and applied using African centred values, standards, and tools (Sebola & Magoboya, 2020). Another means to fully humanize pedagogies at postgraduate level in South Africa, the philosophy of *Ubuntu* needs to be inculcated into both academics and academic developers. *Ubuntu* is viewed as an agent of decolonization in HEIs across South Africa as its core norms and values are rooted in indigenous knowledge systems and African worldviews.

This overall aim of this chapter was to showcase how decolonization and humanization can be achieved within the HEIs of South Africa through the application and use of indigenous knowledge systems and indigenous methodologies. Academics within various fields have attempted to apply indigenous knowledge to their respective fields, but only a handful have the necessary expertise and knowhow, including the methodologies to incorporate this knowledge into finding viable solutions for indigenous communities. The following questions are asked by this chapter:

- Whose reality counts?
- How can we decolonize university pedagogies?
- Which knowledge is vital for university postgraduate education?
- Is indigenous knowledge systems the relevant path for African universities?
- What constitutes decolonized knowledge?
- Which pedagogies are relevant for postgraduate education?
- Are indigenous methodological approaches relevant for postgraduate education?
- How can we learn from indigenous knowledge systems to enhance the pedagogy lens within HEIS?
- Can coaching interventions be applied to humanize postgraduate education?

The above questions should be answered by academics and indigenous scholars who view indigenous knowledge as a system of achieving a decolonized education and pedagogies in Africa generally and South Africa in particular. Decolonization is about bringing forth the previously marginalized indigenous knowledge and the voices of communities forth. The main theoretical concept that underpins decolonization is humanizing pedagogy (Zembylas, 2018). This resulted in higher education institutions (HEIs) focusing only on western models of teaching, learning, and supervising postgraduate research. This monopolizing of pedagogies resulted in the ignorance of African worldviews by these institutions. Lack of valuing indigenous knowledge systems as another form of knowledge has resulted in academic staff neglecting other avenues that can be applied to humanize pedagogy, especially at postgraduate level. Thereof, the call for decolonized and humanized pedagogies in postgraduate education is vital and key in addressing social justice.

Literature Review

This section of the chapter provides the ontological basis for the paper to pinpoint what has been done and achieved previously by other scholars on the topic, and it stems from the reality that has transpired within the higher education sphere of South Africa from the initial time of #feesmustfall to the contemporary stance of higher education. The section is presented in two sub-sections under the literature review section.

Understanding the Call to Decolonize

Ndhovu-Gatsheni (2013) posits that there is a need to appreciate decoloniality as a process of liberatory thought and practice. Therefore, it is vital to encourage the rethinking of decolonization in postgraduate education pedagogies as this will propel expressions of enactments aimed at challenging the mainstream pedagogies and institutional culture in postgraduate education. Notably, this decolonization should acknowledge diversity, ethics, languages, and the creation of synergy between the old and new (Mahabeer, 2018). The transformation agenda remains at the heart of debates of higher education in South Africa (Blignaut, 2020). Subsequently, a call for culturally responsive and cognisant pedagogies at postgraduate

Decolonising, Humanising Pedagogy in South African Education

level in stressed. This is because this transformation that is rooted in indigenous knowledge, pedagogy, and way of knowing advances social justice in higher education. Maistry (2021) posits that the South African education cannot fully transform if it does not enact and centre social justice in its business. Cherrington et al (2018) positions decolonization as a framework for critiquing and renewing the education transformation project. It is vital to decolonize postgraduate education at South African universities because decolonization is about epistemological disobedience premised on power, knowledge and being (Ndhovu, Gatsheni, 2013; Cherington et al, 2018). This decolonization and this epistemological disobedience are aimed at disrupting prevailing power structures and institutional cultures to shed some light on democratized practices of postgraduate education (Keet et al, 2017).

Decolonization is about bringing forth the previously marginalized indigenous knowledge and the voices of communities forth. The main theoretical concept that underpins decolonization is humanizing pedagogy (Zembylas, 2018). Zembylas points out that there is a link between decolonization and the humanization of higher education and that this link lies with pedagogical praxis. Therefore, universities need to reflect critically on what it means to decolonize and humanize postgraduate education and pedagogy. This reflection should deeply focus on reclaiming humanity in knowing and knowledge-making. Additionally, Cherrington et al (2018) point out that humanizing pedagogy can be reconceptualised to decolonial and social transformative frameworks that challenge existing colonial powers within the academy.

Understanding the Nature and Implications of Indigenous Knowledge Systems (IKS) for Higher Education

For the study and its nature, it is important to define what indigenous knowledge is in order to link it to indigenous knowledge systems. Therefore, indigenous knowledge refers to understandings, skills and philosophies developed by local communities with long histories and experiences of interaction with their natural surroundings. Indigenous knowledge and the people who are intrinsically linked to it cannot be separated. It is relevant to events in the biological, physical, social, cultural and spiritual realms. In addition, Bruchac (2014:3) added by saying that:

"Indigenous knowledge can be defined as a network of knowledge, beliefs, and traditions intended to preserve, communicate, and contextualize Indigenous relationships with culture and landscape over time. One might distinguish "knowledge" as factual data, "belief" as religious concepts, and "tradition" as practice, but these terms are often used imprecisely and interchangeably to describe Indigenous epistemologies. Indigenous pieces of knowledge are conveyed formally and informally among kin groups and communities through social encounters, oral traditions, ritual practices, and other activities. They include: oral narratives that recount human histories; cosmological observations and modes of reckoning time; symbolic and decorative modes of communication; techniques for planting and harvesting; hunting and gathering skills; specialized understandings of local ecosystems; and the manufacture of specialized tools and technologies (e.g., flint-knapping, hide tanning, pottery-making, and concocting medicinal remedies)".

Indigenous knowledge is thought to possess several unique characteristics. Firstly, Maher (2000) points out that it is placed in a specific context and that it embodies the native people's way of life, social interactions, and natural surroundings. Since it is localized, there is no claim to universality; yet this does not imply that the area is isolated from the rest of the world. Rather, it suggests that it is useful for

285

the local community's survival in day-to-day life. Secondly, it is holistic knowledge because it addresses all dimensions of human beings. Thirdly, it derives from diverse and multiple sources of indigenous knowledge such as:

- old knowledge that has existed for generations in the specific community like historical events, ancestral wisdoms and genealogies of the clan;
- empirical knowledge that has been learned through careful and daily observations, and
- revealed knowledge acquired through dreams, visions, and spiritual institutions (Maher, 2000:67–68)

These commonalities, according to Higgs (2003), are defined by Warren (1991: 24–25), who asserts that "Indigenous knowledge is the local knowledge - knowledge that is unique to a given culture or society. Indigenous knowledge contrasts with the international knowledge system generated by universities, research institutions and private firms. It is the basis for local-level decision making in agriculture, healthcare, food preparation, education, natural resource management, and a host of other activities in rural communities".

Based on the discussions above, Indigenous Knowledge System (IKS) can be defined as ways of (relational) knowing and living that have evolved among societies that were first native to a place. These additional ideas, skills, and beliefs were developed by societies that have a long history of interacting with the environment. Rural and indigenous people can make decisions about essential aspects of daily life with the assistance of local knowledge. A complex cultural system that also encompasses language, categorization systems, resource-use traditions, social interactions, ritual, and spirituality depends on this information. These many ways of knowing create the foundation for locally appropriate sustainable development and are important components of the global cultural diversity (Onwu & Mosimege, 2004; Von der Porten et al., 2016).

Based on the above definition, the study argues that the African practices and knowledge that a local indigenous group accumulates over many generations of residence in a particular region can be broadly described as African indigenous Knowledge systems. African Indigenous Knowledge Systems (AIKS) have a rich history since for many millennia they have influenced and defined the way of life for Africans (Kaya & Seleti, 2013). It is due of the nature of the 'way of life' that African indigenous knowledge systems continue to be reassessed and seen as an inspirational source of sustainable development methods. Thus, according Tamburro (2013), AIKS can contextualize any knowledge area to the setting in which it is provided (Msila, 2009).

Saurombe (2018) added that in linking it to higher education, African indigenous knowledge systems can be viewed as a call to adapt curricula and syllabi to ensure that teaching and learning is adapted to African realities and conditions. Thus, teaching of African indigenous knowledge systems can be a viable tool in the decolonisation and Africanisation of the curriculum. Kaya and Seleti (2013) support that transforming education in Africa would be truly meaningful if Africans realise the importance of that which belongs to the continent. The higher education system in Africa, and South Africa in particular, is still overly academic and removed from the problems African local communities face in terms of development. The higher education system's relevance might increase with the incorporation of indigenous African knowledge systems (Saurombe, 2018). This is because AIKS approaches education and knowledge production holistically and from a community-based perspective. Yet to facilitate the integration process, we need an African indigenous theoretical framework of knowledge. The framework should

Decolonising, Humanising Pedagogy in South African Education

make clear the value of indigenous African languages in the creation and dissemination of knowledge in the age of globalization.

The experiences of several higher educational institutions in South Africa demonstrate the need for a robust institutional support system for sustained integration. The interrogation on the role of African indigenous knowledge systems in promoting the relevance of higher education in South Africa and Africa at large is based on the argument that although the use of what is considered to be indigenous knowledge in Africa goes back to the history of humankind in the continent, its current promotion in education and other spheres of community livelihood and development is a recent phenomenon (Kaya & Seleti, 2013; Bhuda, 2021). Observations from a few South African higher education institutions show the necessity of a strong institutional support system for a long-term integration (Kaya & Seleti, 2013; Bhuda, 2021). The expectations of this current study are that postgraduate students within African universities need to work to decolonize measures that exist within personal and professional domains: self-decolonization and the indigenous community. For non-indigenous postgraduate students, valuing indigenous culture should be comparable to maintaining indigenous people's worldviews, affirmative research paradigms and methodologies. Donald (2012) stated that although non-indigenous scholars do not identify themselves as indigenous, they can shift toward greater compassion for colonization-related historical and current battles and create improvement in the research process, which also enables indigenous researcher's space to use or potentially improve indigenous philosophies (Kovach, 2009; Smith, 2012).

Research Methodology

This chapter applies a qualitative document analysis (QDA), focusing on various scholarly published papers about indigenous knowledge, indigenous epistemologies and methodologies, Ubuntu philosophy and indigenous knowledge systems. This method provided background information as well as historical insight and qualitative data on African indigenous education, pedagogies, philosophies, and decolonization of knowledge. It focuses mainly on Ubuntu philosophy, indigenous research methodologies, indigenous pedagogies, and humanizing pedagogies. It further focuses on the decolonization and indigenization of postgraduate education and research by indigenous and non-indigenous scholars. The data for this research was collected through a comprehensive literature review of academic articles, books, and reports.

The data acquired is reported herein as subtopics/themes within the chapter. The data provides that decolonizing, indigenizing, and humanizing postgraduate education does not, however, mean rejecting other Euro-Western methodologies, but rather being critical and open to research cultures and encouraging their collaboration and expertise in the research process (Chilisa, 2012; Smith, 1999). The paper's argument, however, is that African indigenous philosophies are culturally sensitive, requiring postgraduate students and researchers to advance cultural reactivity using theoretical frameworks that perceive, share relational responsibility, multiple realities, indigenous systems, and beliefs. Alternatively, Chilisa (2012) proposed that indigenous research methodologies that are part of African indigenous philosophies are influenced by indigenous knowledge systems. The situated learning theory and social learning theory are deemed relevant theories for underpinning this study.

The expectations of this study are that postgraduate student within African universities need to work to decolonize measures that exist within personal and professional domains: self-decolonization and the indigenous community. For non-indigenous postgraduate students, valuing indigenous culture should be comparable to maintaining indigenous people's worldviews, affirmative research paradigms and methodologies. Donald (2012) stated that although non-indigenous scholars do not identify themselves as indigenous, they can shift toward greater compassion for colonization-related historical and current battles and create improvement in the research process, which also enables indigenous researcher's space to use or potentially improve indigenous philosophies (Kovach, 2009; Smith, 2012).

Findings and Discussions

This section presents the findings together with the discussions of the findings following a qualitative document analysis (QDA). This chapter presents the case for decolonization and humanization of pedagogies within higher education institutions (HEIs) of South Africa. An indigenous paradigmatic lens is applied to present these finding and ground them based on indigenous knowledge systems (IKS).

The Significance of Decolonization Within the Education Sphere

The process through which imperial states develop and rule over foreign areas, frequently overseas, is known as colonialism, which is being undone through the process of decolonization or decolonisation. Decolonization refers to re writing against the continuous colonialism and colonial mentalities that permeate all institutions and systems of government. Decolonization does, in fact, call for the adoption of an Indigenous perspective and the centrality of Indigenous lands, Indigenous sovereignty, and Indigenous ways of thinking (Bhuda, 2021).

Decolonization involves reflecting on the structure of educational institutions, and their role within the larger society. It is also important to confront the power relations within these institutions. Who controls knowledge is one question to consider. What part do they play? How did they get this position? What keeps them in power? Learning to be an ally and to stand in solidarity with one another among a varied community of students is a crucial component of decolonization, as is doing so with employees as well as other students. In the context of higher education, decolonization entails tearing down institutional practices and policies that support white supremacist, Western ideologies.

Western institutions are frequently considered as the standard? for the ideal university in non-Western countries, which contributes to the dominance of Western epistemology there as well (Nandy 2000). This has prompted numerous individuals to stress the significance of "*decolonizing the mind*" and the pursuit of cognitive fairness in higher education research and courses (Sousa-Santos, 2007). Others warn against the risk of focusing on the epistemic aspects of decolonization at the expense of more tangible battles for restitution of land and other benefits (Tuck & Yang 2012). These, however, are not mutually exclusive, and calls for decolonization from both viewpoints as well as more are being made by students, professors, and activists all over the world in Western and Westernized universities, within former imperial metropoles, settler colonial nations, and formerly colonized countries.

Figure 1 demonstrates how having an education system that is cantered in the voices of indigenous peoples is necessary for the process of decolonizing education and undoing colonial practices. In the school systems that the indigenous pupils attend, the voices of indigenous peoples must be supported and heard. Indigenous voices and agency must be prioritized in education since Indigenous people are the authorities in their own lives. For those who want to honour indigenous people, it is important to use an indigenous lens when investigating indigenous people, their knowledge and why it is important in education. Using an indigenous lens will mean honouring indigenous worldviews which is a way to create an understanding about indigenous people and their perspectives. Recognizing the contributions made by indigenous people in education is a step toward them reclaiming the power that was taken away

Figure 1. Decolonization in education
(source, researchers).

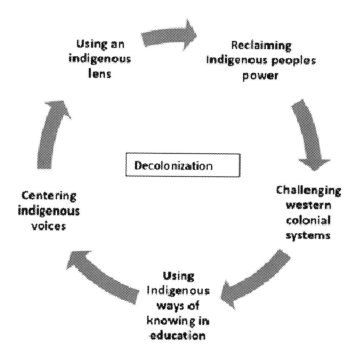

from them by western scholars, systems and methods that viewed their ways of life as too primitive and beneath a formal education system. By reclaiming their power in education, indigenous people are challenging the long-standing western systems and perception that indigenous knowledge and people are obsolete and static. Consequently, it is the opinion of this study that African intellectuals should assist Africa in closing the knowledge gap caused by the dominance and marginalization of African people's knowledge systems for more than four centuries by rejecting the use of the dominant western world view of knowing and knowledge production as the only method of knowing in formal education.

Positioning Decolonization in the Research Agenda: Reflections for Postgraduate Education

Decolonizing education also means decolonizing research that involves indigenous people whose knowledge has been deemed inappropriate to be part of the education system (Bhuda & Koitsiwe, 2022). Decolonizing research entails giving the community's opinions and viewpoints centre stage throughout the investigation. It is crucial for academics to think critically about strategies that can improve the health outcomes of indigenous people. These problems are crucial, and they may be especially pertinent to research in the Global South and the African setting in which we operate (Zavala, 2013). Nhemachena et al. (2016) claim that research among African indigenous people has frequently not improved the health of those who were studied.

Africa genuinely experiences a current crisis due to its material wealth, cultural artefacts, and expertise (Nhemachena et al., 2016). The emphasis is shifted from the goals of the non-Indigenous researcher to the agenda of the Indigenous people when research is decolonized, particularly when it makes use of Indigenous viewpoints, knowledge, and technique (McGregor, 2018; Rix et al., 2018). Indigenous people now have the opportunity to express their own worldviews without feeling as inferior or undervalued as in the past thanks to research on decolonization. Researchers have conducted a lot of studies on Indigenous peoples without decolonizing their research training. Indigenous researchers such as Wilson (2008), Battiste (2001), Kovach (2010), Lavallée (2009), Smith (1999), and others contend that Western research that has not undergone decolonization might be characterized as oppression of Indigenous people. However, they warn researchers that if decolonization is not respected and/or considered in Western research, it might have serious negative effects on many Indigenous people, including economic inequity, displacement, loss of traditional lifestyles, and major harm. According to Smith (1999), decolonizing research training can alter both the researcher and the research. She contends that the decolonization of research will enable Indigenous ways of knowing and being to reclaim power, opening new opportunities for research to advance social justice. This section's main claim is that, when working with Indigenous communities, decolonizing research training is effective and culturally suitable for both the participant's community and the researcher. It also questions the established western methods for studying indigenous people and their knowledge. For indigenous people to communicate their worldviews, which ought to be a part of the formal educational system, decolonizing research returns authority to them.

Decolonization Within the South African Context

There are students in South Africa who view the cultural imposition of higher education as symbolic violence and are upset that since 1994, the year of the first democratic elections, not much has changed to challenge white dominance. Despite how problematic it may be to question the "cultural arbitraries" of the curriculum (Luke, 2018), this is exactly what students are doing. Given that they have had limited formal educational access to texts and knowledge valued outside of the predominately Western and European traditions of study, it is not unexpected that they are frequently unsure about what should be chosen instead. The anger students have been feeling towards the South African Higher education system was experienced during the *#FeesMustFall* movement of 2015 when students protested over more than economic freedom (Luescher & Mugume, 2017). They further indicated that indigenous languages had to be used as a medium of instruction in higher institutions and their indigenous knowledge recognised. It is therefore this studies argument that South Africa the students are often marginalized in higher education come from the country's overwhelming black majority where indigenous languages and culture are taken as a priority. Therefore the #Feesmustfall movement was simply black students recognizing and challenging the existing powers and privileges the social class have in higher education.

Initially, in 2015, people had perceptions that the *#FeesMustFall* movement by students was mainly focused on the financial struggles of historically disadvantaged black students in South Africa. Students at the University of Cape Town called for the removal of Cecil John Rhodes' statue from its elevated position overlooking the campus' mountainside during the same year, using the *#RhodesMustFall*. Rhodes, a prototypical exploitative colonizer linked to "racist, plunder, white supremacy, colonialism, pillaging, dispossession, and the oppression of black people" (Masondo, 2015), came to represent the lack of change in South African higher education institutions (HEIs). The #FeesMustFall campaign served as another outlet for the nationwide call to decolonize higher education (2015–2017).

The study agrees with Janks (2019) that apartheid divided people based on their race, ethnicity, and language in addition to colonizing black people. Although though South Africa takes pride in being a democratic nation, colonial ways of doing in higher education still exist today. The authors of this research argue that all students who enrol in higher education institutions must adjust to a new environment and learn new ways of being, doing, speaking, writing, and interacting. This point was reinforced by (Janks, 2019) who claimed that decolonization of education was soon to be acted up by black students who acted using the *#FeesMustFall* and *#RhodesMustFall* movements.

Janks (2019) further added that black students have had to adapt to academic terminology as well as various institutional, social, pedagogical, and literacy practices for a very long time. Lopez & Rugano. (2018) stated that black students in South Africa find this adjustment to be much more difficult because they are frequently the first members of their families to pursue higher education, their dispositions and tastes frequently diverge from the urban, middle-class, white cultural norms that are prevalent, and their languages are not commonly used in academic settings. Decolonizing South Africa's higher education institutions entails recognizing those who were previously marginalized by apartheid, choosing to embrace and recognize their own cultures (indigenous knowledge), telling their own histories, learning from books written by Africans, and managing institutions in accordance with African values rather than Eurocentric models (Plessis, 2021). According to the claim made in this study, the *#FeesMustFall* and #Rhodesmustfall movements served as a reminder to South Africans of the divisions and exclusion that still exist today in higher education and training.

Indigenous Knowledge Systems as an Agent of Decolonization in Postgraduate Education

Indigenous knowledge systems (IKS) refer to knowledge that is developed by a given community (Mahlangu & Garutsa. 2019). It is knowledge that is acquired, owned, and used by a close group of people within a locality as compared to western or modern knowledge systems that is generated by universities, government research centre and private industry (Mapara, 2009). This knowledge is subjected to ridicule, de-privileging, and marginalization within the knowledge production process. This is mainly because indigenous knowledge through the application of western epistemology is denied legitimacy and suppressed by the colonial education (Mzamane, 2003). Additionally, not much has been explained or shared about how indigenous knowledge has contributed to the academic scholarship. This marginalization of IK therefore excludes indigenous knowledge in the knowledge economy by universities thereby applying a monoculturalistic approach to postgraduate education (Yunkaporta, 2007).

Universities have failed to respond to the particular social problems Africa is facing (Mahlangu & Garutsa, 2019). This is because these institutions shy away from applying an African based epistemological foundation to deal with complex social problems. This therefore has an impact on postgraduate education where students are being fed western dominant knowledge, epistemologies, and methodologies to deal with complex African centred problems. Keet and Porteus (2010) support the above and posit that the use of vernacular terminology has a deep humanizing function in innovative learning and teaching processes as opposed to the subjugation of local languages, values, and experiences in monocultural epistemology. Therefore, IKS is deemed as an agent for decolonizing and humanizing pedagogy at postgraduate level. This is because humanizing pedagogy through IKS builds resonance between students' real-life experiences, their histories and teaching, learning and research processes of the university as an investment to be returned by the collaborative growth of socially engaged students and a socially engaged relevant university (Mahlangu & Garutsa, 2019).

Higher education pedagogical practices in South Africa continue to draw from the Western Eurocentric views, which undermine and dismiss indigenous philosophies such as *Ubuntu* as false assumptions and a simple illegitimate African thinking (Letseka, 2014). Such negative assumptions about African indigenous knowledge systems result in students from African cultures feeling unwelcomed and alienated in higher education (Ndlovu-Gatsheni, 2018). There is a need for epistemic freedom. This means that the methodology and pedagogy that is embedded in indigenous knowledge should be stressed by universities at postgraduate level (Chilisa, 2012). Additionally, universities should embrace epistemic freedom for postgraduate education as epistemic freedom is a process that involves enactment of decolonizing research whereby the formerly colonized people, women and indigenous peoples remove their knowledge from the margins of the knowledge economy (Chilisa, 2016).

Kaya and Seleti (2013) point out that the basic problem is that the educational structures inherited from colonialism are based on cultural values different from those existing in most African indigenous societies. The lack of relevance is perpetuated by continued social, economic, and technological ties between African countries and their former colonizers. Indigenous knowledge systems are therefore viewed as a bridge for African intellectuals to help close the gap created over four hundred years of domination and marginalization of African people's knowledge system in education. This can be affected within the postgraduate education by academics rejecting the utilization of dominant western worldviews of knowing and knowledge production as the only way of knowing.

The above statement is supported by Ngugi wa Thiong'o (1986) in his seminal work on: "Decolonizing the mind". He made it clear that African indigenous knowledge should not only be seen as an "alternative" knowledge but as one domain of knowledge among others. The implication for higher education is that research in Africa can no longer be conducted with local communities and People as if their views and personal experiences are of no significance.

Ubuntu as an African Philosophy for Humanizing Pedagogy

Postgraduate education was dehumanized previously due to colonialism and apartheid in South Africa. The dehumanizing of education made indigenous people and students feel isolated from their own education system (Maluleka, 2020). It is within this isolation that a call for humanizing of postgraduate educate is made. The application of African philosophies is vital for underpinning this humanization. *Ubuntu* is a South African philosophy that is concerned with the culture of society. Spencer-Oatey (2012) points out that this culture that is interlinked to *Ubuntu* refers to a set of traditions, norms and values that are shared by a group of people or community. This philosophy also views a university as a community that is diverse. This is a space whereby people from all walks of life come together for collective learning. However, many students at postgraduate level come across challenges of dehumanized education and pedagogy.

Ngubane and Makua (2021) argue that *Ubuntu* as a pedagogy for postgraduate education provides an alternative to the current pedagogies that draw from European theories for teaching and learning in South African higher education. The application of *Ubuntu* and being culturally sensitive enables students and staff at postgraduate level to embrace each other's knowledge, beliefs, morals, customs and any other capabilities and habits learnt (Ford & Moore, 2004). Therefore, the curriculum and pedagogy at postgraduate level should be made culturally responsive. (Maluleke, 2020) posits that indigenous students in previously colonized countries have been experiencing a loss of identity, culture, humanness, and way

Decolonising, Humanising Pedagogy in South African Education

of life within the higher education sphere, especially at postgraduate level. This shows that curricula and pedagogy at postgraduate level requires attention.

The route that higher education can follow to re-humanize postgraduate education is to take the humanist approach (Mahabeer, 2018). This humanist approach is embedded in African philosophy, and it is concerned with changing curricula and pedagogy at postgraduate level to make it locally and contextually relevant. This section makes argument that *Ubuntu* as an African philosophy amongst others, and it can be viewed as the first attempt/step to humanize postgraduate education and drive a curriculum that is culturally sensitive. *Ubuntu* is explained by West (2014) as a combination of *ubu-* which means *being* or *be-ing or becoming* and *–ntu* represents *being* taking concreate form. This is a philosophy termed from one of the Nguni languages of the Bantu languages and it is translated as humanness or being human. It's phrased as follows: *Umtu ngumtu ngabantu* meaning a person is a person though other people. This philosophy is befitting to be applied to humanize postgraduate education as academic staff and postgraduate students can apply this philosophy which embraces culture sensitivity and diversity and respect of each other's differences.

Ubuntu is a source of African ontology and epistemology, and applying these enables postgraduate students to contextualize their education and consider African education that reflects and sustains national priorities, aims and aspirations (Nasongo & Musungu, 2011; Louw, 2006). Therefore, a bottom-up approach to achieving the above which centres on the African indigenous communities in the creation, sharing and dissemination of knowledge will be affected. Also, applying and following Ubuntu in postgraduate education will enable students to use their own powers, efforts, abilities, and resources to promote their county without relying heavily on outsiders.

Relevance of Indigenous Pedagogies and Methodologies for Post-Graduate Education in South African Universities

The South African universities education landscape has since developed and changed drastically from the dispensation in 1994. However, arguments are that not much has been done to fully inculcate and identify relevant decolonial methodologies and pedagogies at the same universities as they are still reliant on the colonial methodologies that have since been used to drive the African universities. Paringatai (2019) supports the above statement by pointing out that historically, institutions of higher learning have been domains of western education theory and philosophy. These western epistemologies and theories have been entrenched so much in education that they have been made central to knowledge acquisition through teaching, learning and research. Furthermore, these epistemologies have further dictated the development of pedagogies to be used in these HEIs. Battiste (2002) posits that the use of these western epistemologies and paradigms has resulted in the worldviews, languages, teachings, and experiences of the indigenous populations being left out in the margins of the knowledge economy. Indigenous academic and scholars have now ventured into a new epistemological transition whereby their overall aim is to transform HEIs' pedagogies (Paringatai, 2019). This transformation sees these indigenous academics forging ways to restore and advance the much-neglected indigenous knowledge and teachings. This is mainly because indigenous scholars have seen the necessity of indigenous education as a key driver to sustainability (Cote-Meek & Moeke-Pickering, 2016). This therefore reflects that for decoloniality to be experienced and implemented in postgraduate education of African universities, then there must be an avenue made available to inculcate indigenous/decolonial frameworks in higher education. Decoloniality is a huge aspect of African and indigenous worldview which is enshrined in the African principles of

293

being, knowing and teaching. Therefore, a full underpinning of indigenous worldviews, its incorporation as well as critical analysis to understand the world and its influences is paramount (Cote-Meek & Moeke-Pickering, 2016). Shirley (2017) posits that as the indigenous communities envision the future, it is without question that the indigenous youth play a significant role in sustaining the indigenous lifeways and communities thereby placing these youth at the forefront of invoking sustainable development through the navigation of socio-cultural, environmental, political, and economic issues while simultaneously preserving IKS.

The transformation of pedagogies and methodologies to advance relevant indigenous pedagogies and methodologies in African education is key to achieving sustainable education in HEIs. The transformed pedagogies can engage the heart and mind of students/youth in HEIs which will in turn drive and promote social change in African communities. Therefore, indigenous values and epistemologies can be used to affirm and empower the African youth in HEIs thereby maiming them uncover sustainable solutions to the ever-changing demands of society and develop these youth to become critically conscious and aware (smith, 1999; Shirley, 2017). A term, indigenous social justice pedagogy as articulated by Shirley (2017) gives space for academics to understand this concept or phrase as a framework for *rethinking* the process of education for indigenous students. She further unpacks this phrase by pointing out that the primary focus of this indigenous social justice pedagogy is on reframing the curriculum and pedagogy that aims to preserve and privilege indigenous epistemologies while concurrently promoting nation building in indigenous communities.

Changing the Pedagogy Lens at the North-West University: Lessons Leant Through Indigenous Knowledge Systems

Postgraduate pedagogy is central to the acquisition, assimilation and sharing of knowledge. Therefore, to achieve the above three elements, postgraduate pedagogy by university staff should actively participate in the knowledge society and economy (Ngulube, 2021). Additionally, it is vital to note that the relationship between the supervisors and students at postgraduate level should be equivalent. This is because an uneven relationship has brought about pedagogy or supervision models that are notoriously vague with no common nomenclature (Lahenius & Ikavalko, 2014; Ngulube, 2021) and highly grounded in the western epistemologies and methodologies. Postgraduate pedagogy in South African universities which is western based has led to calls for humanized and decolonized postgraduate pedagogies within south African universities.

The call for humanized and decolonized pedagogy therefore led to universities such as the North west University (NWU) to implement various mechanisms and approaches to ground itself in African principles. Additionally, implementation of indigenous centered pedagogy which embraces African values are developed and implemented to provide postgraduate students and staff the opportunity to fully explore new pedagogical approaches. Postgraduate pedagogy that is grounded within indigenous epistemologies and methodologies is bent towards the caring attitude afforded by supervisors (Gumbo, 2019). The element of care (*Botho/Ubuntu*) is at the centre and heart of the indigenous knowledge systems scholars at the NWU. Therefore, academic engagements within the IKS Centre and NWU embraces this principle as the institution understand that it serves students who hail from indigenous environments which are deeply enshrined in *Botho/Ubuntu*. This principle can be adopted and applied universally by other institutions even though it's rooted in African culture (Mabovula, 2011).

Decolonising, Humanising Pedagogy in South African Education

The Afrikology philosophy as one of the profound philosophies, is also one means applied to humanize postgraduate pedagogy. Afrikology positions postgraduate pedagogy and education at the centre of sustainability in terms of knowledge production (Moichela, 2017). Afrikology affords the staff and students to apply a transdisciplinary approach to unearth tacit knowledge that can be applied to deal with issues that society comes across. In essence, decolonizing and humanizing pedagogy at the NWU is achieved by implementing and applying the above-mentioned strategies. These can be summarized as follows:

- A humane supervision practice that recognizes everyone's voice;
- Application of *botho/Ubuntu* principle;
- Use of proper nomenclature that each discipline embraces;
- Application of indigenous epistemologies and methodologies that embraces the caring attitude;
- Application of Afrikology philosophy which makes space for a transdisciplinary approach in postgraduate studies.

The North-West University (NWU) is the first university in South Africa to incorporate IKS into research, teaching, learning and community engagement (Kaya & Seleti, 2013). This incorporation saw the university having a fully fletched programme based on IKS in the year 2001. This endeavour by the NWU was taking into cognisance the IKS Policy of 2004. Therefore, the NWU can be viewed as the first institution that brought about the pedagogical change that is much needed in the decolonial agenda of HEIs in South Africa. A study conducted by Mmola (2010) on students and lecturer's perceptions towards the IKS programme at the NWU and cited/presented by Kaya & Seleti (2013) bared the following results:

"More than 80% of the respondent students had the opinion that lecturers who incorporated indigenous African cultural elements, especially the use of the local language, that is, Setswana, into their teaching practices were highly appreciated by students. They also indicated that such lecturers made them experience a feeling of autonomy by getting the opportunity to learn university education using their own language. Interviews with both respondent students and lecturers (the majority of them being Setswana speaking) revealed that the lecturers who used Setswana in their teaching and interaction with students, incorporated local community practices into lessons, utilised culturally relevant material, were very much appreciated by students".

Further interviews with various academic leaders from different departments that incorporated IKS modules in their teaching programmes showed the following results:

"That when IKS was systemically and holistically included into the curriculum, student achievement improved. This was because students could relate what was taught with their own home and community experiences. The respondent academic leaders also indicated that the building of strong relationships between students, researchers, lecturers with student families and local communities created meaningful and positive learning outcomes for students".

This is evident that the incorporation of indigenous pedagogies in HEIs teaching, learning, research, and community engagement activities can indeed bear positive fruits for the country's mission of social cohesion and nation building. A need to move from a Eurocentric approach of teaching and learning and the inculcation of indigenous pedagogies that are enshrined in attaining social justice would provide the basis for indigenous innovations that can be adopted and applied to address the challenges face d by society today. Shirley (2017) supports this argument by pointing out that the first step in decolonization requires the rediscovery of indigenous histories to uncover and examine the extent to which colonization affected the indigenous communities' history, culture, language, identities, land and resources.

Coaching Interventions as a Way of Humanizing Postgraduate Education

Postgraduate supervision is a complex process that involves political pressure, adherence to policy, evolving pedagogy and prolonged supervisor-student relationships (Keane, 2016). Maintaining these relationships for the period prescribed by universities sometimes comes with a lot of challenges both to students and supervisors. The coaching pedagogy as discussed by (Middleton, 2015) is based on depending on self-awareness, improving cultural intelligence and communication. This pedagogy has its own principles and those are relevant in the postgraduate education as they level the power relations between the supervisor and the student.

Coaching pedagogy can be used to humanize postgraduate education as it can further foster the relationship between the supervisor and student and ensure accountability (Keane, 2016). In the context of South Africa Keane (2016) points out that coaching tools should be introduced. He argues that these tools at postgraduate level can open spaces for culturally sensitive dialogue that contributes to the surfacing of issues of privilege, ethnicity and race. Therefore, considering this approach for postgraduate education could assist students in developing resilience, self-confidence, self-efficacy and learning more about how they can chart their own path (Wadee et al, 2010).

Keane (2016) provides the following three coaching tools that can be used in postgraduate education:

- an informal learner-centred agreement on how the relationship can be set up to best serve both student and supervisor;
- a self-assessment tool to provide a snapshot of areas of development or concern or achievement;
- a 'values' worksheet that provides a way of better understanding one's working style and motivation.

Coaching interventions can be used in conjunction with other processes of questioning, listening, and setting goals. This is because coaching tolls can provide a holistic support to postgraduate students and deepen self-refection and encourage more equitable communication between the supervisor and the student thereby promoting accountability.

CONCLUSION AND RECOMMENDATIONS

Indigenous Knowledge Systems (IKS) are a social capital that universities need to tap into to decolonize and humanize their postgraduate education. Decolonization should be viewed as a vehicle to inculcate the African worldviews, epistemology, and methodologies in postgraduate education. Culture sensitiveness is vital between the students at postgraduate level and the academics. The western dominant models of teaching, learning, and researching at postgraduate level should be blended with the African centred models to harmonize the two knowledge systems for the development and better good of serving the communities in which these universities exist. Postgraduate education should be holistic and provide a merger between theory and practice especially since these students are expected to develop the communi-

Decolonising, Humanising Pedagogy in South African Education

ties which are mainly marginalized by universities and governments. Postgraduate education curriculum must respond to the culture of the people being taught. Knowledge transmitters should put the culture of students at the centre of lecturer room activities. Ubuntu as an agent of decolonization in South Africa should lead to self-resilience and the liberation of previously colonized communities. Ubuntu philosophy which serves as a pedagogy that draws from IKS should be embraced with understanding and dignity.

REFERENCES

Asante, M. K. (1999). *The painful demise of Eurocentrism: An Afrocentric response to critics.* Africa World Press.

Battiste, M. (2001). Decolonizing the university: Ethical guidelines for research involving indigenous populations. In L. M. Findlay & P. M. Bidwell (Eds.), *Pursuing Academic Freedom: "Free and Fearless"?* (pp. 190–203). Purich Press.

Bhuda, M., & Koitsiwe, M. (2022). The Importance of Underpinning Indigenous Research Using African Indigenous Philosophies: Perspectives From Indigenous Scholars. In *Handbook of Research on Protecting and Managing Global Indigenous Knowledge Systems* (pp. 223–248). IGI Global. doi:10.4018/978-1-7998-7492-8.ch013

Bhuda, M. T. (2021). Making a Case for Indigenous Education Systems in South Africa. *African Journal of Development Studies, 2021*(si2), 67.

Blignaut, S. (2020). Transforming the curriculum for unique challenges faced by South Africa. *Curriculum Perspectives.* doi:10.100741297-020-00104-6

Bruchac, M. M. (2014). Indigenous knowledge and traditional knowledge. In C. Smith (Ed.), *Encyclopedia of Global Archaeology* (pp. 3814–3824). Springer Science and Business Media. doi:10.1007/978-1-4419-0465-2_10

Cherrington, A. M., Botha, M., & Keet, A. (2018). 'Decolonising' Education Transformation. *South African Journal of Education, 38*(4), 1–4.

Chilisa, B. (2012). *Indigenous Research Methodologies.* Sage publications.

Chilisa, B. (2016). *Indigenous research methodologies* (2nd ed.). Sage.

Cote-Meek, S. and Moeke-Pickering, T., (2017) Indigenous Pedagogies and Transformational Practices. *Talking Back, Talking Forward: Journeys in Transforming Indigenous Educational Practice.*

Du Plessis, P. (2021). Decolonisation of education in South Africa: Challenges to decolonise the university curriculum. *South African Journal of Higher Education, 35*(1), 54–69. doi:10.20853/35-1-4426

Ford, D. Y. & Moore, J. L. (2004). Creating responsive gift understanding of culture is the first step. *Fall, 27*(4), 34–39.

Gumbo, M. T. (2019). Online or offline supervision? Postgraduate supervisors state their position at university of South Africa. *South African Journal of Higher Education*, *33*(1), 92–110. doi:10.20853/33-1-2673

Heleta, S. (2018). Decolonizing knowledge in South Africa: Dismantling the 'pedagogy of big lies'. *Ufahamu. Journal of African Studies*, *40*(2).

Higgs, P., Higgs, L. G., & Venter, E. (2003). Indigenous African knowledge systems and innovation in higher education in South Africa: Perspectives on higher education. *South African Journal of Higher Education*, *17*(2), 40–45.

Janks, H. (2019). The decolonization of higher education in South Africa: Luke's writing as gift. *Curriculum Inquiry*, *49*(2), 230–241. doi:10.1080/03626784.2019.1591922

Kassam, K., & Maher, S. (2000). Indigenous, Cartesian, and cartographic: visual metaphors of knowledge in Arctic (tundra) and sub-Arctic (taiga) communities. In J. Xu (Ed.), *Links between cultures and biodiversity: proceedings of the Cultures and Biodiversity Congress* (pp. 785–811).

Kaya, H. O., & Seleti, Y. N. (2013). African indigenous knowledge systems and relevance of higher education in South Africa. *International Education Journal: Comparative Perspectives, 12*(1).

Keane, M. (2016). Coaching interventions for postgraduate supervision courses: Promoting equity and understanding in the supervisor–student relationship. *South African Journal of Higher Education*, *30*(6), 94–111. doi:10.20853/30-6-720

Keet, A., & Porteus, K. (2010). Life, Knowledge, Action: The Grounding Programme at the University of Fort Hare. *Report on the Pilot July–December 2009*. UFH. http://wvw.ufh.ac.za/files/Appendix_6.pdf

Keet, A., Sattarzadeh, S. D., & Munene, A. (2017). An awkward, uneasy (de)coloniality higher education and knowledge otherwise. *Education as Change*, *21*(1), 1–12. doi:10.17159/1947-9417/2017/2741

Kovach, M. (2009). *Indigenous Methodologies: Characteristics, Conversations, and Contexts*. University of Toronto Press.

Kovach, M. E. (2010). *Indigenous methodologies: Characteristics, conversations, and contexts*. University of Toronto Press.

Lahenius, K., & Ikävalko, H. (2014). Joint supervision practices in doctoral education–A student experience. *Journal of Further and Higher Education*, *38*(3), 427–446. doi:10.1080/0309877X.2012.706805

Lavallee, L. F. (2009). Practical application of an Indigenous research framework and two qualitative Indigenous research methods: Sharing circles and Anishnaabe symbol- based reflection. *International Journal of Qualitative Methods*, *8*(1), 21–40. doi:10.1177/160940690900800103

Le Grange, L. (2016). Decolonising the university curriculum. *South African Journal of Higher Education*, *30*(2), 1–12.

Leiden Ndlovu-Gatsheni S.J. (2013). Why decoloniality in the 21st century? *The Thinker: For Thought Leaders*.

Letseka, M. (2014). *Ubuntu* and justice as fairness. *Mediterranean Journal of Social Sciences*, 5(9), 544–551. doi:10.5901/mjss.2014.v5n9p544

Lopez, A. E., & Rugano, P. (2018). Educational leadership in post-colonial contexts: What can we learn from the experiences of three female principals in Kenyan secondary schools? *Education Sciences*, 8(3), 99. doi:10.3390/educsci8030099

Louw, D. J. (2006). The African concept of ubuntu and restorative justice. In D. Sullivan & L. Tifft (Eds.), *Handbook of restorative justice: A global perspective* (pp. 161–173). Routledge.

Luke, A. (2018). Pedagogy as gift. In Critical Literacy, Schooling, and Social Justice (pp. 272- 296). Routledge. doi:10.4324/9781315100951-13

Mabovula, N. N. (2011). The erosion of African communal values: A reappraisal of the African Ubuntu philosophy. *Inkanyiso*, 3(1), 38–47. doi:10.4314/ijhss.v3i1.69506

Mahabeer, P. (2018). Curriculum decision-makers on decolonising the teacher education curriculum. *South African Journal of Education*, 38(4), 1–13. doi:10.15700aje.v38n4a1705

Mahlangu, P. M., & Garutsa, T. C. (2019). A Transdisciplinary Approach and Indigenous Knowledge as Transformative Tools in Pedagogical Design: The Case of the Centre for Transdisciplinary Studies, University of Fort Hare, *Africa. Education Review*, 16(5), 60–69. doi:10.1080/18146627.2016.1251293

Maistry, S. (2021). Curriculum theorising in Africa as a social justice project: Insights from decolonial theory. In K. G. F. Kehdinga & B. K. Khoza (Eds.), *Curriculum theory, curriculum theorising and theories: The African theorising perspective* (pp. 133–147). Sense.

Maluleka, K. J. (2020). Humanising higher education through a culturally responsive curriculum. *South African Journal of Higher Education*, 34(6), 137–149. doi:10.20853/34-6-3764

Mapara, J. (2009). Indigenous Knowledge Systems in Zimbabwe: Juxtaposing Postcolonial Theory. *The Journal of Pan African Studies*, 3(1), 139–155.

Masondo, S. (2015). Rhodes Must Fall campaign gains momentum at UCT. City Press. https://www.news24.com/SouthAfrica/News/Rhodes-Must-Fall-campaign-gains- momentum- at-UCT-20150323 date of access: 15 February 2023

McGregor, D. (2018). Indigenous research: Future directions. In D. McGregor, J.-P. Restoule, & R. Johnston (Eds.), Indigenous research: Theories, practices, and relationships (pp. 296–310). Canadian Scholars.

Middleton, J. (2015). *Cultural intelligence: CQ: The competitive edge for leaders crossing borders.* Bloomsbury.

Mmola, S. (2010). *A survey of perceptions of IKS students and IKS lecturers on IKS programme at North-West University (Mafikeng Campus).* [Unpublished manuscript, IKS Programme: North-West University].

Moichela, K. Z. (2017). *Integration of indigenous knowledge systems in the curriculum for basic education: possible experiences of Canada* (Doctoral dissertation).

Msila, V. (2009). Africanisation of education and the search for relevance and context. *Educational Research Review*, 4(6), 310–315.

Mugume, T., & Luescher, T. M. (2017). Student representation and the relationship between student leaders and political Parties: The case of Makerere University. *South African Journal of Higher Education, 31*(3), 154–171. doi:10.20853/31-3-639

Mzamane, V. Z. (2003). Toward a Pedagogy for Liberation: Education for National Culture in South Africa. In I. M. Nkomo (Ed.), *Pedagogy of Domination: Toward Democratic Education in South Africa.* Africa World Press.

Nandy, A. (1981). *The Intimate Enemy: Loss and Recovery of Self Under Colonialism.* Oxford University Press.

Nandy, A. (2000). Recovery of indigenous knowledge and dissenting futures of the university. *The university in transformation: Global perspectives on the futures of the university*, 115-123.

Nasongo, J. W., & Musungu, L. L. (2009). The implications of Nyerere's theory of education to contemporary education in Kenya. *Educational Research Review, 4*(4), 111–116.

Ndlovu-Gatsheni, S. J. (2013). Why decoloniality in the 21st century? *The Thinker: For Thought Leaders, 48*, 10–15.

Ndlovu-Gatsheni, S. J. (2018). *Epistemic freedom in Africa: Deprovincialization and decolonization.* Routledge. doi:10.4324/9780429492204

Ngubane, N. I., & Makua, M. J. (2021). Intersection of Ubuntu pedagogy and social justice: Transforming South African higher education. *Transformation in Higher Education, 6*, 8. doi:10.4102/the.v6i0.113

Ngulube, P., (2021). Postgraduate Supervision Practices In Education Research And The Creation Of Opportunities For Knowledge Sharing. *Problems of Education in the 21st Century, 79*(2), 255-272.

Nhemachena, A., Mlambo, N., & Kaundjua, M. (2016). The notion of the "field" and the practices of researching and writing Africa: Towards decolonial praxis. *Africology, 9*(7), 15–36.

Nhemachena, A., Mlambo, N., & Kaundjua, M. (2016). The notion of the "field" and the practices of researching and writing Africa: Towards decolonial praxis. *Africology, 9*(7), 15–36.

Onwu, G., & Mosimege, M. (2004). Indigenous knowledge systems and science and technology education: A dialogue. *African Journal of Research in Mathematics. Science and Technology Education, 8*(1), 1–12.

Paringatai, K. (2019). Indigenous pedagogies in practice in universities. In Migration, Education and Translation (pp. 199-212). Routledge. doi:10.4324/9780429291159-15

Rix, E. F., Wilson, S., Sheehan, N., & Tujague, N. (2018). Indigenist and decolonising research methodology. In P. Liamputtong (Ed.), *Handbook of research methods in health social sciences* (pp. 253–267). Springer. doi:10.1007/978-981-10-2779-6_69-1

Saurombe, A. (2018). The teaching of indigenous knowledge as a tool for curriculum transformation and Africanisation. *Journal of Education, 138*, 160.

Sebola, M., & Mogoboya, M. J. (2020). Re-imagining Africanisation of sustainable epistemologies and pedagogies in (South) African higher education: A conceptual intervention. *South African Journal of Higher Education, 34*(6), 237–254. doi:10.20853/34-6-4078

Shahjahan, R. A., Estera, A. L., Surla, K. L., & Edwards, K. T. (2022). "Decolonizing" curriculum and pedagogy: A comparative review across disciplines and global higher education contexts. *Review of Educational Research, 92*(1), 73–113. doi:10.3102/00346543211042423

Shirley, V. J. (2017). Indigenous Social Justice Pedagogy: Teaching into the Risks and Cultivating the Heart. *Critical Questions in Education, 8*(2), 163–177.

Smith, L. T. (1999). *Decolonizing methodologies: Research and indigenous peoples.* Zed Books.

Sousa Santos, B. D. (2007). Beyond abyssal thinking: From global lines to ecologies of knowledges. *Review - Fernand Braudel Center, 30*, 45–89.

Spencer-Oatey, H. (2012). What is culture? A compilation of quotations. *GlobalPAD Core Concepts.* GlobalPAD Open House. http://www.warwick.ac.uk/globalpadintercultural

Tamburro, A. (2013). Including decolonization in social work education and practice. *Journal of Indigenous Social Development, 2*(1).

Tuck, E., & Yang, K. W. (2012). Decolonization is not a metaphor. *Decolonization, 1*(1), 1–40.

Von der Porten, S., de Loë, R. C., & McGregor, D. (2016). Incorporating indigenous knowledge systems into collaborative governance for water: Challenges and opportunities. *Journal of Canadian Studies. Revue d'Etudes Canadiennes, 50*(1), 214–243. doi:10.3138/jcs.2016.50.1.214

Wa Thiong'o Ngugi. (1986). *Decolonizing the Mind.* Heinemann.

Wadee, A. A., Keane, M., Dietz, T., & Hay, D. (2010). Effective PhD supervision mentoring and coaching. 2nd Edition. South Africa-Netherlands research Programme on Alternatives in Development SANPAD. Amsterdam: Rosenberg Publishers.

Warren, D. M. (1991). *Using indigenous knowledge in agricultural development. World Bank Discussion.* The World Bank.

West, A. (2014). Ubuntu and business ethics: Problems, perspectives and prospects. *Journal of Business Ethics, 121*(1), 47–61. doi:10.100710551-013-1669-3

Wilson, S. (2008). *Research is ceremony: Indigenous research methods.* Fernwood.

Yunkaporta, T. (2009). *Aboriginal Pedagogies at the Cultural Interface.* [PhD thesis, James Cook University, Townsville].

Zavala, M. (2013). What do we mean by decolonizing research strategies? Lessons from decolonizing, indigenous research projects in New Zealand and Latin America. *Decolonization, 2*(1), 55–71.

Zembylas, M. (2018). Decolonial possibilities in South African higher education: Reconfiguring humanising pedagogies as/with decolonising pedagogies [Special issue]. *South African Journal of Education, 38*(4), 1699. doi:10.15700aje.v38n4a1699

KEY TERMS AND DEFINITIONS

Decolonization: The process of undoing the colonial legacies.

Indigenous Knowledge Systems: The combination of knowledge systems encompassing technology, social, economic, and philosophical learning, education, and governance systems.

Indigenous Methodologies: A deep pursuit of questioning one's epistemological underpinnings; of questioning what knowledge and approach is favoured in research.

Pedagogy: The method and practice of teaching, especially as an academic subject or theoretical concept.

Ubuntu: The notion of humanity towards others (I am because you are).

Chapter 16

Integration of Indigenous Knowledge Into Library and Information Science Teaching Practices:
A Systematic Review of the Global Literature

Mousin Omarsaib
https://orcid.org/0000-0002-7274-7635
Durban University of Technology, South Africa

Nalindren Naicker
Durban University of Technology, South Africa

Mogiveny Rajkoomar
Durban University of Technology, South Africa

ABSTRACT

Indigenous knowledge is an emerging theme in humanistic scholarly conversations. Therefore, the purpose of this study was to present a global perspective of teaching practices related to indigenous knowledge in the Library and Information Science (LIS) field as it lends itself to a humanistic approach. The aim was to identify how indigenous knowledge is integrated into the LIS curriculum. Preferred Reporting Items for Systematic Reviews and Meta-Analyses methodology was used to review the literature. Key findings revealed that integrated teaching practices and indigenous knowledge are still emerging topics at LIS schools. The study recommends academics from LIS schools earnestly contribute to global literature by sharing their knowledge on teaching practices 'vis-a-vis' indigenous knowledge. Globally, this would ensure LIS academics tread common ground in integrating indigenous knowledge into the curriculum by using appropriate teaching practices. Ultimately, developing future LIS graduates as custodians of indigenous knowledge in industry.

DOI: 10.4018/978-1-6684-7024-4.ch016

Copyright © 2023, IGI Global. Copying or distributing in print or electronic forms without written permission of IGI Global is prohibited.

INTRODUCTION

Globally, higher education institutions have been key drivers of societal, political and economic change (De Wit & Altbach, 2020). Historically, the blueprint that drove these changes at higher education institutions emanated from Western ideologies. The rich knowledge that existed in less privileged higher education institutions of the world was suppressed within curriculums dictated through colonial idiosyncrasies (Davids & Waghid, 2021). Decades were spent in this fashion wherein a colonial approach mandated what was taught, learned and researched in previously disadvantaged higher education institutions. Colonialism is defined as the domination of one group of people over another in terms of territory, jurisdiction, culture, language, education, and economy (Murrey, 2020). Today, the after effects of colonialism within previously disadvantaged higher education systems still exist (Patel, 2021). This reverberates subtly in the type of curriculums being designed at higher education institutions with limited focus on localizing teaching, learning, and research. However, Mayblin and Turner (2020) posit that curriculum change is imminent as scholars are vigorously addressing disparities that historically underpinned higher education systems juxtapose colonialism. Therefore, the term decolonization cannot be overstated. Decolonization challenges and addresses injustices of the past (Ghosh et al, 2021). The decolonized approach is resolute in localizing education in previously disadvantaged tertiary institutions, globally. Further, according to Cross (2020), decolonization adopts a retrospective approach. It aims to contextualize teaching, learning and research to suit the needs of previously disadvantaged communities. It also creates opportunities to benchmark and learn from other higher education systems on a global scale. Thus, decolonization has the potential to create cutting-edge social, economic and political independence from first-world superpowers.

Currently, at higher education institutions, there is also a process wherein curriculums are being decolonized to suit workplace graduate outcomes as needed in local industries (Ramnund-Mansingh & Reddy, 2021). One such field wherein decolonization has prominently featured is Library and Information Science (LIS). Within the LIS sector, topics attached to a decolonized approach include critical pedagogy, open access, digital preservation, intellectual property, open educational resources, and knowledge management (Masenya, 2022). However, a topic that far supersedes any other in the LIS field is indigenous knowledge. Library and Information Science experts are honing into indigenous knowledge and the role of libraries in preserving this vital resource. Worldwide, there is an emphasis on the LIS sector and its role in protecting and preserving indigenous knowledge for the benefit of society. Therefore, this subject is topical in nature and is gaining momentum within the LIS field.

However, to understand the significance of indigenous knowledge it is important to determine who are indigenous people (Jessen et al, 2022). The term indigenous people are widely used in the literature, though, there are no standardized definitions that can be adopted and approved within academia. Cobo (1986) presents one of the most cited definitions related to indigenous people. The definition aligns indigenous people to nations that were invaded and colonized leading to a loss of culture, territory, ethnic identity, education, artifacts, communities, and legal systems. Over recent years the preservation of indigenous knowledge has become vulnerable due to globalization (Kohsaka & Rogel, 2021). Consequently, indigenous knowledge is fast becoming lost and erased from modern society. Therefore, libraries have a pivotal role to play in creating an environment to preserve indigenous knowledge (Christen & Anderson, 2019). Fundamentally, indigenous knowledge provides resourceful information on many issues such as health, politics, economy, and culture that can benefit society if preserved and made accessible. It also protects historical prestige and the cultural heritage of indigenous communities (Tom et al, 2019). This allows individuals to trace the roots of their origin within civil society in the modern world. Ultimately, this helps an individual create a connection with an enriching societal, cultural, and historical background. Moreover, it ensures indigenous people maintain an identity and do not lose touch with character traits or lineage because of globalization.

The publicity related to indigenous knowledge within the LIS sector over the past decade has been remarkable (Hangshing, 2019). Efforts are being made to conscientize librarians from both public and academic sectors on the importance of indigenous knowledge through the literature. There are also initiatives such as conferences, seminars, and workshops to engage librarians on the importance of indigenous knowledge. However, there seems to be a dearth of indigenous knowledge covered in the curriculum at LIS schools (Littletree, 2020). Moreover, teaching practices of academics in LIS schools when designing, delivering, and assessing content on indigenous knowledge are met with scarcity in the literature. This chapter aims to review the literature, identify, and present a global perspective in relation to indigenous knowledge and LIS teaching practices between 2019-2023. The systematic review endeavours to shed light on how LIS academics are integrating indigenous knowledge into the curriculum when teaching. Further, it focuses on the types of methods, activities, and assessments used when teaching indigenous knowledge as a module in LIS schools at higher education institutions.

LITERATURE ON INDIGENOUS KNOWLEDGE AND LIBRARY AND INFORMATION SCIENCE (LIS)

Indigenous knowledge emerged as a topic in the LIS field during the 20th century (Ball & Lar-Son, 2021). Initially, LIS experts aimed to capture historical collections and preserve them to protect the heritage of indigenous communities. The gathering of indigenous knowledge was therefore seen as an ad hoc project using informal systems and processes. However, experts began noticing the value of indigenous knowledge as it gained impetus appearing more often in the LIS literature (Abidogun & Falola, 2020). Consequently, during the 21st century, the literature in relation to indigenous knowledge began expanding rapidly. Many fields such as psychology, health, engineering, and law also extracted valuable data from indigenous knowledge to use in practice as a solution to problems (Gartuala et al 2020, Schmidt 2019, Thornton & Bhagwat, 2020).

Globally, there is a wealth of literature illustrating the incorporation of indigenous knowledge as a vital trend in libraries (Montgomery et al., 2021). Juxtapose, the literature is scarce in relation to LIS programmes introducing a module to prepare graduates as indigenous librarians (Jimenez et al., 2023). Therefore, this study used Preferred Reporting Items for Systematic Reviews and Meta-Analyses (PRISMA) to explore how academics integrate indigenous knowledge into their teaching practices at LIS schools, globally. This knowledge is critical as it can bridge the gap between knowledge and practice for LIS professionals and academics. Thus, a holistic approach was charted to explore the literature underpinned by PRISMA methods. The aim was to navigate the literature through the lens of academics in LIS who supposedly teach indigenous knowledge in developing and developed economies of the world.

In Canada, Ball and Lar-Son (2021) penned an essay highlighting the implementation, growth, and development of a LIS indigenous knowledge course at the University of Alberta. The study provided valuable insights into pedagogical underpinnings when teaching indigenous knowledge to students. The course structure according to the essay included clear learning objectives, measurable student learning outcomes, and a variety of teaching methods. Field trips were organized to local indigenous communities wherein students learned from elders through storytelling programmes. Additionally, small group discussions with indigenous communities during these field trips proved useful for sharing knowledge in art creation techniques and deliberations about traditional spaces within the Canadian context. The facilitator also supported these field trips by creating podcast interviews and YouTube videos apart from scholarly articles. This was developed to support students who grasped concepts better through visual resources. There were three major assignments and weekly reflections related to indigenous knowledge for students. These assignments compromised writing a research paper, developing a library programme, and creating a display for student research day on indigenous knowledge.

Whilst the Canadian context demonstrated LIS schools beginning to actively engage students in learning about indigenous knowledge, however, this scenario did not exist in India. Hangshing (2019) highlights in a study titled *"Towards Indigenous Librarianship: Indian Perspective"*, that there is minimal focus on indigenous knowledge within the LIS curriculum. The study unearthed that indigenous knowledge in India is overlooked. There is a lack of interest in indigenous knowledge not only from LIS schools but also from librarians in general. Therefore, although India is rich in indigenous knowledge there are no policies, systems, or guidelines to preserve this heritage. The support for a rich history of indigenous knowledge is currently unfounded in India. Thus, this can result in indigenous knowledge within the Indian context being lost in the near future due to neglect, undervalued and stagnant LIS practices.

Komeiji et al. (2021) provide a commentary on the Hawaiian natural resource management principles (kapu, kūlana, waiwai, and lele). Hawaiian communities are deeply rooted in these principles as it is associated with their genealogy. The belief in Hawaai is that indigenous people are physically and spiritually born on these Islands. Therefore, preserving this knowledge is critical to Hawaiian identity as it is engrained within natural resource management principles. The library systems in Hawaii are hence geared towards sustaining heritage as the communities are intimately connected to history. Although, the commentary depicts a sustainable preservation system, there is no alignment with LIS schools in Hawaii or neighboring countries teaching librarians how to provide access to or preserve indigenous knowledge. This knowledge is preserved because of the drive from Hawaiians rather than the LIS sector. Within the African context, a bibliometric analysis of indigenous knowledge published in the LIS sector presented interesting findings (Maluleka & Ngulube, 2019). The bibliometric analysis highlighted that Africa has been focusing on the role of information professionals in relation to the preservation of indigenous knowledge. The study also unearthed through research intense databases such as Web of Science and Scopus that South African researchers affiliated with higher academic institutions contributed the most to indigenous knowledge in Africa. The contributions of Africa as a continent are truly commendable. Researchers are addressing issues such as traditional ecological knowledge, indigenous knowledge systems, indigenous knowledge, and traditional knowledge. Still, there is little research on how indigenous knowledge is incorporated and taught at LIS schools in Africa, despite the continent's literature focusing on the role of information professionals, preservation and the high levels of contributions to the field.

In a Sudanese study, the objectives were to assess the awareness, management, and preservation skills of librarians related to indigenous knowledge (Sharief et al., 2021). The study also explored challenges when using information and communication technologies to manage indigenous knowledge. The aim was to develop a national indigenous knowledge strategy. A structured questionnaire and semi-structured interviews were used to assess Sudanese librarians. The findings revealed that, although Sudanese librarians had a positive impression of indigenous knowledge there was a dearth of skills to manage and preserve such collections. The recommendations included LIS departments' need to play an active and leading role in the professional development of academic librarians in relation to indigenous knowledge. Library and

Information Science schools need to introduce indigenous knowledge into the curriculum, offer courses wherein librarians can learn about indigenous knowledge from practical training, and include courses with information and communication technologies for the digital preservation of indigenous knowledge.

Compared to the African and Asian perspectives, when literature was scanned from the global North, countries such as America and Canada are actively involved in indigenous librarian programmes (Gopal, 2021). It is reasonable enough to assert that LIS schools in these regions have been instrumental in driving indigenous knowledge into the profession (Ball &Lar-Son, 2021). Noteworthy, to mention although there is a shortage of academics within LIS programmes on how to teach indigenous knowledge in America and Canada, this gap was identified, leading to LIS schools employing indigenous information professionals from industry on a contractual basis to teach. This is important as *experience is the biggest teacher*. Information professionals from the industry have an understanding and hands-on practice in indigenous knowledge. Juxtapose, it also begs to question, why is there a lack of LIS academics in relation to indigenous knowledge at these higher education institutions in the global North. Furthermore, LIS communities have also remained self-critical affirming that there are only eight accredited library programmes covering indigenous knowledge in varying degrees within their curriculums in the global North.

Similarly, in the Oceania region, Gosart et al. (2021), theorized the term 'indigeneity' to promote the importance of indigenous librarianship within the LIS field. This theory advocates that a revision of the traditional theory of librarianship is key as it maintains Western ideologies. The change would mean principles of indigenous knowledge can be included when revising the LIS curriculum. Gosart et al., (2021) further suggest that it would be most appropriate to repatriate indigenous knowledge and preservation through the active involvement of communities of practice themselves. Thus, worldwide, indigenous knowledge is seen through the research lens of essays, conceptual papers and communities of practices in the LIS field. In most instances, these contributions highlight how a cohort of information professionals is working with indigenous communities to access and preserve knowledge. However, currently, the literature is lacking as to how academics are integrating indigenous knowledge within the curriculum at LIS schools. There is minimal literature available as to what teaching methods, activities, and assessments are used to prepare future LIS graduates on how to manage indigenous knowledge in the industry. Hence, globally, there is a gap related to academics and the transfer of indigenous knowledge in the LIS programmes through teaching and learning (Samson & Gigoux, 2016). There is clearly a need to focus on LIS schools and the integration of indigenous knowledge into the curriculum. It is important to ascertain as to the most suitable teaching practices used at LIS schools aligned with indigenous knowledge. Library and Information Science academics should be emphatic in sharing this knowledge through publications as this can enhance teaching, learning and research of indigenous communities for the profession. Furthermore, it will help LIS academics to mould graduates with the relevant tools to promote, access, use and preserve indigenous knowledge in the industry.

Preferred Reporting Items for Systematic reviews and Meta-Analyses is a clearly formulated question that uses systematic and explicit methods to identify, select, collect, analyze, and critically appraise relevant research data from the studies that are included in the review (Moher et al., 2010). Preferred Reporting Items for Systematic Reviews and Meta-Analyses refer to the use of statistical techniques in a systematic review to integrate research data (Moher et al., 2010). It includes a 27-item checklist, ensuring, ensuring transparency in the reporting of a review (Sohrabi et al., 2021). A systematic review as defined, described, and demonstrated through PRISMA was used in this study. Preferred Reporting Items for Systematic Reviews and Meta-Analyses were used to identify, scan and delve into the LIS literature.

Scientific publications related to indigenous knowledge in relation to integration and teaching practices at LIS schools over the past five years were explored to ascertain the necessary data.

This chapter aimed to explore the integration of indigenous knowledge into LIS programmes globally and how it is taught at LIS schools. Library and Information Science academics need to have a germane understanding when teaching indigenous knowledge to students. The systematic reviews intended to explore the teaching methods used in LIS schools related to indigenous knowledge. The search strategies used, and the source selected, replicated the PRISMA statement. This was aligned with the research questions whilst engaging with the extant literature on indigenous knowledge and LIS schools. Therefore, in keeping with a global perspective the criteria did not exclude country or author bias unless there was a substantive reason too as discussed in the methods section.

RESEARCH QUESTIONS

Based on the scanned literature and the gap identified, the purpose of this systematic review is to unravel studies focused on the integration of indigenous knowledge into LIS teaching practices. Aligned with the research objectives, the following researched questions were formulated:

RQ1 Is indigenous knowledge as a module been integrated into the curriculum at LIS schools in the literature between 2018-2022?

RQ2 What practices and methods are being implemented by LIS academics when teaching indigenous knowledge at LIS schools?

METHODOLOGY

This section outlines the methods undertaken to explore and systematically review existing literature in relation to indigenous knowledge being integrated into LIS programmes and teaching practices. Indigenous knowledge and integration into the LIS teaching sector are emerging themes as discussed earlier in the literature section. Therefore, the purpose of this chapter was to review contributions made by LIS academics on the integration of indigenous knowledge into the curriculum and the methods used to teach LIS students. Tharani (2021) states, stages used in PRISMA statement are defining research questions, conducting a literature search for identifying, screening, and selecting relevant articles, coding and analyzing articles, and reporting results. These criteria as described in PRISMA are rigorously implemented in this systematic review. Omarsaib et al., (2022) concur that when using PRISMA criteria, it is critical that quality and transparency are strictly adhered to through every stage. Further, the findings in this systematic review contain the analysis of the results through these stringent stages of PRISMA methods. The analysis is facilitated qualitatively, and it was then categorized using the PRISMA statement as a master template. Thus, in alignment with the research questions the searches were documented using PRISMA eligibility criteria (Zibani et al., 2021).

INCLUSION CRITERIA

The systematic retrieval process used a combination of search terms incorporating the primary search term of indigenous knowledge/library and information science, indigenous knowledge/indigenous librarianship, and indigenous knowledge/teaching practices. Other secondary terms used included LIS programmes, integration, and information science. The literature reviewed when conducting these searches was not limited to developed or developing higher education institutions. In determining the articles to be included a three-stage screening and selection criteria was used as framed within the PRISMA protocols (Moher et al. 2010). The searches were conducted between March 2022 and October 2022. The results were revised and updated in December 2022 and January 2023.

EXCLUSION CRITERIA

Articles that were excluded are publications in dialects other than English and published prior to 2019. Other exclusions included book reviews, editorials, book chapters, books, and commentaries. The eligibility of selected articles was determined once the abstract, introduction, and findings sections were read. Concurrently, articles were scanned for duplications. This exercise guided through the stages of PRISMA resulting in the exclusion of 302 articles, resulting in a data set of 79 articles. In-depth reading and analysis of the remaining articles resulted in 59 articles being excluded. These articles were excluded because there did not reflect indigenous knowledge being integrated into the LIS curriculum. Further, there was a dearth of information on teaching practices aligned with indigenous knowledge in these articles. The practicality of how the selection process unfolded is represented through a PRISMA flow diagram in Figure 1.

SELECTED DATABASES

An iterative process using a systematic search strategy for publications associated with the integration of indigenous knowledge and teaching practices in the LIS curriculum charted a clear path in identifying relevant databases as defined through PRISMA protocols. In terms of PRISMA the selected databases were relevant to the LIS field. Databases were explored using a formulated search strategy using a primary and secondary combination of terms. The databases searched include Web of Science, Scopus, Library, Information Science & Technology Abstracts (LISTA), and ProQuest. The searches using these databases were restricted to articles published in the English language between 2018-2022 using PRISMA information flow diagram as illustrated in Figure 2. The articles then went through a screening process once downloaded using referencing management software, EndNote. The EndNote tool was able to filter duplicates and outline the final step of the three-stage screening process. This process resulted in 381 records. Consequently, a total of 381 articles between the years 2018-2022 were retrieved, captured, and organized using EndNote. During the eligibility screening using PRISMA, 302 articles were excluded after further refinements. The eligibility criteria applied when excluding these records include currency, relevance, accuracy, and context. The remaining 79 articles examined resulted

Figure 1. PRISMA flow diagram of literature retrieval
(Adapted from Moher et al., 2010)

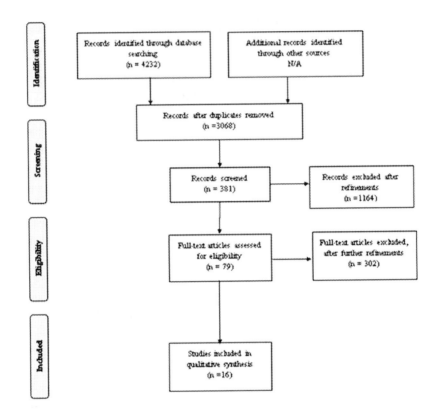

in the synthesis and selection of 16 records aligned to indigenous knowledge being integrated into LIS programmes and teaching practices, globally. Thus, the systematic use of the PRISMA statement alleviated issues related to bias and subjectivity for the exploration of this topic. In Figure 1. PRISMA flow diagram related to the breakdown of sources accessed and refinements are presented.

LATENT DIRICHLET ALLOCATION (LDA)

This unsupervised machine learning algorithm was used to perform topic modelling through clustering. The algorithm was implemented on python version 3.11 using anaconda3 as the platform and jupyter notebook as the integrated development environment (IDE). The selected articles were concatenated using python code and then preprocessed before executing the algorithm and obtaining results.

FINDINGS

The final data set in Table 1 provides a global overview of developed and developing knowledge economies related to the integration of indigenous knowledge with the LIS curriculum and teaching practices. This includes Canada, Sudan, and New Zealand amongst other countries. Sixteen articles explicitly addressed

Integration of Indigenous Knowledge Into LIS Teaching Practices

Table 1. Summarized findings

Study Identity	Author	Publication journal	Methodology
SI1	Ball, T., & Lar-Son, K. (2021).	*Libraries and the Academy*	Reflective essay
SI2	Cooke, N. A (2020).	*Communications in Information Literacy*	Perspective essay
SI3	Edwards, A. (2019).	*Partnership: The Canadian Journal of Library and Information Practice and Research*	Reflective essay
SI4	Frayne, A. (2022).	*IFLA journal*	Rhetorical analysis
SI5	Gopal, P. (2021).	*Textual Practice*	Reflective essay
SI6	Gosart, U. (2021).	*IFLA journal*	Components of advocacy
SI7	Guzik, E., Griffin, B., & Hartel, J. (2020).	*Journal of Education for Library and Information Science*	Case study
SI8	Hangshing, J. (2019).	*Library Philosophy and Practice*	Reflective essay
SI9	Hill, H., Harrington, M., Rothbauer, P., & Pawlick Potts, D. (2021).	*ALISE 2021 Juried Papers*	Perspective essay
SI10	Jimenez, A., Vannini, S., & Cox, A. (2023).	*Journal of Documentation*	Conceptual paper
SI11	Komeiji, K., Long, K., Matsuda, S., & Paikai, A. (2021).	*IFLA journal*	Perspective essay
SI12	Lilley, S. (2018).	*Journal of the Australian Library and Information Association*	Epistemological approach
SI13	Lilley, S. (2021).	*IFLA journal*	Perspective essay
SI14	Maluleka, J. R., & Ngulube, P. (2019).	*Publishing Research Quarterly*	Bibliometric analysis
SI15	Sharief, O. A. E., Mudawi, M. S. E., & Mohamed, R. A. (2021).	*IFLA journal*	Quantitative and qualitative approaches
SI16	Sulyman, A. S., Amzat, B. O., & Taiwo, M. A. (2022).	*Library Philosophy & Practice*	Perspective essay

the pressing need for indigenous knowledge to be integrated into the LIS curriculum, globally (S11, SI2, SI3, SI4, SI7, SI8, SI9, SI10, SI11, SI12, SI13, SI14, SI15, SI16). Article SI12 has contributed to the knowledge base related to academic integration and indigenous knowledge related to the LIS curriculum. However, only SI1 and SI9 included teaching practices with integration of indigenous knowledge into the LIS programme.

Figure 2 illustrates that currency, relevance, accuracy, and context were the criteria applied when selecting databases for searching indigenous knowledge, LIS schools, and teaching practices for the systematic review process. Library, Information Science, and Abstracts were chosen for their relevance and authority within the LIS field. Web of Science and Scopus reflect suitability as globally these are widely used citation databases. There are authoritative abstract databases and house records from several high-powered research platforms from engineering to social sciences. Additionally, ProQuest was selected to expand the sources explored aligned to indigenous knowledge and integration within LIS programmes.

Figure 2. Search strategies

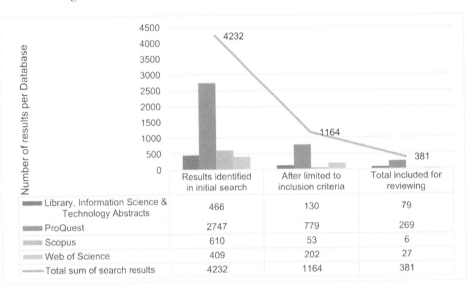

Articles related to indigenous knowledge, teaching practices, and integration into LIS programmes were scanned worldwide between the year 2018 – 2022/23. Figure 3 illustrates the earliest publication related to the systematic searching of the literature is in 2018. The article SI12 – Table 1 published in 2021 presents the importance of the interdisciplinary need of understanding and integrating the local *Māori* culture into society in New Zealand. In 2019 articles point to the importance of indigenous knowledge being embedded into the LIS curriculum – SI3 and SI8 in Table 1. In the same year, article – SI14 a bibliometric analysis in Table 1 contributes widely to indigenous knowledge and the LIS sector, however, there is a lack of pointing to integration into LIS programmes. It is not until 2021, in articles SI1 and SI9 - Table 1, that there is a focus on teaching practices being integrated into the LIS programme in the literature. The analyzed results in Table 1, Figure 2, and Figure 3 point to an emerging theme in indigenous knowledge within the LIS sector of magnanimous importance and value. Yet, LIS programmes on a global scale are still grappling with implementation into the curriculum and therefore there is a dearth of knowledge illustrating teaching practices. Thus, globally there are limited findings when the literature is scanned and explored on the integration and teaching practices of indigenous knowledge within LIS programmes (Gosart, 2021). In general, LIS schools have reached a tipping point in relation to indigenous knowledge and how to teach the content to future librarians (Jimenez & Vannini, 2023). LIS academics need to embrace indigenous knowledge to translate the pedagogy into teaching methods in the classroom. There must be a significant shift in thinking at LIS schools related to integration of indigenous knowledge into the curriculum (Lilley, 2021).

DISCUSSIONS OF FINDINGS

This systematic review explored the integration of indigenous knowledge within LIS programmes, worldwide, using PRISMA. Literature was scanned and delved into, to ascertain the teaching practices of LIS academics at higher education institutions in relation to indigenous knowledge. The purpose for inspecting

Figure 3. Number of publications 2018 – 2022/2023

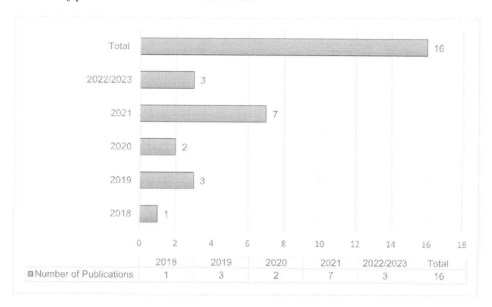

the literature so intensely using PRISMA was to determine the active engagement of LIS programmes to indigenous knowledge since it is an emerging theme within the sector. The literature explored was able to find published articles on indigenous knowledge and librarians aligned to work-based practices. However, sources pointing to LIS programmes integrating indigenous knowledge were met with scarcity. Hence, teaching practices also rarely existed in the literature juxtaposed LIS programmes. Each article was reviewed against the backdrop of indigenous knowledge, integration, and teaching practices in LIS programmes. Indigenous knowledge as a theme is discussed extensively in the LIS sector -Table 1. This seems to be the current focus in LIS. However, the integration and teacher practices as themes remain unexplored as LIS programmes grapple with introducing indigenous knowledge into the curriculum. Indefinitely, this is a gap within the LIS knowledge base.

Recently, researchers have identified the transformative nature of indigenous knowledge and the need for LIS programmes to integrate this topic into the curriculum (Edwards 2019, Guzik et al., 2020, Lilley, 2021, Sharief et al., 2021). In a literature review, Lilley (2021) found that, an important aspect of this is to ensure that indigenous content not only exists in a stand-alone course but is also incorporated into all courses which are part of the qualification offered. If educators do not have any indigenous faculty members, they should seek specialist assistance from the wider profession or from indigenous specialists elsewhere in their institutions of learning. The addition of indigenous content recognizes the importance and legitimacy of indigenous knowledge and the service and resource needs associated with these. Its inclusion provides non-indigenous students with the opportunity to gain an understanding of these needs, why they are important, and what role they can have in ensuring that Indigenous peoples are able to successfully access and use the services required. The role of LIS courses is crucial and therefore library schools need to include modules to prepare graduates. This is a key step in the right direction as it will bridge the gap between LIS programmes and the workplace. Further, LIS graduates will benefit and gain extensive knowledge on indigenous knowledge. Ultimately, a graduate will be skilled in converting theory from such programmes into practice in public, academic, and specialized libraries.

Similarly, findings in a reflective essay, Hangshing (2019) indicate that active engagement is needed to conscientize LIS academics, indigenous librarians and practitioners on their role within the LIS sector to understand the significance of indigenous knowledge. Additionally, LIS schools need to include indigenous knowledge within the professional programme. Lilley (2021) also posits the importance of meaningful conversations and discussions between stakeholders in LIS programmes are important as there stimulate reflection about the profession. Cooke (2020), agrees, LIS programmes need to formalize the integration of indigenous knowledge into the curriculum. This can lead to a shift if needed in policies, practices, and systems to integrate indigenous knowledge into the LIS curriculum. Jimenez et al., (2023) in a conceptual paper also found that although libraries are contributing to indigenous knowledge a holistic approach is necessary to integrate indigenous knowledge into LIS programmes.

Interestingly, Ball and Lar-Son (2021) describe through a reflective essay the growth and development of a course on indigenous knowledge at the University of Alberta's School of Library and Information Studies. A credit-bearing course was introduced covering a host of relevant topics such as digital preservation, data sovereignty, traditional knowledge, culture, society, and technology in relation to indigenous knowledge. These topics were chosen for the curriculum through an all-inclusive approach with local indigenous communities and future LIS graduates. Further, students had to complete three major assignments as assessments for the course. There were also weekly reflection activities for students to complete as different subject matter was being unpacked through the curriculum on indigenous knowledge. The findings revealed that there is a pressing need for the LIS sector to connect with indigenous communities through meaningful discussion programmes, collections, and services. Further, this approach conscientized academics to become familiar with indigenous collections and decolonize the LIS syllabus to suit the local population.

Juxtapose, in Africa Maluleka and Ngulube (2019) conducted a bibliometric analysis of publishing patterns in Africa. The study revealed that the Southern tip of the continent contributed the most to indigenous knowledge. A detailed analysis of Scopus and Web of Science databases also indicated the vast amount of literature emanating from the LIS field in Africa in relation to indigenous knowledge. Currently, the focus in Africa has been on the preservation of indigenous knowledge as information professionals. This is noteworthy, however, the literature from Africa lacks in providing a deeply rooted understanding of the role LIS programmes or academics play in including indigenous knowledge into the curriculum. Currently, there is limited literature that aligns with teaching practices and indigenous knowledge in LIS programmes in Africa (Sharief et al., 2021). Historically, African countries are seen as developing economies and are therefore in many ways disadvantaged because of colonialism. Therefore, Gopal (2021), posits indigenous knowledge must be revived into the curriculum at higher education institutions in Africa and not just preserved through information professionals as there is rich history in African literature.

In Hawaii, Komeiji et al., (2021), detailed a perspective essay on the rich indigenous heritage of local communities. The study revealed indigenous knowledge is embedded and sustained in Hawaiian communities because of the active role of the citizens. However, there is no alignment of indigenous knowledge to LIS University courses in the Hawaiian Islands or in neighbouring countries. Hence, systems and processes associated with indigenous knowledge are community-driven projects housed in public libraries. Indigenous communities and the LIS sector both need each other. Therefore, collaboration is necessary to ensure the viable sustainability of indigenous knowledge. Nevertheless, the protection of indigenous knowledge through community structures is complementary. Hence, as way a forward for

Integration of Indigenous Knowledge Into LIS Teaching Practices

Hawaiian communities there should engage and have robust discussions with stakeholders from the LIS sector, particularly academics to integrate indigenous knowledge into meaningful programmes.

The benefit of associating Indigenous knowledge is seen through the lens of Māori indigenous people in New Zealand using an epistemological approach with LIS schools (Lilley, 2018). Library and Information Science programmes in New Zealand have embedded indigenous knowledge of Māori into the curriculum. The course prepares future graduates to work in libraries, tribal repositories, and cultural centres. This kind of approach promotes indigenous knowledge in the modern world. However, it would be advantageous to the global LIS sector if literature from New Zealand can include teaching practices and methods used in indigenous knowledge LIS programmes. This information was unavailable in the current literature in relation to indigenous knowledge. The impact of indigenous knowledge on LIS programmes at higher education institutions cannot be overstated. However, there must be policies, structures, and strategies governing the formalized rollout of indigenous knowledge into LIS programmes, worldwide. Currently, this seems to be the challenge as depicted in the literature reviewed using the PRISMA method. Globally, the integration of indigenous knowledge and teaching practices of academics is limited in LIS courses according to this study. However, this limitation is viewed from an anglophone context, since only studies that were written in English were sourced in this study. Therefore, one can assume that there could be discussions on how this topic can be introduced into the curriculum from other dialects in African and Asian languages. Every context would be unique in terms of indigenous knowledge and articulation into LIS programmes as the cultural and social norms of every community are diverse, globally. However, the LIS field celebrates diversity, and therefore as information professionals, it is important to embrace indigenous knowledge or run the risk of losing rich heritage due to negligence. Gosart (2021) agrees, stating that this is an opportunity to revolutionize the LIS curriculum. Other factors to be considered include intellectual freedom and postgraduate research of indigenous knowledge in LIS programmes (Frayne, 2022, Sulyman, 2022). Barriers such as graduates knowing how to organize and disseminate a diverse collection of indigenous knowledge responsibly need to be broken.

Hill et al., (2021), present changes made to the LIS curriculum to introduce indigenous knowledge in Canada as advised through the Truth and Reconciliation committee. The changes included students engaging in critical self-reflection activities and indigenous pedagogy. The purpose of adapting this teaching approach was to allow students and LIS academics the opportunity to internalize the topic. This is an important method of teaching and learning as it promotes dialogue and critical thinking as indigenous knowledge is underpinned in past injustices and inequalities of Western oppression (Freire, 2018). Therefore, critical self-reflection in activities and dialogue helps both the oppressed and oppressors shift to rebuild humane relationships in modern society. Further, within the Canadian context, students were also prompted to develop a proposal as to how indigenous knowledge can be promoted, preserved, and integrated into a library setting. The projects proposed by LIS students included collection development and decolonization, designing a LibGuide, developing a specialized indigenous collection, creating, and ratifying a policy document related to indigenous knowledge, and encouraging a project to deal with reconciliation in a library. Thus, these types of challenges in reinventing standard procedures, practices, and pedagogies aligned to indigenous knowledge within the Canadian context, can provide future LIS programmes in the world, opportunities to benchmark, critically evaluate, and find the most suitable methods to endorse indigenous knowledge into their curriculum.

Figure 4 shows the results of the unsupervised machine learning algorithm, Latent Dirichlet Allocation. The model was able to derive 4 latent topics from the corpus of 16 selected journal papers on the

Figure 4. Topics modelling produced by latent dirichlet allocation (LDA)

```
[(0,
  '0.010*"knowledge" + 0.009*"libraries" + 0.008*"research" + '
  '0.008*"information" + 0.007*"library" + 0.007*"rights" + 0.005*"freedom" + '
  '0.005*"lis" + 0.005*"statement" + 0.005*"university"'),
 (1,
  '0.015*"māori" + 0.010*"knowledge" + 0.009*"library" + 0.007*"indigenous" + '
  '0.007*"hawaiian" + 0.005*"information" + 0.005*"hawai" + 0.005*"resources" '
  '+ 0.004*"university" + 0.004*"access"'),
 (2,
  '0.012*"decolonisation" + 0.006*"europe" + 0.005*"colonial" + '
  '0.005*"university" + 0.005*"also" + 0.004*"colonialism" + 0.003*"fanon" + '
  '0.003*"european" + 0.003*"even" + 0.003*"knowledge"'),
 (3,
  '0.028*"indigenous" + 0.016*"knowledge" + 0.013*"library" + '
  '0.009*"information" + 0.006*"students" + 0.006*"libraries" + '
  '0.005*"librarianship" + 0.005*"lis" + 0.004*"course" + 0.004*"librarians"')]
```

integration of indigenous knowledge into library and information science teaching practices. Figure 4 also illustrates the keywords and their relative weights from the selected papers.

Figure 5 shows the word clouds per topic of the 16 selected papers. The word cloud in Figure 5 shows color-coded topics. Topic 0 is represented in blue. Topic 1 is in orange, Topic 2 is represented in green, and Topic 3 is represented in red. The words that have prominence throughout the corpus are slightly larger in size. The following themes can be derived from each topic: Indigenous Knowledge (Topic 0), Integrating Indigenous Knowledge into Library Information Science (Topic 1), Decolonisation of University Education (Topic 2), and Transforming Indigenous Knowledge from Communities (Topic 3).

Figure 5. Word clouds per topic

Integration of Indigenous Knowledge Into LIS Teaching Practices

Figure 6 shows a massive world cloud for the corpus of 16 selected journal papers collectively. Featuring prominently in the literature are the words "Indigenous", "knowledge", "library", "information", "university", "research", "decolonisation", "western", "traditional" and "values". Figure six shows that the papers selected were accurate in the sense that it emphasizes Indigenous Knowledge and shows the link to Library Information Science.

Figure 7 established the words "indigenous", "libraries", "knowledge", "lis", "university", "students" and "information are the most frequent terms used overall in the selection of 16 journal papers. The inter-topic distance map shows 4 distinct topics chosen from the 16 selected journal papers.

Figure 6. World cloud for all 16 publications

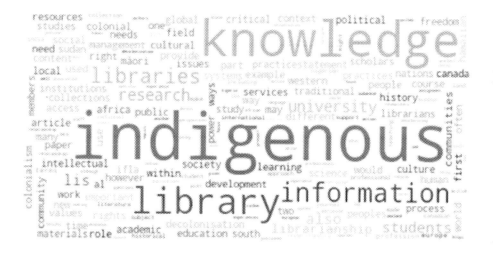

Figure 7. Visualisation of the topics and most salient terms

CONCLUSION AND RECOMMENDATIONS

This chapter aimed to identify and present a global perspective of teaching practices adopted at Library and Information Science (LIS) schools in relation to indigenous knowledge. It sought to address the research questions as outlined in this chapter. The findings revealed that indigenous knowledge is still an emerging theme at LIS schools. Therefore, globally, there is limited literature in the LIS knowledge base in relation to the integration and teaching practices of indigenous knowledge as assumed from Anglophonic literature. However, PRISMA methods indicate that experts are advocating for the integration of indigenous knowledge into LIS programmes. The current focus according to articles presented in this systematic review is on the pressing need for LIS schools to integrate indigenous knowledge into the curriculum. These discussions and dialogues at LIS schools need to be formalized into the curriculum before we lose ground in retaining invaluable rich knowledge from the historical past of indigenous communities. The role of LIS programmes is pivotal as there can equip graduates with the necessary knowledge and skills to access, preserve and disseminate indigenous knowledge. However, LIS schools have not found viable solutions as to how indigenous knowledge can be integrated into the course. Therefore, LIS schools globally need to contribute and share their knowledge on curriculum changes including teaching practices related to indigenous communities. This can help LIS academics to tread common ground in integrating indigenous knowledge into LIS programmes and adopt relevant teaching practices in the classroom.

REFERENCES

Abidogun, J. M., & Falola, T. (2020). *The Palgrave handbook of African education and indigenous knowledge.* Springer. doi:10.1007/978-3-030-38277-3

Ball, T., & Lar-Son, K. (2021). Relationality in the classroom: Teaching indigenous LIS in a Canadian context. *portal. Portal (Baltimore, Md.), 21*(2), 205–218. doi:10.1353/pla.2021.0012

Cobo, J. R. M. (1986). *Study of the problem of discrimination against indigenous populations.* UUN.

Cross, M. (2020). Decolonising universities in South Africa: Backtracking and revisiting the debate. In *Transforming Universities in South Africa* (pp. 101–130). Brill. doi:10.1163/9789004437043_006

Davids, N., & Waghid, Y. (2021). *Academic activism in Higher Education: a living philosophy for social justice* (Vol. 5). Springer Nature. doi:10.1007/978-981-16-0340-2

De Wit, H., & Altbach, P. G. (2021). Internationalization in higher education: Global trends and recommendations for its future. *Policy Reviews in Higher Education, 5*(1), 28–46. doi:10.1080/23322969.2020.1820898

Edwards, A. (2019). Unsettling the future by uncovering the past: Decolonizing academic libraries and librarianship. *Partnership. The Canadian Journal of Library and Information Practice and Research, 14*(1). doi:10.21083/partnership.v14i1.5161

Frayne, A. (2022). Transcribing public libraries as revitalized ethical spaces. *IFLA Journal, 48*(3), 410–421. doi:10.1177/03400352221074716

Integration of Indigenous Knowledge Into LIS Teaching Practices

Freire, P. (2018). *Pedagogy of the oppressed*. Bloomsbury publishing USA.

Gartaula, H., Patel, K., Shukla, S., & Devkota, R. (2020). Indigenous knowledge of traditional foods and food literacy among youth: Insights from rural Nepal. *Journal of Rural Studies, 73*, 77–86. doi:10.1016/j.jrurstud.2019.12.001

Ghosh, B., Ramos-Mejía, M., Machado, R. C., Yuana, S. L., & Schiller, K. (2021). Decolonising transitions in the Global South: Towards more epistemic diversity in transitions research. *Environmental Innovation and Societal Transitions, 41*, 106–109. doi:10.1016/j.eist.2021.10.029

Gopal, P. (2021). On Decolonisation and the University. *Textual Practice, 35*(6), 873–899. doi:10.1080/0950236X.2021.1929561

Gosart, U. (2021). Indigenous librarianship: Theory, practices, and means of social action. *IFLA Journal, 47*(3), 293–304. doi:10.1177/0340035221991861

Guzik, E., Griffin, B., & Hartel, J. (2020). Multimedia Approaches to Learning the Foundations of Library and Information Science. *Journal of Education for Library and Information Science, 61*(1), 126–154. https://doi.org/10.3138/jelis.61.1.2018-0003. doi:10.3138/jelis.61.1.2018-0003

Hangshing, J. (2019). Towards indigenous librarianship: Indian perspective. *Library Philosophy and Practice*, 1-16.

Hill, H., Harrington, M., Rothbauer, P., & Pawlick Potts, D. (2021). Decolonizing & indigenizing LIS. *ALISE 2021 Juried Papers*, 1-6.

Jessen, T. D., Ban, N. C., Claxton, N. X., & Darimont, C. T. (2022). Contributions of Indigenous Knowledge to ecological and evolutionary understanding. *Frontiers in Ecology and the Environment, 20*(2), 93–101. doi:10.1002/fee.2435

Jimenez, A., Vannini, S., & Cox, A. (2023). A holistic decolonial lens for library and information studies. *The Journal of Documentation, 79*(1), 224–244. doi:10.1108/JD-10-2021-0205

Kohsaka, R., & Rogel, M. (2021). Traditional and local knowledge for sustainable development: Empowering the indigenous and local communities of the world. In *Partnerships for the Goals* (pp. 1261–1273). Springer. doi:10.1007/978-3-319-95963-4_17

Komeiji, K., Long, K., Matsuda, S., & Paikai, A. (2021). Indigenous resource management systems as models for librarianship: I waiwai ka 'āina. *IFLA Journal, 47*(3), 331–340. doi:10.1177/0340035221991561

Lilley, S. (2018). Interdisciplinarity and Indigenous Studies: A Māori Perspective. *Journal of the Australian Library and Information Association, 67*(3), 246–255. doi:10.1080/24750158.2018.1497348

Lilley, S. (2021). Transformation of library and information management: Decolonization or Indigenization? *IFLA Journal, 47*(3), 305–312. doi:10.1177/03400352211023071

Littletree, S., Belarde-Lewis, M., & Duarte, M. (2020). Centering relationality: A conceptual model to advance indigenous knowledge organization practices. *Knowledge Organization, 47*(5), 410–426. doi:10.5771/0943-7444-2020-5-410

Masenya, T. M. (2022). Decolonization of Indigenous Knowledge Systems in South Africa: Impact of Policy and Protocols. [IJKM]. *International Journal of Knowledge Management, 18*(1), 1–22. doi:10.4018/IJKM.310005

Mayblin, L., & Turner, J. (2020). *Migration studies and colonialism.* John Wiley & Sons.

Moher, D., Liberati, A., Tetzlaff, J., & Altman, D. G. (2010). Preferred reporting items for systematic reviews and meta-analyses: The PRISMA statement. *International Journal of Surgery, 8*(5), 336–341. doi:10.1016/j.ijsu.2010.02.007 PMID:20171303

Montgomery, L., Hartley, J., Neylon, C., Gillies, M., & Gray, E. (2021). *Open knowledge institutions: reinventing universities.* MIT Press. doi:10.7551/mitpress/13614.001.0001

Murrey, A. (2020). Colonialism. In A. Kobayashi (Ed.), *International Encyclopedia of Human Geography* (2nd ed., pp. 315–326). Elsevier. doi:10.1016/B978-0-08-102295-5.10804-2

Omarsaib, M., Rajkoomar, M., Naicker, N., & Olugbara, C. T. (2022). Digital pedagogies for librarians in higher education: A systematic review of the literature. *Information Discovery and Delivery*, 1–13.

Patel, L. (2021). *No study without struggle: Confronting settler colonialism in higher education.* Beacon Press.

Ramnund-Mansingh, A., & Reddy, N. (2021). South African specific complexities in aligning graduate attributes to employability. *Journal of Teaching and Learning for Graduate Employability, 12*(2), 206–221. doi:10.21153/jtlge2021vol12no2art1025

Samson, C., & Gigoux, C. (2016). *Indigenous peoples and colonialism: Global perspectives.* John Wiley & Sons.

Schmidt, H. (2019). Indigenizing and decolonizing the teaching of psychology: Reflections on the role of the non-Indigenous ally. *American Journal of Community Psychology, 64*(1-2), 59–71. doi:10.1002/ajcp.12365 PMID:31355969

Sharief, O. A. E., Mudawi, M. S. E., & Mohamed, R. A. (2021). Indigenous knowledge in Sudan: Perceptions among Sudanese librarians. *IFLA Journal, 47*(3), 361–374. doi:10.1177/03400352211013839

Sohrabi, C., Franchi, T., Mathew, G., Kerwan, A., Nicola, M., Griffin, M., Agha, M., & Agha, R. (2021). *PRISMA 2020 statement: What's new and the importance of reporting guidelines* (Vol. 88). Elsevier.

Sulyman, A. S., Amzat, B. O. & Taiwo, M. A. (2022). Indigenisation of Nigerian Librarianship through Indigenous Knowledge: Exploring its Possibilities. *Library Philosophy & Practice*, 1-17.

Tharani, K. (2021). Much more than a mere technology: A systematic review of Wikidata in libraries. *Journal of Academic Librarianship, 47*(2), 102326. doi:10.1016/j.acalib.2021.102326

Thornton, T. F., & Bhagwat, S. A. (2020). *The Routledge handbook of indigenous environmental knowledge.* Routledge. doi:10.4324/9781315270845

Tom, M. N., Sumida Huaman, E., & McCarty, T. L. (2019). *Indigenous knowledges as vital contributions to sustainability* (Vol. 65). Springer.

Zibani, P., Rajkoomar, M., & Naicker, N. (2022). A systematic review of faculty research repositories at higher education institutions. *Digital Library Perspectives*, *38*(2), 237–248. doi:10.1108/DLP-04-2021-0035

KEY TERMS AND DEFINITIONS

Academic Integration: Combining students' academic learning experiences and intellectual developments over a period thereby connecting theory to practice in preparation for work.

Colonialism: Political and economic oppression of one group of people over another.

Decolonization: The process of gaining social, political, and economic independence from a colonial power.

Digital Preservation: Providing access to sources of knowledge and information using both hardware and software.

Indigenous Knowledge: Native societies transfer their experiences using verbal and written mediums of communication through generations related to beliefs, practices, and culture.

Teaching Practices: Effective methods used by teachers to facilitate learning and prepare students for a specific industry.

Chapter 17

The Application of OAIS Model as a Framework for Digital Preservation of Indigenous Knowledge Systems:
The Roles of Educational Managers

Godian Patrick Okenjom
https://orcid.org/0000-0003-1212-2163
University of Calabar, Nigeria

Michael Ekpenyong Asuquo
University of Calabar, Nigeria

ABSTRACT

In a world faced with increased and emerging technology, indigenous knowledge systems seem to be en route to extinction. This is resulting from lack of preservation practices by knowledge experts. This kindled the interest of the researchers to discuss how the OAIS model can be applied in the preservation of indigenous knowledge system and the roles educational managers can also play. The chapter vividly discussed the concept of digital preservation, approaches to digital preservation, components constituting framework for digital preservation and application of the OAIS model as framework for digital preservation of indigenous knowledge systems. The model used as framework for digital preservation of indigenous knowledge system discussed in this chapter is the open archival information system (OAIS) reference model. This model discusses the basis for preserving indigenous knowledge system for a long time and providing necessary access to knowledge holders without restrictions. Appropriate conclusion was made for the study.

DOI: 10.4018/978-1-6684-7024-4.ch017

Copyright © 2023, IGI Global. Copying or distributing in print or electronic forms without written permission of IGI Global is prohibited.

INTRODUCTION

The focus of this chapter is hinged on applying the Open Archival Information System (OAIS) Reference Model for long term digital preservation of documented indigenous knowledge systems (IKS) and the roles of educational managers. Extinction of indigenous knowledge systems resulting from inability of preservation practices adversely affects indigenous knowledge transfer from one generation to another. indigenous knowledge systems aforetime have always been relegated, owing to the fact that indigenous knowledge is seen to be local, primitive, uncivilized and inimical to development. It is also believed that indigenous knowledge hinders technological advancement and hence, continues to suffer devaluation overtime. The idea for erosion of indigenous knowledge systems (IKS) have been observable in many African societies a long time ago (Mdhluli, Mokgoatšana, Kugara & Vuma, 2021). The major essence of relegation and erosion of indigenous knowledge systems credited to high extent of secrecy by holders which makes the hope of such knowledge termed indigenous being circulated to everyone and utilized for common benefit become almost a mirage. Mdhluli, et al (2021) averred that this act of secrecy has negatively contributed immensely with respect to indigenous peoples' way of preserving, managing and disseminating knowledge being threatened with extinction. From ample study of literature, it is observed that, there is little or no evidence indicating indigenous knowledge holder's readiness to warmly accept open debate or discussions on indigenous knowledge preservation as it is seen as cultural heritage reserved to be passed orally from one generation to another (Dlamini & Nokwanda, 2021; Harry & Kanehe, 2006). The essence according to the authors is owed to the constant threat from exploitation, theft, misrepresentation, misuse, and commodification faced by dissemination of indigenous knowledge system. Research interest into indigenous knowledge systems is fairly new. The term "indigenous knowledge" was coined in 1980 by Warren, Brokensha, Werner and Chambers. Warren et al, developed a huge interest into the study of local knowledge or traditional knowledge. This interest made them to sought for a more appropriate terminology to describe traditional or local knowledge. Before their coinage, the term indigenous knowledge was usually referred to as "traditional knowledge" or "local knowledge". It was their interest on how they could describe local people knowledge in a more encompassing way that brought about the idea of the term "indigenous knowledge". Historically, indigenous knowledge system has been seen as one of the essential possessions rural people own and utilize for developing communities (Kugara, 2017). As noted by Gupta (2010), the main obstacle since the initiation of the term "indigenous knowledge" has been the fact that there is no standard process to capturing and documenting indigenous knowledge systems. It is resulting from the claim of Gupta that this chapter advocates for digital preservation of indigenous knowledge system for development and research.

Indigenous knowledge systems have numerous scopes; and these scopes are linguistics, medicine, clinical psychology, botany, zoology, ethology, ecology, climate, agriculture, animal husbandry, and craft skills (Langtone, 2016). Indigenous knowledge is simply a type of knowledge that expresses itself in practice and stems from natural life and belief system. It creates an environment where rural dwellers derive solutions to their problems by applying practical knowledge which is indigenous. Since indigenous people believe so much in deities and spirituality, indigenous knowledge forms the basis for faith and belief system. It provides ample direction for their existence culturally, spiritually and socio-economically. Ihekwoaba, Okwor, Nnadi, Jidere and Obim (2022) added that indigenous knowledge (IK) is advancement and activities of local populations around the world which has grown over a period and which has adjusted to local culture and background. This information is communicated through oration and traditional rites, bonds, beliefs, proverbs from one generation to another, and has overtime time formed the basis for farming activities and a wide diversity of other actions that support societal development.

From the foregoing, the mission and concern of this book chapter is tailored towards sufficiently addressing the Open Archival Information System (OAIS) model as a framework for digital preservation of indigenous knowledge systems and its implication to educational management. Open Archival Information System (OAIS) is a reference model that defines the processes necessary for preservation and access to information objects effectively by establishing a mutual linguistic to describe such objects (José & Carmen, 2016). This model offers the framework for executing tasks effectively, while explaining the basic aspects and systems of information required of the preservation background. For maintaining access to digital information over a period of time, the Open Archival Information System (OAIS) Reference Model has been widely adopted as the foundation for many important digital preservation initiatives (Sibsankar, Mrinal & Ujjal, 2009). This OAIS Reference Model published by the Consultative Committee on Space Data Systems (CCSDS, 2000) of the National Aeronautics and Space Administration (NASA) became an ISO standard in 2003. The OAIS Reference Model is a framework for a universal archival system, which is dedicated to a planned role of preserving and providing access to information digitally. Part of the work involved in the development of a reference model for an 'open archival information system' (OAIS) is the representation of a reliable framework for explaining and analyzing digital preservation issues, providing a comprehensive footing for future quality and serving as a point of reference for merchants who show interest in building digital preservation products and services. The specific objectives of this chapter is tailored towards addressing the following:

- explaining the meaning of digital preservation and indigenous knowledge (systems);
- differentiating the various components constituting framework for digital preservation of indigenous knowledge (systems);
- discussing how the OAIS model can be utilized as a framework for digital preservation of indigenous knowledge systems; and
- state the roles educational managers can play in the preservation of indigenous knowledge system

DIGITAL PRESERVATION

When issues and scholarly discussions are initiated with regards to digital preservation, what come to mind first is the term "Digital". Generally speaking, the term "digital" is associated with discrete values, often binary digits. These values and binary digits do not work in isolation but it becomes realistic and meaningful with technology and computing. The combination of hardware and software components makes it possible for information to be transmitted and processed to data for preservation and subsequent utilization. Mukasa (2012) averred that digital preservation are procedures, actions and management of digital information for a period of time to ensure its sustained access. For The Joint Information Systems Committee (2012), digital preservation is the sequence of engagements needed to guarantee continual and consistent access to accurate digital resources as much as the value remains as it is intended.

According to Roux (2015), there are indications that in a few generations to come, the existence of indigenous knowledge may be inevitable. The sole reason is owed to non-interest of children born in

OAIS Model for Digital Preservation of Indigenous Knowledge Systems

the jet and computer age sitting at the feet of indigents researchers. These children are supposed to learn about the culture, belief systems and local technology of the community or society where there originate from. Rather, they grow with recent technology and build their lives along with the technological dynamics of the century. UNESCO (2021) maintained that preservation of traditional characteristics that are at threat of extinction is a matter of determination and uttermost primacy. This challenge stands out among many observable actions that critically depend on appropriate forecasting and well-organized application, as it has been the matter with digitally preserving irreplaceable indigenous knowledge that is rapidly going to extinction.

One of the major factors in ensuring sustainability to heritage materials like indigenous knowledge is preservation. This preservation has long been managed by the rural people, thereby making the accessibility of important information with regards to indigenous people and communities, whether rural or urban become a futile adventure (Mdhluli, Mokgoatšana, Kugara & Vuma, 2021). According to Mdhluli, et al (2021), this reason is argued to have aided the threat of extinction of indigenous knowledge systems. This is one of the major reason researchers around the world advocates digital preservation of indigenous knowledge and it systems. Lee, Slattery, Lu, Tang and McCrary (2002) appreciated that digital content has many benefits which makes it stress-free to create, handle, circulate, find, and save information digitally. Despite the relevance of paper document, digital content is more reliable to easily accessed by users around the world with enormous challenges. Further, preserving digital documents for a time span is further challenging and difficult, than preserving paper documents (Lee et al, 2002). Perry (2014) lamented on the challenges bedeviling digital preservation of indigenous knowledge systems. It is believed that if these challenges are not immediately and consistently addressed, it will continue to truncate the successful preservation of indigenous knowledge systems digitally. These challenges according Perry (2014), are authenticity and reliability of material, awareness, imbibing new formats of technology, uncertified staff, standardization and copyright and cost issues.

Approaches to Digital Preservation

There are numerous approaches, strategies, frameworks and technologies that can be implemented for effective preservation and management of indigenous knowledge and it system when engaged in digital preservation processes and activities. This will encourage access and utilization of digital contents/objects which are stored over a long period of time. Artut (2021) discussed relevant literature bothering on approaches to digital preservation. These approaches are; technology preservation, technology emulation, information migration and technology encapsulation. This chapter therefore considers a review of the foregoing with regards to digital preservation of indigenous knowledge systems below.

Technology Preservation: The longevity of indigenous people or indigent researchers cannot be overlooked when discussing issues of digital preservation of indigenous knowledge systems, the essence is because there are the reservoir and holders of raw information needed for documentation and preservation of indigenous knowledge systems. For instance, London Parliamentary Archives (2008) maintained that, if a format depends on a certain match of hardware and software for rendering, it should be possible to preserve at least a few working examples of the outdated platform. Technology preservation is the intervening solution of digital preservation problem (Oguche & Aliyu, 2020). Utilizing the approach of technology preservation to document and sustain indigenous knowledge systems can be of great benefit to providing historic information about the conducts of outdated routines and rituals of indigenous people in rural or urban communities. Thibodeau (2002) carried out a study on Overview of

325

Technological Approaches to Digital Preservation and Challenges in Coming Years Digital Preservation: An International Perspective. The chapter debated that technology preservation is not a feasible approach for longitudinal preservation, for the following reasons:

a. The time, rate and space effects for obtaining and conserving enormous quantities of hardware are expensive for most organizations, this makes them either acquire sub-standard equipment or fail in the maintenance of available material resources available;

b. The maintenance of defacing operating system and application software and right authorizations will be gotten and sustained too;

c. The decrease in quantity of machines that can of read certain types of old files becomes eminent as this machines keep degrading overtime and eventually fail;

d. Expertise assistance for both hardware and software also disappear over time due to constant and regular use of the machines;

e. Most of the time, records for preceding computing backgrounds can be challenging to uncover.

Technology Emulation: The essence of digital preservation is not to put into extinct indigenous knowledge systems, but to duplication in a usable digital format the same knowledge and information in a global perspective. This will help users around the world get into the knowledge of researching into this new area of digital preservation of indigenous knowledge around the world. In technology emulation, older documents are not modified to make them match with newer hardware and software but rather, it creates software to run on new computers to allow them render digital documents in their original form through the use of an emulator. By implication, indigenous knowledge can be preserved digitally only when reliable data and information is obtained from holders in its original form without tampering or changing the pattern, design or format. According to Acker (2021), emulation practices are computational processes which permit for one system to replicate the tasks and results of another. An emulator is projected to authentically replicate information, experience with hardware or software, or in a blend. Many authors have maintained that retrieving outdated software with emulation approaches is time and resource consuming, hence, emulation is currently experimented with as a service provision for long-term preservation and archiving (Von, Rechert & Valizada, 2013; Rechert, Von & Welter, 2010). From available literature, there is an indication that there is an increasing occurrence of software preservation in information institutions and concerns about these challenges amongst information professionals, scholarly consideration to the software management practices of archivists has been impeded (Chassanoff & Altman, 2020).

Information Migration: For efficient and effective preservation of indigenous knowledge systems, there must be migration of data, information and technology. It is through migration that reliable and current information is transferred from one process to another. Migration is a concept which is used when discussing issues that bother around digital preservation. Contributing into the concept of migration, Sarmah (2018) stated that migration moves records from one format to another format, involving the actions of migrating data from a legacy system to a new system without impacting active applications and finally redirecting all input/output activity to the new device. Data migration is a multi-step process that begins with an analysis of legacy data and concludes in the loading and reconciliation of data into the new applications. There are some other factors to consider when replacing the old legacy system. There are:

OAIS Model for Digital Preservation of Indigenous Knowledge Systems

a. databases continually develop by requiring supplementary storage capacity
b. establishments switch to high-end servers
c. cost minimization and reduction of complexities by transferring to useable and steady system
d. data requires to be transferable from physical and simulated situations for virtual use
e. availing accurate data for consumption

Digital migration of information/data is primarily targeted at preserving the originality of digital objects with new technologies and provide access to users and other researchers around the world.

Technology Encapsulation: Digital preservation in this chapter aims at preserving indigenous knowledge from the original owners to a more accessible format without attempting to destroy the original information, system or method. This preservation system is digital technology. Technology changes with time, and this change affect both the hardware, software and other accessories of the generation. When information is digitally preserved and the digital preservers do not upgrade both file and system format, the essence of technology encapsulation become defeated as the information preserved aforetime may be obsolete and hence, unusable. Oguche, et al (2020) described encapsulation as the process of assembling all the appropriate resources for the digital object and to maintain the resulting digital object as an entity. This approach encompasses generating the unique request that was used to create the digital object on impending computer platforms. Part of the process of encapsulation may be to transfer the entire data to a more easily documented format. The adequate promotion of technology encapsulation will enhance effective sustainability of indigenous knowledge systems and make it more sustainable for future users and researchers in the area.

COMPONENTS CONSTITUTING FRAMEWORK FOR DIGITAL PRESERVATION OF INDIGENOUS KNOWLEDGE SYSTEMS

Components constituting frameworks for digital preservation stand as a viable structure for preservation of indigenous knowledge systems. These components explain what indigent and alien researchers should do to guarantee the long-term preservation of digital records and information. In a bid to present some discussion on components constituting frameworks for digital preservation of indigenous knowledge systems, Grindley (2010), presented the following as aspects which serve as components constituting framework for digital preservation of IKS, and according to Grindley (2010), these are: policy, emotional, intellectual and strategic components.

a. **Policy Component:** A policy component is such that carries prescribed declaration of path-way or guidance as to how activities or organization will operate for goal achievement in line with the available mandate, interest, programs or functions. As policies and legislative frameworks are developed, the importance of both identifying and protecting indigenous knowledge is receiving increased attention from policy makers the world over (Innocenti, Ross, Maceciuvite, Wilson, Ludwig and & Pempe, 2009). It is the policy component that makes them viable, without a policy framework a digital library is little more than a container for content (Innocenti, et al 2009). Policy framework exists to handle, guide and frame the structure of digital library which performs the task of preserving information digitally for research purposes and as policy reservoir, as well as repository for information which cumulate analog systems of indigenous knowledge preservation.

327

In this chapter, the policy framework interest is on standards for the selection of formats for digital records in connection with the digital preservation policy. Digital objects ideally must have a specified format to enable successful upload or transmission to designated repository or website for archiving. There are a wide range of digital formats required for the preservation of indigenous knowledge systems for facilitation of long term, middle term or short term preservation of digital objects converted from analogue materials. The essence of format maintenance policy is to avoid the danger of digital obsolescence (Procedures for Records Creation, 2021). Digital formats can thousands of different file formats in the preservation process. For best preservation practices, there are recommended standards which are also commonly used required for digital preservation of indigenous knowledge systems. The following formats are considered for text, audio and video files: These formats are carefully standardized as part of policy framework for digital preservation of indigenous knowledge systems.

Table 1. Text file formats

Format	File	Support Level	Best Practices
Microsoft Word	.doc	Bit-Level	To get required output, it is important to convert .doc files to PDF even if it is acceptable for deposit
Microsoft PowerPoint	.ppt	Bit-Level	It is recommended that .ppt files are converted to PDF. It also necessary to disable all macros and other effects.
Microsoft Excel	.xls	Bit-Level	User needs to disable all macros. User may wish to export dataset into a tab-delimited text file (.txt) prior to Deposit
PDF	.pdf	Format	
Rich Text	.rtf	Bit-Level	It is strongly recommended that user converts to PDF
Plain Text	.txt	Format	For best practice, tt is recommended that .txt files be saved using UTF-* (Unicode) character set
XML	.xml	Bit-Level	Assuring top accessible backing, include the DTD with a well-formed XML file that is valid according to the included DTD

Table 2. Image File Formats

Format	File	Support Level	Best Practices
BMP	.bmp	Bit-Level	
GIF	.gif	Format	
JPEG	.jpg	Format	Presently accepted optimum for presentation. Best practice is to save with NO Compression
JPEG2000	.jp2	Bit-Level	More acceptable practice is to save with NO Compression
PNG	.png	Format	
Photoshop	.psd	Bit-Level	Proprietary format that may be best saved as a .jpg and/or .tiff
TIFF	.tif	Format	Presently accepted to be the archival standard. Best practice is to save with NO Compression

Table 3. Audio File Formats

Format	File	Support Level	Best Practices
MPEG	.mp3	Bit-Level	Suggested for presentation of audio files
WAVE	.wav	Format	Presently accepted as best archival standard. Recommended format for capturing digital audio. This format stores all data in an uncompressed format and suggested widely for use as long-term community support

Table 4. Video File Formats

Format	File	Support Level	Best Practices
AVI	.avi	Bit-Level	
MPEG	.mp1, mp2, mp4	Bit-Level	
Quicktime	.mov	Bit-Level	
Windows Media Video	.wmv	Bit-Level	

Source: *Rimkus, Padilla, Popp & Martin (2014),* digital preservation file format policies of ARL member libraries: an analysis

b.   **Emotional Component:** Emotional component constituting framework for digital preservation of indigenous knowledge systems is an importation aspect in digital preservation process. Research findings reveals that individuals, communities and societies from around the world agree that building social and emotional competencies is important to societal growth, but more work needs to be done to forestall the difficulty encountered in the digital preservation of indigenous knowledge (OECD, 2018; Humphrey, 2013). When the emotional well-being of dwellers in rural or urban communities is put into commendable consideration, it becomes a source of motivation to them, which will invariably spur them to divulge more information than normal for intended purposes. In separate studies carried out by Ljubetic and Maglica (2020) and Bowers, Lemberger-Truelove and Brigman (2018), emotional framework for digital preservation of indigenous knowledge systems were approached from five different perspectives; self-awareness, self-management, relationship skills, responsible decision-making and social awareness.

Self-awareness: Indigenous knowledge holders can function effectively in their willingness to divulge certain knowledge considered sacred and concealed. Making them realize and understand the importance of continuous self-reflect to enhance a better understanding of how to systematically conceptualize their world and holistic experiences of the years and how it is appreciated now. Self-awareness is a very nascent skill required by indigenous knowledge holder to help them appreciate the ability to identify emotions, maintain accurate self-perception, identify personal strengths, and maintain healthy self-confidence and self-efficacy. The growth of indigenous knowledge systems and it's improved performance can lead to personal growth and societal development. It then implies that indigent researchers and indigenous knowledge holders may lack certain awareness of themselves and environment. When this happens, it creates a permissible gap for permeation.

Self-management: The importance of managing oneself when it comes to emotional issues cannot be overemphasized. This is because emotion controls behaviour and guides certain actions and decisions one would take when faced with a situation at a time. The embodiment of emotional self-management covers the ability to control impulses, manage stress, exercise self-discipline, maintain motivation for themselves, setting realistic, relevant, and achievable goals. As indigenous knowledge holders observe their environment and situations, they build self-motivation and enthusiasm by creating a situation where their thoughts and attitude reflects the environment they find themselves. Though they could find themselves in some strenuous and stressful situation but they are always determining to build self-confidence knowing their total wellbeing in its entirety depends wholly on knowledge acquired or experienced from their predecessors. Researchers who are indigents who already know the terrain require to carefully and tactfully get closer to the indigents, by giving them vital information that will help build on their psyche on the relevance of preserving indigenous knowledge for future use by generations to come. According to (ASCA, 2012), the idea of digital preservation entails encouraging the creation of realistic and achievable goals for proper preservation of indigenous knowledge systems

Social awareness: The power of diversity makes our dwelling as different people meaningful in an indigenous society. It is important that in a society we take into consideration and respect the opinions and perspective of other people. Understanding the diversity of other people as we live together brings out the best of realization of objectives which is basically living mutually as one people, family and society, this will invariably curb serious and incessant unrest and retard development. Empathy plays a very crucial role in developing harmonious work environments among indigenous people as they strive to make out the best out of their living as natural people who believe so much in the knowledge acquired from their ancestors.

Relationship skills: Building a solid relationship within individuals or group circle forms a very important point in developing and maintaining relationship. It is through working and viable relationships that meaningful contributions and ideas are harnesses for an improved living of the rural or urban indigenous communities. Applying emotional intelligence techniques within a social context creates opportunities to build interpersonal relationships with others. This is achieved through appropriate communication, active listening, partnership, resistance to inappropriate peer pressure, constructive negotiation during conflicts and helping others, as well as asking for help when necessary (Ljubetic & Maglica, 2020).

Responsible decision-making. Decision making builds the confidence of indigenous people to decide what they want to do with the indigenous knowledge acquired overtime. The reason is to enable them secure their heritage as indigenous people. There are components that make decisions responsible. These among others are identify problems and challenges as they come in the daily activities of indigenous people, analyzing circumstances, solving problems, evaluating situations that occur alongside the daily lives of indigenous people, reflecting and practicing within a context of the indigenous people and their practices.

c. **Intellectual Component:** Intellectual component and capabilities harness knowledge specific to information technology and digital systems with problem domains of personal interest to information bothering around indigenous knowledge collation and preservation using digital contents for digital preservation. The prominence and importance of intellectual framework being relevant to digital preservation of indigenous knowledge systems rely heavily on technology and its ware (hardware and software). As stated by Augusto, Nakashima and Aghajan (2010), advances in the smallness of electronics is allowing computing devices with various capabilities and interfaces to become part of our daily life. By being part of our daily lives it makes it easier for us as human to interact with computers and its accessories. Modernized and portable devices like sensors, actuators, and processing units have been reduced so small enabling utilization and compatibility. This technology can be networked and used with the coordination of highly intelligent software to understand the events and relevant context of a specific environment and to take sensible decisions in real-time (Aghajan, 2010). The essential elements of intellectual framework with regards to indigenous knowledge management and digital preservation include engaging in sustained reasoning, managing complexity, testing a solution, managing problems in faulty solutions, etc. (Noun, 2022).

The Elements of intellectual framework for digital preservation of indigenous knowledge system are pertinent to achieving seamless process for digitization of harvested information and data for digital processing and transmission. These elements are:

Intellectual capabilities: Intellectual capabilities of indigenous knowledge researchers is applicable to informed implementation of information technology in difficult but sustained circumstances. These capabilities go beyond particular hardware or software applications of technology. Most of the surveys and experiences shows that these abilities uneasily transmit between problem areas as most individuals are very abreast with technological competencies which influences standard practices in digital preservation processes. This scenario makes intellectual capabilities to be seen as "life skills" that are articulated in the context of information technology.

Fundamental concepts: Fundamentally, the basics which information technology is hinged on expressed. A good knowledge of concepts and meaning about computer and computing activities gives indigenous knowledge researchers leverage and an understanding of how fundamental issues pertaining computing are manipulated and managed for great output. These fundamental concepts have relationship with information and computing and are continuing, resulting that, innovative ideas could become essential in prospect as new information technologies emerges as new knowledge.

Contemporary skills: Skills in relation to digital preservation of indigenous knowledge depicts the effective utilization of specific hardware or software resources to accomplish information processing tasks. Contemporary skills have to do with having the well-without or technical know-how of how computer and its various components are manipulated for the achievement of sustaining digital knowledge for research and development purposes. The benefits of contemporary skills as indigenous knowledge researchers are enormous as it increases and improves proficiency in the skills acquired.

Engage in sustained reasoning: It is a policy that every indigenous knowledge researcher has right to engage in sustained reasoning. Working with indigenous people who are indigenous knowledge holders is quite demanding. Issues and problems that tend to hinder the smooth working with indigenous people needs to always be defined and clarified. It is only when this is achieved that a reasonable success can be recorded in the process of information assemblage and transmission. This can be achieved through a broad knowledge of information technology. Through technology, a wide range of formulated strategies for problem solving can be generated and applied as test of implementation strategy for possible solution to problems envisaged and tackled.

Test a solution: In getting reliable solution to problems and challenged experience while engaged in indigenous knowledge systems research, there is a need to test several solutions. The essence is because there is no particular formalized method that can be used to solve a problem. Solving problems or challenges depends on situations, timing and environment. For instance, considering the scope, nature, and circumstances under which a technological result is envisaged to function can be challenging. That is the major reason testing a solution should involve the consideration of a proposed solution whether it meets the design goals and works under varied situations or not. Testing a solution involves identifying the areas that are most likely to cause failure in the implementation phase of the tested solution, because some fixes to problems may introduce more problems often than not, exceptional care is necessary to fix (or manage) the initial flaws before introducing a new solution or implementing a tested solution.

d. **Strategic Component:** Over the years indigenous knowledge holders has continued to manage and preserve its information and knowledge in various traditionally accepted ways like signs, symbols and objects. As the changing world evolves with new advances, skills and technological development, these generations that hold such knowledge termed indigenous, continue to pass away by death without any emerging plan to preserve this knowledge termed indigenous for generations to come. It is the worry researchers have over the years on how indigenous knowledge can be digitally preserved for posterity. This forms the embryo of this review. The challenges of preserving and maintaining access to digital resources over time continues to emerge. This is the area where strategic framework comes in, to utilize technical and infrastructural capacities and systems to strengthen digital preservation of indigenous knowledge systems. According to London Parliamentary Archives (2008), there are nascent ideas/structures that encompasses strategic framework when it concerns digital preservation of indigenous knowledge, these are digital record, digital asset, digital resource, digitization, digital preservation, digital archaeology, digital repository, metadata, etc. these frameworks come together to form a strong whole for preservation of indigenous knowledge digitally for present and future purposes. UNITAR (2021) added that Science and technology are key elements for sustaining any goal oriented strategy like the strategic framework for digital preservation of indigenous knowledge systems (IKS). The use of technology-based and innovative solutions for preservation of indigenous knowledge will continue to play an important role in supporting better informed and evidence-based decision-making processes by researchers around the world. However, implementing strategic objectives for digital preservation of indigenous knowledge contents cannot be done without acknowledging certain assumptions, risks and challenges.

Building a viable strategic framework for digital preservation of indigenous knowledge systems is of immense importance to achieving relevant goals and objectives for knowledge expansion and appreciation. There certain values and achievement that strategic frame can achieve if well managed as knowledge builders. Strategic framework for digital preservation of indigenous knowledge systems can serve the purpose of:

- ensuring that the long-term digital memory required for preservation of indigenous knowledge systems is used for digitization to avoid inaccessible, loss or compromise;
- helping researchers to offer easy access to online resources, for leisure, educational purposes, entrepreneurship and effective management and accountability;
- prevention of wastage minor or major projects for online repository hosting and maintenance for public access in a conducive environment
- introducing best practices in digital preservation strategies of indigenous knowledge systems within extant policies that guide digital preservation practices around the world through sharing of experiences, collaborating with suitable partners and influencing technological developments.

THE APPLICATION OF OAIS MODEL AS FRAMEWORK FOR DIGITAL PRESERVATION OF INDIGENOUS KNOWLEDGE SYSTEMS

The application of OAIS model as framework for digital preservation of indigenous knowledge systems is discussed in this study. The Open Archival Information System (OAIS) model takes the obligation to reserve information and make it accessible for a particular group of people for utilization. An archival information system is 'an archive, involving an organization of societies and structures, that has acknowledged the obligation to preserve information and make it available for a Designated Community (Ball, 2006). Ball (2006) averred that the OAIS model is set in the perspective of manufacturers (who produce the information to be archived), users (who retrieve the information) and management (the wider organization hosting the OAIS).

The OAIS Reference Model was developed by the Consultative Committee for Space Data Systems (CCSDS) as a work item under the ISO Technical Committee 20, Sub-committee 13. It is a framework for accepting and applying concepts needed for long-term digital information preservation. The idea of preserving digital information for long-term calls for a concern about changing technologies which may affect digitized information overtime (José & Carmen, 2016; Sawyer, Reich, Giaretta, Mazal, Huc, Nonon-Latapie & Peccia, 2002). The OAIS model accepts that it is more difficult to preserve information digitally that is written or inked on paper or film because the associated technology is determined by obsolescence which poses information loss hazards (José & Carmen, 2016). The model approaches this as an organizational, legal, industrial, scientific and cultural issue, not just a technological one, cautioning that overlooking the hitches posed by the preservation of information in digital form would lead to its loss. The purpose of discourse on the activities of OIS model is to preserve the content information in a way understandable to the appropriate community within the knowledge base of that community. This entails coordinating the access tools with the knowledge of the users, without mislaying sight of how this knowledge evolve (Lee, 2010).

THE FUNCTIONAL MODEL OF OPEN ARCHIVAL INFORMATION SYSTEM

The functional model of open archival information system is composed of seven main functional entities and the interfaces between them: management, data management, preservation planning, access, archival storage and ingest (Lee, 2010). The functional model of the open archival information system (OAIS) is described around the producer (indigenous knowledge holders), consumer (indigent researchers) and management (digital preservation experts), these three entities constitute the environment in which an OAIS operates and interacts.

Lavoie (2014) explicitly described the functional components of the Open Archival Information System (OAIS) model as follows:

- **Management:** The management function is liable for managing the daily operations of the OAIS. It coordinates the actions of the other five high-level OAIS functional entities. Management functions as the dominant core for the OAIS's internal and external interactions: it interacts directly with the five other OAIS high-level services – Ingest, Archival Storage, Data Management, Preservation Planning, and Access, as well as the OAIS's external stakeholders – Producers, Consumers, and Management.

- **Data Management:** Data Management function does the job of maintaining the databases of descriptive metadata by recognizing and explaining the archived information in aiding the OAIS's finding aids. It also directs the managerial data supporting the OAIS's internal system actions, such as system activities or access statistics. The primary functions of Data Management include retaining the databases for which it is responsible; execution queries on the databases and producing reports in response to requests from other functional units within the OAIS; and directing updates to the databases as new information reaches, or existing information is improved. The method through which data management is achieved using the OAIS supporting search and recovery of the OAIS's archived content, and running of the OAIS's internal operations.

- **Preservation Planning:** Preservation Planning is in charge for strategizing methods of preservation, as well as suggesting suitable reviews to the approach in response to changing conditions in the OAIS environment. This plan monitors the external environment for changes and risks that could impact the OAIS's ability to preserve and maintain access to the information in its custody, such as innovations in storage and access technologies, or shifts in the scope or expectations of the Designated Community.

- **Access:** The Access function manages the processes and services by which Consumers (Designated Community) locate, request, and receive delivery of items residing in the OAIS's archival store. It is in charge for executing any security or access control machineries associated with the archived content. The Access function characterizes the OAIS's interface with its customers, hence, it is the major tool by which the OAIS meets its responsibility to make its archived information available to the user community.

- **Archival Storage:** Archival Storage deals with the aspect of archival system that manages the long-term storage and maintenance of digital materials trusted to the OAIS. It is responsible for ensuring that archived content resides in appropriate storage system or path like online, near-line, offline – and that the bit streams encompassing the preserved information remain complete over time through media refreshment or format migration.

- **Ingest:** Ingest explains the set of processes responsible for accepting information submitted by producers of information (indigenous knowledge systems) and preparing it for inclusion in the archival store for users. Some of the related activities executed by Ingest includes receiving of information conveyed to the OAIS by a Producer; authentication that the information received is virus free and complete; transformation of the submitted information into a form fit for storage and management within the archival system; extraction and/or creation of descriptive metadata to support the OAIS's search and retrieval tools and finding aids; and transfer of the submitted information and its associated metadata to the archival store.

Relating this model to educational management and preservation of indigenous knowledge systems, formal education today has taken a large part of Nigerian educational system. This has led to the relegation of traditional education system where parents pass indigenous knowledge to other generations through oral tradition using proverbs, myths and stories, learning through culture, elders, specific names, traditional African science and technology. It is impeccable to state that without documentation of the said traditional knowledge by educational managers and knowledge producers digitally, the threat of extinction of indigenous and traditional knowledge might take its full course in some near future to come. The application of the open archival information system (OAIS) model by educational managers

OAIS Model for Digital Preservation of Indigenous Knowledge Systems

has been well discussed in this chapter as a framework for digital preservation of indigenous knowledge system for producers, consumers and information users.

THE ROLES OF EDUCATIONAL MANAGERS

Educational managers have a functional role to play when it comes to knowledge economy in terms of knowledge acquisition, storage, retrieval and dissemination. These roles are discussed aligning with the functional entities of the Open Archival Information System (OAIS).

- **The role of educational managers in knowledge management:** Educational managers manage both human and material resources. Indigenous knowledge being an important resource for information development and educational system needs to be adequately managed for posterity without altering its original quality and meaning. This can be achieved by successfully coordinating continuous increase in knowledge investments such as education and knowledge production. It is when they is proper management that planning, organizing, staffing, directing, coordinating, reporting, and budgeting can be achieved in preservation of knowledge acquired from indigenous knowledge holders. Educational managers in performing their functions communications with relevant stakeholders to enable them achieve a seamless digital preservation of data and information gotten from indigenous communities.
- **The role of educational managers in data management:** Educational managers in coordinating and organizing data useful to educational management strategically sustains databases of descriptive metadata explaining the archived information in backing of the framework used for this dialogue. Primarily, educational managers maintain the databases for which it is liable for executing queries and producing reports in response to requests from other functional entities related to educational management. It is this relationship that support updates to the databases as new information arrives for appropriate reform for utilization and storage.
- **The role of educational managers in preservation planning**: Every piece of information requires preservation. The essence of preservation is to enable generations to come benefit from archived knowledge and build on own to suit purpose and eminent times. Educational managers have a major role to play in addressing the planning process for preservation of indigenous knowledge systems, this achievable through meaningful suggestion of appropriate revisions to the strategy in response to evolving technology and information user demands. The preservation plan monitors the external setting for changes and risks that could impact the preservation processes and suggest best practices in innovations, access technologies and expectations of the designated community where indigenous knowledge is harvested from.
- **Role of educational managers in providing access to preserved knowledge**: One of most important aspects of digital preservation of indigenous knowledge system is providing access to indigent knowledge providers without altering its original form. One of the major reasons indigenous knowledge access is embodied in secrecy is because of fear of alteration in the peoples' culture and customs. This access function manages the processes and services by which indigenous knowledge holders locate, request, and receive delivery of items residing in the archival store by managers. Information availability is key to access in preserved indigenous.

335

- **Role of educational managers in archival storage:** as important as getting indigenous knowledge is to the development of educational management, the long-term preservation and maintenance of digital materials is paramount. Educational managers ensue that information at their disposal is properly managed and preserved appropriately through recommended and appropriate technologies and archival storage systems like online, near-line or offline systems.
- **Role of educational managers in indigenous knowledge ingest:** For proper preservation of indigenous knowledge gotten from indigent knowledge holders, there are criteria, standards and processes responsible for accepting information for submission and preparation for archiving. Educational managers receive information necessary for educational development and transmits it to validators who are preservation experts using emerging technologies for screening from virus and other unprotected actions that affect seamless preservation processes. The transformation process is then made possible for suitability and storage within the archival system in archival store.

RECOMMENDATIONS

The major remedy to extinction of indigenous knowledge systems is total embrace to emerging technologies. Through preservation of indigenous knowledge digitally, African traditions, customs and traditional practices will continue to be available to users for further knowledge production and dissemination. Based on literature reviewed, the following recommendations are made:

- Educational managers should enhance the propagation of frameworks necessary for digital preservation of indigenous knowledge by applying these indigenous knowledge indices to real classroom experience very often with materials, information, experience and data acquired.
- The assimilation of African indigenous knowledge systems (AIKS) educational system should be encouraged to provide opportunities for development of educational management
- Students should be provided with prospect to acquire suitable communal and unrestricted attitudes and values for viable livelihood by helping students to learn through culture as indigenous knowledge systems is stored in various cultural methods like folk stories, songs, folk drama, legends, proverbs, myths, etc.
- Cultural resources should be utilized these in educational management can be very effective in bringing indigenous knowledge systems to bare for students in educational management and the field of education in general Kaya & Seleti, 2013).

CONCLUSION

Indigenous people have continued to survive through indigenous knowledge acquire from forefathers and through experience, this knowledge system covers a wide range of life activities like farming, healthcare, culture and spiritual life. These aspects of life are usually transferred from one generation to another orally. It is often difficult to get informing on how this local and indigenous people survive using the knowledge acquired from past generations. The reason is hinged on their belief that if vital information containing indigenous knowledge is revealed, aliens will rob them of their cultural heritage and make them proliferated with unknown culture. For the sake of sustainability, the advocacy for digital preservation remains a valid means through which indigenous knowledge can be preserved digitally for the future. Achieving this purpose requires the application of a framework for digital preservation. As discussed in this chapter, the Open Archival Information System (OAIS) model was used as the framework for digital preservation of indigenous knowledge systems. Application of this framework to preservation of indigenous knowledge system will enhance the successful archiving of indigenous knowledge systems digitally for a long time without losing it value.

REFERENCES

Acker, A. (2021). Emulation practices for software preservation in libraries, archives, and museums. *Journal of the Association for Information Science and Technology, 72*(9), 1148–1160. doi:10.1002/asi.24482

American School Counselor Association. (2012). *ASCA National Model: A framework for school counseling programs* (3rd ed.). ASCA.

Artut, S. (2021). *Conservation of Technological artworks. In technological arts Preservation.* Sabancı University Sakıp Sabancı Museum (SSM), Turky. https://www.sakipsabancimuzesi.org

Augusto, J. C., Nakashima, H., & Aghajan, H. (2010). *Ambient Intelligence and Smart Environments: A State of the Art.* CiteSeer. https://citeseerx.ist.psu.edu/document? repid=rep 1&type=pdf&doi=ca53 e5830538d1f18feb1995045a40e94db5553b.

Ball, A. (2006). Briefing Paper: the OAIS Reference Model. UKOLN, University of Bath.

Bowers, H., Lemberger-Truelove, M., & Brigman, G. (2018). A Social-Emotional Leadership Framework for School Counselors. *Professional School Counseling, 21*(1b), 1–10. doi:10.1177/2156759X18773004

Chassanoff, A., & Altman, M. (2020). Curation as "interoperability with the future": Preserving scholarly research software in academic libraries. *Journal of the Association for Information Science and Technology, 71*(3), 325–337. doi:10.1002/asi.24244

Dlamini, P. P., & Nokwanda, K. N. (2021). Preservation of traditional medicinal knowledge: Initiatives and techniques in rural communities in KwaZulu-Natal. *Library Philosophy and Practice (e-journal).* https://digitalcommons.unl.edu/libphilprac/4824

Elias, M. J. (2003). Academic and Social-Emotional Learning. Educational Practices Series – 11. Geneva, Switzerland: International Academy of Education and International Bureau of Education.

Grindley, N. (2010). Frameworks for e-Content. *Decoding the Digital Conference, DPC/Preservation Advisory Centre, BL.* Joint Information Systems Committee.https://www.dpconline.org/docs/miscellaneous/events/491-decoding grindley- pdf/file

Handayani, R. D., Wilujeng, I., & Prasetyo, Z. K. (2018). Elaborating Indigenous Knowledge in the Science Curriculum for the Cultural Sustainability. *Journal of Teacher Education for Sustainability, 20*(2), 74–88. doi:10.2478/jtes-2018-0016

Harry, D., & Kanehe, L. M. (2006) Asserting Tribal Sovereignty over Cultural Property: Moving Towards Protectio8n of Genetic Material and Indigenous Knowledge. *Seattle Journal for Social Justice, 5*(1). https://digitalcommons.law.seattleu.edu/sjsj/vol5/iss1/13

Humphrey, N. (2013). *Social and emotional learning: A critical appraisal.* Sage. doi:10.4135/9781446288603

Ihekwoaba, E. C., Okwor, R. N., Nnadi, C. U., Jidere, U. U., & Obim, I. E. (2022). Sustaining Indigenous knowledge through the digitization of information on Herbal Medicinei n Medical libraries in Nigeria: Problems and Prospects. *Library Philosophy and Practice (e-journal), 7316.* https://digitalcommons.unl.edu/libphilprac/7316

Innocenti, P., Ross, S., Maceciuvite, E., Wilson, T., Ludwig, J., & Pempe, W. (2009). Assessing Digital Preservation Frameworks: the approach of the SHAMAN project. *International ACM Conference on Management of Emergent Digital Eco Systems (MEDES'09), Proceedings of the International Conference on Management of Emergent Digital Eco Systems.* ACM. https://strathprints.strath.ac.uk/70503/1/Innocenti_etal_ MEDES_2009_Assessing_digital_preservation_frameworks_the_approach_of_the_SHAMAN project.pdf

José, R. C., & Carmen, D. (2016). Open Archival Information System (OAIS): Lights and shadows of a reference model. *Investigación Bibliotecológica, 30*(69), 227–253.

Kaya, H. O., & Seleti, Y. N. (2013). African indigenous knowledge systems and relevance of higher education in South Africa. *The International Education Journal: Comparative Perspectives, 12*(1), 30–44.

Kugara, S. L. (2017). *Witchcraft belief and criminal responsibility: A case study of selected areas in South Africa and Zimbabwe* [Doctoral dissertation, University of Venda].

Langtone, M. (2016). A moral compass that slipped: Indigenous knowledge systems and rural development in Zimbabwe. *Cogent Social Sciences, 2,* 1266749. doi:10.1080/23311886.2016.1266749

Lanzano, C. (2013). Kind of knowledge is "indigenous knowledge"? Critical insights from a case study in Burkina Faso. *Transcience, 4*(2), 1–16.

Lavoie, B. (2014). *The Open Archival Information System (OAIS) Reference Model: Introductory Guide* (2nd ed.). The Digital Preservation Coalition. doi:10.7207/twr14-02

Lee, C. A. (2010). *Open Archival Information System (OAIS) Reference Model. Encyclopedia of Library and Information Sciences* (3rd ed.). Taylor & Francis. doi:10.1081/E-ELIS3-120044377

Lee, K. H., Slattery, O., Lu, R., Tang, X., & McCrary, V. (2002). The State of the Art and Practice in Digital Preservation. *Journal of Research of the National Institute of Standards and Technology, 107*(1), 93–106. doi:10.6028/jres.107.010 PMID:27446721

Library Technology Reports. (2008). Preservation Practices. *Tech Source.* www.techsource.ala.org https://journals.ala.org/index.php/ltr/article/viewFile/4223/4806

Ljubetic, M., & Maglica, T. (2020). Social and emotional learning in education and care policy in Croatia. [IJERE]. *International Journal of Evaluation and Research in Education, 9*(3), 650–659. doi:10.11591/ijere.v9i3.20495

London Parliamentary Archives. (2008). *A digital preservation strategy for parliament.* Parliamentary Archives: House of Parliament London SW1A 0PW. https://www.parliament.uk/globalassets/documents/upload/digital-preservation- strategy- final-public-version.pdf

Mdhluli, T., Mokgoatšana, S., Kugara, S., & Vuma, L. (2021). Knowledge management: Preserving, managing and sharing indigenous knowledge through digital library. *HTS Teologiese Studies / Theological Studies, 77*(2). . doi:10.4102/hts.v77i2.6795

Nakata, M., Byrne, A., Nakata, V., & Gardiner, G. (2005). Indigenous Knowlege, the Library and Information Service Sector and Protocols. *Australian Academic and Research Libraries, 36*(2), 1–25.

National Open University of Nigeria. (2022). *Indigenous Knowledge Management.* NOUN Press.

OECD. (2018). The future of education and skills. *Education, 2030.* https://www.oecd.org/education/2030/

Oguche, D., & Aliyu, A. (2020). Towards a National Framework for Digital Preservation in Nigeria: Technologies and Best Practices. Information Impact. *Journal of Information and Knowledge Management, 11*(4), 146–155. doi:10.4314/iijikm.v11i4.14

Perry, S. R. (2014). *Digitization and digital preservation: a review of the literature.* Scholar Works. http://scholarworks.sjsu.edu/cgi/viewcontent.cgi?article=1170&context=slissrj

Procedures for Records Creation. (2021). *Digital Preservation Policy.* Heriot-Watt University, Edinburgh: United Kingdom. https://www.hw.ac.uk/documents/digital-preservation-procedures-records- creation.pdf

Rechert, K., Von, S. D., & Welte, R. (2010). Emulation based services in digital preservation. *Proceedings of the 10th Annual Joint Conference on Digital Libraries,* (pp. 365–368). ACM. 10.1145/1816123.1816182

Rimkus, K., Padilla, T., Popp, T., & Martin, G. (2014). Digital Preservation File Format Policies of ARL Member Libraries: An Analysis. *D-Lib Magazine : the Magazine of the Digital Library Forum, 3/4*(20), 1–11. doi:10.1045/march2014-rimkus

Roux, A. (2015). *Indigenous knowledge in a virtual context: Sustainable digital preservation. A literature review.* Unisa Library (SP PD6). https://core.ac.uk/display/188775692? utm_source=pdf&utm_medium=banner&utm_c ampaign=pdf-decoration-v1

Sarmah, S. S. (2018). Data Migration. *Science and Technology, 8*(1), 1–10. doi:10.5923/j.scit.20180801.01

Sarumaha, M. S. (2019). Educational Management Based on Indigenous Knowledge (Narrative Studies of Culture of Indigenous Knowledge in South Nias). *Advances in Social Science, Education and Humanities Research, 410*(1), 150–133.

Sawyer, D., Reich, L., Giaretta, D., Mazal, P., Huc, C., Nonon-Latapie, M., & Peccia, N. (2002). *The Open Archival Information System (OAIS) Reference Model and its Usage.* UNC. https://ils.unc.edu/callee/p4020-lee.pdf

Settee, P. (2007). *Pimatisiwin: Indigenous knowledge systems, our time has come.* [Master's thesis, University of Saskatchew].

Sibsankar, J., Mrinal, K., & Ujjal, M. (2009). *Digital Preservation with Special Reference to the Open Archival Information System (OAIS) Reference Model: An Overview.* 7th International CALIBER-2009, Pondicherry University.

Thibodeau, K. (2002). Overview of Technological Approaches to Digital Preservation and Challenges in Coming Years Digital Preservation: An International Perspective. *Conference Proceedings.* CLIR. https://www.clir.org/PUBS/reports/pub107/pub107.pdf

UNESCO. (2021). *Documentary heritage at risk: Policy gaps in digital preservation.* International Advisory Committee of the UNESCO Memory of the World Programme. https://en.unesco.org/sites/default/files/documentary_ heritage_at_risk_policy_gaps_in_digital_preservation_en.pdf

UNITAR. (2021). Strategic Framework 2018-2021. United Nation Institute for Training and Research (UNITAR). UNITAR. https://unitar.org/sites/default/files/media/publication/doc/unitar_strategicframework_web-new.pdf

Von, S. D., Rechert, K., & Valizada, I. (2013). *Towards emulation-as-a-service: Cloud services for versatile digital object access.* IJDC. doi:10.2218/ijdc.v8i1.250

ADDITIONAL READING

Ezeanya-Esiobu, C. (2019). *Indigenous knowledge and education in Africa.* Frontiers in African Business Research, Los Angeles: USA. https://library.oapen.org/bitstream/id/bc50d2c2- 78d3-4252-aef4-fbfabb7c8116/10068 86.pdf

Maemura, E., Moles, N., & Becker, C. (2017). Organizational assessment frameworks for digital preservation: A literature review and mapping. *Journal of the Association for Information Science and Technology, 68*(7), 1619–1637. doi:10.1002/asi.23807

Plockey, F. D. (2015). Indigenous Knowledge Production, Digital Media and Academic Libraries in Ghana. *The Journal of Pan African Studies, 8*(4), 32–44.

KEY TERMS AND DEFINITIONS

Digital Preservation: Digital preservation is an innovative activity that consists of varied levels of actions involving technical approaches with the help of computer and its accessories like the hardware and software components of the computer for ensuring that analogue resources are easily converted to digital resources for a long period of time for researchers and general purpose.

Emotional Framework: Emotional framework takes into consideration the well-being and personality of indigenous people as it relates to how they develop and succeed in their pattern of living and behaviour as indigenous people.

Indigenous Knowledge: Indigenous knowledge is a native group of activities that cover a wider range of aspects like language, norms, behaviors, farming and healthcare systems held by indigents for survival which is passed from generation to generation.

OAIS Model for Digital Preservation of Indigenous Knowledge Systems

Intellectual Framework: Intellectual framework explains the intellectual capability of researchers in converting indigenous knowledge systems into digital data made accessible to all over a long period of time.

Policy Framework: Policy framework are guiding principles which gives the process of digital preservation necessary information required for harvesting indigenous knowledge from indigenous people within extant laws.

Strategic Framework: Strategic framework is the tact involved in coordinating all relevant resources required for smooth transmission of indigenous knowledge systems to enable successful preservation of information and material digitally.

Chapter 18

Indigenous Research and Data Management in Electronic Archives:
A Framework for African Indigenous Communities

Valentine Joseph Owan
https://orcid.org/0000-0001-5715-3428
University of Calabar, Nigeria & Ultimate Research Network, Nigeria

Joseph Ojishe Ogar
https://orcid.org/0000-0003-0970-7283
Federal University Ndufu-Alike, Nigeria

Patience Okwudiri Nwosu
https://orcid.org/0009-0008-2406-8882
Taraba State University, Jalingo, Nigeria

Victor Ubugha Agama
University of Calabar, Nigeria & Ultimate Research Network, Nigeria

Anjali Verma
Government Degree College, Lahar, India

Favour-Ann Kyrian Nwoke
Alex Ekweme Federal University, Nigeria

ABSTRACT

This chapter introduces a framework for indigenous research and data management in electronic archives that aligns with indigenous worldviews and practices. It discusses indigenous communities' challenges in owning and controlling their data and the need for a culturally relevant framework for managing indigenous data in electronic archives. The proposed eight-step framework emphasises community control, data sovereignty, and ethical data management practices; and includes key components such as community engagement, informed consent, and culturally relevant metadata standards. Best practices for data sharing and partnership building with non-indigenous institutions are also discussed, as well as the steps for implementing the framework and the role of stakeholders in the process. Evaluation metrics for measuring the framework's success are proposed. The chapter concludes by emphasising the importance of community control and ethical data management practices in preserving and protecting indigenous cultural heritage and identity in electronic archives.

DOI: 10.4018/978-1-6684-7024-4.ch018

Indigenous Research and Data Management in Electronic Archives

INTRODUCTION

Indigenous data management in electronic archives has significant implications for indigenous communities, research, and society (Smith, 2021). It is crucial to empower indigenous communities to take ownership and control of their data, ensuring that their cultural heritage and knowledge are preserved and protected for future generations (Kim et al., 2019; Ruhanen & Whitford, 2019). This promotes self-determination and reinforces the value of indigenous knowledge systems and practices. In addition, it enables researchers to conduct more culturally sensitive and ethical research by engaging with indigenous communities and gaining a deeper understanding of their knowledge, culture, and values (Anderson & Cidro, 2019; Hyett et al., 2019; Mashford-Pringle & Pavagadhi, 2020). Furthermore, indigenous data management in electronic archives promotes knowledge sharing and collaboration between indigenous and non-indigenous communities, contributing to recognising and appreciating indigenous knowledge and perspectives. This can help bridge the gap between indigenous and non-indigenous communities and promote social cohesion (Gupta et al., 2023). By acknowledging the importance of indigenous data and collaborating with indigenous communities, non-indigenous institutions can help to rebuild trust and support broader societal goals of reconciliation and social justice (McGregor et al., 2023).

A framework for indigenous research and data management in electronic archives is therefore, needed to be guided by indigenous worldviews and practices. This chapter proposes an 8-step framework that includes indigenous data collection, curation/processing, analysis/synthesis, storage, security/backup, retrieval, sharing/communication, and reuse. The framework is guided by community control, data sovereignty, and ethical data management practices that align with indigenous worldviews and practices. The chapter thus discusses best practices for indigenous data management in electronic archives, emphasising the importance of developing data-sharing protocols and establishing partnerships between indigenous communities and non-indigenous institutions.

CONCEPT OF INDIGENOUS RESEARCH AND DATA

Indigenous research is an approach that values and respects indigenous knowledge, perspectives, and ways of knowing. It involves collaborating with indigenous peoples to promote self-determination and empower indigenous communities. Smith (2021) argues that a critical examination of research practices and the impact of colonialism on indigenous peoples is necessary for indigenous research. This approach recognises the importance of oral traditions, community-based knowledge and the use of indigenous languages in research (Wilson, 2020). In addition, indigenous research requires a culturally sensitive approach that respects indigenous protocols and values. This includes obtaining free, prior and informed consent from indigenous communities before conducting research while also ensuring that research benefits the community, and protecting the privacy and confidentiality of research participants (Bassey & Owan, 2023; Owan et al., 2023). Smith (2021) emphasises that a decolonising approach to research must challenge the dominant research paradigm and promote indigenous knowledge and ways of knowing.

On the other hand, indigenous data refers to the information generated, collected and analysed by indigenous communities for their purposes and decision-making processes. This data is based on indigenous knowledge systems, cultural practices and ways of knowing and often includes traditional ecological knowledge, oral histories, and other forms of knowledge that are not typically captured in

Western-style data collection methods (Smith, 2021). Indigenous data has gained increasing recognition in recent years as a way to empower indigenous communities to take ownership of their data and use it for their purposes. This has been partly driven by concerns about the exploitation of indigenous data by non-indigenous researchers and institutions and the need to support indigenous self-determination and governance (Oguamanam, 2020). Indigenous data sovereignty is a related concept that refers to the right of indigenous peoples to control the collection, ownership, and use of their data. This includes the right to determine how data is collected and who has access to it, as well as the right to use data for their purposes and to protect it from exploitation (Kukutai & Taylor, 2016).

TYPES OF INDIGENOUS DATA

There are several types of indigenous data which include:

- **Traditional Knowledge**

This type of data encompasses the knowledge, practices, and beliefs passed down through generations of indigenous peoples. It often includes environmental knowledge, such as traditional land management practices, medicinal plants, and wildlife behaviour (Walter & Suina, 2019). It can also include cultural knowledge, ceremonial practices, language and art. Traditional knowledge is often based on a deep understanding of the natural world and reflects indigenous perspectives and values.

- **Oral Histories**

Oral histories are a type of indigenous data that are transmitted through verbal narratives and story-telling from one generation to the next. This type of data often includes stories, legends, and myths that explain the origins of the world and the values and beliefs of indigenous communities. Oral histories can provide insight into the historical and cultural contexts in which indigenous communities exist and can serve as a way to preserve cultural knowledge.

- **Indigenous Language Data**

Indigenous language data refers to indigenous languages' words, grammar, and syntax. This data type is often used to understand indigenous peoples' linguistic and cultural heritage. Many indigenous languages are endangered or have been lost, so the preservation and study of language data are crucial for the continuation of indigenous cultures (Ruckstuhl, 2022).

- **Community-Based Research Data**

Community-based research data is produced through research projects collaborating with indigenous communities. This type of data often reflects the perspectives and priorities of indigenous peoples and can be used to address community needs and concerns, and it is often guided by reciprocity, respect, and shared decision-making principles (Arxer, 2019; Jason & Glenwick, 2016).

Indigenous Research and Data Management in Electronic Archives

- **Genealogical Data**

Genealogical data is a type of indigenous data that relates to family histories and lineages. This type of data is often used to understand indigenous communities' social and cultural structures, kinship systems, and inheritance practices. Genealogical data can establish legal and cultural connections to traditional lands and territories (Gavrilov et al., 2002; Liu et al., 2017).

- **Environmental Data**

Environmental data refers to indigenous peoples' observations and knowledge about their natural environment. This type of data is often used to inform environmental management and conservation efforts. indigenous communities have a long history of living in a close relationship with the natural world, and their knowledge can be invaluable for understanding ecological systems and developing sustainable practices.

- **Artistic and Cultural Data**

Artistic and cultural data includes a range of creative expressions, such as music, dance, and visual arts. This type of data often reflects indigenous communities' cultural traditions and values. It can provide insight into indigenous peoples' histories, beliefs, and practices and serve as a means of cultural expression and preservation.

CONCEPT OF ELECTRONIC ARCHIVES

Electronic archives refer to collections of digital records that are preserved and made available for future access and use (Owan, 2022). The International Council on Archives described electronic archives as a set of digital records, preserved for their long-term value, authenticity and reliability, and made accessible to users over time (ICA, 2017). Electronic archives can include various types of digital content such as text documents, images, audio and video recordings and data sets. Electronic archives are becoming increasingly important as more information is being created and stored in digital format, and as the need for long-term preservation of this information becomes more pressing. However, the electronic archives must be authentic, reliable, usable and have the integrity to be valuable to society. Thus, electronic archives are typically managed using specialised software to ensure the integrity and authenticity of digital records and provide search, retrieval and access control mechanisms.

Types of Electronic Archives

The following are types of electronic archives:

- **Digital Document Archives**

Digital document archives store digital versions of physical documents such as books, manuscripts, photographs, maps, and other primary source materials. They are often used by scholars and researchers studying history, literature, and other humanities subjects. These archives allow users to access primary source materials from anywhere worldwide, which can be especially useful for researchers who cannot visit physical archives. Digital document archives also help preserve physical materials that may be fragile or deteriorating, ensuring they are available for future generations (Matlala, 2019).

- **Web Archives**

Web archives capture and preserve web pages and other online content, providing a snapshot of how the internet looked at a particular point in time, and are created by web crawlers, which automatically scan and capture web pages and other online content (Vlassenroot et al., 2019). These archives are important for researchers studying social, cultural and political phenomena documented online, such as the development of social media or the evolution of online activism.

- **Multimedia Archives**

Multimedia archives store audio and video recordings, photographs, and other digital media. Multimedia archives are used in various fields, including journalism, film studies, and anthropology. These archives may be organised by subject, date or other criteria and often include metadata such as descriptions and tags that make it easier to find specific media files. Multimedia archives also play an important role in preserving cultural heritage, as they allow for the preservation and sharing of traditional music, dance, and other forms of artistic expression.

- **Social Media Archives**

Social media archives are typically created by web crawlers or other automated tools that capture content from social media platforms such as Twitter, Facebook, and Instagram (Anderson, 2020; Pehlivan et al., 2021). These archives capture and preserve social media content, including posts, comments and other interactions, and are used by researchers studying topics such as social movements, political campaigns, public opinion as well as journalists and other media professionals to track breaking news and monitor public sentiment.

- **Research Data Archives**

These archives store data from scientific studies and other research projects. Scientists and researchers in various fields, including biology, physics, and social sciences, use research data archives. They may be organised by discipline or topic, often including metadata describing the data and its sources. Research data archives help to ensure that scientific data is available for future studies and can be used to verify or build upon existing research (Bossaller & Million, 2022).

- **Institutional Archives**

Institutional archives store digital records and documents related to the activities of an institution such as a university or government agency, and are often used for administrative purposes such as tracking budgets, personnel records and other institutional data. These archives may also include reports, policy documents and other materials documenting the institution's activities.

- **Personal Archives**

Personal archives store personal digital records such as email correspondence, photographs and personal documents. Individuals or families may create and maintain personal archives to preserve history and memories and may include family photographs, personal journals and other materials documenting the individual's or family's life and experiences.

ELECTRONIC ARCHIVES AND INDIGENOUS DATA MANAGEMENT: THE NEXUS

Electronic archives and indigenous data management are two concepts that have become increasingly important in recent years. The nexus between these two concepts lies in ensuring that indigenous data is managed in a culturally appropriate manner and that electronic archives do not further perpetuate historical injustices. Indigenous data management is a critical issue because data collected from indigenous communities have historically been used to dispossess them of their land, culture, and rights (Cormack & Kukutai, 2022). The collection of this data has often been done without the informed consent of the communities, and the data has been used to justify discriminatory policies and practices. As a result, indigenous communities have become increasingly distrustful of external researchers and institutions that collect and use their data (Figueiredo et al., 2020). The field of indigenous data sovereignty has emerged in response to these issues (Rainie et al., 2019; Walter et al., 2021). This field recognises that indigenous communities have the right to own, control and govern their data. Indigenous data sovereignty involves working with indigenous communities to ensure that their data is collected, managed and analysed culturally appropriately. This approach requires a recognition of the importance of indigenous knowledge systems and a commitment to building relationships of trust and respect with indigenous communities.

Electronic archives can play an important role in supporting indigenous data sovereignty. The digitisation of information can make it more accessible to indigenous communities and help to preserve their cultural heritage. However, the digitisation of information can also be a source of concern if it is done without the appropriate cultural protocols and consent from indigenous communities. Electronic archives must be designed and implemented to respect indigenous data sovereignty and support community goals. One way to ensure electronic archives are designed and implemented culturally is to involve indigenous communities. Indigenous communities should be involved in planning, designing, and implementing electronic archives that relate to their data, and this involvement should be based on the principles of informed consent and respect for cultural protocols. Indigenous communities should also be consulted on issues such as access, storage, and use of their data in electronic archives. These communities should also be involved in decisions about using digital technologies and tools to manage, analyse and preserve their data.

Another important issue related to electronic archives and indigenous data management is the protection of privacy and confidentiality. Indigenous communities can control their data and decide who can access it. Electronic archives must thus be designed with appropriate security measures to protect the privacy and confidentiality of indigenous data and this includes using encryption and access controls to prevent unauthorised access and ensuring that data is only used for purposes agreed upon by the community.

IMPORTANCE OF INDIGENOUS DATA MANAGEMENT IN ELECTRONIC ARCHIVES

The following are some reasons why managing indigenous data in electronic archives is important:

- **Complete Data Security**

Regarding indigenous data and knowledge, complete data security is particularly important as this information may be sensitive and sacred to the community. Storing this information in physical files can be risky as they may be lost, damaged or accessed by unauthorised persons. Digital archival provides a secure way of storing indigenous data and knowledge, ensuring that it is protected and only accessible to authorised individuals (Hunter, 2005). With digital archival, you can encrypt and password-protect files, use firewalls and antivirus software to protect against cyber threats, and backup files to prevent data loss (Maina, 2012). This level of security is crucial for protecting the integrity of indigenous data and knowledge and ensuring its long-term preservation.

- **Simpler to Manage**

The digital archival of indigenous data or knowledge in digital archives allows for easier sharing and collaboration between individuals and organisations. Physical documents may be limited to one location, making it difficult for individuals in different locations to access the same information. With digital archives, access to data is not limited by location, and multiple users can access the same data simultaneously, regardless of location (Müngen, 2022). This makes it easier for indigenous communities to collaborate and share their knowledge with others who may be interested in learning from them. In addition, the ease of access and sharing allows for better protection of indigenous data or knowledge from unauthorised use, as access can be controlled and monitored. Thus, digital archival simplifies managing and sharing indigenous data/knowledge while providing better protection against misuse.

- **Cost Saving**

Digital archival can also result in significant cost savings (Boczar et al., 2023; Jahn et al., 2020; Pillen & Eckard, 2023). Indigenous communities may have limited resources and budget constraints, which makes it challenging to maintain and preserve physical documents. By switching to digital archival, indigenous communities can reduce inventory and stationery costs and save on the expenses of transporting physical documents to different locations. This is especially important for preserving indigenous knowledge across different regions or communities. Moreover, digital archival can also help reduce the costs of managing and preserving physical documents. Indigenous communities can easily organise, store, and retrieve digital documents without worrying about physical storage limitations or damage due to environmental factors. This makes it easier for indigenous communities to access and share their knowledge, supporting their cultural preservation and development efforts.

Indigenous Research and Data Management in Electronic Archives

- **Collaborative Access and Editing**

Digital archives make it easier for multiple users to access and edit the same document simultaneously (Goldin et al., 2022), even in different locations (Cannelli & Musso, 2022; Jaillant, 2022; Jaillant & Rees, 2023). This allows for more efficient collaboration among individuals and teams working on a project. For example, multiple indigenous communities and organisations can collaborate on a digital archive to share their knowledge and preserve their cultural heritage.

- **Improved Search and Retrieval**

Digital archives use advanced search algorithms, making locating specific documents or data easier. Users can search for documents using keywords, tags, or other metadata (Owan, 2022), and this makes it easier to find relevant information quickly and efficiently.

OVERVIEW OF EXISTING FRAMEWORKS AND MODELS FOR INDIGENOUS DATA MANAGEMENT

Indigenous data management is a complex and evolving field that requires consideration of cultural, ethical and legal factors. Recently, there has been an increased focus on developing culturally appropriate, respectful, and effective frameworks and models for indigenous data management. This chapter reviewed existing frameworks and models for indigenous data management and discuss their key features and limitations.

The National Aboriginal Health Organization (NAHO) in Canada developed one of the earliest frameworks for indigenous data management. The framework is known as the Ownership, Control, Access, and Possession (OCAP) principles that guides indigenous communities and organisations in managing their data in a culturally appropriate and respectful manner (Kukutai & Taylor, 2016). The OCAP principles emphasise the importance of respecting indigenous communities' ownership and control of data, ensuring that data is accessible to community members, and protecting the confidentiality of personal and sensitive data (First Nations Information Governance Centre, 2014).

Another key framework for indigenous data management is the Te Mana Raraunga framework developed by the Maori Data Sovereignty Network in New Zealand (Maori Data Sovereignty Network, 2019). This framework is based on the principles of mana (authority), tiaki (guardianship) and kaitiakitanga (stewardship) and emphasises the importance of respecting Maori cultural values and practices in data management. The framework guides on issues such as data governance, data ownership, and data sharing and emphasises the importance of community involvement in decision-making processes (Maori Data Sovereignty Network, 2019).

In addition to these frameworks, several models for indigenous data management have been developed in specific contexts. For example, Canada's Inuvialuit Settlement Region (ISR) has developed a data management model emphasising community involvement in data collection, analysis and interpretation (Inuvialuit Regional Corporation, 2017). The model involves establishing a community-based data management system controlled by the community and providing access to data relevant to the community's needs and interests.

349

Another model for indigenous data management is the Indigenous Data Sovereignty model developed by the Aboriginal and Torres Strait Islander Data Archive in Australia (Aboriginal and Torres Strait Islander Data Archive, 2021). This model emphasises the importance of indigenous self-determination in data management and calls for developing indigenous-led data governance structures grounded in indigenous cultural values and practices.

Despite the growing number of frameworks and models for indigenous data management, some key challenges and limitations still need to be addressed. One of the main challenges is the lack of resources and capacity for indigenous communities and organisations to implement these frameworks and models effectively (Kukutai & Taylor, 2016). This can result in a lack of standardisation and consistency in data management practices, limiting the usefulness and comparability of data across different contexts. Another challenge is balancing the competing demands of data protection and sharing (First Nations Information Governance Centre, 2014). Indigenous communities are often concerned about using their data by external researchers or government agencies and may be hesitant to share data outside the community. However, data sharing is also important for promoting collaboration and knowledge exchange and can help to address health and social disparities. Another challenge is that indigenous data management's ethical and legal considerations constantly evolve and newer frameworks and models are needed to reflect these changes. Furthermore, the impact of globalisation and digitalisation on indigenous communities is complex and multifaceted, and newer frameworks and models are needed to address the challenges and opportunities that arise from these trends.

A FRAMEWORK FOR INDIGENOUS RESEARCH AND DATA MANAGEMENT

The framework developed in this chapter has eight broad steps, including indigenous data collection, indigenous data curation/processing, indigenous data analysis/synthesis, indigenous data storage, indigenous data security/backup, indigenous data retrieval, indigenous data sharing/communication, and indigenous data reuse. These steps were extracted from the 16 data management practices in previous work (Owan & Bassey, 2019), and the five data management practices in another (Odigwe et al., 2020). The eight steps were selected to develop the framework in this chapter carefully due to their applicability in indigenous data management systems.

Step 1: Indigenous Data Collection

Indigenous data collection refers to the process of collecting and analysing data that is relevant to indigenous communities, and this data can be used for various purposes, including improving policies, programs, and services that affect indigenous peoples. Indigenous data collection typically involves working with indigenous communities to understand their specific needs and priorities and ensuring that data is collected in a culturally appropriate and respectful manner. This may involve developing partnerships with indigenous organisations, using indigenous research methodologies, and involving indigenous community members in all stages of the data collection process. Generating data requires appropriate methods and instruments to ensure the validity of study findings (Sileyew, 2020). It is crucial to collect data accurately, as erroneous data can lead to misleading research results (Owan & Bassey, 2019). To collect accurate data, researchers and their teams must have the necessary skills and knowledge, while

Indigenous Research and Data Management in Electronic Archives

respondents or the studied phenomena must provide truthful details. The framework to guide indigenous data collection is presented in Table 1.

Step 2: Indigenous Data Curation/Processing

Data curation refers to the process of selecting, organising, and maintaining data for use in research, analysis, or other purposes. It involves ensuring that data is consistent, accurate, and high-quality. Data curation involves several steps, including cleaning, normalisation, and integration. The data collection process may result in not immediately usable data, requiring data cleaning to improve data quality (Owan & Bassey, 2019). Subsequently, meaningful information can be derived through data analysis, leading to potential problem resolution or improvement (Banerjee et al., 2013). On the other hand, data processing is manipulating, transforming, and analysing data to derive insights or create useful information. Data processing involves several steps, including transformation and visualisation (French, 1996). Table 2 presents a framework that can be used to direct the curation and processing of indigenous data.

Step 3: Indigenous Data Analysis/Synthesis

Data analysis is organising and interpreting data to extract valuable insights or information. It involves breaking down the data into its components or categories better to understand each (Owan & Bassey, 2019). Soler et al. (2016) describe data synthesis as combining diverse data sets from various sources, such as incorporating newly collected data with pre-existing data from different providers, to create a larger and more comprehensive dataset. Therefore, indigenous data analysis/synthesis refers to analysing and synthesising data collected from indigenous communities or relevant to indigenous peoples' experiences and perspectives. The goal is to gain a more comprehensive understanding of the studied issues and ensure that the findings contribute to positive outcomes for indigenous communities. A framework is provided in Table 3 that can guide the analysis and synthesis of indigenous data.

Table 1. A framework for indigenous data collection

Stakeholders	Activity/Expectation
Research team	The research team establish protocols and guidelines for data collection that prioritise the community's cultural traditions and knowledge systems. They work with community elders and knowledge keepers to collect data using culturally appropriate methods.
Indigenous community	The indigenous community is at the centre of this framework as their cultural traditions and knowledge systems are prioritised in the data collection process. They guide the research team in collecting, storing, and sharing data. The community also has the power to decide whether to participate in the research, and their consent must be obtained before any data collection can occur.
Elders and knowledge keepers	Elders and knowledge keepers are crucial stakeholders in this framework as they hold the community's cultural knowledge and traditions. They provide the research team with all relevant information through storytelling or responding to questions seeking further insights into their history, activities and practices.
Government agencies	Government agencies play a role in this framework by providing funding and support for the research project. They also ensure that the project follows ethical guidelines and standards for data collection, storage, and sharing. Government agencies are expected to perform supervisory and oversight functions.
Academia	Academia provides expertise and knowledge in data collection, analysis, and interpretation. Academia is expected to provide technical support to the research team, such as instrument development and validation, ensuring adherence to ethical standards.

Table 2. A framework for indigenous data curation and processing

Stakeholders	Activity/Expectation
Research team	The research team plays a critical role in this stage, as they are responsible for organising and processing the data using indigenous data curation tools and techniques. They must have expertise in indigenous data curation and be sensitive to the cultural context of the data.
Indigenous community	The indigenous community has a stake in curating and processing the data as it is their knowledge being represented. Community members can help identify the data types that are most important and relevant to their community. This can involve specifying the topics, issues, and questions the data should address.
Data managers	Data managers can work with indigenous communities to develop data management plans that outline how the data will be collected, organised, stored, and shared. Data managers can help ensure the quality and integrity of indigenous data by implementing quality control measures, such as data cleaning and validation procedures. They must have expertise in data management and indigenous data curation to ensure that the data is treated with respect and sensitivity.
Technology providers	Technology providers may be involved in this stage as they provide tools and platforms for the organisation and processing of the data. They must ensure their tools are culturally appropriate and respect indigenous knowledge systems.
Funding agencies	Funding agencies play a role in this stage as they support the curation and processing of the data. They may require that the data is organised and processed in a way consistent with best practices for indigenous data curation.

Table 3. A framework for indigenous data analysis and synthesis

Stakeholders	Activity/Expectation
Research team	The research analyses data using methods appropriate for indigenous research, such as community-based participatory research (CBPR) or two-eyed seeing. They also synthesise the data collected from indigenous communities to generate insights that are relevant and meaningful to them. This may involve identifying patterns, themes, or trends in the data and interpreting these findings in the context of indigenous knowledge systems and experiences.
Indigenous community	The indigenous community ensure that their perspectives are represented in the research. This can include participating in focus groups, workshops, or interviews to help interpret the data. The indigenous community validates the findings to ensure that the insights generated are accurate and meaningful. This process can involve reviewing reports or other materials and providing feedback to the research team.
Elders and knowledge keepers	The elders and knowledge keepers provide a cultural and spiritual lens. They ensure that the data is analysed respectfully and ethically and that the findings are interpreted within the community's cultural context. Their insights can also help to identify gaps in the data or areas where further research is needed. Elders and knowledge keepers provide valuable guidance in interpreting the data, particularly about traditional knowledge and practices. They contextualise the findings and ensure they are interpreted consistently with the community's values and beliefs.
Academia	In this stage, Academia provides technical expertise in data analysis and synthesis. This may involve using specialised software and statistical techniques to analyse large datasets or developing novel methods for analysing qualitative data. Academics also collaborate with elders and knowledge keepers to incorporate their insights and perspectives into the analysis process and ensure that the findings are presented in a culturally appropriate and respectful manner. Academics bridge the gap between indigenous communities and mainstream scientific communities by presenting research findings in a way that is accessible to both groups. This may involve using plain language summaries or visualisations to help communicate complex data to a broader audience.

Step 4: Indigenous Data Storage

Indigenous data storage refers to the various methods and systems used to store, manage, and protect data collected from or relevant to indigenous communities. Storing research data for future reference is a crucial process that enables researchers to retrace their steps in case of errors in analysis (Owan & Bassey, 2019). This includes traditional and modern storage methods like paper records, digital files, and cloud-based solutions. Data sovereignty is a key concept in indigenous data storage (Hummel et

Indigenous Research and Data Management in Electronic Archives

al., 2021; Lovett et al., 2019), which recognises the right of indigenous peoples to control and manage their data. However, the framework developed in Table 4 provides a guide for storing indigenous data in electronic archives.

Step 5: Indigenous Data Security/Backup

Data security involves implementing protective measures to prevent unauthorised access to private data across various platforms, such as computer systems, databases, websites, and mobile devices (Owan & Bassey, 2019). To ensure data security, it is necessary to consider physical security, network security, and the security of computer systems and files to prevent unauthorised access, modification, disclosure,

Table 4. A framework for indigenous data storage in electronic archives

Stakeholders	Activity/Expectation
Research team	The research team stores indigenous data in electronic archives after obtaining informed consent from participants. They ensure that the data are collected, managed, and stored culturally appropriately. The research team provides appropriate safeguards to protect participants' privacy and confidentiality. The research team collaborates with indigenous communities to ensure that the data is being stored and managed in a way that aligns with the values and beliefs of the community. This may involve engaging with elders and knowledge keepers to gain insights into traditional knowledge systems and cultural protocols.
Indigenous community	The indigenous community must be involved in the decision-making process around the storage and use of the data, and their informed consent should be obtained before any data is collected or stored. The community works with the research team to establish policies and practices that align with the community's values and beliefs and develop protocols for accessing and using the data. They should have access to information about the data storage and management processes and be informed about any potential risks or benefits associated with using their data. The community should also be involved in the ongoing management and governance of the data, including decisions around access and use. They should have a say in how the data is used and can revoke consent or limit access to the data if they feel that their privacy or cultural protocols are being compromised.
Data managers	Data managers ensure that the data is stored securely, with appropriate measures to prevent unauthorised access, loss, or theft. This may include implementing encryption and access control measures, regular backups, and disaster recovery planning. Data managers must document the data to make it easy to understand and use. This may include providing detailed metadata, documentation of the data collection process, and information on any relevant cultural protocols or ethical considerations. Data managers must ensure that the data is accessible to authorised users while also taking steps to protect the privacy and confidentiality of the data. This may involve implementing access controls, requiring users to sign confidentiality agreements, or providing remote access to the data through secure networks. Data managers must maintain the data over time, with appropriate measures to ensure its long-term preservation and accessibility. This may include regular data integrity checks, migration to new storage systems, and monitoring ongoing data usage and access.
Technology providers	Technology providers ensure that the electronic archives they provide are secure and confidential. This means implementing access controls, encryption, and firewalls to prevent unauthorised access, data breaches, and cyber-attacks. Technology providers ensure that the electronic archives are reliable, and the data is not lost or corrupted. This means providing redundant storage, backups, and disaster recovery plans to ensure that data can be recovered in case of a system failure or other disaster. Technology providers ensure that the electronic archives support appropriate data formats relevant to the indigenous communities' specific needs. This may include supporting languages, data structures, and data types relevant to indigenous communities. Technology providers must ensure that the electronic archives are accessible to the indigenous communities and that they can easily access and retrieve their data. Technology providers must ensure that the electronic archives are sustainable over time and can support the long-term storage and retrieval of indigenous data. This may include ongoing support, maintenance, and updates to ensure the archives remain relevant and useful to the indigenous communities.
Funding agencies	Funding agencies provide adequate funding to ensure indigenous data is properly stored and managed in electronic archives. This will enable researchers to access the data for future research purposes.

or destruction of data (Parker, 2012). Data backup enables researchers to safeguard research data against loss (Abduldayan et al., 2021). This involves storing the data across multiple files, locations, and media to ensure its availability during a disaster. Backup can be done manually using physical storage options or electronically through various online storage systems such as email, Google Drive, and cloud storage services (Owan & Bassey, 2019). In Table 5, a framework offering guidance on the security and backup of indigenous data in electronic archives has been developed.

Step 6: Indigenous Data Retrieval

Data retrieval allows authorised individuals to regain access to previously stored data, which can be used for various purposes such as verification, data reuse, error checking, observation, and reference (Owan

Table 5. A framework for indigenous data security and backup in electronic archives

Stakeholders	Activity/Expectation
Research team	The research team classify the indigenous data and ensure that access to it is restricted to authorised individuals only. They also implement access control measures such as password protection, encryption, and two-factor authentication to prevent unauthorised data access. The research team ensure that indigenous data are regularly backed up to prevent loss in case of a disaster. The research team ensures the electronic archives are regularly updated and upgraded to prevent vulnerabilities and ensure compatibility with new technologies. The team also ensures that any software or hardware used in the archives is patched and updated.
Indigenous community	The indigenous community asserts its ownership and control over the indigenous data ensuring that the data are being used in a manner that respects its cultural and intellectual property rights. The indigenous community gives informed consent and is consulted about using and sharing the indigenous data. The community should know who can access the data and for what purposes. The indigenous community should be vigilant in protecting the indigenous data from unauthorised access, use, and sharing. The indigenous community educate and raise awareness about the importance of indigenous data and its protection. The community should inform its members about the rights and responsibilities of using and sharing data.
Data managers	Data managers design and implement appropriate security measures to protect indigenous data. These measures may include access controls, firewalls, encryption, and intrusion detection systems. Data managers establish and implement regular backup and disaster recovery procedures to ensure indigenous data is protected and recoverable during a disaster or system failure. Data managers ensure that access to indigenous data is limited to authorised individuals only. The data storage infrastructure should be robust, reliable, and scalable to accommodate the growth of indigenous data. Access to the data should be controlled through authentication mechanisms, such as usernames and passwords. Data managers should provide training and awareness programs for personnel managing and using indigenous data.
Technology providers	Technology providers design and implement secure systems to protect indigenous data. The systems should use the latest security technologies and best practices to safeguard the data from unauthorised access, use, and disclosure. The systems should be scalable and flexible enough to accommodate indigenous data's growth and changing needs. Technology providers provide training and awareness programs for data managers and other personnel managing and using indigenous data.
Funding agencies	Funding agencies provide sufficient resources to support the development and maintenance of electronic archives. This includes the hardware, software, and staffing cost necessary to ensure the security and backup of indigenous data. Funding agencies develop clear policies and guidelines for the ethical use of indigenous data. Funding agencies ensure backup copies of indigenous data are created and stored in their directories or repositories in multiple locations to protect against data loss due to hardware failures, natural disasters, or other events.
Data Users	Data users comply with the security policies established by the funding agencies or institutions responsible for the electronic archives. Data users must understand the sensitivity of the data they are working with and treat it accordingly. Indigenous data may contain sensitive information about cultural practices, beliefs, and identities. Therefore, data users should be careful to protect this data from unauthorised access, loss, or theft. Data users should promptly report security incidents or breaches to the appropriate authorities. This can help minimise the incident's impact and prevent future incidents from occurring.

Indigenous Research and Data Management in Electronic Archives

& Bassey, 2019). Indigenous data retrieval refers to accessing, recovering, and utilising data collected, generated, or preserved by indigenous communities. The retrieval of indigenous data can serve several purposes, including the preservation of cultural heritage, the advancement of indigenous research and education, and the empowerment of indigenous communities. Principles of cultural respect, ethical considerations, and community engagement guide the process of indigenous data retrieval. Table 6 presents a framework that can assist in retrieving indigenous information from electronic archives.

Step 7: Indigenous Data Sharing/Communication

Sharing data benefits individual researchers and the scientific community (Longo & Drazen, 2016; Tenopir et al., 2011). According to Soler et al. (2016), data can be shared within the research team with external collaborators and can also be made publicly available. Indigenous data sharing and communication refer to the exchange of information between indigenous communities and individuals and other stakeholders such as researchers, policymakers, and governments. It involves sharing data, knowledge, and information collected, produced, or held by indigenous peoples and communities. Table 7 provides a framework for indigenous data sharing and communication in electronic archives.

Step 8: Indigenous Data Reuse

Data reuse refers to using previously collected data for different purposes, such as validating prior research findings or addressing new problems (Owan & Bassey, 2019). Researchers often reuse data from public repositories, especially for similar studies conducted in different locations (Park & Wolfram, 2017).

Table 6. A framework for indigenous data retrieval from electronic archives

Stakeholders	Activity/Expectation
Research team	The research team identifies the electronic archives that contain relevant indigenous information. This may involve searching online databases, archives, libraries, and other repositories. The research team determine if the archives have access restrictions or require permissions to retrieve the information. If access or permissions are required, the team must obtain them before proceeding. The research team must review the archives and identify the specific indigenous information relevant to their research objectives. This may involve searching for specific keywords, topics, or themes. Depending on the type of information and the archive, the research team may need to use different retrieval techniques. The research team ensures they follow the appropriate cultural protocols when retrieving indigenous information. The research team must document the retrieval process to ensure transparency and reproducibility. This may include documenting the search terms, the date and time of retrieval, the sources consulted, and any issues encountered. Once the indigenous information has been retrieved, the research team must analyse and interpret it in the appropriate cultural and historical contexts. This may involve working with community members and cultural authorities to ensure that the analysis and interpretation are respectful and accurate.
Indigenous community	Indigenous communities can start by identifying the electronic archives that contain their relevant indigenous information. Indigenous communities can establish partnerships and collaborations with research institutions, archives, and other organisations to retrieve their indigenous information. Indigenous communities can use appropriate legal and ethical frameworks to protect their rights and interests in retrieving their indigenous information. Indigenous communities can use appropriate retrieval techniques to access their indigenous information from electronic archives. This may involve working with research institutions and archives to use appropriate search terms, metadata, and other techniques to retrieve relevant information. Indigenous communities can document the retrieval process to ensure transparency and reproducibility. This may include documenting the search terms, the date and time of retrieval, the sources consulted, and any issues encountered.
Data managers	If data managers, technology providers, funding agencies and other users are interested in retrieving indigenous data from electronic archives, then the process is the same as for the research team above.

Table 7. A framework for indigenous data sharing and communication in electronic archives

Stakeholders	Activity/Expectation
Research team	The research team must obtain informed consent from the indigenous communities before sharing or communicating their data. The research team must acknowledge the source of the data and give credit to the indigenous communities for their contributions. This includes appropriate attribution in any publications, reports, or presentations using the data.
Indigenous community	The indigenous community provides informed consent for sharing and communicating their data. The indigenous community review and approve any data-sharing agreements before they are finalised. The indigenous community provide feedback and guidance on the use of the data. This includes providing input on any publications, reports, or presentations that use the data and providing guidance on appropriate language and terminology.
Government agencies	Government agencies respect the rights of indigenous communities when sharing and communicating their data. This includes recognising and upholding the United Nations Declaration on the Rights of Indigenous Peoples, which affirms the right of Indigenous peoples to control their data and determine how it is used. Government agencies must take measures to protect the privacy and confidentiality of indigenous data. This includes implementing appropriate security measures, such as access controls and encryption, to ensure the data is not accessed or used inappropriately.
Academic institutions	Academic institutions must recognise and respect the sovereignty of indigenous communities when sharing and communicating their data. This includes acknowledging their right to control their data and determine how it is used. Academic institutions must develop policies that guide sharing and communication of indigenous data. These policies should be developed in consultation with indigenous communities and reflect their cultural protocols and values.
Data managers	Data managers respect the rights of indigenous communities when sharing and communicating their data. Data managers provide appropriate access and use agreements that reflect the rights and interests of the indigenous communities. These agreements should include provisions for data ownership, intellectual property rights, and the appropriate use and dissemination of the data. Data managers ensure that the data is of high quality and integrity and accurately reflects the indigenous communities' cultural and linguistic practices.
Data Users	Data users recognise and respect the sovereignty of indigenous communities when using their data. This includes acknowledging their right to control their data and determining how it is used. Data users follow appropriate protocols and guidelines for the use of indigenous data. This includes seeking approval from the indigenous community before using their data and complying with any agreed-upon data use restrictions. Data users acknowledge the source of the data and provide appropriate attribution to the indigenous community that provided it.

Data can have a longer lifespan than the research projects produced, allowing for continued analysis and reuse by other researchers even after the initial funding has ended (Owan & Bassey, 2019). However, it is important to note that the reuse of indigenous data must be done ethically and respectfully, fully considering the rights and interests of the indigenous peoples or communities involved. Table 8 provides a framework for indigenous data reuse in electronic archives.

PRINCIPLES AND VALUES GUIDING THE FRAMEWORK

The indigenous data management framework is guided by a set of principles and values that are important to indigenous communities. These principles and values reflect indigenous peoples' unique cultural and historical context and their relationship to data. Here are some of the principles and values that guide the framework:

- *Self-determination:* Indigenous communities have the right to determine how their data is collected, used, and shared. The framework respects and prioritises indigenous ownership and control over the data.

Indigenous Research and Data Management in Electronic Archives

Table 8. A framework for indigenous data reuse in electronic archives

Stakeholders	Activity/Expectation
Research team	Researchers should obtain informed consent from the indigenous community or individuals who are the custodians of the data. Researchers should collaborate with indigenous communities and involve them in the research process. This may include co-designing research questions, co-analysing the data, and co-authoring research outputs. Researchers should acknowledge the sources and ownership of the data and ensure that appropriate credit is given to the indigenous community or individuals who have contributed to the data.
Indigenous community	Indigenous communities establish ownership and control of their data and have a say in how it is used and shared. Indigenous communities monitor who has access to their data and how it is used. This may involve setting up review committees or working with trusted intermediaries to manage access to the data. Indigenous communities should ensure that the reuse of their data in electronic archives benefits the community and is not exploitative.
Data managers	Data managers ensure that indigenous data is stored securely, and that confidentiality and privacy are maintained before reuse. Data managers implement appropriate metadata standards that accurately describe the indigenous data and ensure it can be easily discovered and accessed. Data managers implement appropriate data curation and preservation practices to ensure that the indigenous data is properly curated and preserved for future generations. Data managers ensure that the reuse of indigenous data in electronic archives complies with ethical and legal requirements, including informed consent, intellectual property rights, and data protection regulations.
Data Users	Data users respect indigenous communities' ownership and control of indigenous data. Data users acknowledge the source of the indigenous data and cite the original researchers or indigenous community from which the data was obtained. Data users should use indigenous data ethically and follow relevant guidelines and legal requirements. Data users should use the indigenous data responsibly to contribute to the well-being of the indigenous community. This may involve ensuring that the research benefits the indigenous community, respecting the cultural and spiritual significance of the data, and ensuring that the research is conducted in a culturally appropriate manner.

- *Indigenous knowledge:* Indigenous knowledge is valued and respected in the framework. The framework recognises that indigenous knowledge systems are diverse and complex and important for understanding the relationships between indigenous peoples, their environments, and their cultures.
- *Community engagement:* The framework is designed to engage indigenous communities in all stages of the data management process. Community members are involved in developing protocols and guidelines for data collection, processing, storage, retrieval, sharing, and reuse.
- *Cultural safety:* The framework promotes cultural safety by recognising indigenous peoples' unique cultural and historical context. The framework is designed to be sensitive to indigenous communities' cultural values and traditions and promote the well-being and safety of indigenous individuals and communities.
- *Respect for indigenous intellectual property rights:* The framework recognises the importance of indigenous intellectual property rights and seeks to protect them. Indigenous communities have the right to control their data, and the framework ensures that data is shared and reused in a way that respects these rights.
- *Trust and transparency:* The framework is designed to be transparent and trustworthy, with clear protocols and guidelines for all stages of the data management process. indigenous communities can trust that their data is being managed in a way that respects their rights and values.
- *Reciprocity:* The framework recognises that indigenous data management is two-way, with benefits flowing both ways. Indigenous communities may share their data with others, but they also have the right to benefit from using their data. The framework ensures that benefits are shared fairly and equitably.

EVALUATION METRICS FOR MEASURING THE SUCCESS OF THE FRAMEWORK

Several metrics can be used to evaluate the framework's success in managing indigenous data in electronic archives. These metrics include:

- **Data quality:** The quality of the data collected, processed, and analysed can be evaluated based on criteria such as accuracy, completeness, and relevance.
- **Data security:** The security of the data can be evaluated based on criteria such as access controls, encryption, and backup and recovery procedures.
- **Data accessibility:** The accessibility of the data can be evaluated based on criteria such as ease of retrieval, availability of metadata, and compliance with relevant data-sharing policies and guidelines.
- **Cultural and ethical considerations:** The framework's success can also be evaluated based on criteria related to cultural and ethical considerations, such as the involvement of the indigenous community in the data collection process, respect for the privacy and dignity of individuals involved, and acknowledgement of the source and ownership of the data.
- **User satisfaction:** The satisfaction of users, such as researchers and community members, with the framework, can be evaluated through surveys or interviews to assess ease of use, appropriateness, and effectiveness.
- **Impact:** These impact of the framework on research, education, and community development can be evaluated by tracking the number of publications, presentations, and other outputs that use the data, as well as by assessing the benefits and outcomes of the research and other activities enabled by the framework.

CONCLUSION AND RECOMMENDATIONS

This chapter contributes to indigenous data management in electronic archives by proposing a comprehensive framework that reflects indigenous worldviews and practices. The framework provides an 8-step approach that includes key components such as community engagement, informed consent, and the development of culturally relevant metadata standards. The chapter concludes that indigenous data management in electronic archives offers valuable contributions to the empowerment of indigenous communities, ethical research practices, knowledge sharing, and reconciliation efforts. Indigenous data management in electronic archives has important implications for indigenous communities, research, and society. It empowers indigenous communities to own and control their data, allowing for preserving their cultural heritage and promoting self-determination. Researchers benefit from a better understanding of indigenous knowledge and practices, leading to more culturally sensitive and ethical research. Knowledge-sharing between indigenous and non-indigenous communities promotes social cohesion and ethical data management practices contribute to reconciliation efforts. Future research should focus on the ethical, legal, and social implications of indigenous data management, developing best practices and standards, and greater recognition and support within society. Future research should also focus on further exploring and refining these practices while addressing the broader societal implications and ensuring

Indigenous Research and Data Management in Electronic Archives

the recognition and support of indigenous data management within the field. Based on the framework developed in this chapter, it is recommended that iindigenous communities should participate in training programs to gain a comprehensive understanding of indigenous data management practices, ethical considerations and technical skills. Researchers and digital archivists should facilitate and conduct training programs, sharing expertise and knowledge on data management practices with indigenous communities. Indigenous communities should engage in collaborative governance processes by actively participating in the development and implementation of data management frameworks, policies, and decision-making.

REFERENCES

Abduldayan, F. J., Abifarin, F. P., Oyedum, G. U., & Alhassan, J. A. (2021). Research data management practices of chemistry researchers in federal universities of technology in Nigeria. *Digital Library Perspectives*, *37*(4), 328–348. doi:10.1108/DLP-06-2020-0051

Anderson, K., & Cidro, J. (2019). Decades of doing: Indigenous women academics reflect on the practices of community-based health research. *Journal of Empirical Research on Human Research Ethics; JERHRE*, *14*(3), 222–233. doi:10.1177/1556264619835707 PMID:31018813

Anderson, K. E. (2020). Getting acquainted with social networks and apps: Capturing and archiving social media content. *Library Hi Tech News*, *37*(2), 18–22. doi:10.1108/LHTN-03-2019-0011

Banerjee, A., Bandyopadhyay, T., & Acharya, P. (2013). Data analytics: Hyped-up aspirations or true potential? *Vikalpa*, *38*(4), 1–12. doi:10.1177/0256090920130401

Bossaller, J., & Million, A. J. (2022). The research data life cycle, legacy data, and dilemmas in research data management. *Journal of the Association for Information Science and Technology*, 1–6. doi:10.1002/asi.24645

Cormack, D., & Kukutai, T. (2022). Indigenous Peoples, Data, and the Coloniality of Surveillance. In *New Perspectives in Critical Data Studies: The Ambivalences of Data Power* (pp. 121–141). Springer International Publishing. doi:10.1007/978-3-030-96180-0_6

Figueiredo, A., Rocha, C., & Montagna, P. (2020). Data collection with indigenous people: Fieldwork experiences from Chile. In *Researching peace, conflict, and power in the field: Methodological challenges and opportunities* (pp. 105–127). Springer International Publishing. doi:10.1007/978-3-030-44113-5_7

French, C. (1996). *Data processing and information technology* (10th ed.). Cengage Learning Business Press. https://bit.ly/3LXxLAC

Gupta, N., Martindale, A., Supernant, K., & Elvidge, M. (2023). The CARE Principles and the Reuse, Sharing, and Curation of Indigenous Data in Canadian Archaeology. *Advances in Archaeological Practice*, *11*(1), 76–89. doi:10.1017/aap.2022.33

Hummel, P., Braun, M., Tretter, M., & Dabrock, P. (2021). Data sovereignty: A review. *Big Data & Society*, *8*(1), 2053951720982012. doi:10.1177/2053951720982012

Hyett, S. L., Gabel, C., Marjerrison, S., & Schwartz, L. (2019). Deficit-based indigenous health research and the stereotyping of indigenous peoples. *Canadian Journal of Bioethics, 2*(2), 102–109. doi:10.7202/1065690ar

International Council on Archives. (2017). *Electronic Records*. (Web Source). ICA. https://www.ica.org/en/what-archive

Kim, S., Whitford, M., & Arcodia, C. (2019). Development of intangible cultural heritage as a sustainable tourism resource: The intangible cultural heritage practitioners' perspectives. *Journal of Heritage Tourism, 14*(5-6), 422–435. doi:10.1080/1743873X.2018.1561703

Kukutai, T., & Taylor, J. (2016). *Indigenous data sovereignty: Toward an agenda*. ANU press., doi:10.22459/CAEPR38.11.2016

Longo, D. L., & Drazen, J. M. (2016). Data sharing. *The New England Journal of Medicine, 374*(3), 276–277. doi:10.1056/NEJMe1516564 PMID:26789876

Lovett, R., Lee, V., Kukutai, T., Cormack, D., Rainie, S. C., & Walker, J. (2019). Good data practices for Indigenous data sovereignty and governance. In A. Daly, S. K. Devitt, & M. Mann (Eds.), *Good data* (pp. 26–36). Institute of Network Cultures. http://bit.ly/3LTVJNo

Mashford-Pringle, A., & Pavagadhi, K. (2020). Using OCAP and IQ as frameworks to address a history of trauma in Indigenous health research. *AMA Journal of Ethics, 22*(10), 868–873. doi:10.1001/amajethics.2020.868 PMID:33103649

Matlala, E. (2019). Long-term preservation of digital records at the University of KwaZulu-Natal archives. *Journal of the South African Society of Archivists, 52*, 95–109. https://www.ajol.info/index.php/jsasa/article/view/189859

McGregor, D., Latulippe, N., Whitlow, R., Gansworth, K. L., McGregor, L., & Allen, S. (2023). Towards meaningful research and engagement: Indigenous knowledge systems and Great Lakes governance. *Journal of Great Lakes Research, 49*, S22–S31. doi:10.1016/j.jglr.2023.02.009

Odigwe, F. N., Bassey, B. A., & Owan, V. J. (2020). Data management practices and educational research effectiveness of university lecturers in South-South Nigeria. *Journal of Educational and Social Research, 10*(3), 24–34. doi:10.36941/jesr-2020-0042

Oguamanam, C. (2020). Indigenous peoples, data sovereignty, and self-determination: Current realities and imperatives. *The African Journal of Information and Communication, 26*(26), 1–20. doi:10.23962/10539/30360

Owan, V. J. (2022). A data mining algorithm for accessing research literature in electronic databases: Boolean operators. In T. Masenya (Ed.), *Innovative technologies for enhancing knowledge access in academic libraries* (pp. 140–155). IGI Global. doi:10.4018/978-1-6684-3364-5.ch009

Owan, V. J., & Bassey, B. A. (2019). Data management practices in Educational Research. In P. N. Ololube & G. U. Nwiyi (Eds.), *Encyclopedia of institutional leadership, policy, and management: A handbook of research in honour of Professor Ozo-Mekuri Ndimele* (Vol. 2, pp. 1251–1265). Pearl Publishers International Ltd.. doi:10.13140/RG.2.2.16819.04647

Park, H., & Wolfram, D. (2017). An examination of research data sharing and reuse: Implications for data citation practice. *Scientometrics*, *111*(1), 443–461. doi:10.100711192-017-2240-2

Parker, D. B. (2012). Toward a New Framework for Information Security? In S. Bosworth, M. E. Kabay, & E. Whyne (Eds.), *Computer security handbook* (pp. 3.1–3.23). John Wiley & Sons, Ltd., doi:10.1002/9781118851678.ch3

Pehlivan, Z., Thièvre, J., & Drugeon, T. (2021). Archiving social media: the case of Twitter. In *The Past Web: Exploring Web Archives* (pp. 43–56). Springer International Publishing. doi:10.1007/978-3-030-63291-5_5

Rainie, S. C., Kukutai, T., Walter, M., Figueroa-Rodríguez, O. L., Walker, J., & Axelsson, P. (2019). Indigenous data sovereignty. In T. Davies, S. B. Walker, M. Rubinstein, & F. Perini (Eds), *The state of open data: Histories and horizons*. African Minds and International Development Research Centre. https://library.oapen.org/handle/20.500.12657/24884

Ruhanen, L., & Whitford, M. (2019). Cultural heritage and Indigenous tourism. *Journal of Heritage Tourism*, *14*(3), 179–191. doi:10.1080/1743873X.2019.1581788

Sileyew, K. J. (2020). Research design and methodology. In E. Abu-Taieh, A. El Mouatasim, & I. H. Al Hadid (Eds.), *Cyberspace* (pp. 1–12). IntechOpen., doi:10.5772/intechopen.85731

Smith, L. T. (2021). *Decolonising methodologies: Research and indigenous peoples*. Bloomsbury Publishing. https://bit.ly/3zaudU6

Soler, A. S., Ort, M., & Steckel, J. (2016). *An Introduction to Data Management. (Version 4)* [Reader]. BEFmate, GFBio. https://bit.ly/3LSkSry

Tenopir, C., Allard, S., Douglass, K., Aydinoglu, A. U., Wu, L., Read, E., Manoff, M., & Frame, M. (2011). Data Sharing by Scientists: Practices and Perceptions. *PLoS One*, *6*(6), 1–21. doi:10.1371/journal.pone.0021101 PMID:21738610

Vlassenroot, E., Chambers, S., Di Pretoro, E., Geeraert, F., Haesendonck, G., Michel, A., & Mechant, P. (2019). Web archives as a data resource for digital scholars. *International Journal of Digital Humanities*, *1*(1), 85–111. doi:10.100742803-019-00007-7

Walter, M., Lovett, R., Maher, B., Williamson, B., Prehn, J., Bodkin-Andrews, G., & Lee, V. (2021). Indigenous data sovereignty in the era of big data and open data. *The Australian Journal of Social Issues*, *56*(2), 143–156. doi:10.1002/ajs4.141

Wilson, S. (2020). *Research is ceremony: Indigenous research methods*. Fernwood publishing. http://bit.ly/3TKxPWa

ADDITIONAL READING

Briggs, J. (2005). The use of indigenous knowledge in development: Problems and challenges. *Progress in Development Studies*, *5*(2), 99–114. doi:10.1191/1464993405ps105oa

Carroll, S. R., Rodriguez-Lonebear, D., & Martinez, A. (2019). Indigenous data governance: Strategies from United States Native Nations. *Data Science Journal*, *18*(1), 31. doi:10.5334/dsj-2019-031 PMID:34764990

Ruckstuhl, K. (2022). Trust in scholarly communications and infrastructure: Indigenous data sovereignty. *Frontiers in Research Metrics and Analytics*, *6*, 81. doi:10.3389/frma.2021.752336 PMID:35098013

Walter, M., & Suina, M. (2019). Indigenous data, indigenous methodologies and indigenous data sovereignty. *International Journal of Social Research Methodology*, *22*(3), 233–243. doi:10.1080/136455 79.2018.1531228

Yu, P. L. (2018). The New Data Makers: Indigenous Innovations in Cultural Heritage Management. In P. L. Yu, C. Shen, & G. Smith (Eds.), *Relevance and Application of Heritage in Contemporary Society* (pp. 115–124). Routledge. doi:10.4324/9780203702277-12

KEY TERMS AND DEFINITIONS

Cultural Heritage: Refers to the artefacts, practices, and traditions that are inherited from past generations and preserved as a cultural legacy. Cultural heritage includes tangible and intangible elements, such as artefacts, historical sites, language, music, and storytelling.

Electronic Archives: This refers to a collection of digital data, documents, and records preserved for long-term storage and access. Electronic archives can include various types of digital data, such as text, images, audio, and video.

Indigenous Data: This refers to the data that relates to or originates from Indigenous peoples, communities, cultures, or knowledge systems. This data often includes cultural, ecological, and linguistic information and is unique to Indigenous communities and their experiences.

Indigenous Research: Indigenous research is a type of research that is carried out by and with Indigenous peoples, communities, and knowledge systems. It emphasises the importance of Indigenous knowledge, perspectives, and values in shaping research questions, methodology, and outcomes.

Metadata: Data that provides information about other data. Metadata can include information about the context, structure, format, and content of digital data and is used to help organise and manage digital collections. In Indigenous data management, metadata can include information about data's cultural and historical significance and ownership and access.

Chapter 19
Time Travel and Paradoxes:
Could Libraries Be an Alternative?

Adebowale Jeremy Adetayo
Adeleke University, Nigeria

ABSTRACT

The purpose of this chapter was to gain a deeper understanding of the paradoxes surrounding time travel, and to explore how students view libraries as a source of knowledge for both the past and the future. A survey research design was adopted, and the results were analyzed using descriptive statistics. Of the 384 surveyed, the findings revealed that students occasionally use libraries for research purposes, both for exploring the past and envisioning the future. This indicates support for libraries as a viable alternative solution to the paradoxes of time travel. Although students held the belief that time travel will be possible in the future, they also expressed support for government funding of libraries, to make them more suitable for historical and futuristic research. Therefore, it is recommended that government funding be made available to libraries, with the aim of equipping them with state-of-the-art technologies that will enhance their suitability for research.

INTRODUCTION

The contemporary understanding of time and causality in secular circles is rooted in the ground-breaking theory of general relativity developed by renowned theoretical physicist Albert Einstein. Einstein's theory revolutionized our perception of gravity, proposing that it is not a force that travels through space but rather a fundamental aspect of space-time itself. Through his theory, Einstein seamlessly merged the concepts of space and time into a single entity known as "space-time," offering a comprehensive and unparalleled description of their interrelated functioning. For decades, scientists have been on a quest to explore the feasibility of time travel through the lens of general relativity. Despite numerous efforts, no tangible progress has been made, and all attempts remain confined to mathematical equations on paper, with no concrete evidence of successful time travel. In light of this, some prominent scientists have declared time travel impossible due to two crucial factors. The first is the requirement for the exotic matter - matter with negative energy - to construct a functional time machine (Curiel, 2017). Unfortunately,

DOI: 10.4018/978-1-6684-7024-4.ch019

Copyright © 2023, IGI Global. Copying or distributing in print or electronic forms without written permission of IGI Global is prohibited.

this type of matter starkly contrasts the positive energy that surrounds us in our daily lives, making it difficult to obtain. According to quantum physics, there is a possibility that negative matter can form in small quantities, albeit only briefly (Ford & Roman, 1995).

The second reason cited for the alleged impossibility of time travel is rooted in the paradoxes that seem to arise when contemplating such an idea. The concept of time travel appears to defy logic, and these inconsistencies take the form of time travel paradoxes (Hauser & Shoshany, 2020). To illustrate this point, let us consider the following scenario. If I were to travel back in time five minutes using my time machine and then proceed to destroy it immediately upon arriving in the past, I would no longer be able to utilize the time machine five minutes later. However, suppose I cannot use the device. In that case, I cannot travel back in time to destroy it in the first place. This creates a paradoxical situation where the machine is destroyed and not destroyed simultaneously, defying logical explanations (Shoshany, 2022). These paradoxes only further complicate the already perplexing idea of time travel.

In light of the paradoxes associated with time travel, various attempts have been made to eliminate these inconsistencies, yet none have resulted in successful time travel. This has led theoretical physicist Stephen Hawking to put forth the "chronology protection conjecture," which postulates that time travel should be inherently impossible (Hawking, 1992). Instead of completely dismissing the idea of time travel due to these paradoxes, a different approach could be to look towards a well-established institution that has withstood the test of time and can bring the concept of time itself to us without the need for physically reversing time and space. This institution is the library, a repository of knowledge and history that has remained steadfast through countless challenges and wars. Based on this background, the chapter investigates the paradoxes of time travel and how students perceive libraries as a knowledge hub of the past and future. The aim of this chapter was to critically analyze the intricacies and conflicting concepts surrounding time travel, and to investigate how students utilize libraries as a source of knowledge for the past and future, as an alternative to time travel. To accomplish this aim, the chapter conducted a comprehensive examination of several key areas, including:

- Students' beliefs regarding the potential discovery of time travel
- The frequency of library usage by students for researching the past
- The frequency of library usage by students for exploring the future
- Students' support for funding libraries as a possible "time machine"

CONCEPT OF TIME TRAVEL

The foundation for time travel lies in understanding space-time, an idea formulated by Albert Einstein. During the late 19th century, experiments showed that light was an exceptional phenomenon, always traveling at the same speed regardless of the observer's frame of reference. French physicist and mathematician Henri Poincaré theorized that this constant velocity of light might be an unbreakable limit. Concurrently, other scientists investigated how objects change their size and mass based on their momentum. All of these ideas culminated in Einstein's 1905 theory of special relativity, which posited that space and time must be integrated into a single framework to preserve the constant speed of light for all observers (Mann, 2021). However, it was not solely Einstein who proposed this idea. German mathematician Hermann Minkowski is credited with the insight that space and time are interwoven into a single entity. In 1916, Einstein's general theory of relativity provided further insight into the nature of space

Time Travel and Paradoxes

and time, revealing that they are pliable and respond to the presence of matter and energy by changing, such as warping, bending, expansion, and compression. With the help of some hypothetical form of exotic energy, it becomes possible for space and time to curve back on themselves like circles, making it feasible for an individual to travel forward in a linear path while still arriving at the starting point in both space and time (Krauss, 2017). Despite over a hundred years of exploration and contemplation, the concept of time travel remains a subject that physicists have yet to comprehend fully.

TIME TRAVELLING WITH LIBRARIES

Libraries are significant cultural institutions that serve as repositories for records, written materials, legends, and literature, preserving the history of a specific place and time and the intellectual pursuits, breakthroughs, and innovative ideas of culture (Landauer, 2019). In a sense, libraries function as a time machine, allowing us to revisit the past, enhance our present understanding, and anticipate the future. The history of libraries can be traced back to the 7th century B.C. and the royal library of Assyrian monarch Ashurbanipal in Nineveh, present-day Iraq. The library contained around 30,000 cuneiform tablets organized by subject, including numerous literary texts such as the ancient "Epic of Gilgamesh," which dates back 4,000 years.

Another landmark library was the Library of Alexandria, a symbol of intellectual excellence in the ancient world. It is said to have housed an impressive collection of around 500,000 papyrus scrolls, including literary masterpieces and writings covering history, law, mathematics, and science. Some of the most renowned thinkers and scholars of the ancient world worked or studied at the Museum and Library of Alexandria. One such individual was Erasistratus, a Greek who lived between 325 and 250 B.C. He was an assistant to Herophilus, the founder of the anatomy school in Alexandria, and was renowned for his contributions to anatomy and medicine. Erasistratus was the first person to distinguish between motor and sensory nerves, and he gave names to the trachea and the tricuspid valve in the heart based on his study of veins and arteries that led to the heart .The Alexandria Museum and Library was a hub for intellectual pursuit and advancement in ancient times. It attracted some of the most brilliant minds of the era, including Euclid and Archimedes, who made significant contributions to mathematics and physics. Euclid, known as the "Father of Geometry," lectured at the Museum, sharing his knowledge and insights with students. Meanwhile, Archimedes is considered the most original mathematical thinker of the ancient world, studied and later taught at the Museum. Archimedes made seminal contributions to hydrostatics, engineering, and mathematics and even invented practical devices, such as the Archimedean screw, which was widely used for water-lifting purposes. Moreover, Eratosthenes, the first person to accurately calculate the Earth's circumference, served as the librarian at Alexandria. The Museum and library played a pivotal role in advancing knowledge and learning in the ancient world, attracting some of the brightest minds of the time and serving as a hub for intellectual growth and discovery.

Libraries have always been at the forefront of intellectual advancement and cultural preservation. One such library was the Library of Pergamum in present-day Turkey, which housed over 200,000 scrolls from the third century B.C. Another essential library was the House of Wisdom in Baghdad, Iraq, founded in the early ninth century A.D. The House of Wisdom was a hub of intellectual activity, attracting some of the brightest minds in the Middle East who came to study and translate its vast collection of books into Arabic. For centuries, the House of Wisdom was a center of learning and innovation in the Islamic world (Andrews, 2018). These examples demonstrate the vital role that libraries have played in shaping

365

human history and advancing our knowledge and understanding of the world. Libraries have long served as vital institutions during times of war. During World War I and II, mobile camp libraries emerged in various regions, including the United States, Europe, and even as far as Siberia. These libraries were managed by dedicated volunteer librarians, who were tasked with preserving and circulating the collections, removing outdated books, and acquiring new additions.

Over 1,000 librarians stepped up during World War I to offer their services, which only increased during World War II. As they neared the end of the war, many soldiers considered their future careers and found that libraries provided a valuable source of skills training for various occupations (Bennett, 2017). Libraries have evolved to play a crucial role in the rapidly advancing technological landscape. In today's world, libraries have transformed into hubs for testing and exploring new and cutting-edge technologies. Implementing makerspaces within libraries is a prime example of how libraries reinvent themselves to serve the community's needs better and prepare individuals for the ever-evolving job market. By making these technologies readily available to the public, libraries empower individuals to educate themselves and gain the necessary skills for future employment opportunities (Jochumsen et al., 2015). With their innovative approach, libraries continue to serve as vital resources for the community, bridging the gap between the present and the future.

MENTAL TIME-TRAVELING: UNVEILING ANCIENT INDIGENOUS KNOWLEDGE THROUGH LIBRARIES

Indigenous knowledge systems are repositories of ancient wisdom, encompassing the deep understanding of the natural world, traditional practices, cultural beliefs, and social structures developed by indigenous communities over generations (Bruchac, 2014). These knowledge systems provide a unique window into the past, allowing individuals to mentally "time-travel" and connect with the rich heritage of ancient indigenous cultures. Libraries, as custodians of knowledge, play a crucial role in unveiling and preserving this ancient indigenous knowledge, serving as portals to the past and facilitating the experience of "mental time-traveling."

- **Preservation and Accessibility of Ancient Indigenous Knowledge**

Preserving and accessing ancient indigenous knowledge pose significant challenges due to factors such as cultural assimilation, language loss, and the erosion of traditional practices (United Nations Press, 2019). However, libraries have emerged as key institutions in preserving and making accessible this valuable knowledge. Through their collections and resources, libraries provide a gateway to the past, allowing individuals to delve into the wisdom and traditions of ancient indigenous cultures.

- **Ancient Manuscripts and Oral Traditions**

Libraries house a wealth of resources that enable individuals to engage in mental time-traveling and explore ancient indigenous knowledge. Ancient manuscripts, written by indigenous scholars and sages, provide insights into the cosmologies, philosophies, and practical wisdom of bygone eras. These manuscripts offer a direct connection to the intellectual heritage of indigenous civilizations and allow individuals to mentally transport themselves to different time periods. In addition to written texts, librar-

366

Time Travel and Paradoxes

ies also preserve and share the oral traditions of indigenous communities (Kays, 2022). Oral histories, passed down through generations, contain narratives, legends, and ancestral knowledge that offer a unique window into ancient indigenous cultures. Through oral tradition collections, libraries enable individuals to immerse themselves in the stories and experiences of past generations, bridging the gap between the present and the distant past.

- **Cultural Artefacts and Exhibitions**

Libraries often curate exhibitions and displays that showcase cultural artefacts related to indigenous knowledge (IFLA, 2020; Pilot, 2013). These artefacts, such as tools, artwork, and ceremonial objects, provide tangible links to ancient indigenous practices and beliefs. By carefully selecting and presenting these artefacts, libraries create immersive experiences that allow individuals to mentally travel back in time, gaining a deeper understanding of the ancient indigenous worldviews and traditions.

- **Collaborative Partnerships and Indigenous Perspectives**

To ensure the accurate representation and respectful treatment of ancient indigenous knowledge, libraries must collaborate closely with indigenous communities, knowledge holders, and cultural authorities. Engaging in dialogue and actively seeking indigenous perspectives help libraries incorporate diverse voices and worldviews into their collections and exhibitions. By involving indigenous communities in the interpretation and presentation of ancient indigenous knowledge, libraries promote cultural authenticity and offer a more comprehensive experience of mental time-traveling. By embracing the concept of mental time-traveling, libraries can ensure the continuity of ancient indigenous knowledge and foster a deeper appreciation for the cultural heritage of indigenous peoples.

ESTABLISHING LIBRARIES AS A TIME MACHINE

To fully realize the potential of libraries as a knowledge time machine, a collaborative effort must be made by all stakeholders involved. Governments have a crucial role in ensuring libraries' longevity and continued success as knowledge hubs through legislative support, funding, and staffing. Through these efforts, libraries can serve as a valuable resource for current and future generations, offering access to the past and providing a glimpse into the future. As the adage goes, "Those who do not learn from history are doomed to repeat it." To that end, libraries must receive the necessary financial and technological resources to fulfil their potential as the cornerstone of knowledge and learning (Adetayo et al., 2022).

The libraries of today have become a hub for exploring and experimenting with cutting-edge technologies such as cloud computing (Frederick, 2016), artificial intelligence (Liang, 2020), robots (Asemi et al., 2020), 3D printers (Moorefield-Lang, 2014), internet of things (Massis, 2016), and virtual and augmented realities (Oyelude, 2017). These advancements have transformed libraries into a center of innovation and creativity, attracting inventors and scholars in their quest for knowledge. To ensure that libraries continue to serve as makerspace, where the future is forged and imagined, government and big tech organizations must come together collectively. This can be achieved through government initiatives such as legislation, financing, and staffing and through partnerships with tech companies to facilitate the release or development of new technologies that will make libraries the ultimate solution to the time travel paradoxes.

METHODOLOGY

This chapter utilized a descriptive survey research design to thoroughly understand students' utilization of libraries for exploring both the past and future. This approach was chosen as libraries offer a valuable resource for conducting research, despite the current impossibility of time travel. The descriptive survey research design allowed for an in-depth examination of the students' usage patterns towards utilizing libraries to research historical and future events and trends.

Population and Sampling Size

The participants of this chapter were students enrolled at Adeleke University at the time of the research. The student population, consisting of 3457 individuals, served as the target population for the chapter. To ensure representativeness, a sample size of 517 participants was selected through a lottery method, which is a type of simple random sampling technique, equating to 15% of the total student population. The use of simple random sampling was a crucial aspect of the chapter, as it ensured that each individual in the population had an equal chance of being selected for the sample. This approach minimized the potential for bias in the results and ensured that the findings truly reflected the experiences of the entire student population rather than just a select subset.

Instrumentation

The data for this chapter was collected through a self-administered questionnaire that aimed to gather participants' perceptions and insights on the subject matter. The questionnaire was developed specifically to address the research objectives of the chapter, with each item carefully crafted to elicit meaningful responses. Before administering the questionnaire to the participants, a comprehensive pretesting was conducted to evaluate its clarity and feasibility. This step was crucial in ensuring the accuracy and reliability of the participants' responses. Any areas of improvement identified through the pretesting phase were promptly addressed through modifications to the questionnaire. As a result of these modifications, the questionnaire was refined to effectively capture participants' perceptions and experiences, leading to high-quality data that accurately reflected their views. Using a well-designed and pretested questionnaire was critical to the chapter's success, as it ensured that the data collected was of a high standard and directly relevant to the research objectives.

Method of Data Collection

This chapter's data collection method involved the distribution of a self-administered questionnaire to the participants. Participants were asked to complete and return the questionnaire within a specified timeframe, and proactive measures were taken to maximize participation and follow-up with non-responders. To ensure the confidentiality and trust of the participants, it was emphasized that the information they provided would only be used for academic research purposes and would not be shared with any third

Time Travel and Paradoxes

parties. This assurance was crucial in fostering the participants' cooperation, ultimately resulting in a high response rate of 74.3%, which gives 384 participants. This response rate is acceptable for survey research, as it provided a large enough sample to make valid inferences about the population of interest. The high response rate was attributed to the proactive measures taken to encourage participation and follow-up with non-responders, which was crucial in obtaining accurate and reliable data for the chapter. A self-administered questionnaire and a high response rate ensured that the data collected was representative of the participants' perspectives and experiences, providing valuable insights into the research subject.

Method of Data Analysis

The data analysis process employed in this chapter leveraged the power of descriptive statistics to gain insights into the participants' perceptions and experiences. The collected data were analyzed using various statistical techniques, including frequency counts, percentages, mean, and standard deviation scores. By employing a systematic approach to data analysis, the chapter was able to accurately capture the participants' perceptions and experiences, ultimately leading to a deeper understanding of the research subject. This approach was essential in achieving the research objectives and providing valuable insights that will contribute to the field.

Ethical Considerations

To ensure ethical conduct, informed consent was obtained from each participant, and the confidentiality of their responses was guaranteed. The chapter complied with ethical standards for education research, prioritizing protecting participant rights, dignity, and well-being. The voluntary nature of participation was emphasized, and efforts were made to minimize any potential harm. All data collected was kept confidential and used solely for academic research purposes. The ethical principles adhered to throughout the chapter reflect the highest standards of ethical conduct in research.

FINDINGS OF THE STUDY

The findings of the present chapter are presented comprehensively and in detail in the following section. Utilizing descriptive statistics, a thorough analysis has been conducted, and the results are depicted through the use of Table 1 to Table 5. These tables provide a clear and in-depth visualization of the findings, offering a rich and fluent representation of the results of the chapter.

The results of the chapter, as depicted in Table 1, indicate a significant disparity in gender representation among the respondents. A large majority of 62.2% of the participants were female, while a relatively smaller proportion of 37.8% was male. Additionally, the age distribution of the participants showed a skewed pattern, with a predominant group of 51.8% falling under the age of 20. On the other hand, the age group between 26 and 30 years was the least represented, making up only 3.4% of the sample.

The results presented in Table 2 offer intriguing insights into the beliefs and perceptions of students regarding time travel. The findings reveal a widespread belief among students that time travel will be a reality.

The findings presented in Table 3 offer an insightful view into using libraries as a resource for researching the past. The results revealed an occasional overall usage of libraries for this purpose, with

Table 1. Demographics of respondents

Gender	Frequency (N=384)	Percent
Female	239	62.2
Male	145	37.8
Age Group		
30 & Above	82	21.4
26 to 30	13	3.4
21 to 25	90	23.4
20 & Below	199	51.8

Table 2. Time travel discovery

Indicators	Frequency (384)	Percent
No	138	35.9
Yes	246	64.1

Table 3. Usage of libraries for researching the past

Indicators	Frequency	Percent
Never	47	12.2
Rarely	129	33.6
Occasionally	153	39.8
Often	55	14.3
Mean	**2.56**	
Std. Deviation	**0,883**	

Table 4. Usage of libraries for researching the future

Indicators	Frequency	Percent
Never	54	14.1
Rarely	125	32.6
Occasionally	139	36.2
Often	66	17.2
Mean	**2.57**	
Std. Deviation	**0.934**	

Table 5. Funding of libraries by the government as a time machine

Indicators	Frequency	Percent
No	23	6.0
Yes	361	94.0

Time Travel and Paradoxes

a mean score of 2.56. A closer examination of the data shows that the most significant proportion of students (39.8%) use the library occasionally when researching the past. In comparison, a substantial number 33.6% rarely utilize the library for this purpose. The data highlights a moderate usage of libraries among students, with 14.3% often relying on libraries when conducting historical research. However, a relatively small group of 12.2% does not use the library.

The findings presented in Table 4 offer a fascinating view into using libraries as a resource for exploring the future. The results revealed an occasional overall usage of libraries for this purpose, with a mean score of 2.57. A closer examination of the data indicates that the most significant proportion of students (36.2%) use the library occasionally when researching the future. In comparison, 32.6% rarely utilize the library for this purpose. The data also highlights a moderate usage of libraries among students, with 17.2% often relying on libraries when researching future possibilities. However, a relatively small group of 14.1% does not use the library.

The findings presented in Table 5 offer a powerful glimpse into students' views on the role of libraries in exploring both the past and the future. The results reveal that 94.0% of students support the idea that government investment is necessary to equip libraries with the technologies and resources required to make them a hub for exploring the past and future. These results highlight the importance of libraries as a source of information and knowledge and their role in shaping future perspectives and influencing the way students envision the future. The findings presented in Table 5 provide valuable insights into students' opinions on the part of libraries in exploring the past and future and offer a rich and detailed picture of the views of this critical demographic.

DISCUSSIONS OF FINDINGS

The findings of the chapter show that students widely believe that time travel will become a reality. This is a significant discovery as it reflects their imagination, curiosity, and optimism toward advancements in technology and science. The result underscores the exciting prospect of exploring new realms and experiencing past and future events, which has long captivated the human imagination. Additionally, it sheds light on students' views on the power of human knowledge and innovation to unlock the mysteries of time. The result is intriguing and provides a deeper understanding of the perspectives of young people on science and technology. The findings further indicate that students utilize libraries to research the past. This result is backed up by Modak (2021), who found similar usage in Nabadwip for exploring the local history of Sri Chaitanya Mahaprabhu. This chapter also found that users prefer to expand their knowledge of Sri Chaitanya Mahaprabhu through various information sources. These results contribute to a greater understanding of the use of libraries as a resource for conducting historical research and the critical role they play in preserving cultural heritage and knowledge. The occasional usage of libraries in this chapter highlights their ongoing relevance in the digital age and the significance of preserving and maintaining physical libraries for future generations. Despite the advancement of technology, physical libraries still play an essential role in providing access to historical information and preserving cultural knowledge. This chapter highlights the importance of libraries as a resource for researching the past and the need to protect and maintain these institutions.

The chapter further delves into the role of libraries in supporting history research. Bhar (2015) underscores the significance of libraries in this regard, highlighting how they can collect, organize, and disseminate relevant information about a place's local history to meet users' needs. MacRitchie (2017), in a review of the book "Local History Reference Collections for Public Libraries" by Marquis and Waggener, notes the authors' strong suggestion for public libraries to create a local history reference collection, differentiating it from an archival collection. The authors also identify the need for local history librarians to have a platform for exchanging ideas, suggesting that a web-based approach, such as a wiki, would be ideal. However, Daniel (2012) offers a different perspective, proposing that librarians and historians should collaborate to educate students on how to research the past. This proposal recognizes the importance of training the next generation of researchers in effectively using libraries and other resources for historical research.

The findings show that students occasionally use libraries as a resource for exploring the future. This highlights the ongoing significance of libraries as sources of information and knowledge and the need to preserve and maintain these institutions for future generations. Schulte et al. (2018) have noted that as teaching shifts towards more student-centred and authentic learning experiences, with a focus on preparing students for the future workplace, librarians have an opportunity to collaborate with academic staff using their skills in information management, digital literacy, scholarly communication, and technology. Today's libraries have become centres of innovation and creativity, attracting both inventors and scholars with cutting-edge technologies such as cloud computing (Frederick, 2016), artificial intelligence (Liang, 2020), 3D printers (Moorefield-Lang, 2014), the Internet of Things (Massis, 2016), and virtual and augmented realities (Oyelude, 2017). These advancements have transformed libraries into makerspaces, where the future is forged and imagined.

According to Olayinka (2022), the current state of public libraries in the country is deplorable, with inadequate facilities, insufficient funding, and understaffing being the primary causes. This has led to a call from the Non-Academic Staff Union of Educational and Associated Institutions to encourage private-sector investment in public libraries to enhance education in the country. The results of this chapter reveal that students strongly support government investment in libraries to equip them with the latest technologies and resources. This overwhelming support for government investment highlights the continued significance of libraries in the ever-evolving technological landscape and the need to preserve and upgrade their capabilities and resources.

CONCLUSION AND RECOMMENDATIONS

The chapter highlights the continued relevance of libraries as critical resources for exploring and understanding both the past and future. The results have important implications for library practice and policies, particularly concerning ensuring that these institutions are equipped with the necessary resources and technology to support the needs and demands of their users. The chapter highlights the importance of government investment in libraries, enabling these institutions to continue serving as a hub of knowledge and innovation. By establishing the library as a knowledge time machine, students and researchers alike can use these resources to deepen their understanding of history and explore new frontiers of knowledge. Ultimately, libraries have the potential to play an even more significant role in advancing the boundaries of human knowledge and understanding, and we must invest in these institutions to support their continued growth and evolution.

Recommendations:

- ***Enhanced Collaboration between Libraries and Educational Institutions:*** Libraries should foster stronger partnerships with educational institutions, particularly history departments, to provide tailored resources, training, and support for students and researchers. Collaborative efforts can improve the integration of library resources and services into the curriculum and promote the effective use of libraries for historical research.
- ***Continued Investment in Library Infrastructure and Resources***: Governments and funding bodies should recognize the vital role of libraries in preserving cultural heritage and knowledge. Adequate investment is necessary to upgrade library infrastructure, acquire new technologies, and expand collections, ensuring that libraries can meet the evolving needs and expectations of users.
- ***Promotion of Digital Literacy Skills:*** Libraries should play an active role in promoting digital literacy skills among users. This includes providing training programs, workshops, and resources that enable individuals to effectively navigate and utilize digital platforms, databases, and online resources for historical research and time travel exploration.
- ***Creation of Collaborative Platforms***: Libraries can establish collaborative platforms, such as online forums or wikis, where users, librarians, historians, and experts can exchange ideas, share resources, and collaborate on historical research projects. These platforms can facilitate knowledge sharing, interdisciplinary collaboration, and the co-creation of historical narratives.
- ***Emphasis on Outreach and Public Engagement:*** Libraries should actively engage with the community by organizing events, exhibitions, and workshops that highlight the significance of historical research. These efforts can enhance public awareness, appreciation, and utilization of library resources while fostering a sense of ownership and pride in cultural heritage.

Future Research Directions

- ***Exploring the Role of Virtual Libraries:*** With the advancements in technology, virtual libraries and digital resources are becoming increasingly popular. Future research could investigate the effectiveness and user experience of virtual libraries in facilitating indigenous knowledge exploration and historical research. This could involve studying the accessibility, usability, and impact of virtual libraries compared to physical libraries.
- ***Understanding the Impact of Emerging Technologies***: As libraries continue to incorporate cutting-edge technologies such as artificial intelligence, virtual reality, and 3D printing, it is important to examine the impact of these technologies on the user experience and the effectiveness of historical research. Future research could focus on evaluating the benefits and limitations of these technologies in supporting indigenous knowledge exploration and addressing potential challenges that may arise.

REFERENCES

Adetayo, A. J., Suleiman, A. I., & Ayodele, M. O. (2022). Leveraging Digital Infopreneurship for Financial Well-Being of Academic Librarians: The Nigerian Perspective. *Library Philosophy and Practice (e-Journal)*. https://digitalcommons.unl.edu/libphilprac/6652

Andrews, E. (2018, August 22). *8 Legendary Ancient Libraries*. HISTORY. https://www.history.com/news/8-impressive-ancient-libraries

Asemi, A., Ko, A., & Nowkarizi, M. (2020). Intelligent libraries: A review on expert systems, artificial intelligence, and robot. *Library Hi Tech*, *39*(2), 412–434. doi:10.1108/LHT-02-2020-0038

Bennett, K. D. (2017, May 8). *How libraries served soldiers and civilians during WWI and WWII*. OUPblog. https://blog.oup.com/2017/05/libraries-soldiers-world-war/

Bhar, D. (2015). Literature Review on Local History Collection, Its Various Sources and Roles of Libraries by Dhritiman Bhar : SSRN. *Calcutta University Journal of Information Studies*. https://papers.ssrn.com/sol3/papers.cfm?abstract_id=3198824

Bruchac, M. M. (2014). Indigenous Knowledge and Traditional Knowledge. In *Encyclopedia of Global Archaeology* (pp. 3814–3824). Springer. doi:10.1007/978-1-4419-0465-2_10

Curiel, E. (2017). A Primer on Energy Conditions. In *Towards a Theory of Spacetime Theories* (pp. 43–104). Birkhäuser. doi:10.1007/978-1-4939-3210-8_3

Daniel, D. (2012). Teaching Students How to Research the Past: Historians and Librarians in the Digital Age. *The History Teacher*, *45*(2), 261–282.

Ford, L. H., & Roman, T. A. (1995). Averaged energy conditions and quantum inequalities. *Physical Review. D*, *51*(8), 4277–4286. doi:10.1103/PhysRevD.51.4277 PMID:10018903

Frederick, D. E. (2016). Libraries, data and the fourth industrial revolution (Data Deluge Column). *Library Hi Tech News*, *33*(5), 9–12. doi:10.1108/LHTN-05-2016-0025

Hauser, J., & Shoshany, B. (2020). Time travel paradoxes and multiple histories. *Physical Review. D*, *102*(6), 064062. doi:10.1103/PhysRevD.102.064062

Hawking, S. W. (1992). Chronology protection conjecture. *Physical Review. D*, *46*(2), 603–611. doi:10.1103/PhysRevD.46.603 PMID:10014972

IFLA. (2020, May 20). *Gateways to Cultural Diversity: Libraries as multicultural hubs*. IFLA. https://blogs.ifla.org/lpa/2020/05/20/gateways-to-cultural-diversity-libraries-as-multicultural-hubs/

Jochumsen, H., Skot-Hansen, D., & Hvenegaard Rasmussen, C. (2015). Towards Culture 3.0 – performative space in the public library. *International Journal of Cultural Policy*, *23*(4), 512–524. doi:10.1080/10286632.2015.1043291

Kays, J. (2022, April 19). *Native Voices: Oral Histories Help Preserve Indigenous Heritage*. Explore Magazine. https://explore.research.ufl.edu/native-voices-oral-histories-help-preserve-indigenous-heritage.html

Krauss, L. M. (2017, May 10). *What Einstein and Bill Gates Teach Us About Time Travel*. NBC News. https://www.nbcnews.com/storyline/the-big-questions/what-einstein-bill-gates-teach-us-about-time-travel-n757291

Landauer, L. B. (2019). *The Development of Libraries in the Ancient World*. Encyclopedia. https://www.encyclopedia.com/science/encyclopedias-almanacs-transcripts-and-maps/development-libraries-ancient-world

Time Travel and Paradoxes

Liang, X. (2020). Internet of Things and its applications in libraries: A literature review. *Library Hi Tech, 37*(2), 251–261. doi:10.1108/LHT-01-2018-0014/FULL/XML

MacRitchie, J. (2017). Book reviews: Local History Reference Collections for Public Libraries. *The Electronic Library, 35*(1), 209–210. doi:10.1108/EL-12-2015-0246

Mann, A. (2021, May 20). What is space-time? *Live Science.* https://www.livescience.com/space-time.html

Massis, B. (2016). The Internet of Things and its impact on the library. *New Library World, 117*(3–4), 289–292. doi:10.1108/NLW-12-2015-0093

Modak, S. (2021). Local history collection on Sri Chaitanya Mahaprabhu in the Public Libraries in Nabadwip. *Library Philosophy and Practice (e-Journal).* https://digitalcommons.unl.edu/libphilprac/6217

Moorefield-Lang, H. M. (2014). Makers in the library: Case studies of 3D printers and maker spaces in library settings. *Library Hi Tech, 32*(4), 583–593. doi:10.1108/LHT-06-2014-0056

Olayinka, C. (2022). NASU seeks government, private investment in library services. *The Guardian.* https://guardian.ng/appointments/nasu-seeks-government-private-investment-in-library-services/

Oyelude, A. A. (2017). Virtual and augmented reality in libraries and the education sector. *Library Hi Tech News, 34*(4), 1–4. doi:10.1108/LHTN-04-2017-0019

Pilot, J. (2013). Developing Indigenous Knowledge Centres. *Australian Academic and Research Libraries, 36*(2), 37–43. doi:10.1080/00048623.2005.10721247

Schulte, J., Tiffen, B., Edwards, J., Abbott, S., & Luca, E. (2018). Shaping the Future of Academic Libraries: Authentic Learning for the Next Generation. *College & Research Libraries, 79*(5), 685–696. doi:10.5860/crl.79.5.685

Shoshany, B. (2022, April 24). Time travel could be possible, but only with parallel timelines. *The Conversation.* https://theconversation.com/time-travel-could-be-possible-but-only-with-parallel-timelines-178776

United Nations Press. (2019, April 22). *Indigenous People's Traditional Knowledge Must Be Preserved, Valued Globally, Speakers Stress as Permanent Forum Opens Annual Session.* UNP. https://press.un.org/en/2019/hr5431.doc.htm

ADDITIONAL READING

Adetayo, A., Ajayi, K., & Komolafe, R. (2022). Wars and Sanctions: Do Libraries Have a Role to Play? *The Reference Librarian, 63*(3), 102–117. doi:10.1080/02763877.2022.2100559

Friedrich, M., Müller, P., & Riordan, M. (2017). Practices of historical research in archives and libraries from the eighteenth to the nineteenth century. *History of Humanities, 2*(1), 3–13. doi:10.1086/690570

Lewis, D. (2016). The paradoxes of time travel. *Science Fiction and Philosophy: From Time Travel to Superintelligence,* 357-369.

Sarkhel, J. K. (2017). Strategies of indigenous knowledge management in libraries. *Qualitative and Quantitative Methods in Libraries*, 5(2), 427–439.

Summit, J. (2019). *Memory's Library: Medieval Books in Early Modern England*. University of Chicago Press.

KEY DEFINITIONS AND TERMS

Libraries: Libraries are institutions that collect, organize, and provide access to information resources such as books, periodicals, and other materials. They are often used for research, education, and entertainment purposes, and they can be found in many different settings, such as schools, universities, public buildings, and online. Libraries play an essential role in preserving cultural heritage and promoting lifelong learning.

Paradoxes: A paradox is a statement or situation that appears to be self-contradictory or absurd, but in reality, it may be true. Paradoxes often challenge our assumptions and expectations about how things should be, and they can be found in many areas of human inquiry, including philosophy, mathematics, and science.

Space-time: Space-time is the four-dimensional continuum in which all physical events occur. It combines the three dimensions of space and the one dimension of time into a single mathematical model that describes the behavior of objects and events in the universe. Space-time is a fundamental concept in physics, especially in the theory of relativity.

Time Travel: Time travel is the hypothetical ability to move through time in a way different from the normal flow of time experienced by most people. The concept of time travel has been explored in science fiction and in theories of physics, such as general relativity.

Compilation of References

Abbacan-Tuguic, L., & Galinggan, R. (2016). Earthenware: The art of traditional pottery of Pasil Kalinga. *International Journal of Advanced Research in Management and Social Sciences*, 5(6), 774–784. http://bitly.ws/BkCv

Abduldayan, F. J., Abifarin, F. P., Oyedum, G. U., & Alhassan, J. A. (2021). Research data management practices of chemistry researchers in federal universities of technology in Nigeria. *Digital Library Perspectives*, 37(4), 328–348. doi:10.1108/DLP-06-2020-0051

Abdul-Mumin, K. H. (2016). Village midwives and their changing roles in Brunei Darussalam: A qualitative study. *Women and Birth; Journal of the Australian College of Midwives*, 29(5), 73–81. doi:10.1016/j.wombi.2016.04.002 PMID:27105748

Abebe, R., Aruleba, K., Birhane, A., Kingsley, S., Obaido, G., Remy, S. L., & Sadagopan, S. (2021, March). Narratives and counternarratives on data sharing in Africa. In *Proceedings of the 2021 ACM conference on fairness, accountability, and transparency* (pp. 329-341). ACM. 10.1145/3442188.3445897

Abidogun, J. M., & Falola, T. (2020). *The Palgrave handbook of African education and indigenous knowledge*. Springer. doi:10.1007/978-3-030-38277-3

Abubakar, S. (2021). Youth empowerment as a tool for socio-economic changes in Nigeria. *International Journal of Youth Economy*, 5(1), 19–27. doi:10.18576/ijye/050103

Achi, O. M., & Ukwuru, M. (2015). Cereal-Based Fermented Foods of Africa as Functional Foods. *International Journal of Microbiology and Application.*, 2(4), 71–83.

Acker, A. (2021). Emulation practices for software preservation in libraries, archives, and museums. *Journal of the Association for Information Science and Technology*, 72(9), 1148–1160. doi:10.1002/asi.24482

Adebimpe, O. (2015). Pottery production, an entrepreneurship perspective for job creation and poverty alleviation. A case study of Dada pottery, Okelele, Ilorin, Kwara State, Nigeria. *Journal of Economics and Sustainable Development*, 6(2), 172–178.

Adedoyin, O. B., & Soykan, E. (2020). Covid-19 pandemic and online learning: The challenges and opportunities. *Interactive Learning Environments*, 1–13. doi:10.1080/10494820.2020.1813180

Adegbite, W. (2003). Enlightenment and attitudes of the Nigerian elite on the roles of languages in Nigeria. *Language, Culture and Curriculum*, 16(2), 185–196. doi:10.1080/07908310308666667

Adekannbi, J., Olatokun, W. M., & Ajiferuke, I. (2014). *Predictors of traditional medical knowledge transmission and acquisition in South-West Nigeria*. Sage. http://idv.sagepub.com/content/ early/2014/12/09/0266666914561534.full. pdf+html

Adesina, O. A., Taiwo, A. E., Akindele, O., & Igbafe, A. (2021). Process parametric studies for decolouration of dye from local 'tie and dye industrial effluent using moringa oleifera seed. *South African Journal of Chemical Engineering*, *37*, 23–30. doi:10.1016/j.sajce.2021.03.005

Adetayo, A. J., Suleiman, A. I., & Ayodele, M. O. (2022). Leveraging Digital Infopreneurship for Financial Well-Being of Academic Librarians: The Nigerian Perspective. *Library Philosophy and Practice (e-Journal)*. https://digitalcommons.unl.edu/libphilprac/6652

Adjei, K., Asante, A. E., & Adu-Gyamfi, V. E. (2015). Life, death and eternity: The role of pottery in some cultural practices among the Akans of Ghana. Online International Journal of Arts and Humanities, 4(4), 55-61. https://bit.ly/3LKP0Fh

Adu, K. K. (2016). *Framework for digital preservation or electronic government in Ghana* [Doctoral thesis, University of South Africa, UNISA, South Africa]

Adu-Gyamfi, S., & Anderson, E. (2019). Indigenous medicine and traditional healing in Africa: A systematic synthesis of the literature. *Philosophy. Social and Human Disciplines*, *1*, 69–100.

Adyanga, F. A. (2014). *African Indigenous Science in Higher Education in Uganda*. [Unpublished PhD Thesis, Ontario Institute for Studies in Education, University of Toronto]

Adyanga, F. A., & Romm, N. R. (2022). Reflections Upon our Way of Invoking an Indigenous Paradigm to Co-Explore Community Mobilization against Irresponsible Practices of Foreign-Owned Companies in Nwoya District, Uganda. *Qualitative Report*, *27*(7). Advance online publication. doi:10.46743/2160-3715/2022.5147

Adyanga, F. A., & Romm, N. R. A. (2016). Researching Indigenous science knowledge integration in formal education: Interpreting some perspectives from the field. *International Journal of Educational Development*, *3*(1), 1–14.

Afful-Arthur, P., Kwafoa, P. N. Y., Ampah-Johnston, M., & Mensah, V. (2022). Managing and accessing Indigenous for national development: The role of academic libraries in Ghana. *Information Development*, *38*(4), 535–548. doi:10.1177/02666669211009916

Afolayan, A. (1984). The English language in Nigerian education as an agent of proper multilingual and multicultural development. *Journal of Multilingual and Multicultural Development*, *5*(1), 1–22. doi:10.1080/01434632.1984.9994134

African Regional Intellectual Property Organization. (2019). *Swakopmund Protocol on the Protection of Traditional & Expressions of Folklore*. ARIPO. https://www.aripo.org/wp-content/uploads/2019/06/Swakopmund-Protocol-on-the-Protection-of-Traditional knowledge -and-Expressions-of-Folklore-2019.pdf Accessed 12 March 2023.

Agariya, A. K., Johari, A., Sharma, H. K., Chandraul, U. N. S., & Singh, D. (2012). The role of packaging in brand communication. *International Journal of Scientific and Engineering Research*, *3*(2), 1–13.

Agbor, A. M., & Naidoo, S. (2016). A review of the role of African traditional medicine in the management of oral diseases. *African Journal of Traditional, Complementary, and Alternative Medicines*, *13*(2), 133–142. doi:10.4314/ajtcam.v13i2.16

Agrawal, A. (1995). Dismantling the Divide between Indigenous and Scientific Knowledge. *Development and Change*, *26*(3), 413–439. doi:10.1111/j.1467-7660.1995.tb00560.x

Agrawal, A. (2002). Indigenous knowledge and the politics of classification. *International Social Science Journal*, *54*(173), 287–297. doi:10.1111/1468-2451.00382

Aikawa, N. (2004). An historical overview of the preparation of the UNESCO International Convention for the Safeguarding of the Intangible Cultural Heritage. *Museum International*, *56*(1-2), 137–149. doi:10.1111/j.1350-0775.2004.00468.x

Compilation of References

Akena, F. A. (2012). Critical Analysis of the Production of Western Knowledge and Its Implications for Indigenous Knowledge and Decolonization. *Journal of Black Studies, 43*(6), 599–619. doi:10.1177/0021934712440448

Akena, F. A. (2022in press). Education transformation post Covid-19 in Uganda, implications for Indigenous Knowledge Systems: The conversational approach. In *A. Fymat, N. R.A. Romm & Kapalanga J. (2022). Covid-19 pandemic: Perspectives across Africa.* Tellwell publishing.

Akinrotoye, K. P. (2014). Effects of fermented palm wine on some diarrhoeagenic bacteria. *Elite Research Journal of Biotechnology and Microbiology, 2*(1), 4–14.

Akintonde, M. A. (2013). Typology and geography of outdoor sculpture in southwestern Nigeria. *Research on Humanities and Social Sciences, 3*(10), 120-129. https://core.ac.uk/download/pdf/234673566.pdf

Akinwale, A. A. (2012). Digitisation of indigenous knowledge for natural resources management in Africa. *Proceedings of the AERN Summit.* SCECSAL. https://www.scecsal.org/publications/papers2016/034_sraku_latey_2016.pdf

Akpan, I. J., & Ibidunni, A. S. (2021). Digitization and technological transformation of small business for sustainable development in the less developed and emerging economies: A research note and call for papers. *Journal of Small Business and Entrepreneurship,* 1–7. doi:10.1080/08276331.2021.1924505

Akullo, D., Kanzikwera, R., Birungi, P., Alum, W., Aliguma, L., & Barwogeza, M. (2007). *Indigenous Knowledge in Agriculture: a case study of the challenges in sharing knowledge of past generations in a globalized context in Uganda.* IFLA.

Al-Emran, M., Mezhuyev, V., Kamaludin, A., & Shaalan, K. (2018). The impact of knowledge management processes on information systems: A systematic review. *International Journal of Information Management, 43,* 173–187. doi:10.1016/j.ijinfomgt.2018.08.001

Alemu, G., Stevens, B., Ross, P., & Chandler, J. (2012). Linked data for libraries: Benefits of a conceptual shift from library-specific record structures to RDF-based data models. *New Library World, 113*(11/12), 549–570. doi:10.1108/03074801211282920

Alexander, C. (2011). *Linking Indigenous and Scientific Knowledge of Climate Change.* America Institute of Biological Sciences: University of California Press. doi:10.1525/bio.2011.61.6.10

Alfred, R. (2009). June 24, 1993: Concert Goes Live on Net. *Wired.* https://www.wired.com/2009/06/dayintech-0624/ (Accessed: 14 December 2022).

Alharahsheh, H. H., & Pius, A. (2020). A review of key paradigms: Positivism vs interpretivism. *Global Academic Journal of Humanities and Social Sciences, 2*(3), 39–43.

Alimba, J. O., & Mgbada, J. U. (2003). Socio-economic consequences of technological change on the rural non-farm Igbo women entrepreneurs of south-eastern Nigeria: Implications for farm and non-farm linkages. *ATPS Working Paper Series No. 40.* African Technology Policy Studies Network. https://www.africaportal.org/documents/17076/working_paper_series_40.pdf

Aluma, J. R. (2010). Integration of indigenous knowledge (IK) agriculture and health development processes in Uganda. *Journal of Sustainable Development in Africa, 10*(3), 12–26.

American School Counselor Association. (2012). *ASCA National Model: A framework for school counseling programs* (3rd ed.). ASCA.

Amhag, L., Hellström, L., & Stigmar, M. (2019). Teacher educators' use of digital tools and needs for digital competence in higher education. *Journal of Digital Learning in Teacher Education, 35*(4), 203–220. doi:10.1080/21532974.2019.1646169

379

Amzat, J., & Abdullahi, A. A. (2008). Role of traditional healers in the fight against HIV/AIDS. *EthnoMed.*, *2*(2), 153–159.

Andermann, J. (2010). State Formation, Visual Technology and Spectatorship: Visions of Modernity in Brazil and Argentina. *Theory, Culture & Society*, *27*(7), 161–183. doi:10.1177/0263276410384749

Anderson, B. (2006). *Imagined Communities: Reflections on the Origin and Spread of Nationalism* (2nd ed.). Verso.

Anderson, K. E. (2020). Getting acquainted with social networks and apps: Capturing and archiving social media content. *Library Hi Tech News*, *37*(2), 18–22. doi:10.1108/LHTN-03-2019-0011

Anderson, K., & Cidro, J. (2019). Decades of doing: Indigenous women academics reflect on the practices of community-based health research. *Journal of Empirical Research on Human Research Ethics; JERHRE*, *14*(3), 222–233. doi:10.1177/1556264619835707 PMID:31018813

Andrews, D. H., & Goodson, L. A. (1980). A comparative analysis of models of instructional design. *Journal of instructional development, 3*(4), 2-16.

Andrews, E. (2018, August 22). *8 Legendary Ancient Libraries*. HISTORY. https://www.history.com/news/8-impressive-ancient-libraries

Anjum, M. (2013). *Artisanal craft pottery in South Asia (and Ethiopia) and the potential for expanding markets locally and globally* [Doctoral dissertation, Royal College of Art, United Kingdom].

Ansah, E. K., Moucheraud, C., Arogundade, L., & Rangel, G. W. (2022). Rethinking integrated service delivery for malaria. *PLOS Global Public Health*, *2*(6), e0000462. https://www.ncbi.nlm.nih.gov/pmc/articles/PMC10021790/. doi:10.1371/journal.pgph.0000462 PMID:36962405

Anthony-Euba, P., & Towobola, W. (2014). Entrepreneurship for sustainable development: A Case for present-day Ìjàyè pottery tools genre. *Journal of Poverty. Investment and Development*, *5*, 112–117.

Anyaoku, E. N., Nwafor-Orizu, O. E., & Eneh, E. A. (2015). Collection and Preservation of Traditional Medical Knowledge: Roles for Medical Libraries in Nigeria. *Journal of Library and Information Science*, *3*(1), 33–43. https://obianujunwafor-orizu.com/collection-and-preservation-of-traditional-medical-knowledge-roles-for-medical-libraries-in-nigeria/. doi:10.15640/jlis.v3n1a2

Anyogu, F., & Ibekwe, C. S. (2020). A Comparative Exposition of Customary Law Marriage in Nigeria and South Africa. [*IJOCLLEP*]. *International Journal of Comparative Law and Legal Philosophy*, *2*(2), 60–74.

Apeh, A. A., & Opata, C. C. (2019). The oil palm wine economy of rural farmers in Nigeria: Evidence from Enugu Ezike, south-eastern Nigeria. *Rural History*, *30*(2), 111–128. doi:10.1017/S0956793319000062

Ardolino, M., Rapaccini, M., Saccani, N., Gaiardelli, P., Crespi, G., & Ruggeri, C. (2018). The role of digital technologies in the service transformation of industrial companies. *International Journal of Production Research*, *56*(6), 2116–2132. doi:10.1080/00207543.2017.1324224

Areo, A. (2014). Women involvement in handmade pottery and marketing concept strategy. *Journal of Economics and Sustainable Development*, *5*(6), 150–159. https://core.ac.uk/download/pdf/234646323.pdf

Areo, M. O., & Kalilu, R. O. R. (2013). Adire in southwestern Nigeria: Geography of the centres. *African Research Review*, *7*(2), 350–370. doi:10.4314/afrrev.v7i2.22

Arnoldi, M. J. (2006). Youth festivals and museums: The cultural politics of public memory in postcolonial Mali. *Africa Today*, *52*(4), 55–76. doi:10.1353/at.2006.0037

Compilation of References

Arnoldi, M. J., Kéita, D., & Sidibé, S. (2021). The national museum of Mali, 1960–present: Protecting and promoting the national cultural heritage. In R. Silverman, G. Abungu, & P. Probst (Eds.), *National museums in Africa* (pp. 139–158). Routledge., doi:10.4324/9781003013693-8

Art. 231 da Constituição Federal de 88 (1988) *Constituição Federal de 1988.* Brazil: Brazilian Goverment. https://www.jusbrasil.com.br/topicos/10643688/artigo-231-da-constituicao-federal-de-1988

Artut, S. (2021). *Conservation of Technological artworks. In technological arts Preservation.* Sabancı University Sakıp Sabancı Museum (SSM), Turky. https://www.sakipsabancimuzesi.org

Aryal, A., Morley, C. G., & McLean, I. G. (2018). Conserving elephants depend on a total ban of ivory trade globally. *Biodiversity and Conservation, 27*(10), 2767–2775. doi:10.100710531-018-1534-x

Arya, R. (2021). Cultural appropriation: What it is and why it matters? *Sociology Compass, 15*(10), e12923. doi:10.1111oc4.12923

Asante, M. K. (2005b). Afronography. Encyclopedia of black studies, 76-77.

Asante, E. A., Opoku-Asare, N. A., & Wemegah, R. (2015). Indigenous pottery at Sirigu: Dialogue on materials, methods and sociocultural significance. *Craft Research, 6*(1), 31–56. doi:10.1386/crre.6.1.31_1

Asante, M. K. (1991). The Afrocentric idea in education, spring. *The Journal of Negro Education, 60*(2), 170–180. doi:10.2307/2295608

Asante, M. K. (1999). *The painful demise of Eurocentrism: An Afrocentric response to critics.* Africa World Press.

Asante, M. K. (2007c). An Afrocentric Manifesto: Toward an African Renaissance. *Polity.*

Asante, M. K. (2013d). *The African American people: A global history.* Routledge. doi:10.4324/9780203145807

Asemi, A., Ko, A., & Nowkarizi, M. (2020). Intelligent libraries: A review on expert systems, artificial intelligence, and robot. *Library Hi Tech, 39*(2), 412–434. doi:10.1108/LHT-02-2020-0038

Ashby, M. F. (2013). *Materials and the environment* (2nd ed.). Elsevier.

Asmah, A. E., Frimpong, C., & Asinyo, B. K. (2013). Enhancing the Value of Indigenous pottery products with surface decoration methods & macramé. *Arts and Design Studies, 8,* 1-9. http://bitly.ws/BkCvhttp://bitly.ws/Bm5x

Asmah, A. E., Mateko, M. M., & Daitey, S. T. (2016). Tourist art: A prime phase of Sirigu art. *European Journal of Research in Social Sciences, 4*(2), 1–14. http://bitly.ws/BmyD

Asrani, P., Patial, V., & Asrani, R. K. (2019). 14 - Production of Fermented Beverages: Shedding Light on Indian Culture and Traditions. In A. M. Grumezescu & A. M. B. T.-P. & M. of B. Holban (Eds.), Production and management of beverages (pp. 409–437). Woodhead Publishing. https://doi.org/ doi:10.1016/B978-0-12-815260-7.00014-6

Asrar-ul-Haq, M., & Anwar, S. (2016). A systematic review of knowledge management and knowledge sharing: Trends, issues, and challenges. *Cogent Business & Management, 3*(1), 1127744. doi:10.1080/23311975.2015.1127744

Asuquo, M. E., Ekpoh, U. I., & Udeh, K. V. (2022). Politics of managing university education with emerging technologies in the covid – 19 pandemic era: Perspectives of academic staff in Cross River State, Nigeria. *Global Journal of Educational Research, 21*(2), 87–97. doi:10.4314/gjedr.v21i2.1

Audet, C. M., Gobbo, E., Sack, D. E., Mlemens, E. M., Ngobeni, S., Mkansi, M., Ailu, M. H., & Wanger, R. G. (2020). Traditional healers use of personal protective equipment: A qualitative study in rural South Africa. *BMC Health Services Research, 20*(1), 655. doi:10.118612913-020-05515-9 PMID:32669101

Augusto, J. C., Nakashima, H., & Aghajan, H. (2010). *Ambient Intelligence and Smart Environments: A State of the Art*. CiteSeer. https://citeseerx.ist.psu.edu/document? repid=rep 1&type=pdf&doi=ca53e5830538d1f18feb1995045a4 0e94db5553b.

Awada, G. (2016). Effect of WhatsApp on critique writing proficiency and perceptions toward learning. *Cogent Education, 3*(1), 1264173. doi:10.1080/2331186X.2016.1264173

Awuor, P. (2013). Integrating Indigenous Knowledge for Food Security: Perspectives from Millennium Village Project at Bar-Sauri in Nyanza Province in Kenya. *Paper presented to the African Research and Resource Forum (ARRF) held in Kampala Uganda, on 16 – 17 November 2011.*

Ayittey, G. (2006). *Indigenous African Institutions*. Transnational Publishers Inc. doi:10.1163/ej.9781571053374.i-586

Ayuba, Z. (2009) *Adaptation of aspect of Garin Bah traditional pottery into contemporary ceramic* [M. A thesis, University of Nigeria, Nsukka]. http://bitly.ws/BbIY

Babatunde, S., El-Gohary, H., & Edwards, D. (2021). Assessment methods in entrepreneurship education, challenges and opportunities in developed and developing nations: A comparative study of Nigeria and England. *Education + Training, 63*(7/8), 1092–1113. doi:10.1108/ET-12-2020-0368

Bal, E. (2007). They ask if we eat frogs: Garo ethnicity in Bangladesh (IIAS/ISEAS series on Asia). Leiden, The Netherlands: Singapore: International Institute for Asian Studies; Institute of Southeast Asian Studies.

Bal, E. (2010). Taking root in Bangladesh: States, minorities and discourses on citizenship. *The Newsletter* (Special issue: Indigenous India), 53, 24–25

Bal, E. (1999). *Manderangni Jagring: Images of the Garo(s) in Bangladesh*. University Press.

Bal, E. (2007). Becoming the Garos of Bangladesh: Policies of exclusion and the ethnicization of a 'tribal' minority. *South Asia, 30*(3), 439–455. doi:10.1080/00856400701714062

Bal, E. W. (2000). *They ask if we eat frogs: social boundaries, ethnic categorisation, and the Garo people of Bangladesh*. Eburon.

Ball, A. (2006). Briefing Paper: the OAIS Reference Model. UKOLN, University of Bath.

Ballard, H. L., Robinson, L. D., Young, A. N., Pauly, G. B., Higgins, L. M., Johnson, R. F., & Tweddle, J. C. (2017). Contributions to conservation outcomes by natural history museum-led citizen science: Examining evidence and next steps. *Biological Conservation, 208*, 87–97. doi:10.1016/j.biocon.2016.08.040

Ball, T., & Lar-Son, K. (2021). Relationality in the classroom: Teaching indigenous LIS in a Canadian context. *portal. Portal (Baltimore, Md.), 21*(2), 205–218. doi:10.1353/pla.2021.0012

Balogun, T., & Kalusopa, T. (2022). Web archiving of indigenous knowledge systems in South Africa. *Information Development, 38*(4), 658–671. doi:10.1177/02666669211005522

Bandhari, H., & Yasunobu, K. (2009). What is Social Capital? A Comprehensive Review of the Concept. *Asian Journal of Social Science, 37*(3), 480–510. doi:10.1163/156853109X436847

Bandura, A. (1977). *Social Learning Theory*. General Learning Press.

Bandyopadhyaya, H. (1966). *Bangiya Sabdakosh*. Sahitya Akademii.

Banerjee, A., Bandyopadhyay, T., & Acharya, P. (2013). Data analytics: Hyped-up aspirations or true potential? *Vikalpa, 38*(4), 1–12. doi:10.1177/0256090920130401

Compilation of References

Bao, X., Huang, Y., Jin, Z., Xiao, X., Tang, W., Cui, H., & Chen, X. (2021). Experimental investigation on mechanical properties of clay soil reinforced with carbon fiber. *Construction & Building Materials, 280*, 122517. doi:10.1016/j.conbuildmat.2021.122517

BARCIK (Bangladesh Resource Centre for Indigenous Knowledge). (2006). *Our agriculture, our lives: Shifting agriculture & livelihood struggles of Adivasi Garo in Modhupur* [In Bangla.]. BARCIK.

Barker, S. K. (2007). New opportunities for research libraries in digital information and knowledge management: Challenges for the mid-sized research library. *Journal of Library Administration, 46*(1), 65–74. doi:10.1300/J111v46n01_05

Barnett, W. K., & Hoopes, J. W. (1995). *The emergence of Pottery. Technology and innovation in ancient societies.* Smithsonian Institution Press.

Battiste, M. (2001). Decolonizing the university: Ethical guidelines for research involving indigenous populations. In L. M. Findlay & P. M. Bidwell (Eds.), *Pursuing Academic Freedom: "Free and Fearless"?* (pp. 190–203). Purich Press.

Bein, A. (1993). Cataloging of materials in African languages. *Cataloging & Classification Quarterly, 17*(1-2), 97–114. doi:10.1300/J104v17n01_07

Bennett, K. D. (2017, May 8). *How libraries served soldiers and civilians during WWI and WWII.* OUPblog. https://blog.oup.com/2017/05/libraries-soldiers-world-war/

Bereda, J. E. (2015). *A model to facilitate the Integration of Indigenous Knowledge Systems in the management of HIV & AIDS within a Primary Health Care context in Limpopo Province, South Africa.* North-West University.

Berg, I. (2007). Meaning in the making: The potter's wheel at Phylakopi, Melos (Greece). *Journal of Anthropological Archaeology, 26*(2), 234–252. doi:10.1016/j.jaa.2006.10.001

Bhar, D. (2015). Literature Review on Local History Collection, Its Various Sources and Roles of Libraries by Dhritiman Bhar : SSRN. *Calcutta University Journal of Information Studies.* https://papers.ssrn.com/sol3/papers.cfm?abstract_id=3198824

Bhebhe, S. (2018). Interrogating myths surrounding sex education in Zimbabwean schools: Lessons to be learned from Ndebele traditional literature/oral traditions. *Oral History Journal of South Africa, 6*(1), 18. doi:10.25159/2309-5792/3322

Bhuda, M. T. (2021). Making a Case for Indigenous Education Systems in South Africa. *African Journal of Development Studies, 2021*(si2), 67.

Bhuda, M., & Koitsiwe, M. (2022). The Importance of Underpinning Indigenous Research Using African Indigenous Philosophies: Perspectives From Indigenous Scholars. In *Handbook of Research on Protecting and Managing Global Indigenous Knowledge Systems* (pp. 223–248). IGI Global. doi:10.4018/978-1-7998-7492-8.ch013

Bibi, F., Abbas, Z., Harun, N., Perveen, B., & Bussmann, R. W. (2022). Indigenous knowledge and quantitative ethnobotany of the Tanawal area, Lesser Western Himalayas, Pakistan. *PLoS One, 17*(2), e0263604. https://journals.plos.org/plosone/article?id=10.1371/journal.pone.0263604. doi:10.1371/journal.pone.0263604 PMID:35192648

Bienkowski, P., & Millard, A. (2010). *Dictionary of the ancient near east.* University of Pennsylvania Press.

Birch, T. (2020). 'The invisible fire': Indigenous sovereignty, history and responsibility. In *Sovereign Subjects* (pp. 105–117). Routledge. doi:10.4324/9781003117353-11

Biswas, S. K., Majumder, N. M. & Po, L. T. (2015). An ethnographic exploration of the Lyngam ethnic community in Bangladesh. *Sociology and Anthropology 3(*3), 179-185. Horizon Research Publishing. doi:10.13189/sa.2015.030305

383

Biyela, N., Oyelude, A., & Haumba, E. (2016). Digital preservation of Indigenous Knowledge (IK) by cultural heritage institutions: a comparative study of Nigeria, South Africa and Uganda. HDL. http://hdl.handle.net/20.500.11910/10196

Blake, J. (2000). On Defining the Cultural Heritage. *The International and Comparative Law Quarterly*, *49*(1), 61–85. doi:10.1017/S002058930006396X

Bleie, T. (2005). *Tribal peoples, nationalism, and the human rights challenge: The Adivasis of Bangladesh*. University Press.

Blignaut, S. (2020). Transforming the curriculum for unique challenges faced by South Africa. *Curriculum Perspectives*. doi:10.100741297-020-00104-6

Boadle, A. (2022) *Indigenous protest camp erected in Brazilian capital to press land rights*. Reuters.https://www.reuters.com/world/americas/indigenous-protest-camp-erected-brazilian-capital-press-land-rights-2022-04-05/

Boamah, E. (2018). Relative advantages of digital preservation management in developing countries. *New Review of Information Networking*, *23*(1-2), 83–98. doi:10.1080/13614576.2018.1544088

Boamah, E., & Liew, C. L. (2017). Conceptualizing the digitization and preservation of indigenous knowledge: The importance of attitudes. *Lecture Notes in Computer Science*, *10647*, 65–80. Advance online publication. doi:10.1007/978-3-319-70232-2_6

Boikhutso, D. N. (2012). *Methods of Indigenous Knowledge Preservation in South Africa*. Tshwane University of Technology.

Bollweg, L., Lackes, R., Siepermann, M., & Weber, P. (2020). Drivers and barriers to the digitalisation of local owner-operated retail outlets. *Journal of Small Business and Entrepreneurship*, *32*(2), 173–201. doi:10.1080/08276331.2019 .1616256

Bosancic, B. (2016). Information in the knowledge acquisition process. *The Journal of Documentation*, *72*(5), 930–960. doi:10.1108/JD-10-2015-0122

Bossaller, J., & Million, A. J. (2022). The research data life cycle, legacy data, and dilemmas in research data management. *Journal of the Association for Information Science and Technology*, 1– 6. doi:10.1002/asi.24645

Bouchenaki, M. (2007). A Major Advance Towards A Holistic Approach to Heritage Conservation the 2003 Intangible Heritage Convention. *International Journal of Intangible Heritage*, *2*(105–109), 51–78.

Bountouri, L. (2017). Archives in the digital age: standards, policies and tools. United Kingdom: Chandos Publishing (Oxford) Ltd.

Bovill, C. (2017). A Framework to Explore Roles Within Student-Staff Partnerships in Higher Education: Which Students Are Partners, When, and in What Ways? *International Journal for Students as Partners*, *1*(1). Advance online publication. doi:10.15173/ijsap.v1i1.3062

Bowers, H., Lemberger-Truelove, M., & Brigman, G. (2018). A Social-Emotional Leadership Framework for School Counselors. *Professional School Counseling*, *21*(1b), 1–10. doi:10.1177/2156759X18773004

Boyd, D. (2007). Why Youth Heart Social Network Sites: The Role of Networked Publics in Teenage Social Life. *Berkman Center for Internet and Society at Harvard University*, *7641*(2007–16). doi:10.31219/ doi:osf.io/22hq2

Bradford, S. (2002). Mário Juruna. *The Guardian*.https://www.theguardian.com/news/2002/aug/03/guardianobituaries1

Bratianu, C., & Orzea, I. (2010). Organizational knowledge creation. *Management & Marketing, 5*(3).

Brennen, J. S., & Kreiss, D. (2016). Digitalisation. *The international encyclopedia of communication theory and Philosophy*, 1-11. https://doi.org/ doi:10.1002/9781118766804.wbiect111

Compilation of References

Breunig, P., Franke, G., & Nüsse, M. (2008). Early sculptural traditions in West Africa: New evidence from the Chad Basin of north-eastern Nigeria. *Antiquity, 82*(316), 423–437. doi:10.1017/S0003598X00096915

Broadhead, L. A., & Howard, S. (2011). Deepening the debate over 'sustainable science': Indigenous perspectives as a guide on the journey. *Sustainable Development (Bradford), 19*(5), 301–311. doi:10.1002d.421

Brown, A. (2008). *Digital preservation guidance Note 1: Selecting file formats for long-term preservation*. CDN. https://cdn.nationalarchives.gov.uk/documents/selecting-file-formats.pdf

Bruchac, M. M. (2014). Indigenous knowledge and traditional knowledge. In C. Smith (Ed.), *Encyclopedia of Global Archaeology* (pp. 3814–3824). Springer Science and Business Media. doi:10.1007/978-1-4419-0465-2_10

Burbanks, S. (2014). *Afrocentricity published in the encyclopaedia of identity*. https://www.researchgate.net/publication/268148430

Burling, R. (1963). *Rengsanggri: Family and kinship in a Garo village*. Pennsylvania University Press. doi:10.9783/9781512814972

Burling, R. (1997). *The strong women of Modhupur*. Dhaka University Press.

Burnard, P. (1991). A method of analysing interview transcripts in qualitative research. *Nurse Education Today, 11*(6), 461–466. doi:10.1016/0260-6917(91)90009-Y PMID:1775125

Burrison, J. A. (1997). The living tradition of English country pottery. *Folk Life, 36*(1), 25–39. doi:10.1179/043087797798238198

Busari, D., & Odetoyinbo, O. (2021). Homegrown; Home inspired: The resilience of traditional hand-built pottery production in Ìjàyè, Abéòkúta, Southwest Nigeria. *African Identities, 2021*, 1–17. doi:10.1080/14725843.2021.1940839

Byron, I. P. (2022). The protection of traditional knowledge under the sui generis regime in Nigeria. *International Review of Law Computers & Technology, 36*(1), 17–27. doi:10.1080/13600869.2021.1997086

Cajete, G. (2000). *Native science: Natural laws of interdependence*. Clear Light Publishers.

Camacho, L. D., Gevaña, D. T., Carandang, A. P., & Camacho, S. C. (2016). Indigenous knowledge and practices for the sustainable management of Ifugao forests in Cordillera, Philippines. *The International Journal of Biodiversity Science, Ecosystem Services & Management, 12*(1-2), 5–13. doi:10.1080/21513732.2015.1124453

Camara, J. (2022) *Entenda os motivos para o conflito entre indígenas guarani kaiowá e polícia em Amambai (MS)*. Mato Grosso do Sul, G1. https://g1.globo.com/ms/mato-grosso-do-sul/noticia/2022/06/26/entenda-os-motivos-para-o-conflito-entre-indigenas-guarani-kaiowa-e-policia-em-amambai-ms.ghtml

Cámara-Leret, R., & Bascompte, J. (2021). Language extinction triggers the loss of unique medicinal knowledge. *Proceedings of the National Academy of Sciences of the United States of America, 118*(24), e2103683118. doi:10.1073/pnas.2103683118 PMID:34103398

Carneiro da Cunha, M. (1992). *'Legislação indigenista no século XIX', Uma compilação (1808-1889)*. CPI-SP/Edusp.

Carr, A., Ruhanen, L., & Whitford, M. (2016). Indigenous peoples and tourism: The challenges and opportunities for sustainable tourism. *Journal of Sustainable Tourism, 24*(8-9), 1067–1079. doi:10.1080/09669582.2016.1206112

Carroll, S. R., Garba, I., Plevel, R., Small-Rodriguez, D., Hiratsuka, V. Y., Hudson, M., & Garrison, N. A. (2022). Using indigenous standards to implement the CARE principles: Setting expectations through tribal research codes. *Frontiers in Genetics, 13*, 823309. doi:10.3389/fgene.2022.823309 PMID:35386282

Carvalho, G. O. (2000). The politics of indigenous land rights in Brazil. *Bulletin of Latin American Research, 19*(4), 461–478. doi:10.1016/S0261-3050(00)00032-2

Cassidy, L., Wilk, J., Kgathi, D. L., Bendsen, H., Ngwenya, B. N., & Mosepele, K. (2011). Indigenous knowledge, livelihoods, and government policy in the Okavango Delta, Botswana. In Kgathi, D.L. Ngwenya, B.N. and Darkoh, M.B.K. (Eds). Rural Livelihoods, Risk and Political Economy of Access to Natural Resources in the Okavango Delta, Botswana. Nova Science Publishers.

Chang'a, L. B., Yanda, P. Z., & Ngana, J. (2010). Indigenous Knowledge in Seasonal Rainfall Prediction in Tanzania. *Journal of Geography and Regional Planning, 3*(4), 20–34.

Chassanoff, A., & Altman, M. (2020). Curation as "interoperability with the future": Preserving scholarly research software in academic libraries. *Journal of the Association for Information Science and Technology, 71*(3), 325–337. doi:10.1002/asi.24244

Chauke, O. R. (2022). ORATURE IN AN AFRICAN CONTEXT: VATSONGA AS A CASE IN POINT. *Journal of Positive Psychology and Well-being*, 67-74.

Chaves, L. (2022) *The challenges Lula will face to eradicate illegal deforestation in Amazonia by 2028.* InfoAmazonia. https://infoamazonia.org/en/2022/11/11/the-challenges-lula-will-face-to-eradicate-illegal-deforestation-in-amazonia-by-2028/ (Accessed: 14 December 2022).

Chen, S.-S. (2007). Digital preservation: Organisational commitment, archival stability, and technological logical continuity. *Journal of Organizational Computing and Electronic Commerce, 17*(3), 205–215. doi:10.1080/10919390701294012

Cherrington, A. M., Botha, M., & Keet, A. (2018). 'Decolonising' Education Transformation. *South African Journal of Education, 38*(4), 1–4.

Cherry, A. &Mukunda, K. (2015). A case Study in Indigenous Classification: Revising and Reviving the Brian Deer Scheme, *Catalouging and Classification Quartely, 53*(5-6), 548-567.

Cherry, A., & Mukunda, K. (2015). A case study in indigenous classification: Revisiting and reviving the Brian Deer scheme. *Cataloging & Classification Quarterly, 53*(5-6), 548–567. doi:10.1080/01639374.2015.1008717

Chikodi Mole, A. J., & Obidike, N. A. (2015). Overcoming challenges of electronic collection development in university libraries: A study of three Nigerian university libraries. *Library Collections, Acquisitions & Technical Services, 39*(3-4), 73–81. doi:10.1080/14649055.2016.1231564

Chilisa, B. (2012). *Indigenous Research Methodologies.* Sage publications.

Chilisa, B. (2012). *Indigenous research methodologies.* Sage.

Chimalakonda, S., & Nori, K. V. (2020). An ontology-based modeling framework for design of educational technologies. *Smart Learn. Environ., 7*(1), 28. doi:10.118640561-020-00135-6

Chin, K. Y., Lee, K. F., & Chen, Y. L. (2018). Using an interactive ubiquitous learning system to enhance authentic learning experiences in a cultural heritage course. *Interactive Learning Environments, 26*(4), 444–459. doi:10.1080/10494820.2017.1341939

Chisaka, J. W. (2019). *The use of traditional herbal medicines among palliative care patients at Mulanje Mission Hospital, Malawi.* Master's thesis, Faculty of Health Sciences, University of Cape Town, South Africa]. https://open.uct.ac.za/handle/11427/31511

Compilation of References

Chisenga, J. (2002). Indigenous knowledge: Africa's opportunity to contribute to global information content. *South African Journal of Library and Information Science, 68*(1), 16–22.

Chisita, C. T. (2011). Role of libraries in promoting the dissemination and documentation of indigenous agricultural information: Case study of Zimbabwe. *IFLA WLIC. San Juan, Puerto Rico*, 10-11. In *Paper Of World Library And Information Congress: 77th IFLA General Conference And Assembly.* IFLA. https://www.ifla.org/past-wlic/2011/78-chisita-en.pdf Accessed 23 February 2023.

Chisita, C. T., Rusero, A. M., & Shoko, M. (2016). 18 Leveraging Memory Institutions to Preserve Indigenous Knowledge in the Knowledge Age. Indigenous Notions of Ownership and Libraries. *Archives and Museums, 166*, 273.

Chisita, C. T., Rusero, A. M., & Shoko, M. (2016). Leveraging Memory Institutions to Preserve Indigenous Knowledge inthe Knowledge Age. In *Indigenous Notions of Ownership and Libraries* (p. 273). Archives and Museums. doi:10.1515/9783110363234-021

Chouliaraki, L. (2006) The Spectatorship of the Suffering. SAGE Publications Ltd. doi:10.4135/9781446220658

Christen, K. (2015). Tribal archives, traditional knowledge, and local contexts: Why the "s" matters. *Journal of western archives,6*(1), 1-21

Cicalo, A. (2018). Goodbye "Racial Democracy"? Brazilian Identity, Official Discourse and the Making of a "Black" Heritage Site in Rio de Janeiro. *Bulletin of Latin American Research, 37*(1), 73–86. doi:10.1111/blar.12636

Claire, C., Lefebvre, V., & Ronteau, S. (2020). Entrepreneurship as practice: Systematic literature review of a nascent field. *Entrepreneurship and Regional Development, 32*(3-4), 281–312. doi:10.1080/08985626.2019.1641975

Claxton, M. (2010). Indigenous Knowledge and Sustainable Development. A lecture on Cropper Foundation, UWI, St Augustine, Trinidad, Tobago, September, 2010.

Cobb, A. (2011). *Incorporating indigenous knowledge systems into climate change discourse.* Colorado conference on earth system Governance: Crossing boundaries and Building Bridges.

Cobo, J. R. M. (1986). *Study of the problem of discrimination against indigenous populations.* UUN.

Cocq, C. (2022). Revisiting the digital humanities through the lens of Indigenous studies—Or how to question the cultural blindness of our technologies and practices. *Journal of the Association for Information Science and Technology, 73*(2), 333–344. doi:10.1002/asi.24564

Coleman, A. (2013). Preservation of knowledge in traditional medical practices through information communication technology: A case study in South Africa. *Indilinga, 12*(1), 52–61.

Coleman, J. S. (1990). *Foundations of social theory.* Harvard University Press.

Colombari, R., & Neirotti, P. (2022). Closing the middle-skills gap widened by digitalisation: How technical universities can contribute through Challenge-Based Learning. *Studies in Higher Education, 47*(8), 1585–1600. doi:10.1080/03075079.2021.1946029

Conway, P. (2010). Preservation in the age of Google: Digitalization, digital preservation, and dilemmas. *The Library Quarterly: Information, Community. Policy, 80*(1), 61–79. doi:10.1086/648463

Copyright and Neighbouring Rights Act Chapter 26:05 (2004) Available https://media.zimlii.org/files/legislation/akn-zw-act-2000-11-eng-2004-09-10.pdf Accessed 13 July 2023

Copyrights and Neighbouring Rights Act, 2018. Act No. 4. https://wipolex-res.wipo.int/edocs/lexdocs/laws/en/sz/sz017en.pdf

387

Corcoran, N., & Duane, A. (2018). Using Social Media to Enable Staff Knowledge Sharing in Higher Education Institutions. *AJIS. Australasian Journal of Information Systems*, *22*. Advance online publication. doi:10.3127/ajis.v22i0.1647

Cormack, D., & Kukutai, T. (2022). Indigenous Peoples, Data, and the Coloniality of Surveillance. In *New Perspectives in Critical Data Studies: The Ambivalences of Data Power* (pp. 121–141). Springer International Publishing. doi:10.1007/978-3-030-96180-0_6

Correa, C. M. (2001). Traditional and intellectual property. Geneva: The Quaker United Nations Office (QUNO), 17.

Cossa, J. A. (2009). African Renaissance and globalization: A conceptual analysis. *Ufahamu. Journal of African Studies*, *36*(1).

Cote-Meek, S. and Moeke-Pickering, T., (2017) Indigenous Pedagogies and Transformational Practices. *Talking Back, Talking Forward: Journeys in Transforming Indigenous Educational Practice.*

Council of Canadians Academies. (2015). Leading in the digital world: Opportunities for Canada's memory institutions. The expert panel on memory institutions in the digital revolution. Canada: Ottawa.

Craft Ghar. (n.d.). *Khurja Pottery and Ceramics & Jaipur Blue Pottery.* Craft Ghar. https://www.craftghar.com/blogs/handicrafts-of-india/khurja-pottery-and-ceramics-jaipur-blue-pottery

Craith, M. N. (2008). Intangible Cultural Heritages. *Anthropological Journal on European Cultures*, *17*(1), 54–73. doi:10.3167/ajec.2008.01701004

Cross, M. (2020). Decolonising universities in South Africa: Backtracking and revisiting the debate. In *Transforming Universities in South Africa* (pp. 101–130). Brill. doi:10.1163/9789004437043_006

Cuaton, G. P., & Su, Y. (2020). Local-indigenous knowledge on disaster risk reduction: Insights from the Mamanwa indigenous peoples in Basey, Samar after Typhoon Haiyan in the Philippines. *International Journal of Disaster Risk Reduction*, *48*, 101596. doi:10.1016/j.ijdrr.2020.101596

Curiel, E. (2017). A Primer on Energy Conditions. In *Towards a Theory of Spacetime Theories* (pp. 43–104). Birkhäuser. doi:10.1007/978-1-4939-3210-8_3

Custódio, L. (2017). *Favela Media Activism Counterpublics for Human Rights in Brazil* (1st ed.). Lexington Books.

Damgaard, M. (2018). 'Cascading corruption news : Explaining the bias of media attention to Brazil' s political scandals'. *Opinião Pública*, *24*(1), 114–143. http://dx.doi./10.1590/1807-01912018241114. doi:10.1590/1807-01912018241114

Daniel, D. (2012). Teaching Students How to Research the Past: Historians and Librarians in the Digital Age. *The History Teacher*, *45*(2), 261–282.

Dapar, M. L. G., Alejandro, G. J. D., Meve, U., & Liede-Schumann, S. (2020). Quantitative ethnopharmacological documentation and molecular confirmation of medicinal plants used by the Manobo tribe of Agusan del Sur, Philippines. *Journal of Ethnobiology and Ethnomedicine*, *16*(1), 1–60. doi:10.118613002-020-00363-7 PMID:32138749

Das, T. K., & Islam, H. Z. (2005). Psycho-social dimensions of ethnicity: The situation of Garo community in Bangladesh. Dhaka. *Asian Affairs*, *27*(3), 45–54.

Davenport, T., & Kalakota, R. (2019). The potential for artificial intelligence in healthcare. *Future Healthcare Journal*, *6*(2), 94–98. doi:10.7861/futurehosp.6-2-94 PMID:31363513

Daves, S., & Ebbe, K. (1995). *Traditional Knowledge and Sustainable Development.* World Bank. https://documents1.worldbank.org/curated/en/517861468766175944/pdf/multi-page.pdf

Compilation of References

Davids, N., & Waghid, Y. (2021). *Academic activism in Higher Education: a living philosophy for social justice* (Vol. 5). Springer Nature. doi:10.1007/978-981-16-0340-2

Davis, S. H. (1977). *Victims of the miracle : development and the Indians of Brazil* (1st ed.). Cambridge University Press.

De Sutter, E., Borry, P., Geerts, D., & Huys, I. (2021). Personalized and long-term electronic informed consent in clinical research: Stakeholder views. *BMC Medical Ethics*, 22(1), 1–12. doi:10.118612910-021-00675-7 PMID:34332572

De Wit, H., & Altbach, P. G. (2021). Internationalization in higher education: Global trends and recommendations for its future. *Policy Reviews in Higher Education*, 5(1), 28–46. doi:10.1080/23322969.2020.1820898

Deck, A., & Marasciulo, M. (2022) TikTok's biggest Chinese competitor bets big on Brazil. Rest of World. https://restofworld.org/2022/tiktok-competitor-kwai-brazil/ (Accessed: 27 March 2022).

Decuypere, M., Grimaldi, E., & Landri, P. (2021). Introduction: Critical studies of digital education platforms. *Critical Studies in Education*, 62(1), 1–16. doi:10.1080/17508487.2020.1866050

Dei, G. J. S., & Hall, L. B. L., & Rosenberg, D. G (2000). Indigenous knowledge in global contexts: multiple readings of our world. Toronto Canada: University of Toronto Press.

Dei, G. J. S. (2008). Indigenous knowledge studies and the next generation: Pedagogical possibilites for anti-colonial education. *Australian Journal of Indigenous Education*, 37(S1), 5–13. doi:10.1375/S1326011100000326

Demssie, Y. N., Biemans, H. J., Wesselink, R., & Mulder, M. (2020). Combining indigenous knowledge and modern education to foster sustainability competencies: Towards a set of learning design principles. *Sustainability (Basel)*, 12(17), 6823. doi:10.3390u12176823

Denbow, J., & Thebe, P. C. (2006). *Culture and Customs of Batswana*. Greenwood Press.

Department of Science and Technology (DST). (2004). *Indigenous Knowledge Systems*. DST.

Department of Science and Technology (DST). (2016). Protection, promotion, development and management of indigenous knowledge systems bill. South Africa: Pretoria.

Development in Ethiopia. (●●●). Ethiopian. *Journal of Social Sciences and Humanities*, 18(1), 121–144. doi:10.1314/ejossah.v18i1.5

Dlamini, P. (2016). *The use of information and communication technologies to manage indigenous knowledge in KwaZulu-Natal, South Africa*. [PhD, Dissertation, Department of Library and Information Science, University of Zululand, South Africa]. https://uzspace.unizulu.ac.za/server/api/core/bitstreams/f6a73311-71d8-4bd0-8652-c9655efad417/content

Dlamini, P. P., & Nokwanda, K. N. (2021). Preservation of traditional medicinal knowledge: Initiatives and techniques in rural communities in KwaZulu-Natal. *Library Philosophy and Practice (e-journal).*https://digitalcommons.unl.edu/libphilprac/4824

Dlamini, P., & Ocholla, D. N. (2018). Information and communication technology tools for managing indigenous knowledge in KwaZulu-Natal Province, South Africa. *African Journal of Library Archives and Information Science*, 28(2), 137–153.

Dogara, P. D., Yashim, A. B., & Peter, Y. L. (2022). Enhancing Information Service Delivery through Effective Information Repackaging in Colleges of Education Libraries. *Niger Delta Journal of Library and Information Science*, 3(1).

Dougherty, A. (2011). Live-streaming mobile video: Production as civic engagement. *Mobile HCI 2011 - 13th International Conference on Human-Computer Interaction with Mobile Devices and Services*, (pp. 425–434). IEEE. 10.1145/2037373.2037437

Doyle, A. M., Lawson, K., & Dupont, S. (2015). *Indigenization of knowledge organization at the Xwi7xwa Library.* University of British Columbia.

Doyle, M. A., Lawson, K., & Dupont, S. (2015). *Journal of Library and Information Studies, 13*(2), 107–134.

Drinot, P. (2011). Website of memory: The war of the Pacific (1879-84) in the global age of YouTube. *Memory Studies, 4*(4), 370–385. doi:10.1177/1750698011409290

Drong, S. (2004). *Eco-park project threats to evict 25,000 Garos.* Indigenous People's Forum.

Drumheller, A., & Kaminitz, M. (1994). Traditional care and conservation, the merging of two disciplines at the national museum of the American Indian. *Studies in Conservation, 39*(2), 58–60. doi:10.1179ic.1994.39.Supplement-2.58

Du Plessis, P. (2021). Decolonisation of education in South Africa: Challenges to decolonise the university curriculum. *South African Journal of Higher Education, 35*(1), 54–69. doi:10.20853/35-1-4426

Dube, L., Ngulube, P., & Mhlongo, M. (2015). Towards a cartography of indigenous knowledge systems in library and information science training and education in Anglophone eastern and southern Africa. *Indilinga, 14*(2), 145–168.

Dumbrill, G. C., & Grren, J. (2008). Indigenous Knowledge in the Social Work Academy. *Social Work Education, 27*(5), 489–503. doi:10.1080/02615470701379891

Duncan, C., & Wallach, A. (2019). The Museum of Modern Art as Late Capitalist Ritual: An Iconographie Analysis. In D. Preziosi & C. Farago (Eds.), *Grasping the World* (pp. 483–499). Routledge. doi:10.4324/9780429399671-31

Duranti, L. (2010). The long-term preservation of the digital heritage: A case study of universities' institutional repositories. *JLIS.it. 1*(1), 157–168.

Durie, M. (2005). Indigenous knowledge within a global knowledge system. *Higher Education Policy, 18*(3), 301–312. doi:10.1057/palgrave.hep.8300092

Duvelle, C. (2017). Aventuras y desventuras de una hermosa Convención Internacional. *Revista Andaluza de Antropología, 12*(12), 31–47. doi:10.12795/RAA.2017.12.02

Easa, N. F. (2012). *Knowledge management and the SECI model: A study of innovation in the Egyptian banking sector.* University of Striling.

Ebhuoma, E. E., & Simatele, D. M. (2019). 'We know our Terrain': Indigenous knowledge preferred to scientific systems of weather forecasting in the Delta State of Nigeria. *Climate and Development, 11*(2), 112–123. doi:10.1080/1756552 9.2017.1374239

Ebijuwa, A. S., & Mabawonku, I. (2015). Documentation and use of indigenous knowledge by practitioners of alternative healthcare in Oyo State, Nigeria. *African Journal of Library Archives and Information Science, 25*(1).

Edwards, A. (2019). Unsettling the future by uncovering the past: Decolonizing academic libraries and librarianship. *Partnership. The Canadian Journal of Library and Information Practice and Research, 14*(1). doi:10.21083/partnership.v14i1.5161

Eichler, J. (2021). Intangible cultural heritage, inequalities and participation: Who decides on heritage? *International Journal of Human Rights, 25*(5), 793–814. doi:10.1080/13642987.2020.1822821

Eje, A. E., Udie, E. A., & Vincent, C. A. (2021). Making Agricultural Education more Practicable: The need for its curriculum restructuring in Nigeria.[AJRD]. *Academic Journal of Research and Development, 15*(2), 52–64.

Compilation of References

Ekaette, S. O., Owan, V. J., & Agbo, D. I. (2019). External debts and the financing of education in Nigeria from 1988 – 2018: Implication for effective educational management.[JERA]. *Journal of Educational Realities, 9*(1), 1–14. doi:10.5281/zenodo.4320606

Ekong, C. E. (2018). Rethinking the preservative relevance of pottery to the development of Nigeria. *Humanities Report, 8*(1), 59–72.

Ekpoh, U. I., & Asuquo, M. E. (2018). Management techniques and sustainability of post-basic education in Calabar Education Zone of Cross River State, Nigeria. *African Journal of Studies in Education, 12*(2), 39–53. https://scholar.google.com/scholar?cluster=8570829484364958859&hl=en&oi=scholarr

Elebute, A., & Odokuma, E. (2016). Arts and crafts as veritable sources of economic empowerment for marginalised people in Nigeria. *International Journal of Development and Economic Sustainability, 4*(3), 11–24. http://bitly.ws/B9Le

Elias, M. J. (2003). Academic and Social-Emotional Learning. Educational Practices Series – 11. Geneva, Switzerland: International Academy of Education and International Bureau of Education.

Esosuakpo, S. (2020). Restructuring ceramic production for wealth creation, security and sustainable development through the construction of Kick Wheel. *UJAH: Unizik Journal of Arts and Humanities, 21*(4), 118–134. doi:10.4314/ujah.v21i4.7

Eyong, C. T. (2007). Indigenous knowledge and sustainable development in Africa: Case study on Central Africa. *Tribes and Tribals, Special, 1,* 121-139. https://www.researchgate.net/publication/208152935_Indigenous_Knowledge_and_Sustainable_Development_in_Africa_Case_Study_on_Central_Africa

Ezeanya-Esiobu, C. (2019), Indigenous Knowledge and Education in Africa. *Frontiers in African Business Research.*

Ezenagu, N. (2020). Heritage resources as a driver for cultural tourism in Nigeria. *Cogent Arts & Humanities, 7*(1), 1734331. doi:10.1080/23311983.2020.1734331

Fahm, A. O., Azeez, A. L., Imam-Fulani, Y. O., Mejabi, O. V., Faruk, N., Abdulrahaman, M. D., Olawoyin, L. A., Oloyede, A. A., & Surajudeen-Bakinde, N. T. (2022). ICT enabled Almajiri education in Nigeria: Challenges and prospects. *Education and Information Technologies, 27*(3), 3135–3169. doi:10.100710639-021-10490-7 PMID:34539214

Faklaris, C. (2016). Legal and Ethical Implications of Mobile Live-Streaming Video Apps. In *Proceedings of the 18th International Conference on Human-Computer Interaction with Mobile Devices and Services Adjunct.* New York City: ACM. 10.1145/2957265.2961845

FAO. (2012). *Gender and climate change research in agriculture and food security for rural development training guide.* FAO. https://www.fao.org/docrep/013/i2050e/i2050e00.htm

FAO. (2014). *Second International Conference on Nutrition; Better Nutrition-better lives.* FAO.

Fatuyi, O. A. (2018). Technological Shift and Consequences for Pottery Practices in South-Western Nigeria. *International Journal of Sciences, 7*(06), 93–102. doi:10.18483/ijSci.1284

Faust, B. (2007). Implementation of tacit knowledge preservation and transfer methods: Preservation-and-Transfer-Methods. *Fraser Health.* https://www.fraserhealth.ca/media/Implementation-of-Tacit-Knowledge

Federal Republic of Nigeria (FRN). (2008). *National Policy on Education.* NERDC Press.

Fenton, J. A. (2016). Masking and money in a Nigerian metropolis: The economics of performance in Calabar. *Critical Interventions, 10*(2), 172–192. doi:10.1080/19301944.2016.1205364

Fernandez, M.E. (1994). Gender and indigenous knowledge. *Indigenous knowledge and development monitor, 2*(3), 6-7.

Fernández-Llamazares, Á., & Cabeza, M. (2018). *Rediscovering the potential of indigenous storytelling.* Wiley.

Figueiredo, A., Rocha, C., & Montagna, P. (2020). Data collection with indigenous people: Fieldwork experiences from Chile. In *Researching peace, conflict, and power in the field: Methodological challenges and opportunities* (pp. 105–127). Springer International Publishing. doi:10.1007/978-3-030-44113-5_7

Flavia Costa Netto, A. (2022) *SOS POVO HUNI KUIN DO ALTO RIO PURUS – ACRE.* Vakinha. https://www.vakinha.com.br/vaquinha/sos-povo-huni-kuin-no-acre

Ford, D. Y. & Moore, J. L. (2004). Creating responsive gift understanding of culture is the first step. *Fall, 27*(4), 34–39.

Ford, L. H., & Roman, T. A. (1995). Averaged energy conditions and quantum inequalities. *Physical Review. D, 51*(8), 4277–4286. doi:10.1103/PhysRevD.51.4277 PMID:10018903

Forutnani, S., Nowkarizi, M., Kiani, M. R., & Aski, H. R. M. (2018). The role of rural libraries in preserving the indigenous knowledge of rural residents: The case of South Khorasan Province. *World Journal of Science. Technology and Sustainable Development, 15*(3), 245–256. doi:10.1108/WJSTSD-12-2017-0044

Francis, O. M., Ifeanyieze, F. O., Ikehi, M. E., Ojiako, C. C., Okadi, A. O., Nwankwo, C. U., & Ekenta, L. U. (2019). Vocational agriculture and entrepreneurship aspirations among university students in Nigeria. *International Journal of Training Research, 17*(3), 220–237. doi:10.1080/14480220.2019.1690744

Frayne, A. (2022). Transcribing public libraries as revitalized ethical spaces. *IFLA Journal, 48*(3), 410–421. doi:10.1177/03400352221074716

Frederick, D. E. (2016). Libraries, data and the fourth industrial revolution (Data Deluge Column). *Library Hi Tech News, 33*(5), 9–12. doi:10.1108/LHTN-05-2016-0025

Fredriksson, M. (2021). India's Traditional Knowledge Digital Library and the Politics of Patent Classifications. *Law and Critique.* Doi.org/10.1007/s10978-021-09299-7 PMID:36915708

Fredriksson, M. (2022). Balancing community rights and national interests in international protection of knowledge: A study of India's Traditional Digital Library. *Third World Quarterly, 43*(2), 352–370. doi:10.1080/01436597.2021.2019009

Freeman, L., & Vazquez Llorente, R. (2021). Finding the Signal in the Noise. *Journal of International Criminal Justice, 19*(1), 163–188. doi:10.1093/jicj/mqab023

Freire, P. (2018). *Pedagogy of the oppressed.* Bloomsbury publishing USA.

French, C. (1996). *Data processing and information technology* (10th ed.). Cengage Learning Business Press. https://bit.ly/3LXxLAC

Friday, A., & Oghenerioborue, U. P. (2023). Cultural Riddles and Performance in Modern African Societies. *Randwick International of Social Science Journal, 4*(1), 118–131. doi:10.47175/rissj.v4i1.633

Fruth, M., & Teuteberg, F. (2017). Digitization in maritime logistics—What is there and what is missing? *Cogent Business & Management, 4*(1), 1411066. doi:10.1080/23311975.2017.1411066

FUNAI. (2023). *PL 490/07 e marco temporal colocam em risco os direitos dos povos indígenas.* Fundação Nacional dos Povos Indígenas. https://www.gov.br/funai/pt-br/assuntos/noticias/2023/201cpl-490-07-e-marco-temporal-colocam-em-risco-os-direitos-dos-povos-indigenas201d-alerta-presidenta-da-funai (Accessed: 29 May 2023).

Gabrys, J. (2022). *Instrumental Citizens: How to Retool Action.* University of Minnesota Press. https://manifold.umn.edu/projects/citizens-of-worlds

Compilation of References

Gain, P. (1989). The History of Mandis. *Dhaka Journal*, (January-February), 19–25.

Gain, P. (1998). *Forest and forest people of Bangladesh. Bangladesh: Land Forest and Forest people, Society for Environment and Human Development*. SEHD.

Gain, P. (2011). *Survival on the fringe: Adivasis of Bangladesh*. Society for Environment and Human Development.

Gain, P. (Ed.). (1995). *Bangladesh Land Forest and Forest People*. SEHD.

Galloway, K. (2010). *Advance guard: climate change impacts, adaptation, mitigation and Indigenous peoples*. UNUIAS.

Garrett, R. D., Cammelli, F., Ferreira, J., Levy, S. A., Valentim, J., & Vieira, I. (2021). Forests and Sustainable Development in the Brazilian Amazon: History, Trends, and Future Prospects. *Annual Review of Environment and Resources, 46*(1), 625–652. doi:10.1146/annurev-environ-012220-010228

Gartaula, H., Patel, K., Shukla, S., & Devkota, R. (2020). Indigenous knowledge of traditional foods and food literacy among youth: Insights from rural Nepal. *Journal of Rural Studies, 73*, 77–86. doi:10.1016/j.jrurstud.2019.12.001

Gaura, A. S., Honjia, M. A., & Baoshan, G. E. (2019). MNC strategy, knowledge transfer context and knowledge flow in MNEs. *Journal of Knowledge Management, 23*(9), 1885–1900. doi:10.1108/JKM-08-2018-0476

Gelfand, J. A. (1984). Infections in burn patients: A paradigm for cutaneous infection in the patient at risk. *The American Journal of Medicine, 76*(5, 5A), 158–165. doi:10.1016/0002-9343(84)90259-6 PMID:6372465

Gelfand, M. (1979). *Growing up in Shona society: from birth to marriage*. Mambo Publishers.

Ghimire, P. (2021). The digitalisation of Indigenous Knowledge in Nepal—Review Article. *Acta Inform. Malays, 5*(2), 42–47. doi:10.26480/aim.02.2021.42.47

Ghosh, B., Ramos-Mejía, M., Machado, R. C., Yuana, S. L., & Schiller, K. (2021). Decolonising transitions in the Global South: Towards more epistemic diversity in transitions research. *Environmental Innovation and Societal Transitions, 41*, 106–109. doi:10.1016/j.eist.2021.10.029

Gibbons, J. A., Hammersley, M., & Atkinson, P. (1986). Ethnography: Principles in Practice. *Contemporary Sociology, 15*(3), 451. Advance online publication. doi:10.2307/2070079

Gilmore, R. O., Kennedy, J. L., & Adolph, K. E. (2018). Practical solutions for sharing data and materials from psychological research. *Advances in Methods and Practices in Psychological Science, 1*(1), 121–130. doi:10.1177/2515245917746500 PMID:31157320

Ginsburg, F. (1992). Indigenous Media: Faustian Contract or Global Village? In G. E. Marcus (Ed.), Rereading Cultural Anthropology. Duke University Press., Available at http://read.dukeupress.edu/books/book/chapter-pdf/664756/9780822397861-019.pdf, Retrieved May 2, 2022, from.

Gittell, R. J., & Vidal, A. (1998). *Community organizing: Building social capital as a development strategy*. Sage Publications, Inc. doi:10.4135/9781452220567

Gladman Chibememe, G, Dhliwayo, M, Gandiwa, E, Mtisi, S, Muboko, N, & Kupika, O.L (2014). *Review of National Laws & policies that support or undermine Indigenous peoples and Local Communities*. Natural Justice. naturaljustice.org/wp-content/uploads/2015/09/Zimbabwe-Legal-Review.pdf .

Glaser, B. G., & Strauss, A. L. (1967). *The discovery of grounded theory: Strategies for qualitative research*. Aldine De Gruyter.

Glasson, G. E., Mhango, N., Phiri, A., & Lanier, M. (2010). Sustainability science education in Africa: Negotiating indigenous ways of living with nature in the third space. *International Journal of Science Education, 32*(1), 125–141. doi:10.1080/09500690902981269

Goldman, M.J., Turner, M.D. & Daly, M. (2018). A critical political ecology of human dimensions of climate change: Epistemology, ontology, and ethics. *Wiley Interdisciplinary Reviews: Climate Change, 9*(4), p.e526.

Goodwin Gómez, G. (2006). Computer Technology and Native Literacy in the Amazon Rain Forrest. In L. Everlyn Dyson, M. Hendriks, & S. Grant (Eds.), *Information Technology and Indigenous People* (1st ed., pp. 17–20). Information Science Publishing., doi:10.4018/978-1-59904-298-5.ch013

Gopal, P. (2021). On Decolonisation and the University. *Textual Practice, 35*(6), 873–899. doi:10.1080/0950236X.2021.1929561

Gorjestani, N. (2000). Indigenous knowledge for development: Opportunities and challenges.*The UNCTAD Conference on Traditional Knowledge in*Geneva.The World Bank.

Gosart, U. (2021). Indigenous librarianship: Theory, practices, and means of social action. *IFLA Journal, 47*(3), 293–304. doi:10.1177/0340035221991861

Govender, N., Mudaly, R., & James, A. (2013). Indigenous knowledge of custodians of Zulu culture–Implications for multilogical dialogue in the academy. *Alternation (Durban), 20*(1), 154–177.

Government of Uganda. (2003) The National Library Act, 2003, Kampala Uganda Government of Uganda (2023) Museum and Monument Act,2023, Kampala Uganda

Grande, S., San Pedro, T., & Windchief, S. (2015). Indigenous peoples and identity in the 21st century: Remembering, reclaiming, and regenerating. *Multicultural perspectives on race, ethnicity, and identity*, 105-122.

Greenhow, C., & Askari, E. (2017). Learning and teaching with social network sites: A decade of research in K-12 related education. *Education and Information Technologies, 22*(2), 623–645. doi:10.100710639-015-9446-9

Gregory, S. (2015). *Ubiquitous witnesses : who creates the evidence and the live (d) experience of human rights violations ?* Taylor and Francis. . doi:10.1080/1369118X.2015.1070891

Gregory, S. (2022) *TikTok Must Not Fail Ukrainians.* WIRED.https://www.wired.com/story/tiktok-must-not-fail-ukrainians/

Grenier, L. (1998). *Working with indigenous knowledge: A guide for researchers.* IDRC.

Greyling, E., & Zulu, S. (2010). Content development in an indigenous digital library: A case study in community participation. *IFLA Journal, 36*(1), 30–39. doi:10.1177/0340035209359570

Grey, S. (2014). Indigenous Knowledge. In A. C. Michalos (Ed.), *Encyclopedia of Quality Life and Well-Being Research* (pp. 3229–3233). Springer. doi:10.1007/978-94-007-0753-5_1448

Grindley, N. (2010). Frameworks for e-Content.*Decoding the Digital Conference, DPC/Preservation Advisory Centre, BL.* Joint Information Systems Committee.https://www.dpconline.org/docs/miscellaneous/events/491-decoding grindley- pdf/file

Guadalupe, M. R. (2002). Indigenous Rights in Democratic Brazil. *Human Rights Quarterly, 24*(2), 487–512. https://www.jstor.org/stable/20069611. doi:10.1353/hrq.2002.0028

Gumbo, M. T. (2019). Online or offline supervision? Postgraduate supervisors state their position at university of South Africa. *South African Journal of Higher Education, 33*(1), 92–110. doi:10.20853/33-1-2673

Compilation of References

Gundhlanga, E. S., & Makaudze, G. (2012). Indigenous Knowledge Systems: Confirming Legacy of Civilization and Culture on the African Continent.[PJSS]. *Prime Journal of Social Science, 1*(4), 72–77.

Gupta, N., Martindale, A., Supernant, K., & Elvidge, M. (2023). The CARE Principles and the Reuse, Sharing, and Curation of Indigenous Data in Canadian Archaeology. *Advances in Archaeological Practice, 11*(1), 76–89. doi:10.1017/aap.2022.33

Guzik, E., Griffin, B., & Hartel, J. (2020). Multimedia Approaches to Learning the Foundations of Library and Information Science. *Journal of Education for Library and Information Science, 61*(1), 126–154. https://doi.org/10.3138/jelis.61.1.2018-0003. doi:10.3138/jelis.61.1.2018-0003

Hakim, G., & Chishti, M. (2010). *The traditional healer's handbook: a classic guide to the medicine of Avicenna*. Healing Arts Press.

Hammersmith, J. A. (2007). *Converging Indigenous and Western Knowledge Systems: Implications for Tertiary Education*. [Unpublished Doctoral Thesis. University of Pretoria: South Africa].

Handayani, R. D., Wilujeng, I., & Prasetyo, Z. K. (2018). Elaborating Indigenous Knowledge in the Science Curriculum for the Cultural Sustainability. *Journal of Teacher Education for Sustainability, 20*(2), 74–88. doi:10.2478/jtes-2018-0016

Hangshing, J. (2019). Towards indigenous librarianship: Indian perspective. *Library Philosophy and Practice*, 1-16.

Hanna de Almeida Oliveira, P. (2012). *The social impacts of large projects on Indigenous Peoples, University of Groningen*. University of Groningen., doi:10.1016/B978-0-12-373932-2.00298-2

Hanna, P., Langdon, E. J., & Vanclay, F. (2016). Indigenous rights, performativity and protest. *Land Use Policy, 50*, 490–506. doi:10.1016/j.landusepol.2015.06.034

Happel, H., Maalej, W., & Seedorf, S. (2010). *Applications of Ontologies in Collaborative Software Development.* . doi:10.1007/978-3-642-10294-3_6

Haque, M., Chowdhury, A. B. M., Shahjahan, M., Harun, M., & Dostogir, G. (2018). Traditional healing practices in rural Bangladesh: A qualitative investigation. *BMC Complementary and Alternative Medicine, 18*(1), 1–15. doi:10.118612906-018-2129-5 PMID:29448941

Haron, H., & Hamiz, M. (2014). An Ontological Framework to Preserve Malay Indigenous Health Knowledge. *Journal of Computational and Theoretical Nanoscience, 20*(1), 226–230.

Harris, F. (2015). Understanding human remains repatriation: Practice procedures at the British Museum and the natural history museum. *Museum Management and Curatorship, 30*(2), 138–153. doi:10.1080/09647775.2015.1022904

Harry, D., & Kanehe, L. M. (2006) Asserting Tribal Sovereignty over Cultural Property: Moving Towards Protectio8n of Genetic Material and Indigenous Knowledge. *Seattle Journal for Social Justice,5*(1). https://digitalcommons.law.seattleu.edu/sjsj/vol5/iss1/13

Hassim, A., Heywood, M., & Berger, J. (2007). *Health and democracy: A guide to human rights, health law and policy in post-apartheid South Africa*. ALP. http://www.alp.org.za/publications/healthanddemocracy/Chapter7.pdf

Haumba, E. N., & Kaddu, S. (2017). Documenting and disseminating agricultural indigenous for sustainable food security in Uganda. *University of Dar es Salaam. Library Journal, 12*(1), 66–86.

Hauser, J., & Shoshany, B. (2020). Time travel paradoxes and multiple histories. *Physical Review. D, 102*(6), 064062. doi:10.1103/PhysRevD.102.064062

Hawking, S. W. (1992). Chronology protection conjecture. *Physical Review. D, 46*(2), 603–611. doi:10.1103/PhysRevD.46.603 PMID:10014972

Hedstrom, M. L., & Montgomery, S. (1998). *Digital preservation needs and requirements in RLG member institutions.* Research Libraries Group.

Heleta, S. (2018). Decolonizing knowledge in South Africa: Dismantling the 'pedagogy of big lies'. *Ufahamu. Journal of African Studies, 40*(2).

Herrera-Franco, G., Montalván-Burbano, N., Carrión-Mero, P., Apolo-Masache, B., & Jaya-Montalvo, M. (2020). Research trends in geotourism: A bibliometric analysis using the scopus database. *Geosciences, 10*(10), 379. doi:10.3390/geosciences10100379

Higgs, P., Higgs, L. G., & Venter, E. (2003). Indigenous African knowledge systems and innovation in higher education in South Africa: Perspectives on higher education. *South African Journal of Higher Education, 17*(2), 40–45.

Hill, H., Harrington, M., Rothbauer, P., & Pawlick Potts, D. (2021). Decolonizing & indigenizing LIS. *ALISE 2021 Juried Papers*, 1-6.

Hisayasu, L. (2019). *Mediated Memory and the Internet : Indigenous Protagonism in Brazil.* Danube University.

Höchtl, J., Parycek, P., & Schöllhammer, R. (2016). Big data in the policy cycle: Policy decision making in the digital era. *Journal of Organizational Computing and Electronic Commerce, 26*(1-2), 147–169. doi:10.1080/10919392.2015.1125187

Hoelle, J. (2017). Jungle beef: Consumption, production and destruction, and the development process in the Brazilian Amazon. *Journal of Political Ecology, 24*(1), 743. doi:10.2458/v24i1.20964

Hoe, S. L. (2006). Tacit knowledge, Nonaka and Takeuchi SECI model and informal knowledge processes. *International Journal of Organization Theory and Behavior, 9*(4), 490–502. doi:10.1108/IJOTB-09-04-2006-B002

Höijer, B. (2004). The discourse of global compassion: The audience and media reporting of human suffering. *Media Culture & Society, 26*(4), 513–531. doi:10.1177/0163443704044215

Holston, J. (2008). *Insurgent Citizenship: Disjunctons of Democracy and Modernity in Brazil.* Princton University Press.

Holtorf, C. (2018). Embracing change: How cultural resilience is increased through cultural heritage. *World Archaeology, 50*(4), 639–650. doi:10.1080/00438243.2018.1510340

Hornbeck, S. E. (2015). Elephant ivory: An overview of changes to its stringent regulation and considerations for its identification. *Objects Spec. Group Postprints AIC, 22*, 101–121.

Horsthemke, K. (2017). Indigenous (African) Systems, Science, and Technology. In A. Afolayan & T. Falola (Eds.), *The Palgrave Handbook of African Philosophy.*, doi:10.1057/978-1-137-59291-0_38

Hostettmann, K., Marston, A., Ndjoko, K., & Wolfender, J. L. (2000). The potential of African plants as a source of drugs. *Current Organic Chemistry, 4*(10), 973–1010. doi:10.2174/1385272003375923

Hue, N. V., Chung, N. D., Hang, V. T. T., Be, P. T., & Nga, T. T. P. (2022). Factors affecting the fermentation process of Vietnamese traditional wine (" men la" wine) using" Ba Nang" wine starter. *African Journal of Food, Agriculture, Nutrition and Development, 22*(5), 20317–20330. doi:10.18697/ajfand.110.21480

Huiberts, E., & Joye, S. (2019). Who cares for the suffering other? A survey-based study into reactions toward images of distant suffering. *The International Communication Gazette, 81*(6–8), 562–579. doi:10.1177/1748048518825324

Compilation of References

Hummel, P., Braun, M., Tretter, M., & Dabrock, P. (2021). Data sovereignty: A review. *Big Data & Society, 8*(1), 2053951720982012. doi:10.1177/2053951720982012

Humphrey, N. (2013). *Social and emotional learning: A critical appraisal.* Sage. doi:10.4135/9781446288603

Hunter, J. (2005). The Role of Information Technologies in Indigenous Knowledge Management. *Australian Academic and Research Libraries, 36*(2), 109–124. doi:10.1080/00048623.2005.10721252

Hunter, L. B. (2019). Live streaming and the perils of proximity. *International Journal of Performance Arts and Digital Media, 15*(3), 283–294. doi:10.1080/14794713.2019.1671697

Hussein, H. (2022). Interview Method. In M. R. Islam, N. A. Khan, & R. Baikady (Eds.), *Principles of social research methodology.* Springer. doi:10.1007/978-981-19-5441-2_14

Hutchings, A., Scott, A. H., Lewis, G., & Cunningham, A. B. (1996). *Zulu medicinal plants: An inventory.* University of Natal Press. https://pubs.acs.org/doi/10.1021/np970084y

Hyett, S. L., Gabel, C., Marjerrison, S., & Schwartz, L. (2019). Deficit-based indigenous health research and the stereotyping of indigenous peoples. *Canadian Journal of Bioethics, 2*(2), 102–109. doi:10.7202/1065690ar

Ibrahim, Y. (2010). Distant Suffering and Postmodern Subjectivity: The Communal Politics of Pity. *Nebula, 7*(1/2), 122–135. http://content.ebscohost.com/ContentServer.asp?T=P&P=AN&K=51594697&S=R&D=hlh&EbscoCont ent=dGJyMNHX8kSeqLE4y9fwOLCmr0ueprRSsa64TbWWxWXS&ContentCustomer=dGJyMPPZ8oTn2LmF39/ sU+Pe7Yvy%5Cnhttp://search.ebscohost.com/login.aspx?direct=true&db=hlh&AN=51594697&si

Ibrahim, Y. (2020). *Technologies of Trauma: Flesh Witnessing to Livestreaming Online.* Human Arenas. doi:10.100742087-020-00120-y

Ifijeh, G., Iwu-James, J., & Osinulu, I. (2015). From binding to digitization: Issues in newspaper preservation in Nigerian academic libraries. *Serials Review, 41*(4), 242–249. doi:10.1080/00987913.2015.1103153

IFLA. (2020, May 20). *Gateways to Cultural Diversity: Libraries as multicultural hubs.* IFLA. https://blogs.ifla.org/ lpa/2020/05/20/gateways-to-cultural-diversity-libraries-as-multicultural-hubs/

IFLA. (2023)IFLA statement on Indigenous Traditional Knowledge. IFLA. https://www.ifla.org/publications/ifla-statement-on-indigenous-traditional-knowledge

IFLA/UNESCO. (2010). *Manifesto for Digital Libraries.* National Library of the Netherlands.

Ihekwoaba, E. C., Okwor, R. N., Nnadi, C. U., Jidere, U. U., & Obim, I. E. (2022). Sustaining Indigenous knowledge through the digitization of information on Herbal Medicinei n Medical libraries in Nigeria: Problems and Prospects. *Library Philosophy and Practice (e-journal),* 7316. https://digitalcommons.unl.edu/libphilprac/7316

IIo, P. I. (2012). Acquisition, preservation and accessibility of indigenous knowledge in academic libraries in Nigeria: The place of ICT. *Ikenga: International Journal of Institute of African Studies, 14*(1), 468–487.

Ijisakin, E. T. (2019). Printmaking in Nigeria: Its evolution and developmental history. *Academic Journal of Interdisciplinary Studies, 8*(2), 247–260. doi:10.2478/ajis-2019-0036

Ijisakin, E. T. (2021). Printmaking and cultural imagination in contemporary Nigerian art. *Critical Arts, 35*(1), 1–16. doi:10.1080/02560046.2020.1856900

Ikegwu, J. U. (2014). The value of palm wine tapping in the food production practices of Igbo-land: a case study of Idemili south local government area, Anambra state. *Research on Humanities and Social Sciences, 4*(6), 49-54. https:// iiste.org/Journals/index.php/RHSS/article/view/11891

Ingram Irving, S. J. (2011). *From Food Production to Food Security: Developing Interdisciplinary, Regional Level Research.* [Doctoral Thesis, Wageningen University: The Netherlands].

Innocenti, P., Ross, S., Maceciuvite, E., Wilson, T., Ludwig, J., & Pempe, W. (2009). Assessing Digital Preservation Frameworks: the approach of the SHAMAN project. *International ACM Conference on Management of Emergent Digital Eco Systems (MEDES'09), Proceedings of the International Conference on Management of Emergent Digital Eco Systems.* ACM. https://strathprints.strath.ac.uk/70503/1/Innocenti_etal_ MEDES_2009_Assessing_digital_preservation_frameworks_the_approach_of_the_SHAMAN project.pdf

Instefjord, E., & Munthe, E. (2016). Preparing pre-service teachers to integrate technology: An analysis of the emphasis on digital competence in teacher education curricula. *European Journal of Teacher Education, 39*(1), 77–93. doi:10.1080/02619768.2015.1100602

Intellectual Property Laws Amendment Act, No. 28. https://www.gov.za/sites/default/files/gcis_document/201409/37148gon996act28-2013.pdf

International Council on Archives. (2017). *Electronic Records.* (Web Source). ICA. https://www.ica.org/en/what-archive

International Federation of Library Associations and Institutions. (2002). IFLA Statement on Indigenous Traditional Knowledge. IFLA. http://ifla.queenslibrary.org/III/eb/sitk03.html

Irivwieri, G. O. (2009). Arts and crafts as a springboard for sustainable development and industrialisation in Nigeria. *International Journal of Creativity and Technical Development, 1*(1-3), 1–18. https://www.academia.edu/8151930/Arts_and_crafts

Isife, E.E. (2023). African environmental ethics and the challenge of decolonizing science and technology for Africa's growth and development. *AKU: An African Journal of Contemporary Research, 4*(1).

Islam, M. (2008). *The changing Garo Adivasi culture of Bangladesh: a case study of marriage rituals.* [Unpublished MPhil dissertation, University of Tromso].

Islam, N. (2008). Bangladesh. In B. Roberts & T. Kanaley (Eds.), *Urbanization and Sustainability in Asia.* Asian Development Bank.

Istvandity, L. (2021). How does music heritage get lost? Examining cultural heritage loss in community and authorised music archives. *International Journal of Heritage Studies, 27*(4), 331–343. doi:10.1080/13527258.2020.1795904

Jacksi, K., Zeebaree, S. R., & Dimililer, N. (2018). LOD explorer: Presenting the web of data. (IJACSA). *International Journal of Advanced Computer Science and Applications, 9*(1), 45–51. doi:10.14569/IJACSA.2018.090107

James-Gilboe, L. (2005). The challenge of digitization: Libraries are finding that newspaper projects are not for the faint of heart. *The Serials Librarian, 49*(1-2), 155–163. doi:10.1300/J123v49n01_06

James, P. B., Wardle, J., Steel, A., & Adams, J. (2018). Traditional, complementary and alternative medicine use in Sub-Saharan Africa: A systematic review. *BMJ Global Health, 3*(5), e000895. doi:10.1136/bmjgh-2018-000895 PMID:30483405

Janks, H. (2019). The decolonization of higher education in South Africa: Luke's writing as gift. *Curriculum Inquiry, 49*(2), 230–241. doi:10.1080/03626784.2019.1591922

Jasmine, B., Singh, Y., Onial, M., & Mathur, V. B. (2016). Traditional systems in India for biodiversity conservation. *Indian Journal of Knowledge, 15*(2), 304–312.

Jengcham, S. (1994). *Bangladesher Garo Sampradai.* Bangla Academy. (In Bengali)

Compilation of References

Jessen, T. D., Ban, N. C., Claxton, N. X., & Darimont, C. T. (2022). Contributions of Indigenous Knowledge to ecological and evolutionary understanding. *Frontiers in Ecology and the Environment, 20*(2), 93–101. doi:10.1002/fee.2435

Jimenez, A., Vannini, S., & Cox, A. (2023). A holistic decolonial lens for library and information studies. *The Journal of Documentation, 79*(1), 224–244. doi:10.1108/JD-10-2021-0205

Jimoh, S. O., Ikyaagba, E. T., Alarape, A. A., Obioha, E. E., & Adeyemi, A. A. (2012). The role of traditional laws and taboos in wildlife conservation in the Oban Hill Sector of Cross River National Park (CRNP), Nigeria. *Journal of Human Ecology (Delhi, India), 39*(3), 209–219. doi:10.1080/09709274.2012.11906513

Jiri, O., Mafongoya, P. L., & Chivenge, P. (2015). Indigenous knowledge systems, seasonal 'quality and climate change adaptation in Zimbabwe. *Climate Research, 66*(2), 103–111. doi:10.3354/cr01334

Jochumsen, H., Skot-Hansen, D., & Hvenegaard Rasmussen, C. (2015). Towards Culture 3.0 – performative space in the public library. *International Journal of Cultural Policy, 23*(4), 512–524. doi:10.1080/10286632.2015.1043291

Johnson, P. (2018). *Fundamentals of collection development and management.* American Library Association.

Johnston, B. R., Hiwasaki, L., Klaver, I. J., Castillo, A. R., & Strang, V. (Eds.). (2012). *Water, cultural diversity, and global environmental change: Emerging trends, sustainable futures?* (pp. XI–XXI). Springer. doi:10.1007/978-94-007-1774-9

Jordan, S., Zabukovšek, S. S., & Klančnik, I. Š. (2022). Document Management System–A Way to Digital Transformation. *Naše gospodarstvo/Our economy, 68*(2), 43-54. doi:10.2478/ngoe-2022-0010

José, R. C., & Carmen, D. (2016). Open Archival Information System (OAIS): Lights and shadows of a reference model. *Investigación Bibliotecológica, 30*(69), 227–253.

Kaari, M. F., & Ombaka, O. (2019). Indigenous knowledge and applications of clay among rural communities in western Kenya. *International Journal of Development and Sustainability, 8*(4), 264–283. https://isdsnet.com/ijds-v8n4-01.pdf

Kacunguzi, D. T. (2019). Preservation of Endangered Indigenous Knowledge: The Role of Community Libraries in Kampala –Uganda.[QQML]. *Qualitative and Quantitative Methods in Libraries, 8*, 61–72.

Kaddu, S., & Chisita, C. (2009). *The Challenges of Repackaging Traditional in the Context of Intellectual Property Rights: Case of Zimbabwe and Uganda.* Uganda Christian University.

Kaggwa, B., Kyeyune, H., Munanura, E. I., Anywar, G., Lutoti, S., Aber, J., Bagoloire, L. K., Weisheit, A., Tolo, C. U., Kamba, P. F., & Ogwang, P. E. (2022). Safety and efficacy of medicinal plants used to manufacture herbal products with regulatory approval in Uganda: A cross-sectional study. *Evidence-Based Complementary and Alternative Medicine, 2022*, 1–21. doi:10.1155/2022/1304839 PMID:35463071

Kamal, K. J., Manjit, S. S., & Gurvinder, K. S. (2007). *Knowledge sharing among academic staff: A case study of Business School in Klang Valley, Malaysia.* USCI. https://www.ucsi.edu.my/cervie/ijasa/volume2/pdf/08A.pdf

Kamau, E. C., & Winter, G. (2009). Protecting TK amid disseminated Knowledge–A new task for ABS regimes? A Kenyan legal view. In Genetic Resources, Traditional Knowledge and the Law (pp. 177-204). Routledge.

Kamwendo, G., & Kamwendo, J. (2014). Indigenous Knowledge Systems and Food Security: Some examples from Malawi. *Journal of Human Ecology (Delhi, India), 48*(1), 97–101. doi:10.1080/09709274.2014.11906778

Kansiime, M., Mulema, J., Karanja, D., Romney, D., & Day, R. (2016). *Crop pests and disease management in Uganda: Status and investment needs. Final report.* CAB International, Wallingford, UK.

Kasere, S. (2010). *CAMPFIRE: Zimbabwe's Tradition of Caring.* UN System. https://www.unsystem.org/ngls/documents/publications.en/voices.africa/number6/vfa6.08.htm

Kashim, I. B., Adelabu, O. S., Fatuyi, S. A., & Fadairo, O. O. (2013). Bridging the Gap: Artistry of Felicia Adepelu, Potter of Igbara-Odo, Ekiti State, Nigeria. *Critical Interventions*, *7*(1), 50–64. doi:10.1080/19301944.2013.10781426

Kassam, K., & Maher, S. (2000). Indigenous, Cartesian, and cartographic: visual metaphors of knowledge in Arctic (tundra) and sub-Arctic (taiga) communities. In J. Xu (Ed.), *Links between cultures and biodiversity: proceedings of the Cultures and Biodiversity Congress* (pp. 785–811).

Kastellec, M. (2012). Practical limits to the scope of digital preservation. *Information Technology and Libraries*, *31*(2), 63–71. doi:10.6017/ital.v31i2.2167

Kavada, A., Treré, E., & Kavada, A. (2019). Live democracy and its tensions : Making sense of livestreaming in the 15M and Occupy livestreaming in the 15M and Occupy. *Information Communication and Society*, *0*(0), 1–18. doi:10.1080/1369118X.2019.1637448

Kawooya, D., Kakungulu, R., & Akubu, J. (2010). Uganda. *Access to Knowledge in Africa: The role of copyright*, 281-316.

Kaya, H. O. (2014). Revitalizing African indigenous ways of knowing and knowledge production. *Restoring Indigenous Self-Determination*, 105.

Kaya, H. O., & Seleti, Y. N. (2013). African indigenous knowledge systems and relevance of higher education in South Africa. *International Education Journal: Comparative Perspectives*, *12*(1).

Kaya, H. O., & Seleti, Y. N. (2013). African indigenous knowledge systems and relevance of higher education in South Africa. *The International Education Journal: Comparative Perspectives*, *12*(1), 30–44.

Kaya, H., & Seleti, Y. N. (2013). African Indigenous Knowledge Systems and Relevance of Higher Education in South Africa. *International Education Journal: Comparative Perspectives*, *12*(1), 30–44.

Kays, J. (2022, April 19). *Native Voices: Oral Histories Help Preserve Indigenous Heritage*. Explore Magazine. https://explore.research.ufl.edu/native-voices-oral-histories-help-preserve-indigenous-heritage.html

Kazembe, T., & Mashoko, D. (2008). Should traditional medicine practised in Chivi, Zimbabwe, be included in school curricula? *Zimbabwe Journal of Educational Research*, *20*(1), 49–69.

Keane, M., Khupe, C., & Seehawer, M. (2017). Decolonising methodology: Who benefits from indigenous knowledge research? *Educational Research for social change*, *6*(1), 12-24.

Keane, M. (2016). Coaching interventions for postgraduate supervision courses: Promoting equity and understanding in the supervisor–student relationship. *South African Journal of Higher Education*, *30*(6), 94–111. doi:10.20853/30-6-720

Keane, M., Khupe, C., & Seehawer, M. (2017). Decolonizing methodology: Who benefits from indigenous knowledge research? *Educ. Res. Soc. Change*, *6*(1), 12–24. doi:10.17159/2221-4070/2017/v6i1a2

Keet, A., & Porteus, K. (2010). Life, Knowledge, Action: The Grounding Programme at the University of Fort Hare. *Report on the Pilot July–December 2009*. UFH. http://wvw.ufh.ac.za/files/Appendix_6.pdf

Keet, A., Sattarzadeh, S. D., & Munene, A. (2017). An awkward, uneasy (de)coloniality higher education and knowledge otherwise. *Education as Change*, *21*(1), 1–12. doi:10.17159/1947-9417/2017/2741

Kennedy, G., & Davis, B. (2006). *Electronic communication systems* (4th ed.). McGraw-Hill.

Kepe, T. (2010). Secrets that kill: Crisis, custodianship and responsibility in ritual male circumcision in the Eastern Cape Province, South Africa. *Social Science & Medicine*, *70*(5), 732–740. doi:10.1016/j.socscimed.2009.11.016 PMID:20053494

Compilation of References

Khalala, G., Botha, A., & Makitla, I. (2016). *Process as an element of UX in collecting Indigenous Knowledge: A case study in South Africa. In 2016 IST-Africa Week Conference.* IEEE.

Khan, D., & Banerjee, S. (2020). Revitalising ancient Indian clay utensils and their impact on health. *International Journal of All Research Education and Scientific Methods*, 8(7), 357–360. https://www.researchgate.net/publication/343678519

Khan, M. S. A., & Ahmad, I. (2019). Herbal medicine: current trends and future prospects. In *New look to phytomedicine* (pp. 3–13). Academic Press., doi:10.1016/B978-0-12-814619-4.00001-X

Khan, M., & Rahman, A. U. (2019). A systematic approach towards web preservation. *Information Technology and Libraries*, 38(1), 71–90. doi:10.6017/ital.v38i1.10181

Khanyile, N. C., & Dlamini, P. (2021). Preservation of traditional medicinal knowledge: Initiatives and techniques in rural communities in KwaZulu-Natal. *Library Philosophy and Practice*, 1-19. https://digitalcommons.unl.edu/libphilprac/4824

Kiggundu, J. (2007). Intellectual property law and the protection of indigenous knowledge. In I. Mazonde & P. Thomas (Eds.), *Indigenous knowledge systems and intellectual property in the twenty-first century; perspectives from Southern Africa* (pp. 26–47). Dakar Codesria.

Kijazi, A. L., Chang'a, L. B., Liwenga, E. T., Kanemba, A., & Nindi, S. J. (2013). The use of indigenous knowledge in weather and climate prediction in Mahenge and Ismani Wards, Tanzania. Proceedings of the first *Climate Change Impacts, Mitigation and Adaptation Programme Scientific Conference*.

Kim, J. (2020). Learning and teaching online during Covid-19: Experiences of student teachers in an early childhood education practicum. *International Journal of Early Childhood*, 52(2), 145–158. doi:10.100713158-020-00272-6 PMID:32836369

Kim, S., Whitford, M., & Arcodia, C. (2019). Development of intangible cultural heritage as a sustainable tourism resource: The intangible cultural heritage practitioners' perspectives. *Journal of Heritage Tourism*, 14(5-6), 422–435. doi:10.1080/1743873X.2018.1561703

King, L., & Schielmann, S. (2004). *The Challenge of indigenous education: practice and perspectives. Project: Indigenous education.* UNESCO.

Kissock, T. (2020a). Bolsonaro's Congressional Cheerleaders in the Global Post-Truth Era: Demagoguery as communication, and YouTube as the tool. UCL: University College London. doi:10.13140/RG.2.2.27059.96800/1

Kissock, T. (2020b). *Jungle Drones: Can Indigenous drone projects in Latin America and the Caribbean be more sustainable?* Tom Kissock. https://www.tomkissock.com/post/jungle-drones-indigenous-drone-projects

Kissock, T. (2020c). Live Streaming: A confirmation of community and exercise of citizenship. | by Tom Kissock-Mamede. *Medium.* https://medium.com/@tomkissock-mamede/live-streaming-a-confirmation-of-community-and-exercise-of-citizenship-d615f71e1244

Kissock, T. (2021). *Why the English-speaking world should take notice of Brazil's #3JForaBolsonaro Movement.* LatAMDialogue. https://www.latamdialogue.org/post/why-the-english-speaking-world-should-take-notice-of-brazil-s-3jforabolsonaro-movement (Accessed: 25 March 2022).

Kittipanya-Ngam, P., & Tan, K. H. (2020). A framework for food supply chain digitalisation: Lessons from Thailand. *Production Planning and Control*, 31(2-3), 158–172. doi:10.1080/09537287.2019.1631462

Kohsaka, R., & Rogel, M. (2021). Traditional and local knowledge for sustainable development: Empowering the indigenous and local communities of the world. In *Partnerships for the Goals* (pp. 1261–1273). Springer. doi:10.1007/978-3-319-95963-4_17

Kolawole, O. D. (2015). Twenty reasons why local knowledge will remain relevant to development. *Development in Practice*, *25*(8), 1189–1195. doi:10.1080/09614524.2015.1078777

Kolawole, O. D. P., Wolski, B., Ngwenya, B., & Mmopelwa, G. (2014). Ethno-meteorology and scientific weather forecasting: Small farmers and scientists' perspectives on climate variability in the Okavango Delta. *Climate Risk Management*, *4*(5), 43–58. doi:10.1016/j.crm.2014.08.002

Komeiji, K., Long, K., Matsuda, S., & Paikai, A. (2021). Indigenous resource management systems as models for librarianship: I waiwai ka 'āina. *IFLA Journal*, *47*(3), 331–340. doi:10.1177/0340035221991561

Konaré, A. O. (1981). Birth of a museum at Bamako, Mali. *Museum International*, *33*(1), 4–8. doi:10.1111/j.1468-0033.1981. tb01936.x

Kovach, M. (2009). *Indigenous Methodologies: Characteristics, Conversations, and Contexts*. University of Toronto Press.

Kovach, M. E. (2010). *Indigenous methodologies: Characteristics, conversations, and contexts*. University of Toronto Press.

Kozhakhmet, S., & Nazri, M. (2017). Governing Knowledge Sharing Behavior in Post-Soviet Kazakhstan. *Journal of Workplace Learning*, *29*(3), 1–18. doi:10.1108/JWL-06-2016-0053

Kozol, W. (2015). *Distant Wars Visible* (1st ed.). University of Minnasota Press. doi:10.5749/minnesota/9780816681297.001.0001

Kramer, J. (2013). Möbius museology: Curating and critiquing the multiversity galleries at the museum of anthropology at the University of British Columbia. *The International Handbooks of Museum Studies*, 489-510. doi:10.1002/9781118829059. wbihms421

Krauss, L. M. (2017, May 10). *What Einstein and Bill Gates Teach Us About Time Travel*. NBC News. https://www. nbcnews.com/storyline/the-big-questions/what-einstein-bill-gates-teach-us-about-time-travel-n757291

Kristoffersen, A. E., Broderstad, A. R., Musial, F., & Stub, T. (2019). Prevalence, and health-and sociodemographic associations for visits to traditional and complementary medical providers in the seventh survey of the Tromsø study. *BMC Complementary and Alternative Medicine*, *19*(1), 1–11. doi:10.118612906-019-2707-1 PMID:31711478

Krtalic, M., & Hassenay, D. (2012). Exploring a framework for comprehensive and successful preservation management in libraries. *The Journal of Documentation*, *68*(3), 353–377. doi:10.1108/00220411211225584

Kruglikova, G. A. (2020). Use of information technologies in the preservation and popularizing of cultural heritage. *International Scientific Conference: "Digitalization of Education: History, Trends, and Prospects.* (pp. 446-450). IEEE. 10.2991/assehr.k.200509.081

Kugara, S. L. (2017). *Witchcraft belief and criminal responsibility: A case study of selected areas in South Africa and Zimbabwe* [Doctoral dissertation, University of Venda].

Kukutai, T., & Taylor, J. (2016). *Indigenous data sovereignty: Toward an agenda*. ANU press., doi:10.22459/ CAEPR38.11.2016

Kumar, K. A. (2010). Local Knowledge and Agricultural Sustainability: A Case Study of Pradhan Tribe in Adilabad District. *Centre for Economic and Social Studies*, *15*(6), 1–38.

Kurin, R. (2004). Safeguarding Intangible Cultural Heritage in the 2003 UNESCO Convention: A Critical Appraisal. *Museum International*, *56*(1-2), 66–77. doi:10.1111/j.1350-0775.2004.00459.x

Kusimi, Donkor, A. K., Ayivor, J. S., Kyeremeh, K., & Kusimi, J. M. (2020). The lifecycle of pottery art processes and production in Mpraeso, Ghana. *Dearte*, *55*(3), 70–94. doi:10.1080/00043389.2020.1805849

Compilation of References

Kyarisimire, S. (2010). The role of indigenous knowledge in conservation of Uganda's National Parks (Bwindi). Kampala: Royal Geographical Society London: IT Publications.

Lahenius, K., & Ikävalko, H. (2014). Joint supervision practices in doctoral education–A student experience. *Journal of Further and Higher Education, 38*(3), 427–446. doi:10.1080/0309877X.2012.706805

Lal, J. J., Sreeranjit, K. C. V., & Indira, M. (2003). Coconut palm. In B. Caballero (Ed.), *Encyclopedia of Food Sciences and Nutrition* (2nd ed., pp. 1464–1475). Academic Press. doi:10.1016/B0-12-227055-X/00263-7

Lalonde, D. (2021). Does cultural appropriation cause harm? *Politics, Groups & Identities, 9*(2), 329–346. doi:10.108 0/21565503.2019.1674160

Landauer, L. B. (2019). *The Development of Libraries in the Ancient World.* Encyclopedia. https://www.encyclopedia. com/science/encyclopedias-almanacs-transcripts-and-maps/development-libraries-ancient-world

Land, C. (2015). *Decolonizing solidarity: dilemmas and directions for supporters of indigenous struggles.* Zed Books.

Langlois, J. (2022) For the Kayapó, a Long Battle to Save Their Amazon Homeland. *Yale Enviroment 360.* https://e360. yale.edu/features/for-the-kayapo-a-long-battle-to-save-their-amazon-homeland.

Langtone, M. (2016). A moral compass that slipped: Indigenous knowledge systems and rural development in Zimbabwe. *Cogent Social Sciences, 2,* 1266749. doi:10.1080/23311886.2016.1266749

Lanzano, C. (2013). Kind of knowledge is "indigenous knowledge"? Critical insights from a case study in Burkina Faso. *Transcience, 4*(2), 1–16.

Lata, N., & Owan, V. J. (2022). Contemporary trends and technologies in research libraries: An overview. In T. Masenya (Ed.), *Innovative technologies for enhancing knowledge access in academic libraries* (pp. 40–56). IGI Global., doi:10.4018/978-1-6684-3364-5.ch003

Latif, S. S. (2010). *Integration of African traditional health practitioners and medicine into the health care management system in the province of Limpopo.* University of Stellenbosch.

Latulippe, N., & Klenk, N. (2020). Making Room and moving over: Co-production, Indigenous Sovereignty and the Politics of global environmental change decision-making. *Current Opinion in Environmental Sustainability, 42,* 7–14. doi:10.1016/j.cosust.2019.10.010

Lau, J. (2009). Mexican libraries, archives and museums: a snapshot. In P. Elis (Ed.), *Encyclopedia of Library and Information Science* (3rd ed., pp. 1–40). Taylor & Francis. https://core.ac.uk/download/pdf/16292208.pdf

Lavallee, L. F. (2009). Practical application of an Indigenous research framework and two qualitative Indigenous research methods: Sharing circles and Anishnaabe symbol- based reflection. *International Journal of Qualitative Methods, 8*(1), 21–40. doi:10.1177/160940690900800103

Lavoie, B. (2014). *The Open Archival Information System (OAIS) Reference Model: Introductory Guide* (2nd ed.). The Digital Preservation Coalition. doi:10.7207/twr14-02

Lazaro Ortiz, S., & Jimenez de Madariaga, C. (2022). The UNESCO convention for the safeguarding of the intangible cultural heritage: A critical analysis. *International Journal of Cultural Policy, 28*(3), 327–341. doi:10.1080/10286632 .2021.1941914

Lazer, D., Kennedy, R., King, G., & Vespignani, A. (2014). The Parable of Google Flu: Traps in Big Data Analysis. *Science, 343*(6176), 1203–1205. doi:10.1126cience.1248506 PMID:24626916

Le Grange, L. (2016). Decolonising the university curriculum. *South African Journal of Higher Education, 30*(2), 1–12.

403

Leal de Oliveira, A., Ruy Bragatto, J., & Montenegro de Souza Lima, M. (2023). *A Inconstitucionalidade Do Marco Temporal: Riscos E Ameaças À Tutela Dos Povos Indígenas Originários Do Brasil, Revista Direitos Sociais e Políticas Públicas*. UNIFAFIBE. doi:10.25245/rdspp.v10i3.1349

Lee, C. A. (2010). *Open Archival Information System (OAIS) Reference Model. Encyclopedia of Library and Information Sciences* (3rd ed.). Taylor & Francis. doi:10.1081/E-ELIS3-120044377

Lee, K. H., Slattery, O., Lu, R., Tang, X., & McCrary, V. (2002). The State of the Art and Practice in Digital Preservation. *Journal of Research of the National Institute of Standards and Technology, 107*(1), 93–106. doi:10.6028/jres.107.010 PMID:27446721

Lee, N., & Rodríguez-Pose, A. (2021). Entrepreneurship and the fight against poverty in US cities. *Environment and Planning A. Environment & Planning A, 53*(1), 31–52. doi:10.1177/0308518X20924422

Leiden Ndlovu-Gatsheni S.J. (2013). Why decoloniality in the 21st century? *The Thinker: For Thought Leaders.*

Lemma, M., & Hoffmann, V. (2005). The Agricultural Knowledge System in Tigray, Ethiopia: Empirical Study about its Recent History and Actual Effectiveness. *The Global Food and Product Chain: Dynamics, Innovations, Conflicts, Strategies, Tropentag 2005.* Stuttgart-Hohenheim. http://www.tropentag. de/2005/proceedings/node152.html#2487

Letseka, M. (2014). *Ubuntu* and justice as fairness. *Mediterranean Journal of Social Sciences, 5*(9), 544–551. doi:10.5901/mjss.2014.v5n9p544

Levy, M., Shibata, T., & Shibata, H. (2022). *Wild clay: Creating ceramics and glazes from natural and found resources.* Bloomsbury Publishing.

Liana, R. (2011). An Ontology-Based Framework for Modeling User Behavior. A Case Study in Knowledge Management. *IEEE Transactions on Systems, Man, and Cybernetics. Part A, Systems and Humans, 41*(4), 772–783. doi:10.1109/TSMCA.2011.2132712

Liang, X. (2020). Internet of Things and its applications in libraries: A literature review. *Library Hi Tech, 37*(2), 251–261. doi:10.1108/LHT-01-2018-0014/FULL/XML

Library Technology Reports. (2008). Preservation Practices. *Tech Source.* www.techsource.ala.orghttps://journals.ala.org/index.php/ltr/article/viewFile/4223/4806

Likalu, M., Abdulla, R., Selamat, M. H., Ibrahim, H., & Nor, M. Z. M. (2010). A framework of collaborative knowledge management system in open source software development environment. *Computer and Information Science, 3*(1), 81–90. doi:10.5539/cis.v3n1p81

Lilley, S. (2018). Interdisciplinarity and Indigenous Studies: A Māori Perspective. *Journal of the Australian Library and Information Association, 67*(3), 246–255. doi:10.1080/24750158.2018.1497348

Lilley, S. (2021). Transformation of library and information management: Decolonization or Indigenization? *IFLA Journal, 47*(3), 305–312. doi:10.1177/03400352211023071

Lira, M. G., Davidson-Hunt, I. J., & Robson, J. P. (2022). Artisanal products and land-use land-cover change in indigenous communities: The case of mezcal production in Oaxaca, Mexico. *Land (Basel), 11*(3), 387. doi:10.3390/land11030387

Littletree, S., Belarde-Lewis, M., & Duarte, M. (2020). Centering relationality: A conceptual model to advance indigenous knowledge organization practices. *Knowledge Organization, 47*(5), 410–426. doi:10.5771/0943-7444-2020-5-410

Liverman, D. M., & Vilas, S. (2006). Neoliberalism and the Environment in Latin America. *Annual Review of Environment and Resources, 31*(1), 327–363. doi:10.1146/annurev.energy.29.102403.140729

Compilation of References

Ljubetic, M., & Maglica, T. (2020). Social and emotional learning in education and care policy in Croatia.[IJERE]. *International Journal of Evaluation and Research in Education, 9*(3), 650–659. doi:10.11591/ijere.v9i3.20495

Ljungqvist, M., & Sonesson, A. (2022). Selling out education in the name of digitalisation: A critical analysis of Swedish policy. *Nordic Journal of Studies in Educational Policy, 8*(2), 89–102. doi:10.1080/20020317.2021.2004665

Locke, J. (2001). *An essay concerning human understanding*. Batoche Books.

Lodhi, S & Miculecky, P. (2011). *Motives and modes of indigenous knowledge management.*

London Parliamentary Archives. (2008). *A digital preservation strategy for parliament*. Parliamentary Archives: House of Parliament London SW1A 0PW. https://www.parliament.uk/globalassets/documents/upload/digital-preservation-strategy- final-public-version.pdf

Longo, D. L., & Drazen, J. M. (2016). Data sharing. *The New England Journal of Medicine, 374*(3), 276–277. doi:10.1056/NEJMe1516564 PMID:26789876

Lopez, A. E., & Rugano, P. (2018). Educational leadership in post-colonial contexts: What can we learn from the experiences of three female principals in Kenyan secondary schools? *Education Sciences, 8*(3), 99. doi:10.3390/educsci8030099

Lor, P. (2004). Storehouses of knowledge? The role of libraries in preserving and promoting indigenous knowledge. *Indilinga, 3*(1), 45–56.

Lor, P. J. (1997). *Guidelines for Legislation for National Library Services (CII-97/WS/7)*. United Nations Educational, Scientific and Cultural Organization.

Louw, D. J. (2006). The African concept of ubuntu and restorative justice. In D. Sullivan & L. Tifft (Eds.), *Handbook of restorative justice: A global perspective* (pp. 161–173). Routledge.

Lovett, R., Lee, V., Kukutai, T., Cormack, D., Rainie, S. C., & Walker, J. (2019). Good data practices for Indigenous data sovereignty and governance. In A. Daly, S. K. Devitt, & M. Mann (Eds.), *Good data* (pp. 26–36). Institute of Network Cultures. http://bit.ly/3LTVJNo

Luke, A. (2018). Pedagogy as gift. In Critical Literacy, Schooling, and Social Justice (pp. 272- 296). Routledge. doi:10.4324/9781315100951-13

Lwoga, E. T., Ngulube, P., & Stilwell, C. (2020). Indigenous knowledge management practices in indigenous organizations in South Africa and Tanzania. In Indigenous Studies: Breakthroughs in Research and Practice (pp. 37-57). IGI Global. doi:10.4018/978-1-7998-0423-9.ch003

Lwoga, E. T., & Ngulube, P. (2009). Managing indigenous and exogenous knowledge through information and communication technologies for poverty reduction in Tanzania. *Indilinga, 8*(1), 95–113.

Lwoga, E. T., Ngulube, P., & Sitwell, C. (2010). Managing indigenous knowledge for sustainable agricultural development in developing countries: Knowledge management approaches in the social context. *The International Information & Library Review, 42*(3), 174–185. doi:10.1080/10572317.2010.10762862

Lwoga, E. T., Ngulube, P., & Stilwell, C. (2010). Understanding indigenous knowledge: Bridging the knowledge gap through a knowledge creation model for agricultural development. *South African Journal of Information Management, 12*(1), 8–16. doi:10.4102ajim.v12i1.436

Mabovula, N. N. (2011). The erosion of African communal values: A reappraisal of the African Ubuntu philosophy. *Inkanyiso, 3*(1), 38–47. doi:10.4314/ijhss.v3i1.69506

Macie, P., & Martins, A. R. O. (2019). Malazi, the palm wine tapper. In D. Pullanikkatil & C. Shackleton (Eds.), *Poverty reduction through non-timber forest products. Sustainable Development Goals Series*. Springer. doi:10.1007/978-3-319-75580-9_17

Mack, E., & Meadowcroft, J. (Eds.). (2009). *Major conservative and libertarian thinkers: John Locke*. Continuum.

MacRitchie, J. (2017). Book reviews: Local History Reference Collections for Public Libraries. *The Electronic Library*, *35*(1), 209–210. doi:10.1108/EL-12-2015-0246

Madsen, C., & Hurst, M. (2019). Digital preservation policy and strategy: where do I start? In J. Myntti & J. Zoom (Eds.), *Digital preservation in libraries: preparing for a sustainable future* (pp. 37–48). ALA.

Magara, E. (2002) *Community based indigenous knowledge: strategy for Uganda*. In Proceedings of the 15th Standing Conference of Eastern, Central and South African Library and Infor-mation Professionals, Johannesburg.

Magara, E. (2015). Integration of indigenous knowledge management into the university curriculum: A case for makerere university. *Indilinga*, *14*(1), 25–41.

Magni, G. (2017). Indigenous and Implications for the sustainable development agenda. *European Journal of Education*, *52*(4), 437–447. doi:10.1111/ejed.12238

Mahabeer, P. (2018). Curriculum decision-makers on decolonising the teacher education curriculum. *South African Journal of Education*, *38*(4), 1–13. doi:10.15700aje.v38n4a1705

Maharasoa, M. M. A., & Maharaswa, M. B. (2004). Men's initiation schools as a form of higher education within the Basotho indigenous knowledge systems: Perspectives on higher education. *South African Journal of Higher Education*, *18*(3), 106–114.

Mahlangu, P. M., & Garutsa, T. C. (2019). A Transdisciplinary Approach and Indigenous Knowledge as Transformative Tools in Pedagogical Design: The Case of the Centre for Transdisciplinary Studies, University of Fort Hare, *Africa. Education Review*, *16*(5), 60–69. doi:10.1080/18146627.2016.1251293

Mahomoodally, M. F. (2013). Traditional medicines in Africa: An appraisal of ten potent African medicinal plants. *Evidence-Based Complementary and Alternative Medicine*, *2013*(1), 14–15. Retrieved October 23, 2019, from https://www.hindawi.com/journals/ecam/2013/617459/. doi:10.1155/2013/617459 PMID:24367388

Mahwasane, N. P. (2017). Library support and the innovative application of Indigenous knowledge systems. *Journal of Sociology and Social Anthropology*, *8*(2), 77–81. doi:10.1080/09766634.2017.1316952

Maina, Gohole, L. S., & Muasya, R. M. (2017). Effects of storage methods and seasons on seed quality of jute mallow morphotypes (Corchorus olitorius) in Siaya and Kakamega counties, Kenya. *African Journal of Food, Agriculture, Nutrition and Development*, *17*(3), 12395–12412. doi:10.18697/ajfand.79.16035

Maistry, S. (2021). Curriculum theorising in Africa as a social justice project: Insights from decolonial theory. In K. G. F. Kehdinga & B. K. Khoza (Eds.), *Curriculum theory, curriculum theorising and theories: The African theorising perspective* (pp. 133–147). Sense.

Maiwada, S., Dutsenwai, S. A., & Waziri, M. Y. (2012). Cultural industries and wealth creation: The case of the traditional textile industry in Nigeria. *American International Journal of Contemporary Research*, *2*(5), 159–165. http://www.aijcrnet.com/journals/Vol_2_No_5_May_2012/17.pdf

Major, N. B., & Leigha, M. B. (2019). Indigenous skills and entrepreneurship education: A critical blend for sustainable development in Nigeria. *Brock Journal of Education*, *7*(2), 140–148. http://bitly.ws/Bb2R

Compilation of References

Majumdar, D. N. (1978). *Culture change in two Garo villages (No. 42)*. Anthropological Survey of India, Government of India.

Makhanya, S. M. (2012). *The traditional healers' and caregivers' views on the role of traditional Zulu medicine on psychosis*. University of Zululand, Maluleka.

Maltoni, S., Silvestri, A., Maritan, L., & Molin, G. (2012). The medieval lead-glazed pottery from Nogara (north-east Italy): A multi-methodological study. *Journal of Archaeological Science, 39*(7), 2071–2078. doi:10.1016/j.jas.2012.03.016

Maluleka, J. R. (2017). *Acquisition, transfer and preservation of indigenous knowledge by traditional healers in the Limpopo province of South Africa*. [Doctoral thesis, University of South Africa, South Africa].

Maluleka, J. R., & Ngoepe, M. (2018). Turning mirrors into windows: Knowledge transfer among indigenous healers in Limpopo province of South Africa. *South African Journal of Information Management, 20*(1), a918. doi:10.4102ajim.v20i1.918

Maluleka, K. J. (2020). Humanising higher education through a culturally responsive curriculum. *South African Journal of Higher Education, 34*(6), 137–149. doi:10.20853/34-6-3764

Mandisvika, G., Chirisa, I., & Bandauko, E. (2015). Post-harvest issues: Rethinking technology for value-addition in food security and food sovereignty in Zimbabwe. *Advances In Food Technology and Nutrifional Sciences–Open Journal, 1*(1), S29–S37. doi:10.17140/AFTNSOJ-SE-1-105

Mann, A. (2021, May 20). What is space-time? *Live Science.* https://www.livescience.com/space-time.html

Mantelli, G., Neiva, J. M. and Ingrams, M. (2022). Deforestation And Climate Change In Brazil. *Legal and policy gaps.*

Mapara, J. (2009). Indigenous Knowledge Systems in Zimbabwe: Juxtaposing Postcolonial Theory. *The Journal of Pan African Studies, 3*(1), 139–155.

Mapara, J. (2009). Indigenous knowledge systems in Zimbabwe: Juxtaposing postcolonial theory. *The Journal of Pan African Studies, 3*(1), 30–68.

Mapara, J. (2009). Indigenous systems in Zimbabwe: Juxtaposing postcolonial theory. *The Journal of Pan African Studies, 3*(1), 139–156.

Maroyi, A. (2018). *Ethnomedicinal uses of exotic plant species in south-central Zimbabwe*. Research Gate. https://www.researchgate.net/publication/236636386_Traditional_use_of_medicinal_plants_in_south-central_Zimbabwe_Review_and_perspectives

Marques, J. (2022) *Mendonça trava julgamento do STF sobre desmatamento na Amazônia - 06/04/2022 Ambiente.* Folha.https://www1.folha.uol.com.br/ambiente/2022/04/mendonca-indicado-de-bolsonaro-trava-julgamento-do-stf-sobre-desmatamento-na-amazonia.shtml (Accessed: 8 April 2022).

Martinez, C. (2011). Digital Ayayote Rattle: The design of a portable, low-cost digital media system for a mediated Xican Indo Resolana. In Nicola Bidwell and Heike Winschiers-Theophilus (Eds.), *Proceedings of IKT2011: Embracing Indigenous Knowledge Systems in a New Technology Design Paradigm.* Indigenous Knowledge Technology Conference.

Martini, M. (2018). *Online distant witnessing and live-streaming activism : Emerging differences in the activation of networked publics.* Sage. . doi:10.1177/1461444818766703

Martiniello, G. (2015). Food sovereignty as praxis: Rethinking the food question in Uganda. *Third World Quarterly, 36*(3), 508–525. doi:10.1080/01436597.2015.1029233

Marx, K. (1986). *Karl Marx: The Essential Writings*. Westview Press.

Masango, C. A. (2010). Indigenous traditional knowledge protection: Prospects in South Africa's intellectual property framework? *South African Journal of Library and Information Science*, *76*(1), 74–80. doi:10.7553/76-1-88

Masango, C. A. (2020). Indigenous knowledge codification of African traditional medicine: Inhibited by status quo based on secrecy? *Information Development*, *36*(3), 327–338. doi:10.1177/0266666919853007

Masenya, T. M. (2018). *A Framework for preservation of digital resources in academic libraries in South Africa.* [PhD thesis, University of South Africa].

Masenya, T. M. (2022). Decolonization of Indigenous Knowledge Systems in South Africa: Impact of Policy and Protocols.[IJKM]. *International Journal of Knowledge Management*, *18*(1), 1–22. doi:10.4018/IJKM.310005

Masenya, T. M. (2022). Digital Preservation of Indigenous Knowledge in South African Rural Communities. In R. Tshifhumulo & T. Makhanikhe (Eds.), *Handbook of Research on Protecting and Managing Global Indigenous Knowledge Systems* (pp. 317–340). IGI Global. doi:10.4018/978-1-7998-7492-8.ch017

Masenya, T. M., & Ngulube, P. (2019). Digital preservation practices in academic libraries in South Africa in the wake of the digital revolution. *South African Journal of Information Management*, *21*(1), a1011. doi:10.4102ajim.v21i1.1011

Mashford-Pringle, A., & Pavagadhi, K. (2020). Using OCAP and IQ as frameworks to address a history of trauma in Indigenous health research. *AMA Journal of Ethics*, *22*(10), 868–873. doi:10.1001/amajethics.2020.868 PMID:33103649

Masoga, M. A. (2017). Critical reflections on selected local narratives of contextual South African indigenous knowledge. In P. Ngulube (Ed.), *Handbook of research on theoretical perspectives on indigenous knowledge systems in developing countries*. IGI Global. doi:10.4018/978-1-5225-0833-5.ch014

Masoga, M. A., & Shokane, A. L. (2020). Socio-economic challenges faced by traditional healers in Limpopo province of South Africa: Conversations from below. *Alternative*, *00*(0), 1–8. doi:10.1177/1177180120956718

Masondo, S. (2015). Rhodes Must Fall campaign gains momentum at UCT. City Press. https://www.news24.com/SouthAfrica/News/Rhodes-Must-Fall-campaign-gains- momentum- at-UCT-20150323 date of access: 15 February 2023

Massis, B. (2016). The Internet of Things and its impact on the library. *New Library World*, *117*(3–4), 289–292. doi:10.1108/NLW-12-2015-0093

Matenge, S. T. P., Van der Merwe, D., De Beer, D., Bosman, M. J. C., & Kruger, A. (2012). Consumers' beliefs on indigenous and traditional foods and acceptance of products made with cow pea leaves. *African Journal of Agricultural Research*, *7*(14), 2243–2254.

Mathew, R. M. (1985). Social analysis of information production and consumption: the new challenges and tasks of Third World Countries. In A. I. Mikhalov (Ed.), *Theoretical problems of informatics: social aspects of modern informatics* (pp. 37–47). All Union Institute for Scientific and Technical Information.

Matlala, E. (2019). Long-term preservation of digital records at the University of KwaZulu-Natal archives. *Journal of the South African Society of Archivists*, *52*, 95–109. https://www.ajol.info/index.php/jsasa/article/view/189859

Matshameko, Y., Kebonye, N. M., & Eze, P. N. (2022). Ethnopedological knowledge and scientific assessment of earthenware pottery-making soils of southern Botswana for natural resource management. *Geoderma Regional*, *31*, e00580. doi:10.1016/j.geodrs.2022.e00580

Maundu, P. (1995). Methodology for collecting and sharing indigenous knowledge WLEDGE: A case study. *Indigenous and Development Monitor*, *3*(2), 3–5.

Compilation of References

Mawere, M. (2015). Indigenous knowledge and public education in sub-Saharan Africa. *Africa Spectrum, 50*(2), 57–71. doi:10.1177/000203971505000203

Mayblin, L., & Turner, J. (2020). *Migration studies and colonialism*. John Wiley & Sons.

Mazzocchi, F. (2006). Western science and Knowledge: Despite their variations, different forms can learn from each other. *EMBO Reports, 7*(5), 463–466. doi:10.1038j.embor.7400693 PMID:16670675

Mbadiwe, N., Adikaibe, B. E., Achor, J., Okoye, O., Onodugo, O., Anyim, O., Ijoma, U., Orah-Okpala, C., Ugwu, C., & Onodugo, N. (2021). Alcohol use in selected low-income neighbourhoods in Enugu, Southeast Nigeria. *Annals of Medical and Health Sciences Research, 11*, 1555–1560.

Mba, E. H., Ekpo, A. S., Ozim, E. C., & Oladeinde, S. O. (2019). Assessment of traditional palm wine tapping practice: Effect on vegetation in Nasarawa State, Nigeria. *International Journal of Environment and Climate Change, 9*(12), 841–851. doi:10.9734/ijecc/2019/v9i1230165

Mbeki, T. (2005). Goals of higher education in Africa. *USA/Africa Dialogue, 588.*

Mbeki, T. (1998). *Africa, the time has come*. Tafelberg.

Mbilinyi, D., & Mwabungulu, E. M. (2020). The fate of indigenous knowledge: The role played by libraries in Tanzania. *Information Development, 36*(4), 489–502. doi:10.1177/0266666919871088

McClellan, J. E. III, & Dorn, H. (2006). *Science and technology in world history: An Introduction*. JHU Press.

McCoy, T. (2021). Cunhaporanga Tatuyo became a TikTok star by sharing glimpses of her life in a remote indigenous community in the Amazon. *The Washington Post.*https://www.washingtonpost.com/world/interactive/2021/brazil-indigenous-tik-tok-star/

McCoy, S. I., Ralph, L. J., Wilson, W., & Padian, N. S. (2013). Alcohol production as an adaptive livelihood strategy for women farmers in Tanzania and its potential for unintended consequences on women's reproductive health. *PLoS One, 8*(3), e59343. doi:10.1371/journal.pone.0059343 PMID:23527167

McGaw, L. J., Omokhua-Uyi, A. G., Finnie, J. F., & Van Staden, J. (2022). Invasive alien plants and weeds in South Africa: A review of their applications in traditional medicine and potential pharmaceutical properties. *Journal of Ethnopharmacology, 283*, 114564. doi:10.1016/j.jep.2021.114564 PMID:34438034

McGinnis, G., Harvey, M., & Young, T. (2020). Indigenous knowledge sharing in Northern Australia: Engaging digital technology for cultural interpretation. *Tourism Planning & Development, 17*(1), 96–125. doi:10.1080/21568316.2019.1704855

McGregor, D. (2018). Indigenous research: Future directions. In D. McGregor, J.-P. Restoule, & R. Johnston (Eds.), Indigenous research: Theories, practices, and relationships (pp. 296–310). Canadian Scholars.

McGregor, D., Latulippe, N., Whitlow, R., Gansworth, K. L., McGregor, L., & Allen, S. (2023). Towards meaningful research and engagement: Indigenous knowledge systems and Great Lakes governance. *Journal of Great Lakes Research, 49*, S22–S31. doi:10.1016/j.jglr.2023.02.009

McIntosh, S. K. (2022). Igbo-Ukwu at 50: A symposium on recent archaeological research and analysis. *African Archaeological Review, 39*(4), 369–385. doi:10.100710437-022-09495-5 PMID:36405395

McKnight, K., O'Malley, K., Ruzic, R., Horsley, M. K., Franey, J. J., & Bassett, K. (2016). Teaching in a digital age: How educators use technology to improve student learning. *Journal of Research on Technology in Education, 48*(3), 194–211. doi:10.1080/15391523.2016.1175856

McPherson, E. (2018). Risk and the Pluralism of Digital Human Rights Fact-Finding and Advocacy. In K. Land, M. and D. Aronson, J. (eds) Human Rights New Technologies for Human Rights Law and Practice. Cambridge University Press. doi:10.1017/9781316838952.009

Mdhluli, T. D., Mokgoatšana, S., Kugara, S. L., & Vuma, L. (2021). Knowledge management: Preserving, managing and sharing indigenous knowledge through digital library. *Hervormde Teologiese Studies, 77*(2), a6795. doi:10.4102/hts.v77i2.6795

Meissner, O., & Buso, D. L. (2007). Traditional male circumcision in the Eastern Cape-scourge or blessing? *South African Medical Journal, 97*(5), 71–373. PMID:17599221

Menton, M., Milanez, F., Souza, J. M. A., & Cruz, F. S. M. (2021). The COVID-19 pandemic intensified resource conflicts and indigenous resistance in Brazil. *World Development, 138*, 105222. doi:10.1016/j.worlddev.2020.105222

Mertala, P. (2020). Paradoxes of participation in the digitalisation of education: A narrative account. *Learning, Media and Technology, 45*(2), 179–192. doi:10.1080/17439884.2020.1696362

Méry, S., Anderson, P., Inizan, M. L., Lechevallier, M., & Pelegrin, J. (2007). A pottery workshop with flint tools on blades knapped with copper at Nausharo (Indus civilisation, ca. 2500 BC). *Journal of Archaeological Science, 34*(7), 1098–1116. doi:10.1016/j.jas.2006.10.002

Middleton, J. (2015). *Cultural intelligence: CQ: The competitive edge for leaders crossing borders.* Bloomsbury.

Minishi-Majanja, M. K. (2012). *Educating a changeling: The paradox of library and information science in Africa.* Inaugural Lecture, University of South Africa. https://uir.unisa.ac.za/bitstream/handle/laugural%

Mji, G. (2019). *Opting for a walk without limbs: the avoidance of Stellenbosch University to be an African University.* Stellenbosch University Library Auditorium.

Mmola, S. (2010). *A survey of perceptions of IKS students and IKS lecturers on IKS programme at North-West University (Mafikeng Campus).* [Unpublished manuscript, IKS Programme: North-West University].

Modak, S. (2021). Local history collection on Sri Chaitanya Mahaprabhu in the Public Libraries in Nabadwip. *Library Philosophy and Practice (e-Journal).* https://digitalcommons.unl.edu/libphilprac/6217

Mohanty, C. T. (2003). *Feminism without borders: Decolonizing theory, practicing solidarity.* Duke University Press.

Moher, D., Liberati, A., Tetzlaff, J., & Altman, D. G. (2010). Preferred reporting items for systematic reviews and meta-analyses: The PRISMA statement. *International Journal of Surgery, 8*(5), 336–341. doi:10.1016/j.ijsu.2010.02.007 PMID:20171303

Moichela, K. Z. (2017). *Integration of indigenous knowledge systems in the curriculum for basic education: possible experiences of Canada* (Doctoral dissertation).

Moichela, K. Z. 2017. *Integration of indigenous systems in the curriculum for basic education: possible experiences of Canada* [Doctoral dissertation, University of South Africa]. https://core.ac.uk/download/pdf/162048463.pdf

Mokgobi, M. G. (2014). Understanding traditional African healing. *African Journal for Physical Health Education, Recreation and Dance, 20*(sup-2), 24-34.

Mokgobi, M. G. (2014). Understanding traditional African healing. *African Journal of Physical Health Education Recreation and Dance, 20*(2), 24–34. PMID:26594664

Mokhesi, T., & Modjadji, P. (2022). Usage of Traditional, complementary and alternative medicine and related factors among patients receiving healthcare in Lesotho. *The Open Public Health Journal*, *15*(1), e187494452202090. doi:10.2174/18749445-v15-e2202090

Montgomery, L., Hartley, J., Neylon, C., Gillies, M., & Gray, E. (2021). *Open knowledge institutions: reinventing universities*. MIT Press. doi:10.7551/mitpress/13614.001.0001

Monyela, M. (2021). Call Us by Our Names: The Need to Establish Authority Control Standards for Non-Roman Names. *Library Philosophy and Practice*, *1*(1), 1–10.

Monyela, M. (2022). Knowledge organisation in academic libraries: The Linked Data approach. In T. M. Masenya (Ed.), *Innovative Technologies for Enhancing Knowledge Access in Academic Libraries* (pp. 71–88). IGI Global. doi:10.4018/978-1-6684-3364-5.ch005

Moorefield-Lang, H. M. (2014). Makers in the library: Case studies of 3D printers and maker spaces in library settings. *Library Hi Tech*, *32*(4), 583–593. doi:10.1108/LHT-06-2014-0056

Morgan, H. (2020). Best practices for implementing remote learning during a pandemic. *The Clearing House: A Journal of Educational Strategies, Issues and Ideas*, *93*(3), 135–141. doi:10.1080/00098655.2020.1751480

Morris, B. (2010). Indigenous knowledge. *The Society of Malawi Journal*, *63*(1), 1–9.

Mortensen, M. (2015). Connective witnessing: Reconfiguring the relationship between the individual and the collective. *Information Communication and Society*, *18*(11), 1393–1406. doi:10.1080/1369118X.2015.1061574

Mosoti, Z., & Masheka, B. (2010). Knowledge management: The case for Kenya. *The Journal of Language. Technology & Entrepreneurship in Africa*, *2*(1), 107–133.

Mothibe, M. E & Sibanda, M. (2019). *African Traditional Medicine: South African Perspective*. InTech. . doi:10.5772/intechopen.83790

Mothibe, M. E., & Sibanda, M. (2019). African traditional medicine: South African perspective. *Traditional and Complementary Medicine*, 1-27. https://www.intechopen.com/chapters/65475

Mothoagae, I. D. (2017). The transfusion of bogwera in Luke 2:21 in the 1857 English-Setswana bible. *Theological Studies*, *73*(3), 1–9. doi:10.4102/hts.v77i1.6914

Motsamayi, M. F. (2019). *Sotho-Tswana'Difala vessels in selected South African museums: challenges in descriptions and catalogues* [Doctoral dissertation, University of Kwa Zulu Natal, Durban. South Africa]

Motsa, Z. (2017). When the lion tells the story: A response from South Africa. *Higher Education Research & Development*, *36*(1), 28–35. doi:10.1080/07294360.2017.1249070

Mposhi, A., Manyeruke, C., & Hamauswa, S. (2013). The importance of patenting traditional medicines in Africa: The case of Zimbabwe. *International Journal of Humanities and Social Science*, *3*(2), 236–246.

Msila, V. (2009). Africanisation of education and the search for relevance and context. *Educational Research Review*, *4*(6), 310–315.

Msuya, J. (2007). Challenges and opportunities in the protection and preservation of indigenous knowledge in Africa. *International Journal of Information Ethics*, *7*, 1–8.

Mteti, S. H. (2016). Engendering pottery production and distribution processes among the Kisi and Pare of Tanzania. *International Journal of Gender and Women's Studies*, *4*(2), 127–141. doi:10.15640/ijgws.v4n2a11

Muchineripi, P. C. (2008). *Feeding Five Thousand: The case for indigenous crops in Zimbabwe*. African Research Institute.

Mugabe, J., Kameri-Mbote, P., & Mutta, D. (2001). *Knowledge, genetic resources, and intellectual property protection: towards a new international regime*. International Environmental Law Research Centre. https://www.ielrc.org/content/w0105.pdf.

Mugovhania, N. G. (2012). The androgynic pedagogic approach in the study and teaching of performing arts in South Africa. *Journal of Sociological Studies*, 2(12), 908–917. http://bitly.ws/B9nk

Mugume, T., & Luescher, T. M. (2017). Student representation and the relationship between student leaders and political Parties: The case of Makerere University. *South African Journal of Higher Education*, 31(3), 154–171. doi:10.20853/31-3-639

Muguti, T., & Maposa, S. R. (2012). Indigenous Weather Forecasting: A phenological study engaging the Shona of Zimbabwe. *Journal of African Studies*, 4(2), 102–112.

Muhammed, N., Chakma, S., Hossain, M. F., Masum, M., Hossain, M., & Oesten, G. (2011). A case study on the Garo ethnic people of the Sal (Shorea robusta) forests in Bangladesh. *International Journal of Social Forestry.*, 4, 179–193.

Mujere, N., Chanza, N., Muromo, T., Guurwa, R., Kutseza, N., & Mutiringindi, E. (2023). Indigenous Ways of Predicting Agricultural Droughts in Zimbabwe. In *Socio-Ecological Systems and Decoloniality: Convergence of Indigenous and Western* (pp. 51–72). Springer International Publishing.

Mukred, M., Yusof, Z. M., Alotaibi, F. M., Asma'Mokhtar, U., & Fauzi, F. (2019). The key factors in adopting an electronic records management system (ERMS) in the educational sector: A UTAUT-based framework. *IEEE Access : Practical Innovations, Open Solutions*, 7, 35963–35980. doi:10.1109/ACCESS.2019.2904617

Müller, K. (2007). *The Potter's Studio Handbook*. Quarry Books.

Murrey, A. (2020). Colonialism. In A. Kobayashi (Ed.), *International Encyclopedia of Human Geography* (2nd ed., pp. 315–326). Elsevier. doi:10.1016/B978-0-08-102295-5.10804-2

Mutula, S. M., & Tsvakai, M. (2002). Historical perspectives of cataloguing and classification in Africa. *Cataloging & Classification Quarterly*, 35(1-2), 61–77. doi:10.1300/J104v35n01_05

Muzah, G. (2016). *Legal protection of Knowledge*. Lessons from Southern Africa. In WIPO-WTO COLLOQUIUM PAPERS.

Myemana A. (2004). *Should Christians undergo the Circumcision Rite?* East London: 3 Eden Ministries.

Mzamane, V. Z. (2003). Toward a Pedagogy for Liberation: Education for National Culture in South Africa. In I. M. Nkomo (Ed.), *Pedagogy of Domination: Toward Democratic Education in South Africa*. Africa World Press.

Nahotko, M. (2020). OPAC development as the genre transition process, PART 1: OPAC generations historical development. *Annals of Library and Information Studies*, 67(2), 107–117.

Nakashima, D., & Roué, M. (2002). Indigenous KNOWLEDGE, peoples, and sustainable practice. Encyclopedia of global environmental change, 5, 314-324.

Nakata, M., & Langton, M. (2005). Australian indigenous knowledge and libraries (p. 188). UTS ePRESS.

Nakata, M. (2013). The rights and blights of the politics in Indigenous higher education.[). Routledge.]. *Anthropological Forum*, 23(3), 289–303. doi:10.1080/00664677.2013.803457

Compilation of References

Nakata, M., Byrne, A., Nakata, V., & Gardiner, G. (2005). Indigenous Knowlege, the Library and Information Service Sector and Protocols. *Australian Academic and Research Libraries, 36*(2), 1–25.

Nanashaitu, U. (2017). The indigenous Yoruba pottery: Processes and products. *Research on Humanities and Social Sciences, 7*(20), 52–63.

Nandy, A. (2000). Recovery of indigenous knowledge and dissenting futures of the university. *The university in transformation: Global perspectives on the futures of the university*, 115-123.

Nandy, A. (1981). *The Intimate Enemy: Loss and Recovery of Self Under Colonialism*. Oxford University Press.

Nasongo, J. W., & Musungu, L. L. (2009). The implications of Nyerere's theory of education to contemporary education in Kenya. *Educational Research Review, 4*(4), 111–116.

Nassauer, A., & Legewie, M. N. (2022) Video Data Analysis: How to use 21st century video in the social sciences. Sage Publishing.

National Open University of Nigeria. (2022). *Indigenous Knowledge Management*. NOUN Press.

Navei, N. (2021). Cultural tourism potentials of Daŋi traditional pottery art. *International Journal of Innovative Research and Development, 10*(9), 153–165. doi:10.24940/ijird/2021/v10/i9/JUL21044

Ndiribe, M. O., & Aboh, S. C. (2022). Multilingualism and marginalisation: A Nigeria diversity approach. *International Journal of Multilingualism, 19*(1), 1–15. doi:10.1080/14790718.2020.1818752

Ndlovu-Gatsheni, S. J. (2013). Why decoloniality in the 21st century? *The Thinker: For Thought Leaders, 48*, 10–15.

Ndlovu-Gatsheni, S. J. (2015). Decoloniality as the future of Africa. *History Compass, 13*(10), 485–496. doi:10.1111/hic3.12264

Ndlovu-Gatsheni, S. J. (2018). *Epistemic freedom in Africa: Deprovincialization and decolonization*. Routledge. doi:10.4324/9780429492204

Ndubuisi, C. (2022). The Oye-Ekiti Christian art workshop and the fusion of the European Catholic tradition and Nigerian indigenous art in three Lagos churches. *Art in Translation*, 1-25. https://doi.org/ doi:10.1080/17561310.2022.2120343a

Nduka, S. C., & Oyelude, A. A. (2019). Goge Africa: Preserving Indigenous Knowledge Innovatively through Mass Media Technology. *Preservation. Digital Technology & Culture, 48*(3-4), 120–128. doi:10.1515/pdtc-2019-0007

Nekesa, A. W., & Oyelude, A. A. (2016). Standing Conference of Eastern, Central, and Southern African Library Associations XXII 2016. *The International Information & Library Review, 48*(3), 228–231. doi:10.1080/10572317.2016.1205430

Nelson, H. E., & NO, R. (2015). *Challenges of documenting and disseminating agricultural indigenous knowledge for sustainable food security in Soroti District*. Kampala: Makerere University.

Ngara, R., Rutsate, J., & Mangizvo, R. V. (2014). Shangwe Indigenous Knowledge Systems: An Ethno metrological and Ethno musicological Explication. *International Journal of Asian Social Sciences, 4*(1), 81–88.

Ngozi, O. R., Ihekwoaba, E. C., & Ugwuanyi, F. C. (2014). Strategies for Enhancing Information Access to Traditional Medical Practitioners to Aid Health Care Delivery in Nigeria. *Library Philosophy and Practice*, 0_1.

Ngubane, N. I., & Makua, M. J. (2021). Intersection of Ubuntu pedagogy and social justice: Transforming South African higher education. *Transformation in Higher Education, 6*, 8. doi:10.4102/the.v6i0.113

Ngulube, P., (2021). Postgraduate Supervision Practices In Education Research And The Creation Of Opportunities For Knowledge Sharing. *Problems of Education in the 21ˢᵗ Century, 79*(2), 255-272.

413

Ngulube, P. (2002). Managing and preserving indigenous knowledge in the knowledge management era: Challenges and opportunities for information professionals. *Information Development*, *18*(2), 95–102. doi:10.1177/026666602400842486

Ngulube, P. (2003). Using the SECI knowledge management model and other tools to communicate and manage tacit indigenous knowledge. *Innovation*, *27*(1), 21–30.

Ngulube, P. (2004). Using the SECI knowledge management and other tools to communicate and manage tacit indigenous knowledge. *Innovation*, *27*(1), 21–30. doi:10.4314/innovation.v27i1.26484

Nhemachena, A., Mlambo, N., & Kaundjua, M. (2016). The notion of the "field" and the practices of researching and writing Africa: Towards decolonial praxis. *Africology*, *9*(7), 15–36.

Nicholas, G. (2022). Protecting Indigenous heritage objects, places, and values: Challenges, responses, and responsibilities. *International Journal of Heritage Studies*, *28*(3), 400–422. doi:10.1080/13527258.2021.2009539

Nnama-Okechukwu, C. U., & McLaughlin, H. (2022). Indigenous knowledge and social work education in Nigeria: Made in Nigeria or made in the West? *Social Work Education*, ●●●, 1–18. doi:10.1080/02615479.2022.2038557

Noah, E. A., & Çağnan, Ç. (2021). A Study of Vernacular Architecture In Relation To Sustainability; the Case of Northern Nigeria. *YDÜ Mimarlık Fakültesi Dergisi*, *3*(1), 21–35.

Noaman, A. Y., Ragab, A. H. M., Madbouly, A. I., Khedra, A. M., & Fayoumi, A. G. (2017). Higher education quality assessment model: Towards achieving the educational quality standard. *Studies in Higher Education*, *42*(1), 23–46. doi:10.1080/03075079.2015.1034262

Nonaka, I. (1994). A dynamic theory of organizational knowledge creation. *Organization Science*, *5*(1), 14–37. doi:10.1287/orsc.5.1.14

Nonaka, I., & Konno, N. (1998). The concept of "Ba": Building a foundation for knowledge creation. *California Management Review*, *40*(3), 40–54. doi:10.2307/41165942

Nonaka, I., & Nishiguchi, T. (2001). *Knowledge emergence: Social, technical, and evolutionary dimensions of knowledge creation*. Oxford University Press.

Nonaka, I., & Takeuchi, H. (1995). *The knowledge-creating company: How Japanese companies create the dynamics of innovation*. Oxford university press.

Noonan, J. (2014). Radical Philosophy and Social Criticism. *International Critical Thought*, *4*(1), 10–20. doi:10.1080/21598282.2014.878143

Noronha, M., Pawar, V., Prajapati, A., & Subramanian, R. B. (2020). A literature review on traditional herbal medicines for malaria. *South African Journal of Botany*, *128*, 292–303. doi:10.1016/j.sajb.2019.11.017

Nortey, S., & Bodjawah, E. K. (2018). Designers' and indigenous potters' collaboration towards innovation in pottery production. *Journal of Desert Research*, *16*(1), 64–81. doi:10.1504/JDR.2018.091153

Ntombana, L. (2011). Should Xhosa male initiation be abolished? *International Journal of Cultural Studies*, *14*(6), 631–640. doi:10.1177/1367877911405755

Ntuli, P. (1999). The missing link between culture and education: are we still chasing Gods that are not our own? In M. W. Makgoba (Ed.), *African renaissance*. Mafube-Tafelberg.

Nugraha, A. S., Damayanti, Y. D., Wangchuk, P., & Keller, P. A. (2019). Anti-infective and anti-cancer properties of the Annona species: Their ethnomedicinal uses, alkaloid diversity, and pharmacological activities. *Molecules (Basel, Switzerland)*, *24*(23), 4419. doi:10.3390/molecules24234419 PMID:31816948

Compilation of References

Nwankwo, E., Oguamanam, C., & Obieluem, U. (2018). Sustainable safety and preservation mechanisms for cross river monoliths. *Journal of Tourism and Heritage Studies, 7*(2), 52–62. doi:10.33281/JTHS20129.2017.2.5

Nwashindu, V., & Onu, A. (2019). Palm wine economy and labour migrants of mgbowo community of Igbo society. *International Journal of Research in Arts and Social Sciences, 12*, 202–228.

Nwokoma, A. (2012). Nigeria Indigenous Knowledge Application in ICT Development, School of Information Communication; American University of Nigeria, Yola, Adamawa state, Nigeria. *Journal of Education and Social Research, 2*(7).

Nyiringango, G. (2019). *Assessing Changes in Knowledge about and Self-efficacy for Neonatal Resuscitation Among Rwandan Nurses and Midwives after a Mentorship Process* (Doctoral dissertation, The University of Western Ontario (Canada).

Nyota, S., & Mapara, J. (2008). Shona Traditional children's games and play songs as indigenous ways of knowing. *The Journal of Pan African Studies, 2*(4), 184–202.

Nyumba, J. B. (2006). *The role of the library in promoting the application of indigenous knowledge (ik) in development projects*. IFLA.

O'Dora-Hoppers, C. (Ed.). (2002). *Indigenous Knowledge and the Integration of Knowledge Systems: Towards a Conceptual and Methodological Framework*. New Africa Books.

Ochieng, A., Koh, N. S., & Koot, S. (2023). Compatible with Conviviality? Exploring African Ecotourism and Sport Hunting for Transformative Conservation. *Conservation & Society, 21*(1), 38–47. doi:10.4103/cs.cs_42_21

Ocholla, D. N. (2007). Marginalized knowledge: An agenda for indigenous knowledge development and integration with other forms of knowledge. *International Journal of Information Ethics, 7*(9), 237–247.

Odede, I. (2020). African traditional medicine research between 1998 and 2018: an informetrics analysis in South Africa. Mousaion: South African Journal of Information Studies, 38(1).

Odigwe, F. N., Bassey, B. A., & Owan, V. J. (2020). Data management practices and educational research effectiveness of university lecturers in South-South Nigeria. *Journal of Educational and Social Research, 10*(3), 24–34. doi:10.36941/jesr-2020-0042

Odigwe, F. N., Offem, O. O., & Owan, V. J. (2018). Vocational training duration and university graduates' job performance in Cross River State, Nigeria. *International Journal of Current Research, 10*(7), 72024–72028. doi:10.5281/zenodo.4320545

Odigwe, F. N., & Owan, V. J. (2019). Trend analysis of the Nigerian budgetary allocation to the education sector from 2009 – 2018 with reference to UNESCO'S 26% Benchmark. *International Journal of Educational Benchmark, 14*(1), 1–14. doi:10.5281/zenodo.4458703

Odora-Hoppers, C. A. (Ed.). (2002). *Indigenous knowledge and the integration of knowledge systems: towards a philosophy of articulation*. New Africa Books.

OECD. (2018). The future of education and skills. *Education, 2030*. https://www.oecd.org/education/2030/

Oguamanam, C. (2020). Indigenous peoples, data sovereignty, and self-determination: Current realities and imperatives. *The African Journal of Information and Communication, 26*(26), 1–20. doi:10.23962/10539/30360

Oguche, D., & Aliyu, A. (2020). Towards a National Framework for Digital Preservation in Nigeria: Technologies and Best Practices. Information Impact. *Journal of Information and Knowledge Management, 11*(4), 146–155. doi:10.4314/iijikm.v11i4.14

Ogundipe, O. O. (2005). *The Librarianship of Developing Countries: The Librarianship of Diminished Resources*. Ikofa Press.

Ogunyoku, T. A., Nover, D. M., McKenzie, E. R., Joshi, G., & Fleenor, W. E. (2011). Point-of-use drinking water treatment in the developing world: Community acceptance, project monitoring and revision. *International Journal for Service Learning in Engineering. Humanitarian Engineering and Social Entrepreneurship, 6*(1), 14–32. doi:10.24908/ijsle.v6i1.3207

Ohaja, M., & Murphy-Lawless, J. (2017). Unilateral collaboration: The practices and understandings of traditional birth attendants in southeastern Nigeria. *Women and Birth; Journal of the Australian College of Midwives, 30*(4), 165–e171. doi:10.1016/j.wombi.2016.11.004 PMID:27889258

Okafor, N. (1975). Preliminary microbiological studies on the preservation of palm wine. *The Journal of Applied Bacteriology, 38*(1), 1–7. doi:10.1111/j.1365-2672.1975.tb00493.x

Okonkwo, E. E., Ukaegbu, M. O., & Eyisi, A. P. (2016). A documentation of some traditional aspects of wood consumption in Anaocha, Nigeria. *SAGE Open, 6*(2), 2158244016649417. doi:10.1177/2158244016649417

Okonkwo, I. E. (2014). Students' perception of ceramics education in Nigeria tertiary institutions. *African Research Review, 8*(2), 217–234. doi:10.4314/afrrev.v8i2.13

Okonya, J. S., & Kroschel, J. (2013). Indigenous Knowledge of Seasonal Weather Forecasting: A Case Study in Six Regions of Uganda. *Agricultural Sciences, 4*(12), 641–648. doi:10.4236/as.2013.412086

Okorafor, C. N. (2010). Challenges confronting libraries in documentation and communication of indigenous knowledge in Nigeria. *The International Information & Library Review, 42*(1), 8–13. doi:10.1080/10572317.2010.10762837

Okoye, J., & Oni, K. (2017). Promotion of indigenous food preservation and processing knowledge and the challenge of food security in Africa. *Journal of Food Security, 5*(3), 75–87.

Okwoche, A. S., & Okonkwo, E. E. (2021). Contemporary Process of Pottery Making in Yala Local Government of Cross River State. *American Journal of Aerospace Engineering, 8*(1), 1–8. doi:10.11648/j.ijmpem.20210601.11

Okwoche, A. S., Okonkwo, E. E., & Oyong, T. A. (2021). Ethnographic studies of Bakor stone monolith and their implication to tourism development. *Lakhomi Journal Scientific Journal of Culture, 2*(4), 171–187. doi:10.33258/lakhomi.v2i4.556

Oladejo, M. T. (2019). Challenges of technical and vocational education and training in Nigerian history. *Makerere Journal of Higher Education, 11*(1), 67–81. doi:10.4314/majohe.v11i1.6

Olalere, F. E. (2019). Effects of ecological process on indigenous pottery as a cultural tourism product: A case of Zulu pottery. *African Journal of Hospitality, Tourism and Leisure, 8*(5), 1–11. http://bitly.ws/BmuMa

Olasebikan, M. K. (2022). Socio-economic impacts of pottery business to the people of Isan Ekiti from 1960-2000. *Sapientia Global Journal of Arts. Humanities and Development Studies, 5*(3), 73–80.

Olayinka, C. (2022). NASU seeks government, private investment in library services. *The Guardian.* https://guardian.ng/appointments/nasu-seeks-government-private-investment-in-library-services/

Olorunfemi, S. O. (2023). The Ado of Rural-Urban Migration: Implication on Food Security in Akutupa-Kiri, Kogi State, Nigeria. In A. A. Popoola, H. H. Magidimisha-Chipungu, & L. Chipungu (Eds.), *Handbook of Research on Managing the Urban-Rural Divide Through an Inclusive Framework* (pp. 167–187). IGI Global. doi:10.4018/978-1-6684-6258-4.ch010

Omarsaib, M., Rajkoomar, M., Naicker, N., & Olugbara, C. T. (2022). Digital pedagogies for librarians in higher education: A systematic review of the literature. *Information Discovery and Delivery*, 1–13.

Compilation of References

Onayade, O.A., Onayade, O.A. and Sowofora, A.(1996). Wound Healing with Plants: The African perspective in IOCD Chemistry. *Biology and Pharmacologic properties of African medicinal plants.*

Ongachi. (2017). Traditional pottery techniques towards poverty eradication in Emuhaya constituency, Vihiga County, Kenya. *International Journal of Economics, Commerce and Management, 5*(12),868-877. http://bitly.ws/BSag

Ong, J. C. (2015). Witnessing distant and proximal suffering within a zone of danger: Lay moralities of media audiences in the Philippines. *The International Communication Gazette, 77*(7), 607–621. doi:10.1177/1748048515601555

Onwu, G., & Mosimege, M. (2004). Indigenous knowledge systems and science and technology education: A dialogue. *African Journal of Research in Mathematics. Science and Technology Education, 8*(1), 1–12.

Onyango, G., & Ondiek, J. O. (2021). Digitalisation and integration of sustainable development goals (SGDs) in public organisations in Kenya. *Public Organization Review, 21*(3), 511–526. doi:10.100711115-020-00504-2

Oppong, P. K. (2018). *The influence of packaging and brand equity on over-the-counter herbal medicines in Kumasi, Ghana. (Doctor of Philosophy, School of Management, IT and Governance).* University of KwaZulu-Natal., https://ukzn-dspace.ukzn.ac.za/handle/10413/17127

Orduña-Malea, E. (2021). Dot-science top level domain: Academic websites or dumpsites? *Scientometrics, 126*(4), 3565–3591. doi:10.100711192-020-03832-8

Orton, C., & Hughes, M. (2013). *Pottery in archaeology.* Cambridge University Press., doi:10.1017/CBO9780511920066

Osabohien, R. (2023). ICT adoption and youth employment in Nigeria's agricultural sector. *African Journal of Economic and Management Studies.* doi:10.1108/AJEMS-03-2022-0111

Osasona, C. O. (2007). Indigenous art and Nigerian contemporary residential architecture. *WIT Transactions on the Built Environment, 95,* 129–139. doi:10.2495/STR070131

Oseni, I. O., & Oyelade, A. O. (2023). Effect of capital expenditure on unemployment rate in Nigeria. *African Journal of Economic Review, 11*(3), 1–12.

Ovharhe, O. J., Ebewore, S. O., & Alakpa, S. O. E. (2022). Rural-urban migration of farmers in Delta and Edo States, Nigeria: Policy implications. *Migration and Development, 11*(2), 163–173. doi:10.1080/21632324.2020.1806601

Owan, V. J. (2022). A data mining algorithm for accessing research literature in electronic databases: Boolean operators. In T. Masenya (Ed.), *Innovative technologies for enhancing knowledge access in academic libraries* (pp. 140–155). IGI Global. doi:10.4018/978-1-6684-3364-5.ch009

Owan, V. J., Agurokpon, D. C., & Udida, U. J. (2021). Curriculum restructuring and job creation among Nigerian graduates: The mediating role of emerging Internet applications. *International Journal of Educational Administration, Planning, &[IJEAPR]. Research, 13*(2), 1–16. doi:10.5281/zenodo.5886422

Owan, V. J., Ameh, E., & Anam, E. G. (2023). Collaboration and institutional culture as mediators linking mentorship and institutional support to academics' research productivity. *Educational Research for Policy and Practice, 22*(2), 1–26. doi:10.100710671-023-09354-3

Owan, V. J., & Bassey, B. A. (2019). Data management practices in Educational Research. In P. N. Ololube & G. U. Nwiyi (Eds.), *Encyclopedia of institutional leadership, policy, and management: A handbook of research in honour of Professor Ozo-Mekuri Ndimele* (Vol. 2, pp. 1251–1265). Pearl Publishers International Ltd.. doi:10.13140/RG.2.2.16819.04647

Owan, V. J., Duruamaku-Dim, J. U., Okon, A. E., Akah, L. U., & Agurokpon, D. C. (2022a). Joint mediation of psychosis and mental stress on alcohol consumption and graduates' job performance: A PLS structural equation modeling. *The International Journal of Learning in Higher Education, 30*(1), 89–111. doi:10.18848/2327-7955/CGP/v30i01/89-111

Owan, V. J., Emanghe, E. E., Denwigwe, C. P., Etudor-Eyo, E., Usoro, A. A., Ebuara, V. O., Effiong, C., Ogar, J. O., & Bassey, B. A. (2022b). Curriculum management and graduate programmes' viability: The mediation of institutional effectiveness using PLS-SEM approach. *Journal of Curriculum and Teaching, 11*(5), 114–127. doi:10.5430/jct.v11n5p114

Owan, V. J., Ndibe, V. C., & Anyanwu, C. C. (2020). Diversification and economic growth in Nigeria (1981–2016): An econometric approach based on ordinary least squares (OLS). *European Journal of Sustainable Development Research, 4*(4), em0131. Advance online publication. doi:10.29333/ejosdr/8285

Owiny, S. A., Mehta, K., & Maretzki, A. N. (2014). The use of social media technologies to create, preserve, and disseminate indigenous knowledge and skills to communities in East Africa. *International Journal of Communication, 8,* 234–247. https://ijoc.org/index.php/ijoc/article/view/1667

Oyadonghan, J. C., Eke, F. M., & Fyneman, B. (2016). Information repackaging and its application in academic libraries. *International Journal of Computer Science and Information Technology Research, 4*(2), 217–222.

Oyelude, A. A. (2017). Virtual and augmented reality in libraries and the education sector. *Library Hi Tech News, 34*(4), 1–4. doi:10.1108/LHTN-04-2017-0019

p'Bitek, O. (1964). Fr. Tempels' Bantu Philosophy. *Transition,* (13), 15–17. doi:10.2307/2934418

Pal, S. K. (2021). Reviving Pottery Industry by Solving Problems: A Study in a Developing Economy. *IOSR Journal of Business and Management, 23*(7), 44–49. http://bitly.ws/BmWP

Palvia, S., Aeron, P., Gupta, P., Mahapatra, D., Parida, R., Rosner, R., & Sindhi, S. (2018). Online education: Worldwide status, challenges, trends, and implications. *Journal of Global Information Technology Management, 21*(4), 233–241. doi:10.1080/1097198X.2018.1542262

Panda. (2019). Traditional clay pottery of Odisha, India. *Indian Journal of Traditional Knowledge, 18*(2), 325–332. http://bitly.ws/BSfo

Parashar, R., Hulke, S., & Pakhare, A. (2018). Learning styles among first professional Northern and central India medical students during digitization. *Advances in Medical Education and Practice, 1-5,* 1–5. Advance online publication. doi:10.2147/AMEP.S182790 PMID:30588146

Paringatai, K. (2019). Indigenous pedagogies in practice in universities. In Migration, Education and Translation (pp. 199-212). Routledge. doi:10.4324/9780429291159-15

Parker, D. B. (2012). Toward a New Framework for Information Security? In S. Bosworth, M. E. Kabay, & E. Whyne (Eds.), *Computer security handbook* (pp. 3.1–3.23). John Wiley & Sons, Ltd., doi:10.1002/9781118851678.ch3

Park, H., & Wolfram, D. (2017). An examination of research data sharing and reuse: Implications for data citation practice. *Scientometrics, 111*(1), 443–461. doi:10.100711192-017-2240-2

Partha, P. (2018). Indigenous climate calendar: Changes and challenges. *Peoples' Preface, 9.*

Pasteur, K. (2011). *From Vulnerability to Resilience: A Framework for Analysis and Action to build Community Resilience.* Practical Action Publishing. doi:10.3362/9781780440583

Patel, L. (2021). *No study without struggle: Confronting settler colonialism in higher education.* Beacon Press.

Compilation of References

Paul, C. (2022). MANAGEMENT PRACTICES IN AGRIBUSINESS FIRMS. *European Journal of Information and Management*, *1*(1), 11–20.

Pehlivan, Z., Thièvre, J., & Drugeon, T. (2021). Archiving social media: the case of Twitter. In *The Past Web: Exploring Web Archives* (pp. 43–56). Springer International Publishing. doi:10.1007/978-3-030-63291-5_5

Peltzer, K., Preez, N. F., Ramlagan, S., & Fomundam, H. (2008). Use of traditional complementary and alternative medicine for HIV patients in KwaZulu-Natal, South Africa. *BMC Public Health*, *8*(1), 1–14. doi:10.1186/1471-2458-8-255 PMID:18652666

Pendergrass, K. L., Sampson, W., Walsh, T., & Alagna, L. (2019). Toward environmentally sustainable digital preservation. *The American Archivist*, *82*(1), 165–206. doi:10.17723/0360-9081-82.1.165

Perry, S. R. (2014). *Digitization and digital preservation: a review of the literature*. Scholar Works. http://scholarworks.sjsu.edu/cgi/viewcontent.cgi?article=1170&context=slissrj

Peters, E. E. (2021). Implication of early pottery practice by women in Nigeria: A focus on women pottery practice in Akwa Ibom state. *Academicia: An International Multidisciplinary Research Journal*, *11*(1), 474–481. doi:10.5958/2249-7137.2021.00067.7

Peters, J. D. (2009). Witnessing. In P. Frosh & A. Pinchevski (Eds.), *Media Witnessing* (1st ed., pp. 23–42)., doi:10.1057/9780230235762_2

Peterson, S., & Peterson, J. (2003). *The craft and art of clay: a complete potter's handbook*. Laurence King Publishing.

Pfister, P., & Lehmann, C. (2022). Digital value creation in German SMEs–a return-on-investment analysis. *Journal of Small Business and Entrepreneurship*, ●●●, 1–26. doi:10.1080/08276331.2022.2037065

Piauí, R. (2022). *Revista piauí on Twitter: "In Brazil, the coup will be live-streamed. Piauí analyzed 181 of Jair Bolsonaro's live streams and can now show, in video, how the president has prepared his supporters to discredit tomorrow's election. A crash course on coup-mo, Revista Piauí*. Twitter. https://twitter.com/revistapiaui/status/1576199768031756288

Pillay, N. (2013). Free, prior and informed consent of indigenous peoples. Foreword to the Manual for National Human Rights Institutions, 1-2.

Pilot, J. (2013). Developing Indigenous Knowledge Centres. *Australian Academic and Research Libraries*, *36*(2), 37–43. doi:10.1080/00048623.2005.10721247

Pionke, L., & Browdy, T. (2008). Communities of practice in action-the implementation and use of an enterprise-wide information system, *Proceedings of the 5th International conference on intellectual capital and knowledge management*, New York: Institute of Technology.

Planet Ark. (2004). *Where Are All The Dead Animals? Sri Lanka Asks*. Reuters Limited. www.planetark.com

Plockey, F. D. D. (2014). The role of Ghana public libraries in the digitization of indigenous knowledge: Issues and Prospects. *The Journal of Pan African Studies*, *6*(10), 20–36.

Plockey, F. D. D. (2015). Indigenous knowledge production, digital media, and academic libraries in Ghana. *The Journal of Pan African Studies*, *8*(4), 32–44.

Pontes, F. (2022). *Após descida do rio, indígenas recolhem produtos descartados por comerciantes - Amazônia Real, Amazonia Real*. Amazon IA Real. https://amazoniareal.com.br/apos-descida-do-rio-indigenas-recolhem-produtos-descartados-por-comerciantes/ (Accessed: 15 April 2022).

Prakash, S., Kumar, M., Kumari, N., Thakur, M., Rathour, S., Pundir, A., & Mekhemar, M. (2021). Plant-based antioxidant extracts and compounds in the management of oral cancer. *Antioxidants*, *10*(9), 1358. doi:10.3390/antiox10091358 PMID:34572990

Preservica. (2016). *How Preservica works*. Preservica. http://preservica.com/ preservica-works.

Pretorius, E. (1994). *Traditional healers. South African health review* (5th ed.). Health Systems Trust.

Procedures for Records Creation. (2021). *Digital Preservation Policy*. Heriot-Watt University, Edinburgh: United Kingdom. https://www.hw.ac.uk/documents/digital-preservation-procedures-records- creation.pdf

Putnam, R. (2007). E pluribus Unum Diversity and community in the twenty-first century. *Scandinavian Political Studies*, *30*(2), 137–174. doi:10.1111/j.1467-9477.2007.00176.x

Quayle, A. F., & Sonn, C. C. (2019). Amplifying the voices of indigenous elders through community arts and narrative inquiry: Stories of oppression, psychosocial suffering, and survival. *American Journal of Community Psychology*, *64*(1-2), 46–58. doi:10.1002/ajcp.12367 PMID:31365131

Quintanilla, M., Guzmán León, A., & Josse, C. (2022) *Amazonia Against the Clock, A Regional Assessment on where and how to protect 80% by 2025*. Amazonia.

Rahat, M. (2022). *Problematic video-streaming: a short review*. Science Direct. . doi:10.1016/j.cobeha.2022.101232

Rahman, M. (2006). The Garos: struggling to survive in the valley of death.

Rainie, S. C., Kukutai, T., Walter, M., Figueroa-Rodríguez, O. L., Walker, J., & Axelsson, P. (2019). Indigenous data sovereignty. In T. Davies, S. B. Walker, M. Rubinstein, & F. Perini (Eds), *The state of open data: Histories and horizons*. African Minds and International Development Research Centre. https://library.oapen.org/handle/20.500.12657/24884

Rajasekaran, B. (1993). *A framework for incorporating indigenous knowledge systems into agricultural research and extension organizations for sustainable agricultural development in India. Iowa State University*. [Doctoral thesis, Lowa State University, Lowa. United States]

Rajasekaran, B. (1993). A framework for incorporating indigenous knowledge systems into agricultural research, extension, and NGOs for sustainable agricultural development. *Studies in Technology and Social Change 21*. Ames, IA: Technology and Social Change Program, Iowa State University. http://www.iss.nl/ikdm/IKDM/IKDM/1-3/articles/rajasekaran.html

Rajeswari, R., Umadevi, M., Rahale, C. S., Pushpa, R., Selvavenkadesh, S., Kumar, K. S., & Bhowmik, D. (2012). Aloe vera: The miracle plant and its medicinal and traditional uses in India. *Journal of Pharmacognosy and Phytochemistry*, *1*(4), 118–124.

Rakemane, D., & Mosweu, O. (2021). Challenges of managing and preserving audio-visual archives in archival institutions in Sub Saharan Africa: A literature review. *Collection and Curation*, *40*(2), 42–50. doi:10.1108/CC-04-2020-0011

Ramnund-Mansingh, A., & Reddy, N. (2021). South African specific complexities in aligning graduate attributes to employability. *Journal of Teaching and Learning for Graduate Employability*, *12*(2), 206–221. doi:10.21153/jtlge2021vol-12no2art1025

Ramokgopa, G. (2013). *Speech by Deputy Minister Gwen Ramokgopa at the inauguration of the Interim Traditional Health Practitioners Council of South Africa*. Minister Gwen Ramokgopa.

Ramos, A. R. (1998). *Indigenism: ethnic politics in Brazil* (1st ed.). University of Wisconsin Press.

Ramose, M. B. (2004). *In search of an African identity*. South African Journal of Education.

Compilation of References

Ranjan, P., & Singh, B. K. (2020). Conservation of Traditional Knowledge in India and Need of Knowledge Networks. In *First International Conference on Bridging Traditional Knowledge to Modern Science–2020*. Research Gate.

Rao, T. Y., & Lal, B. S. (2010). Rural artisans-indigenous technology: An empirical study on village potters in Warangal. *Indian Journal of Development Research and Social Action*, *5*(1), 309–317.

Raseroka, H. K. (2002). From Africa to the world – the globalisation of indigenous knowledge systems: setting the scene. In From Africa to the World – the Globalisation of Indigenous Knowledge Systems. *Proceedings of the 15th Standing Conference of Eastern, Central and Southern African Library and Information Associations*. Library and Information Association of South Africa.

Ray, S. (2023). Weaving the links: Traditional Knowledge into modern science. *Futures*, *145*, 103081. doi:10.1016/j.futures.2022.103081

Rechert, K., Von, S. D., & Welte, R. (2010). Emulation based services in digital preservation.*Proceedings of the 10th Annual Joint Conference on Digital Libraries*, (pp. 365–368). ACM. 10.1145/1816123.1816182

Reimers, E. (2020). Secularism and religious traditions in non-confessional Swedish preschools: Entanglements of religion and cultural heritage. *British Journal of Religious Education*, *42*(3), 275–284. doi:10.1080/01416200.2019.1569501

Renne, E. P. (2020). Reinterpreting Adire cloth in northern Nigeria. *Textile History*, *51*(1), 60–85. doi:10.1080/00404969.2020.1747372

Ribeiro, D. (1975). *Configurações histórico-culturais dos povos americanos*. Global Editora e Distribuidora Ltda.

Ribeiro, D. (1977). *Os índios e a civilização*. Editora Vozes.

Rice, P. M. (2015). *Pottery analysis: A sourcebook*. University of Chicago press.

Riggs, E. M. (2005). Field-based education and indigenous knowledge: Essential components of geoscience education for Native American communities. *Science Education*, *89*(2), 296–313. doi:10.1002ce.20032

Rimkus, K., Padilla, T., Popp, T., & Martin, G. (2014). Digital Preservation File Format Policies of ARL Member Libraries: An Analysis. *D-Lib Magazine : the Magazine of the Digital Library Forum*, *3/4*(20), 1–11. doi:10.1045/march2014-rimkus

Ristovska, S. (2016). Strategic witnessing in an age of video activism. *Media Culture & Society*, *38*(7), 1034–1047. doi:10.1177/0163443716635866

Ritter, T., & Pedersen, C. L. (2020). Digitization capability and the digitalisation of business models in business-to-business firms: Past, present, and future. *Industrial Marketing Management*, *86*, 180–190. doi:10.1016/j.indmarman.2019.11.019

Rix, E. F., Wilson, S., Sheehan, N., & Tujague, N. (2018). Indigenist and decolonising research methodology. In P. Liamputtong (Ed.), *Handbook of research methods in health social sciences* (pp. 253–267). Springer. doi:10.1007/978-981-10-2779-6_69-1

Robertson, G. L. (2013). *Food packaging: Principles and practice* (3rd ed.). CRC Press.

Robinson, D. (2020). T202. Multicast: Has Its Time Finally Arrived? [Video] YouTube. *Streaming Media West*. https://www.youtube.com/watch?v=KG-ecsdmodI&list=PL_tg9vfNLui1vnqdPEHFdM3S_b8zc3RW1&index=14

Robinson, D. (2010). *Confronting biopiracy: challenges, cases, and international debates*. Routledge. doi:10.4324/9781849774710

Rojas, D., de Azevedo Olival, A., & Alves Spexoto Olival, A. (2021). Despairing Hopes (and Hopeful Despair) in Amazonia. In B. Junge, (Ed.), *Precarious Democracy* (1st ed., pp. 129–141). Rutgers University Press., doi:10.36019/9781978825697-012

Rosoff, N. B. (2005). Integrating native views into museum procedures: Hope and practice at the national museum of the American Indian. In N. B. Rosoff (Ed.), *Museums and source communities* (pp. 83–90). Routledge. doi:10.4324/9780203987834-14

Ross, S. (2007). *Digital Preservation, Archival Science and Methodological Foundations for Digital Libraries, Keynote Address at the 11th European Conference on Digital Libraries (ECDL)*. Budapest: HATII at the University of Glasgow.

Roux, A. (2015). *Indigenous knowledge in a virtual context: Sustainable digital preservation. A literature review.* Unisa Library (SPPD6). https://core.ac.uk/display/188775692?utm_source=pdf&utm_medium=banner&utm_campaign=pdf-decoration-v1

Ruberg, B., & Brewer, J. (2022). Digital Intimacy in Real Time : Live Streaming Gender and Sexuality. *Television & New Media*, *00*(0), 1–8. doi:10.1177/15274764221084071

Ruhanen, L., & Whitford, M. (2019). Cultural heritage and Indigenous tourism. *Journal of Heritage Tourism*, *14*(3), 179–191. doi:10.1080/1743873X.2019.1581788

Ruhinirwa, F. W., Katabulawo, P., Atukwase, R. B., Otiti, R., & Musingo, D. (2019). *Using indigenoUs knowledge to connect FaMilies with natUre For conservation in Uganda.* IZE JOURNAL.

Ruusalepp, K. I., & Dobreva, M. (2013). *Innovative digital preservation using social search in agent environments: State of art in digital preservation and multi-agent systems.* Durafile. http://www.durafile.eu

Sage Rauchberg, J. (2022). '#Shadowbanned. In P. Paromita (Ed.), *LGBTQ Digital Cultures* (1st ed., p. 196). Routledge. doi:10.4324/9781003196457-15

Sagsan, M. (2009). Knowledge management discipline: Test for an undergraduate program in Turkey. *Electronic Journal of Knowledge Management*, *7*(5), 627–636.

Saldaña, J. (2021). The coding manual for qualitative researchers. *Sage (Atlanta, Ga.).*

Sallaz, J. J. (2018). Is a Bourdieusian Ethnography Possible? In T. Medvetz & J. J. Sallaz (Eds.), *The Oxford Handbook of Pierre Bourdieu* (pp. 1–24). Oxford University Press. doi:10.1093/oxfordhb/9780199357192.013.21

Salzar, J. F. (2006). Indigenous Peoples and the Cultural Construction of Information and Communication Technology (ICT) in Latin America. In L. Everlyn Dyson, M. Hendriks, & S. Grant (Eds.), *Information Technology and Indigenous People* (1st ed., pp. 14–27). Information Science Publishing. doi:10.4018/978-1-59904-298-5.ch002

Samson, C., & Gigoux, C. (2016). *Indigenous Peoples and Colonialism: Global Perspectives* (1st ed.). Polity Press.

Samson, C., & Gigoux, C. (2016). *Indigenous peoples and colonialism: Global perspectives.* John Wiley & Sons.

Samuel, O., Lina, J., & Ifeanyi, O. (2016). Production of vinegar from oil-palm wine using Acetobacter aceti isolated from rotten banana fruits. *Universal Journal of Biomedical Engineering*, *4*(1), 1–5. doi:10.13189/ujbe.2016.040101

San Nicolas Roca, T., & Parrish, J. (2013). *Using Social Media to Capture and Convey Cultural Knowledge: A Case of Chamorro People.System Sciences (HICSS), 2013 46th Hawaii International Conference.* IEEE. 10.1109/HICSS.2013.593

Sangha, K., Baijnatha, H., & Street, R. (2020). Spirostachys Africana: A review of phytochemistry, traditional and biological uses and toxicity. *Indilinga*, *19*(2), 176–188.

Sangma, S. (2010). *Bangladesh indigenous peoples' Forum.* Indigenous People's Forum.

Sangma, U. (1998). *Adibashi Barta.* Tribal Welfare Association, Sunamgonj, Sylhet. (In Bengali)

Compilation of References

Sarah, E. A. (2015). The Role of Libraries in Preserving indigenous knowledge in primary healthcare in Nigeria. *International Journal of digital library services, 5*(2), 43-54.

Sarmah, S. S. (2018). Data Migration. *Science and Technology, 8*(1), 1–10. doi:10.5923/j.scit.20180801.01

Sarumaha, M. S. (2019). Educational Management Based on Indigenous Knowledge (Narrative Studies of Culture of Indigenous Knowledge in South Nias). *Advances in Social Science, Education and Humanities Research, 410*(1), 150–133.

Saurombe, A. (2018). The teaching of indigenous knowledge as a tool for curriculum transformation and Africanisation. *Journal of Education, 138*, 160.

Savithramma, N., Yugandhar, P., & Lingarao, M. (2014). Ethnobotanical studies on Japali Hanuman theertham-a sacred grove of Tirumala hills, Andhra Pradesh, India. *J Pharm Sci Res, 6*, 83–88.

Sawyer, D., Reich, L., Giaretta, D., Mazal, P., Huc, C., Nonon-Latapie, M., & Peccia, N. (2002). *The Open Archival Information System (OAIS) Reference Model and its Usage.* UNC. https://ils.unc.edu/callee/p4020-lee.pdf

Saxena, S., Saini, S., Samtiya, M., Aggarwal, S., Dhewa, T., & Sehgal, S. (2021). Assessment of Indian cooking practices and cookwares on nutritional security: A review. *Journal of Applied and Natural Science, 13*(1), 357–372. doi:10.31018/jans.v13i1.2535

Scaff, L. A. (2021). Max Weber. In P. Kivisto (Ed.), *The Cambridge Handbook of Social Theory* (pp. 124–144). Cambridge Univeristy Press.

Schmidt, H. (2019). Indigenizing and decolonizing the teaching of psychology: Reflections on the role of the non-Indigenous ally. *American Journal of Community Psychology, 64*(1-2), 59–71. doi:10.1002/ajcp.12365 PMID:31355969

Scholtes, F. (2009). *Status quo and prospects of smallholders in the Brazilian sugarcane and ethanol sector: Lessons for development and poverty reduction.* University of Bonn, Center for Development Research (ZEF). http://hdl.handle.net/10419/88388

Schulte, J., Tiffen, B., Edwards, J., Abbott, S., & Luca, E. (2018). Shaping the Future of Academic Libraries: Authentic Learning for the Next Generation. *College & Research Libraries, 79*(5), 685–696. doi:10.5860/crl.79.5.685

Schwandt, T. A., & Gates, E. F. (2018). Case study methodology. In N. K. Dezin & Y. S. Lincoln (Eds.), *The Sage handbook of qualitative research* (5th ed., pp. 341–358). Sage publications.

Schwarcz, M. L. & Starling, H. (2019) Brazil a biography. First. Farrar, Straus and Giroux.

Sebata, T. P. (2015). *The role of traditional healers in the treatment of HIV and AIDS in Tsetse Village: The case of Mahikeng in the North West Province.* [Maters of Arts in indigenous Knowledge system masters thesis, North-West University, Potchefstroom].

Sebola, M., & Mogoboya, M. J. (2020). Re-imagining Africanisation of sustainable epistemologies and pedagogies in (South) African higher education: A conceptual intervention. *South African Journal of Higher Education, 34*(6), 237–254. doi:10.20853/34-6-4078

Seidu, R. K., Howard, E. K., Apau, E., & Eghan, B. (2022). Symbolism and conservation of indigenous African textiles for museums. Handbook of Museum Textiles, 1, 239-265. doi:10.1002/9781119983903.ch13

Sekiwu, D., Akena, F. A., & Rugambwa, N. O. (2022). Decolonizing the African University Pedagogy Through Integrating African Indigenous Knowledge and Information Systems. In *Handbook of Research on Transformative and Innovative Pedagogies in Education* (pp. 171–188). IGI Global. doi:10.4018/978-1-7998-9561-9.ch010

Senanayake, S. G. (2006). Indigenous knowledge as a key to sustainable development. *Journal of Agricultural Science, 2*(1).

423

Senanayake, S. G. J. N. (2006). Indigenous knowledge as a key to sustainable development. *Journal of Agricultural Sciences*, *2*(1), 87–94. doi:10.4038/jas.v2i1.8117

Sen, S., & Chakraborty, R. (2017). Revival, modernization and integration of Indian traditional herbal medicine in clinical practice: Importance, challenges and future. *Journal of Traditional and Complementary Medicine*, *7*(2), 234–244. doi:10.1016/j.jtcme.2016.05.006 PMID:28417092

Seroto, J. (2011). Indigenous education during the pre-colonial period in southern Africa. *Indilinga African Journal of Indigenous Systems*, *10*(1), 77–88.

Session, F. T. (2022). Intergovernmental Committee on Intellectual Property and Genetic Resources. *Traditional Knowledge and Folklore*. ABS. https://abs.igc.by/wp-content/uploads/2022/07/Glossary-of-key-terms-wipo_grtkf_ic_43_inf_7.pdf

Settee, P. (2007). *Pimatisiwin: Indigenous knowledge systems, our time has come*. [Master's thesis, University of Saskatchew].

Shabalala, D. B. (2017). Intellectual Property, Knowledge, and Traditional Cultural Expressions in Native American Tribal Codes. *Akron Law Review*, *51*, 1125.

Shahjahan, R. A., Estera, A. L., Surla, K. L., & Edwards, K. T. (2022). "Decolonizing" curriculum and pedagogy: A comparative review across disciplines and global higher education contexts. *Review of Educational Research*, *92*(1), 73–113. doi:10.3102/00346543211042423

Shanhong, T. (2000). *Knowledge management in libraries in the 21st century*. IFLA. https://www.ifla.org/IV/ifla66/papers/057-110e.htm.

Sharief, O. A. E., Mudawi, M. S. E., & Mohamed, R. A. (2021). Indigenous knowledge in Sudan: Perceptions among Sudanese librarians. *IFLA Journal*, *47*(3), 361–374. doi:10.1177/03400352211013839

Sharma, I. P., Kanta, C., Dwivedi, T., & Rani, R. (2020). Indigenous agricultural practices: A supreme key to maintaining biodiversity. *Microbiological Advancements for Higher Altitude Agro-Ecosystems & Sustainability*, 91-112.

Sharma, P., Kharkwal, A. C., Kharkwal, H., Abdin, M. Z., & Varma, A. (2014). A review on pharmacological properties of Aloe vera. *International Journal of Pharmaceutical Sciences Review and Research*, *29*(2), 31–37.

Shimray, S. R., & Ramaiah, C. K. (2018). *Digital preservation strategies: an overview*. www.researchgate.net/publication/327221006_Digital_Preservation_Strategies_An_Overview/link/5b80da10a6fdcc5f8b6592f4/download

Shintani, N. (2016). The effects of computer-mediated synchronous and asynchronous direct corrective feedback on writing: A case study. *Computer Assisted Language Learning*, *29*(3), 517–538. doi:10.1080/09588221.2014.993400

Shipley, J. W. (2017). From primitivism to Pan-Africanism: Remaking modernist aesthetics in postcolonial Nigeria. *Ghana Studies*, *20*(1), 140–174. doi:10.3368/gs.20.1.140

Shiri, A., Howard, D., & Farnel, S. (2022). Indigenous digital storytelling: Digital interfaces supporting cultural heritage preservation and access. *The International Information & Library Review*, *54*(2), 93–114. doi:10.1080/10572317.2021.1946748

Shirley, V. J. (2017). Indigenous Social Justice Pedagogy: Teaching into the Risks and Cultivating the Heart. *Critical Questions in Education*, *8*(2), 163–177.

Shoko, K., & Shoko, N. (2013). Indigenous Weather Forecasting Systems: A case study of biotic weather forecasting indicators for ward 12 and 13 in Mberengwa District, Zimbabwe. *Asian Social Science*, *9*(3), 285–297. doi:10.5539/ass.v9n5p285

Shonge, R. (2018). An Analysis of the Zimbabwe National Intellectual Property Policy and Implementation Strategy (2018-2022). *African Journal of Intellectual Property*, *3*(1), 45–60.

Shoshany, B. (2022, April 24). Time travel could be possible, but only with parallel timelines. *The Conversation*. https://theconversation.com/time-travel-could-be-possible-but-only-with-parallel-timelines-178776

Sibsankar, J., Mrinal, K., & Ujjal, M. (2009). *Digital Preservation with Special Reference to the Open Archival Information System (OAIS) Reference Model: An Overview*. 7th International CALIBER-2009, Pondicherry University.

Sileyew, K. J. (2020). Research design and methodology. In E. Abu-Taieh, A. El Mouatasim, & I. H. Al Hadid (Eds.), *Cyberspace* (pp. 1–12). IntechOpen., doi:10.5772/intechopen.85731

Sillitoe, P., & Marzano, M. (2009). Future of indigenous knowledge research in development. *Futures*, *41*(1), 13–23. doi:10.1016/j.futures.2008.07.004

Sindiga, I., Nyaigotti-Chacha, C., & Kanunah, M. P. (Eds.). (1995). *Traditional medicine in Africa*. East African Publishers.

Singh, H. B., Yaipharembi, N., Huidrom, E., & Devi, C. A. (2023). Knowledge, Beliefs, and Practices Associated with Ethnic People of Manipur, North East India in Conservation of Biodiversity. In *Traditional Ecological of Resource Management in Asia* (pp. 61–75). Springer International Publishing.

Singh, J., Flaherty, K., Sohi, R. S., Deeter-Schmelz, D., Habel, J., Le Meunier-FitzHugh, K., Malshe, A., Mullins, R., & Onyemah, V. (2019). Sales profession and professionals in the age of digitization and artificial intelligence technologies: Concepts, priorities, and questions. *Journal of Personal Selling & Sales Management*, *39*(1), 2–22. doi:10.1080/08853134.2018.1557525

Si, S., Yu, X., Wu, A., Chen, S., Chen, S., & Su, Y. (2015). Entrepreneurship and poverty reduction: A case study of Yiwu, China. *Asia Pacific Journal of Management*, *32*(1), 119–143. doi:10.100710490-014-9395-7

Sithole, J. (2007). The challenges faced by African *libraries and information centres in documenting and preserving indigenous knowledge. IFLA Journal*, *33*(2), 117–123. doi:10.1177/0340035207080304

Siyanbola, W. O., Egbetokun, A. A., Oluseyi, I., Olamade, O. O., Aderemi, H. O., & Sanni, M. (2012). Indigenous technologies and innovation in Nigeria: Opportunities for SMEs. *American Journal of Industrial and Business Management*, *2*(2), 18846. doi:10.4236/ajibm.2012.22009

Smith, L. T. (2021) Decolonizing Methodologies: Research and Indigenous Peoples was Third. Zed Books. doi:10.5040/9781350225282

Smith, L. T. (2021). *Decolonising methodologies: Research and indigenous peoples*. Bloomsbury Publishing. https://bit.ly/3zaudU6

Smith, L. T. (1999). *Decolonizing methodologies: Research and indigenous peoples*. Zed Books.

Sobowale, T. O., Olarinde, O. J., Uzzi, F. O., & Sunday, O. S. (2020). Creative Welded Metal Art: A Means to Financial Sustainability. *KIU Journal of Humanities*, *5*(1), 77–86.

Sodi, T., Mudhovozi, P., Mashamba, T., Radzilani-Makatu, M., Takalani, J., & Mabunda, J. (2011). Indigenous healing practices in Limpopo Province of South Africa: A qualitative study. *International Journal of Health Promotion and Education*, *49*(3), 101–110. doi:10.1080/14635240.2011.10708216

Sohrabi, C., Franchi, T., Mathew, G., Kerwan, A., Nicola, M., Griffin, M., Agha, M., & Agha, R. (2021). *PRISMA 2020 statement: What's new and the importance of reporting guidelines* (Vol. 88). Elsevier.

Soler, A. S., Ort, M., & Steckel, J. (2016). *An Introduction to Data Management. (Version 4)* [Reader]. BEFmate, GFBio. https://bit.ly/3LSkSry

Sousa Santos, B. D. (2007). Beyond abyssal thinking: From global lines to ecologies of knowledges. *Review - Fernand Braudel Center, 30*, 45–89.

Spencer-Oatey, H. (2012). What is culture? A compilation of quotations. *GlobalPAD Core Concepts.* GlobalPAD Open House. http://www.warwick.ac.uk/globalpadintercultural

Sraku-Lartey, M., Acquah, S. B., Brefo, S. S., & Djagbletey, G. D. (2017). Digitization of indigenous knowledge on forest foods and medicines. *IFLA Journal, 43*(2), 187–197. doi:10.1177/0340035216681326

Srinivasan, R., Boast, R., Furner, J., & Becvar, K. M. (2009). Digital museums and diverse cultural knowledge: Moving past the traditional catalogue. *The Information Society, 25*(4), 265–278. doi:10.1080/01972240903028714

Starkey, L. (2020). A review of research exploring teacher preparation for the digital age. *Cambridge Journal of Education, 50*(1), 37–56. doi:10.1080/0305764X.2019.1625867

Stevens, A. (2008). A different way of knowing: Tools and strategies for managing indigenous knowledge. *Libri, 58*(1), 25–33. doi:10.1515/libr.2008.003

Stout, D., Toth, N., Schick, K., & Chaminade, T. (2008). Neural correlates of early stone age toolmaking: Technology, language and cognition in human evolution. *Philosophical Transactions of the Royal Society of London. Series B, Biological Sciences, 363*(1499), 1939–1949. doi:10.1098/rstb.2008.0001 PMID:18292067

Stuart, J., O'Donnell, A. W., Scott, R., O'Donnell, K., Lund, R., & Barber, B. (2022). Asynchronous and synchronous remote teaching and academic outcomes during COVID- 19. *Distance Education, 43*(3), 408–425. doi:10.1080/01587 919.2022.2088477

Sulyman, A. S., Amzat, B. O. & Taiwo, M. A. (2022). Indigenisation of Nigerian Librarianship through Indigenous Knowledge: Exploring its Possibilities. *Library Philosophy & Practice*, 1-17.

Sunday, O. O., Oyeniran, G., & Akeju, A. A. (2022). Community Participation in Conservation and Management of Cultural Heritage Resources in Yoruba Ethnic Group of South Western Nigeria. *SAGE Open, 12*(4), 21582440221130987. doi:10.1177/21582440221130987

Svotwa, E. J., Manyanhaire, I. O., & Makanyire, J. (2007). Integrating Traditional Knowledge Systems with Agriculture and Disaster Management: A Case for Chitora Communal Lands. *Journal of Sustainable Development in Africa, 9*(3), 59–60.

Szulanski, G., Ringov, D., & Jensen, R. J. (2016). Overcoming stickiness: How the timing of knowledge transfer methods affects transfer difficulty. *Organization Science, 27*(2), 304–322. doi:10.1287/orsc.2016.1049

Tabuti, J. R. S. (2004). *Locally used plants in Bulamogi County, Uganda: Diversity and modes of utilization. Medicinal, edible, fodder, and firewood species.* Semantic Scholar.

Tabuti, J. R. S., & Van Damme, P. (2012). Review of indigenous knowledge in Uganda: Implications for its promotion. *AFRICA FOCUS, 25*(1), 29–38. doi:10.1163/2031356X-02501004

Tagba, P., Osseyi, E., Fauconnier, M. L., & Lamboni, C. (2018). Aromatic composition of" sodabi", a traditional liquor of fermented oil palm wine. *Advance Journal of Food Science and Technology : AJFST, 14*(1), 15–22. doi:10.19026/ajfst.14.5421

Tajul. (2011). Local Genius of Mambong Pottery in Kelantan, Malaysia. *International Journal of Humanities and Social Science, 1*(21), 147–155. http://bitly.ws/Bmbh

Compilation of References

Tamburro, A. (2013). Including decolonization in social work education and practice. *Journal of Indigenous Social Development, 2*(1).

Tanyanyiwa, I. V., & Chikwanha, M. (2011). The role of indigenous knowledge systems in themanagement of forest resources in Mugabe area, Masvingo, Zimbabwe. *Journal of Sustainable Development in Africa, 13*(3), 132–149.

Tapfuma, M., & Hoskins, R. (2016). Visibility and accessibility of indigenous knowledge on open access institutional repositories at universities in Africa. In P. Ngulube (Ed.), *Handbook of Research on Theoretical Perspectives on Indigenous Knowledge Systems in Developing Countries* (pp. 248–266). IGI Global. doi:10.4018/978-1-5225-0833-5.ch011

Tarugarira, G. (2017). Dimensions of totemic history and its related accessories among the Gumbo-Madyirapazhe clan of Gutu, Zimbabwe. *DANDE Journal of Social Sciences and Communication, 2*(1).

Taye, M. M. (2010). Understanding Semantic Web and Ontologies: Theory and Applications. *Journal of Computing, 2*(6).

Taylor, C. (1992). Modernity and the rise of the public sphere. The Tanner Lectures on Human Values. *Delivered at Stanford University, 25*(February), 1992.

Taylor, J., & Gibson, L. K. (2017). Digitization, digital interaction and social media: Embedded barriers to democratic heritage. *International Journal of Heritage Studies, 23*(5), 408–420. doi:10.1080/13527258.2016.1171245

Tebes, J. K., Champine, R. B., Matlin, S. L., & Strambler, M. J. (2019). Population health and trauma-informed practice: Implications for programs, systems, and policies. *American Journal of Community Psychology, 64*(3-4), 494–508. doi:10.1002/ajcp.12382 PMID:31444915

Tella, R. D. (2007). Towards promotion and dissemination of indigenous knowledge: A case of NIRD. *The International Information & Library Review, 39*(3-4), 185–193. doi:10.1080/10572317.2007.10762748

Tenopir, C., Allard, S., Douglass, K., Aydinoglu, A. U., Wu, L., Read, E., Manoff, M., & Frame, M. (2011). Data Sharing by Scientists: Practices and Perceptions. *PLoS One, 6*(6), 1–21. doi:10.1371/journal.pone.0021101 PMID:21738610

Tharani, K. (2021). Much more than a mere technology: A systematic review of Wikidata in libraries. *Journal of Academic Librarianship, 47*(2), 102326. doi:10.1016/j.acalib.2021.102326

The Constitution of Zimbabwe. Amendment (N0.20) 2013.

The Copyright and Neighbouring Rights Act, 2006. https://www.aripo.org/wp-content/uploads/2018/12/Uganda-Copyright-Act.pdf

Thibodeau, K. (2002). Overview of Technological Approaches to Digital Preservation and Challenges in Coming Years Digital Preservation: An International Perspective. *Conference Proceedings*. CLIR. https://www.clir.org/PUBS/reports/pub107/pub107.pdf

Thiong'o, N. (1986). *Decolonising the mind: The politics of language in African literature*. J. Currey.

Thomas, A., & Gupta, V. (2022). The role of motivation theories in knowledge sharing: An integrative theoretical reviews and future research agenda. *Kybernetes, 51*(1), 116–140.

Thorburn, E. D. (2017). Social reproduction in the live stream. *TripleC, 15*(2), 425–440. doi:10.31269/triplec.v15i2.774

Thornton, T. F., & Bhagwat, S. A. (2020). *The Routledge handbook of indigenous environmental knowledge*. Routledge. doi:10.4324/9781315270845

Tjiek, L. T. (2006). Desa informasi: The role of digital libraries in the preserving and dissemination of indigenous knowledge. *The International Information & Library Review, 38*(3), 123–131. doi:10.1080/10572317.2006.10762713

Tom, M. N., Sumida Huaman, E., & McCarty, T. L. (2019). *Indigenous knowledges as vital contributions to sustainability* (Vol. 65). Springer.

Torres, F. L., & Medina, C. L. (2021). Cuentos Combativos: Decolonialities in Puerto Rican Books About María. *Journal of Literacy Research*, *53*(2), 242–264.

Tran Ba, L., Le Van, K., Van Elsacker, S., & Cornelis, W. M. (2016). Effect of cropping system on physical properties of clay soil under intensive rice cultivation. *Land Degradation & Development*, *27*(4), 973–982. doi:10.1002/ldr.2321

Triplett, K. (2000). *Handbuilt ceramics: pinching, coiling, extruding, molding, slip casting, slab work*. Lark books.

Truter, I. (2007). African traditional healers: Cultural and religious beliefs intertwined in a holistic way. *South African Pharmaceutical Journal. Suid-Afrikaanse Tydskrif vir Apteekwese*, *7*(8), 56–60.

Tuck, E., & Yang, K. W. (2012). Decolonization is not a metaphor. *Decolonization*, *1*(1), 1–40.

Tumuhairwe, G. K. (2013). *Analysis of library and information science/studies (lis) education today: The inclusion of indigenous knowledge and multicultural issues in lis curriculum*. IFLA.

Turner, S. (1994). *The Social Theory of Practices: Tradition, Tacit Knowledge, and Presuppositions* (1st ed.). Polity Press.

Turner, V. (1980). Social Dramas and Stories about Them. *Critical Inquiry*, *7*(1), 141–168. https://www-jstor-org.ezp. lib.cam.ac.uk/stable/1343180?seq=1. doi:10.1086/448092

Tyburski, E., Mak, M., Sokołowski, A., Starkowska, A., Karabanowicz, E., Kerestey, M., Lebiecka, Z., Preś, J., Sagan, L., Samochowiec, J., & Jansari, A. S. (2021). Executive dysfunctions in schizophrenia: A critical review of traditional, ecological, and virtual reality assessments. *Journal of Clinical Medicine*, *10*(13), 2782. doi:10.3390/jcm10132782 PMID:34202881

Udensi, J. (2010). Information repackaging-a necessity in Nigerian Libraries. Modern Library and information science for information professionals in Africa. Ibadan. Textlinks Publishers.

Uganda. (2006). *The Uganda National Culture Policy: A Culturally vibrant, cohesive and Progressive Nation*. Ministry of Gender, Labour & Social Development.

Ugboma, J. (2021). *Thicken Soups in a Flash with a Nigerian Evwere Clay Pot*. http://bitly.ws/BbMV

Ugwuogu, U. O. (2015). Expectations and challenges of information repackaging in Nigerian Academic Libraries. *International Journal of Learning and Development*, *5*(2), 56–64.

Ukwueze, F. (2012). The role of information and communication technology in the development of indigenous technical/ vocational knowledge. *Ikenga International Journal of Institute of African Studies,NN*, *12*(2), 233–248.

Umoru-Oke, N. (2017). Apprenticeship system in indigenous Yoruba pottery art of Nigeria. *International Journal of Small Business and Entrepreneurship Research*, *5*(4), 29–34. http://bitly.ws/BbzI

UNESCO (2021) *GLOBAL ACTION PLAN OF THE INTERNATIONAL DECADE OF INDIGENOUS LANGUAGES (IDIL2022-2032)*. UNESCO.

UNESCO. (2016). *Global Education Monitoring report. Indigenous knowledge and implications for sustainable development agenda*. UNSECO.

UNESCO. (2021). *Documentary heritage at risk: Policy gaps in digital preservation*. International Advisory Committee of the UNESCO Memory of the World Programme. https://en.unesco.org/sites/default/files/documentary_ heritage_at_ risk_policy_gaps_in_digital_preservation_en.pdf

Compilation of References

UNESCO. I. (2020). *Basic texts of the 2003 Convention for the Safeguarding of the intangible cultural heritage.* UNESCO. https://ich.unesco.org/doc/src/2003_Convention_Basic_Texts-_2022_version-EN_.pdf Accessed 11 March 2023.

UNITAR. (2021). Strategic Framework 2018-2021. United Nation Institute for Training and Research (UNITAR). UNITAR. https://unitar.org/sites/default/files/media/publication/doc/unitar _strategicframework_web-new.pdf

United Nations Press. (2019, April 22). *Indigenous People's Traditional Knowledge Must Be Preserved, Valued Globally, Speakers Stress as Permanent Forum Opens Annual Session.* UNP. https://press.un.org/en/2019/hr5431.doc.htm

United Nations. (2008). United Nations Declaration on the Rights of Indigenous Peoples. UN. https://www.un.org/esa/socdev/unpfii/documents/DRIPS_en.pdf Accessed 18 February 2023.

Uriah, L., Dungrit, C., & Rhoda, G. (2014). Locally made utensils as potential sources of heavy metals contamination of water: A case study of some pots made in Nigeria. *American Journal of Environmental Protection, 3*(6-2), 35-41. doi:10.11648/j.ajep.s.2014030602.16

Urt, J. N. (2016). How Western Sovereignty Occludes Indigenous Governance: The Guarani and Kaiowa Peoples in Brazil. *Contexto Internacional, 38*(3), 865–886. doi:10.15900102-8529.2016380300007

Uzogara, S. G., Agu, L. N., & Uzogara, E. O. (1990). A review of traditional fermented food condiments and beverages in Nigeria. Their benefits and possible problems. *Ecology of Food and Nutrition, 24*(4), 267–288. doi:10.1080/03670 244.1990.9991145

Van Wyk, B. E. (2011). The potential of South African plants in the development of new medicinal products. *South African Journal of Botany, 77*(4), 812–829. doi:10.1016/j.sajb.2011.08.011

Van Wyk, B., & Higgs, P. (2004). Towards an African philosophy of higher education: Perspectives on higher education. *South African Journal of Higher Education, 18*(3), 196–210.

Vassev, E., & Hinchey, M. (2015). Knowledge Representation for Adaptive and Self-aware Systems. In: Wirsing, M., Hölzl, M., Koch, N., Mayer, P. (eds) Software Engineering for Collective Autonomic Systems. Lecture Notes in Computer Science. Springer, Cham. doi:10.1007/978-3-319-16310-9_6

Veloso Ferreira, L. (2022). *Brasileiros pelo Brasil completa 3 meses com mais de 900 mil pessoas atendidas,* Fundação Banco do Brasil. https://fbb.org.br/pt-br/component/k2/conteudo/brasileiros-pelo-brasil-completa-3-meses-com-mais-de-900-mil-pessoas-atendidas

Venkanna, E. (2018). Perspectives of digital libraries in medical education. *IJARIIE,* 4(1), 2395-4396. http://ijariie.com/AdminUploadPdf/PERSPECTIVES_OF_DIGITAL_LIBRARIES_IN_MEDICAL_EDUCATION_ijariie7279.pdf

Verdery, K. (1999). *The Political Lives of Dead Bodies: Reburial and Post socialist Cahange* (1st ed.). Colombia University Press.

Vidal, L. B. (1986) 'A questão indígena', Carajás: desafio político, ecologia e desenvolvimento, p. 222.

Villén-Pérez, S., Anaya-Valenzuela, L., Conrado da Cruz, D., & Fearnside, P. M. (2021). Mining threatens isolated indigenous peoples in the Brazilian Amazon. *Global Environmental Change, 72,* 102398. doi:10.1016/j.gloenvcha.2021.102398

Viriri, A., & Mungwini, P. (2009). Down but not out: Critical insights in traditional Shona metaphysics. *The Journal of Pan African Studies, 2*(9). https://www.academia.edu/7946155/Down_But_Not_Out_Critical_Insights_in_Traditional_Shona_Metaphysics

Virtanen, P. K. (2015). Indigenous social media practices in Southwestern Amazonia. *AlterNative: An International Journal of Indigenous Peoples,* 11, 4, 350.

Vlassenroot, E., Chambers, S., Di Pretoro, E., Geeraert, F., Haesendonck, G., Michel, A., & Mechant, P. (2019). Web archives as a data resource for digital scholars. *International Journal of Digital Humanities, 1*(1), 85–111. doi:10.100742803-019-00007-7

Vlieghe, J. (2016). Education, Digitization and Literacy training: A historical and cross-cultural perspective. *Educational Philosophy and Theory, 48*(6), 549–562. doi:10.1080/00131857.2015.1044928

Von der Porten, S., de Loë, R. C., & McGregor, D. (2016). Incorporating indigenous knowledge systems into collaborative governance for water: Challenges and opportunities. *Journal of Canadian Studies. Revue d'Etudes Canadiennes, 50*(1), 214–243. doi:10.3138/jcs.2016.50.1.214

Von, S. D., Rechert, K., & Valizada, I. (2013). *Towards emulation-as-a-service: Cloud services for versatile digital object access.* IJDC. doi:10.2218/ijdc.v8i1.250

Vygotsky, L. S. (1962). *Thought and Language.* MIT Press. doi:10.1037/11193-000

Vygotsky, L. S. (1978). *Mind in Society: The development of higher psychological processes.* Harvard University Press.

Wa Thiong'o Ngugi. (1986). *Decolonizing the Mind.* Heinemann.

Wadee, A. A., Keane, M., Dietz, T., & Hay, D. (2010). Effective PhD supervision mentoring and coaching. 2nd Edition. South Africa-Netherlands research Programme on Alternatives in Development SANPAD. Amsterdam: Rosenberg Publishers.

Walter, M., Lovett, R., Maher, B., Williamson, B., Prehn, J., Bodkin-Andrews, G., & Lee, V. (2021). Indigenous data sovereignty in the era of big data and open data. *The Australian Journal of Social Issues, 56*(2), 143–156. doi:10.1002/ajs4.141

Wane, N. N. (2008). Mapping the field of indigenous knowledge in anti-colonial discourse: A transformative journey in education. *Race, Ethnicity and Education, 11*(2), 183–197. doi:10.1080/13613320600807667

Warraich, N. F., & Rorissa, A. (2018). Adoption of linked data technologies among university librarians in Pakistan: Challenges and prospects. *Malaysian Journal of Library and Information Science, 23*(3), 1–13. doi:10.22452/mjlis.vol23no3.1

Warren, D. M. (1991). *Using indigenous knowledge in agricultural development. World Bank Discussion.* The World Bank.

Waungana, E. (1984). Children's story telling and reading activities in Zimbabwe, Library Work for Children and Young Adults in the Developing Countries. *Proceedings of the IFLA/UNESCO Pre-Session Seminar in Leipzig, GDR,* München.

Waziri, A. F., & Aliero, B. L. (2004). Soil physicochemical properties under two different species of range land grasses at Gangam rangeland, Shagari local government area, Sokoto State.[SAN]. *Bulletin of Science Association of Nigeria, 26*, 274–281.

Weber, M. (1992). The Protestant Ethic and the Spirit of Capitalism. Journal of Geophysical Research. Routledge.

West, A. (2014). Ubuntu and business ethics: Problems, perspectives and prospects. *Journal of Business Ethics, 121*(1), 47–61. doi:10.100710551-013-1669-3

Westerlund, D. (2006). *African indigenous religions and disease causation.* Brill. https://brill.com/display/title/12074

Whaanga, H., Bainbridge, D., Anderson, M., Scrivener, K., Cader, P., Roa, T., & Keegan, T. T. (2015). He Matapihi Mā Mua, Mō Muri: The ethics, processes, and procedures associated with the digitization of indigenous knowledge—The Pei Jones collection. *Cataloging & Classification Quarterly, 53*(5-6), 520–547. doi:10.1080/01639374.2015.1009670

Whitson, J. (2021). Indigenizing instagram: Challenging settler colonialism in the outdoor industry. *American Quarterly*, *73*(2), 311–334. doi:10.1353/aq.2021.0029

WHO (World Health Organization). (2013). *Traditional medicine definitions*. WHO. www,synergy.com.kurt.

WHO. (1978). *Declaration of Alma Ata. International conference on primary health care, Alma-Ata, USSR, 6-12 September 1978*. Geneva: WHO. https://cdn.who.int/media/docs/default-source/documents/almaata-declaration-en. pdf?sfvrsn=7b3c2167_2 Accessed 12 March, 2023.

Whyte, K. (2017). What do indigenous knowledges do for indigenous peoples? M. Nelson and D. Shilling (eds) Keepers of the Green World: Traditional Ecological Knowledge and Sustainability. Cambridge University Press.

Williamson, B., Eynon, R., & Potter, J. (2020). Pandemic politics, pedagogies and practices: Digital technologies and distance education during the coronavirus emergency. *Learning, Media and Technology, 45*(2), 107–114. doi:10.1080 /17439884.2020.1761641

Wilson, S. (2020). *Research is ceremony: Indigenous research methods*. Fernwood publishing. http://bit.ly/3TKxPWa

Wilson, T. D., & Walsh, C. (1996). *Information behaviour: An interdisciplinary perspective*. Sheffield: University of Sheffield department of information studies.

Wilson, S. (2008). *Research is ceremony: Indigenous research methods*. Fernwood.

Wilson, T. D. (1999, August1). Models in information behaviour research. *The Journal of Documentation, 55*(3), 249–270. doi:10.1108/EUM0000000007145

Winschiers-Theophilus, H., Jensen, K., & Rodil, K. (2012). Locally situated digital representation of indigenous knowledge: Co-constructing a new digital reality in rural Africa. In Strano, M. Hrachovec, H. Sudweeks, F. and Ess, C. (Eds.), Proceedings Cultural Attitudes Towards Technology and Communication 2012, Murdoch University.

WIPO. (2017). *Protect and Promote Your Culture: A practical guide to intellectual property for Indigenous Peoples and local communities*. World Intellectual Property. https://www.wipo.int/edocs/pubdocs/en/wipo_pub_1048.pdf

WIPO. (2018). *Glossary: Key Terms Related to Genetic Resources, Knowledge, and Traditional Cultural Expressions*. WHO. https://www.wipo.int/meetings/en/doc_details.jsp?doc_id=410022,

Wittman, H., Desmarais, A., & Wiebe, N. (2010). The origins and potential of food sovereignty. *Food sovereignty: Reconnecting food, nature and community*, 1-14.

World Council of Indigenous Peoples (WCIP) (1998). *World Council of Indigenous Peoples Report*. WCIP.

World Health Organisation (WHO). (2013). *Traditional medicine. Geneva: publication*. WHO. https://www.who.int/ mediacentre/ factsheet s/2003/fs134/en/

World Health Organisation. (2008). *Male circumcision policy, practices and services in the Eastern Cape Province of South Africa: Case study*. WHO. https://www.malecircumcision.org/sites/default/files/document_library/South_Africa_MC_case_study_May_2008_002_0.pdf

World Health Organization (WHO). (2008). [- *Primary Health Care: Now More Than Ever. Geneva*.]. *World Health Report*. WHO.

World Intellectual Property Organisation (WIPO). (2012). Traditional and Intellectual Property – Background Brief. WHO. https://www.wipo.int/pressroom/en/briefs/traditional_ip.html

World Intellectual Property Organization. (2003). *Intellectual property and traditional cultural expressions/folklore* (Vol. 913). WIPO.

Wroe, F. C. R. (1994). Microwave-assisted firing of ceramics. In *Proceedings of the Institute of Energy Conference held in London, UK,* (pp. 43-53). IEEE. 10.1016/B978-0-08-042133-9.50007-1

WSIS (World Summit on the Information Society). (2013). *WSIS Forum 2013 13-17 May, Geneva.* WSIS. https://www.itu.int/net/wsis/implementation/2013/forum/

Wutete, O. (2014). *The Role of Indigenous Knowledge in Agriculture and Environmental Conservation: The Case of Gutu District, Zimbabwe.* [Unpublished Doctoral Thesis, Fort Hare University: South Africa].

Wynberg, R. (2023). Biopiracy: Crying wolf or a lever for equity and conservation? *Research Policy, 52*(2), 104674. doi:10.1016/j.respol.2022.104674

Yadav, V., & Goyal, P. (2015). User innovation and entrepreneurship: Case studies from rural India. *Journal of Innovation and Entrepreneurship, 4*(1), 1–20. doi:10.118613731-015-0018-4

Yannus, F. (2017). Preservation of indigenous knowledge by public libraries in Westcliff. Chatsworth, Durban. University of Western Cape.

Yanou, M. P., Ros-Tonen, M., Reed, J., & Sunderland, T. (2023). Local and practices among Tonga people in Zambia and Zimbabwe: A review. *Environmental Science & Policy, 142,* 68–78. doi:10.1016/j.envsci.2023.02.002

Young, J. O. (2005). Profound offence and cultural appropriation. *The Journal of Aesthetics and Art Criticism, 63*(2), 135–146. doi:10.1111/j.0021-8529.2005.00190.x

Young, J. O. (2010). *Cultural appropriation and the arts.* John Wiley & Sons.

Yuan, H., Ma, Q., Ye, L., & Piao, G. (2016). Traditional medicine and modern medicine from natural products. *Molecules (Basel, Switzerland), 21*(5), 559. doi:10.3390/molecules21050559 PMID:27136524

Yunkaporta, T. (2009). *Aboriginal Pedagogies at the Cultural Interface.* [PhD thesis, James Cook University, Townsville].

Yunnus, F. (2017). *Preservation of indigenous knowledge (IK) by public libraries in Westcliff, Chatsworth.* The University of Western Cape.

Yussif, I., Adu-Gyamfi, V. E., & Tabi-Agyei, E. (2018). Documentation of some identified traditional pottery decorative techniques in Northern Ghana. *Asian Research Journal of Arts & Social Sciences, 6*(3), 1–11. doi:10.9734/ARJASS/2018/41149

Yusufali, S. S. (2021). A Values-Based, Holistic Approach towards School Mission in a US Islamic School. Retrieved from https://ir.lib.uwo.ca/oip/204

Zaim, H., Muhammed, S., & Tarim, M. (2019). Relationship between knowledge management processes and performance: Critical role of knowledge utilization in organisations. *Knowledge Management Research and Practice, 17*(1), 24–38. doi:10.1080/14778238.2018.1538669

Zavala, M. (2013). What do we mean by decolonizing research strategies? Lessons from decolonizing, indigenous research projects in New Zealand and Latin America. *Decolonization, 2*(1), 55–71.

Zembylas, M. (2018). Decolonial possibilities in South African higher education: Reconfiguring humanising pedagogies as/with decolonising pedagogies[Special issue]. *South African Journal of Education, 38*(4), 1699. doi:10.15700aje.v38n4a1699

Zhang, X., & Luther, C. A. (2020). Transnational news media coverage of distant suffering in the Syrian civil war: An analysis of CNN, Al-Jazeera English and Sputnik online news. *Media, War & Conflict, 13*(4), 399–424. doi:10.1177/1750635219846029

Zhao, Y. (2020) Analysis of TikTok's Success Based on Its Algorithm Mechanism. *Proceedings - 2020 International Conference on Big Data and Social Sciences, ICBDSS 2020*, (pp. 19–23). IEEE. 10.1109/ICBDSS51270.2020.00012

Zibani, P., Rajkoomar, M., & Naicker, N. (2022). A systematic review of faculty research repositories at higher education institutions. *Digital Library Perspectives, 38*(2), 237–248. doi:10.1108/DLP-04-2021-0035

Ziff, B. H., & Rao, P. V. (Eds.). (1997). *Borrowed power: Essays on cultural appropriation.* Rutgers University Press.

Zimu-Biyela, A. N. (2016). *The management and preservation of indigenous knowledge in Dlangubo village in Kwazulu-Natal, South Africa.* [Doctoral Dissertation, University of South Africa, Pretoria]. http://hdl.handle.net/10500/22968

Zimu-Biyela, A. A. N. (2021). What is the role of libraries in disseminating about South African intellectual property laws in rural communities? *South African Journal of Library and Information Science, 87*(2), 21–29. doi:10.7553/87-2-1956

Zola, F. C., Colmenero, J. C., Aragão, F. V., Rodrigues, T., & Junior, A. B. (2020). Multicriterial model for selecting a charcoal kiln. *Energy, 190*, 116377. doi:10.1016/j.energy.2019.116377

Zondi, N. B. (2019). *A dissection of the Protection, Promotion, Development and Management of Indigenous Knowledge Systems Act 6 of 2019: substantive issues and foreseeable consequences for creative industries in South Africa* [Minor Dissertation, University of Cape Town]. http://hdl.handle.net/11427/36221

Zuma-Netshiukhwi, G., Stigter, K., & Walker, S. (2013). Use of Traditional Weather/Climate Knowledge by farmers in the South-Western Free State of South Africa: Agro metrological Learning by Scientists. *Atmosphere (Basel), 4*(4), 383–410. doi:10.3390/atmos4040383

About the Contributors

Tlou Maggie Masenya holds a PhD in Information Science from University of South Africa and completed Masters in Information Technology at the University of Pretoria. She has seven years of work experience in academia, in the field of Information Science and Technology. She is currently a Senior Lecturer in the Department of Information Systems at Durban University of Technology. She also worked as a Senior Lecturer at University of South Africa and University of Zululand. She supervises Masters and PhD students and also serves as an external examiner for postgraduate studies. She published book chapters and articles in peer-reviewed accredited journals. She is currently reviewing articles for South African Journal of Information management, South African Journal of Library and Information Science, Mousaion, Research Metrics and Analytics Journal, Journal of South African Society of Archivists and IGI-Global book chapters. Her areas of expertise encompass ICT4D, Digital Preservation, Technopreneurship, Digital entrepreneurship, Knowledge Management, Indigenous Knowledge System, Disruptive Technologies . She is planning to be an editor for books that cover some of these arrears.

***

Adebowale Jeremy Adetayo is an academic staff of Adeleke University. His research interest is Library Science, Social media, Knowledge Management, and Business Information Management. He has published many articles in reputable journals and currently working on projects relating to pandemics, vaccines and virtual learning. He is a graduate of Babcock University.

Francis Akena Adyanga, PhD. is a Senior Lecturer at Kabale University in the Faculty of Education. He is also the Faculty Dean of the Faculty of Education. Francis obtained his PhD. from the University of Toronto in 2014. In 2015, he taught at the University of Toronto and was later a postdoctoral fellow at the College of Education, University of South Africa (UNISA) Pretoria in 2016/2017. He is a passionate educator with keen teaching and research interest in Indigenous Knowledge, Social and Environmental Justice Education, Education in Emergencies and Post Emergencies Contexts and Global Citizenship Education.

Kealeboga Aiseng holds a PhD in African Languages and Linguistics from the University of the Witwatersrand. He is a lecturer in the department of journalism and media studies at Rhodes University, Makhanda. Aiseng's research interests are sociolinguistics, language policy, African popular culture, new media and film studies. He has published articles in local and international journals. He also serves on numerous journal editorial boards.

About the Contributors

Michael Ekpenyong Asuquo received his B.Ed(Sc.), M.Ed and P.hD in 2009, 2014 and 219 respectively from the University of Calabar, Nigeria. He is currently a Lecture in the same institution. He has over forty (40) publications in both local and international reputable Journals. His research area is educational leadership, management and administration.

Monicca Thulisile Bhuda is a culture activist, a Children's book author, an indigenous scholar and a lecturer at the University of Mpumalanga. She holds a Bachelor's degree (hons) in Indigenous knowledge Systems, a Master's degree in Indigenous Knowledge Systems, and a PhD in social sciences with indigenous knowledge systems,. All of her qualifications have been obtained from the North-West University. Dr Bhuda specialises in African indigenous knowledge systems. She has been featured on numerous media platforms such as TV, Radio, Magazines and Newspapers that were based on her interests as an indigenous scholar and on Indigenous Knowledge Systems. Her interests include decolonization of education, promotion of indigenous languages, indigenous knowledge preservation, protection, management and dissemination.

Kamulegeya Grace Bugembe is an academician and researcher at Makerere University School of Computing and IT (SCIS) with teaching experience of 12 years. He obtained his PhD in 2022 from (Makerere University and MSc in Computer Science (University of Cape Town), Higher Diploma in Computer Science(University of the Witwatersrand), and, BSc computer science and Mathematics (Makerere University).He also works as a consultant software architect, Software project manager, and Software solutions lead for the last 6 years. He has considerable experience in applied software engineering, software innovation, and commercialization of software innovations in the nascent ecosystem of East Africa. He is a certified Java programmer and mentors many young software engineers in various technology start-ups in hubs that include Makerere Innovations and Incubation Center (MIIC). He is also a seasoned judge in technology and ICT-related innovations in Uganda and Africa. As a seasoned academic and researcher, he is passionate about advancing the applied software engineering discipline in Uganda through professionalizing the nascent software industry and through practice in ideation, innovation, architecting, implementation, and enabling the adoption and commercialization of software-enabled solutions). He holds Ph.D. in Software Engineering with a focus on measurements and metrics in software start-ups in the East African ecosystem. He has several publications related to software start-ups.

Collence Takaingenhamo Chisita is a Senior lecturer and Researcher based at the Durban University of Technology (DUT) in South Africa

Felicia Agbor-Obun Dan holds a Ph.D and an M.Ed. degrees in Health Education. She is a thorough breed educationalist as she further holds the Nigerian Certificate in Education and a Bachelor of Science degree in Physical and Health Education from Federal College of Education Obudu and the prestigious University of Calabar, Calabar, respectively.. Dr Felicia is an astute lecturer in the Department of Human Kinetic & Health Education of the University of Calabar, Calabar where she lectures School health Services, adult and adolescence health, Community health and current trends in Health Education. Prior to joining the University of Calabar in 2017, she was a public servant with Cross River State Secondary Education Board where she taught Physical and Health Education in various Secondary Schools in Calabar. She had carried out various academic research works and her publications in reputable International and local Journals. Dr Felicia is poised to contributing her best towards the development, growth

435

About the Contributors

and wellbeing of our society and educational sector of our nation; through team work and harmony in achieving set goals and targets. She is married with kids.

Aidam Benjamin Ekereke is a post graduate student of the University of Calabar, Calabar, Nigeria. His area of interest is school_ based assessment, measurement and evaluation.

Sarah Kaddu holds a Bachelor of Library & Information Science, Master of Arts in Information Studies, and a Ph.D. in Information Science. Currently, President, Uganda Library & Information Association (ULIA); Former Secretary-General, ULIA; President, SCECSAL (Standing Conference for Eastern, Central and Southern Africa), AfLIA East Africa Representative; Treasurer, AfLIA, Executive member IFLA Africa section, Reviewer, IFLA/ OCLC Jay Jordan Early Career Fellowship programme, and a Library & Information Science Educator.

Tom Kissock is a PhD student in the Department of Sociology at the Univerisyt of Cambridge. Tom has fifteen years of experience as a Director and Executive Producer working and researching digital video outside of academia for the BBC, YouTube, NBC, Cisco, and CBS. He has also researched video witnessing and human rights abuses in the fourth sector. His MSc at UCL used Video Data Analysis to track how populist political actors in Brazil built misinformation and election campaigns by strategising the cross-sharing video assets to avoid journalistic questioning as a symbolic accountability mechanism. His PhD at the University of Cambridge explores how Indigenous activists use video streaming platforms to produce knowledge and subsequently how non-indigenous people value those knowledges through the process of witnessing in real-time.

Jeffrey Kurebwa is a holder of a PHD in Public Administration. He is currently working as a Lecturer in the Department of Peace and Governance at Bindura University of Science Education in Zimbabwe. His research interests are in Gender Studies, Local governance and community development.

Claire Clement Lutaaya Nabutto, PhD is a lecturer at the East African School of Library and Information Science, College of Computing and Information Science at Makerere University. Claire obtained her PhD in 2015 from the University of Kwazulu -Natal . Her research interests include bibliometrics, Academic librarianship, Collection management and curriculum development in Library and Information Science. I am also passionate about teaching, research and learning new trends in Information Science through exchange programs with professionals in my field.

Mothusiotsile Edwin Maditsi is a PhD candidate at the North-West University (Mahikeng campus). He holds a BA (Hons) in Indigenous Knowledge Systems (IKS) degree from the North-West University (NWU), a Master of IKS degree also from the NWU and currently a PhD candidate at the NWU. During his Master's degree journey he served as a full member of PRIMCO in which he was appointed as a researcher for the project leader. He has participated and facilitated some community engagement activities for and on behalf of the IKS Centre at National and local level.Ssome of the community engagement activities entails; IK Act of 2019 and BCP public awareness workshops across the country; IK Act regulations public consultations across the country and a host of other IKS related activities. He is now appointed as a lecturer under the nGAP at the Indigenous Knowledge Systems Centre (NWU Mahikeng). In his PhD he is focusing on decolonizing community engagement using the NWU as a

About the Contributors

case study and he is supervised/promoted by Prof SA Materechera. Otsile is a member of South African Higher Education Community Engagement Forum (SAHECEF). Since assuming his position as a lecturer, he has shown dedication and commitment in decolonizing the teaching and learning activities within the higher education sector. This has seen him attend and present papers at the NWU's annual teaching and learning conference. In 2022, Otsile has since been appointed by the IKS Centre Director to coordinate the third leg of the centre which is community engagement and stakeholder relations, a position that he is still currently serving in.

Nalindren Naicker Ha PhD [Information Systems & Technology]; MSc [Information Systems]; Hons BSc (Computer Science); BSc (Computer Science). Currently serves as acting head of the Information Systems Department at the Faculty of Accounting and Informatics. He is currently involved with the supervision of PhD and Masters students at the Department of Information Systems. Prof. Naicker has been the recipient of the National Research Foundation grant for continued research in machine learning and ICT related projects in South Africa. He is a member of the ICT and Society Research Group at the Faculty of Accounting and Informatics.

Patience Nwosu is a lecturer in the Department of Educational Foundations, Taraba State University Jalingo Taraba State. She was the pioneer Head of the Department of Educational Administration and planning, which has now metamorphosed into Educational Foundations. Dr Nwosu is currently a senior lecturer and a member of the Taraba State University Senate, representing the Faculty of Education. She has attended conferences and workshops internationally and domestically and has also published in reputable journals. She is a member of the World Educators Forum, Association for the Advancement of Knowledge, National Association for Educational Administration and planning, Teachers' Registration Council, and Commonwealth Council for Educational Administration and Management, among many others. She has vast research interests such as educational work environment and worker productivity, educational leadership, work stress management, and educational finance.

Godian Patrick Okenjom received his B.Ed(English) in 2010 in University of Calabar, M.Ed, in 2012 in University of Nigeria, Nsukka and Ph.D in 2018 respectively from Ebonyi State University, Abakaliki-Nigeria respectively. He is currently a Lecturer in the Department of Educational Management, University of Calabar-Cross River State-Nigeria. He has over thirty (30) publications in both local and international reputable Journals. His research areas are educational leadership, management and administration.

Ovat Okpa received his B.Ed, 2005, M.Ed, 2010 and Ph.D in 2015 respectively from the University of Calabar. He is currently a Senior Lecturer in the Department of Educational Management, University of Calabar-Cross River State-Nigeria. He has over forty (40) publications in both local and international reputable Journals. His research area is educational leadership, policy studies, pedagogy, management, funding and administration of higher education.

Mousin Omarsaib has a PhD [Information Systems - LIS], MIS [Information Studies], Hons BA [Information Science]. Currently employed as a Subject Librarian and a guest lecturer for the library and Department of Information Systems respectively at the Durban University of Technology in South Africa. He has been instrumental at the Durban University of Technology libraries in pioneering blended learning, online teaching, and mentoring of library staff. He has mentored and trained staff at various levels imparting pertinent skills for their professional development in multimodal environments. His interest includes using digital tools such as learning management systems, Microsoft applications, immersive learning techniques, gamification, active learning styles for multimodal teaching environments. His research interest include digital pedagogies, e-learning, gamification, indigenous knowledge and meta-literacies.

Mercy Valentine Owan is a promising postgraduate student of higher education at the University of Calabar in Nigeria. She is also a research assistant at the Ultimate Research Network (URN). Her research interests lie in educational management, particularly in educational leadership, quality assurance, policy analysis, and management within tertiary institutions. She has demonstrated her proficiency and dedication to the field through her successful publications, both nationally and internationally. Her research work and publications provide valuable insights into addressing educational management and leadership challenges in higher education, making her a respected and accomplished scholar in her field.

Valentine Joseph Owan is a postgraduate student of Research, Measurement and Evaluation in the Department of Educational Foundations of the University of Calabar, Calabar, Nigeria. He is the founder of the Ultimate Research Network (URN) and a mentor to numerous scholars. His interests include item-response theory, research and statistics, structural equation modelling, program evaluation, quantitative research methodology, Rasch measurement theory, and higher education. Due to his early interest in research, Owan has published internationally and domestically in many leading journals. He is an established reviewer for several Web of Science and Scopus-indexed journals.

Mogiveny Rajkoomar has an educational background as follows: PhD (LIS); MIM; BInfo; BA; HED. She currently serves as a Senior lecturer and Programme coordinator in the Information Systems Department at the Durban University of Technology. She is passionate about Teaching, Learning and Research. She is currently involved in the supervision of PhD and Masters Students in the fields of information science, information management, information systems and information technology. She is currently the Acting Faculty Research coordinator for the Faculty of Accounting and Informatics. She serves on the following committees: Information and Technology Committee; Library Committee; Higher Degrees Committee, Institutional Research and Innovation Committee, Institutional Research Ethics Committee, Faculty Research Ethics Committee, Scholarship Committee and Conference funding Committee . Her research interest is in information and communication technologies, e-learning, digital pedagogies; cloud computing; carbon literacy and decision support systems.

Nina Olivia Rugambwa, PhD. is a lecturer in the Department of Library and Information Science, School of Computing and Information Science at Kyambogo University in Kampala Uganda. She is both an educationist and Information scientist and has 12 years of teaching experience in university settings. Nina obtained her PhD in 2020 from Makerere University. She is passionate about teaching and research. Her research interests are; information seeking behavior, Indigenous Knowledge Management, Academic librarianship, Health information and informatics and curriculum design and development. Nina is also a student mentor at Makerere University MasterCard Foundation program. She coaches young people to excel and succeed in their academic endeavors. This is a voluntary service that she has offered to her community since 2016 to date.

Index

A

A Farming System 177
Academic Integration 311, 321
Activism 263-264, 266-272, 275, 278-279, 318, 346
African Indigenous Knowledge 29, 40, 83, 123-125, 178-185, 187, 189-191, 194, 219, 222-224, 235, 286-287, 292, 298, 336, 338
Africans 2, 32, 36, 70, 74, 145, 186, 190, 196, 198-199, 204-205, 208, 220, 222-223, 283, 286, 291
Afrocentric Model 68, 70-71, 86
Afrocentricity 70, 81, 218, 283
Agricultural indigenous knowledge 159-160, 162-164, 166, 172-173, 193
Archives 34, 36, 39, 70, 79, 82, 114-115, 127, 156, 180, 210, 212, 219, 221, 224, 232, 246, 251-252, 258-259, 275, 325, 332, 337, 339, 342-343, 345-349, 353-358, 360-362, 375

B

Batswana. 123, 125, 128-131, 136, 140
Best practices 27, 29, 80, 97, 101, 124, 255, 262, 332, 335, 339, 342-343, 358
Bogwera 123-126, 128-141
Brazil 262-268, 270-271, 274-280

C

Cataloguing 181, 186, 190, 220, 225-227, 231, 233, 235, 262
Challenges 1, 3, 18-21, 36-39, 41, 43, 45-46, 55-57, 61-64, 67, 83, 85, 87, 90-92, 95-100, 102, 107, 113-115, 117-119, 122-129, 133, 138-139, 153, 157, 159-160, 164, 174, 178, 181, 187, 190, 193-194, 197, 213, 215-216, 227, 229, 233-234, 236, 238, 241, 249, 254, 257, 259, 275, 292, 296-297, 301, 304, 306, 315, 325-326, 330-332, 340, 342, 350, 359, 361, 364, 366, 373

Clay pot 1-5, 8-10, 12-18, 20-21, 25-26, 50
Collection Development and Collection Management 195
Collection Management 178, 184-185, 189, 195
Colonialism 29, 35-37, 70, 136, 196, 198-199, 202, 204-205, 223, 249, 266, 280-281, 288, 290, 292, 300, 303-304, 314, 320-321, 343
Cultural Heritage 1-2, 13, 34, 37, 46-47, 61-62, 87, 89-92, 97, 99-102, 107, 112, 115-116, 122, 129, 140, 197, 200, 203, 206-207, 216-217, 224-225, 229-233, 236-237, 241, 243, 248-250, 253-254, 256-258, 260-261, 304, 323, 336, 342-344, 346-347, 349, 355, 358, 360-362, 367, 371, 373, 376
cultural transmission 110-112, 119
Culture 2-3, 18, 26-27, 29, 33-34, 36, 41, 46, 48, 51, 61, 64, 67, 70, 72, 74, 86, 88-89, 94-98, 104, 111-113, 115, 119, 122-124, 128-134, 136-137, 139-140, 150, 156, 160-161, 164-165, 172, 174, 177, 179, 189, 191, 193-195, 197-198, 200-201, 203, 208-209, 217-219, 222, 224, 228, 230, 236, 241, 244, 248-250, 252, 259, 261, 274, 277, 279, 284-287, 290, 292-294, 296-297, 300-301, 304, 312, 314, 321, 323, 325, 334-336, 339, 343, 347, 365, 374

D

data analytics 342, 359
data sovereignty 314, 342-344, 347, 349-350, 352, 359-362
Decision-Making 89-91, 94, 96, 116-117, 119, 159-161, 168, 177, 205, 209, 213, 329-330, 332, 343-344, 349, 359
Decolonization 28, 35-36, 40, 191, 282-285, 287-291, 296-298, 300-302, 304, 315, 319-321
Digital Preservation 27-29, 31, 34, 36, 38, 41-42, 70-71, 78-79, 81, 83, 85-86, 99, 140-141, 219, 227, 231-234, 255-256, 258, 261, 303-304, 307, 314, 321-333, 335-341

Digital technologies 27-29, 31-33, 38, 42, 78, 91, 93-94, 99, 103, 123-125, 127-139, 141, 238, 347

Digital Transformation 27-28, 38, 42, 93, 258

Digital transformation era 27-28, 38

Digitization 68, 87, 90-91, 93-98, 100-103, 126-127, 139-141, 223, 228, 331-332, 338-339

Distillation 43-48, 51, 55-57, 60-63

Distilled Spirits 45, 53, 67

Documentation 2, 25, 32, 37-38, 69-70, 78, 93, 115, 118, 127, 139-140, 145, 156, 159, 162-164, 179-180, 186, 188, 190, 194, 197, 212, 221, 223, 225, 227, 230-232, 235-238, 246-254, 256, 259, 319, 325, 334

E

Ecological expertise 105, 110

Ecosystem 99, 107, 110-111, 120, 122

Educational Management 64, 87, 90, 94, 96-97, 103, 324, 334-336, 339

Electronic Archives 342-343, 345, 347-348, 353-358, 362

Emotional Component 329

Emotional Framework 329, 340

Emulation 322, 325-326, 337, 339

Entrepreneurship 1-3, 17, 21, 23-26, 43-46, 62-64, 66-67, 82, 98-99, 102, 157, 332

Ephemeral 266, 281

Explicit Knowledge 29, 87, 145-147, 164

F

farming systems 110, 159-160, 184

Fermentation 50-51, 54, 56, 58, 60-62, 64, 67

Food Security 28, 65, 116, 121, 159-163, 172-174, 177, 193, 213-214, 223, 235, 259

Fourth Industrial revolution 374

G

Garo people 105-115, 118-121

Gutu district 159-160, 166, 169, 172, 176

H

historical research 236, 238, 246-248, 371-373, 375

Huni Kuin 262, 265-268, 270-274, 276

I

Implication 25, 64-65, 87, 95-96, 190, 259, 292, 324, 326

Indegenous knowledge 219

Indegenous knowledge preservation 219

Indigenous 1-5, 8, 11-14, 17-18, 20-46, 49, 51, 56, 60-62, 66-71, 75-76, 78, 80-93, 95-97, 99-107, 110-125, 127-132, 136, 138-147, 149-166, 168-240, 246, 248-282, 284-286, 288-345, 347-362, 366-367, 373-376

Indigenous Arts 2, 26, 236-239, 246, 248-256

Indigenous Clay Pot Production 1-3, 8, 12-13, 17-18, 20-21, 26

Indigenous Communities 18, 23, 26-33, 35-38, 42, 88, 92, 113-118, 141, 172, 186, 196, 200, 202-203, 206, 210, 236, 238, 250, 253-256, 263-264, 266, 268, 270, 284, 290, 293-294, 296, 304-307, 314, 318, 330, 335, 342-345, 347-352, 355-359, 362, 366-367

Indigenous Data 200, 271, 342-345, 347-362

Indigenous Knowledge (IK) 41, 68-69, 80, 88, 158, 174, 177, 179, 195, 219, 231, 237, 323

Indigenous Knowledge Collection Development 178, 183, 186, 191, 195

Indigenous Knowledge Systems 25, 27, 29, 31, 33-35, 37-40, 70, 83-84, 88, 101, 105, 116-117, 123-124, 126-127, 129-132, 138-141, 155, 159-161, 164, 166, 173-176, 179-180, 184-185, 187-188, 190-193, 196, 200-201, 207, 213, 222-225, 231, 233-235, 258, 260, 282-288, 291-292, 294, 296-302, 306, 320, 322-339, 341, 343, 347, 357, 360, 366

Indigenous Medicinal Knowledge 70-71, 80, 142-147, 149-155, 179

Indigenous Medicinal Knowledge Owners 142-145, 149-150, 152-154

Indigenous Methodologies 282, 284, 298, 302, 362

Indigenous Pottery 2, 12, 22, 24, 26

Indigenous Practices 33, 43-44, 46, 62, 67, 92, 125, 127-128, 163, 194, 196, 367

Indigenous Research 212, 269-270, 287, 297-299, 301, 342-343, 350, 355, 361-362

Indigenous traditional knowledge system 105

Instagram 262-263, 265, 267-268, 270-272, 281, 346

Intellectual Framework 330-331, 341

K

Knowledge 2-3, 14, 21, 23-42, 45, 57, 62, 66-73, 75-84, 86-132, 136-141, 144-147, 149-166, 169-201, 203-235, 237-238, 249-252, 257-262, 266-270, 274-275, 280, 282-345, 347-350, 355, 357-367, 371-376

Knowledge Acquisition 90, 143, 156, 158, 293, 335

440

Index

Knowledge Management (KM) 177

Knowledge Sharing 28-29, 31, 39-40, 42, 91, 99, 112-113, 146, 156, 224, 258, 300, 343, 358, 373

knowledge sovereignty 196, 200, 211

Knowledge Transfer 30, 39, 127, 143, 145, 157-158, 274, 323

L

Libraries 31, 33-36, 40-42, 68, 70-71, 75, 77-83, 85-86, 99-101, 115, 127, 139-141, 156, 158, 163, 176, 178-190, 193-194, 196, 199, 209-212, 215-216, 218-219, 221, 224, 227, 231-235, 238, 246, 258, 261, 275, 304-305, 313-315, 317-318, 320, 329, 337-340, 360, 363-376

Library and Information Science programmes 315

Linked Data 228, 231, 233-235

Live Streaming 262, 277-278, 280

Lived experiences 116, 178, 181-182

Livestreaming 262-266, 269-270, 273-274, 277, 281

Local Knowledge 68-69, 71, 80, 86, 94, 101, 110, 175, 204, 235, 286, 319, 323

M

Medical Libraries 68, 70-71, 75, 77-81, 86, 231, 338

Metadata 34, 79, 182-183, 185-186, 189, 225-228, 235, 252, 254, 261, 269, 332, 334-335, 342, 346, 349, 358, 362

Metadata Management Software 261

Methodology 31, 40, 47, 64, 66, 71, 128, 147, 159, 164, 166, 181, 193, 199, 204, 214, 223, 262, 269, 287, 292, 300, 303, 308, 361-362, 368

Museums 34, 36-37, 115, 117, 127, 129, 180, 210, 212, 221, 224, 233, 237, 240, 247-248, 253, 256, 258-260, 275, 337

O

OAIS 34, 322-324, 333-335, 337-340

Open Access 260-261, 304

Opportunities 2-3, 15, 17, 28-29, 32, 34-37, 39, 41, 43-46, 48, 57, 62-64, 77, 90-91, 93-94, 96, 98, 112-114, 116, 119, 123-124, 126-131, 138-139, 189, 225, 234, 237, 248, 250, 257, 260, 290, 300-301, 304, 315, 330, 336, 350, 359, 366

P

Palm Wine Production 43-45, 47-49, 51, 55-56, 58, 61-63, 67

Paradoxes 101, 363-364, 368, 374-376

Pedagogy 187, 194, 282-285, 291-302, 304, 312, 315, 319

Policy Component 327

Policy Framework 327-328, 341

pottery 1-5, 8-9, 12, 14-26, 208, 220, 236-237, 244, 259

Preservation 27-29, 31-32, 34, 36-43, 65, 69-71, 78-79, 81-83, 85-87, 90-91, 93, 96, 98-100, 102, 107, 112-118, 120, 122, 125-126, 133, 137, 139-141, 156, 158-159, 161, 163-164, 166, 169-173, 179-181, 184, 187-188, 191, 193, 196-197, 210, 216, 219, 223, 227-238, 247-249, 251, 253, 255-256, 258-261, 263, 274, 303-304, 306-307, 314, 321-341, 344-346, 348, 355, 360, 365-366

Preservation of traditional knowledge 118, 163

production 1-5, 7-9, 11-24, 26, 30, 32, 34, 37, 43-48, 50-51, 55-58, 61-67, 93, 99, 101, 106, 140, 157, 160, 169, 171, 174, 190-191, 193, 204, 210, 221, 237, 241, 244, 267, 276-277, 283, 286, 289, 291-292, 295, 335-336, 340

Public University Libraries 178, 180-182, 184, 187

Q

Quantum Computing 363

R

Reflection 262, 269, 271, 281, 285, 298, 314

repackaging indigenous knowledge 196, 218

Repackaging Indigenous Knowledge Refers 218

research 1-3, 11, 21-25, 28-29, 31-32, 34-35, 37, 40-45, 47-48, 63-66, 68, 71, 79, 81-84, 89-91, 93-94, 98-101, 103, 109-111, 115, 118-119, 121, 124, 127-129, 139-140, 142, 147-149, 155, 157, 163, 166, 173-176, 178-184, 186-187, 190-194, 197-200, 202-205, 210, 212-217, 223-224, 226, 228, 230, 232, 234-238, 246-248, 255-260, 262-263, 265, 268-275, 280-282, 284, 286-293, 295, 297-302, 304, 306-308, 311, 315, 317-319, 321, 323, 327, 329, 331, 337-340, 342-344, 346, 350-352, 354-356, 358-363, 368-369, 371-376

Resource Description Framework 221, 228, 235

rural communities 23, 26, 34, 46, 62, 66, 69, 80, 83, 124, 150, 159-161, 172-173, 218, 258, 286, 337

S

senior Library staff 178, 182, 184-185

Space-time 363-364, 375-376

standardisation 236, 350

Strategic Framework 332, 340-341

sustainable development 21-23, 29, 35, 38, 41, 43, 64, 66, 82, 89, 98, 102, 115-117, 120, 127, 140, 156, 160-162, 174, 176, 179-180, 185, 187, 190-192, 214, 237, 258, 261, 276, 286, 294, 319

T

Tacit knowledge 42, 80, 92, 104, 144, 146-147, 152-153, 155-156, 158, 160, 280, 295

Teaching Practices 295, 303, 305, 307-316, 318, 321

technologies 3, 17, 27-35, 37-40, 42, 45, 68, 70-71, 77-78, 80, 82, 90-91, 93-95, 98-101, 103, 123-141, 156, 160, 163, 219, 228-229, 231, 233-238, 252-253, 260, 263, 265, 277-278, 285, 306-307, 325, 327, 331, 333-336, 339, 347, 360, 363, 366-368, 371-373

Technology Preservation 325-326

Time Travel 363-365, 368-371, 373-376

Tradition 22, 24, 26, 31, 36, 42, 89, 92, 106, 109, 111-113, 120, 130, 132-133, 136-137, 167, 203, 208, 213, 219, 221-222, 229, 242-243, 280, 285, 334, 367

Traditional Ecological Knowledge 86, 107, 115, 119-120, 122, 197, 217, 306, 343

Traditional Knowledge 24, 35, 39, 67, 70-71, 73, 79, 87, 96, 99, 104-106, 108, 110-113, 115, 117-119, 124, 127, 138, 141, 156, 161, 163, 176, 193, 196-197, 199-201, 203-211, 213, 215-216, 218, 229, 232-233, 235, 238, 251-252, 297, 306, 314, 323, 334, 344, 374-375

Traditional medicinal knowledge 68, 71-73, 75-78, 80, 83, 86, 143-144, 146, 149-152, 158, 337

Traditional medicinal knowledge practitioner 150, 158

Traditional Medicine 32, 35-36, 41, 68-71, 74-81, 83-86, 88, 105-106, 112, 131, 139, 144, 151-153, 157-158, 163, 202, 205, 213, 216, 225

Traditional practices 43, 45, 61-63, 88, 96, 104, 107, 111, 113, 117-118, 122-124, 163, 222, 237, 249, 251, 336, 366

Traditional Tools 1-2, 13-15, 21, 26

Transmission 29, 32, 34, 69, 105, 110-113, 116-117, 119, 124, 143-146, 149, 155, 158, 164, 190, 200, 210, 238, 251, 263, 281, 328, 331, 341

U

Ubuntu 201, 282-283, 287, 292-295, 297, 299-302

Uganda 83, 168-169, 172, 174-176, 178-185, 187-189, 191-194, 196, 198-207, 210, 213-216, 225, 231, 233

V

Video 33, 48, 78, 94, 123-124, 130, 252, 263-274, 276, 279, 281, 328-329, 345-346, 362

vocational career 1, 3, 17, 21

W

Witnessing 202, 263, 266-270, 272-274, 277-279, 281

Z

Zimbabwe 83, 159-160, 168-169, 175-176, 196, 198-199, 201-208, 210, 212-214, 216-217, 221, 234, 299, 338

Recommended Reference Books

IGI Global's reference books are available in three unique pricing formats:
Print Only, E-Book Only, or Print + E-Book.

Order direct through IGI Global's Online Bookstore at
www.igi-global.com or through your preferred provider.

ISBN: 9781668437384
EISBN: 9781668437407
© 2022; 343 pp.
List Price: US$ 215

ISBN: 9781668433645
EISBN: 9781668433669
© 2022; 317 pp.
List Price: US$ 215

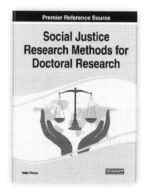

ISBN: 9781799884798
EISBN: 9781799884804
© 2022; 397 pp.
List Price: US$ 215

ISBN: 9781799885535
EISBN: 9781799885559
© 2022; 277 pp.
List Price: US$ 215

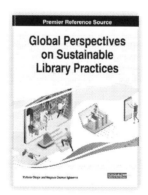

ISBN: 9781668459645
EISBN: 9781668459652
© 2023; 376 pp.
List Price: US$ 240

ISBN: 9781668438817
EISBN: 9781668438824
© 2022; 663 pp.
List Price: US$ 415

Do you want to stay current on the latest research trends, product announcements, news, and special offers?
Join IGI Global's mailing list to receive customized recommendations, exclusive discounts, and more.
Sign up at: **www.igi-global.com/newsletters.**

Publisher of Timely, Peer-Reviewed Inclusive Research Since 1988

www.igi-global.com   Sign up at www.igi-global.com/newsletters   facebook.com/igiglobal   twitter.com/igiglobal   linkedin.com/igiglobal

Ensure Quality Research is Introduced to the Academic Community

Become an Evaluator for IGI Global Authored Book Projects

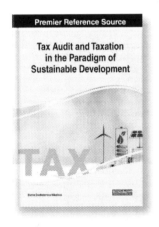  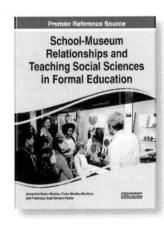 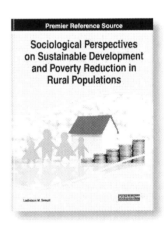

The overall success of an authored book project is dependent on quality and timely manuscript evaluations.

Applications and Inquiries may be sent to:
development@igi-global.com

Applicants must have a doctorate (or equivalent degree) as well as publishing, research, and reviewing experience. Authored Book Evaluators are appointed for one-year terms and are expected to complete at least three evaluations per term. Upon successful completion of this term, evaluators can be considered for an additional term.

If you have a colleague that may be interested in this opportunity, we encourage you to share this information with them.

Easily Identify, Acquire, and Utilize Published
Peer-Reviewed Findings in Support of Your Current Research

IGI Global OnDemand

Purchase Individual IGI Global OnDemand Book Chapters and Journal Articles

For More Information:
www.igi-global.com/e-resources/ondemand/

Browse through 150,000+ Articles and Chapters!

Find specific research related to your current studies and projects that have been contributed by international researchers from prestigious institutions, including:

- Accurate and Advanced Search
- Affordably Acquire Research
- Instantly Access Your Content
- Benefit from the InfoSci Platform Features

"*It really provides* an excellent entry into the research literature of the field. *It presents a manageable number of* highly relevant sources *on topics of interest to a wide range of researchers. The sources are* scholarly, but also accessible *to 'practitioners'.*"

- Ms. Lisa Stimatz, MLS, University of North Carolina at Chapel Hill, USA

Interested in Additional Savings?

Subscribe to
IGI Global OnDemand *Plus*

Learn More

Acquire content from over 128,000+ research-focused book chapters and 33,000+ scholarly journal articles for as low as US$ 5 per article/chapter (original retail price for an article/chapter: US$ 37.50).

7,300+ E-BOOKS. ADVANCED RESEARCH. INCLUSIVE & AFFORDABLE.

IGI Global e-Book Collection

- **Flexible Purchasing Options** (Perpetual, Subscription, EBA, etc.)
- Multi-Year Agreements with **No Price Increases** Guaranteed
- **No Additional Charge** for Multi-User Licensing
- No Maintenance, Hosting, or Archiving Fees
- Continually Enhanced & Innovated **Accessibility Compliance Features** (WCAG)

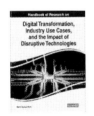

Handbook of Research on Digital Transformation, Industry Use Cases, and the Impact of Disruptive Technologies
ISBN: 9781799877127
EISBN: 9781799877141

Handbook of Research on New Investigations in Artificial Life, AI, and Machine Learning
ISBN: 9781799886860
EISBN: 9781799886877

Handbook of Research on Future of Work and Education
ISBN: 9781799882756
EISBN: 9781799882770

Research Anthology on Physical and Intellectual Disabilities in an Inclusive Society (4 Vols.)
ISBN: 9781668435427
EISBN: 9781668435434

Innovative Economic, Social, and Environmental Practices for Progressing Future Sustainability
ISBN: 9781799895909
EISBN: 9781799895923

Applied Guide for Event Study Research in Supply Chain Management
ISBN: 9781799889694
EISBN: 9781799889717

Mental Health and Wellness in Healthcare Workers
ISBN: 9781799888130
EISBN: 9781799888147

Clean Technologies and Sustainable Development in Civil Engineering
ISBN: 9781799898108
EISBN: 9781799898122

Request More Information, or Recommend the IGI Global e-Book Collection to Your Institution's Librarian

For More Information or to Request a Free Trial, Contact IGI Global's e-Collections Team: eresources@igi-global.com | 1-866-342-6657 ext. 100 | 717-533-8845 ext. 100

Are You Ready to
Publish Your Research ?

IGI Global offers book authorship and editorship opportunities across 11 subject areas, including business, computer science, education, science and engineering, social sciences, and more!

Benefits of Publishing with IGI Global:

- Free one-on-one editorial and promotional support.
- Expedited publishing timelines that can take your book from start to finish in less than one (1) year.
- Choose from a variety of formats, including Edited and Authored References, Handbooks of Research, Encyclopedias, and Research Insights.
- Utilize IGI Global's eEditorial Discovery® submission system in support of conducting the submission and double-blind peer review process.
- IGI Global maintains a strict adherence to ethical practices due in part to our full membership with the Committee on Publication Ethics (COPE).
- Indexing potential in prestigious indices such as Scopus®, Web of Science™, PsycINFO®, and ERIC – Education Resources Information Center.
- Ability to connect your ORCID iD to your IGI Global publications.
- Earn honorariums and royalties on your full book publications as well as complimentary content and exclusive discounts.

Learn More at: www.igi-global.com/publish
or Contact IGI Global's Aquisitions Team at: acquisition@igi-global.com

Printed in the United States
by Baker & Taylor Publisher Services